The Gospel and the Gospels

The Gospel and the Gospels

Edited by

Peter Stuhlmacher

WILLIAM B. EERDMANS PUBLISHING COMPANY
GRAND RAPIDS, MICHIGAN

Copyright © 1991 by Wm. B. Eerdmans Publishing Co.
255 Jefferson Ave. S.E., Grand Rapids, Mich. 49503
All rights reserved
Printed in the United States of America

Originally published as *Das Evangelium und die Evangelien. Vorträge vom Tübinger Symposium 1982* © J. C. B. Mohr (Paul Siebeck) 1983. The essays by E. Earle Ellis, Robert Guelich, Graham N. Stanton, I. Howard Marshall, and James D. G. Dunn appeared in English in *Das Evangelium und die Evangelien*. "Literary, Theological, and Historical Problems in the Gospel of Mark" by Martin Hengel and "The Portrayal of Peter in the Synoptic Gospels" by Reinhard Feldmeier are reprinted from *Studies in the Gospel of Mark*, English translation © 1985 John Bowden. Used by permission of Augsburg Fortress Publishers. The rest of the essays were translated by John Vriend.

Library of Congress Cataloging-in-Publication Data

Evangelium und die Evangelien. English.
The Gospel and the Gospels / edited by Peter Stuhlmacher.
p.   cm.
Translation of: Das Evangelium und die Evangelien.
Chiefly papers of a symposium held at the Tübinger Evangelische Stift, Sept. 13-18, 1982.
Includes bibliographical references and indexes.
ISBN 0-8028-3688-7
1. Bible. N.T. Gospels—Criticism, interpretation, etc.—Congresses.   I. Stuhlmacher, Peter.   II. Title.
BS2555.2.E8713   1991

226'.06—dc20   90-48026
                                                                                 CIP

Contents

Contributors

Abramowski, Luise, Prof. Dr. theol., FBA, Church History, Brunnstrasse 18, 7400 Tübingen.

Betz, Otto, Prof. emeritus Dr. theol., New Testament, Rappenberghalde 11, 7400 Tübingen.

Dihle, Albrecht, Prof. Dr. phil., Dr. theol.h.c., Classical Philology, Schillingsrotter Platz 7, 5000 Köln 51.

Dunn, James D. G., MA, BD, Ph.D., Professor of Divinity (New Testament), Department of Theology, Abbey House, Palace Green, Durham DH1 3RS.

Ellis, Earle E., Prof., Southwestern Baptist Theological Seminary, P.O. Box 22000, Ft. Worth, TX 76122.

Feldmeier, Reinhard, Dr. theol., New Testament, Finkenstrasse 7, 8806 Neuendettelsau.

Gerhardsson, Birger, Prof. Dr. teol., New Testament, Teologiska Institutionen, Theologicum, Sandgatan 1, S-223 50 Lund.

Guelich, Robert A., MA, S.T.B., Dr. theol., Prof., Fuller Theological Seminary, Pasadena, CA 91182.

Hengel, Martin, Prof. Dr. theol., Dr. teol.D.h.c., D.D., FBA, New Testament, Schwabstrasse 51, 7400 Tübingen.

Hofius, Otto Friedrich, Prof. Dr. theol., New Testament, Kleisstrasse 1, 7400 Tübingen.

Lampe, Peter, Prof. Dr. theol., New Testament, Union Theological Seminary, 3401 Brook Road, Richmond, Virginia 23227, U.S.A.

Luz, Ulrich, Prof. Dr. theol., New Testament, Marktgasse 21, CH-3177 Laupen.

Marshall, I. Howard, MA, BD, Ph.D., Prof., 132 Deeside Gardens, Aberdeen AB1 7PX, Scotland.

Pesch, Rudolf, Prof. Dr. theol., New Testament, Herzog-Heinrich-Strasse 18, 8000 München 2.

Polag, Athansius, Dr. theol., Abtei St. Matthias, Matthiasstrasse 85, 5500 Trier.

Stanton, Graham N., MA, BD, Ph.D., Professor of New Testament Studies, King's College London, Strand, London WC2R 2LS, England.

Stuhlmacher, Peter, Prof. Dr. theol., New Testament, Untere Schillerstrasse 4, 7400 Tübingen.

Abbreviations

AB	Anchor Bible
AGG	Abhandlungen der Gesellschaft der Wissenschaften, Göttingen
ALBO	Analecta Lovaniensia biblica et orientalia
AnBib	Analecta Biblica
ANRW	*Aufstieg und Niedergang der römischen Welt*
ARW	Archiv für Religionswissenschaft
ATD	Das Alte Testament Deutsch
AThANT	Abhandlungen zur Theologie des Alten und Neuen Testaments
BAGD	W. Bauer, W. F. Arndt, and F. W. Gingrich, *A Greek-English Lexicon of the New Testament and Other Early Christian Literature,* second edition revised and augmented by F. W. Gingrich and F. W. Danker, 1979
BBB	Bonner biblische Beiträge
BBE	Beiträge zur biblischen Exegese
BETL	Bibliotheca ephemeridum theologicarum Lovaniensium
BEvTh	Beiträge zur Evangelischen Theologie
BGU	Aegyptische Urkunden aus den Museen zu Berlin: Griechische Urkunden, 1895-1933
BHTh	Beiträge zur historischen Theologie
Billerbeck	(H. Strack and) P. Billerbeck, *Kommentar zum Neuen Testament aus Talmud und Midrasch,* 1924ff.
BJRL	*Bulletin of the John Rylands Library*
BK	Biblischer Kommentar
BR	*Biblical Research*
BWANT	Beiträge zur Wissenschaft vom Alten und Neuen Testament
BZ	*Biblische Zeitschrift*
BZNW	Beiheft zur Zeitschrift für die Neutestamentliche Wissenschaft
CBNT	Coniectanea Biblica, Novum Testamentum
CBQ	*Catholic Biblical Quarterly*
CBQMS	*Catholic Biblical Quarterly* Monograph Series
CIG	*Corpus Inscriptionum Graecarum*
CIJ	*Corpus Inscriptionum Judaicarum*
CN	Coniectanea Neotestamentica
CSCO	Corpus Scriptorum Christianorum Orientalium

CW	*Die Christliche Welt*
DACL	*Dictionnaire d'archéologie chrétienne et liturgie*
DBS	*Dictionnaire de la Bible. Supplément*
DLZ	*Deutsche Literaturzeitung*
EKK	Evangelisch-katholischer Kommentar
ET	English translation
EuA	*Erbe und Auftrag*
EvTh	*Evangelische Theologie*
EWNT	*Exegetisches Wörterbuch zum Neuen Testament,* ed. H. Balz and G. Schneider, 1980ff.
EVV	English versions (of the Bible)
ExpT	*Expository Times*
FRLANT	Forschungen zur Religion und Literatur des Alten und Neuen Testaments
HDB	*Dictionary of the Bible,* ed. J. Hastings, et al., 1898ff.
HNT	Handbuch zum Neuen Testament
HTK	Herders theologischer Kommentar zum Neuen Testament
HZ	*Historische Zeitschrift*
ICC	International Critical Commentary
JBL	*Journal of Biblical Literature*
JJS	*Journal of Jewish Studies*
JK	*Junge Kirche*
JR	*Journal of Religion*
JSHRZ	Jüdische Schriften aus hellenistisch-römischer Zeit
JSJ	*Journal for the Study of Judaism*
JSNT	*Journal for the Study of the New Testament*
JSS	*Journal of Semitic Studies*
JTS	*Journal of Theological Studies*
KEK	Kritisch-exegetischer Kommentar
KlT	Kleine Texte
LCL	Loeb Classical Library
LXX	Septuagint
NAWG	*Nachrichten der Akademie der Wissenschaften in Göttingen*
NCBC	New Century Bible Commentary
NF	Neue Folge
NICNT	New International Commentary on the New Testament
NIGTC	New International Greek Testament Commentary
NovT	*Novum Testamentum*
NS	new series
NTA	Neutestamentliche Abhandlungen
NTD	Das Neue Testament Deutsch
OGIS	*Orientis Graeci Inscriptiones Selectae,* ed. W. Dittenberger, 1903ff.
Ord. Korr.	Ordens-Korrespondenz
ÖTK	Oekumenischer Taschenbuch Kommentar
PRE	*Paulys Realencyclopädie der classischen Altertumswissenschaft*

PS	Patrologia Syriaca
QD	Quaestiones Disputatae
RE	*Realencyclopädie für protestantische Theologie*
RGG	*Die Religion in Geschichte und Gegenwart*
RHPR	*Revue d'histoire et de philosophie religieuses*
RNT	Regensburger Neues Testament
RSR	*Religious Studies Review*
SBB	Stuttgarter biblische beiträge
SBLDS	Society of Biblical Literature Dissertation Series
SBM	Stuttgarter biblische Monographien
SBS	Stuttgarter Bibelstudien
SHAW.PH	Sitzungsberichte der Heidelberger Akademie der Wissenschaften. Philosophisch-historische Klasse
SNTSMS	Society for New Testament Studies Monograph Series
ST	*Studia Theologica*
TDNT	*Theological Dictionary of the New Testament,* ed. G. Kittel and G. Friedrich, 1964ff.
ThB	Theologische Bücherei
ThBeitr	Theologische Beiträge
ThBT	Theologische Bibliothek Töpelmann
Theol. Lit. Dienst	Theologischer Literaturdienst
ThGl	*Theologie und Glaube*
ThLZ	*Theologische Literaturzeitung*
ThQ	*Theologische Quartalschrift*
ThRev	*Theologische Revue*
ThViat	*Theologia Viatorum*
TR	*Theologische Rundschau*
TRE	*Theologische Realencyclopädie*
TU	Texte und Untersuchungen
TZ	*Theologische Zeitschrift*
USQR	*Union Seminary Quarterly Review*
UTB	Uni-Taschenbücher
WdF	Wege der Forschung
WMANT	Wissenschaftliche Monographien zum Alten und Neuen Testament
WTJ	*Westminster Theological Journal*
WuD	*Wort und Dienst*
WUNT	Wissenschaftliche Untersuchungen zum Alten und Neuen Testament
ZDPV	*Zeitschrift der deutschen Palästina-Vereins*
ZNW	*Zeitschrift für die neutestamentliche Wissenschaft*
ZTK	*Zeitschrift für Theologie und Kirche*

Preface

Thanks to the assistance of the Deutsche Forschungsgemeinschaft, the Ministerium für Wissenschaft und Kunst of Baden-Württemberg, and the Evangelische Landeskirche in Württemberg, an international scholarly symposium on the theme "The Gospel and the Gospels" was convened in the premises of the Tübinger Evangelische Stift. The participants were from Germany and other countries and were for the most part New Testament exegetes, but also included Church historians and classical scholars. The goal of the symposium was to uncover lines of convergence in the study of the biblical Gospels and so to give a new impulse to Gospel research, which is to some extent becoming directionless. It is hoped that this goal has been reached.

With three exceptions the contributions contained in this volume are the papers submitted by the participants, delivered by them in Tübingen, and revised for publication. Reinhold Feldmeier's short contribution on the Peter tradition in the Synoptics is a supplement that Martin Hengel wished to have added to his own treatment of the problems of the Gospel of Mark. Peter Lampe and Ulrich Luz have contributed a summary of the discussion at the symposium; the questions raised in their summary have been considered by the participants in the revision of their papers for publication, though these questions were not discussed at the symposium. Robert A. Guelich has supplied, in addition to the paper that he gave at the symposium, an Introduction to the volume, which discusses the significance of the concerns expressed by the symposium's participants for the broader context of New Testament studies, particularly for the English-speaking world.

The participants in the symposium have agreed to dedicate this volume to their colleague Otto Betz of Tübingen. Otto Betz was born June 6, 1917. He received his S.T.M. from Oberlin College, Oberlin, Ohio, and his Dr. Theol. from (the Protestant Faculty of Theology in) Tübingen, Germany. He is a specialist not only in the New Testament, but also in ancient Judaism and the Qumran scrolls. In 1961 his *Habilitationsschrift* was accepted at Tübingen. In 1962 he returned to the U.S. to teach at Chicago Theological Seminary, where he stayed until 1967. He then returned to Tübingen and taught New Testament studies at the Protestant Faculty of Theology until his retirement in 1983. He is now Emeritus Professor of New Testament and still active in both research and publication. Professor Betz's main books are *Offenbarung und Schriftforschung in der Qumransekte* (Tübingen: J. C. B. Mohr [Paul Siebeck], 1960), *Der Paraklet* (Leiden/Köln: E. J. Brill, 1963), *What Do We Know about Jesus?* (London: SCM, 1967), *Jesus—Der Messias Israels* (Tübingen: J. C. B. Mohr [Paul Siebeck], 1987), and *Jesus—Der Herr der Kirche* (Tübingen: J. C. B. Mohr [Paul Siebeck], 1990). We give our respects to him with the highest collegial regards and with all good wishes for a retirement that continues to be profitable both in relation to scholarship and personally.

There are many to thank. First the president of the University of Tübingen, Adolf Theis, who with his research department energetically supported the plans for the symposium. Then the faculty of Protestant theology and its dean at that time, Dr. Luise Abramowski, for their assistance with the preparations for the Tübingen meeting. Also Ephorus Dr. Friedrich Hertel, with his coworkers in the Evangelische Stift, for a pleasant living and working environment, for which all the participants in the symposium have been most grateful and which made a substantial contribution to the success of the whole project. Then also the institutions that financed the symposium.

But thanks are owed above all to the participants in the symposium, who came to Tübingen, presented papers, and revised them for publication in a timely manner. Research assistants Dr. Karl-Theodor Kleinknecht, Mr. (now Dr.) Scott Hafemann, and Dr. Rainer Riesner are deserving of thanks for organizing the symposium and bringing it to a successful conclusion. Dr. Riesner aided me untiringly in the preparation of this volume for publication. Dr. Hafemann prepared the index of biblical and other ancient writings. Both of them, with Dr. Karl-Heinz Schlaudraff, took part in correcting the manuscript. Gisela Kienle patiently and carefully carried out all the necessary typing and work in the office.

I thank Martin Hengel and Otfried Hofius, my colleagues in the faculty of Protestant theology, for accepting the volume into the scholarly series edited by them. J. C. B. Mohr (Paul Siebeck), of Tübingen handled the typesetting and printing of that edition in an impressive manner.

The English edition would not have been possible were it not for the initiative of E. E. Ellis and the kind accommodation of Wm. B. Eerdmans Publishing Co. My sincere thanks go to them as they do to J. M. Whitlock, M.Th., who helped me proofread the creditable translations by John Vriend.

May this symposium volume now also meet with a response in English-speaking countries and make its contribution to the renewal of attention to and consideration of questions involving the formation of the (synoptic) Gospels and their value as sources for our knowledge of Jesus' message and ministry and early Christian tradition.

Peter Stuhlmacher
September, 1983 / October, 1990

Introduction

Robert A. Guelich

1. The issues surrounding "the gospel and the Gospels" have formed a major part of New Testament studies for the last two centuries. These concerns extend beyond the academic and ultimately lead to the question of the content and meaning of the gospel, a question that penetrates to the very core of the Christian faith. Since the publication by G. E. Lessing in 1774-78 of "fragments" from Herrmann Samuel Reimarus's unpublished *Apologie oder Schutzschrift für die verknüftigen Verehrer Gottes,* the relationship of the person and teaching of Jesus from Nazareth to the Christ of the Gospels has led not only to the question who Jesus was but also what the Gospels are. While much of nineteenth-century New Testament scholarship engaged in the debate over the "historical Jesus," based in part on the nature and character of the Gospels and their sources, much of twentieth-century New Testament scholarship, using the historical and literary-critical tools of source, form, redaction, and literary criticism, has focused attention on the Gospels themselves. Yet this investigation of the Gospels has had significant implications for Jesus-of-history and Christ-of-faith debate.

    1.1 During this period a rigorous historicism guided by a "purely historical" concern has dominated New Testament studies and has deconstructed the Gospels by identifying their constituent form-critical units and reconstructing the respective *Sitze im Leben* in the life of the early Church. R. Bultmann's influential and unrivaled *History of the Synoptic Tradition* (English translation, 1963) stands as the premier illustration of this approach. N. Perrin's *Rediscovering the Teaching of Jesus* (1967) illustrates the next logical step by pursuing how and what one can know about Jesus' teaching from this supposedly historically complex body of materials. The general consensus of this form-critical approach found relatively little of the Gospel tradition originating with Jesus and essentially confirmed J. Weiss's and A. Schweitzer's conclusion that

Jesus and his message of "the gospel of the Kingdom" arose out of apocalyptic strands within first-century Judaism. This "gospel" represented not only a different "gospel" from that of the early Church and Paul but even from that of the Gospels.

1.2 The examination of the rise and development of the Jesus-tradition has been renewed with vigor in the USA by the establishment of the Jesus Seminar in 1985 under the leadership of Robert Funk. The form-critical methodology employed incorporates refinements from both a sociological and literary-critical standpoint. Yet the fundamental assumptions of form criticism about the Gospel tradition and its development still obtain unquestioned. The Jesus Seminar has as its agenda to inventory and examine sayings attributed to Jesus by ranking them as: (a) sayings clearly coming from Jesus, (b) sayings originating in the primitive community, and (c) sayings whose origins are too much in dispute to assign with confidence. In Funk's own words, this group of scholars is "going to inquire simply, rigorously after the *voice* of Jesus, after what he really said" (*Foundations and Facets Forum* 1.1 [1985] 7). In the process the other voices in the tradition are also evaluated literarily and historically. Ultimately, after a subsequent examination of the non-sayings material of the Gospels, the work is to culminate in a new history of the Gospel tradition.

Although it is too soon to know where this examination of the Jesus-tradition will lead, the *Myth of Innocence* (1987) by B. Mack, a charter member of the Jesus Seminar, does indicate a major break with the picture of Jesus set against apocalyptic Judaism that has prevailed since Weiss. For Mack, Jesus stands more in line with the peripatetic Hellenistic cynic philosophers than appearing as an eschatological prophet. Mack sees Jesus combining a Hellenistic ethos with a religious piety energized by a concern for Jewish ethical and theocratic ideals (pp. 62-74). The Jesus of the Gospels, on the other hand, is traceable ultimately to the evangelist Mark. According to Mack, Mark combined the Christ myth of the Hellenistic Christ cults with the Jesus-traditions of the Jesus movements to create the story that "was to give to Christian imagination its sense of radical and dramatic origin in time" (p. 355). Not unlike W. Schmithals (see pp. 9-12 below), Mack attributes the "origin for the Christian view of Christian origins" to the genius of the writer of Mark's Gospel (p. 357).

1.3 One can see that the radical form-critical approach, which has dominated Gospels studies for most of this century, has led in two directions. On the one hand, form criticism with its isolation of literary forms as units combined with a rigorous socio-historical pursuit of the traditional units' *Sitze im Leben* has contributed further to the deconstruction of the Gospels as literary units in the examination of their constituent traditional elements. On the other hand, redaction criticism, which examines the Gospels as literary products reflecting their own theological nuances, accepts the results of radical form criticism and responds to it by attributing more and more creativity to the evangelist, who appears to have operated in a historical vacuum unaware of or unconcerned about the supposed "history" behind these units. In each case, the result is an even greater divergence of the Christ(s) of the Gospels from the Jesus of history. This disengagement of Jesus and his message—whether apocalyptic or cynic in nature—from the gospel of the early Church, Paul, and the Gospels still dominates many circles of New Testament studies. In other words, the historical-critical questions of the Gospels continue to raise anew the question of the gospel.

2. The work and results of the historical-critical approach to the question of "the gospel and the Gospels" has engendered two negative responses. First, there are those who for confessional reasons disdain the use of the historical-critical tools and, second, those who disdain the use of the historical-critical tools as irrelevant or illegitimate from a literary-critical understanding of the Gospels as texts.

2.1 On the one side, though modern Gospels study has been dominated in one way or another by the quest for the historical Jesus or the Jesus behind the Gospels, the legitimacy of this quest has constantly come into question from those who eschew a "critical" reading of the Gospels because of their confessional stance regarding the very nature of Scripture. The Gospels are God-given, Spirit-inspired, thus reliable historical records of Jesus' ministry, and any use of historical-critical methods to examine and interpret them assumes that they are more or less than a Spirit-inspired snapshot or transcript of Jesus' ministry. Consequently, this approach limits one's investigations of the Gospels to textual, lexical, and grammatical issues. The issues that give rise to this volume on *The Gospel and the Gospels* simply do not exist for this approach. Indeed, the disastrous disjunction of the Jesus of history from the Christ of faith for the gospel of Paul, the early Church, and the Gospels, combined with the lack of consensus among those using historical-critical methods concerning "the assured results of scholarship," confirms the "high" view of Scripture and the conviction that a "critical" reading of the Gospels is futile.

One does not, however, solve problems in general, including those behind *The Gospel and the Gospels,* by denying or ignoring them. Nor should one necessarily attribute the deleterious results of radical New Testament criticism to the historical-critical tools themselves. One must distinguish a historical-critical school of thought with its radical historicism from the historical-critical method, which seeks to use literary and historical tools to examine the Gospels, which must be taken seriously precisely as literary and historical documents. A supposedly "high" view of the Scriptures that eschews the historical-critical method fails, in reality, to take the Gospels seriously as Gospels. By reading what was intended by the writer to be a verbal *portrait* of Jesus as if it were a historical *snapshot,* one asks both too much and too little of the Gospels and distorts their actual message — at the risk of distorting the gospel they portray.

2.2 On the other side, a more recent challenge to a historical-critical reading of the Gospels has emerged, stemming more from literary-critical than confessional concerns. A quick scanning of a recent program for the annual meeting of the American Academy of Religion and the Society of Biblical Literature will demonstrate how extensive this approach has become in American biblical studies. In part this challenge has risen out of the tenuous character of historical pursuits and the failure to arrive at a fixed consensus concerning historical questions. For some the quest for historical answers only leads to a multiplicity of theories and more questions while taking one further and further from the Gospels as texts. Despairing of ever resolving the "age-old questions" and overwhelmed by the plethora of conflicting "answers," these scholars have chosen to move back to the surer ground of the texts as texts.

This approach does reflect a concern for the text as a whole, a welcome shift from looking at the trees, i.e., the discrete units comprising the Gospels, to the forest, the Gospels themselves as literary texts. Literary questions regarding implied author and reader, plot, characters, and narrative time and space pursue an understanding of the text as a whole. Questions focusing on rhetoric ask about the design and desired effect of the text. Reader-response questions ask about the text as viewed by the reader. These literary approaches shift the perspective from the text perceived as a window through which one views the past to the text itself as the object perceived as a whole. Consequently, for many who follow this trend in Gospel studies, the issues behind *The Gospel and the Gospels* are at best irrelevant, at worst illegitimate.

Both the approach of those whose confessional assumptions control their reading of the Gospels as historical documents and that of those whose literary-critical concerns control their literary reading of the text collapse the time between the text and the reader. The former closes the hermeneutical gap between the text then and now by an unquestioned acceptance of the Gospels as a direct historical replay of Jesus and his ministry recorded for the reader's information about the what, when, where, and how of Jesus' ministry. The latter closes the hermeneutical gap by letting the text take on a life of its own for the reader, regardless of where the reader then or now stands on the stage of history.

Furthermore, both approaches ignore the historical gap between Jesus' ministry and the text—the former by collapsing the time between Jesus and the text so that the text takes us back to Jesus, the latter by ignoring the gap as irrelevant and starting with the text as the given. In doing so, each fails to address the question of the Gospels as the gospel by failing to take seriously the uniqueness of the texts as "Gospels."

3. It is the firm conviction of the writers in this volume that one must address the historical-critical questions about the Gospels as literary documents, questions that inevitably lead to the question of the relationship of the documents to Jesus and his message in view of their very nature as "Gospels." The question is, however, both a historical question that calls for a critical look at the underlying assumptions controlling the use of the historical-critical method as well as a theological question that poses the more fundamental question about the relationship of the "Gospels" to the "gospel" and ultimately about the essence of the "gospel" as such. One cannot distinguish between the Jesus of history and the Christ of faith and relegate the one to historical inquiry and the other to a somewhat optional theological reflection.

3.1 P. Stuhlmacher's initial essay introduces the theme of the volume. Turning first to the methodological issue of form criticism, he recognizes its legitimacy as a critical tool for working in the Gospels but questions some of the fundamental assumptions that have controlled its use and thus its results from the outset. He then offers in thesis fashion observations about the well-known problems of the relationship of John and Paul to the Jesus/Gospel-tradition. He concludes with a look at the word "gospel" and its tradition and suggests that its roots may well extend to Jesus' ministry as viewed in the light of Isaiah's promise.

3.2 E. Ellis's contribution focuses specifically on the "state of the art" of Gospels criticism. He first raises questions about the philosophical or closed "worldview" controlling much of modern biblical criticism, raises again the crucial issue of the literary relationship of the Gospels to each other and the nature of their supposed sources, and extends Stuhlmacher's critique of the fundamental assumptions of form criticism. He concludes with his own suggestion of a more circumscribed corporate ("apostolic") nature of the preservation, use, and development of the tradition that would preclude ascribing any radical redactional innovation on the part of an evangelist like Schmithals's or Mack's Mark.

3.3 Ellis's suggestion of a corporate participation in the traditional process sets the stage for Gerhardsson's essay on "The Path of the Gospel Tradition." Beginning with the phenomena of the concrete Jesus-texts found almost exclusively in the Gospels and the freer proclamation and teaching based on but not reproductive of that Jesus-tradition as found from Acts to Revelation, Gerhardsson concludes by use of analogies drawn especially from Judaism that the Jesus-tradition was an independent or "isolated" tradition valued for its own sake. Therefore, rather than being a distillation of the early Church's preaching and teaching, as assumed by classical form criticism, it was used along with the Scriptures as a given in the worship, catechetical teaching, and study of the early Church.

Gerhardsson traces the Jesus-tradition to Jesus' role as teacher and to the role of the disciples—the "Twelve" in Jerusalem—as the preservers, shapers, interpreters, and transmitters of this tradition. Recognizing the value of form criticism in arranging materials in formal units, he adds his own critique of the fundamental assumptions of form criticism about the relationship between form and history, that is, about the question of *Sitz im Leben*. He acknowledges that the Jesus-texts exhibit a degree of fluidity arising from differences in memory, interpretative adaptations, variations in translation, omissions, additions, changes, etc. Therefore, for him the task of historical criticism is to examine the Jesus-tradition for probable post-Easter interpretations, changes, additions, and secondary creations—but beginning from the assumption, which the evidence points to, "that Jesus said and did what they say he said and did." The historical-critical burden of proof lies on those regarding material as secondary rather than on those regarding it as primary.

4. Following this methodological critique of the assumptions of classical form criticism, three essays look more closely at parts of the Jesus-tradition. A. Polag looks at Q, which, he concludes, "gives us words of Jesus with the least amount of editing by comparison with other strands of tradition" (p. 100). Then R. Pesch takes another look at Mark 14:12-26 as "the oldest tradition of the early Church," and O. Hofius looks at the agrapha to gain further perspective on the scope and nature of the Jesus-tradition.

4.1 Polag directs his attention to Q and, contrary to the contemporary trend in Q studies, disclaims any theological center for Q based on formal or theological motifs. Catchwords serve as the primary device for arranging materials that lack form-critical homogeneity. No particular text within Q emerges as having a redactional prominence in the light of which the other texts are to be viewed confessionally. Rather, for Polag, "the genesis of the collection lies in the teaching activity of Jesus" (p. 102), whose person unites the collection.

Yet the collection does not merely reflect the significance of Jesus as the teacher of the disciples or of the early community. It reflects the disciples' pre-Easter experience, an experience authenticated by Easter, with Jesus and his teaching, which elicited a decision about God's saving action in history, resulting in new conduct. One might say that it represents their own experience of the gospel of God through Jesus in these sayings. So "when the churches structured their Jesus-tradition in a way resembling the sketch of Acts 10:36-43, the texts of Q were then coordinated with other traditions which had a more comprehensive view of the work of God in Jesus" (p. 105). Q then became part of the Gospels. These texts had long been transmitted "with a view toward a personal relationship to Jesus" (p. 105). Therefore, "these texts were not transmitted for the purpose of conveying information but in order to make personal experience possible" (p. 105). Instead of a rival gospel devoid of the death and resurrection of Jesus that arises or stems from a particular early Christian community, the core of Q "goes back to the pre-Easter circle of disciples and hence . . . the genesis of the collection lies in the teaching activity of Jesus" (p. 102). Consequently, the Q tradition can only have had, according to Polag, a complementary role in the life of any church.

4.2 In several previous works, R. Pesch has suggested that the passion narrative behind Mark's Gospel represents "the oldest tradition of the early Church," originating in the Aramaic-speaking early Church of Jerusalem before A.D. 37. He defends on literary-critical, tradition-critical, and form-critical grounds his claim that the pre-Markan passion narrative was transmitted as an entire complex of connected events rather than constructed of isolated episodes, a claim that has gained in prevalence in contemporary studies of Mark's passion narrative. In particular, he demonstrates that 14:22-25 is the oldest tradition of the Lord's Supper and represents form-critically a narrative report rather than a cult-etiological legend. Furthermore, he argues that instead of having an independent existence as a separate traditional unit, this passage has its original *Sitz im Leben* in the passion narrative context of 14:12-26, which reflects the events of Jesus' ministry.

In so doing, Pesch shows that the claim that an early Jewish Christian community in Jerusalem or elsewhere had an "unpauline gospel" with no reference to the cross lacks any historical basis. In fact, the Lord's Supper tradition in Mark indicates that Jesus himself, not the early Church, provided the earliest interpretation of the redemptive significance of his death. What Pesch refers to in his title as "the gospel in Jerusalem" could well be seen then as "the gospel of Jesus," showing once again the proximity of Jesus and his ministry to the Gospel tradition. As he notes in conclusion, one cannot play historical and kerygmatic interests against each other, as has been done so often in New Testament studies, without destroying "the unbreakable linkage between history and kerygma (between events and their theological interpretation as God's action, interpretation distilled in the tradition) . . ." (p. 148).

4.3 In a third essay focusing on the Jesus-tradition O. Hofius examines the agrapha, an agraphon being "a saying attributed to the earthly Jesus which has not been transmitted in the oldest version of the four canonical Gospels" (p. 336). Though we have numerous such sayings, Hofius concurs with J. Jeremias that the number of these sayings on the level of the sayings of Jesus in the Synoptic Gospels is very small—only nine. He then questions on a tradition-historical basis five of these, leaving only four that are indisputable. This state of affairs differs markedly from what one might think based on a recent spate of books dealing with other "Gospels," not to mention the elevation of the Gospel of Thomas and other early Christian documents to nearly canonical status.

The implications of Hofius's study, along with those of Gerhardsson, Polag, and Pesch, bode ominously for the assumptions of classical form criticism about the development and proliferation of Jesus' sayings in the life of the Church in the period between Jesus and the written Gospels. For example, these data provide little evidence that sayings from the exalted Christ received by early Christian prophets were transferred at some point in the tradition to the status of sayings of the earthly Jesus. Furthermore, the fact that most of the agrapha can be shown to be so tendentious and so incongruent with the Jesus-tradition as to lie beyond serious consideration or to be derivative from existing materials rather than novel creations underscores the lack of evidence "that the early Church freely, on a large scale, and without inhibitions, produced sayings of the earthly Jesus" (p. 359). Indeed, the contents of the Gospels, while certainly not an exhaustive collection of Jesus' sayings, do stand out as distinctive not only in terms of their relative scarcity in the rest of the New Testament (cf. Gerhardsson) but in the early Christian world of the first and second centuries.

5. If, as these essays have argued, one cannot detach the Jesus-tradition so readily from Jesus and his ministry, what can we say about the claim that the content of Jesus' message ("gospel") stands in tension with the message ("gospel") of the New Testament, in particular with that of the Gospels and Paul? O. Betz and P. Stuhlmacher address the question of Jesus' and Paul's gospel respectively.

5.1 Betz, to whom this volume is dedicated, traces the roots of the term "gospel" to its usage in the Old Testament and Jewish tradition rather than usage in Hellenism in general or in the imperial cult in particular. By examining the "gospel" terminology in the Synoptics, he argues that the verb ("to proclaim the gospel") in Luke and the noun in Matthew ("the gospel of the Kingdom") and Mark ("the gospel") correspond to each Gospel's respective portrait of Jesus' ministry. These portraits in turn reflect the nuances of the prophetic hope or "message of great joy" of Isa. 52:7; 56:1; 61:1-2; 52:13–53:12 (cf. 42:6 and 49:8). Furthermore, he maintains that the terminology of the Gospels originated not from the early Church but from Jesus' own ministry, who used "the verb *biśśar* = εὐαγγελίζεσθαι for his preaching of the dawning kingdom" (cf. Isa. 52:7; 61:1-2). Even the noun *beśorah* = εὐαγγέλιον in Mark 14:9, when viewed against the background of Isa. 53:1, "could also have been used by him" (p. 74, cf. pp. 70-71). Consequently, Mark's "gospel of the suffering Messiah" (cf. Isa. 52:13–53:12), Matthew's "gospel of the Kingdom" with the accompanying "righteousness" (Isa. 52:7; 56:1), and Luke's portrait of the anointed messenger sent to "speak . . . of the realization of the kingdom of God" (Isa. 61:1-2; 52:7) all have their counterpart in deutero-Isaiah's promise. This deutero-Isaianic background offers the connecting link in Jesus' own ministry between "the proclamation of the kingdom . . . and the announcement of the suffering and atoning sacrifice of Jesus' life . . ." (p. 74). Consequently, the Gospels of Matthew, Mark, and Luke simply develop motifs of Jesus' own "gospel of the Kingdom."

5.2 P. Stuhlmacher looks more closely at the "Pauline Gospel." Convinced that Paul's understanding of the Gospel had its origin in his Damascus road experience of the risen Son of God, Stuhlmacher demonstrates how this experience represented both a *conversion* from a Pharisaic, Torah-zealous persecutor of the followers of Jesus Christ to a Torah-critical follower of Christ Jesus and a *call* to proclaim obediently the "good news" about what God had done redemptively in his Son. As Paul himself says, he received his gospel through a revelation (Gal. 1:11-12).

According to Stuhlmacher's discussion of Gal. 1:13-16 and II Cor. 4:4-6, Paul in this Damascus revelation "was illumined by the knowledge that Christ was not a messianic seducer and false prophet but the Lord, by the will of God, and the 'end' (τέλος) of the law as a way of salvation (Rom. 10:4)" (p. 155). "The glory of Christ" seen in the vision was "inseparable from Jesus' death on the cross; to Paul it seemed to be the glorification and heavenly vindication of the Son of God who was . . . condemned to die an accursed death on the cross" (p. 158). Consequently, Paul's gospel concentrated quite naturally on the death and resurrection of Christ as the "decisive events of salvation" with the inevitable consequence of subordinating the traditions about Jesus' life and ministry to the tradition of the passion (p. 158).

This gospel, however, did not stand in material tension with the early Church gospel traditions as he received them during his time in Damascus, Jerusalem, and Antioch. As seen in I Cor. 15:3ff.; 11:23-26; Rom. 3:25-26; 4:25 and 8:3; Phil. 2:6-11, "he adopts them to the extent that they accommodate his knowledge of Christ and aid him in preaching Christ in the way in which God has instructed him and in which he has experienced Christ before the city walls of Damascus" (p. 157). This Jerusalem tradition as seen, for example, in I Cor. 15:3ff. echoes Jesus' own interpretation of his death as heard in the Lord's Supper tradition and behind Mark 10:45. Only at the point of the implications for the law of Christ's atonement do the differences emerge between Paul and his Jewish-Christian "opponents." Even here Stuhlmacher maintains that Paul arrived at his distinctively dialectical view of the law based in part on his own understanding of "his" gospel and in part on the knowledge of the Jesus-tradition (p. 168).

After demonstrating the correspondence between Paul's gospel and that of the early Church, particularly the traditions emanating from Jerusalem, Stuhlmacher looks again at the apparent difference between Paul's conceptual expression of the "gospel" and the narrative expression of the "gospel" in the

New Testament Gospels, a difference he suggests may be traceable to Peter and seen most clearly in Mark. For Mark the "gospel" corresponds to the later missionary use of "gospel" to refer to the story of Jesus (e.g. 1:1; 14:9), which may have arisen from Peter's own "relationship to the earthly Jesus and his role as initial witness to the resurrection," which enabled him to base his missionary message ("gospel") more directly on Jesus and his ministry (p. 171). Acts 15:7 and 10:36-43 would appear to support such a Petrine expression of the gospel.

> Stated positively: in Acts 10:36-43 (+ 15:7) we catch sight of the gospel (of Peter) which was just as much εὐαγγέλιον τοῦ θεοῦ as that of Paul; it has connections with Paul's gospel and nevertheless makes a different use of the narrative of Jesus' history than Paul does . . . [Paul] focused on the cross and resurrection of Jesus. . . . The Church needs both forms of proclamation to preserve, and ever to regain afresh, its identity as Church of Jesus Christ. (p. 172)

6. To what extent, however, do the Gospels as Gospels support such an understanding of the gospel? Three essays look more closely at the Gospels from the standpoint of literary genre, a question that ultimately has to do with the "context of expectation" in which one ought to read them.

6.1 In "The Gospel Genre" this writer finds the key to the genre question in Mark 1:1. The evangelist's opening words designate the story that follows as "the *gospel* of Jesus Messiah, Son of God" whose "beginning," as described in 1:4-15, takes place "just as was written by Isaiah the prophet" (1:2a). By explicitly setting "the beginning of the gospel of Jesus Messiah, Son of God" against the backdrop of Isaiah, Mark connects "the gospel about Jesus Messiah" to the Old Testament Jewish roots for "gospel" (e.g. Isa. 52:7; 61:1). At the same time, in 1:14-15 Jesus' own proclamation is summarized as "the gospel from God" that announces the fulfillment of time and the coming of the God's rule in keeping with Isa. 52:7. Therefore, in Mark the story about the proclaimer of the gospel from God (1:14) becomes itself the proclaimed gospel about Jesus Messiah, Son of God (1:1).

> Mark's achievement . . . lies in selecting, arranging, and bringing together the traditional narrative and sayings units or blocks around the traditional framework of the gospel as seen behind Acts 10:36-43 and putting it in writing. To the extent that Mark first put the "gospel" in *written* form, he created a new *literary* genre, the gospel. (p. 202)

Mark's literary achievement, however, does not lie, as argued for instance by Schmithals and Mack, in Mark creatively developing "the story of Jesus" that now serves as the "gospel" and offers the framework for Matthew's and Luke's Gospel. Though Mark's work may well have spawned the *literary* genre of *Gospel,* the evangelist neither created the *gospel* of Jesus Messiah, Son of God (cf. Schmithals and Mack) nor the use of narrative or story as a way of expressing the gospel. Rather, as has been argued before, the tradition underlying Acts 10:34-43 (pp. 198-202) suggests an existing pattern of early Christian "gospel" preaching in narrative form. This pattern corresponds to the basic structure of Mark's narrative, a pattern that Stuhlmacher and Hengel trace to a "Petrine gospel."

Formally and *materially* the Gospels do stand without adequate parallels in the literary world. As such, they constitute a special literary genre, though limited in number (four canonical and several apocryphal) and time (a generation or so before and after the turn of the first century), and provide a "context of expectation" for understanding and interpreting the gospel of the Gospels.

6.2 L. Abramowski looks more closely at Justin's reference to the Gospels as "Memoirs of the Apostles" and explores the background and function of this designation. First, she notes that the expression occurs twice in the *First Apology* (66.3; 67.3) and thirteen times in the *Dialogue with Trypho* (98-107, an anti-Gnostic exposition of Ps. 22 [LXX 21]). Second, she identifies the designation *apomnemoneumata* as referring to a distinctive literary genre of " 'memories' of a significant person" or "memoirs of a master philosopher" (pp. 327-28, e.g. Xenophon's *Memorabilia* of Socrates), the usage of which not only underscores the written character of the Gospels but elevates them to a certain literary status (p. 327).

But why this designation, since Justin also used the term "Gospel" (εὐαγγέλιον) to refer to a written work (e.g. *Apol.* 66.3, *Dial.* 10.2; 100.1)? Abramowski finds her primary clue in *Dial.* 98-107. She argues:

> If the issue is that Christ must be acknowledged as the one who really suffered . . . then it is natural for Justin, who hints at the idea of Socrates as a forerunner of Jesus, to adopt a heading which applies especially to memories of one who was condemned to death for his convictions. (p. 328)

In other words, Socrates offers an appropriate literary and personal parallel for Justin's debate with the Gnostics. At the same time, "the chief function of the memoirs of the apostles in the exposition of the twenty-first psalm consists in the fact that they document as having *happened* that which is predicted in the psalm . . ." (p. 332). So by accenting the written character of the "apostles' memories of events" as memoirs, Justin underscores the motif of the Old Testament promise (in the psalm) and fulfillment in Christ ("Memoirs of the Apostles") and supplies proofs against the Gnostics of the suffering and death by crucifixion of Jesus as the Christ (p. 332). Accordingly Abramowski concludes that Justin himself coined the phrase "Memoirs of the Apostles" on anti-Gnostic grounds (p. 334). In his apologetic writings, then, he "takes over the title already formed in that discussion" and uses it in "a descriptive section

(*Apol.* 66 and 67)" to accent in this "somewhat neutral application" the "writtenness" of the Gospels (p. 334).

6.3 A. Dihle in "The Gospels and Greek Biography" returns to the broader question of the Gospels as "biography," in particular as related to Greek biography. Beginning with the genre issue, he notes that many kinds of literary and subliterary works can be "biographical" in a nontechnical sense in that they, the Gospels included, may reflect biographical interests without constituting a full-fledged "biography" in the technical sense of a distinct literary genre. Then Dihle shows that Plutarch's *Lives* "possess a highly developed literary form and hence . . . they [and following literary parallels] distinguish themselves from all other extant biographical accounts in Greek literature" (p. 371) as distinctively "biographical" in this more technical sense. Furthermore, Greek biography focuses primarily on "the realization of morally appraised ways of conduct" (p. 369), a concern that leaves its mark in early Christian hagiography rather than in the Gospels.

The Gospels do not exhibit this moral concern or orientation to character found in Greek biography (pp. 378-39). They are, indeed, marked by a particular historical perspective that sets them off from Greek biography.

> Precisely those elements which one could, in the message of the early Church, most quickly describe as biographical acquire a special historical, more precisely, a salvation-historical, meaning. . . . On this view the life of Jesus appears as a decisive segment of a salvation-history which began in the remote past and continues in the future. (p. 380)

> One must therefore claim the canonical Gospels . . . as witnesses for a special kind of historical thought, which separates them from Greek biography, despite the interests of both in biographical details. (p. 381)

In short, the Gospels with their distinctive theological-historical perspective differ from Greek biography with its anthropological-moral perspective, despite the fact that their more broadly defined "biographical" interests and anecdotal styles may appear quite similar.

Dihle's conclusions indicate that the Gospel genre emerged from the content or message of the Gospels rather than from the influence of an existing literary model. Consequently, the Gospel genre has significant implications not only for one's reading of the "biographical" character of the Gospels but for one's reading of their "historical" character as well.

7.1 This historical perspective of the Gospels is accented by M. Hengel's comprehensive essay "Literary, Theological, and Historical Problems in the Gospel of Mark," the first of four essays on the Gospels of Mark, Matthew, Luke, and John. Like Pesch and Stuhlmacher, Hengel rejects as incongruous with the nature of the Gospels the disjunction between kerygma and history.

> In his account, which *retells a past event,* Mark expresses in detail what
> Paul seeks to express in extremely concentrated form, focused on a single
> point, through the aorists of his confessional formulas and the reference
> to the cross of Jesus . . . . (p. 222, italics added)

Mark "preaches by narrating; he writes history and in so doing proclaims"
(p. 224).

Hengel's thesis might well be summarized accordingly: Mark's role as
evangelist was neither that of a mere collector of traditional units nor that of an
ingenious creator of the Jesus story but that of "a theological teacher who
himself must have been a master of the word and an authority in early Christianity," "a disciple of the greatest apostolic authority [Peter] in the earliest
Church" (p. 243). In keeping with Papias's testimony, Hengel traces the source
and narrative style of Mark's "gospel" to Peter, "the authoritative mediator of
the Jesus-tradition in the mission churches from Antioch to Rome" (p. 246).
Indeed, he even suggests that Mark's use of "gospel" (1:1) to describe his
narrative goes back to Peter, in whose preaching the story of Jesus "will have
played a much greater role . . . than with Paul" (p. 247).

Hengel also suggests a more fundamental reason for the use of "gospel"
for the Jesus story by Mark and ultimately Peter. The reason lies in the
relationship of the story of Jesus to the story of Moses in which Judaism gave
expression to "a historical saving event: the exodus from Egypt under the
leadership of Moses and the handing down of the Torah to Israel through Moses"
(p. 248). According to Hengel, the story of Jesus as found in Mark stands in a
typological antitypical relationship with the story of Moses. "In other words,
the story of Jesus as the eschatological saving event, as gospel, stands in a
relationship of tension with the story of Moses as 'saving event' for Israel, or
with the Torah as 'saving' message" (p. 250). This Jesus story as gospel
mediated through Mark and developed by Matthew and Luke

> would then also be influenced to some degree by Petrine tradition,
> making it the third significant corpus in the New Testament alongside
> the Pauline corpus and the Johannine corpus. The designation εὐαγγέ-
> λιον would then perhaps go back to this Petrine understanding of the
> gospel. (p. 251)

7.2 G. Stanton in "Matthew as a Creative Interpreter of the Sayings of
Jesus" examines several Matthean sayings of Jesus drawn from Mark and Q and
"expanded" by Matthew for clues about how the first evangelist handled his
tradition. A consistent pattern emerges in which the evangelist draws on themes
emphasized elsewhere to expand and *"elucidate"* the tradition for his community, without creating *de novo* sayings of Jesus. Stanton concludes that Matthew
is "creative but not innovative" in his handling of the tradition, a trait he traces

also to "other stages in the transmission of gospel traditions" (p. 271). Matthew's conservative use of the tradition reflects his view that

> Jesus is (almost) τὸ εὐαγγέλιον (or ὁ λόγος) τῆς βασιλείας, and for that reason (among others) the words of Jesus are to be treasured carefully; they are elucidated by the evangelist so that they can be appropriated by his community and used in its proclamation (28:20a). (p. 272)

7.3 In "Luke and his 'Gospel'" I. H. Marshall approaches Luke's Gospel from the broader perspective of the author's primary purpose in writing Luke-Acts. After establishing the need to view Luke-Acts as a unity, he questions the adequacy of thinking about Luke as a "Gospel"-writer as such, since "his distinctive contribution to the New Testament is a two-part work that links together the story of Jesus and the story of the experience of salvation and the gathering of the Church as the confirmation of the gospel of salvation" (p. 292). Based on the clues from threads running through both works, Marshall concludes:

> Luke's main purpose was to confirm the kerygma/catechetical instruction heard by people like Theophilus with a fuller account of the basis of the kerygma in the story of Jesus, as handed down by faithful witnesses, and in the continuing story of the way in which through the activity of the witnesses the Church, composed of Jews and Gentiles, came into existence. (p. 291)

The continuity between the ministry of Jesus (Luke) and the witness of the Church (Acts) is apparent in the common teaching about salvation, christology, eschatology, and mission.

In other words, Luke writes what he considered to be a historical account about " 'how we got here' " (p. 291). "It is historical events with which Luke is concerned, but historical events which bring salvation" as seen by the formation of the community of the saved (p. 282). These "historical events are those to which testimony is borne by witnesses" (p. 282). Again Marshall, like Stuhlmacher, Pesch, and Hengel, explicitly rejects the prevailing dichotomy between history and kerygma. "Deed and word, event and witness belong together in Luke as well as in the rest of the New Testament" (p. 282).

7.4 Finally, J. D. G. Dunn argues that one can best understand the fourth Gospel as a finished product "in its own terms, within its own context" (p. 300). In "Let John Be John" Dunn takes his primary clue for determining the appropriate historical context from the *distinctiveness* of John, found above all in John's christology (cf. John 20:31!) but also in the depiction of "the Jews," "the official representatives of Judaism, the religious authorities who determine matters of faith and polity for the people" (p. 302). The latter designation together with its adversarial tone points to late "first-century Judaism," a view supported by John's distinctive christology, which leads to this adversarial relationship between Jesus and "the Jews."

According to Dunn, John's *"Jesus is from above,* and because he is from above, *he brings and embodies the truth,* the true knowledge of God and of heavenly things" (p. 311). Two points are of particular importance: first, John's claim of a *"heavenly origin"* of Jesus the Messiah and, second, "John's claim for *a closeness of continuity* between Father and Son which is more than simply identity of will or function . . ." (p. 312). This christology redefines the meaning of Jesus as Messiah and Son of God (cf. John 20:31).

> In presenting Jesus as the Messiah, the Son of God who is also the Son of Man, the fourth evangelist wants to persuade his readers of *a heavenly origin* for Jesus the Messiah which goes back to the beginning of time, and of *a closeness of continuity* between Father and Son which is more than simply identity of will or function. (p. 313)

Dunn then traces the source of this christology to the Wisdom/Logos that sets the interpretive framework for what follows. Both the "precosmic existence with God" and "its close identity with God" as "God himself, God in his self-manifestation" belong to Wisdom/Logos in Jewish backgrounds.

> The key then to understanding the Johannine distinctives in his presentation of Jesus as Messiah, Son of God, and Son of Man, is to see these titles primarily as *an elaboration of the initial explicit identification of Jesus as the incarnate Wisdom/Logos*—an identification taken over certainly from earlier Christian tradition, but expounded in John's own distinctive fashion. (p. 315)

This elaboration sets John apart from the earlier Christian tradition and explains the adversarial relationship of "the Jews" for his community. On the one hand, John's distinctiveness derives from earlier Christian tradition and is found not so much in his *"content"* as in "the *way* in which he formulates it, [in] the *degree of development* of the Jesus-tradition . . ." designed to express the truth of Jesus in the Johannine community, which was set in the context of late first-, early second-century Judaism (pp. 321-22). Yet John's freedom knows its bounds. He not only preserves Jesus-tradition parallel to that of the Synoptics but he chooses to use the same Gospel format as was laid down by Mark.

On the other hand, John's distinctive christology shows that while John and the Christian community were focusing on Jesus, the rabbis were focusing on the law (p. 315). The characteristics of Wisdom applied to Jesus by John are applied to the law. Furthermore, " 'the Jews' recognized that so to identify Christ with Wisdom/Logos, the self-expression of God, was to make Jesus equal with God (5:18), was to make him . . . *God* (10:33)" (p. 316). This view posed a threat for "the Jews" to the unity of God and raised the fundamental question of monotheism. The adversarial relationship, therefore, reflected in John by "the Jews" toward Jesus comes into clearer focus and supports the late first-century setting within the debates of Judaism for this Gospel.

This reading of John's Gospel as a whole finds congruity with the Jesus-tradition underlying the Synoptics without exploring more closely the relationship of John to that tradition. Even in its bold development of Jesus as Messiah, Son of God, Son of Man this distinctive christology hardly offers a contrary gospel to that of the Synoptics or Paul. But as with the distinctives of the gospel according to Matthew, the gospel according to Mark, the gospel according to Luke, expressed respectively in their Gospels, along with the Pauline gospel expressed in his letters, Dunn asks that we also "let John's Gospel be John's gospel—both *gospel* and *John's* Gospel" (p. 322).

8. These essays reflect the independent work of a group of German, British, and American scholars who for various reasons have argued for a greater confidence in the Gospel tradition as a reliable witness to Jesus and his ministry. They have found a radical historical criticism that leaves the Church either with a minimalist Jesus divorced from the Christ of the Gospels or a creative evangelist whose "Gospel" became the "gospel" of the Church divorced from the person and ministry of Jesus incompatible with the evidence. At the same time, the very nature of the materials requires one to avoid, in Gerhardsson's words, "a narrow-minded biblicism or a general credulity with regard to the assertions of the New Testament documents" (p. 96). One might also add that the nature of the materials requires one to go beyond the Gospels as texts, since the very nature of the Gospel genre forces one into a historical-critical mode not only with reference to the Gospels themselves but to the very content of the gospel itself, whether Petrine, Marcan, Matthean, Lucan, Johannine, or Pauline, anchored as it is in the historical person and work of Jesus of Nazareth.

The Theme:
The Gospel and the Gospels

Peter Stuhlmacher

New Testament research has not yet succeeded in constructing an understanding, one established and universally recognized by scholars in the field, of the status of the sources of the Jesus-tradition and the course of its development, of the final composition of the four canonical Gospels and their interrelationships, or of the history of the word "gospel." The complexity of the material and the ambiguity of the available historical sources provide a certain explanation for the multiplicity of the competing scholarly hypotheses and force one to leave many questions open. Still, even when we grant this, it is meaningful in a new research situation to inquire into the existing lines of convergence in the treatment of our theme. Precisely this was the goal of the Tübingen symposium in September, 1982.

Currently we have facing us a new research situation because the following problems need to be restudied: (1) Following the triumph of the form- and redaction-critical Gospels research since 1920, we must today also take account of the well-founded criticism of some of the tradition-historical premises of form criticism. The resulting new view of the course and credibility of the synoptic tradition is (2) to be linked as much as possible with a parallel picture of the formation of the Johannine tradition. (3) The question of what position Paul assumed toward the gospel tradition must be further explored, and, finally, (4) in the light of the perspectives resulting from a comprehensive view of the synoptic, Johannine, and Pauline tradition, the history of the word "gospel," as well as of its transmission, must be rethought.

At Tübingen the following essay was intended to be introductory and claimed only to stimulate discussion. In the course of the symposium the questions raised were sometimes answered and at other times remained open and controversial. For example, the question of the influence of early Christian prophets upon the gospel tradition requires still further study, and the Johannine

1

problem could only be touched upon and is scheduled to be the subject of its own symposium.

1. Toward a Critique of Form Criticism

The form-critical examination of the Gospels undertaken programmatically by M. Dibelius and R. Bultmann, with its focus on the history of the tradition, proceeded from five fundamental assumptions:

1. As long as the early Christian communities and transmitters of tradition after Jesus' death and the events of Easter believed that the end of the world with the parousia of the Son of Man would be imminent, they had neither the inclination nor the time to develop a fixed literary Jesus-tradition. The fixation and elaboration of this tradition could only occur after this expectation of Christ's imminent return *(Naherwartung)* subsided.[1]

2. The tradition fixed in the four canonical Gospels that have come down to us is fed, roughly speaking, from a double source: on the one hand, from the recollection of the words and deeds of Jesus as it was kept alive in the circle of Jesus' disciples; on the other, from the deposit of preaching and teaching materials newly formed in the post-Easter mission churches. These churches not only adopted and condensed the traditions of the disciples of Jesus but also to a considerable degree enlarged, reinterpreted, and recast them to suit their own concrete missionary interests. The laws of the growth of this tradition are to be understood on the analogy of folk tradition.[2]

3. In the fixation of the small units of which the synoptic tradition is composed the oral and written forms correspond exactly; the formation of the material must not be understood in individual-literary terms but in anonymous-sociological terms.[3]

---

1. M. Dibelius, *From Tradition to Gospel,* ET 1934, 9:

The company of unlettered people which expected the end of the world any day had neither the capacity nor the inclination for the production of books, and we must not predicate a true literary activity in the Christian Church of the first two or three decades.

2. M. Dibelius, op. cit., 7, 8:

[O]ur enquiry is not directed towards the personality of the authors, nor towards their literary dexterity; rather the issue is concerned with laws which operate as formative factors in popular tradition. The ultimate origin of this Form is primitive Christian life itself. To understand the categories of popular writings as they developed in the sphere of unliterary people we must enquire into their life and, in our special case, which deals with religious texts, into the customs of their worship.

Quite similarly R. Bultmann, in *The History of the Synoptic Tradition,* ET 1963, 4ff.

3. M. Dibelius, op. cit., 7:

[T]he popular writings with which we are concerned have no such an individual source. The style which it is our part to observe is "a sociological result." . . . [U]nder the word "style"

4. The geographical and chronological framework which serves to hold together the individual gospel narratives is not based on primary historical recollection. It is not an original component of the tradition but the result of the redactional activity of the evangelists.[4]

5. The present form of the gospel tradition is not only the result of a long process of transmission and redaction but also the product of subsequent historicizing, a process which occurred in the course of time over a wide area. Words (in the style of Rev. 3:20; 16:15) originally uttered by early Christian prophets in the name of the exalted Christ were deemed equal in the churches to words of the earthly Jesus which had come down by tradition, and were finally incorporated in the gospel tradition without being especially marked.[5]

For form criticism these assumptions yielded the thesis—one that has meanwhile been applied in a large number of exegetical variations—that in the Gospels we have what are essentially post-Easter compilations in which the material of the tradition which goes back to the time of Jesus must first be expressly shown to be such by historical analysis. E. Käsemann, in his well-known essay on "The Problem of the Historical Jesus," could therefore state:

> With the work of the Form-Critics as a basis, our questioning has sharpened and widened until the obligation now laid upon us is to investigate and make credible not the possible inauthenticity of the individual unit of material but, on the contrary, its genuineness. The issue today is not whether criticism is right but where it is to stop.[6]

---

must be understood the whole way of speaking which, at least in the case of popular writing, is determinative of its category, for the lowly people who use this style write according to laws which are independent of the individual personality.

4. K. L. Schmidt, *Der Rahmen der Geschichte Jesu,* 1964, v:

My research in specific units will show that the question concerning the value of the topography and chronology in the gospels is, in general, to be answered in the negative. . . . The earliest Jesus-tradition is pericope-tradition, hence the transmission of individual scenes and sayings which for the most part were handed down in the Church without established chronological and topographical markings. Much that looks chronological and topographical is but the framework which was added to the individual units.

5. R. Bultmann, op. cit., 127f.:

We can see with complete clarity what the process of reformulation of such dominical sayings was like in sayings like Rev. 16:15 . . . or like Rev. 3:20. . . . They could very easily have gained currency at first as utterances of the Spirit in the Church. Sometimes the ascended Christ would assuredly have spoken in them—as in Rev. 16:15—and it would only be gradually that such sayings would come to be regarded as prophecies by the Jesus of history. The Church drew no distinction between such utterances by Christian prophets and the sayings of Jesus in the tradition, for the reason that even the dominical sayings in the tradition were not the pronouncements of a past authority but sayings of the risen Lord, who is always a contemporary for the Church.

6. Ernst Käsemann, *Essays on New Testament Themes,* ET 1964, 15-47; the quotation is from p. 34.

In the same article Käsemann expresses the view that till now has been shared by many exegetes, namely that "all passages in which any kind of Messianic title occurs [are] kerygma shaped by the community."[7] At the same time he asserts the utter impossibility of reconstructing a life of Jesus from the Gospels. But conversely, neither is he "prepared to concede that, in the face of these facts, defeatism and scepticism must have the last word and lead us on to a complete disengagement of interest from the earthly Jesus."[8] Rather, with regard to the Gospels, it is to be observed that, "out of the obscurity of the life story of Jesus, certain characteristic traits in his preaching stand out in relatively sharp relief."[9] This determination is decisive for Käsemann because for him "[t]he Gospel is tied to him who, both before and after Easter, revealed himself to his own as the Lord, by setting them before the God who is near to them and thus translating them into the freedom and responsibility of faith."[10]

This form-critical position, radical as it is both in its analysis of detail and in its overall perspective, has for some considerable time now been opposed by another which, while it affirms the form-critical analysis of the gospel tradition, to be sure, conducts it on the basis of quite different historical presuppositions from those of Dibelius, Bultmann, and their disciples. This position was first articulated by H. Riesenfeld[11] and B. Gerhardsson[12] and has been further elaborated from diverse starting points but with the same basic thrust by Gerhardsson[13] himself and R. Riesner,[14] on the one hand, and by H. Schür-mann,[15] E. Earle Ellis,[16] G. Stanton,[17] and others, on the other.

Riesenfeld's and Gerhardsson's main focus is on the proclamation and teaching of the earthly Jesus. Both proceed from the assumption that Jesus did not just occasionally and spontaneously utter his parables and preaching *logia* but that, in the same way as a Jewish teacher of the law, he had his disciples

7. Ibid., 43.
8. Ibid., 45f.
9. Ibid., 46.
10. Ibid. For the same judgment, cf. G. Bornkamm, *Jesus of Nazareth,* ET 1960, 24ff.
11. H. Riesenfeld, *The Gospel Tradition and its Beginnings: A Study in the Limits of "Formgeschichte,"* 1954.
12. B. Gerhardsson, *Memory and Manuscript: Oral Tradition and Written Transmission in Rabbinic Judaism and Early Christianity,* 1961.
13. B. Gerhardsson, *The Origins of the Gospel Traditions,* ET 1979. See also Gerhardsson's contribution to the present volume, "The Path of the Gospel Tradition."
14. R. Riesner, *Jesus als Lehrer,* 1981.
15. H. Schürmann, "Die vorösterlichen Anfänge der Logientradition. Versuch eines form-geschichtlichen Zugangs zum Leben Jesu," in *Traditionsgeschichtliche Untersuchungen zu den synoptischen Evangelien,* 1967, 39-65. Cf. also Schürmann's study ". . . und Lehrer," in his *Orientierungen am Neuen Testament, Exegetische Aufsätze,* 1978, 116-56, esp. 117ff., 126ff.
16. E. E. Ellis, "New Directions in Form Criticism," in his *Prophecy and Hermeneutic in Early Christianity,* 1978, 237-53.
17. G. N. Stanton, "Form Criticism Revisited," in *What About the New Testament? Essays in Honour of C. Evans,* ed. M. D. Hooker and C. Hickling, 1975, 13-27.

learn them by heart and thus literally imprinted them on their minds. For both of these Swedish scholars this view yields a chain of tradition and of transmitters of tradition reaching from Jesus through his disciples to the post-Easter Church in analogy to the rabbinic tradition. To be sure, variants of translation and interpretation are to be expected and to be exegetically established in this process of transmission; also, supplementary material added to the tradition results from within the faith perspective of the post-Easter Church which acknowledged Jesus as Messiah and Son of God; but taking the material as a whole we must reckon with the fact that it "has been preserved with respect and care."[18]

This view of the formation of the synoptic tradition has been widely rejected on the ground that Jesus clearly distinguished himself and his circle of disciples from the rabbinate and the way rabbis ran their schools. R. Riesner, responding to this wholesale rejection, has in *Jesus als Lehrer* given a fresh account of Jewish education and of the teaching activity of Jesus. Following Martin Hengel's study of Jesus as a messianic teacher of wisdom and the beginnings of christology,[19] Riesner stresses that Jesus was active as messianic wisdom teacher. According to him, the decisive motive for the compilation and preservation of the Jesus-tradition lies in the teaching activity of Jesus himself and in the interest his person and preaching evoked among his followers and sympathizers. What we have in the Jesus-tradition is "not the wild growth of a popular tradition but a cultivated tradition of teaching."[20]

H. Schürmann and E. E. Ellis by no means question whether Jesus acted as preacher and teacher. Their main interest, however, lies in the development of the form-critical analysis of the Gospels itself. Both exegetes proceed from the classic form-critical premise that for every text that has been formed and consciously handed down there must also have been a circle of traditioners guided by specific goals and interests (and vice versa). However, instead of looking for the circle of these traditioners (by means of critical *Formgeschichte*) above all in the (late) postresurrection Church or even in part in the Hellenistic Church, Schürmann and Ellis reckon with the fact that the preresurrection circle of Jesus' disciples must already have been concerned with gathering up and transmitting the Jesus tradition, since during his lifetime Jesus had already given the disciples a share of the proclamation of the kingdom of God (cf. the synoptic tradition of the sending out of the disciples, Matt. 10:1-16). Since that preresurrection circle of disciples was partly identical with the circle of apostles and associates of Jesus which, according to Acts 1:12-26, constituted

---

18. Gerhardsson, *Origins* (n. 13), 80.
19. "Jesus als messianischer Lehrer der Weisheit und die Anfänge der Christologie," in *Sagesse et religion (Colloque de Strasbourg, Octobre, 1976), 1979*, 148-88.
20. R. Riesner, op. cit. (n. 14), 502.

the early Church, there again emerges a chain of tradition which appears to make further inquiry into the Jesus-tradition in the Synoptics quite promising. This inquiry is the more likely to yield results the earlier the written fixation of the tradition can be put. Ellis assumes that established (written) fixations already occurred in the time of Jesus.[21]

Added to these tradition-historical reflections comes the critical observation that the process, postulated by radical form-criticism, of the subsequent historicizing of "countless 'I' sayings of the Christ who revealed himself through the mouth of prophets"[22] is by no means verifiable with an adequate degree of historical certainty. F. Neugebauer and D. Hill have pointed out that postresurrection words of prophecy in the New Testament tradition are for the most part expressly identified as words of the ascended Christ (cf. e.g. Matt. 28:17ff.; II Cor. 12:9; Rev. 3:20; 16:15, etc.).[23] J. D. G. Dunn has expressed his agreement with this assertion. Without fundamentally denying the possibility that *logia* of Jesus were formed by prophets, he has focused our attention also on the confrontations which early Christian churches had with false prophets. In the context of these confrontations it is hard to think, says Dunn, that prophetic sayings were incorporated uncontrolled into the body of the tradition that came down from the time of Jesus, and Käsemann's hypothesis must "be dismissed as a considerable oversimplification and overstatement."[24]

In the face of these weighty argumentations the following remarks need to be made concerning the five basic assumptions of classic form criticism:

On assumption 1: Since the discovery of the Qumran texts the view that "near-expectation" and the formation of a literary tradition are mutually exclusive is obsolete. The Essenes, precisely on the basis of "near-expectation," were intensely active in literary production and in the cultivation of tradition. That which can be historically established for the Qumran texts must also be considered possible for the circle of Jesus' followers and the early Church. Hence the fixation and transmission of the Jesus-tradition can be viewed positively, from a tradition-historical perspective, as existing from the beginning!

On assumption 2: Jesus did not maintain a real center of instruction, nor

21. Ellis, in his essay "New Directions in Form Criticism" (see n. 16), pleads, for example, for the position that Luke 10:25-37 "may have been formulated and transmitted within the pre-resurrection circle of disciples as a teaching piece contrasting Jesus' ethic to that of other Jewish groups in terms of his radically new interpretation of Scripture: 'you have heard it said . . . but I say' " (*Prophecy and Hermeneutic,* 250).

22. E. Käsemann, "Is the Gospel Objective?" in his *Essays on New Testament Themes,* ET 1964, 60.

23. Cf. F. Neugebauer, "Geistsprüche und Jesuslogien," *ZNW* 53, 1962, 218-28; and D. Hill, "On the Evidence for the Creative Role of Christian Prophets," *NTS* 20, 1973-74, 262-74.

24. J. D. G. Dunn, "Prophetic 'I'-sayings and the Jesus-Tradition: The Importance of Testing Prophetic Utterances within Early Christianity," *NTS* 24, 1977-78 (175-98), 197.

was he, like a Jewish rabbi, primarily busy with the exposition of the Torah. He did, however, teach and work as a "messianic wisdom teacher" (M. Hengel). Already before his resurrection he sent out his disciples to preach (for a time) and in the last phase of his ministry initiated them into the meaning of his death. Since the leadership circle of the primitive Church in Jerusalem derived from the circle of Jesus' disciples and his family, one must, with regard to the gospel tradition, reckon with a continuum which was not a fortuitous coincidence but deliberately cultivated, a continuum which leads from the time of Jesus to the post-Easter Church. Insofar as additions, new interpretations, and redactional activity can be shown to be present in the gospel tradition, they are to be judged on the analogy of the way Old Testament and early Jewish prophecy, the Essenes, and the rabbinate related to tradition; the example of the Hellenistic schools must also be injected into this evaluation. On balance, a much larger part of the gospel tradition could represent historically trustworthy material than has been originally assumed by classic form criticism.

On assumption 3: The parallelism between the oral and the written reproduction of the Jesus-tradition, a parallelism especially called into question by E. Güttgemanns's *Candid Questions concerning Gospel Form Criticism* (1979), can be maintained on the basis of the fundamental data of Jewish (and Greek) school practices. A purely sociological approach to forms and style is, however, questionable. We owe the fixation and transmission of the material of the synoptic tradition to primitive Christian teachers; but for them, coming as they did from the tradition of the Old Testament, a freer (rhetorical and literary) association with the forms was possible.[25]

On assumption 4: A comparison of the synoptic (and Johannine) rendering of the Gospel with compilations of tradition such as the so-called *logia*-source (Q), The Gospel of Thomas, and the "Sayings of the Fathers" (Pirke Aboth) leads one to give new consideration to the astonishing mass of history-reporting narrative units and historical framework—which stands out by comparison with these collections of sayings—of the Jesus-history in the Gospels (so G. N. Stanton[26]). The historical interest of the Gospels in the words, actions, and fate of Jesus, observed by J. Roloff in another connection,[27] prohibits us, with reference to the

---

25. Cf. G. Von Rad, *Old Testament Theology* II, 33-49 (esp. 48f.).

26. In his essay on form criticism (see n. 17) Stanton writes (15):

When we look at roughly comparable rabbinic traditions such as Pirqe Aboth or at the Gospel of Thomas, we are immediately struck by the amount of narrative material about Jesus which is found in the traditions on which Mark drew and which the Marcan framework extends rather than contrasts, as seems to have happened in some circles in the early church. Indeed, on the grounds of the criterion of dissimilarity which is so beloved of many form critics, the framework of Mark emerges with strong claims to historicity!

27. Cf. J. Roloff, *Das Kerygma und der irdische Jesus. Historische Motive in den Jesus-Erzählungen der Evangelien,* 1970. The aim of Roloff's investigation is "to examine to what extent

gospel tradition, from playing the historic and kerygmatic interests against each other; from an early stage, the history of the words, deeds, and fate of Jesus is narrated in the Jesus-tradition as redemptive and revelational, a sequence of events which forms the foundation for the present and future of the traditioners.

On assumption 5: As the Johannine sayings concerning the Paraclete (esp. John 14:25f. and 16:12f.) make particularly plain, and Luke 24:25ff. and II Cor. 4:5f. also prove, it was not until the Easter events and the reception of the Spirit that the Christian Church saw itself placed in a position where it could truly understand and proclaim Jesus as Messiah and Son of God. The reception of the Spirit and the faith-understanding created by it therefore constitute a most essential impulse for the compilation, completion, and transmission of the Jesus-tradition! In the face of reports such as Matt. 23:34ff.; Acts 11:27; 13:1; I Cor. 12:10, 28; Rom. 12:6, etc., the activity of early Christian prophets cannot be denied. We lack historical evidence, however, for the position that a large part of the synoptic Jesus-*logia* go back to originally post-Easter words of prophecy which were later identified consciously or unconsciously with the words of the earthly Jesus. As much as in the power of the Spirit the preresurrection tradition was freshly interpreted and shaped, so little does this process of redaction justify the hypothesis of creative additions to the words of Jesus (*Gemeindebildunden*) on a grand scale by Christian prophets.

With regard to these overall findings one may summarize the situation in the words of W. G. Kümmel to the effect that the synoptic tradition as a whole deserves "critical sympathy" rather than fundamental historical distrust.[28] Until the destruction of Jerusalem the tradition was subject to the constant scrutiny of eyewitnesses and the control of the tradition-consciousness of the churches, a consciousness sensitized against false prophecy. Hence in distinguishing between the Jesus-tradition and the Church-tradition one must be at pains not simply and flatly to assume the possibility and reality of secondary tradition and

---

a historicizing mode of viewing the history of Jesus has shaped the Jesus-tradition of the Gospels from the start and has noticeably influenced the pre-literary and literary process of transmission that can be surveyed by us" (47).

28. W. G. Kümmel, "Jesu Antwort an Johannes den Täufer. Ein Beispiel zum Methodenproblem in der Jesusforschung," in his *Heilsgeschehen und Geschichte* II, 1978 (177-200), 187f., states that

> until the opposite has been proven we have the right and duty to trust the intent of the author of the sources and when historical criticism commands us to do the opposite we must be able to make intelligible the rise of sources which are not historically useful in their alleged sense. Recently H. I. Marrou [in *Über die historische Erkenntnis*, 1973] has made exceptionally clear that the appropriate attitude of the historian toward his sources is not methodical distrust but sympathy. . . .

> Accordingly, when it seems warranted from the perspective of historical science to approach the synoptic Jesus-tradition with *critical sympathy*, the decisive question remains nevertheless whether we have adequate *criteria* by which to penetrate the oldest layer of the tradition.

redaction but to explain them as exactly as possible in historical terms of where and how. Only when this attempt is made is the distinction between the original Jesus-material and the creation of the Church exegetically convincing.

The studies and commentaries on the synoptic tradition submitted on the basis of these premises by R. Guelich,[29] M. Hengel,[30] I. H. Marshall,[31] R. Pesch,[32] A. Polag,[33] H. Schürmann,[34] G. N. Stanton,[35] and others justify the hope that we are making progress toward a more satisfying answer, with regard to both tradition history and biblical theology, to the question of the origin and editorial purpose of the Synoptics than was possible on the basis of radical form-critical analysis of tradition.

In the German research situation one cannot express this hope without entering a discussion on the completely contrary critique of form criticism and view of the synoptic problem which W. Schmithals has developed in his commentary on Mark,[36] his essay "Kritik der Formkritik,"[37] and in his article on the synoptic Gospels in the *Theologische Realenzyklopädie*.[38] By his work Schmithals wishes to eliminate a disturbing inconsistency in Bultmann's starting point in Gospels research and at the same time to seal off the path by which the Christian kerygma is based on the so-called historical Jesus, a path he considers theologically disastrous.

In his *Theology of the New Testament* Bultmann had posited that, according to the theological standards to be derived from Paul and John, the Christian faith needed no support in the person and message of the earthly Jesus beyond the mere fact of his coming and crucifixion. Jesus' message was for Bultmann therefore no more than a (decisive) presupposition for the theology of the New Testament, not an essential part of it.[39] Earlier, however, in his *History of the Synoptic Tradition*, Bultmann had concluded that in the synoptic tradition a

29. R. Guelich, *The Sermon on the Mount*, 1982.

30. M. Hengel, "History Writing in Antiquity and in Earliest Christianity," in his *Acts and the History of Earliest Christianity*, ET 1979, 1-68, esp. 40-49.

31. I. H. Marshall, *The Gospel of Luke*, 1978; idem, *Last Supper and Lord's Supper*, 1980.

32. R. Pesch, *Das Markusevangelium* I and II, [3]1980; idem, *Das Evangelium der Urgemeinde*, 1979; idem, *Das Abendmahl und Jesu Todesverständnis*, 1978.

33. A. Polag, *Die Christologie der Logienquelle*, 1977; idem, *Fragmenta Q*, 1979.

34. From Schürmann's voluminous literary production I will only mention, as representative, his large commentary on Luke: *Das Lukasevangelium* I, 1969.

35. G. N. Stanton, "The Origin and Purpose of Matthew's Gospel: Matthean Scholarship since 1945," *ANRW* II, 25/2, 1983.

36. W. Schmithals, *Das Evangelium nach Markus* I and II, 1979.

37. *ZTK* 77, 1980, 149-85 (hereafter "Kritik").

38. *TRE* X, 570-626, esp. 603ff.

39. *Theology of the New Testament* I, ET 1951, 3:

The message of Jesus is a presupposition for the theology of the New Testament rather than a part of that theology itself. For New Testament theology consists in the unfolding of those ideas by means of which Christian faith makes sure of its own object, basis, and consequences.

certain amount of authentic Jesus-tradition had been handed down! Besides, he had not scrupled to write a most interesting book on Jesus[40] in which he transcended in part the critical standards of authenticity of his *History of the Synoptic Tradition.* From within this altogether ambivalent state of affairs a number of Bultmann's disciples—E. Käsemann,[41] E. Fuchs,[42] G. Bornkamm,[43] and others—have nevertheless—over Bultmann's objections![44]— with admirable consistency renewed the inquiry into the historical Jesus.

In order to be able to advance without fear of exegetical contradiction his theological thesis of the independence of the Christ-kerygma from the figure and history of the historical Jesus, Schmithals bade farewell to the methodological starting point of his teacher and to the theologically ambiguous analysis of the Synoptics practiced in the school of Bultmann. Instead of dissecting, in the manner of form criticism, the synoptic tradition further into individual pericopes, and then analyzing their history in terms of form-historical categories, Schmithals again argued for a primarily literary(-critical) approach to the large units of the synoptic tradition and of the Gospels as a whole. In his opinion, until the destruction of Jerusalem there was generally no fixed oral or written Jesus-tradition: the early Christian mission initially worked rather with the Old Testament and a concise catechism, not with Jesus-traditions.

Within the reach of the Synoptics only the early *logia*-tradition (= Q^1), which Schmithals (following S. Schulz[45]) traced back to a circle of adherents of Jesus residing in Galilee or Syria, had pre- and early postresurrection roots. "Q^1," according to Schmithals, constitutes a "pre-churchly" collection of "non-kerygmatic and non-Christological Jesus-tradition,"[46] in which the kerygma of Jesus' passion and resurrection is missing. That circle of adherents viewed Jesus as an eschatological prophet who died a martyr's death (cf. Luke 13:34 par.); by this time it expected the Son of Man, announced by Jesus (but not identical with its dead prophet), to come as the eschatological judge of the world.

In his Gospel Mark occasionally mentions this collection in order to demonstrate the identity of the messiah Jesus with the earthly teacher and prophet Jesus to whom this circle adhered.[47] The main body of the Gospel of Mark is formed by the "basic document" *(Grundschrift),* narrated with literary

---

40. R. Bultmann, *Jesus,* ET 1964.

41. Cf. E. Käsemann's programmatic article on "The Problem of the Historical Jesus" mentioned in n. 6.

42. Cf. E. Fuchs, *Studies of the Historical Jesus,* ET 1964.

43. Cf. G. Bornkamm, *Jesus of Nazareth* (see n. 10).

44. Cf. Bultmann's "The Primitive Christian Kerygma and the Historical Jesus," in *The Historical Jesus and the Kerygmatic Christ,* ed. C. E. Braaten and R. A. Harrisville, 1964, 15-42.

45. S. Schulz, *Q—Die Spruchquelle der Evangelisten,* 1972.

46. *Kritik,* 184.

47. *Evangelium nach Markus* I, 56.

completeness and brilliance, which was composed shortly after AD 70 (probably in Antioch) by the biblical John Mark (or an anonymous author). From his hand, as the first, stem the miracle stories, the "framed" *logia* of the Lord, the parables of Jesus, and the passion narrative! This basic document serving as a "handbook for mission among the God-fearers"[48] and written by John Mark was intended "to protect the confession(s) of the early Church from the misunderstanding that the issue in the Christ-event was an occurrence comparable to the oriental myths of dying and rising gods." The handbook "instead unmistakably allows the message of the gospel to be a witness to a unique historical action of redemption by God, that is, a witness to the eschatological once-for-all act of divine redemption."[49] After the disorders of the Jewish War another writer, unknown to us by name, met the traditioners of Q^1 and, to win them for faith in Christ, joined some material from Q^1 together with the "basic document" of John Mark, under the theme of the messianic-secret theory, to form what we today know as the Gospel of Mark.

The result of this analysis of tradition, taken as a whole, is as follows: The tradition which the evangelist worked into the framework of his "basic document" emerges, tradition-historically, "as a poetic product of the kerygma"; on the other hand, "the unkerygmatic and unchristological Jesus-tradition of the early *logia* . . ." is seen to be "pre-churchly. There never was such a thing as a *churchly* tradition of the so-called historical Jesus. Therefore, Bultmann—like Karl Barth—with his rejection of the search for the historical Jesus *as opposed to* his *History of the Synoptic Tradition,* turns out in the end to be historically and theologically correct."[50]

However theologically consistent Schmithals's general design may be, it does not allow itself, to any remotely satisfying degree, to be inserted into the dates available to us of the history of early Christianity. We have no historical information whatever of a Galilean or Syrian group of Jesus-adherents without a christology or a kerygma of passion and resurrection. The poetic "basic document" allegedly composed by John Mark around the year AD 70 is an entity which cannot be brought into agreement with the history of the origin and transmission of the Jesus-tradition that was traced by Gerhardsson, Riesner, Schürmann, and others and confirmed from the perspective of the history of religion. Also, Schmithals's theologically determined understandings of Paul's message and of the fourth Gospel is highly questionable: tradition-historically, Paul is demonstrably "a messenger of Jesus" (so A. Schlatter; see below), and the fourth Gospel, by choosing the grand category of "Gospel," by its precise

48. Ibid., I, 46.
49. Ibid., I, 45 (italicized in the original).
50. *Kritik,* 184f. (italicized in the original).

topography and Paraclete-sayings, demonstrates that it does not aim to unfold a kerygma independent of the history of Jesus (see below). Although the critique of form criticism offered by Schmithals is interesting in several details, it offers no solution to the problem of tradition as a whole that suggests that we deviate from the course of inquiry sketched above.

2. The Problem of the Johannine Tradition

One cannot treat the problems of the synoptic tradition without at the same time keeping in view the fourth Gospel and the letters of John. As always, we are at least as far removed from a solution to the Johannine riddle as we are from a generally acknowledged answer to the synoptic problem. Hence, the following series of propositions is only designed to suggest certain perspectives to be kept in mind in the present research context.

1. The uniqueness and uniformity of the Johannine idiom, the striking arrangement of the material, and the—in some cases—conspicuous glosses in the fourth Gospel (cf. e.g. 13:12-27, 34ff.; 19:35; ch. 21 passim) indicate that the Johannine writings arose in a Johannine school that is comparable to other schools in antiquity.[51]

2. Historically, the Johannine school maintained two defensive fronts: one against the synagogue, which thrust the members of the circle of John from its ranks (cf. John 9:22, 34; 12:42; 16:2), and the other against docetists from their own ranks (cf. 1:14; 6:52ff.; 19:34f. with I John 4:1-3; 5:5-8). Besides, in the letters of John a certain tension between Johannine itinerant missionaries and churches led by bishops (?) shows up. It is evident from John 1:35ff. and 3:22-24 + 4:1-3 that the disciples of Jesus deemed most authoritative in John's writings were those who came out of the circle of John the Baptist's adherents. Hence the roots of the Johannine school reach back to a Palestinian-Jewish and synagogal milieu.

3. In its particular situation the Johannine school formed a particular concept of tradition. In the fourth Gospel one grasps it especially in the figure of the Beloved Disciple, in the Paraclete-sayings, and in the amazing (in the framework of the New Testament) multiple references to the inscripturation of the Johannine tradition (John 20:30f.; 21:24f.). In the letters of John one may point, in this connection, especially to the teaching imparted "from the beginning" (I John 2:7, 24; 3:11) and to the significance of the confession of Christ (4:2f.; 5:5-10).

4. According to John 13:23-26; 19:26f., (34f.); 20:3-10, and 21:7, 20-24,

51. Cf. R. A. Culpepper, *The Johannine School,* 1975.

the Beloved Disciple is the guarantor and crown witness, superior in many ways even to Peter, of the Johannine tradition. The tradition he vouched for represented the unique interpretation of God given by Jesus himself: the interpretation of God through the only begotten Son of God is revealed to the Johannine circle in the testimony of the disciple who was especially beloved by Jesus (cf. John 1:18 and 3:16 with 13:23; 19:26f., 34f.). The fourth Gospel does not inform us who that Beloved Disciple was. In light of John 21:2 it is historically more likely in my opinion that the figure of the Beloved Disciple was historically identified by the Johannine circle itself, and that his testimony was so highly regarded precisely for that reason, than that we are dealing here with a symbolic guarantor-figure who was subsequently injected into the framework of tradition. The identification of the Beloved Disciple with the John who was one of the sons of Zebedee, an identification which has become customary in the Church, has until now not been satisfactorily verified from the sources.

5. The Johannine Paraclete-sayings (John 14:16, 26; 15:26; 16:7; I John 2:1) are emphatically related (John 14:25f. and 16:12f.) to the question of what is to be taught and handed down: the Paraclete set the Johannine school on the way of the authentic memory of Jesus and so qualifies it to receive the perfect teaching which initiates faith and eternal life (20:31). There is a striking parallelism between Jesus, the Paraclete, and the Beloved Disciple (cf. 14:16f.; 16:12f. with 19:34f.; 21:24f.) that points to the fact that the teaching and tradition guaranteed by the Beloved Disciple were of the greatest importance for the Johannine school.[52] The historical analogy which presents itself is that of the Teacher of Righteousness and the Essenes' understanding of tradition.[53]

6. In the Johannine tradition, the preresurrection time of Jesus and the time of the Church that is called to give witness after Easter are linked together by means of the figure of the Beloved Disciple and the idea of the Paraclete. The witness of Jesus, the full understanding of the word and person of Jesus generated in the Church by the Spirit-Paraclete, and the Church's Spirit-borne witness to the world appear as a comprehensive unity. The Johannine tradition is inherently more than the witness concerning the way and word of the earthly Jesus; it is the written attestation of the earthly Jesus as the Logos and Son of God who is ever present to the Church.

7. Accordingly, the real interest of the Johannine school's tradition, in both the fourth Gospel and the letters of John, lies in the focal pronouncements of its christology: Jesus' preexistence and true divine Sonship (John 1:1-18); his saving self-communication in word and sacrament (6:52-58, 66-69); his being

---

52. Cf. ibid., 267f.
53. Cf. J. Roloff, "Der Johanneische 'Lieblingsjünger' und der Lehrer der Gerechtigkeit," *NTS* 15, 1968-69, 129-51.

the bread of life (6:35, 41, 48), the good Shepherd (10:11, 14), the resurrection and the life (11:25), and the way, the truth, and the life (14:6); his mission-crowning redemptive death (19:30, 34f.); his resurrection (ch. 20); and his entry before God as Paraclete (I John 2:1). Over against these themes the communication and preservation of historical details from Jesus' life and the transmission of authentic Jesus-*logia* (including parables!) recede in John. To be sure, that such units (and *logia*) also occur in the Johannine tradition (cf. esp. John 13:3ff.; 18:15ff., and the astonishingly exact place indications in John) must not be flatly denied.[54]

8. The origin of the Beloved Disciple in the circle of Jesus' disciples, a circumstance which this Gospel itself stresses, and the literary character of John's Gospel (esp. in the succession of scenes beginning with 6:5ff.; feeding of the five thousand + 6:16ff.; walking on the water + 6:66ff.; Peter's confession—cf. Mark 6:35ff., 45ff.; 8:27ff.) suggest the assumption that the Johannine school possessed knowledge of parts of the synoptic tradition. This is true especially for the tradition of Mark, but also for Lucan traditions concerning the person and passion of Jesus.[55] The Johannine school, however, assumed the freedom to add new material to this tradition (cf. e.g. 2:1-11; 5:1-9; 9:1-7), to recast it (cf. e.g. 2:14-17; 4:46-54), to comment on it in special revelational discourses, and to place parts of it in totally new contexts (cf. only the placing at the beginning of the cleansing of the temple in 2:14ff., and the special Johannine passion chronology).

9. In addition to these findings one is struck in John by a number of pronouncements which can be taken as corrections and conscious instances of new interpretation of the synoptic picture of Jesus: In the place of the tradition (which Luke 2:19 traces back to Mary[56]) of the virgin birth of Jesus in Bethlehem, the fourth Gospel offers only the prologue, which sets forth the preexistence of Jesus, and the unusually strong statement of 6:42. In the place of the synoptic story of the Transfiguration (Mark 9:2ff. par.), John places the entire course of Jesus up to and including his crucifixion under the aspect of glorification (cf. esp. 12:23, 28 and 17:1ff., 10). While John's Gospel merely hints at Jesus' agony in the garden of Gethsemane, it emphasizes Christ's determination consciously to enter upon his passion (12:27ff.). In John, as distinct from the Synoptics, Jesus emphatically addresses his disciples as his "friends" (cf. 15:15). In place of the synoptic crossbearing scene (Mark 15:21

---

54. A recent and extremely instructive study of John's topography is that of B. Schwank, "Ortskenntnisse im Vierten Evangelium?" in *EuA* 57, 1981, 427-42.

55. Cf. C. K. Barrett, *The Gospel According to St. John*, 1978, 42-54.

56. The verb συντηρέω in Luke 2:19 means "to keep in the memory" and may, as in *Test. Lev.* 6:2 and in Josephus, *BJ* 2.142, be colored by tradition-historical usage. Cf. H. Riesenfeld, *TDNT* VIII, 151.

par.) we find in John the remark that "they took Jesus, and he went out bearing his own cross, to the place called the place of a skull" (19:17). If one adds to this material the new Johannine dating of the death of Jesus on the day of preparation for the Passover festival together with the Spirit-buttressed Johannine understanding of the tradition and remembers that the prologue (1:1-18) literally transcends the infancy narratives of Matthew and Luke with respect to christology, one may perhaps posit the thesis that over against the Synoptics John's Gospel aims to offer the true μαρτυρία or ἀκοὴ ἀπ' ἀρχῆς (cf. John 21:24; I John 1:1). The view of the ancient Church that the fourth Gospel seeks not to supersede but to supplement and complete the Synoptics[57] has still today something in its favor!

10. What we have before us in the fourth Gospel and the Johannine school is a cultivated continuum of tradition. It presupposes parts of the synoptic tradition and, from within the pneumatic consciousness of a special primitive Christian schooling, carries it forward in order to elevate the historic tradition concerning Jesus into the dimension of completed revelation. The process is reminiscent of the sovereign updating of the biblical tradition in the Book of Jubilees or the Temple Scroll of Qumran. This new formation of a tradition becomes linguistically apprehensible in the esoteric idiom and the textual and stylistic forms favored by the Johannine circle.

11. For our knowledge and understanding of the earthly Jesus we are to a special degree dependent on the tradition embodied in the synoptic Gospels. The Johannine tradition deepens our christological understanding of Jesus, of his work and purpose, and carries it beyond the level of the knowledge of merely historical facts. The Johannine tradition points back toward the synoptic, and the latter points forward to the Johannine.

12. The Johannine tradition shows the extent of the possibilities of the so-called primitive Christian *Gemeindebildungen* in the sphere of the transmission of Jesus-tradition, and indicates where their criteria lie and what purpose they are designed to serve. They stem from a specific tradition-complex, favor certain forms of expression and style, and present themselves as further interpretations of already existing tradition. They owe their existence to proven apostolic-prophetic traditioners, and were understood and received in the context of a specific school or congregation as words of the Spirit who brought Jesus back to their remembrance. These structural peculiarities need to be observed when one asserts, or seeks to demonstrate, the presence of these "church-formations."

---

57. This is already the case in the Muratorian Canon, ll. 9ff. In this connection cf. H. F. von Campenhausen, *The Formation of the Christian Bible*, ET 1972, 248, n. 213.

3. Paul and the Gospel Tradition

This is not the place to report at length on Paul's gospel as a whole (see my essay, "The Pauline Gospel," in the present volume). At the beginning of our reflections on the theme of "the Gospel and the Gospels," however, it is already helpful to involve the letters of Paul. It has always struck students of the New Testament that in his letters Paul only rarely makes use of the gospel tradition. Conclusions drawn from this have been that the apostle chose to ignore the Jesus-tradition,[58] that in his lifetime the tradition concerning Jesus still bore, so to speak, an apocryphal character,[59] or that the gospel tradition and the Pauline legacy represented two fundamentally different primitive Christian streams of tradition.[60] With regard to these hypotheses we must call attention to a number of historical contexts and phenomena which must be recognized if one is not to draw false conclusions from Paul about the value and position of the gospel tradition.

1. It is historically quite unlikely that Paul would have had no knowledge of the Jesus-tradition that was "at home" in Jerusalem, Antioch, or Damascus! Since in German scholarship Lucan historiography has been restored to a certain position of honor by M. Hengel[61] and J. Roloff,[62] one may somewhat more candidly than before argue as follows: Already as a persecutor of the church of Christ in Jerusalem and Damascus Paul was confronted with the fact that the

---

58. Cf. e.g. G. Bornkamm, *Jesus of Nazareth,* 16f.:

> The primitive Christian proclamation confines itself so exclusively to this history—a history which shatters the horizon of all events confined to this world and shifts the ages, that it can pass over the pre-Easter life and work of Jesus to an extent which seems astonishing to us (II Cor. v.16). Doubtless [!] Paul and the authors of other New Testament writings knew extremely little of the detail which is known to us from the Gospels.

H. Conzelmann is even more definite in "Jesus von Nazareth und der Glaube an den Auferstandenen," in *Der historische Jesus und der kerygmatische Christus,* ed. H. Ristow and K. Matthiae, 1962 (188-99), 189:

> The Gospels present the faith in the form of a historical narrative. Paul, on the other hand, ignores the life of Jesus, reducing it to a mathematical point, namely, that he was truly human, was crucified, and rose again. This he does, not out of difficulty—because he knew so little about Jesus—but in the sense of a deliberate theological program (II Cor. 5:15); in this manner he denies that the object of faith is concretely visible (II Cor. 4:18; 5:7).

59. W. Schmithals, "Paulus und der historische Jesus," in his *Jesus Christus in der Verkündigung der Kirche,* 1972 (36-59), 49:

> More important . . . is the observation that until the middle of the second century our Gospels and the "historical" Jesus-tradition that preceded them had a pronounced apocryphal character. "Apocryphal" not in the sense that the Church for some theological reasons pushed them into concealment. . . . The idea is rather that the concealment must have been original.

60. Thus esp. U. Wilckens, "Jesusüberlieferung und Christuskerygma—Zwei Wege urchristlicher Überlieferungsgeschichte," *ThViat* 10, 1965-66, 310-39.

61. M. Hengel, "History Writing" (cf. n. 30), 59-68.

62. J. Roloff, *Die Apostelgeschichte,* 1981.

circle around Stephen, appealing to Jesus, expressed criticism of the temple and the Mosaic law (Acts 6:14), and that Christians acknowledged as the messianic king exalted by God to his right hand precisely that Jesus whom a short time before the Sanhedrin had condemned as blasphemer and "messianic" deceiver of the people[63] and who on orders of Pilate had died the accursed death on the cross before the walls of Jerusalem. After his calling as apostle outside of Damascus Paul appropriated for himself the confession of the persecuted Christians and in so doing fundamentally changed his picture of Jesus. In II Cor. 5:16 he wrote: " . . . even though we once regarded Christ from a human point of view, we regard him thus no longer!" This statement is formulated in terms of a theology of conversion and says nothing whatever to support the alleged lack of interest of Paul in the earthly Jesus.[64] In his encounter with Peter, with the members of the Stephen circle who were driven from Jerusalem and went to Antioch (Acts 11:19), and with James the brother of Jesus, Paul had ample opportunity in his lifetime to gain firsthand information concerning Jesus and the Jesus-tradition.

2. All the letters of Paul that have reached us, the short as well as the long, date from after the Council at Jerusalem. In all his letters except the one to Philemon Paul had to defend his person and teaching against hostile criticism, and this is the case also in Romans (cf. Rom. 3:8; 16:17ff.). Hence one must examine very closely the historical situation out of which Paul wrote in order not to misconstrue the character of the Pauline letters that have come down to us. Right up to the Jerusalem Council Paul seems to have had generally positive contacts with the "pillars" at Jerusalem. The same is true for Barnabas and the Antioch circle of early Christian prophets and teachers. At the Jerusalem Council Paul and Barnabas succeeded in getting the consent of the Jerusalem "pillars" for the Antiochian "gospel to the uncircumcised" (Gal. 2:7) and for the Gentile mission based at Antioch, in which Gentiles who were baptized were received without circumcision. Then, after the Jerusalem Council, in Antioch and beyond, fundamental differences concerning the issue of law-observance surfaced between Paul, the emissaries of James, Peter, Barnabas, and the people at Antioch (cf. Gal. 2:11ff.). After the so-called Antiochian incident, in Galatia, Corinth, and Rome, as well as in Jerusalem and Antioch, the opponents of Paul appealed to Peter (and James) as the genuinely authoritative and true apostles and started a sort of countermission[65] in the Pauline congregations. As a result

---

63. Cf. A. Strobel, *Die Stunde der Wahrheit*, 1980, 81ff.

64. As H. Lietzmann already correctly stated in *An die Korinther I, II,* 1949 (4th edition), 125; cf. further C. K. Barrett, *The Second Epistle to the Corinthians*, 1973, 171f.

65. M. Hengel, *Acts and the History of Earliest Christianity,* 98:

The best explanation of Paul's opponents in II Corinthians is that they were representatives of a mission sponsored by Peter which was in competition with Paul, especially as

Peter became completely Paul's great missionary rival, and James, the brother of the Lord, became the *éminence grise* in Jerusalem, in terms of whose reaction of acceptance or nonacceptance the work of collection—of fundamental significance to Paul—would be decided (cf. Rom. 15:30ff. and Acts 21:17ff.). These confrontations are reflected in all the letters of Paul that have come down to us. Paul was always compelled, pointedly and with his eyes on the focal points, to stand by his gospel. In his struggles with Peter and his Jewish Christian challengers he made but sparing use of the universally recognized teaching tradition and Jesus-tradition. More quotations from the tradition would certainly have reinforced the old charge that Paul had "learned" his gospel elsewhere, getting it at second hand (Gal. 1:12).

3. With reference to the letters of Paul and their infrequent use of the Jesus-tradition there is in addition, interestingly enough, a situation which characterizes *all* the apostolic and deutero-apostolic letters which have come down to us in the New Testament (as it does also the book of Acts).[66] Truly extensive quotation from the Jesus-tradition occurs in none of these books, not once in the letters of Peter, the letters of John, or in the letter of James. The attempt to reconstruct the Johannine gospel tradition from the three letters of John is just as unpromising as the attempt to glean from Paul's letters the material of Mark or the main texts of the *logia*-source. There is, in my opinion, only one really plausible explanation for this state of affairs: the literary form or category of an apostolic letter calls specifically for only occasional or incidental reference to the Jesus-tradition. Extensive or complete reproduction of the Jesus-tradition simply was not a requirement or concern of epistolary communication. Or to formulate the issue differently: while the apostolic letters unfold the Christ-kerygma in terms of church-related paraklesis, and Luke writes concerning the history of the Church on the basis of his Gospel (Acts 1:1ff.), the gospel tradition is in all likelihood to be regarded as the material of doctrinal proclamation passed on in the form of memorable stories and summaries of doctrine.

4. If one now tests the demonstrable use which Paul makes of the Jesus-tradition by the historical and form-critical criteria just mentioned, the following facts emerge: (1) Beginning with I Thessalonians one can show evidence in Paul's letters both of direct quotation from, and allusion to, the Jesus-tradition (cf. I Thess. 4:16ff.; I Cor. 7:10; 9:14; 11:23ff., and I Cor. 2:8ff.; 13:2; Rom. 12:14; 13:8ff.,

---

Peter-Cephas must already have exercised considerable influence on the Corinthian community (see I Corinthians), which must have caused difficulties for Paul (I Cor. 1.12; 3.22; cf. 15.3).

See also my *Reconciliation, Law, & Righteousness,* ET 1986, 74ff.

66. For the following, cf. L. Goppelt, *Theology of the New Testament* II, ET 1982, 44-46.

etc.). Hence Paul knows more about the Jesus-tradition than his few direct quotations would lead us to suspect.[67] (2) I Cor. 2:8ff.; 11:23ff.; 15:3ff.; and Rom. 15:3 show that Paul knows the Jerusalem (Antiochene) tradition of the passion, that he presupposes it as familiar in his churches, and that he argues from it as valid Christian doctrine. (3) I Cor. 7:10; 9:14; and 11:23 also show that the sayings of the Lord had great authority for the apostle, not only in the sphere of ethical admonition, but also in an ecclesiological connection. (4) I Thess. 2:15; I Cor. 11:23ff.; 15:3ff.; and Gal. 3:1 make it very likely that during his (sometimes lengthy) times of missionary teaching in the churches Paul told the story of Jesus' accursed death on the cross, of the night of the betrayal together with the passion, and of Jesus' resurrection and appearances, and thus himself to a degree employed the Jesus-tradition for purposes of mission and teaching.

5. If one takes these facts together with the polemical and apologetic emphasis in Paul's letters, one finds that the Pauline mission and message of the gospel of justification did not in any way hinder the progress of the gospel tradition but rather presupposed and promoted it. Hence the situation in the letters of Paul cannot be adduced as argument against the view of the history of the transmission of the gospel tradition sketched above. The history of the synoptic (and Johannine) tradition appears to be the history of the didache of Jesus as in the course of the first century it took shape as the essential content of teaching and preaching. This didache completes the apostolic paraklesis and, like it, serves to identify and unfold the saving message of Jesus' mission, death on the cross, and resurrection.

4. The History of the Word "Gospel" and of Its Tradition

As before, with regard to the history of the word "gospel" (εὐαγγέλιον) we face a choice. With regard to the verb εὐαγγελίζεσθαι there is some agreement that it is rooted in the Semitic language field of early Judaism and the Old Testament; but the origin and function of the word "gospel" is still explained in different ways. G. Strecker has only recently stated: "The primary rootage of the substantive 'εὐαγγέλιον' in the Greek-Hellenistic tradition is evident. Precisely in that way the new content that came with the Christian message was intelligibly articulated in the surrounding world."[68] The possibility I proposed, namely that

---

67. Of late this has been emphasized by D. C. Allison, Jr., "The Pauline Epistles and the Synoptic Gospels: The Pattern of the Parallels," *NTS* 28, 1982 (1-32), 19ff. Unfortunately Allison's main thesis, namely that in certain sections of his letters Paul bases himself on at least three synoptic passages (Mark 9:33-50; Luke 6:27-38, and the tradition of the sending out of the Twelve), does not stand up under close scrutiny.

68. G. Strecker, εὐαγγέλιον, *EWNT* II (176-86), 180.

"gospel" could be understood as a rendering of (prophetic) "message" (Heb. שמועה and בשורה), hence also in terms of the Semitic idiom of Judaism and the Old Testament,[69] has been rejected as mistaken in method by Strecker.[70]

This state of the debate gives me occasion to recall that, after the publication of the famous calendar inscription of Priene around the turn of the century, A. von Harnack himself initially held the opinion that early Christianity "had simply taken over" this term which was originally coined for Caesar Augustus and "transferred it to Jesus Christ."[71] After examining the body of early Christian materials on this term, however, Harnack soon distanced himself from this initial attempt at interpretation. In an appendix to his work, *The Constitution and Law of the Early Church* (1910), he offered an account of the history of the term "gospel" in the primitive Church.[72] Here he followed a general tradition-historical perspective which finds the word's point of departure in Jesus' message of the kingdom, leading through the primitive Church to Paul and finally becoming the formal designation for the Gospels. It seems to me that if one wishes to explain the history of the word and tradition of εὐαγγέλιον and εὐαγγελίζεσθαι without arbitrary hypotheses and in view of the entire body of New Testament evidence, one must follow Harnack's line of thought. The following is suggestive of this attempt.[73]

1. Jesus himself saw his mission in the light of Isa. 61:1ff. As the Q tradition in Matt. 11:2-6 par. shows, he understood his healing miracles and preaching as fulfillment (esp.) of that Isaianic text. Jesus worked as the messianic evangelist to the "poor" and saw himself in the role of the מבשר mentioned there. His proclamation of the kingdom of God bears the stamp of Isa. 52:7 (cf. Mark 1:15).

Proceeding from this insight one easily arrives at the possibility that already in his lifetime Jesus' message of the kingdom of God (now dawning in his works) was designated as בשורה or שמועה (= the salvation message of God's coming). The very striking semitism in Mark 1:15, πιστεύετε ἐν τῷ εὐαγγελίῳ, as Schlatter already observed,[74] is thus best explained as tradition,[75]

---

69. Cf. my *Das paulinische Evangelium* I, 1968 (hereafter *PaulEv*), 122ff.

70. G. Strecker, "Das Evangelium Jesu Christi," in *Jesus Christus in Historie und Theologie* (Conzelmann Festschrift), ed. G. Strecker, 1975 (503-48), 506f. (= G. Strecker, *Eschaton und Historie*, 1979 [183-228], 186f.).

71. Cf. *PaulEv*, 12.

72. Appendix III, "Gospel," 275-331.

73. What is stated here is an attempt to correct and carry further the outline I gave in *PaulEv*, 207ff., of the history of the Christian tradition. In my essay "The Pauline Gospel," which follows in this volume, I will return to the sketch given here.

74. A. Schlatter, *Der Glaube im Neuen Testament*, 1927, 590. Schlatter compares his formulation with the Targum on Isa. 53:1 (so also O. Betz in "Jesus' Gospel of the Kingdom" in the present volume).

75. R. Schnackenburg, " 'Das Evangelium' in Verständnis des ältesten Evangelisten," in *Orientierung an Jesus,* ed. P. Hoffmann, 1973 (309-24), 320ff.

and the redactional designation of the message of Jesus in Matthew as εὐαγγέ-λιον τῆς βασιλείας becomes historically transparent (cf. Matt. 4:23; 9:35; 24:14). It is perhaps permissible also to read Mark 14:9 as containing an original saying of Jesus: When the message of God's coming in judgment over the world is proclaimed in the future (cf. Rev. 14:6), the deed of the woman who anointed Jesus before his death will be remembered before the judgment throne of God.[76]

According to the synoptic tradition of the sending out of the Twelve (Matt. 10:1-16 par.) Jesus involved his disciples in his preaching and sent them out (for a certain time) to bring the same message as he. The way Luke 9:6 puts it, ἐξερχόμενοι δὲ διήρχοντο κατὰ τὰς κώμας εὐαγγελιζόμενοι καὶ θεραπεύοντες πανταχοῦ, suggests that the missionaries, like Jesus, understood their preaching mandate in light of the m^ebaśśēr tradition of Isa. 61:1ff. and 52:7.

2. In the early Jerusalem Church and the Stephen circle that was a part of it, the words εὐαγγελίζεσθαι and εὐαγγέλιον are simply the translation equivalents for Jesus' "message," equivalents that came naturally from the Septuagint and its rendering of biśśēr with εὐαγγελίζεσθαι. However, these ancient words were given a new and deeper meaning from the context of Easter and the eschatological mission mandate rooted in it.

It is true that εὐαγγελίζεσθαι as a rule retains the general sense of "preach," but in addition it also becomes the *terminus technicus* for the missionary message of the coming of God's rule through the mission, cross, and resurrection of Jesus (cf. Acts 5:42). When Paul calls the *paradosis* of I Cor. 15:3ff. εὐαγγέλιον (I Cor. 15:1), known in Jerusalem as well as in Antioch and Corinth, this may indeed be an older usage he adopted. Also the report about the Apostolic Council in Gal. 2:1-10, according to which τὸ εὐαγγέλιον τῆς ἀκροβυστίας and τῆς περιτομῆς was dealt with, shows that the missionary gospel-terminology, far from being unfamiliar in Jerusalem, was customary there.

3. This terminology seems, however, to have gained its own special importance only in the mission movement which proceeded from the Stephen circle and was carried forward from Antioch, i.e., from within the Hellenistic Jewish mission Christianity which programmatically represented missions to Gentiles. Information about the way this mission Christianity (also represented by Paul) used language comes to us by way of inferences from the letters of Paul, the Book of Acts, and the pre-Marcan tradition.

---

76. J. Jeremias, *Jesus' Promise to the Nations,* ET 1958, 22, and R. Pesch, *Das Markusevangelium* II, [3]1980, 334f. The difficulties involved in this understanding, which stem from the contingent-iterative sense of ὅπου ἐάν, also to be assumed in the Semitic original according to K. Beyer, *Semitische Syntax im Neuen Testament* I, 1962, 196, n. 2, remain unresolved. Hence Mark 14:9 can also be understood in the light of 13:10 in the sense of mission and is presumably so understood by the evangelist.

In I Thess. 1:9f. + 2:2ff.; I Cor. 9:12ff.; 15:1ff.; Rom. 1:1-7 Paul so naturally links the traditions of missionary preaching and materials of Jewish Christian origin with the words εὐαγγέλιον (τοῦ θεοῦ or τοῦ Χριστοῦ) and εὐαγγελίζεσθαι that one may conclude that this word usage had already been established in the Church by Christian missions before his time.

In the word usage of Acts one is struck by the fact that it describes with εὐαγγέλιον the missionary message of Peter (Acts 15:7) as well as that of Paul (Acts 20:24), thus making clear, from Luke's usage, that the mode of speech one finds in Gal. 2:1-10 was in general use. Interestingly enough, however, the verb εὐαγγελίζεσθαι in Acts 10:36ff. is also linked with the preached narrative of Jesus' mission and destiny which Peter presented in the house of Cornelius. That there is a tradition at work here is not only evident from the un-Lucan allusion to Isa. 52:7 (and Nah. 2:1) in v. 36; it is established above all from the circumstance that the text mentions God himself as the messenger of peace through Jesus Christ[77] and that vv. 36ff. follow a midrashic pattern, as G. N. Stanton has shown at some length.[78] Since the λόγος declared by Peter in Acts 10:36-43 is not simply a summary of the Lucan gospel but rather presents a concise version of Mark's Gospel, I am of the opinion, again in company with C. H. Dodd[79] and M. Dibelius,[80] that what we have in Acts 10:36ff. is the fundamental kerygmatic model of the gospel account first offered by Mark. This fundamental model is pre-Pauline or contemporary with Paul and shows not only that in the Church's mission Jesus' resurrection is proclaimed and his return announced but also that the story of the deeds and fate of the earthly Jesus is told, and all this in the framework of scriptural references to the Old Testament.

In the tradition of Mark the additions καὶ τοῦ εὐαγγελίου in Mark 8:35 and ἕνεκεν τοῦ εὐαγγελίου in 10:29 seem to point to the self-understanding and the sense of mission of early Christian missionaries to the Gentiles other than Paul.[81] The idea that before the parousia of the Son of Man "the gospel must first be

---

77. Cf. *PaulEv,* 148, 279, n. 1.

78. G. N. Stanton, *Jesus of Nazareth in New Testament Preaching,* 1974, 70ff.

79. C. H. Dodd, "The Framework of the Gospel Narrative," in his *New Testament Studies,* 1953, 1-11.

80. *From Tradition to Gospel,* 25f., 230f.

81. G. Dautzenberg, "Der Wandel der Reich-Gottes-Verkündigung in der urchristlichen Mission," in *Zur Geschichte des Urchristentum,* ed. by G. Dautzenberg, 1979 (11-32), 21ff., sees behind (what he regards as) the pre-Marcan summary (Mark 1:14f.) an "extra-Palestinian, early Christian missionary movement," the members of which, like the traditioners of Q,

> promoted Jesus' message of the kingdom of God, [and] . . . first went part of the common missionary and theological way with the Palestinian traditioners before and after Q, but then decided, on the basis of a developing understanding of the universal significance of Jesus' proclamation of the kingdom of God, for the mission to the Gentiles (23f.).

This group "formed the concept of εὐαγγέλιον τοῦ θεοῦ" (24) and passed it on to Paul or perhaps to the pre-Pauline missionary Church; in Mark 10:29 (cf. I Cor. 9:23); 13:10; and 14:9 the universal

preached to all nations" (Mark 13:10) also suggests the mindset of those sent to the Gentiles. In Rom. 11:13f., 25ff., Paul adopts this very same view.

4. According to Gal. 1:16, Paul sees his apostolic mandate—which he received directly by God's revelation—as consisting in preaching Christ to the Gentiles. Also, Paul sees himself, in the same way as Peter, the Twelve, James, and those called to be apostles before him, as authorized to preach the gospel by an appearance of Christ. He consistently understands his apostolic office and mandate as parallel to that of the apostles before him and contemporary with him (cf. I Cor. 9:1; 15:8ff.; Rom. 10:14ff.). As far as the content of his gospel is concerned, he has no difficulty accepting the Jewish Christian paradosis with which he has been familiar from his contact with Damascus, Jerusalem, and Antioch. That Paul also knew and cited from Jesus-tradition is a fact on which we already gained clarity earlier in this chapter. What makes Paul's gospel unmistakable and allows the apostle occasionally to speak of "my gospel" (Rom. 2:16; cf. also Gal. 1:11; I Thess. 1:5) is that Paul defines the Christ who arose and was elevated to the right hand of God as the one who was crucified for us (Gal. 3:1; I Cor. 2:2). The content of Paul's gospel is Jesus Christ whom God has made our wisdom, our righteousness and sanctification and redemption (I Cor. 1:30). Whoever believes in this Christ, who in virtue of his atoning death is the end of the law as the way of salvation, is justified apart from the works of the law solely through faith (Rom. 3:28). Paul's gospel of Christ is essentially a gospel of justification! For this gospel he stands, wherever and by whomever any doubt as to its validity might be raised (cf. Gal. 2:2ff., 11ff.; II Cor. 11:1ff.; Rom. 1:16f.). In Paul's work the history of the word εὐαγγέλιον and transmission of the New Testament gospel attains its first culmination.

5. One can only understand the history of the word εὐαγγέλιον correctly if one refuses to elevate Paul's usage to the status of sole criterion. In the post-Pauline period three possible usages of εὐαγγέλιον can be shown to exist:

5.1. In the school of Paul, the apostle's usage remained determinative. Εὐαγγέλιον is the quintessence of the mystery, imparted by the apostle, of promised salvation, i.e., the establishment of peace between God and man and between Jew and Gentile in the mission of Christ, which includes end-time salvation (cf. e.g. Eph. 1:13f.; 2:14–3:7; 6:19f.). Quite similarly for I Peter, the εὐαγγέλιον is the equivalent of the redemptive revelation promised by the prophets and realized in Christ, i.e., of God's eternally abiding word, which through Christ creates life (cf. I Pet. 1:12, 23-25; 4:17).

---

dimension of the preaching of this group becomes clear. I agree with Dautzenberg's perspective but think it would be adequate to make the Stephen circle responsible for the "missionary movement" that he proposes. The language of Mark 1:15 can be traced from the Targum on Isa. 53:1 to Jerusalem (and from there perhaps even to Jesus himself; see n. 74 above).

5.2. Next to this specific usage in the school of Paul and I Peter, the ancient, more open, "message" terminology remained operative: according to Heb. 4:2, 6 the εὐαγγέλιον is simply the message of salvation, imparted to the old and new people of God, to which whoever would be saved must listen. In Rev. 10:7 and 14:6 the same expression means the message of God to the prophets as well as the message of the coming judgment of God proclaimed by the mouth of angels over the whole world.

5.3. To describe the eschatological message of salvation (by Jesus Christ) the early Christian Church also, however, simply used the words ἀγγελία (I John 1:5; 3:11); ἀκοή (Gal. 3:2, 5; Rom. 10:16f., and Heb. 4:2); ῥῆμα (John 6:68; 14:10; 17:8; I Pet. 1:25; Heb. 6:5); μαρτυρία (John 15:26f.; I John 1:2; 4:14; Rev. 1:9, etc.), and above all λόγος (cf. only John 1:1-18; I John 1:1; Jas. 1:18; Heb. 4:12, etc.).

Hence the missionary and preaching terminology of primitive Christianity remained very flexible. There is nowhere any trace of any deliberate accommodation, in this connection, to the εὐαγγέλια of the emperor-cult.[82]

6. The impulse toward writing Gospels resulted when the εὐαγγέλιον was equated with the message concerning Christ. The process becomes very clear in the Gospel of Mark. In an essay on the titles of the Gospels, M. Hengel has shown that the amazingly uniform titles handed down to us are of ancient date and are linked with the use made in the churches of various Gospel manuscripts. In the formulation of these titles Mark 1:1 played a decisive role.[83] If one should ask how Mark's Gospel came to be written, the following attempt at explanation seems to me to be particularly suggestive:

6.1. Mark's concept originated at a time when James and Peter had suffered a martyr's death and, on account of the Jewish War, which was brewing, the Christian community could no longer count on Jerusalem as the bulwark of Jesus-tradition. In this period (i.e., the sixties) the Jesus-tradition, important for mission and catechesis alike, had to be fixed in writing and so preserved for the Church.

6.2. As is evident from Mark 1:1ff., 14f., the Gospel of Mark was designed to define and to concretize the missionary message of salvation by Jesus Christ. It did this by the manner in which the message and history of Jesus appear as

---

82. G. Strecker's opposing view (*EWNT* II, 179f.) cannot be verified.

83. For this essay on the titles of the Gospels, see M. Hengel, *Studies in the Gospel of Mark*, ET 1985, 64-84. In the conclusion of the essay he writes that

it must be asserted that in the present state of our knowledge the titles of the Gospels are by no means late products from the second century but must be very old. With a considerable degree of probability they can be traced back to the time of the origin of the four Gospels between 69 and 100 and are connected with their circulation in the communities. Their ultimate root lies in the terminology of Mark, who was the first to call a writing εὐαγγέλιον Ἰησοῦ Χριστοῦ.

the origin and essential content of the missionary message to be proclaimed over the whole world (1:14f.; 13:10; 14:9). For Mark to recount the history of Jesus' preaching and fate was to reproduce the essential content of the missionary gospel.

6.3. Mark's story, which is told with extraordinary fascination, is built in all likelihood upon extensive collections of authentic tradition. This is true especially of the passion narrative itself (R. Pesch), but also of the parables and the stories of Jesus' miracles.

6.4. As a framework for the materials which came down to Mark (from Peter?) there is, above all, the pre-Lucan preaching or narrative scheme of Acts 10:36ff. According to this scheme the history of Jesus fulfills the prophetic promise recorded in Isa. 52:7 (Nah. 2:1) of God's eschatological message of peace. The history of Jesus appears as gospel of God.

6.5. R. Guelich, in his article " 'The Beginning of the Gospels'—Mark 1:15,"[84] has shown, convincingly in my opinion, that Mark 1:1 and 1:2f. are to be taken together and translated: "Beginning of the gospel of Jesus Christ (the Son of God), as it is written in Isaiah the prophet: Behold. . . ." If this reading is correct it is possible to read 1:2-15 in light of 1:1. But the narrative and teaching scheme of Acts 10:36ff. can also be related to Mark's beginning: it seems the evangelist orients his design to the statement of the gospel in Acts 10:36ff. (probably not accidentally attributed to Peter), which corresponds to the Isaianic promises of Isa. 52:7; 61:1, (God's) gospel of Jesus' mission, saving activity, death, and appearances to the (divinely) appointed missionary Easter witnesses.

6.6. Concerning the missionary catechetical purpose of the Gospels, Matthew (cf. 28:20), Luke (1:4), and John (20:31) followed the example of Mark's Gospel, though they dissociated themselves terminologically from his interesting formulation in Mark 1:1f. In the old Gospel titles, then, the constitutive relationship (according to Mark 1:1 and Acts 10:36ff.) between the gospel of the one salvation message of Jesus Christ and the historical narrative of Jesus' mission, work, passion, and resurrection has been preserved. It has even become the tradition-historical hallmark of the comprehensive genre of "Gospel." The Apostolic Fathers, especially Ignatius of Antioch, constitute proof that the existence of this broad genre did not threaten, but rather enriched, the practical preaching of the gospel.

---

84. *BR* 27, 1982, 5-15. See further his essay in the present volume: "The Gospel Genre."

Gospels Criticism: A Perspective on the State of the Art

E. Earle Ellis

The literary and historical analysis of the synoptic Gospels has pursued four major paths—source criticism, form criticism, tradition criticism, and redaction/composition criticism.[1] All are interrelated and all designed to aid in the reconstruction of the ministry of Jesus and in identifying the particular contributions of the traditioners and of the evangelists.

The task is quite as open as ever since both the quest of the "historical" Jesus[2] and the analysis of the texts remain contested and unresolved. In this context it is difficult if not impossible to set forth in brief compass the present state of the art and one can, at best, only highlight the issues and topics that seem to be most decisive for understanding the present situation and for projecting the future course of research. To my mind these issues are questions of prolegomena, source criticism, and form criticism.

1.

The presuppositions of the investigator govern the historical study of the Gospels more than one might suppose. They include both confessional attitudes

---

1. There are also other emphases e.g. audience criticism: J. A. Baird, *Audience Criticism and the Historical Jesus,* 1969.

2. Cf. J. W. Bowman, *Which Jesus?* 1970; H. K. McArthur, ed., *In Search of the Historical Jesus,* 1969; X. Léon-Dufour, *The Gospels and the Jesus of History,* ET 1968; H. Ristow, ed., *Der historische Jesus und der kerygmatische Christus,* 1961; J. M. Robinson, *A New Quest of the Historical Jesus,* 1959; critiqued by R. P. Martin, "The New Quest of the Historical Jesus," *Jesus of Nazareth, Saviour and Lord,* ed. C. F. H. Henry, 1966, 25-45; A. Schweitzer, *Geschichte der Leben-Jesu-Forschung,* 2 vols., 1966 (1906; partially translated as *The Quest of the Historical Jesus,* 1910).

and methodological assumptions. A cleavage in worldview, *a priori* assumptions that are ultimately confessional in nature, has marked biblical criticism from its beginnings. In the eighteenth century it was characterized by deism on the one hand and theistic (and pietistic) assumptions on the other,[3] assumptions that in recent times have been appropriately labeled Cartesian and non-Cartesian.[4] In the criticism of the Gospels the cleavage has manifested itself most significantly in the approach taken to the Gospel accounts of the miracles of Jesus and of his resurrection from among the dead bodies (ἐκ νεκρῶν). In the nineteenth century a naturalistic-psychological (e.g. H. E. G. Paulus; W. R. Cassels) and naturalistic-mythological (e.g. D. F. Strauss) rationalism contrasted sharply with a supernaturalism that was open to and in principle affirmed the miraculous acts attributed to Jesus by the evangelists.[5]

The difference of worldviews, which are testable but which are not in the final analysis subject to scientific proof, is represented in recent German theology by R. Bultmann and P. Stuhlmacher respectively. For Bultmann, who in this regard stands in the tradition of D. F. Strauss,[6] history and the natural world are a closed continuum of cause and effect, "a self-subsistent unity immune from the interference of supernatural powers."[7] This presupposition had a decisive impact on Bultmann's formulation of the form criticism of the Gospels.[8] On the other hand, Stuhlmacher argues for "an openness to transcendence" and affirms that biblical criticism should be pursued theologically in relation to the third article of the Apostles' Creed: "I believe in the Holy Spirit."[9]

3. Cf. W. G. Kümmel, *The New Testament: The History of the Investigation of its Problems,* ET 1972, 51-62. On its outworking in later criticism cf. the sketch of E. Krentz, *The Historical-Critical Method,* 1975, 55-72.

4. H. Thielicke, *The Evangelical Faith* I, ET 1974, 30-173.

5. Cf. A. Richardson, "History and the Miraculous," *History Sacred and Profane,* 1964, 184-212. On Paulus and Strauss cf. Schweitzer (n. 2); for a rationalist on the British scene cf. W. R. Cassels, *Supernatural Religion,* 1902 (²1874), critiqued by J. B. Lightfoot, *Essays on . . . Supernatural Religion,* ²1893. On the deleterious effects of Cartesian rationalism for other questions cf. F. A. Hayek, *Law, Logic and Liberty* I, 1973, 8-34; III, 1979, 153-76.

6. Rightly, H. Harris, *David Friedrich Strauss and his Theology,* 1973, 272f.; somewhat differently, G. Backhaus, *Kerygma und Mythos bei D. F. Strauss und R. Bultmann,* 1956. Cf. W. G. Kümmel, "Mythische Rede und Heilsgeschehen im Neuen Testament," *Heilsgeschehen und Geschichte* I, 1965, 153-68 (= *Coniectanea Neotestamentica XI in Honorem A. Fridrichsen,* 1947, 109-31).

7. R. Bultmann, "New Testament and Mythology," *Kerygma and Myth,* ET 1953, 7; cf. idem, *Existence and Faith,* ET 1960, 292.

8. Cf. the critique of T. F. Torrance, *Theological Science,* 1969, 327-36, who concludes that Bultmann's approach results in "a travesty of historical method" (330).

9. P. Stuhlmacher, *Schriftauslegung auf dem Weg zur biblischen Theologie,* 1975, 121, 52 (partially translated in *Historical Criticism and Theological Interpretation of Scripture,* 1977, 85); idem, *Vom Verstehen des Neuen Testaments,* 1979, 205-25, where he (219f.) perceives his contribution as a supplement to E. Troeltsch's (*Gesammelte Schriften* II, 1913, 729-53) axioms on "Historical and Dogmatic Method in Theology." I wonder whether Stuhlmacher has fully appreciated the radical difference between himself and Troeltsch, whose own "dogma," as Stuhlmacher rightly sees

This presupposition also has important implications for Gospels criticism. It bears upon the scholar's perception of the sociotheological context of the origin and composition of the Gospels, a matter that will be discussed below, and also affects his conclusions about other matters, for example, the locus of "authenticity" in the Gospels.

If one believes that the exalted Jesus spoke by the Holy Spirit through the gospel traditioners and evangelists, one cannot limit the "authentic" sayings of Jesus to those judged to have a probability of originating in his earthly ministry. The distinction between preresurrection and postresurrection (terms that also imply a confessional *a priori*) elements in the Gospels will continue to be historically and theologically important, but it will not carry the same significance that it does, say, for those who work within Cartesian assumptions. "Authenticity" will be defined rather in terms of the credentials accorded to the documents claiming to impart a knowledge of the word and works of Jesus.

One's worldview, then, enters into one's understanding of the genre of the Gospels. I do not mean here the literary genre as such,[10] nor the more advanced question of their status as canonical Scripture,[11] but rather their status as historical documents and their role (as we hope to show) as prophetic word in and through which the Holy Spirit is speaking. Worldview and historical-literary analysis cannot be separated in any critical study of the Gospels.

Questions of method, which are not unrelated to these theological/philosophical assumptions and attitudes, also form an important part of the prolegomena to Gospels criticism. They include *inter alia* the relation of history and interpretation in the Gospels, the criteria for "placing" a pericope within the transmission of the tradition, and the relationship between the Synoptics and the fourth Gospel. As for the last question it may simply be observed that continental scholarship has tended to assume that the fourth evangelist knew the Synoptics, or at least the Gospel of Mark; Anglo-American writers have, since the work of P. Gardner-Smith, generally rejected any direct relationship between them.[12]

(*Schriftauslegung,* 15) lay fully within a rationalist view of the world as a closed continuum of cause and effect. At root the theses of Stuhlmacher and of Troeltsch are mutually exclusive.

10. On this question some recent studies have given renewed attention to the Gospels as biography. Cf. C. H. Talbert, *What is a Gospel?* 1977; C. W. Votaw, *The Gospels and Contemporary Biographies in the Greco-Roman World,* 1970. Somewhat differently, R. Riesner, *Jesus als Lehrer,* 1981, 29-32; G. N. Stanton, *Jesus of Nazareth and New Testament Preaching,* 1974, 117-36. For a critique of Talbert cf. D. E. Aune, "The Problem of the Genre of the Gospels . . . ," *Gospel Perspectives* II, ed. R. T. France, 1981, 9-60. See the essays in the present volume by L. Abramowski, O. Betz, A. Dihle, R. Guelich, I. H. Marshall, and P. Stuhlmacher.

11. A question that, for the Old Testament, has been addressed by the important book of B. S. Childs, *Introduction to the Old Testament as Scripture,* 1979.

12. The seminal work was P. Gardner-Smith, *St. John and the Synoptic Gospels,* 1938. Cf. also S. S. Smalley, *John: Evangelist and Interpreter,* 1978, 13-22 and the literature cited there; R. E. Brown, *The Gospel according to John* I, 1966, xliv-xlvii; C. H. Dodd, *Historical Tradition in the Fourth Gospel,* 1965, 8f.; D. M. Smith, Jr., "John and the Synoptics," *NTS* 26, 1980, 425-44.

The relation between history and interpretation may be seen in all its problemage in the classical Quest of the "historical" Jesus. The Quest began with the supposition that history could be extracted from the Gospels like a kernel from the husk; it ended with the growing recognition that the process was more like peeling an onion with history and interpretation intermixed at every layer. Interpretation is indeed present at every level of the Gospel traditions and even in the selection of the traditions. This does not mean that the Gospels are less historical since in them, as in every document purporting to give knowledge of the past, history *is* interpretation.

Bernard Lonergan has reminded us that the word "history" is employed in two senses, that which is written and that which is written about.[13] It is history in the former sense that is presented to us by the evangelists or, for that matter, by the modern historian of early Christianity. It provides our only access to the ministry of Jesus, and in it the modern historian is subjectively involved no less (although in a different way) than were the evangelists in their presentation of Jesus' ministry. In important respects history is in the eyes of the reporter. This has at least two consequences for the study of the Gospels. (1) The interpretive mold of the Gospels is the essence of their historical character. To recognize this one need only imagine the situation if, for our knowledge of Jesus, we had only one continuing videotape of his ministry from the baptism to the resurrection appearances. One would have data but hardly meaningful history. (2) The value of modern reconstructions of the ministry of Jesus and of the origin and transmission of gospel traditions will depend in considerable measure upon proper presuppositions and interpretive insights: the historical Jesus will always be the historian's Jesus. However, the importance of a proper historical method is not thereby diminished, and Lonergan gives an instructive presentation of the principles and the process by which the critical historian reconstructs (or should reconstruct) the past.[14] In the Gospels one of the components of the process has involved the attempt to establish criteria for "placing" particular elements in the Gospels within the transmission of the traditions.

Certain criteria by which Gospels material could be proved to originate with the earthly Jesus have received considerable attention. As proposed, they are multiple attestation, absence of "developed" (postresurrection) tendencies, dissimilarity from the idiom or ideas found in Judaism or in early Christianity,

---

Otherwise: C. K. Barrett, *The Gospel according to St. John,* [2]1978, 42-54. On an early date cf. J. A. T. Robinson, *Redating the New Testament,* 1976, 254-311; F. L. Cribbs, "A Reassessment of the Date ... of the Gospel of John," *JBL* 89, 1970, 38-55 and the literature cited there. O. Cullmann, *The Johannine Circle,* ET 1976, 97, also dates the original form of the Gospel as early as the Synoptics. The state of research on John requires separate treatment and cannot be included here.

13. B. Lonergan, *Method in Theology,* 1972, 175.

14. Ibid., 197-234. Cf. also A. Richardson (n. 5), 83-183. On the subjectivity of critical history cf. J. Kenyon, *The History Men,* 1983.

and coherence with other matter established as "authentic."[15] They raise certain probabilities but produce no "assured results," as the devastating critique of M. Hooker has shown.[16] Multiple attestation, say in Mark, Q, and John, establishes the relative earliness of the material, assuming the existence of (independent) sources behind the Gospels, but it does not establish that the material originated in Jesus' ministry. The criterion of dissimilarity is at first blush suggestive, but upon examination it proves to be a weak reed. For it assumes, on the one hand, that a gospel traditioner or a Christian prophetic oracle could not have used a unique idea or expression and, on the other hand, that Jesus would not have used the idiom found in his own society or among his own followers. The criterion of coherence appears to be caught up in a vicious hermeneutical circle: from the Gospels the scholar extracts passages he believes to be "authentic" and then uses the resulting *Jesusbild* to determine the "authenticity" of passages in the Gospels. The absence of "tendencies of a development" most often begs the question, for it only reflects the scholar's assumptions about what the tendencies are. Contrast, for example, A. Schweitzer and his successors with B. H. Streeter's judgment that the tendency of the tradition was to heighten apocalyptic so that the nearer we get to Jesus "the greater is the emphasis on the present, the gradual and the internal aspects of the Kingdom. . . ."[17] It is difficult to fault Professor Hooker's conclusion that the scholar's answers when using these criteria "are very largely the result of his own presuppositions and prejudices."[18] The inadequacies of the above criteria throw greater weight upon the question of the burden of proof. Advocates of the criteria often assumed that Gospel materials should be regarded as postresurrection creations unless proven otherwise. Is this view of the burden of proof in accord with good historical method?

In his classic text on historical method E. Bernheim states that the historian, when he properly fulfills his task, "tests the genuineness and demonstrates the non-genuineness" of his sources.[19] Since the Gospels represent themselves to be an account of the mission and message of the earthly Jesus they, like any other historical documents, should be tested within that context. Equally, the presence of postresurrection elements—the "ungenuine" in Bern-

15. Summarized by McArthur (n. 2), 139-44 (= *Interpretation* 18, 1964, 39-55), who is followed by N. Perrin, *Rediscovering the Teachings of Jesus,* 1967, 39-47.

16. M. Hooker, "On Using the Wrong Tool," *Theology* 75, 1972, 570-81; idem, "Christology and Methodology," *NTS* 17, 1970-71, 480-87. Cf. D. R. Catchpole, "Tradition History," *New Testament Interpretation,* ed. I. H. Marshall, 1977, 165-80 and the literature cited there.

17. B. H. Streeter, "Synoptic Criticism and the Eschatological Problem," *Studies in the Synoptic Problem,* ed. W. Sanday, 1911, 425-36; Schweitzer (n. 2).

18. Hooker ("Tool," n. 16, 581). Cf. also the discussion in E. L. Mascall, *Theology and the Gospel of Christ,* 1977, 87-97 and the literature cited there.

19. E. Bernheim, *Lehrbuch der historischen Methode,* 1965 (1908), 332.

heim's axiom—must be demonstrated and, with careful analysis, can be demonstrated.

In the past generation, however, a critical dogma arose in the form of a methodological thesis: a gospel tradition is to be ascribed, without further ado, to the postresurrection Church unless its origin in Jesus' ministry can be demonstrated.[20] Criticizing this approach, W. G. Kümmel rightly concludes that while one must take full account of the inworking of later elements in the tradition, the burden of proof lies upon those asserting the postresurrection origin of the material since in the Gospels we meet the kerygma in the form of a tradition of the words and deeds of Jesus' preresurrection mission.[21] In this he agrees with Bernheim's axiom: unless the characteristics of genuineness are tested and shown to be lacking and those for ungenuineness established, the evidence of the document in question should be received in the context within which it is given.

The proper assignment of the burden of proof does not relieve the student of the tasks of testing, demonstrating, and then "placing" a particular passage within the transmission and development of the gospel traditions. Tradition criticism and redaction/composition criticism have attempted to do this. Tradition criticism, which seeks to trace the history of a particular tradition in the process of transmission, logically includes redaction/composition criticism, that is, the contribution of the evangelist (or final editor) himself to the present form of a Gospel.[22] In practice it has usually rested on two assumptions, (1) classical form criticism and the traditional two-document source hypothesis and (2) established "tendencies" in transmission based upon them. However, since the first assumption has a doubtful historical basis (as we hope to show below) and the second is equally open to question,[23] the discipline of tradition criticism has become an exercise in uncertainties and can be used only with considerable qualifications.

Redaction/composition criticism goes back at least to William Wrede[24] and one might even say to F. C. Baur.[25] In the English-speaking world its modern form was anticipated in the first part of this century by *inter alia*

20. E. Käsemann, "The Problem of the Historical Jesus" (1954), *Essays on New Testament Themes*, ET 1964, 37; H. Conzelmann, "Jesus Christus," *RGG*[3] III, 623; Robinson (n. 2), 38; Perrin (n. 15), 39.
21. W. G. Kümmel, "Jesusforschung seit 1950," *TR* 31, 1966, 42f.
22. Cf. Catchpole (n. 16), 165-74.
23. Cf. E. P. Sanders, *The Tendencies of the Synoptic Tradition*, 1969, esp. 272-79.
24. W. Wrede, *The Messianic Secret*, ET 1971 (1901), 68, 218, 228f.; the unmessianic (or premessianic) character of Jesus' ministry conflicted with the postresurrection teaching that he was Messiah and was explained by Mark in terms of a concealed messiahship.
25. F. C. Baur, *Das Markusevangelium nach seinem Ursprung und Charakter*, 1851: the Judaizing attitude of Matthew and the opposing Paulinist character of (the original) Luke were brought into "neutrality" by Mark. Cf. Kümmel (n. 3), 139.

B. W. Bacon,[26] R. H. Lightfoot,[27] G. D. Kilpatrick,[28] N. B. Stonehouse,[29] and A. Farrer.[30] Similar work[31] has continued into the present.[32] However, the discipline has received its characteristic shape from German scholars who, with their well-known energy and intensity, have over the past thirty years published a formidable array of titles under the designation of *Redaktionsgeschichte*.[33] In this context it has forged important new paths of investigation but also has presented students with at least three major problems. (1) Like tradition criticism, it has been built upon the twin pillars of classical form criticism and the two-document source hypothesis. As a method of research, then, it is no stronger than the underlying pillars although individual contributions may stand the test of other form-critical and source-critical assumptions. Also, (2) as J. Rhode has shown, there is a considerable diversity of viewpoints even among the scholars of this closely related group. For example, is Matthew's community a universalist Hellenistic Church using traditions of the strict Christian Hebrews (G. Strecker; W. Trilling); or is it still a part of Judaism, a mixed group whose antinomian and legalist extremes Matthew must oppose (G. Barth; G. Bornkamm; R. Hummel)? Is Mark's Gospel an invitation to Christians fleeing the Jewish war to meet the Lord at his parousia in Galilee (W. Marxsen), or does it approach an existential "Johannine" eschatology that has no imminent chronological expectation of the End (J. Schreiber)? Is Luke-Acts an apologetic "salvation history" synthesis of the conflict between Jesus' original apocalyptic message and the fact of the nonappearance of the parousia (H. Conzelmann) or the correction of an earlier view that identified the parousia with Jesus' resurrection (H. W. Bartsch)? Such divergences illustrate the problems present in this discipline, especially in the continuing task of analyzing motives and guidelines by which the evangelists' themes are identified and their background and rationale inferred.

Finally, (3) a Hegelian dialectic reminiscent of W. Wrede and F. C. Baur[34]

---

26. B. W. Bacon, *Studies in Matthew*, 1930.

27. R. H. Lightfoot, *History and Interpretation in the Gospels*, 1935.

28. G. D. Kilpatrick, *The Origins of the Gospel according to St. Matthew*, 1946, 59-139.

29. N. B. Stonehouse, *The Witness of Matthew and Mark to Christ*, 1944; idem, *The Witness of Luke to Christ*, 1951.

30. A. Farrer, *A Study in Mark*, 1951; idem, *St. Matthew and St. Mark*, 1954.

31. E.g., G. N. Stanton, "Matthean Scholarship since 1945," *ANRW* II 25/2, 1983; J. P. Meier, *The Vision of Matthew*, 1979; W. H. Kelber, ed., *The Passion in Mark*, 1976; E. E. Ellis, *Eschatology in Luke*, 1972; I. H. Marshall, *Luke: Historian and Theologian*, 1970; E. Best, *The Temptation and the Passion: Markan Soteriology*, 1965; M. Hooker, *The Son of Man in Mark*, 1967; A. Guilding, *The Fourth Gospel in Jewish Worship*, 1960.

32. Examples of commentaries stressing composition criticism are R. H. Gundry, *Matthew*, 1982; E. E. Ellis, *The Gospel of Luke*, [3]1981; P. Carrington, *According to Mark*, 1960.

33. Cf. the survey of J. Rhode, *Rediscovering the Teaching of the Evangelists*, 1968; cf. also S. S. Smalley, "Redaction Criticism," *New Testament Interpretation* (n. 16), 181-95.

34. See above, nn. 24, 25. Cf. Ellis (n. 31), 17.

continues to play a subtle but influential role in the work of some of the *redaktionsgeschichtlichen* scholars. In its most usual form the apocalyptic expectation of Jesus and the earliest Church *(thesis)* encounters the problem of the delay of the parousia *(antithesis)* and is resolved by a salvation-history theology *(synthesis)* of Luke-Acts (H. Conzelmann) or of all the Gospels (G. Strecker). This dialectical *Denkmethode* fosters, quite apart from the historical questions as such, an inference or implicit assumption that the Gospels are a response to conflict. It also creates *a priori* a caesura between Jesus and the Gospels and thereby imposes a substantive and not only a chronological distance between them.

Further progress in redaction/composition criticism may require, then, both a reassessment of its historical-philosophical assumptions and an appropriate regard for new developments in source and form criticism on which its conclusions are dependent. To these new developments we may now turn our attention.

2.

The relationship of the Gospels to one another was of interest already in the patristic Church,[35] but only in the modern period did it express itself in terms of written sources behind the Gospels. With the supposition of an "original Gospel" *(Urevangelium),* apparently first made by G. E. Lessing in 1784, the history of source criticism of the Gospels began.[36] The contemporaneous theory of J. J. Griesbach posited no written sources, supposing that Luke was dependent on Matthew and Mark dependent on both. While it remained popular until the mid-nineteenth century, the theory of Gospel sources set the trend of the future.

Building chiefly on the work of J. G. Eichhorn (1794), Herbert Marsh of Cambridge gave an important initial impetus to the two-document hypothesis. He argued that in addition to a Hebrew (Aramaic) document of facts (א), used in different recensions by all three Synoptists, there was a second Hebrew (Aramaic) document (ב) "containing a collection of precepts, parables and

---

35. According to Eusebius (*HE* 6.14.5) Clement of Alexandria cites a tradition that the Gospels with genealogies (Matthew and Luke) were written first, that Mark wrote the substance of Peter's preaching during the Apostle's lifetime, and that John, knowing the others, wrote a spiritual Gospel. Augustine (*De consensu evan.* 1.3f.) states the order as Matthew, Mark, Luke, John, with Mark as the epitomizer of Matthew and each one writing with knowledge of his predecessors; Matthew wrote in Hebrew, the others in Greek.

36. The best brief history is W. R. Farmer, *The Synoptic Problem,* [2]1976, who gives an impressive critique of the two-document hypothesis and (less persuasively) argues for Griesbach's theory (199-283). Cf. further Farmer, "The Synoptic Problem," *Perkins Journal* 33, 1980, 20-27. But see also Kümmel (n. 3) and S. Neill, *The Interpretation of the New Testament 1861-1961,* 1964.

discourses" that was used in different copies by (only) Matthew and Luke.[37]
The two documents, later associated respectively with Papias's references to
Mark and Matthew,[38] were identified in the ongoing research with an *Ur-
Markus* (H. J. Holtzmann) or essentially Mark (B. H. Streeter) and with a
sayings (λόγια) source designated Q. In the late nineteenth and early twentieth
century this two-document hypothesis, with variations, became dominant
among Protestant biblical scholars[39] although it was not universally endorsed
either in German[40] or Anglo-American circles.[41] In recent scholarship it has
continued to have a wide following[42] and has become the basis of more
far-reaching reconstructions, so that one may read essays today purporting to
set forth the hypothetical theology of the hypothetical community of the
hypothetical document Q. But can the theory bear the weight of such speculations or of the increasing objections raised against the theory itself?

Criticism of the two-document hypothesis has centered on the alleged
priority of Mark and several objections to the hypothetical source Q.[43] (1) Q has

37. H. Marsh, "The Origin and Composition of our Three First Canonical Gospels," in an
appendix to J. D. Michaelis, *Introduction to the New Testament,* [4]1823 (1799-1801), III, ii, 161-409,
368, 374n. Cf. Kümmel (n. 3), 78.
38. E.g., by C. H. Weisse. Cf. Farmer (n. 36), 17; Kümmel (n. 3), 149-55. Cf. Eusebius, *HE*
2.15.1f.; 3.39.15f.: According to Papias,

> Mark became Peter's interpreter and wrote accurately all that he remembered . . . [from]
> Peter, who gave the teachings, but not making an arrangement of the Lord's sayings
> (λογίων) . . . ; Matthew compiled the sayings (λόγια) in the Hebrew language. . . .

It should be noted that the "sayings" of Matthew no more exclude narrative material than the
"sayings" Mark compiled. Cf. T. Zahn, *Introduction to the New Testament,* ET 1953 ([3]1909), II,
510f.
39. The most influential English-language publications were from an Oxford circle: B. H.
Streeter, *The Four Gospels: A Study of Origins,* 1924; *Oxford Studies in the Synoptic Problem,* ed.
W. Sanday, 1911. Streeter added a special Matthean (M) and a special Lucan (L) source to make a
four-document hypothesis. He (201-22) and others supposed that Q and L were combined to form
a Proto-Luke; cf. V. Taylor, *The Passion Narrative of Luke,* 1972 and the literature cited there. But
see Ellis (n. 32), 26; J. A. Fitzmyer, *The Gospel according to Luke* I, 1981, 89ff.
40. E.g., Zahn (n. 38, II, 607-15; III, 109), who was probably the most erudite New Testament
scholar of his day, gave priority to an Aramaic Matthew (AD 62; based on oral traditions) which was
used by Mark (AD 67); Luke (AD 75) used Mark and "other similar documents" but not Matthew.
Zahn's (II, 400-427) survey of the history of the problem is still instructive. For a somewhat similar
assessment cf. A. Wikenhauser, *New Testament Introduction,* ET 1958, 252f.
41. Farmer (n. 36, 196), J. Chapman (*Matthew, Mark and Luke,* 1937), E. W. Lummis (*How
Luke Was Written,* 1915), H. G. Jameson (*The Origin of the Synoptic Gospels,* 1922), and J. H.
Ropes (*The Synoptic Gospels,* 1934) thought Luke used Matthew. C. F. Burney (*The Poetry of our
Lord,* 1925, 8, 74f.), noting that the parallelisms in Mark vis-à-vis Matthew are often broken and
inferior, concluded that Q was used by all three evangelists. The broken and inferior form of some
Markan explicit midrash patterns vis-à-vis Matthew's also speaks against a simple Matthean
dependence on Mark; cf. E. E. Ellis, *Prophecy and Hermeneutic,* 1978, 159 n., 251f.
42. Recently, Fitzmyer (n. 39), 63-85; cf. H. Conzelmann, "Literaturbericht zu den synoptischen Evangelien," *TR* 37, 1972, 220-72; 43, 1978, 3-51; Cf. A. Polag, *Die Christologie der
Logienquelle,* 1977; see his essay in the present volume.
43. At least one writer, J. M. Rist, *On the Independence of Matthew and Mark,* 1978, is

never been shown to be one document, and (2) its character and limits are difficult if not impossible to establish. (3) It is, some charge, an unnecessary assumption since the synoptic problem can be resolved without invoking such a hypothetical source. The last objection was supported *inter alia* by A. Farrer[44] and, together with an attack on Marcan priority, by B. C. Butler.[45] In recent years it has been pursued persistently by a "task force" of a considerable number of scholars made up largely but not altogether of advocates of a new Griesbach hypothesis.[46]

The denial of the existence of Q on Griesbachian or similar premises, presupposing as it does that Luke used Matthew, involves its own set of problems. It must explain, for example, why Luke shifted the order of so much of his Matthean source and why some of the Matthean matter appears more original in Luke than in Matthew.[47]

The objection to the alleged unity of Q poses a more weighty problem. V. Taylor sought to establish that Q was one document by showing that it had a common order in Matthew and Luke.[48] However, some of the order only reflects that which is common to all three Gospels,[49] and some Q episodes do not in fact have the same order in Matthew and Luke.[50] J. A. Fitzmyer recognizes the force of this and speaks only of "the remnant of a common sequence" observable in the Gospels.[51] But such an admission has already conceded the point: the mixed order/disorder of the Q material in Matthew vis-à-vis Luke speaks not only against Luke's use of Matthew but also against the unity of Q. It is more readily explained by Matthew's and Luke's independent use of several tracts or cycles of tradition,[52] a conclusion that also accords

---

reminiscent of the view of B. F. Westcott (*An Introduction to the Study of the Gospels,* 1888, [1]1860, 192-209) that both Gospels were the product of oral tradition. Cf. also J. W. Wenham, "Synoptic Independence . . . ," *NTS* 27, 1981, 505-15.

44. A. Farrer, "On Dispensing with Q," *Studies in the Gospels,* ed. D. E. Nineham, 1955, 55-86, 85: Matthew amplified Mark and Luke used them both. Cf. also Farrer's student, M. D. Goulder, *Midrash and Lection in Matthew,* 1974, xiii, 452-71.

45. B. C. Butler, *The Originality of St. Matthew,* 1951, 21f., 48, 165, 170f.: Greek Matthew is a translation of a Palestinian Aramaic Matthew and is a direct source of both Mark and Luke. Cf. further D. Wenham, "The Synoptic Problem Revisited," *Tyndale Bulletin* 23, 1972, 3-38, who argues for the secondary character of Mark 4 vis-à-vis Matthew.

46. The major stimulus has come from Farmer's work (n. 36). Cf. B. Orchard, *Matthew, Luke and Mark,* 1976, a forerunner to a synopsis highlighting Griesbach's order; *J. J. Griesbach: Synoptic and Text Critical Studies 1776-1976,* ed. B. Orchard, 1978, and the literature cited there. For a critique of this viewpoint cf. C. M. Tuckett, *The Revival of the Griesbach Hypothesis,* 1983.

47. E.g., the occasion and form of the Lord's Prayer (Luke 11:1-4).

48. V. Taylor, "The Original Order of Q," *New Testament Essays,* ed. A. J. B. Higgins, 1959, 264-69; cf. W. G. Kümmel, *Introduction to the New Testament,* ET [2]1975, 65f.

49. E.g., the sequence Baptist → Temptation.

50. E.g., sayings in Matthew's Sermon on the Mount that are scattered in Luke.

51. Fitzmyer (n. 39), 77.

52. Cf. G. Bornkamm, *RGG*[3], II, 756. However, the close verbal agreement of much of the material suggests written rather than oral sources.

with the form-critical observation that the gospel traditions were first written as short tracts.[53] It is probable that the non-Marcan material common to Matthew and Luke comes from more than one written source.

The objection concerning the uncertain nature and extent of Q is equally serious. The mass of contradictory scholarly opinion about this matter is well summarized by S. Petrie.[54] Q is a single document, a composite document, several documents. It incorporates earlier sources; it is used in different redactions. Its original language is Greek; it is Aramaic; Q is used in different translations. It is the Matthean *logia;* it is not. It has shape and sequence; it is a collection of fragments. It is a Gospel; it is not. It consists wholly of sayings; it includes narrative. It is all preserved in Matthew and Luke; it is not. Matthew's order of Q is correct; Luke's is correct; neither is correct. It is used by Mark; it is not used by Mark.

Traditionally and strictly defined, Q is non-Marcan material common to Matthew and Luke. But such material appears also in episodes of the triple tradition, i.e., those appearing in all three Synoptic Gospels, as can be observed in the so-called minor agreements of Matthew and Luke against Mark.[55] F. Neirynck[56] and others have shown that these agreements are not minor. For a considerable number of triple-tradition episodes they indicate either that all three Gospels are using Q material or that Matthew and Luke (assuming their mutual independence and Marcan priority) are using both Mark and Q material. When these agreements are given their full weight, Q could well be understood as a (derivative of a) primitive Gospel or Gospels postulated by earlier criticism on which all three Synoptics are in one way or another dependent.[57] In the present state of affairs source criticism appears either to have come full circle or to have reached something of an impasse. In any case it is difficult to disagree with M.-É. Boismard's judgment that both the two-source theory and the Griesbach theory are too simple to account for all the literary facts in the Gospels, whether or not one can accept his

53. Cf. Ellis (n. 32), 27ff.

54. S. Petrie, " 'Q' is only What You Make It," *NovT* 3, 1959, 29f.

55. Episodes found in both Mark and Q include teachings (Mark 1:7f.; 3:22-27; 4:10ff., 30ff.; 12:1-12, 18-27, 28-34, 35ff.), narratives (Mark 1:12f.; 6:7-13; 9:2-10; 11:1-10; 15:42-47), and miracles (Mark 4:35-41; 5:21-43; 6:32-44; 9:14-29). The fact was recognized but minimized as a problem by Streeter (n. 39), 295-331. Cf. Farmer (n. 36), 118-52.

56. F. Neirynck, *The Minor Agreements of Matthew and Luke against Mark,* 1974. Cf. T. Schramm, *Der Markus-Stoff bei Lukas,* 1971; E. E. Ellis, "The Composition of Luke 9 and the Sources of its Christology," *Current Issues in Biblical and Patristic Interpretation,* ed. G. F. Hawthorne, 1975, 121-27.

57. W. Schmithals (*Das Evangelium nach Markus,* 1979, I, 43-70) takes this route, positing a primitive source *(Grundschrift)* and Q^1 behind Mark and all three behind Q; Q and Mark are (as in the traditional two-document theory) the sources of Matthew and Luke. For a criticism of Schmithals's theological assumptions and inferences, particularly the caesura he draws between Jesus and the postresurrection period, see the essay below of P. Stuhlmacher.

resolution of the problem.[58] It may be that new developments in the form criticism of the Gospels will enable the student to cast fresh light upon their sources.

3.

Form criticism, going behind the sources of the Gospels, seeks to establish the original setting and to trace the history of the oral and literary forms in which the words and deeds of Jesus were transmitted. To do this it must combine (1) a literary analysis of the Gospels with (2) a historical reconstruction of the sociotheological context *(Sitz im Leben)* of the ministry of Jesus and of his earliest followers and, in the process, (3) rightly relate these two factors to the origin and development of the gospel traditions. Only with the accomplishment of this threefold task can it achieve its goal of a credible historical picture of the beginnings of the gospel tradition, that is, the occasion and causes that gave rise to it and the forms in which it was transmitted.

Beginning about sixty-five years ago with the work of German scholars, form criticism in its initial phase was decisively shaped by R. Bultmann and M. Dibelius.[59] As a method of literary analysis it marked a clear and permanent advance that was, in principle, accepted by almost all New Testament scholars. As it was shaped by its early practitioners, however, it was rejected by a number of scholars for *inter alia* its philosophical assumptions, for its presupposed picture of the ministry of Jesus, and for the influence of both of these factors upon its form-critical analysis.[60] On the philosophical/theological side, for example, Bultmann's "closed" worldview[61] and his quasi-Marcionite attitude toward the Old Testament[62] were hardly without influence on his judgment that the miracle stories and the Old Testament citations and expositions in the Gospels were secondary accretions.[63] Also, the sharp caesura that he drew (also for theological reasons) between Jesus and the earliest Church was not unrelated

58. M.-É. Boismard, "The Two-Source Theory at an Impasse," *NTS* 26, 1980, 1-17.

59. R. Bultmann, *History of the Synoptic Tradition*, ET [5]1963 (1921); M. Dibelius, *From Tradition to Gospel*, ET [2]1965 (1919).

60. On criticisms from the older literature cf. Riesner (n. 10), 6ff.; Ellis (n. 41), 238; E. Güttgemanns, *Candid Questions Concerning Gospel Form Criticism*, ET 1979, 37-52.

61. See above, n. 7.

62. R. Bultmann, "The Significance of the Old Testament for the Christian Faith," *The Old Testament and the Christian Faith*, ed. B. W. Anderson, 1963, 31f.: ". . . to the Christian faith the Old Testament is no longer revelation as it has been, and still is, for the Jews." It "is not in the true sense God's word." Cf. my foreword to the English translation of L. Goppelt, *TYPOS: The Typological Interpretation of the Old Testament in the New*, ET 1982, xif.

63. The suggested alternative that they were a result of his form-critical analysis is altogether unlikely.

to his sceptical attitude to the question of preresurrection traditions in the Gospels.[64]

More important, perhaps, were the historical assumptions on which the classical form criticism was erected. P. Stuhlmacher lists some of them:[65]

1. The gospel tradition began to be fixed only when the early Christian expectation of a soon end to the world faded.
2. It arose from (1) remembrances of Jesus' words and deeds and (2) the preaching and teaching of Christian missioners, both of which were freely elaborated, reinterpreted, and transformed by the Christian communities.
3. Its geographical and chronological framework rested not on historical memories but were wholly the editorial creations of the evangelists.
4. It mixed words of the exalted Jesus through Christian prophets indiscriminately among the traditioned words of the earthly Jesus.

In brief we may characterize these assumptions as delayed fixation, uncontrolled folkloric transmission, dialectical opposition of tradition and redaction, and inclusion of prophetic dominical oracles. To them we may add three more:

5. The tradition had an extended initial period of exclusively oral transmission.
6. It first consisted of isolated units and proceeded progressively toward larger collections.
7. Its progress may be seen and to some extent reconstructed on the basis of the two-document source hypothesis.

Each of these assumptions is open to question. We have observed above some of the problems of the two-document hypothesis. The postulate (point 6) of a uniform and gradual progression from isolated paradigms to larger wholes was recognized by the early form critics to have an exception in the passion story. It also does not accord with the way the evangelists themselves, the final traditioners, handle their sources, omitting and reformulating as well as adding material. There is also some probability of this multifold process in play at earlier stages. For example, some of the independent Old Testament quotations and some of the collected parables in the Gospels are apparently not drawn from isolated units but are the result of the breaking up and reformulation of prior expositions *(midrashim)* containing both biblical citations and parabolic illustrations.[66] Apart from these observed phenomena, if the transmission of the gospel traditions was a controlled process (see below), the whole idea of isolated units gradually coalescing into larger wholes falls by the wayside.

---

64. Cf. Ellis (n. 41), 240 and the literature cited there.
65. Stuhlmacher (n. 57).
66. Ellis (n. 41), 161f., 252. Cf. Sanders (n. 23).

The theory of an initial exclusively oral transmission (point 5) of the tradition was taken over by classical form criticism from J. G. Herder via H. Gunkel[67] and was also, under the influence of B. F. Westcott,[68] a tacit assumption in much of British scholarship. It was thought to be supported (already by Westcott) from the early Christians' expectation, rather imprecise to be sure, of a near-term end of the world. But this was shown to be wrong with the discovery of the library of the Qumran sect, a group that combined an intense apocalyptic expectation with prolific writing. There are other historical objections to a purely oral stage of transmission of gospel traditions.[69] (1) Literacy was widespread in Palestinian Judaism. (2) The occasion that necessitated written teachings in early Christianity, the separation of believers from the teaching leadership, was already present in the earthly ministry of Jesus, in Galilee and also in Judea. (3) The bilingual background of his followers also would have facilitated the rapid written formulation and transmission of at least some of his teachings. (4) Even among the establishment rabbis of the first century the teaching process was apparently not totally oral.[70]

If C. H. Dodd was perhaps too constructive in the schematic "framework of the gospel narrative" that he attributed to the earliest tradition,[71] K. L. Schmidt probably went too far in the other direction when he ascribed virtually the total geographical and chronological framework of the Gospels to the creation of the evangelists (point 3).[72] He went too far particularly (1) in his assumption that the gospel traditions were first transmitted solely (apart from the passion story) as isolated units, (2) in his total reliance on the two-document hypothesis (Marcan priority), and (3) in his *Denkmethode* that imposed *ab initio* a sharp dialectic *(entweder/oder)* between traditional and editorial matter. That is, Schmidt did not give adequate allowance for distinctions between editorial and editorial *de novo*. For example, the central section of Luke (9:51–19:44), the so-called "travel narrative," is as it stands clearly a Lucan editorial arrangement; yet (assuming Luke's dependence on Mark) it is also traditional, being built upon the framework he found in Mark 10–11 (and Q?).[73] Today's students have the task of better distinguishing the evangelists' editorial reworking of traditions from editorial *de novo* and thus, while they can build on the insights of Schmidt, they will need to revise some of his assumptions.

67. Cf. Kümmel (n. 3), 330. See below, n. 78.
68. Westcott (n. 43), 165-84, 207-12.
69. Cf. Ellis (n. 41), 242-47. I did not, as some mistakenly thought, rule out oral transmission altogether, nor did E. Güttgemanns (n. 60), 105, 142f.
70. Cf. J. Neusner in *JSJ* 4, 1973, 56-65; Gerhardsson, *Origins* (n. 93), 22ff.
71. C. H. Dodd, "The Framework of the Gospel Narrative" (1932), *New Testament Studies*, 1953, 1-11; cf. T. W. Manson, *Studies in the Gospels and Epistles*, 1962, 3-27.
72. K. L. Schmidt, *Der Rahmen der Geschichte Jesu*, 1964 (1919).
73. A few episodes in the section appear to have both Q and Marcan *Vorlagen*.

In classical form criticism oral transmission was linked to the further postulate of an uncontrolled and communal, folkloric context with the inevitable conclusion that the fixation of the tradition was both late and unreliable. The lateness of fixation (point 1) should now be reconsidered in the light of (1) the likelihood discussed above of at least some written transmission from the beginning, (2) a greater complex of written sources behind the Gospels than had earlier been supposed, and (3) the observation that the synoptic Gospels (and Acts) display no knowledge of any events after AD 70.

Regarding the last point, at least one event, the destruction of Jerusalem in AD 70, was the subject of several prophecies of Jesus, one that is preserved with elaboration in all three Synoptics and in underlying non-Marcan *Vorlagen.*[74] C. H. Dodd demonstrated that Luke 19:42-44 and 21:20-24 were "composed *entirely* from the language of the Old Testament," i.e., from its picture of the fall of Jerusalem in 586 BC, and were not only not colored by the event of AD 70 but are, in a number of details, actually at odds with that event.[75] With variations[76] Dodd's observation holds true for the other Synoptics' predictions of the destruction of Jerusalem. Since the evangelists elsewhere often reformulate or elaborate Jesus' word in the light of their own situation, the wording of these prophecies gives considerable support to a pre–70 (or about 70) *terminus ad quem* for the publication of the synoptic Gospels.[77]

The uncontrolled transmission of the gospel traditions (point 2), understood largely from the analogy of folk traditions, owed more to J. G. Herder's eighteenth-century romanticism[78] than to an analysis of first-century Jewish practices and rightly raised a number of questions.[79] (1) The limited chronological framework, first of all, does not inspire confidence in the analogy: the development of "holy word" traditions over a few decades in a relatively small and closely knit religious group is quite a different matter from the development of folk traditions over a century or more. (2) The postulate was also at odds with conceptions about the transmission of religious traditions that were present in early Christianity (I Cor. 11:23; 15:1-3) and rabbinic Judaism, as O. Cullmann,

---

74. Mark 13 par. Cf. L. Hartman, *Prophecy Interpreted,* 1966, 172, 226-35; Schramm (n. 56), 171-82. Cf. also Matt. 22:7 (? = Q); 23:37-39 (Q); Luke 19:41-44; 13:33ff. (Q).

75. E.g., "dash your children to the ground" (Luke 19:44; cf. Hos. 10:14); "flee to the mountains" (Luke 21:21). Cf. C. H. Dodd, "The Fall of Jerusalem and the 'Abomination of Desolation' " (1947), *More New Testament Studies,* 1968, 69-83, 79. Items important in AD 66-70 but not present in Luke: factional fighting, famine, cannibalism, fire.

76. There are some allusions to Old Testament references to the fall of Samaria, as there are in Luke (cf. Dodd [n. 75], 74f., 78).

77. Cf. Robinson (n. 12), 13-30, 86-117; E. E. Ellis, "Dating the New Testament," *NTS* 26, 1980, 488.

78. Cf. Güttgemanns (n. 60), 178-91; Kümmel (n. 3), 79-82 .

79. Cf. Riesner (n. 10), 11-17; G. N. Stanton, "Form Criticism Revisited," *What About the New Testament?,* ed. M. Hooker, 1975, 20f.

H. Riesenfeld, B. Gerhardsson, and R. Riesner have shown.[80] Finally, (3) it is difficult if not impossible, in a continuous traditioning process, to account for the transmission from folkloric (communal) oral transmission with its milieu and techniques to the (individual) written result in the Gospels with its milieu and techniques.[81]

On the inclusion of prophetic oracles of the risen Lord (point 4)[82] I believe that the classical form critics were in principle correct. However, the practice was not as extensive as they supposed and must be demonstrated for each passage considered.

The above criticisms of some of the assumptions of classical form criticism are not all of equal force, and they will not be equally persuasive to all. But they do, I believe, reveal fundamental weaknesses that warrant a reassessment of the discipline and a restructuring of it on firmer historical foundations. Such restructuring will need *inter alia* to take fully into account first-century Jewish attitudes and practices regarding the handling of religious tradition as well as the charismatic, prophetic character of the ministry of Jesus and of the primitive Church.

4.

A major obstacle to a satisfying historical reconstruction of gospel origins has been a false dichotomy between Spirit and form, charism and order, that has plagued New Testament studies for several generations. It has a complex background that cannot be detailed here. In brief, it is rooted partly in nineteenth-century philosophy, partly in mistaken inferences: extensive Church structure sometimes drove out the Spirit; therefore powerful, Spirit-carried movements must have driven out structure. But the facts are otherwise.

In the modern Church spiritual power has gone hand in hand with a recognition of order—in the Reformation, the Wesley revivals, and the modern Pentecostal groups and churches. Only on the fringes and extremes of these movements did order give way to *Schwärmerei*. The same was true of the New

---

80. O. Cullmann, "The Tradition" (1953), *The Early Church*, 1956, 57-99; H. Riesenfeld, "The Gospel Tradition and its Beginnings," *TU* 73, 1959, 43-65 = *The Gospel Tradition*, 1970, 1-29; B. Gerhardsson, *Memory and Manuscript*, 1961; Riesner (n. 10).

81. Cf. Güttgemanns (n. 60), 136-39, 200-211.

82. E.g., Matt. 18:20; Luke 11:49ff. (Q), on which cf. E. E. Ellis in *ExpT* 74, 1962-63, 157f.; cf. idem, *Paul's Use of the Old Testament*, ²1981, 107-12; J. D. G. Dunn, "Prophetic 'I' Sayings . . . ," *NTS* 24, 1977-78, 175-98; M. E. Boring, *Sayings of the Risen Jesus*, 1982 (speculatively) and the literature cited there. In addition one should compare here not only Rev. 3:20, etc., but also the "I" sayings in Odes of Solomon 10:4ff.; 17:6-16 *et passim*, in Melito's *Paschal Homily* 101ff. and in the Qumran *Temple Scroll* 29:8ff., *passim*. Otherwise: D. Hill, "On the Creative Role of Christian Prophets," *NTS* 20, 1973-74, 262-74; idem, *New Testament Prophecy*, 1979, 146-85.

Testament Church, where sweeping spiritual power was manifested in the context of ordered ministries. As M. Goguel has rightly noted, even when "the second generation succeeded to the first . . . ministries did not undergo a sharp change. . . . The emphasis in the conception of ministry merely shifted somewhat. We should be stating the problem in terms too narrow if we implied that it was only a question of an institutional ministry being substituted for a charismatic one."[83]

Certainly in the burgeoning Spirit-carried mission of the early Christians, say, of Paul, there was less emphasis on "order." But there was not an absence of it, and there was not the opposition between charism and order that some modern writers have supposed.[84]

The writings of the Qumran sect help us in this matter, as they do in others, to get a clearer picture of the situation in the community of Jesus. At Qumran the Teacher of Righteousness and the highly gifted, Spirit-oriented *maskilim,* who have remarkable affinities with the pneumatics in the Pauline communities, exercised their "prophetic" ministries in the context of a highly structured religious organization.[85]

A candid recognition of the twofold character of the ministry of Jesus and his apostles, charismatic and ordered, has important implications for a proper understanding and reconstruction of the origins of the gospel traditions. On the one hand, Jesus in his activities was, as M. Hengel has rightly emphasized,[86] a charismatic in the fullest sense, whose ministry included a prophetic ἐξουσία[87] and discernment,[88] an experience of visions,[89] and a Spirit-impelled power to a degree that even his family supposed that he was "beside himself" (ἐξέστη).[90] After Pentecost his followers, or certainly the leaders among them, manifested the same spiritual power, zeal, and exalted states.[91] The recognition of early Christianity, including the gospel traditioners, as a self-consciously and intensely prophetic movement[92] is an essential prerequisite to understanding its mission and its literature.

On the other hand, as B. Gerhardsson and more extensively R. Riesner have underscored, Jesus was a teacher who in his upbringing had been schooled

---

83. M. Goguel, *The Primitive Church,* ET 1964 (1947), 119f.

84. Cf. Ellis (n. 41), 10-13. I address this in more detail in *Pauline Theology: Ministry and Society,* 1989, 87ff. See also E. Schweizer, *Church Order in the New Testament,* ET 1979 (1961).

85. Cf. Ellis (n. 41), 57ff.; O. Betz, *Offenbarung und Schriftforschung in der Qumransekte,* 1960, 88-99, 110-42.

86. M. Hengel, *The Charismatic Leader and his Followers,* ET 1981, esp. 63-71.

87. Luke 4:18-21, 24-27 par.; Mark 1:22 par.

88. Mark 5:30; Luke 8:46 (? = Q).

89. Luke 10:18; Mark 9:2-10 (plus Q); Matt. 4:2-11 (Q); cf. John. 1:48.

90. Mark 3:21f.; cf. Acts 10:38.

91. E.g., Acts 4:8; 5:3; 13:1ff., 9ff.; 16:18; 26:12-24; II Cor. 12; cf. Luke 21:15; John 7:38f.

92. Matt. 5:12 (πρὸ ὑμῶν); 10:41; 13:52; Luke 11:49 (Q); 21:15.

in the Scriptures and in their traditional interpretation.[93] In all likelihood he was also knowledgeable in the methods of transmission of religious teaching used in Torah-centric Judaism. As his ministry is represented to us by the Gospels and their sources, he gave revolutionary new interpretations of Scripture, making use of patterns and techniques of exposition *(midrash)* known to us from Philo and rabbinical writings[94] and also employing Hillel's rules of interpretation.[95] His disciples who were sent out "to teach" (Mark 6:30) and the gospel traditioners who transmitted his word and story manifested similar characteristics.

Classical form criticism recognized the presence of "charismatic" and "ordered" elements in the formation of the gospel traditions but, if the arguments above are sound, it failed to provide a satisfactory explanation of their relationship and of the context of their transmission. The question arises, therefore, whether there is an alternative reconstruction which can give a more adequate account of the role and relationship of charism and order in the origin and transmission of the gospel tradition. The approaches of Hengel and Gerhardsson, modified in the light of each other, offer insights and pointers that can facilitate scholarly research in this area. There is also another group of closely analogous traditions that may aid in understanding the way in which the gospel traditions were transmitted. They are the traditions in the New Testament letters and Acts.

5.

In some recent research the Gospels and Epistles are recognized to display affinities that suggest a similar context and process of transmission of their respective traditions. (1) Both are attributed to persons in the same or related apostolic circles. (2) Both are, in part, products of a corporate enterprise in which an apostolic figure as the leading contributor and overseer is aided by and uses traditions composed by others. (3) Both give indications that their traditions were composed by the same or related circles of highly gifted pneumatics, i.e., prophets and teachers.

---

93. Gerhardsson (n. 80), 225ff., 324-35; idem, *The Origins of the Gospel Traditions,* 1979, 67-77; Riesner (n. 10), 206-76. Cf. S. Westerholm, *Jesus and Scribal Authority,* 1978, 126f.

94. E.g., proem and yelammedenu midrashim in Mark 12:1-10 + Q; Mark 12:18-27 + Q; cf. Ellis (n. 41), 157ff., 247-53. Cf. R. T. France, *Jesus and the Old Testament,* 1971; P. Borgen, *Bread from Heaven,* 1965.

95. Inference *a fortiori* (1) and by analogy (2); generalization (3); contextual explanation (7) in Luke 12:24 (קל וחומר); 6:1-5 (גזירה שוה); Mark 12:26 (. . . בניו אב); Matt. 19:4-8 (מענינו . . .). For the rules cf. H. L. Strack, *Introduction to the Talmud and Midrash,* ET 1969, 93f. Further, cf. E. E. Ellis, "Biblical Interpretation in the New Testament Church," *Mikra* (Compendia Rerum Judaicarum ad Novum Testamentum, ed. S. Safrai *et al.,* II/1) (691-725), 692-702.

1. The letters of James, I Peter, and the Pauline corpus were written by
apostles who, on the evidence of Paul and his sometime companion Luke,[96]
worked in a cooperative relationship with one another and shared their common
and/or particular traditions, even as they pursued their different missions and
theological emphases.[97] The letters and the Book of Acts connect their authors
with men who according to second-century sources wrote the synoptic
Gospels,[98] relating both Peter and Paul to Mark[99] and Paul and James to Luke;[100]
Acts puts James and Matthew together in Jerusalem.[101] These relationships are
mentioned in a matter of fact and incidental fashion without apologetic purpose
and have a high degree of historical probability.

More significantly, the letters reveal that Paul (and his congregations)[102]
and Peter[103] and James[104] know a number of synoptic traditions. They rarely

96. On Lucan authorship cf. recently Ellis (n. 32), 40-51; Fitzmyer (n. 39), 35-53. On the
apostolic authorship of these letters cf. F. Mussner, *Der Jakobusbrief,* 1975, 1-23; J. N. D. Kelly,
The Epistles of Peter and Jude, 1969, 30-33. Cf. Robinson (n. 12), *passim* and the literature cited
there; W. C. van Unnik, *Sparsa Collecta II,* 1980, 69-82 (on I Peter).

97. Gal. 1:18; 2:1, 9; I Cor. 3:22–4:1; 9:5; 11:16, 23ff.; 14:33ff.; 15:3-7; Rom. 15:25; Acts
11:29f.; 12:25; 15:6-35; 21:17f.; cf. II Pet 3:15f.; Jude 17f. with I Tim 4:1. Cf. Cullmann (n. 80),
72f.; Gerhardsson (n. 80), 296-302; G. D. Kilpatrick, "Gal 1:18," *New Testament Essays,* ed. A. J. B.
Higgins, 1959, 144-49. This differs, of course, from the theory of the nineteenth-century scholar
F. C. Baur (and his heirs) who, for all his genius, wrongly identified Peter (and James) with Paul's
opponents and made his exegesis too much the servant of his Hegelian philosophy. Cf. Ellis (n. 41),
86-95, 102-24, 230-36; idem (n. 77), 494ff.

98. E.g., Papias (see n. 38); Irenaeus, *Adv. haer.* 3.1.1; Muratorian Canon. For an evaluation
of some second-century traditions see the essays in the present volume by L. Abramowski and
M. Hengel.

99. Col. 4:10f.; II Tim. 4:11; Phlm. 24; I Pet. 5:13; Acts 12:12-25; 13:5, 13; 15:37ff.
Although conceivable, I now think it improbable that the "Hebraist" Mark of Acts and Colossians
is different from the "Hellenist" evangelist and companion of Peter: Mark apparently followed the
pilgrimage of Peter (Acts 10:28) from kosher to lax observance. Cf. V. Taylor, *St. Mark,* [2]1966,
26-31; but see G. Dix, *Jew and Greek,* 1955, 73ff.; Ellis (n. 41), 127 n. See the essay in the present
volume by P. Stuhlmacher.

100. Regarding Paul: Col. 4:14; II Tim. 4:11; Phlm. 24; Acts 16:10-17; 20:5–21:17;
27:1–28:16 ("we"). Regarding James: Acts 21:17f. ("we").

101. Acts 1:13f.; cf. 12:12-17, 25.

102. The fleeting references to Jesus' teachings in I Cor. 7:10; 9:14 (I Tim. 5:18) are hardly
meaningful unless a broader knowledge of them by the congregations is presupposed, as is rightly
observed by Gerhardsson (n. 80), 304ff.; H. Riesenfeld (*The Gospel Tradition,* 1970, 11-18 = *TU*
73 [1959], 51-56), and D. L. Dungan (*The Sayings of Jesus in the Churches of Paul,* 1971, 146-50).
Cf. D. C. Allison, "The Pauline Epistles and the Synoptic Gospels: The Pattern of the Parallels,"
NTS 28, 1982, 1-32; D. Wenham, "The Synoptic Apocalypse," *Gospel Perspectives* (n. 10) II,
345-75. This broader knowledge is confirmed in I Cor. 11:23; 15:3; cf. Col. 2:8; Cullmann (n. 80),
64-69. Otherwise: Goulder (n. 44), 144-70; idem, *The Evangelists' Calendar,* 1978, 227-40, who
thinks that, while Paul knew Marcan traditions, Matthew drew from Paul's letters. More likely is
Dodd's (n. 71, 53-66) view that Matthew and Paul had traditions in common.

103. E.g., I Pet. 1:10f. (Luke 10:24 = Matt. 13:17); 2:7 (Mark 12:10 + Q); 2:12 (Matt. 5:16);
4:13f. (Matt. 5:11f. = Luke 6:22f.).

104. The letter of James shows special affinities with Matthean traditions e.g. Jas. 1:5, 6,
22f.; 2:5, 13; 4:10; 5:12. Cf. Riesenfeld (n. 102); Mussner (n. 96), 47-52; J. B. Mayor, *Epistle of
James,* [3]1910, lxxvff.

cite them as such, apparently because (1) they know their recipients have already received Jesus-traditions that were deliberately transmitted separately as a special kind of tradition[105] and because (2) as prophets who "have the mind of Christ" and apostles who are conscious of being his authorized representatives (שלוחים) and whose teaching is thus his teaching,[106] they have no need to do so. Peter is apparently Paul's source for many such dominical traditions (Gal. 1:18). He, along with others of the Twelve later associated with the writing of Gospels (Matthew, John), played an important role, as Gerhardsson has reminded us, in the initial proclamation and transmission of the teachings of Jesus.[107] But do the Twelve have the special role in the transmission of gospel traditions that Gerhardsson has attributed to them?

The apostles of Jesus Christ are nowhere in the New Testament limited to the Twelve, not even in Luke-Acts.[108] Although the Twelve, the first named apostles, had a "ministry of the Word" that doubtless included the transmission of gospel traditions,[109] they were not the only ones engaged in that activity.[110] According to Luke those who originally "transmitted" (παρέδοσαν) such traditions were "from the beginning eyewitnesses (αὐτόπται) and ministers of the Word," one group with a twofold qualification that went beyond the Twelve and may have included the Seventy.[111] They were very likely, as Luke seems to imply, "men who accompanied (Jesus) . . . beginning from the baptism of John until the day when he was taken up."[112] Although not limited to the Twelve, they are represented as qualified witnesses (μάρτυρες) who had followed (ἀκολουθεῖν) Jesus, had been taught (μαθητεύειν, διδάσκειν) by him, and had in turn taught others. Each of these attributes was, as Gerhardsson has illustrated, characteristic of the pupils of rabbis who were qualified to transmit their master's teachings.[113] However, there are also differences from the rabbinic practice. (1) Jesus' "call to follow" appears to have closer affinities, as we shall

105. See above, n. 102; cf. I Pet. 1:12. See the essay in the present volume by B. Gerhardsson.
106. Cf. I Cor. 2:16; 14:37; K. H. Rengstorf, "ἀπόστολος," *TDNT* I, 1964 (1933), 424-43; C. K. Barrett, "*Shaliaḥ* and Apostle," *Donum Gentilicium*, ed. E. Bammel, 1978, 88-102.
107. Cf. Kilpatrick (n. 97); Gerhardsson (n. 80), 220-25, 329-32; Cullmann (n. 80). Cf. Acts 2:14; 6:2.
108. They include, at least, Cleopas, another apostle, "the eleven and those with them" (cf. Luke 24:9f., 33; 24:13, αὐτῶν, with 24:10, ἀποστόλους), Barsabbas, Matthias, and others (cf. Acts 1:22-26; 10:41; 13:31 with 1:2f.; Luke 24:33-43), and Paul and Barnabas (Acts 14:4, 14). Cf. Ellis (n. 32), 132-35.
109. So, Gerhardsson (n. 80), 242-45; Luke 6:13; Acts 6:4; cf. 2:42.
110. *Pace* Gerhardsson. Cf. W. D. Davies, *The Setting of the Sermon on the Mount*, 1964, 472-76; R. A. Culpepper, *The Johannine School*, 1975, 215-46.
111. Luke 1:2. In my view Luke 10:1f., 17-20 is a traditional piece supplemented (10:3-16) from other sources and not Lucan editorial *de novo*. Mark was probably an adolescent disciple of the earthly Jesus (Mark 14:51f.; cf. Acts 12:12).
112. Acts 1:21f.
113. E.g., Luke 5:11; 11:1; Matt. 13:52; 27:57; 5:1f.; Mark 9:31; 6:30; Acts 1:22; 10:39; cf. Gerhardsson (n. 80), 183ff., 194.

observe below, with a prophetic than with a rabbinic model. And (2) there is some evidence that in the New Testament the transmitters of Jesus-traditions did not work as separate and individual authorities but as part of a corporate or group endeavor. This leads to two further affinities between traditions in the Gospels and in the Epistles.

2. Although the (synoptic) evangelists are probably indentified correctly by the second-century sources,[114] their individual role may be overstated there and indeed, with the possible exception of Luke,[115] it is difficult to assess with any precision. In some of these sources, however, Matthew,[116] Mark,[117] and John[118] are presented as arrangers of gospel traditions whose work, in the case of Mark and John, is then ratified by others. That is, they are participants in a corporate enterprise.

In first-century sources Mark appears similarly as a coworker with Peter and Silas (I Pet. 5:12f.) and earlier with Paul and Barnabas (Acts 13:6). In the latter case he is described as a minister (ὑπηρέτης) in the proclamation of the Word of God, a term that Luke uses earlier of those who transmitted gospel traditions (Luke 1:2). More significantly, Luke represents "the ministry (διακονία) of the Word" in Acts 6:4, which would have included Jesus-traditions, as a corporate activity of the Twelve. And his mention of the "many" who drew up a "narrative" (διήγησις, Luke 1:1) possibly refers to the corporate composition of one document, as the singular may suggest,[119] rather than the individual composition of many narratives. There is then considerable historical evidence that points to the composition of the Gospels and/or their traditions as a group activity. Does the literary criticism of the Gospels support this perception?

114. The arguments against these identifications are conveniently summarized in Kümmel, *Introduction* (n. 48), 49, 95-246, but they are not decisive and often rest on questionable assumptions e.g. that a Palestianian could not write Greek or be ignorant of (or indifferent to) local geography or that an apostle would not use traditions edited by a non-apostle. Of highest probability for Luke and Mark, the tradition was, apart from John, undisputed, is without a satisfactory alternative, and is inherently not improbable: one must resist the modern tendency to assume that in early Christianity only unknowns knew how to write.

115. Cf. H. J. Cadbury, *The Making of Luke-Acts,* 1927. He notes (169-83) parallels between Luke and Josephus on the treatment of sources but gives no attention to possible parallels between them in the use of secretaries and writing assistants (συνεργοί), a matter that remains and needs to be explored. Cf. Josephus, *c. Apion.* 1.50 = 1.9; H. St. J. Thackeray, ed., *Josephus,* 1926-1965, I, xv; II, xv-xix; IV, xiv-xvii. More generally, see the essay in the present volume by I. H. Marshall.

116. "Matthew collected (συνετάξατο) the sayings" (Papias in Eusebius, *HE* 3.39.16).

117. "Mark became Peter's interpreter (ἑρμηνευτής) and wrote"; ". . . Peter ratified (κυρῶσαι) the writing (γραφή) for study" (Papias in Eusebius, *HE* 3.39.15; 2.14f.). "Interpreter" is better understood as "expositor," perhaps a gifted expounder (מליץ, as in 1QH 2:13f.; cf. I Cor. 14:26), than as "translator." Cf. J. Behm, "ἑρμηνεύω," *TDNT* II, 1964 (1935), 663 n.; Ellis (n. 41), 57ff. See above, n. 98.

118. In a garbled reminiscence (?) in the Muratorian Canon: "When (John was) exhorted by his fellow disciples and bishops (to write) . . . , it was revealed to Andrew, one of the apostles, that John was to write all things in his own name, and they were all to certify" *(recognoscentibus).*

119. This point was made by Herbert Marsh (n. 37) almost 200 years ago; he thought that Luke referred to a primitive (Hebrew) Gospel.

As the traditional form and source criticism have shown, despite all their foibles and unresolved problems, the individual evangelist is not the creator *de novo* of the Gospel attributed to him. He is—Mark also[120] at least dependent on sources that are the work of others. For example, Matthew uses special exegetical traditions that appear to reflect the work of a circle of highly skilled prophets and/or teachers (Stendahl),[121] and the same may be said of the cycle of midrashic prophecies and vision-prophecies used by Luke in his infancy narrative (Ellis).[122] Did the evangelist, however, work on his own in the final composition of his Gospel? Luke leaves few if any clues pointing to collaborators even if, given the custom of the day, his use of an amanuensis can be assumed. But John and perhaps Matthew hint at collaboration at the final stage of their composition.[123] Finally, the fact that apart from Luke[124] the Gospels give no pointers to the identity of the author may suggest that he produced his work with the aid of colleagues.

These observations do not confirm Gerhardsson's hypothesis of a college of twelve apostolic traditioners. But they are in accord with a qualified form of that hypothesis and raise probabilities that take us beyond the vague "community formation" theories of classical form criticism. The examination of the transmission of other kinds of tradition in early Christianity may yield still firmer conclusions.

The New Testament letters reflect more than one sociotheological context *(Sitz im Leben),* that of the final composition and that of any preformed traditions within them. In their final form they are not, except perhaps for the Johannines and Hebrews, the product of one creative individual working on his own. Paul's letters disclose the presence of amanuenses[125] and cosenders[126] who, along with

---

120. H. W. Kuhn, *Ältere Sammlungen im Markusevangelium,* 1971; Schmithals (n. 57) I, 34f.; cf. R. Pesch, *Das Markusevangelium* I, 1976, 39: in its arrangement the first half of Mark is determined by pre-Marcan collections of teachings and miracles, the second half by the pre-Marcan passion story. See the essay in the present volume by R. Pesch.

121. K. Stendahl, *The School of St. Matthew,* [2]1968, ixf., 30-35.

122. Luke. 1:5–2:40. Cf. Ellis (n. 32), 27ff., 57f., dependent on A. Schlatter, *Das Evangelium des Lukas,* 1931, 210f.; P. Winter in *NTS* 1, 1954-55, 121; *ZNW* 47, 1956, 217-42; 49, 1958, 65-77; and *BJRL* 37, 1954-55, 328-47.

123. John 19:35; 21:24; Matt. 13:52; cf. O. Cullmann, *The Johannine Circle,* ET 1976, 8-11; Culpepper (n. 110); R. E. Brown, *The Community of the Beloved Disciple,* 1979; Stendahl (n. 121), 204ff.

124. Luke 1:3; Acts 1:1; 16:10 *et passim* ("we").

125. Rom. 16:22; I Cor. 16:21; Gal. 6:11; Col. 4:18; II Thess. 3:17; Phlm. 19. Cf. O. Roller, *Das Formular der Paulinischen Brief,* 1933; Ellis (n. 77), 497ff. Roller (17-20) shows that the amanuensis did not merely take dictation but often had a more substantial influence. This might be expected in New Testament letters if the amanuensis were himself a gifted pneumatic and coworker in ministry.

126. E.g., I Cor. 1:1; II Cor. 1:1; Gal. 1:2; Phil. 1:1; cf. H. Conzelmann in *NTS* 12, 1965-66, 233ff. Some letters may have been primarily composed by the cosender. According to E. G. Selwyn *(First Epistle of St. Peter,* 1946, 17, 369-84) Silas = Silvanus may have been a "joint author" of I-II

the author, had an influence in greater or lesser degree on the form and content of the letter. I Peter similarly reflects the use of an amanuensis (or coauthor)[127] and, judging from the customary writing practice,[128] the same can be assumed for James.[129]

While there is considerable evidence for a corporate participation in the composition of the apostolic letters, it is more difficult to identify traditions within the letters that are composed (1) by others who (2) worked in a group. For one must establish both the context for the writing of traditions within the apostolic missions and also the traditional status of a particular pericope.

The most direct insight into apostolic praxis concerning the formation and transmission of "holy word" traditions is the apostolic decree in Acts 15. Whether the decree is the product of the Jerusalem Council, as is probable,[130] or whether it was appended from another context, it is in either case a contemporary representation of how apostolic traditions were formulated and transmitted. It is the result of discussion and biblical exposition by the teaching leadership (15:6) who, having discerned the will of the Holy Spirit (15:28), commission two prophets among them to write a regulation (and letter)[131] and transmit it to the distant congregation(s). Admittedly, the decree reflects a special situation involving a disagreement between certain evangelists from the Jerusalem mission (15:24) and those from the mission based in Antioch, but *mutatis mutandis* it is not in principle different from regulations formulated in common or within a particular apostle's mission to deal with other questions.

To support this four brief examples must suffice. (1) The household regulations *(Haustafeln)* that are present with variations in letters of different

---

Thessalonians (and I Peter). Less likely, E. Schweizer (*Colossians,* ET 1982, 23-26) and W. H. Ollrog (*Paulus und seine Mitarbeiter,* 1979, 219-33, 241f.) suggest Timothy as the "author" of Colossians, written during Paul's Ephesian imprisonment.

127. I Pet. 5:12. Cf. Selwyn (n. 126). L. Goppelt (*Der Erste Petrusbrief,* 1978, 347ff.) takes Silas to be the author. Cf. Acts 15:22f. (see below, n. 131); Eusebius, *HE* 4.23.11 regarding I Clement; Ignatius, *Ad philad.* 11:2. Cf. Zahn (n. 131 below) II, 535.

128. Even the brief letters of Bar Kokhba (†AD 135) were written through secretaries; Y. Yadin in *IEJ* 11, 1961, 45, 50. According to Roller (n. 125, 7-14, 353-58) to write a page of ca. 150 words on papyrus could take a skilled writer about one hour.

129. Although the relatively good Greek might suggest an amanuensis, it would not be unusual for a Palestinian Jew. Cf. Ellis (n. 41), 245ff.; idem (n. 77), 497 and the literature cited there. The book of Revelation also suggests that John had assistants in its composition: although Jesus (or God) imparts the visions to John, he is said to "make known" or "show" (δεικνύειν) the revelation to his "servants," i.e., John's fellow prophets (Rev. 1:1; 22:6).

130. The problem of its present location arose primarily from the traditional but mistaken equation, Acts 15 = Galatians 2. If the equation Acts 11 = Galatians 2 is followed, that problem is removed. Cf. the perceptive comments of F. F. Bruce, *Commentary on Galatians* (NIGTC), 1982, 3-18, 43-56, 105-28; idem, *The Book of the Acts* (NICNT) ²1988, 282-85; idem, "Galatian Problems," in *BJRL* 51, 1968-69, 292-309; 54, 1971-72, 250-67.

131. Acts 15:23: γράψαντες διὰ χειρὸς αὐτῶν. Cf. T. Zahn, *Die Apostelgeschichte* II, 1921, 534f.

apostles are too similar to have been formed entirely independently. They appear to be particular expressions and elaborations of common principles that have been worked out together or created by one apostle or apostolic circle and shared with others.[132] More significantly, (2) rules concerning the conduct of prophetesses and wives show that it is not a matter of later writers adopting Pauline teachings, as much critical orthodoxy supposes, since they are explicitly stated already by Paul to be the custom in "the churches of God" and "of all the churches of the saints."[133] (3) The listings of virtues and vices, together[134] or separately,[135] also appear to have been a traditional (and traditioned) motif common to the Jacobean, Pauline, Petrine, and Johannine missions. They have an important link with gospel traditions[136] and are rooted in Old Testament exposition (midrash)[137] and in the ethical imperative of "putting off" (ἀποτίθεσθαι) pre-Christian lifestyle and "putting on" (ἐνδύεσθαι) conduct appropriate to believers. While the listings are variously expressed and only loosely parallel, they have sufficient in common to justify the assumption of underlying, commonly shared tradition(s). Some of the lists are introduced with formulas that indicate a cited tradition[138] or are connected with traditions previously delivered.[139] Finally, (4) in certain expositions of the Old Testament different New Testament writers also draw on common traditional interpretations.[140]

These illustrations show, I believe, that the several apostolic missions shared various types of tradition, either jointly formulated (on the analogy of Acts 15) or created individually within one of their circles. And there is some probability that the individuals formulating such pieces worked within a leadership circle (perhaps like that in Acts 13:1-3) which first heard and then helped

132. Eph. 5:22–6:9; Col. 3:18–4:1; Tit. 2:2-10; I Pet. 2:18–3:7. Clement is aware that such rules were observed also in Corinth (I Clem. 1:3). Cf. also Philo, *De decal.* 165-67; Ps.-Phocylides 179-225 (cf. P. W. van der Horst in *ZNW* 69, 1978, 196-200. For various views of the origin and occasion of the *Haustafeln*, not our concern here, cf. J. E. Crouch, *The Origin and Intention of the Colossian Haustafeln,* 1972, 9-31; D. L. Balch, *Let Wives be Submissive: the Domestic Code in I Peter,* 1981.

133. I Cor. 11:16; 14:33; cf. I Tim. 2:11-15; E. E. Ellis, "The Silenced Wives of Corinth," *New Testament Textual Criticism,* ed. E. J. Epp, 1981, 213-20.

134. Rom. 13:12-14; Gal. 5:19-23; Eph. 4:28f., 31f., 5:3-5; Col. 3:5, 8, 12-15; Jas. 3:14–4:2; I Pet. 2:1f., 4:3, 7-9. Cf. S. Wibbing, *Die Tugend- und Lasterkataloge im Neuen Testament,* 1959; H. Conzelmann, *I Corinthians,* ET 1975, 100f. on I Cor. 5:10f.

135. E.g., Phil. 4:8; I Tim. 6:11; II Pet. 1:5-7 (virtues). Rom. 1:29-31; Tit. 3:3; Rev. 9:20f.; 21:8; 22:15 (vices).

136. Mark 7:21f. par.

137. I Pet. 3:9-12; I Tim. 1:9f.

138. Eph. 5:5; I Tim. 1:9f.: τοῦτο γινώσκοντες (εἰδὼς) ὅτι; cf. II Tim. 3:1.

139. I Cor. 6:9 (οὐκ οἴδατε ὅτι); Phil. 4:8f. (μανθάνειν, παραλαμβάνειν).

140. E.g., in the rejected stone typology of Rom. 9:33 and I Pet. 2:6ff. C. H. Dodd (*According to the Scriptures,* 1952, 41ff.) showed that both writers wree dependent on pre-existing tradition. More broadly, the temple typology in Mark 14:58; John 2:19f.; Acts 7:48; 15:16ff.; I Cor. 3:16; Eph. 2:19-22; I Pet. 2:4-8 also is a commonly shared motif rooted in the teachings of Jesus. Cf. Ellis, *Paul's Use* (n. 82), 86-98. Cf. also Rom. 12:19 with Heb. 10:30.

to bring into final form a particular authoritative word for the churches. Who were those who performed this task with such authority that their teachings were incorporated into the apostolic letters?

3. Professor Gerhardsson's conception of a controlled transmission of gospel traditions marked a clear advance beyond earlier form criticism, but his rabbinic analogy has faced a number of problems. One of them is the evident freedom with which the tradition is handled. While there are few if any historical grounds to suppose that the traditioners created events in Jesus' life, as much of classical form criticism assumed, it is clear that, unlike the rabbis, they not only preserved but also altered and elaborated the tradition of Jesus' teachings as well as the description of events.[141] Furthermore, Jesus' call to leave all and follow him appears to have a better analogy in Essene (Qumran) than in rabbinic attitudes.[142] At the same time Jesus' ministry also has affinities with rabbinic practices.[143] It represents a *tertium quid* for which no analogy fully suffices, but in the realm of his teaching and its transmission the prophetic dimension is of decisive significance.

Jesus was certainly perceived by others to be a prophet,[144] a designation that he did not reject but even used of himself with respect both to his teachings and to his destiny to be persecuted and killed.[145] His claim to possess the Spirit is also the assertion of a prophet, and the importance of the prophetic Spirit in his ministry goes beyond the (relatively few) explicit references.[146] The same Spirit is promised to his followers,[147] and the gospel traditioners and the evangelists are very conscious of being heirs of this promise. This is evident from the prominence they give to the Baptist's prophecy (Mark 1:8 par.) and their occasional inclusion of oracles from the risen Jesus.[148] Already in the earthly ministry of Jesus the apostles, in their missions, stand in the role of prophets whether the Spirit has been imparted to them[149] or, perhaps not very different, the Spirit of Jesus is active in their use of his name. Very probably the apostolic traditioners regarded themselves as fulfilling a prophetic role not only

141. E.g., Matt. 4:2-11, as is recognized also by B. Gerhardsson, *The Testing of God's Son,* 1966. It appears to elaborate Jesus' disclosure of a vision experience, like that in Luke 10:18; see above, n. 89.

142. Cf. Hengel (n. 86), 50-60 and the literature cited there. Cf. 1QM 2:7; 3:2; 4:10; CD 4:3f.

143. See above, nn. 94 and 95.

144. Mark 6:15; 8:28; cf. 8:11; 14:65 + Q; Luke 7:39.

145. Mark 6:4 par.; John 4:44; Luke 13:33f.

146. E.g., Matt. 12:28 (Q); cf. Mark 3:28f. + Q; Matt. 11:5 (Q) = Isa. 61:1. Cf. J. Jeremias, *New Testament Theology* I, ET 1971, 75-80; M. A. Chevallier, *Souffle de Dieu,* 1978, 227-39 (the synoptic tradition) and the literature cited there.

147. E.g., Mark 1:8 + Q; Mark 13:11; Luke 21:15; John 7:38f.; 14:17, 26; 16:7.

148. Cf. Luke 11:49-52 (σοφία τοῦ θεοῦ) with Matt. 23:34 (ἐγώ); Ellis (n. 32), 171-74. More generally, Boring (n. 82) and the literature cited there.

149. So, Jeremias (n. 146), 79. Cf. Mark 6:7 + Q.

in their preaching and persecutions[150] but also in their writing as "wise men and scribes," i.e., Scripture teachers,[151] for by the first century the two ancient streams of prophecy and wisdom had merged pretty much into one spiritual type. The role of the prophet included teaching that "made present" previous holy word by reapplication and contemporization.[152] This was at least a part of the task of the gospel traditioners, and it best explains their boldness and confidence both in their christological contemporization and application of Old Testament texts and in their similar handling of the holy word of Jesus.

Traditions in the apostolic letters show similar marks of composition by persons with prophetic gifts. This is already suggested by the high status given to the prophet and prophecy[153] and becomes evident, *exempli gratia,* in hymnic material and certain exegetical traditions. The same kind of christological/ eschatological exposition that appears in gospel traditions recurs in the letters and is, in the words of É. Cothenet,[154] a part of the apostles' prophetic function. The same is true of the revelation of divine wisdom[155] and of mysteries,[156] which is an important aspect of the exposition.[157] Eph. 3:5 ascribes such revelation to Christ's "apostles and prophets." In the light of the status given by Paul to Christian prophets, the reference is not to be limited to (the prophetic function of) apostles[158] but includes the writings of Christian prophets, some of which the apostolic writers use.[159] Examples of such (exegetical) prophetic traditions are the λέγει κύριος quotations,[160] certain πιστὸς ὁ λόγος sayings,[161] and the midrashim in I Cor. 2:6-16[162] and perhaps in Jas. 2:20-26.[163]

Hymnic expression is especially favored in writings of prophets,[164] and

150. Cf. Matt. 5:12 (πρὸ ὑμῶν); Mark 13:11; Luke 21:15; perhaps Mark 14:38.

151. Matt. 13:52; 23:34; cf. Luke 11:49ff.; 21:15; W. C. Allen, *Matthew,* 1907, 154f. Cf. Philo, *De gig.* 5.22; *Q.d. immut.* 1.3: σοφός = προφήτης.

152. Cf. Ellis (n. 41), 52-59, 133-38; Boring (n. 148), 71-78; Riesner (n. 10), 276-98.

153. E.g., Acts 11:27; 15:32; Rom. 12:6; 16:26; I Cor. 12:10, 28; 14:1; Eph. 2:20; 4:11; I Thess. 2:15; I Tim. 1:18; cf. Jas. 5:10; II Pet. 1:19; 3:2. J. Lindblom, *Geschichte und Offenbarungen,* 1968, 162-205.

154. É. Cothenet, "Prophetisme dans le Nouveau Testament," *DBS* 8, 1967-72, 1304.

155. Acts 6:3; I Cor. 3:10; Eph. 3:8-12; Jas. 1:5; cf. II Pet. 3:15; Rev. 13:18.

156. I Cor. 4:1; 13:2; Col. 1:25-28; I Tim. 3:16.

157. Rom. 11:25-27; 11:33-36 (concluding Rom. 9–11); I Cor. 1:18–3:20; Eph. 5:31f.

158. *Pace* Cothenet (n. 154, 1306f.), who apparently takes the καὶ epexegetically. But see above, n. 153.

159. Cf. Rom. 16:26; see above, n. 140.

160. Rom. 12:19 *et passim.* Cf. Ellis (n. 41), 182-87.

161. Probably I Tim. 2:11–3:1a; cf. 4:1, 6 (τοῖς λόγοις τῆς πίστεως).

162. I Cor. 2:6-16 sets forth the role of the pneumatics and is probably a preformed tradition; cf. Ellis (n. 41), 213.

163. Jas. 2:20-26 displays a commentary pattern: Theme (20) + Text (21) + Commentary (22) + Texts (23) + Commentary and Illustration (24f., cf. Josh. 2) + Concluding repetition of the theme (26). Of 53 different words 24 are found only here in James.

164. Cf. K.-P. Jörns, *Das hymnische Evangelium,* 1971 (on hymns in Revelation); D. E. Aune, "The Odes of Solomon and Early Christian Prophecy," *NTS* 28, 1982, 453-55 and the literature cited there.

when it occurs as "the word of Christ" among Colossian "brothers" who, like Paul, teach and admonish one another "in all wisdom," pneumatic, i.e., prophetic activity is clearly in view.[165] Such activity has probably left its literary formulation in some preformed hymns that are used in the Pauline/Petrine letters.[166] There are a few traditions in the Gospels[167] and Epistles[168] where a prophetic-type exposition of the Old Testament is combined with hymnic formulation. Here the mark of the prophet in the formation of early Christian traditions makes its strongest impression.

These observations, if acceptable, indicate that the same apostolic circles were involved in the formation and/or transmission of both gospel and epistolary traditions. They sought to maintain a salvation-history distinction between traditions from the earthly Jesus and those—also mediating "the mind of Christ"—created in the postresurrection mission. As prophets, however, they also "made present" the words of the earthly Jesus. Both concerns, historical distinction and contemporary proclamation, manifested themselves variously in the Gospels. Only in the later apocryphal Gospels was the former finally eclipsed.

The above remarks, necessarily brief, do not establish a thesis. But it is hoped that they have shown something of the progress of research and will encourage others to delineate with greater clarity and detail the process by which, in the good purpose of God, our Gospels came to us.

---

165. Cf. Col. 3:16 with 1:28.

166. E.g., Phil. 2:6-11; I Tim. 3:16; II Tim. 2:11ff.; Tit. 3:3-8a; I Pet. 1:18-21. Perhaps: I Cor. 8:6; Eph. 4:5f.; Col. 1:15-20; I Tim. 6:11f., 15f.; I Pet. 3:18f. Cf. J. T. Sanders, *The New Testament Christological Hymns*, 1971, 17f. *et passim;* O. Hofius, *Der Christushymnus Ph 2, 6-11*, 1976, 80-92 *et passim* and the literature cited there.

167. Luke 1:13-17, 30-33, 46-55, 68-79; 2:29-32; perhaps John 1:1-5. Cf. Burney (n. 41).

168. Rom. 11:33-36; II Cor. 6:14–7:1.

Jesus' Gospel of the Kingdom

Otto Betz

1. The Problem of the Jesus-Tradition: What Do We Know of the Gospel of Jesus?

Not long ago Heinz Zahrnt, in a lead article about a Catholic church convention at Düsseldorf,[1] wrote that the Church has been given a multiplicity of languages, just as this was reported of the first Pentecost at Jerusalem. From the beginning this phenomenon symbolized the variety of confessional expression:

> Not even the New Testament canon constituted a single unified *Formula of Concord*, but a collection of "confessions." Each of these "confessional tendencies" observed the memory of Jesus in its own way: the one voice of God echoing in a chorus of human voices. They all speak of the same revelation of God in Jesus Christ but they speak of it in distinctive ways. The Jewish Christian Matthew speaks of it differently from the Gentile Christian Luke, and John again speaks quite differently from the two of them. Paul has his eye fixed on grace and James focuses mainly on works. "Jewish Christians," "Gentile Christians," "Hellenists," "Samaritans," "Johannine Circle"—each group interprets the Jesus-tradition in terms of their own background and hope and expands it accordingly. And so the process continues throughout the history of the Church. There is no uniformity in it; we are dealing rather with mere fragments of a large confession.

There seems to be no doubt in Zahrnt's mind that this verdict corresponds with the unanimous result of New Testament scholarship. Soon after Jesus' death his gospel is supposed to have become audible through a chorus marred by many dissonants, by way of a "Pentecostal" speech which—in distinction

---

1. *Deutsches Allgemeines Sonntagsblatt*, September 5, 1982, 1: "Von müder Toleranz zum Wettstreit um die Wahrheit."

from that of the first Pentecost—sounded forth in a common language, koine Greek, but which offered a different message with every voice that spoke. On this basis one can never write a unified theology of the New Testament.[2]

But is this correct? Were there actually such grave differences? Was so-called "early catholicism" really needed to tone down and coordinate the tumultuous Spirit and the confusion of the voices of the first witnesses, and so to save the Church from an early decline? This I do not believe. If, for all the pluralism, as the very themes of the symposium on which the present volume is based testify, there had not also been a continuity in Jesus' gospel of the kingdom, a harmony and a unity in the message of the New Testament, Christianity could hardly in such a short time have made its way into the Roman Empire.

In the present essay, the subject of which is the known words of Jesus and not the "unknown" ones with which Otfried Hofius's contribution to this volume deals, I should like briefly to explore the following questions: How does the message of the earthly Jesus concerning the kingdom relate to the gospel of Christ which the Church preached after the resurrection? Are we here dealing with two distinct gospels: the first a Jewish one, a gospel of the Father, the second a specifically Christian one, in which the Son is central; the first, where Jesus appears as brother to the Jews, the second, where trinitarian dogma, irreconcilable with Jewish monotheism, is beginning to show its lineaments? And how does Jesus' gospel of the kingdom relate to his words about the Son of Man, to the person and mission of the proclaimer himself; how does the anticipation of a world-changing coming of God relate to the necessity of Jesus' death?

I would like to begin with the still embattled problem of the origin of the New Testament concept "gospel": does it stem from the world of Hellenism, perhaps from the cult of the ruler,[3] or from the Old Testament and Jewish tradition? Did Jesus himself already describe his kingdom-gospel as "gospel," perhaps utilizing the verb בשר = εὐαγγελίζεσθαι, or even the noun בשורה (Aramaic: בסורתא[4]), perhaps even εὐαγγέλιον as a foreign borrowing?

---

2. In this connection, see my essay, "The Problem of Variety and Unity in the New Testament," in the Festschrift for Dr. Kyung Yun Chun, 1979, and in *Horizons in Biblical Theology* 2, 1980, 3-14; and the sceptical works of E. Käsemann, H. Braun, H. Köster, and others referred to there.

3. Thus again recently G. Strecker, "εὐαγγελίζω, εὐαγγέλιον," in *EWNT* II, 174-86. Strecker attributes the theological usage, esp. of the noun εὐαγγέλιον, to the tradition of the Hellenistic Christian Church, bringing into play the emperor cult with the Priene inscription (*OGIS* II, number 458). Plural εὐαγγελία means, in his opinion, "events of salvation touching on existence"; the singular is "specifically Christian." See esp. Strecker's lengthy contribution, "Das Evangelium Jesu Christi," in the Festschrift for H. Conzelmann, 1975, 503-48. For another view, see the important work by P. Stuhlmacher, *Das Paulinische Evangelium* I, 1968, with illuminating references to the Old Testament and Jewish background and thorough consideration—and rejection—of the Hellenistic materials.

4. Written either with שׁ or ס.

2. The Talmud on the Gospel of Jesus

1. Not only do the first three Gospels create this impression but also a number of rabbinic references. A story is told in b. Shabbat 116a-b in which אונגליון (εὐαγγέλιον) appears as the substance of Christian doctrine—and in the Talmud that means Jesus' teaching—and hence as the counterpart to the Jewish Torah (cf. Luke 16:16); it concerns, to be sure, a short anecdote. The shrewd sister of R. Gamaliel II, Imma Shalom, exposed a supposed Christian philosopher as corruptible and made him look ridiculous when she submitted a fictitious inheritance problem to him for arbitration (cf. Luke 12:13f.). First, the philosopher maintained that from the day the Jews had been driven from their land "the Torah of Moses had been abolished and the אונגליון had come in its place"; according to it, a brother and a sister were entitled to share an inheritance equally. But when he received a bigger bribe from Gamaliel's brother, he changed his decision, for for "further below" one could read: "I אונגליון did not come to detract from the law of Moses but to add to it"; according to the Torah, however, only the brother is entitled to the inheritance.

This information "from the gospel" relates to Matt. 5:17; J. Jeremias even considers the verb "to add" original in preference over the Matthean "to fulfill."[5] Important in the present context is the point that the "philosopher" uses the gospel as a kind of Mishnah from which judicial decisions may be derived; in fact, he maintains that it has replaced the Torah prohibited by Hadrian. On the other hand, אונגליון serves here as the name of a person, one who represents the "I" of the logion in Matt. 5:17,[6] where Jesus asserts his agreement with the law of Moses and the prophets; in Judaism the Torah may also be treated as a person. Finally, in this Aramaic anecdote the Greek word εὐαγγέλιον is treated and ridiculed as a Hebrew phrase: Rabbi Meir (ca. AD 150) called it און גליון = "scroll of evil,"[7] whereas R. Johanan (third century in Palestine) speaks of עוון גליון = "scroll of sins." The first interpretation seems to base itself on a christological component whereas the second relates to a halachic component of this gospel. A similar dual view is suggested also by other rabbinic references to Jesus. According to them, he either issued halachic decisions or presented himself as a divine bearer of salvation.[8]

---

5. J. Jeremias, *New Testament Theology: The Proclamation of Jesus,* ET 1971, 83f. I, however, believe that "to fulfill" is the specifically messianic and hence the original verb when it comes to the validity of Scripture.

6. One is reminded of Mark 8:35 and 10:29, where "the gospel" stands in juxtaposition with Jesus as an equivalent.

7. Accordingly, the gospel is viewed as a book or scroll.

8. On this matter, cf. my study "Probleme des Prozesses Jesu," *ANRW* II, 25/1, 1982, 565-647, esp. 575-79. Eliezer b. Hyrcanus (t. Hullin 2.24) knew of a halachic decision of Jesus. R. Abbahu (y. Taanith 2.165b; b. Sanhedrin 106a) challenged Jesus' messianic-divine authority.

2. There may be a reminiscence of the real content of Jesus' message in still another text of the Talmud, one that is also polemically distorted. In the familiar passage concerning the execution of Jesus (b. Sanhedrin 43a) the extraordinary caution and patience of the Jewish court toward the popular deceiver Jesus is based on the assumption that he is "friendly with the kingdom" (קרוב למלכות הוא). At the root of this reference, which hints at Jesus' relation to godless Rome (המלכות), may well be the message of the kingdom that has come near. The term "gospel" is missing here and is hardly to be expected in this connection.

3. The material which *the first three Gospels* present about Jesus' message is very different. The faithfulness of the tradition is already evident in the fact that the theme of the kingdom, which was central to Jesus, recedes in the preaching of the Church; the term "Son of Man" and the call to discipleship are lacking, as are also the forms of proclamation which are characteristic for the mode of Jesus' teaching: the parable, the beatitude, the brief word of prophecy, and the wisdom saying. Nevertheless there are important lines of continuity leading from the message of Jesus to the post-Easter gospel. They stand out especially where Scripture is quoted, in the utilization and influence of the same Scripture passages, like II Sam. 7:12-14; Pss. 2:7; 110:1; Isa. 52:7; 52:13–53:12; 56:1, etc.[9] It is from such texts, and not, for instance, from Hellenism, that the origin of the word group εὐαγγελ(ίζεσθαι) is to be found, because it is here that not only the terminological equivalent, but also the eschatological reference, as well as the theme of the kingdom, and the role of the anointed in the realization of the kingdom, etc., are given for the gospel. This is true above all for texts like Isa. 52:7 and 61:1 where the verb בשר = εὐαγγελίζεσθαι (otherwise rare in the Old Testament) occurs.

3. Luke: Jesus as the Messianic Messenger of the Kingdom

1. If one proceeds from an Old Testament background one does well to begin with the Gospel according to Luke. At least it comes nearest to the Old Testament situation in one respect. In the Old Testament only the verb εὐαγγελίζεσθαι (cf. Acts 10:36) is employed; as in Isaiah, the noun "good news" is lacking. The verb εὐαγγελίζεσθαι appears in the Gospel 10 times, 2 of these in the passive (cf. the rabbinic בשר, *buśśar*); in Acts it occurs 15 times, and the noun εὐαγγέλιον appears twice.

From the start it is clear that the eschatological event of salvation is both announced and effected by a messenger. According to Luke 4:43 the gospel

9. Cf. my book *Wie verstehen wir das Neue Testament?*, 1981.

preacher Jesus has been sent by God (note how Luke restates here what appears in Mark in terms appropriate to his Gospel); according to 1:19 and 2:10 it is an angel, God's messenger par excellence, who brings the glad tidings. This messenger announces the birth of salvation figures—a fact which is reminiscent of the Hellenistic εὐαγγέλιον.

2. It is further striking that in Luke 3:18 John the Baptist also brings good news to the people;[10] this brief concluding expression follows John's witness to the Messiah and immediately precedes the report of John's imprisonment (3:19f.). Such "glad tidings" seems not to fit the preacher of judgment and repentance.[11] It is perhaps fitting to mention here the picture of the Baptist presented by Flavius Josephus,[12] particularly the positive impression which John's preaching is said to have made on the people: the people who came in droves were "deeply moved"—precisely the thing that alarmed Herod Antipas and led to John's execution (cf. Luke 3:19f.). This presentation suggests that in fact John must have brought an eschatological message of joy, precisely the message concerning the Messiah who was already present but not yet revealed by God as such[13] (Luke 3:16); according to 3:15 some people even questioned whether perhaps John himself was the Christ.

3. Then what distinguished Jesus' gospel from that of the Baptist? From the very beginning Luke makes this clear. Jesus is the Messiah and Son of God (1:32-35); John is not (cf. 3:15), but rather his forerunner in the spirit and power of Elijah (1:17), a prophet (cf. 3:2), the voice of one calling in the wilderness (3:4-6, following Isa. 40:3-5).[14] According to Luke 16:16 he belongs on the side of the law and the prophets; with Jesus began the age of the gospel. From that perspective εὐαγγελίζεσθαι in 3:18 is not used in the full sense of the word— hence the addition of παρακαλεῖν. John is on the threshold of the new age.

4. That which belongs to the real gospel becomes clear in *Jesus' inaugural sermon in Nazareth* (4:16ff.), which occurs in Luke in the place of the summary of the beginning of the work of Jesus in Mark 1:14f. Basic to his message is a text which is particularly important for the Lucan understanding of Jesus'

---

10. Εὐαγγελίζετο τὸν λαόν corresponds to the Hebrew construction in Isa. 61:1f. (בשר ענוים).
11. One may suspect therefore that here the neutral meaning of the verb בשר, which occurs occasionally in the Old Testament and in the rabbis, and which can have bad news as its object, underlies the text. However, in connection with the usage in the remainder of the New Testament and esp. in Luke, where it ordinarily means the message of joy, this interpretation is to be avoided.
12. *Ant.* 18.117f.
13. Cf. the rabbinic view that the Messiah might come at any time since his time had already come, but he had been delayed on account of Israel's sins. For references see Billerbeck IV/2, 857-59.
14. Cf. John 1:31, also Luke 3:4-6, where Isa. 40:3-5 is quoted in full, since in v. 5 the vision of salvation is also promised. According to Matt. 3:2 John not only proclaimed the need to repent but also, like Jesus, that the kingdom of God had come near (cf. 3:2 and 4:17), for which Matthew coined the phrase "the gospel of the kingdom" (4:23; 9:35; 24:14).

gospel: Isa. 61:1f. For Luke this text comprehensively and adequately describes Jesus' mandate, his messianic program. For its interpretation, the real inaugural message, consists in one brief sentence: "Today this Scripture has been fulfilled, in the very moment in which you heard it with your ears" (4:21). The following characteristics of the gospel of the kingdom may be mentioned from the Isaian passage freely cited by Luke:

a. The "evangelist" *has been sent* (4:18); he speaks on instructions from God ("He has sent me . . .").

b. He *has been anointed* with the Spirit of God (4:18), which Luke certainly understood in a messianic sense: the Christ is the real messenger of joy. This implies that he also proclaims himself, usually indirectly in a concealed way through the medium of Scripture, and that with regard to his role as redeemer; but also directly, in the ἦλθον passages, since he has to introduce himself as the messenger of God and to present his mandate. Isa. 61:1f. is the model and legitimating ground for the ἦλθον sayings of Jesus. Also the statement: "I must preach the good news of the kingdom of God to the other cities also, for I was sent for this purpose" (4:43) stands in the shadows of Isa. 61:1 (as well as Isa. 52:7): God is he who sends; the necessity of the mandate (δεῖ) is rooted in this reality as well as in the prophecy of Scripture. As a message from God the gospel is the word of God, just as this is true of the message of the prophets (cf. Isa. 6:8; Deut. 18:15-21). For this reason Jesus' preaching of the gospel in the temple also provoked the question about his ἐξουσία, the issue of delegated authority (Luke 20:1f.).

c. *The addressees of the gospel* are the poor, the meek (עֲנָוִים; v. 18), who expect nothing from themselves or from the world but place all their hope in God (cf. Matt. 5:3).

d. *The theme of the gospel* is redemption, the loosening of bonds, since the beginning of the great year of God's release has been proclaimed (4:19).

e. Luke understands the loosening of bonds to consist above all in *the miraculous healing of infirmities.* The promise of sight for the blind (Isa. 61:1 LXX) is intended literally (7:22). For that reason the messianic gospel is accompanied by miracles. They are expected by the person who inserts himself in his message of joy. Jesus' miraculous action, all his works and deeds, are in accord with the gospel: it can all be expressed in parables (cf. Luke 15).

The gospel speaks therefore of the realization of the kingdom of God. The word is verified by the liberating deed and therefore makes people glad. The unity of word and deed is indicative of the end time; it is messianic. Strictly speaking one can only talk of gospel where prophecy is fulfilled and where there is reference to the liberating future of God in the perfect tense: the Spirit of God is manifest, the feasts can now be celebrated (cf. Nah. 1:15; LXX 2:1). The diction of the prophetic perfect already appears in the Old Testament texts: "the

Lord has anointed me . . . sent me . . ." (Isa. 61:1f.). "Your God reigns!" So reads the pithy and impressive news of the messenger of joy to Zion in Isa. 52:7. This announcement of the enthronement of God is an announcement of victory: the power of chaos has been overcome (51:9); the rulers are defeated (52:5). Also the gospel of the enthronement of Melchizedek (= Michael, the righteous king in heaven) which is proclaimed (1QM 17:6f. and 11QMelch 16 with Isa. 52:7 and 61:1f.) presupposes a decisive victory, namely the dethronement of Belial.[15] The announcement of the elders in heaven is also a gospel: "The Lion of the tribe of Judah, the Root of David, has conquered" (Rev. 5:5). The reference is to the victory over evil (cf. 3:21) attested in Old Testament images.

5. It is of some importance that the glad tidings in Isa. 52:7 have been reproduced in the Targum like this: "The royal rule of God has been revealed!" If one assumes this meaning for the time of Jesus, the linkage of "gospel" and "kingdom" already existed. Next to the message of the self-proclamation and the picture of the messianic messenger announced in Isa. 61:1f. comes the message in Isa. 52:7 whose theme is the "revelation," i.e., the breakthrough of God's rule, which occupies the foreground in Jesus' preaching. The programmatic phrase which sums up the works of Jesus—κηρύσσων καὶ εὐαγγελιζόμενος τὴν βασιλείαν τοῦ θεοῦ (Luke 4:43; 8:1; cf. 16:16)—is totally based on Isa. 52:7: Jesus is the מבשר and משמיע = κηρύσσων; the objects ישועה and שלום explicate the message of joy[16] and qualify the basileia as a liberating seizure of power and the eschatologically revealed rule of God. Further, that Jesus preached the gospel also in Jerusalem (20:1) also has its roots in Isa. 52:7, as does the good news of peace in Acts 10:36.

6. But did *Jesus himself* understand himself to be a מבשר in the sense of the two Isaiah passages?[17] I believe one can confidently answer Yes. In truth Jesus proclaimed the coming of the basileia as the great invitation from God—as the great miracle of salvation—and hence as such he introduced it as gospel in the sense of Isa. 52:7. Also the marks and accompanying phenomena of the

---

15. In 11QMelch 14–18, Isa. 52:7 is utilized, very likely also Isa. 61:1f. (18) where the common term מבשר makes the linkage possible. Cf. Luke 10:18: "I saw Satan fall like lightning from heaven." The "eternal gospel" (Rev. 14:6), i.e., the ever-valid gospel, is an announcement of victory involving the fall of Babylon the great but founded in the cross and resurrection of the Lamb. The imperative "Fear God!" (14:7) is addressed to the peoples ruled by Rome. On בשורה as proclamation of victory cf. II Sam. 18:20, 25, 27; II Kgs. 7:9.

16. In this connection ישועה = σωτηρία (cf. Isa. 52:10) corresponds with the name Jesus (ישוע; Matt. 1:21), the meaning of which anticipates the saving forgiveness of sins, pointing to Isaiah 53. On שלום cf. Isa. 53:5. The rejection of a false peace follows in Matt. 10:34. With reference to a costly peace, cf. my article "Gottes Friede in einer friedlosen Welt," in K. Motschmann, ed., *Flucht aus der Freiheit?* 1982, 13-28.

17. According to A. Harnack (*The Constitution and Law of the Church in the First Two Centuries,* 1910, 324), it is not certain whether Jesus himself used בשרה, since Q is silent on the point.

gospel mentioned in Isa. 61:1f. are realized in his works. Almost all of them appear in *Luke 7:22/Matt. 11:5,* which is a kind of cry of jubilation in the logia document (Q). There Jesus responds to John the Baptist's question whether he really is the one to come: "Go and tell John what you hear and see: the blind receive their sight, the lame walk, lepers are cleansed, the deaf hear, and the poor have good news preached to them!"[18] This joyous exclamation carries allusions to several passages in Isaiah.[19] However, Isa. 61:1f. is predominant, as appears from the healing of the blind and the gospel for the poor.

Here the question concerning the Messiah ("Are you he who is to come?" from Gen. 49:10) is also indirectly, by way of a paraphrase, answered in the affirmative: "I am the one anointed with the Spirit of God, the redeemer authenticated by miraculous deeds referred to in Isa. 61:1f."

In distinction from Isa. 61:1f. and Luke 4:18 the proclamation of the gospel is mentioned in Luke 7:22 par. at the end. By this placement it is not only presented as climactic but also qualified as eschatological: the miraculous deeds are basic to the gospel and mark the "evangelist" as the second, messianic, redeemer. Luke even presents the miracles as taking place before the eyes of John's emissaries (7:21). It is by no means the case that no miracles were expected from the Jewish Messiah—on the contrary. The σημεῖα τῆς ἐλευθερίας (Josephus, *BJ* 2.262) promised by the "prophets" (Jewish messianic pretenders) must be viewed as signals of the dawning year of release (Isa. 61:1f.) and of the eschatological jubilee. They will show that God is with such a redeemer—that he is "the one who was to come"; as "signs" they must correspond to the miracles done by Moses or Joshua. And the Targum on Isaiah 53, which interprets the servant as messianic, finds in v. 8 a description of the miracles "which take place for us in his days—who can tell them?" (cf. IV Ezra 13:49f.; 7:28). In Jesus' miracles the basileia breaks into human life (Luke 11:20, Q) and the bonds of the devil are broken: the sovereign rule of God is realized there where it triumphs over the rule of the devil; at the same time it is the legitimate occasion for preaching the gospel. According to Paul, it is realized not only in word but also in power (I Thess. 1:5); the gospel is (the revelation of) God's power (Rom. 1:16).

Luke has demonstrated the linkage between *gospel* and *miracles* with particular clarity: Women healed by the proclaimer follow him (8:1); the gospel of the disciples who are sent out is verified by miracles (9:6), as later the gospel of the apostles (Acts 8:6, 12; 14:7-15). Luke also incorporates the legitimating effect of miracles in the kerygma: "Jesus of Nazareth, a man attested to you by

---

18. עַנָוִים מְבַשְּׂרִים (*m^ebus̆sarim*).
19. Isa. 29:18f.; 35:5; 42:7, 18. In Pesiqta 106b, 6 (cf. Billerbeck IV/2, 832) Isa. 35:5 is related to the giving of the law on Mt. Sinai and to the messianic future (cf. Ex. 20:18; 24:7).

God with mighty works and wonders and signs which God did through him in your midst" (Acts 2:22), so that after his resurrection and ascension he can be proclaimed as Christ and Lord (2:36). The basis for this linkage between miracles and gospel is the Old Testament meaning of בשורה as announcement of victory (II Sam. 18:20, 25, 27; II Kgs. 7:9), in the messianically understood Isaiah passage (61:1f.) and especially in the works of the earthly Jesus who could therefore proclaim himself, be it indirectly, along with the kingdom, as in his answer to John's question (Matt. 11:5). The pericope is certainly authentic; even Bultmann and his disciples hesitate to apply the verdict *"Gemeindebildung."*[20] Isa. 61:1f. has also been incorporated in the beatitudes for the spiritually poor and those who mourn (Matt. 5:3f.). But this means that Jesus was more than merely a rabbi and prophet, namely the one anointed with the Spirit, the *Christus Exorcista, Christus Victor;* he died for our sins as Messiah (I Cor. 15:3). Thus we also understand that Luke could draw a line separating two epochs between Jesus and John the Baptist (16:16). The gospel does not really begin until Jesus appears on the scene; through him the realization of the basileia begins (17:21). As the Messiah he then also becomes the object of the apostolic gospel (Acts 5:42; 8:35; 17:18).

7. As we mentioned earlier, Luke has Jesus preach the good news also in the temple at Jerusalem in the presence of leading men and members of the Sanhedrin (20:1).[21] In this the Lucan preference for Jerusalem, a scripturally-rooted preference comes out: initially it was the real addressee of the gospel (Isa. 52:7), then it became its point of departure (Isa. 2:3; Acts 1:8). The eschatological role of the Torah which goes forth from Zion (cf. Isa. 2:3) is taken over by the gospel; Jerusalem came to be the bulwark of the apostolic teaching (Acts 2:42).

In Luke 20:1 a second dimension, expressly referred to in Matt. 24:14, is added, namely *the character of the gospel as testimony* (εἰς μαρτυρίαν). Although it is by nature a message of salvation, in the final judgment it may reinforce the indictment and, like the Torah, declare unbelievers guilty. On the other hand it may then act as agent of intercession, as in the case of the unknown woman who anointed Jesus in Bethany (Mark 14:9).

---

20. R. Bultmann, *The History of the Synoptic Tradition,* ET 1963, 126; cf. G. Strecker in the Festschrift for H. Conzelmann, 1975, 513: The question ". . . cannot be answered with certainty." Strecker does, of course, play down the importance of Luke 7:22 with the (unconvincing) argument that εὐαγγελίζεσθαι is not used independently there because it is a citation from the Old Testament (*EWNT* II, 175; cf. Conzelmann Festschrift, 504f., 506, 524f.). However, we are not dealing with a citation, as in Luke 4:18f., but with an allusion that is characteristic for Jesus. On the issue of its authenticity, cf. W. Grundmann, *Das Evangelium nach Matthäus,* 1973[5], 304.

21. According to W. Bachmann, "Jerusalem und der Tempel," BWANT 109, 1980, 287ff., Luke situates Jesus' activity in the temple (Luke 19:45–24:53) more unequivocally than Mark, doing so under the overarching concept of teaching on attitude to law in a manner relevant to the people as a whole and therefore one that required a public place.

This relation of the gospel to the final judgment has still another ground. Because the message promises release to the imprisoned and oppressed, it indicts by implication those who practice violence. Its proclamation may lead to conflict with the—now doomed—tyrannical power. The messenger becomes a witness who must answer for the message with his life; the necessity (δεῖ) to preach the good news (Luke 4:43) may imply *suffering on behalf of the gospel*. The announcement of salvation tacitly implies an eschatological reservation: a time of affliction precedes the end (cf. Mark 8:35; 10:29). Perhaps, in speaking of the εὐαγγέλιον of John the Baptist (3:18), Luke also had in mind the fateful opinion of the people who thought he might be the Messiah (3:15) as well as his imprisonment by Herod (3:19f.). This mistaken estimate of him as Messiah was a factor in John's violent death and brought him closer to the suffering Christ and suffering Servant. His fate made the Baptist appear as a preacher of the new era and set him also "for the fall of many in Israel" (cf. Josephus, *Ant.* 18.118; Luke 2:34). Accordingly, not only the birth of Jesus, but also that of his forerunner was announced through a joyous—and eschatologically relevant— message (1:19; 2:10f.). A miraculous birth and a violent death made the proclaimer into someone proclaimed. The gospel of the birth of the bearers of salvation might call to mind the εὐαγγελία of the emperor cult. But that Luke thought of their violent deaths as a ground for salvation is not part of this picture. For in the εὐαγγέλιον of the angel the newborn Jesus was called σωτήρ; certainly, as in Matt. 1:21, there is an association here with the name Jesus,[22] which points to salvation. Matthew interpreted it as a salvation from sins; would that have been different in Luke? Can the gospel of "Savior" Jesus be abstracted from the cross? People have often expressed the opinion that Luke was silent about the saving significance of the death of Jesus; hence his Christ-message was far removed from the gospel of reconciliation and peace with God. I do not hold to this opinion. Concerning the Baptist it was already prophesied that he would discharge Elijah's office of reconciler (Luke 1:17; Mal. 3:21-24). Further, the risen Christ showed the disciples of Emmaus how in his death on the cross the messianic witness of Moses, the prophets, and the Writings had been fulfilled (Luke 24:44-47). Finally, in his preaching Paul too followed this hermeneutical example of Jesus (Acts 17:2f.). Is it possible then that Luke's understanding of the cross differed from the gospel which Paul adduces (I Cor. 15:1-5) as having been handed down to him and which was "in accordance with Scriptures," a gospel which had been especially molded by Isaiah 53 and accordingly shows the Messiah as having died for our sins? In my opinion, Luke used the verb πάσχειν,[23] whose subject is always Jesus, as a terse reference to Isaiah 53, so

---

22. Cf. Acts 10:38, the end of the verse, where Luke alludes to the name Immanuel.
23. Luke 24:26, 46; Acts 1:3; 3:18; 17:3.

that it implies the atoning character of the cross: it is precisely as the one who suffered on our behalf that Jesus became the Savior (σωτήρ).[24] True, Jesus' suffering is not expressly linked with the verb εὐαγγελίζεσθαι and made into a theme in his Gospel, as, for instance, in Mark 14:9 at the anointing in Bethany; this story is lacking in Luke but has its counterpart in the anointing of Jesus by a woman who is a sinner (7:36-50).

4. Matthew and the Gospel of the Kingdom

1. One must proceed from Luke to Matthew because, in his use of the term "gospel" Matthew seems simpler and more kingdom-related than Mark. True, Matthew only once uses the verb, and that in Jesus' reply to the question of John the Baptist already discussed earlier (11:5 = Luke 7:22). Over against that is the fact that the *noun* εὐαγγέλιον occurs four times: once, as in Mark, at the anointing in Bethany (26:13/Mark 14:9) and three times in the Matthean phrase τὸ εὐαγγέλιον τῆς βασιλείας; each time this phrase occurs as the object of κηρύσσειν (4:23; 9:35; 24:14). Lacking still is the absolute τὸ εὐαγγέλιον which Mark repeatedly uses (cf. 4:17 with Mark 1:15); nor does Matthew use it in the Marcan phrase "for my sake and the gospel's" (cf. 16:25 with Mark 8:35; 19:29 with Mark 10:29). Jesus' proclamation of the kingdom of God was gospel: By means of the phrase κηρύσσειν τὸ εὐαγγέλιον τῆς βασιλείας (cf. 4:23 with Mark 1:19!) Matthew reduces Isa. 52:7 to a concise formula, just as he succeeds in doing that for Dan. 7:13 with the expression "the coming of the Son of man" (24:27). Whereas Luke still kept Isa. 52:7 in its verbal character (4:43; 8:1), the passage now appears in nominal form, but more clearly recognizable as such than, for example, in Mark.

2. Matthew also brought to clear expression *the unity of the gospel and the healing miracles* and thus emphasized the messianic fulfillment character of the good news. This occurs in the redactional, almost identical, summaries of 4:23 and 9:35: "Jesus taught in their synagogues and preached the gospel of the kingdom and healed every disease and every infirmity (among the people)." Preaching the gospel is an extension of Jesus' teaching in the synagogue and is thought of rather as open-air preaching for the people gathered outside accompanied by the redemptive activity which legitimizes it. Also in the activity of the disciples who have been sent out, preaching and miraculous healing form a unity (Matt. 10:7f.; cf. Luke 9:6), though here Matthew does not speak explicitly

---

24. Cf. I. H. Marshall, *Acts,* 1980, 25, n. 1: "Luke does not ignore the atoning significance of the death of Jesus, but he does not go out of his way to stress it." But see the quotation of Isa. 53:7 (LXX) in Acts 8:32f. referring to the Christ as the Lamb that was slain but sees his judgment "lifted" through his humiliation: thus the victory of the slain Lamb is indicated in Rev. 5:5-7.

of "gospel" (cf. 10:23). This linkage of the messianic gospel with miracle (cf. 11:5) may explain why, when he first summarily mentions Jesus' preaching of repentance and the kingdom (4:17) and even more conspicuously when he describes John's preaching (3:2), Matthew does not speak of "gospel"; for there is lacking here the Savior's activity which according to 4:23 and 9:35 belongs to the gospel.

3. It is important that Matthew, too, links Jesus with the Baptist. This is done differently than in Luke, i.e., not in the announcements of the births, but in the context of the *proclamation of the message,* which is admittedly not described as gospel. Its theme, however, is the same in John's case as in that of Jesus: "Repent, for the kingdom is at hand" (3:2; 4:17). Compared with Mark, the brevity and the altered structure of the sentence, which is marked as a call to repentance and based on the coming of the kingdom, stands out (cf. Mark 1:14f.). In fact Matthew has adopted another passage from Isaiah, namely the beginning of trito-Isaiah, where a summary of the preaching of the kingdom of God is offered: "Keep justice, and do righteousness, for soon my salvation will come, and my deliverance be revealed" (Isa. 56:1). If one interprets the theme of Jesus' and John's preaching in terms of this Old Testament foundation, one that Matthew has made clearly recognizable, then the act of repentance corresponds to preparation for the coming of God and as the realization of justice and righteousness and the approaching kingdom of God corresponds to what Isaiah describes as the imminent coming of God's salvation and the revelation of his righteousness.

From the perspective of Isa. 56:1 many a disputed state of affairs is illuminated: 1. The word ἤγγικεν in Matt. 4:17/Mark 1:14 does not mean that the kingdom of God has come (as C. H. Dodd maintains); it means rather that it is near; 2. The righteousness which Matthew underscores as a mark of the kingdom has been taken from Isaiah 56. It is also to be interpreted from the perspective of that passage, and indeed from the Hebrew text, since the Septuagint translates the צדקה of God mentioned there as ἔλεος.

Matthew has made *the righteousness of Isa. 56:1 into the theme of the Sermon on the Mount,* a fact which comes out particularly in the framework of ch. 6. The opening statement, "Be careful not to do your (acts of) righteousness . . . to be seen" (Matt. 6:1), corresponds with Isa. 56:1a; the closing imperative, ". . . seek first his kingdom and his righteousness" (Matt. 6:33), picks up Isa. 56:1b. This means that the better righteousness contrasted in the Sermon on the Mount with that of scribes and Pharisees (Matt. 5:20) has its standard in the saving righteousness of the coming God (Isa. 56:1) and corrects a righteousness to be acquired (זכות) by keeping commandments (Matt. 5:21-48) and by good works (Matt. 6:1-18). Accordingly, Jesus' message of the kingdom has righteousness for its theme, and indeed from within the perspective of Isa. 56:1 as both imperative and indicative: "Keep justice and do righteousness, for soon the righteousness of God will be revealed."

The term "gospel" does not quite fit this appeal, this sequence from the imperative to the indicative, as the lack of it in 4:17 and the Sermon on the Mount indicates. For this reason John the Baptist, who according to Matthew came in "the way of righteousness" (21:32), and who was therefore a kind of "teacher of righteousness," did not yet proclaim "gospel," although he did speak of the kingdom that was near; in his case miracles were also lacking. Only Jesus' preaching fulfilled the conditions of the gospel, a gospel in which the righteousness of God as salvation (Isa. 56:1), and certainly not as the embodiment of merit-creating halacha, is revealed. But in places where Jesus still speaks in the scheme of imperative and indicative and makes righteousness the standard of eschatological conduct, as admission-Torah for the kingdom of God, Matthew avoids the term "gospel."

For *Paul,* however, who also has Isa. 56 in mind when he sees the righteousness of God attested by the law and the prophets (Rom. 3:21f.), the indicative has a fundamental priority because of the cross, so that the righteousness which brings salvation is revealed in the gospel (Rom. 1:16f.). The call to repentance is lacking; the imperative is addressed to believers and filled with the power of the Spirit received in baptism. All the same, with the concept of the salvation-bringing righteousness of God as the supporting pillar, there is a bridge leading from Jesus to Paul.

4. But *did Jesus himself make righteousness the center of his message,* or was this term injected by the theological interest of Matthew?[25] I believe that Isaiah 56 has in fact decisively shaped the message of Jesus. The Isaian scheme of the eschatologically conditioned imperative plus the indicative corresponds to a statement like Matt. 6:14f./Mark 11:15: "For if you forgive people their trespasses, your heavenly Father will also forgive you"; add to this the parable of the wicked servant (Matt. 18:23-25) and the parable of the unjust steward (Luke 16:1-9). Forgiveness is definitely the most momentous constituent of the justice-establishing, helping righteousness of God to which human conduct must correspond. As a result of the redemptive action of Christ the sequence of Isa. 56:1f. is reversed and the indicative placed first.

In the name "Jesus" (ישוע) Matthew already sees an indication of the coming of divine salvation (ישועה in Isa. 56:1), the *gratia preveniens,* which

---

25. Thus G. Strecker, "Biblische Theologie?" in the Festschrift for G. Bornkamm, ed. D. Lührmann and G. Strecker, 1980, 430, n. 23: "No single text in the New Testament can with any certainty be traced back to Jesus himself, not even the verb in Luke 18:9, 14." Beyond that, Strecker has misunderstood the righteousness of God in Matt. 6:33 (also 5:6) as the right attitude of the disciples and as ethical conduct ("Der Weg der Gerechtigkeit," FRLANT 82, 1966[2], 152-57). Nor does he acknowledge the relationship to the Old Testament.

is realized in salvation from sin (1:21). Accordingly, the kingdom of God and the person of Jesus, proclamation and proclaimer, are linked in such a way that the salvation of the basileia is brought and promised by the Messiah. This promise is gospel: "With righteousness" Jesus "judges the poor" (Isa. 11:4), a righteousness which proves itself in the lives of people as the prevenient grace of God. This is evident in the so-called "assailant" saying in Matt. 11:12, where also the negative reaction of people is reported: "From the days of John the Baptist until now the kingdom of heaven breaks into the world, but violent men plunder it." As in Luke 16:16, so here the verb βιάζεσθαι is used in the middle voice. With the liberating power of Jesus' deeds (Matt. 12:28), the rule of God forcefully enters into the stronghold of the evil one (12:29); it is a revelation of the saving righteousness of God (Isa. 56:1), as well as the liberating judgment of the poor (11:4), and can therefore be proclaimed as gospel (Luke 16:16). But violent men (cf. Isa. 11:4[26]) plunder it, make its confessors uncertain, eliminate a prophet like John the Baptist, and blaspheme the Spirit working through Jesus as a demonic power (12:31). That is the very opposite of the doing of righteousness as Isa. 56:1 means it. This also makes manifest that the full revelation and success of the rule and righteousness of God have not yet been realized.

5. In the kairos of a rule that has been initiated but not completed the sustaining role devolves upon *the preaching and doing of the gospel.* According to Matt. 10:23, the disciples will not be done with the proclamation of the kingdom before the Son of Man comes; the term "gospel," which occurs in the parallel passage in Mark (13:10), is lacking in Matthew. The structure and content of this difficult logion of *Naherwartung* in Matt. 10:23 are reminiscent not only of Isa. 56:1 but also of Gen. 49:10. The latter passage was of great importance to the messianism of early Judaism, especially of the Qumran community.[27] People awaited the coming of Shiloh (שִׁילֹה, Gen. 49:10b), whom they took to be the Messiah; until then doing the Torah given by the lawgiver or ruler (המחקק, Gen. 49:10a) was necessary as the preparatory precondition for salvation. In the place of obedience to the Torah, the message of the basileia now comes, which in Matt. 24:14 (cf. Mark 13:10) is called "gospel" and must be brought into the whole inhabited world as a testimony to all nations. Then comes the end, i.e., the appearance of the Son of Man for judgment, a judgment which presupposes the testimony of the gospel (cf. Matt. 25:31-46); in Matt. 10:23, Gen. 49:10 is linked with Dan. 7:13 through the word "come" and Shiloh is related to the Son of Man.

---

26. In Isa. 11:4b one should read עָרִיץ instead of אֶרֶץ. In my opinion there is a word-play between אריסים = "tenants," and אריצים = "men of violence" in the parable of the wicked tenants (Mark 12:1-12).

27. This I have shown in a lecture entitled "Genesis 49:10 in Early Judaism," delivered at a conference of the European Association for Jewish Studies in Oxford (July, 1982).

From within this perspective one can understand the indefatigable zeal of Paul to bring the gospel to all parts of the Roman Empire, and one supposes that the tempo of the proclamation of Jesus and the disciples in Palestine had similar reasons. This obligation to preach based on Gen. 49:10 is also present in John's Gospel, with the component of continuity and the testimonial character of the message being impressed upon the minds of the disciples: Jesus sends the Paraclete who will remind them of his words (14:26) and through them render testimony before the world concerning him (15:26f.); to which is added the keeping of Jesus' commandments (14:21), that is, the love commandment. In the light of Matt. 10:23/Mark 13:10 the promised coming of Jesus (John 14:18-23) must be related also to the parousia and not only to the resurrection.

6. It is important, finally, that Matthew does not describe the gospel referred to in Mark 14:9 at the anointing in Bethany as εὐαγγέλιον τῆς βασιλείας, but only refers to "this gospel" (26:13). And in fact its theme had to be different and had to be related to the person of Jesus. The Son belongs in this gospel which must paradoxically be preached as the good news of the suffering of the Messiah, and that because he saves people from their sins (1:21). "This gospel," to which Matthew already referred at the outset with his explanation of the name Jesus (1:21), accordingly closely resembled the post-Easter, Pauline gospel and according to Mark 14:9 had even been so described by Jesus himself. In John, too, there is the indication of it: in 14:26 the Paraclete reminds the disciples of Jesus' words; in 15:26f. he will bear witness to Jesus along with the disciples (περὶ ἐμοῦ).

5. Mark and the Gospel of the Son of God

1. With respect to "gospel"-terminology, Mark is farthest removed from the soil of the Old Testament. The verb εὐαγγελίζεσθαι is lacking; but the noun εὐαγγέλιον occurs seven times, more often than in Matthew. Striking, further, is his predominantly absolute use of the noun (1:15; 8:35; 10:29; 13:10; 14:9); then the temporal division into present and future proclamation, and finally the christological content. In this regard Mark is unique; the other synoptic evangelists do not follow him. From the very beginning the course is set: "the beginning of the gospel of Jesus Christ, the Son of God"; the phrase already mentioned, "for my sake and the gospel's," points in the same direction (8:35; 10:29); it is a phrase which occurs in the context of discipleship and makes plain its risks.

2. The Marcan summary (1:14f.) is also comparatively lengthy; the noun εὐαγγέλιον occurs two times: ". . . after John was arrested, Jesus came into Galilee, preaching the gospel of God, and saying, 'The time is fulfilled, and the kingdom of God is at hand; repent, and believe in the gospel.'" Accordingly, Jesus does not preach the gospel of "the kingdom of God," as one would

expect;[28] this phrase is lacking in places where it occurs in the parallel evangelists (cf. Mark 1:39 with Matt. 4:23 and Mark 1:38 with Luke 4:43). Mark rather
calls it "the gospel of God," a term which in Rom. 1:1f. describes the apostolic
message of Paul, "which he promised beforehand through his prophets in the
holy Scriptures." In Mark 1:14f., Isa. 52:7 is hardly recognizable and Isa. 56:1
is almost completely concealed. The imperative of the call to repentance follows
the controlling indicative of fulfilled time and a kingdom that is at hand. The
fact of fulfilled time is reminiscent of Luke 4:21 and Gal. 4:4 and allows us to
understand "the gospel of God" thus: God now realizes the witness of the
prophets insofar as it was gospel (cf. Rom. 1:1f.).[29] But the question remains:
what is it that has already been fulfilled, what is the concrete content of
εὐαγγέλιον, the gospel which one must believe (1:15)?

The "gospel" used absolutely and the faith which it requires are also
reminiscent of Paul (cf. I Cor. 15:1f.), but also appear in the Targum on Isa.
53:1, "But who believes our gospel?" (בסורתנא for Heb. שמועתנן). Thus Isaiah
53 becomes the center of the gospel preached beforehand and the key to Mark's
Gospel. That is already true of Paul, who shows in Rom. 10:15f. (but also in
1:16; 4:25; 5:1, 9f.; I Cor. 1:18, 24) that the noun εὐαγγέλιον is especially
derived from Isa. 53:1 (Targum). The same chapter has decisively shaped the
language and content of the message of the cross and resurrection of the
Messiah.[30] When Mark adds to the call to repentance Jesus' summons to faith
in the gospel (1:15) his gospel proves to have a somewhat different content from
Jesus' message of the kingdom in Matthew and Luke. It has a stronger christological stamp: the Messiah preaches a kingdom that has come near (1:14), to be
sure, but brings it closer to the people when he offers his life for them as a ransom
(1:15; 10:45). In his Gospel Mark seeks to show that it is really the Messiah and
Son of God who died for us on a cross (1:1; cf. I Cor. 15:3; Acts 10:36-43); the
death of an ordinary person would have no universal redemptive validity.

Mark therefore offers the passion history of the Messiah—and Son of
God—complete with a lengthy introduction. In the heading (1:1) he already sets

28. Cf. *lectio facilior* in the Koine and the Western text.
29. Cf. I Pet. 1:10-12 and Rev. 10:7: God caused the mystery of the apocalyptic fulfillment
to be preached to his servants, the prophets, as gospel.
30. Paul also uses Isa. 52:7 and Isa. 61:1 as prophecies of gospel-preaching, but now focused
on the ministry of the apostle (Rom. 10:15). Terminologically and in content the gospel of the cross
and resurrection of the Messiah is above all pre-established in Isa. 53:1ff. (Rom. 10:16f.). The
prophetic message of the suffering Servant of God who bears the sins of the people was fulfilled in
Christ's history and can, on account of the atoning, curse-abolishing, and peace-establishing effect
of the death of Jesus, be proclaimed as gospel. Also Paul's vocabulary of faith has been shaped by
Isa. 53, esp. v. 1; hence "faith" and "obedience" toward the gospel (suggested by שמועה), not being
ashamed of the gospel which is a power of God (Rom. 1:16; cf. the Targum on Isa. 53:1), and works
peace with God and reconciliation, etc. (Rom. 5:1; II Cor. 5:18-21; cf. Isa. 53:5). Also a believing
understanding over against an earlier mistaken estimate is expressed in the acknowledgment of the
suffering Servant of God; II Cor. 5:16 must be read in the light of Isa. 53:5.

the course. In conjunction with 1:15 the statement, "the beginning of the gospel of Jesus Christ, the Son of God" (1:1), is reminiscent of Rom. 1:1-4 and the christological attributes of the apostolic gospel mentioned there. Mark was also conscious that this kerygma above all describes and attests as saving event that which is proclaimed in Jesus' passion announcements. Accordingly, Jesus' message of the basileia and the report concerning Jesus, the Son of God, are "gospel" because this Messiah has crowned and completed his work for the kingdom of God with the offering of his life. Faith in the gospel therefore belongs to true repentance (1:15), and to the prediction of suffering belongs the *pro nobis* of Jesus' atoning death, a death to be understood in the light of Isaiah 53. Also the heading above this Gospel, a Gospel which from the start leads toward Jesus' passion, intends to say that Jesus as Messiah died *for us* (I Cor. 15:3), and that God gave up his Son *for us* (Rom. 8:32). True, the passion announcements do not yet qualify as "gospel," because they speak of the future and beyond that apply to a small circle of intimates; still Mark knew that it was precisely those announcements which would become the gospel of the apostles.

4. However, what is meant by "the *beginning* of the gospel"[31] in Mark 1:1? According to Acts 10:37,[32] that beginning started with the works of John the Baptist. So, using the word ἀρχή, Mark shows he regarded the period in which John baptized until the time when Jesus appeared in public as *praeparatio evangelica* (Mark 1:1-13); God himself laid the groundwork for the gospel ministry of the Messiah. He has the Baptist "proclaim" a baptism of repentance for the forgiveness of sins (1:4), since the actual realization of forgiveness only occurs through the work of one mightier than he, just as John's water baptism is oriented to the baptism by the Spirit of that greater one (1:7f.; cf. 1QS 4:20-22). This eschatological act is anticipated in the baptism of Jesus, who is the only one to receive the Spirit from God and hence the anointing to messiahship and who is proclaimed as God's "beloved Son" (1:9-11). Then follows the temptation, in which Jesus proves himself the mightier one in the face of the devil and the wild animals by being the obedient Son (1:12f.).

This "beginning of the gospel" was above all proclaimed beforehand by deutero-Isaiah: the Baptist is one calling in the wilderness according to Isa. 40:3 (Mark 1:2f.); Jesus' baptism with the Spirit and the words of the voice from heaven (1:9-11) are reminiscent of Isa. 42:1; the conquest of temptation (1:12f.) as the victory of the mightier one is reminiscent of Isa. 49:24 (cf. Matt. 12:29); accordingly, in 1:14f., Mark picks up Isa. 52:7; 53:1; (56:1); 61:1 and with them returns to the beginning (1:1).

---

31. Cf. ἀρχὴ τοῦ εὐαγγελίου as the beginning of the mission in Macedonia (Phil. 4:15).

32. In Acts 10:36ff. we encounter the core affirmations of Peter's preaching which underlie Mark's Gospel; they are oriented to the Old Testament and, by way of the "gospel of peace" (10:36), subordinated to Isa. 52:7 and 53:5; cf. v. 38 and Isa. 61:1.

But the influence of Daniel 7 is also present. For the phrase "the mightier one" is an allusion to the Son of man of Dan. 7:13 who overcomes the power of chaos. He demonstrates his authority in that the demons are subject to him (1:27; cf. Dan. 7:10, 14). He is the "Holy One of God" (1:24), i.e., the representative of the Most High (Dan. 7:22, 27); he would gather them to be the people of God's rule. The gospel of God told in the first part of the Gospel (Mark 1–8) serves that goal. But on account of Israel's rejection this ministry must end in the sacrifice of Jesus' life, an act in which the Son of Man follows the example of the Servant of Isaiah 53 (Mark 8:31; 9:31; 10:45; 14:24). Thus the second part of Mark (chs. 9–16) bears the marks of deutero-Isaiah and Daniel as well.

5. The *gospel of the suffering Messiah* begins—symbolically—with the story of John the Baptist. In his life the redemptive necessity of the suffering of the divine messenger is already made clear. Mark speaks of John's "being given over" (1:14) and thus utilizes the word with which he sums up the divinely predetermined suffering of the Son of Man (9:31; 10:33; 14:41; also 14:10, 11, 18, 44). The "beginning of the gospel" ends with the "giving up" of the Baptist, while at the beginning of the second part the Son of Man announces his own "being given up" (9:31) and with the same expression he concludes his announcements to his disciples (14:41). This "being-given-over" formula is derived from Isaiah 53, as the Targum and Rom. 4:25 show. The violent death of John the Baptist is told at length (6:14-29), thus indicating that the fate of the proclaimer is determined by the proclamation, as in Jesus' day people read this fate from the record of the Old Testament prophets.

6. But did *Jesus himself* occasion this usage of the word "gospel," a usage directed toward his atoning death and determined in part by Isaiah 53? J. Jeremias denies this on the ground that, in distinction from the verb בשר, the Hebrew/Aramaic noun בשורה always and exclusively carries a nonreligious meaning; this is not true, he says, of the εὐαγγέλιον of the imperial cult.[33] In the face of the Targum of Isa. 53:1 this is a fateful mistake. There is no doubt whatever that Jesus saw himself as the Servant of Isaiah 53 and from within this understanding took death upon himself as an atoning event. According to Mark 14:9, for the proclamation of this passion history he used the word "gospel," which Isa. 53:1 offered him. In Bethany, speaking of the woman who anointed him, Jesus affirmed: "And truly, I say to you, wherever the gospel is preached in the whole world, what she has done will be told in memory of her" (14:9). In my opinion *the entire history of the anointing is firmly tied in with Isa. 52:13–53:12;* and on this basis I believe that εὐαγγέλιον (Isa. 53:1) is also firmly rooted there.

The difficult expression משחת (Isa. 52:14) served the narrative of Mark 14:1-9 as backdrop. As in the Isaiah scroll of Qumran (1QIsaᵃ), so also in Mark 14

---

33. *New Testament Theology,* 134.

מִשְׁחַת is linked with the verb מָשַׁח = to anoint. In Matt. 6:16-18 Jesus himself utilizes these verbs with an eye toward Isa. 52:14 in a play on words when he recommends that instead of disfiguring their faces (מִשְׁחַת מַרְאֶה) those who fast should anoint them (מִמְשַׁח).[34] In Mark 14:4 ἀπώλεια, meaning "to waste" or "squander" the valuable oil, implies the root מ + שָׁחַת = "to ruin." שָׁחַת = "to ruin" seems here, as in Qumran, also to have been understood as "grave" or "sheol," so that here שָׁחַת מ + signifies the act of "lying in the grave" = ἐνταφιασμός ("burial"). Judas Iscariot believed the anointing (מִמְשַׁח) was an act of squandering (מִשְׁחַת); Jesus, on the other hand, stressed that the woman had done it for his burial (מִשְׁחַת → מִמְשַׁח; Mark 14:8; cf. Isa. 53:9). J. Jeremias considers the history of the anointing and Jesus' words in Mark 14:8 authentic,[35] and denies the authenticity of 14:9, but only on the ground of his mistaken judgment concerning the noun εὐαγγέλιον ≠ בְּשׂוֹרָה. But in terms of Isa. 53:1, this term is the significant conclusion of the narrative oriented to Isa. 52:14; 53:9, 10: As a ministry of clairvoyant love, the anointing in Bethany will pass into the "gospel" (14:9), whose theme, like the message of Isa. 53:1, will be the redemptive suffering of the messianic Servant, his death, burial, and exaltation (cf. Isa. 53:5-12; 52:13f.). This gospel must be preached in the whole world (Mark 14:9), since (Isa. 52:10) all the ends of the earth must see the salvation of God.

Mark recorded this (G)gospel, which was first proclaimed at the communion celebrations of the churches (I Cor. 11:26) and was then supplemented by the message of the earthly Jesus concerning the coming kingdom. He put the word "gospel" as a heading over his work since the primitive Christian/Pauline kerygma is also so labeled (cf. I Cor. 15:1-5) and above all because in the Targum to Isa. 53:1 it is also the introduction to the report on the suffering Servant. Finally, this Gospel is written as a *narrative* concerning Jesus Christ since in Isa. 52:15 the *telling* (סָפַר = ἀναγγέλλειν) and in Isa. 53:8 (LXX, cf. Acts 8:32f.) a διηγεῖσθαι[36] as modes of preaching about the Servant are mentioned; for a long time already the proclamation of the death of Christ occupied the position of the paschal haggadah in the rite of the Lord's Supper.

7. Before Easter, in the period of "discipleship," the message had been restricted to the circle of the disciples and was therefore not yet a "gospel": a public message of great joy. After the Transfiguration, at which Jesus' suffering

---

34 Matt. 6:16-18. In ἀφανίζειν τὸ πρόσωπόν (σου) (v. 16) there is an allusion to the disfigured face (מִשְׁחַת מַרְאֵהוּ) of Isa. 52:14, just as with the anointing of the face (v. 17) in Jesus' statement. In addition, Jesus plays with the words מַרְאֶה = look (or תֹּאַר = appearance in Isa. 52:14) and the verb נִרְאָה = φανεῖσθαι = "to show oneself," "to appear" before men (cf. אִישׁ or בְּנֵי אָדָם in Isa. 52:14). The rendering of מַרְאֶה = πρόσωπον is clearly present in the story of the Transfiguration in Matthew (17:2), which, like Mark 9:2-8, is also influenced by Isaiah 53. Cf. Origen, *Contra Celsum* 1.55, where the clause "your face will not be respected by men" is cited as a characteristic expression of the fourth Servant song.

35. *New Testament Theology*, 284.

36. Cf. Isa. 53:8 (LXX) τὴν γενεὰν αυτοῦ τίς διηγήσεται. This line may have required the inclusion in the Gospels of Jesus' genealogy.

and glorification had as it were been made visible in advance and should have been understood (in light of Isaiah 53) as redemptive-historically necessary, Jesus charged the three eyewitnesses to tell no one what they had seen until the Son of Man should have risen from the dead (Mark 9:9). This command to be silent, in which W. Wrede saw a key to the messianic secret in the Gospels, is rather to be viewed, in light of Isa. 52:15 and 53:1, as a reference to the revelation of the exalted Servant of the Lord and on the basis of the *ordo evangelii:* at Easter the disciples will see what no one has ever told them and understand what they have never heard (Isa. 52:15). Only then could they proclaim the unheard-of as "gospel" which requires faith (Isa. 53:1). The sequence of "vision–gospel proclamation" laid out in the fourth Servant song determines the beginning of the apostolic mission, is established in I Cor. 15:1-5, and incorporated in Mark 9:9.

8. Also the genuinely Marcan phrase "for my sake and the gospel's" (8:35; 10:29) occurs in this context. Why is it that next to the person of Jesus the gospel should also be posited as an object of confession? Because by means of this word, reference is made to the time of proclamation after the death of Jesus. According to Mark 13:10; 14:9, the gospel must be preached to all nations, and that before the parousia. In this period, which begins at Easter, the crucified and risen Son of God is the content of the saving message. People are not to be ashamed of Jesus and his words (Mark 8:38): the kerygma of the crucified Christ enjoys authority equal to that of the teaching of the earthly Jesus.

9. There are, accordingly, two kinds of gospel and several phases of development:

1.a. the prediction of the gospel of God's rule by the prophets of the Old Testament (Isa. 52:7; 61:1f.; Nah. 2:1),

  b. the "beginning of the gospel" (Mark 1:1-13): the ministry of John the Baptist and the preparation of Jesus for messianic service,

  c. the gospel proclaimed by the Messiah concerning the kingdom that has come and in which the prophecies of the great prophets were fulfilled (Mark 1:14),

2.a. the preannounced gospel of the suffering and exalted Servant who is messianically understood (Isa. 52:13–53:12),

  b. the existential adoption of this message by Jesus who foretold the death and resurrection of the Son of Man to his disciples (Mark 8:31; 9:31),

  c. the official proclamation of this gospel of the Messiah and Son of God by the apostles, plus the formation of a passion history for the Lord's Supper at which the death of Jesus is proclaimed (Mark 14:9), and

3. the formation of a "Gospel" in which 1.b., 1.c., and 2.b. are united.

The Gospel of Mark is the history of the fulfillment of the promises of God through Jesus. In the work and passion of the Messiah the realization of the rule of God begins. The Son of Man (= Messiah) establishes the new covenant; at the time of his parousia the kingdom of God will manifest itself in power. The Church therefore believes the gospel of the atoning death of Christ when it hears the call to repentance (Mark 1:15) and awaits the coming of the Son of Man, at which time it expects the full realization of the basileia (Mark 9:1). Under the impact of Jesus-tradition concerning the kingdom of God (Q and their special sources) Matthew and Luke withdrew the Marcan emphasis on the *theologia crucis* and placed Jesus' message of the kingdom at the center. By means of the verb εὐαγγελίζεσθαι used there, they clung to the synopsis of the message about Jesus already available in kerygmatic summaries like Acts 10:36 (following Isa. 52:7).

6. Conclusion

In conclusion, let us return to the questions raised at the outset and try to answer them:

1. Not only the verb εὐαγγελίζεσθαι but also the noun εὐαγγέλιον can best be derived from the Old Testament, particularly from Isa. 52:7; 56:1; 61:1f.; plus Isa. 52:13–53:12 (cf. 42:6 and 49:8). These passages have put a decisive stamp on Jesus' message of the kingdom as well as on the gospel of the cross and resurrection, because it is precisely in these passages that one finds the eschatological gospel of God proclaimed beforehand. The Swabian theologian F. C. Oetinger, who died more than two hundred years ago, offered a paraphrase of Isaiah 40–66 in his book *Etwas Ganzes vom Evangelio* (1739). In these chapters he found a summary of the gospel: of faith (40–49), of righteousness (50–59), and of glory (60–66). Oetinger believed God himself gave this sermon to the world. In an important work entitled *Weil ich dich liebe*[37] W. Grimm demonstrated how closely Jesus' message was tied in with deutero-Isaiah.

One cannot rate highly enough the significance of Isaiah 53 for the New Testament, extending right up to "the lamb that was slain" in Revelation (5:7ff.). The primary reason is that Jesus, by his voluntary suffering, gave a unique interpretation of this song, which he understood as a prophecy of the messianic Servant of God. Hence, that which is specifically Christian does not just begin with the first Easter or with the theology of Paul, but with the earthly Jesus, the author and finisher of faith, in a gospel whose theme is Jesus himself and which can be developed into a coherent narrative by virtue of Isa. 52:15; 53:1-8. To this very day Judaism and Christianity differ fundamentally in their under-

---

37. 1976, published in a second (improved) edition in 1981 under the title *Jesus und Deutero-Jesaja*.

standing of Isaiah 53. Nowhere do the commonality and the characteristic differences come to clearer and more concentrated expression than in the way this song is interpreted in the Targum on the one hand and in the New Testament on the other.

2. It seems to me certain that Jesus himself utilized the verb *biśśar* = εὐαγγελίζεσθαι for his preaching of the dawning kingdom. In the light of Mark 14:9, the noun *b^eśorah* = εὐαγγέλιον, which in my opinion goes back to Isa. 53:1, could also have been used by him, but then as the description of a message which was to be publicly proclaimed only after his death.

3. The question concerning the relationship between the proclamation of the kingdom (which was tied in with the call to repentance) and the announcement of the suffering and the atoning sacrifice of Jesus' life was already implicit in the reception of the Isaianic passages mentioned above: Why is the atoning death of the Servant in Isaiah 53 necessary when, after all, it is God himself who by his coming will bring redemption and the marvelous realization of his royal rule (Isa. 40:3; 52:7; 56:1)? In my opinion, the answer, both in Isaiah and with Jesus, lies in the refusal of the people and their deficient readiness for the coming God: the precondition, the doing of justice as expression of repentance (Isa. 56:1; Mark 1:15), was not being met. The basileia is near, but the people of God distance themselves from it. From this state of affairs arises the necessity of an exceptional deed, namely the "must" of a Servant role for the Messiah who will gather the flock, the "must" of the suffering of the Son of Man who will deliver the gathered saints of the Most High from the bondage of the devil. If the demand for a "better" righteousness was not met from the side of Israel, then the reversal of the imperative and the indicative, i.e., the journey to the cross, would be the only possible and adequate parallel to the forgiving, salvation-bringing righteousness of God. Indeed, this reversal is the revelation of this righteousness, its proof for the cosmic-public character of Golgotha represented by Jews and Romans (Rom. 3:25). As a result the crucifixion of Jesus was proclaimed to be analogous to the events on Sinai, at which, according to the Jews' understanding at the time, the Torah was proclaimed as a law which applied to all the nations. According to I Pet. 2:9; Rev. 1:5-7; 5:7-10, the death of Jesus made possible the fulfillment of the promise of a chosen people and a royal priesthood, a promise given on Sinai, which there presupposed the keeping of the covenant as a condition. To that extent the gospel actually constituted the counterpart to the Torah in a way which the Christian "philosopher" of Imma Shalom sought to clarify in vain. Because through the gospel male and female, Jew and Greek, without distinction, inherit the salvation promised by God (Gal. 3:28; Rev. 5:9f.).

The Path of the Gospel Tradition

Birger Gerhardsson

1.

New Testament studies is a discipline which has to move forward gropingly. We are forced to work with many learned conjectures, to establish the identity of hypothetical sources, and to reconstruct hypothetically the course of events behind these sources. We have to form a total picture of Jesus which is largely hypothetical. In a sense which is not exactly comfortable our discipline is a study of "things that are not seen."

Certainly, we do have something that is completely visible: the New Testament Scriptures: four depictions of the earthly works of Jesus; a theological chronicle about the path of the gospel from Jerusalem to Rome, the world metropolis; twenty-one genuine or fictional letters to early Christian churches or persons; and an apocalypse.

It is also apparent—even striking—that, viewed from a fundamental perspective, these twenty-seven documents fall into two very distinct groups. When we look around for direct quotations from Jesus and concrete stories to see what happened during the period when Jesus did his work on earth, we find them in only one of these groups: the Gospels. One can even push the matter to the extreme and say that the four Gospels aim to furnish us only the words of Jesus and stories about Jesus. To be sure, what they tell us about Jesus is set in the light of Easter and Pentecost and is often stated in relation to post-Easter relationships and questions; they aim nonetheless to offer a picture of what Jesus did and taught during his earthly ministry (cf. Acts 1:1 and Luke 1:1-4). It is also true that the material of John's Gospel represents a vigorous advance, one that borders on free apostolic preaching, but even this Gospel claims that it is portraying that which Jesus did before the eyes of his disciples before his ascension to heaven (20:30; cf. 21:24f.). Here I shall refer to it only incidentally; its peculiar character requires separate treatment.[1]

It is the purpose of the Gospels to furnish only concrete Jesus-texts. When on the other hand we turn to the remaining twenty-three documents, we could say in an equally oversimplifying way that they essentially offer no concrete Jesus-tradition at all. These documents were written in the spirit of Jesus and bear the stamp of his "visions." They contain allusions to his words, reminiscences of him, overlapping pronouncements concerning his person, his life, and his work, above all concerning his death and resurrection, and we encounter summaries and brief formulas. None of these documents, however, aim, in a foundational way, to give their readers a written account of what Jesus "did and taught" during his ministry on earth.

The exceptions are not hard to enumerate. In Acts 20:35 Paul reminds the elders of Ephesus of an (apocryphal) word of Jesus. In I Cor. 11:23-25 Paul aims to remind the Corinthian church of the words of Jesus concerning the elements of the Lord's Supper and to that end he repeats the pericope about Jesus' last meal with his disciples. And in I Cor. 15:3-8 Paul once more repeats a comprehensive text stating the fundamentals of the history of Jesus' passion and resurrection. This text is a marginal case; nevertheless it is a firm instance of a text which restates concrete reminiscences of the work and fate of Jesus on earth.[2]

The old distinction made in the Church between εὐαγγέλιον and ἀπόστολος is terminologically vague and misleading—yet objectively fully justified. Only the evangelists seek to hand down to us a "gospel tradition." In the New Testament the concrete Jesus-tradition, preserved in the form of self-contained small textual units, is present only in the Gospels, only as an "isolated tradition."[3]

How does one explain this? Apostles, prophets, and teachers in early Christianity acted in their public ministry with authority and boldness and spoke freely about Jesus. They were neither forced anxiously to read from written texts nor restricted to commenting on them. In all the documents outside the Gospels we see how freely they spoke about Jesus. Where do we find the real Jesus-tradition?

I can content myself by mentioning a couple of proposed solutions to the problem. One of them amounts to this: The Gospels are quite simply documents

---

1. Cf. J. D. Dunn's essay in the present volume: "Let John Be John—A Gospel for Its Time."

2. A marginal case: on the one hand the episodes referred to are not expanded in narrative form but enumerated in chronological sequence, and on the other, the text does not seem to be complete (provided with an introduction and a conclusion). Cf. my *Memory and Manuscript: Oral Tradition and Written Transmission in Rabbinic Judaism and Early Christianity*, 1961, 299f.

3. In this essay the word "tradition" is used for that which has been handed down, not for the act of transmission. The words "gospel tradition" and "concrete Jesus-tradition" are used synonymously of texts which contain both the words attributed to the earthly Jesus and narratives about him.

that have been composed at a late date, having been written freely and having no firm tradition behind the text. Another proposal is that the synoptic traditions were maintained only in an isolated part of primitive Christianity, in circles with which the other New Testament authors had no real contact.

I consider both theses impossible. It would appear almost inconceivable that the major part of early Christianity would not have been interested in knowing something concrete about Jesus' suffering, death, and resurrection, and beyond that also of his preceding activity, his words and teaching. All the New Testament groups of which we are aware gave their Lord in heaven the name Jesus, a quite ordinary *human* name,[4] and they also knew that he had lived a human life on earth.

We must look for the solution in another direction. The author of Acts intimates that he was familiar with the life and work of Jesus but he does not cite the sources in a way which lets us know that he had a detailed knowledge of Jesus' words and deeds. The author of I John must have been quite familiar at the very least with the Johannine Jesus-tradition—if he is not to be identified with the evangelist John himself—he nevertheless does not even once expressly cite a word from Jesus (the terminology, which is quite general [I John 2:7, 24; 3:11], is telling). There is a division of opinion about how much Paul knew of the Jesus-tradition. Many scholars believe that he had almost no knowledge of it, others think he knew little. I myself am among those who believe he knew several things. He alludes to Jesus' birth and circumcision (Gal. 4:4), his suffering, crucifixion, death, burial, resurrection, and appearance to resurrection witnesses, as well as to specific words of Jesus.[5] However, in his letters he cites the concrete Jesus-tradition only in a few exceptional cases.

We make the following statement of fact: In the New Testament the concrete Jesus-tradition is treated as an *independent entity*. In Acts, the letters, or Revelation it is neither present as quotation nor is it woven into the fabric of the general proclamation and teaching of Christianity. Again, it *is* present in the Gospels, as it is in the older collections which we may assume lie behind the Gospels, but here again only as an isolated tradition. It is also important to state that the example in Acts 20:35 has the character of a reminder of a word which the Church already knew,[6] and that in the two citations of Jesus-tradition in I Corinthians Paul expressly says that already before he had delivered them to the Corinthians and is now compelled to mention them in reminder. In I Cor.

---

4. Interesting observations about the history of the name "Jesus" are made by K. Kjaer-Hansen in *Studier i navnet Jesus*, 1982 (English summary on pp. 369-81).

5. Cf. P. Stuhlmacher's two essays in this volume: "The Theme: The Gospel and the Gospels" and "The Pauline Gospel."

6. The reference to "the words (τῶν λόγων) of the Lord Jesus" can be related to a tractate or a category of Jesus-tradition. Cf. H. H. Wendt, *Die Apostelgeschichte*, KEK, 1913[9], 295.

15:3 he writes that this happened ἐν πρώτοις, hence either "among the most important parts" or "at the beginning."[7]

When I say that the concrete Jesus-tradition is isolated I have in mind three things:

1. It is literarily isolated, for it only occurs in special documents which probably reflect the existence of a special tradition.
2. The entire tradition assembled in these documents deals with Jesus: only he plays a completely independent role in them. No other Jewish teacher or prophet (outside of the Scriptures) is allowed to speak here. John the Baptist does play a role but not an independent one.
3. The disciples of Jesus, headed by Peter of the so-called Twelve, are not allowed to supplement Jesus' teaching with positive contributions under their own name.[8]

It is clear, however, that the Jesus-tradition lies before us *in an edited version*. Jesus' adherents have influenced his words in various ways: when they interpreted them, explicated them, or undertook corrections of the wording; by omissions, additions, and reformulations; and above all when they themselves shaped or reshaped certain narrative traditions. Certain parts—especially the prologues (prehistories, the stories of the baptism and temptation)—seem to be relatively free compositions.[9] There is probably also reason to ask whether certain "disciple-works"—logia and parables formulated in the spirit and style of Jesus (cf. Matt. 13:51, 52)[10]—did not in good faith become a part of the Jesus-tradition.

2.

How are we to picture the path of the concrete Jesus-tradition on its way to the evangelists? Since it is not present in Acts, the letters, or Revelation—neither as completed texts nor as texts in process of becoming—and since it is present in the Gospels only as *Jesus*-tradition and similarly in the older collections

---

7. A more colorless translation of ἐν πρώτοις (like "above all" or "in the first place" and the like) is possible of course but does not seem to me likely here. In the solemn style of the pronouncement, where every step is carefully argued, all the main components are accentuated, also ἐν πρώτοις.

8. On the subject of Jesus as "the sole teacher," cf. my works *Memory and Manuscript*, 332f.; *Tradition and Transmission in Early Christianity*, CN 20, 1964, 40-43; *Die Anfänge der Evangelientradition*, Glauben und Denken 919, 1977, 34f. Cf. also F. Mussner, "Die Beschränkung auf einen einziger Lehrer," in *Israel hat dennoch Gott zum Trost* (Festschrift S. Ben-Chorin), 1979, 33-43 and R. Riesner, *Jesus als Lehrer. Eine Untersuchung zum Ursprung der Evangelien-Überlieferung*, WUNT, 1981, 37-40.

9. Cf. my studies *The Testing of God's Son (Mt 4:1-11 & par.): An Analysis of an Early Christian Midrash*, CB.NT 2/1, 1966, and "Gottes Sohn als Diener Gottes," *ST* 27, 1973, 73-106.

10. Cf. my article "The Seven Parables in Matthew XIII," *NTS* 19, 1972-73 (16-37), 33-36.

which shine through the Gospels, the simplest hypothesis is that *throughout the entire period* the concrete Jesus-tradition was treated as an isolated tradition. G. Kittel already presented this view in a famous statement in 1926.[11]

This statement, however, is but little observed. At this point the impressive form-critical school has obscured this state of affairs by saying that the isolation is only *a secondary phenomenon.* Martin Dibelius and Rudolf Bultmann recognized that in the Gospels the Jesus-tradition is present in its isolated form—later Bultmann could agree with part of Kittel's statement[12]—but they believe that from the beginning it was not so. The evangelists and their predecessors secondarily filtered the Jesus-tradition out of the general preaching of primitive Christianity, the teaching, and the other activity taking place in the service of the gospel. They separated the Jesus-tradition from a general stream of spiritual goods. *From the beginning* the Jesus-traditions have been restated, shaped and reshaped, and partly freely created, within the several activities of primitive Christianity in "typical situations or modes of conduct,"[13] and there they were at home even when people began to bring them together in special collections.

The grounds for this hypothesis are very weak. Our knowledge of the forms of early Christian activity—the typical situations and modes of conduct—is limited: the sources yield only little information. But what we do know we know from Acts, the letters, and Revelation, and there we find, as we noted earlier, no concrete Jesus-traditions, neither in a finished form nor *in statu nascendi.*

The fact is that the form critics did not derive their hypothesis directly from Acts, the letters, and Revelation, but they based themselves on the view of certain students of folklore concerning how popular tradition arises in the life of a people, in "typical situations and modes of conduct" as spiritual goods, and objectifies itself in typical-text-forms before it is eventually written down in various kinds of small literary units ("Kleinliteratur").[14]

---

11. "The *isolation* of the Jesus-tradition is the constitutive feature of the gospel; however, in no period, also in no stage of the formation of the Palestinian tradition, was it lacking." *Die Probleme des palästinischen Spätjudentums und das Urchristentum,* BWANT, third series, 1, 1926, 69.

12. M. Dibelius, *From Tradition to Gospel,* 1934; R. Bultmann, *History of the Synoptic Tradition,* ET 1963, 368f.

13. Bultmann, op. cit., 3.

14. For critical evaluations of form-critical methods, cf. H. Riesenfeld, *The Gospel Tradition and its Beginnings: A Study in the Limits of "Formgeschichte,"* 1957 (now in *The Gospel Tradition,* 1970, 1-29); K. Haacker, *Neutestamentlicher Wissenschaft. Eine Einführung in Fragestellungen und Methoden,* 1981, 48-63; and R. Blank, *Analyse und Kritik der formgeschichtlichen Arbeiten von Martin Dibelius und Rudolf Bultmann,* 1981. For a detailed analysis of so-called "Tendenzen" in the development of tradition, cf. E. P. Sanders, *The Tendencies of the Synoptic Tradition,* SNTSMS 9, 1969. It is interesting to note that the old objections against form criticism which were raised by outside critics since the 1920s, but which were essentially ignored by the representatives of the form-critical school, are now being brought forward even by so pronounced a Bultmann

One thing that is impressive in the total view of the form-critical school, as is well known, is the close link drawn between the origination of the gospel materials and the origination and development of early Christianity itself. The rise and growth of the Church, the religious and theological development on the one hand and the formation of texts on the other, go hand in hand. Form critics point to the fact that the text-forms of the gospel materials are not merely external style forms: the style is "a sociological reality."[15] Accordingly, the several forms of activity of early Christianity produced the different kinds ("Gattungen") of text. And the form of these texts is so distinct and adequate that by them one can tell what function they served and in what "life-situation" they originated.

This hypothesis would have been more illuminating if early Christianity had been a very primitive and exceptionally original movement, one that was uninfluenced by existing culture and forms of activity and by available text models. But that is not the case. All the forms of the activity of early Christianity were already established: preaching, prophecy, admonition, instruction, discussions, worship services, holy meals, community organization, community discipline, etc. And all the early Christian text categories were adapted and of a traditional nature, except for the synthetically written "Gospel,"[16] which came into being only gradually.

A decisive fact is that the several categories of text present in the Jesus-tradition are antecedent to Jesus and early Christianity as *literary* models. One familiar with the holy Scriptures and with the preaching and instruction in the synagogues did not first have to place himself in a certain situation, or experience a certain mode of conduct, in order to formulate a text in terms of a certain literary model. He could freely formulate a text, at his writing desk or wherever, without being bound by the originating fortunes of a given genre. The form-critical hypothesis that the form of the Jesus-tradition reflects a "Sitz im Leben" which shaped it is not only an unproven but also an improbable and unnecessary hypothesis.

It is further of extraordinary importance to observe that the Jews of the New Testament period simply utilized a variety of textual categories side by side. In the Old Testament it is really only the Psalms and Proverbs which exhibit a single genre. In the remaining books a variety of textual kinds are unproblem-

---

disciple as W. Schmithals, "Kritik der Formkritik," *ZTK* 77, 1980, 149-85. The argumentation which Schmithals attributes to me in n. 148 is one that I have never used. On the contrary, I have tended to emphasize that the early Christian traditioners were neither stupid nor ignorant, but men who occupied a leading position in the churches; cf. *Tradition* (n. 8), 25f.; *Die Anfänge* (n. 8), 22.

15. K. L. Schmidt, "Formgeschichte," *RGG*² II, 1928, 639, approvingly cited by Dibelius, op. cit., 7; cf. Bultmann: "a sociological concept and not an aesthetic one," op. cit., 4.

16. Cf. R. Guelich's essay in the present volume, "The Gospel Genre."

atically used side by side. The same is true of the ancient oral collections of traditional material with which we are familiar, even of the Mishnah! The genres occur side by side in the same text and may also form innumerable hybrids. This too shows how the hypothesis that the different kinds of text in the Gospels are always rooted in specific *Sitze im Leben* is far removed from reality.

3.

When I work with the letter of James, the best example we have of early Christian parenesis, I get the impression that textual transmission possibly occurs as an *independent* act. In James we see clearly how the author, though he speaks in his own name, nevertheless admonishes his readers in conventional ways. He spontaneously forgets his own motifs, phrases, and words from the Jesus-tradition and the rest of the early Christian traditions (with their rich borrowings from the Jewish and Hellenistic traditions of parenesis). But he does not quote. Even quotations from Scripture occur sparingly and are usually only fragmentary. The same is true of the other parenetic passages in the New Testament. Hence the thesis of Dibelius[17] that the words of Jesus were preserved within the framework of early Christian parenesis proves to be unfounded.

It is important, generally speaking, to raise the following question: Where in the operational sphere of early Christianity did people use *real texts,* logia, parables, narratives, and the like, which were recited as complete units and not just used as a final court of appeal or fragmentarily?[18] Only three particular contexts come to mind. *First,* I can imagine that people found it natural to recite Jesus-texts *in the worship services.* The pericope concerning the Lord's Supper was probably used at sacred meals. Possibly, the basic summary of the passion history was utilized (cf. I Cor. 11:26). People probably also deemed it appropriate to recite other pericopes about Jesus as ready-made self-contained texts on the model of the synagogue readings from the law and the prophets, but probably from memory, not as a reading from a book.[19]

Second, it is also possible that certain memorized Jesus-texts—the logia

---

17. *From Tradition to Gospel,* 233-65.

18. By a "text" I here mean a self-contained independent utterance—oral or written—both the content *and the form* of which have intrinsic value.

19. From Riesenfeld's brief presentation in *The Gospel Tradition* (see n. 14) one may get the impression that in his opinion recitation in the worship services was the *sustaining* Sitz im Leben of the Jesus-tradition; cf. esp. 22ff. That, however, is hardly Riesenfeld's view. For my part, in *Memory and Manuscript* (n. 2), I have expressed the notion that early Christianity worked "with the word" (holy Scripture and the Jesus-tradition; see following note) and that the transmission of texts occurred independently, by acts which for the sake of clarity must be separated from the many *practical uses* of the transmitted texts. As one *form of use* among others I described recitation in a worship setting as one possibility ("not impossible"), 324-35, esp. 335.

first of all—were employed in the *catechetical instruction* of the early Church, even though this cannot be documented.

Third, I believe that there existed *a direct study* both of the words of Jesus and of the stories of his deeds and his fate—a study in groups or alone. In early Christianity believers were "occupied with" the holy Scriptures for their own sake in order to participate in divine revelation which was profitable for wisdom, for consolation, for teaching, for reproof, for correction, and for training in righteousness (II Tim. 3:16; cf. II Tim. 2:15-17). It is not hard to imagine that in this study people also used Jesus-texts in order to examine[20] them in isolation or in smaller or larger groups.

For the rest, it is hard to imagine contexts in which entire texts were used. We do see, of course, how the Jesus-texts were used in the New Testament by Paul, for instance. Only in two instances does he cite an entire text or a large segment of a text. In other places where he argues about halachic or other theological questions he is able to reproduce sayings of Jesus in his own words, to summarize them, or to refer to them by way of a text-fragment. I have in mind, for example, I Cor. 7:10 (the question of divorce); I Cor. 9:14 (the right of a preacher to material support); and I Thess. 4:15 (the question of the parousia).[21]

With their dynamic insight into the Jesus-tradition the form critics were able to speak of the "Sitz im Leben" of the elements of the tradition and mean by it the "point of origin and conservation in the community."[22] One cannot accept such an unclear hypothesis, however, if one is convinced that in the Jesus-tradition one is dealing with *texts.* Then the following state of affairs emerges: In ever-recurring situations, for example in repeated controversies with outsiders who attacked the teaching or the practice of early Christianity, the churches needed guidelines. However, one did not need a text in order to read it to others. One needed the point of a text, an authoritative teaching from a text, a decisive norm, a convincing argument, the solution to a problem, or whatever it may have been. But not a *text.* When a text was formulated, say a narrative of the type categorized as a dispute, this certainly did not happen in the situation of controversy itself. And once the text was available as text, people did not use it in controversies *as text,* in order to read it together; what people needed was the *content.*

20. Cf. e.g. how the Bereans worked with the Scriptures (Acts 17:10ff.). On the issue of how we should picture the various forms of "laboring in the word" in early Christianity, see *Memory and Manuscript,* 191-335; cf. *Tradition* (n. 8), 40. Unfortunately in this essay I cannot develop this subject. See, however, Otto Betz, "Jesus' Gospel of the Kingdom," in the present volume.

21. *Die Anfänge* (cf. n. 8), 25-31.

22. Bultmann (n. 12), 11.

4.

When in the fifties I became interested in the riddle of the two types of presentation in the New Testament, the Jesus-texts plus the free proclamation and teaching about Jesus, I was struck by the fact that in the Jewish material of antiquity there is a corresponding duality. In the targums and especially in the midrashic literature, in the haggadah and other material which somehow ties into the holy Scriptures, we see how imaginatively and freely, and on how many levels, the Jewish teachers were able to utilize their sacred texts. Still, despite the long period of this free utilization, the wording of the texts remained totally unchanged. The wording was preserved with extraordinary exactness, apart from a few minute changes (תיקוני סופרים and the like). The question which posed itself was: Where do we see this precise text-preservation happening and how does this happen? Three contexts suggest themselves:

1. The reading of the text in worship services. Here the text was read without any change.
2. The study in the elementary Scripture-schools. There the students learned to read the text as it stood without changing it.

Besides this there was a third context, the absolutely most important one:

3. There was an intentional and professional practice of text-preservation. Trained writers copied the Scriptures and corrected them precisely in accordance with the prototype or model. As a result there existed text-preservation and transmission as a recognized independent act, not just as an element in the framework of a general practical use of Scripture.[23]

The next question which arose was: How do things stand with regard to oral transmission? In this context we encounter a similar duality: in part, there was a rich and flourishing spiritual tradition with free interpretations, free variations, free creations from scratch; but, in part, there were also units which seemed to be transmitted as fixed texts, not as a dynamic spiritual tradition on a larger scale.[24]

And how were they transmitted? Here too I found that acts of intentional transmission of a self-contained text occurred, as well as similar acts of reception, even when the whole process took place orally. When the teacher passed on such a text he did not necessarily do this with the deeper intent "to console, to teach, to admonish, and to warn" his pupils. Simply to transmit such an important text to a pupil was valuable in itself. The text might be a point of

23. Cf. *Memory* (n. 2), 33-70.
24. In this case the texts were much more diverse than the written ones.

departure for one's own grounding in the truth, for a joint exercise in interpretation, for teaching on the part of the teacher, or for some other purpose. However, the transmission of a text was an act with intrinsic value. Hence there was good reason to make a distinction between acts of transmission as such and the various uses which were made of the text transmitted—also with reference to the oral tradition.

Textual transmission tended to take place in various ways. The teacher might pass on a single text or also a smaller or larger collection of texts. What made the text a fixed one was that the teacher knew it by heart and that the students were also expected to memorize it. It was only by this act that a student could be said to have received it, and not just that he heard it. The text might also be written down in a notebook, but that did not make much difference. In that case, too, one had to memorize the text; the writing was only a "memorandum," a ὑπόνημα.[25]

But this does not stand in the way of the fact that the text *can be changed.* If he wants to and *when he possesses the authority to do it,* the teacher can undertake to make a change (or more than one) in a text.[26] But also in this case the pupil receives it in a fixed form, namely in the new wording.

This is the result of the study of *rabbinic traditions.* We have every reason to start there. It is only in this material that we find so many clear pieces of information that we can draw a concrete and explicit picture of how people went to work in teaching and transmitting the materials. Once we have a grasp of this process—and I believe that we must have very *concrete* mental images of how this proceeded—we can go on to the generally concise indications we find in other material and ask ourselves if this material was transmitted in the same manner.[27]

Most of what I sketched of the rabbinic techniques of teaching and transmission reflects the situation in the fully developed rabbinic schools after

25. With regard to the unofficial written notices, cf. R. O. P. Taylor, *The Groundwork of the Gospel,* 1946; *Memory,* 157-63; E. E. Ellis, "New Directions in Form Criticism," in *Jesus Christus in Historie und Theologie* (Festschrift H. Conzelmann), 1975, 299-315; W. O. Walker, Jr. (ed.), *The Relationships Among the Gospels, An Interdisciplinary Dialogue,* 1978, 123-92; *Anfänge,* 18-20; Riesner, *Jesus als Lehrer* (cf. n. 8), 491-98.

26. Cf. *Memory,* 77f., 97f., 103-12, 120f., 152f.; *Tradition* (cf. n. 8), 38-40. Today I regret I did not discuss in greater detail the different types of textual changes in the rabbinic writings and the corresponding early Christian material. That would have been worthwhile.

27. By his form-critical analyses of rabbinic materials J. Neusner in many respects advanced tradition research. I have in mind particularly *The Rabbinic Traditions about the Pharisees before 70* III, 1971, and *Early Rabbinic Judaism,* Studies in Judaism in Late Antiquity 13, 1975, 71, 136. My main objection to Neusner's picture of the course of tradition is that he has too one-sidedly built it on an analysis of the rabbinic texts without sufficiently taking account of Near Eastern and Hellenistic Old Testament and non-rabbinic Jewish materials. I personally regret that Neusner refuses to see anything new in my study "Memory" but speaks of it as a summary of what others have done. Cf. *Exploring the Talmud* I: *Education,* ed. H. Z. Dimitrowsky, 1976, xxvif.

the fall of the temple in the year 70 and the total destruction of Jerusalem in the year 135. What surfaced was a rather polished technique. Nevertheless, it seemed to make sense to institute a comparison. For it was clear that in essence the rabbis made use of pedagogical devices which were very ancient. It was not the rabbis who discovered memorization. Nor was it the rabbis who began making a distinction between the inculcation of a text and its interpretation. Nor were the rabbis the first to discover that a shorter text is easier to inculcate than a longer one, that a more graphic and more urgent text is easier to retain than an ordinary flow of words, that rhythmic sentences are not so quickly forgotten as unrhythmic ones, that one should recite in cantillating tones, that people remember things better if they are zealously repeated, etc. Even several of the mnemonic devices of the rabbis are very ancient.

All this I have laid out in my study *Memory and Manuscript* (1961), adding certain clarifications in *Tradition and Transmission in Early Christianity* (1964).[28] Many colleagues were pleased with my book, but all too many have completely rejected it—with queries, bits of data, isolated observations, and all the rest. Sad to say, already at an early stage the debates took an unfortunate turn.[29]

I have never pictured two four-cornered blocks, one rabbinical and the other early Christian, and said: these two are twins. I have never said that Jesus was only a rabbi, still less that he was a rabbi of the late Tannaitic type; that the disciples built a rabbinic academy in Jerusalem and that the gospel tradition was a ready-made entity which Jesus drilled into the disciples' memories and which they only had to repeat and to explicate. Nor have I ever said that the Mishnah and the Gospels resembled each other as two eggs in a tray.

What I did say is that Jesus, despite his incomparable grandeur, taught his disciples, and that clearly in the traditional style *as far as the external form is concerned.* I have said that his disciples, when they were still in training, must have memorized weighty sayings of Jesus. I have also said that the Twelve, probably after Jesus' death, were for several years residents of Jerusalem and functioned there as an authoritative body of teachers. And that as such they very likely "labored in the Word"—the holy Scriptures and the Jewish tradition—in a way which resembled somewhat the labor in the Word that occurred in other Jewish groups, as for example the leading figures of the Qumran community or the Pharisees.[30]

---

28. See nn. 2 and 8.

29. Often an all too simple picture of my thesis was sketched, which people could then dispatch with equally simple counter-arguments. Both kinds of simplification then, partly without further discussion, made their way into the footnotes of handbooks. *Habent sua fata libelli.* With regard to the debates, cf. *Tradition,* in toto; *Anfänge,* 65-69 (bibliography); P. H. Davids, "The Gospels and Jewish Tradition: Twenty Years after Gerhardsson," in *Gospel Perspectives,* ed. R. T. France and D. Wenham, I, 1980, 75-97; Riesner, *Jesus als Lehrer* (cf. n. 8), *passim,* esp. §§ 3-4.

30. Cf. my brief historical sketch in *Memory and Manuscript,* 324-35. Cf. how I presented

There is no reason for making a simple block comparison between the fully developed educational system of the rabbis and the activity of Jesus or that of early Christianity. Rabbinical forms of instruction, in almost all cases, in instance after instance, are traditional, ancient, and national. That is what I have maintained throughout this period[31] and this is now what R. Riesner has independently demonstrated with much evidence from pre-Christian sources in his important book *Jesus als Lehrer* (1981).[32]

More use can be made of the comparative material, Jewish as well as Hellenistic, than Riesner, I, and others[33] have made of it. Now already, however, we know enough to take element after element in the practice of the ancient teachers—and also of the prophets; there is no reason to overlook them—and to ask: Was the Jesus-tradition perhaps transmitted in a similar way? To what extent did Jesus himself and the early Christian authorities utilize the ancient forms of oral instruction and oral transmission? Was this the case throughout early Christianity or only in parts of it?[34] Over the whole period or only gradually? It is certain that many problems that were insurmountable until now could be satisfactorily explained if they were viewed in the light of the materials consulted.

It belongs to the subject that the transmitting *persons* are of interest: Peter, the three pillars, the Twelve, Paul, etc.; and how they were linked with the chain of tradition which glimmers through. The form critics do not think much of the information which the ancient Church provides concerning the concrete persons behind the Gospels, not even of the personal references in the New Testament. The notion of the creative community makes all this uninteresting. This depersonalization has had a contagious effect right into the present. It still regularly happens that people blithely speak of "Church-constructions" and of traditions "which circulated in the churches," instead of asking who it is who has formulated, reformulated, or transmitted a text.

_____

Luke's view of things ("The Witness of Luke"), ibid., 208-61, and *Paul's* view ("The Evidence of Paul"), 262-323. In the ensuing discussion people have clearly understood especially the *Lucan* perspectives as though they were my own. With reference to the debates about the place of Jerusalem in early Christianity, cf. among others B. Holmberg, *Paul and Power: The Structure of Authority in the Primitive Church as Reflected in the Pauline Epistles*, 1978; J. D. G. Dunn, "The Relationship Between Paul and Jerusalem According to Galatians 1 and 2," *NTS* 28, 1982, 461-78 (= *Jesus, Paul and the Law: Studies in Mark and Galatians,* 1990, 108ff.).

31. *Memory,* 76-78; *Tradition,* 13-21; *Anfänge,* 16-19.

32. Cf. n. 8.

33. Cf. e.g. R. A. Culpepper's presentation of a variety of Hellenistic and Jewish school-forms: *The Johannine School: An Evaluation of the Johannine-School Hypothesis based on an Investigation of the Nature of Ancient Schools,* SBLDS 26, 1975.

34. Cf. e.g. U. Wilckens's notion of the double tradition-historical currents of Jesus-memories in early Christianity, *Tradition de Jésus et kérygme du Christ: la double histoire de la tradition au sein du Christianisme primitif, RHPR* 47, 1967, 1-20.

5.

At least briefly I should show how I picture the path of the synoptic tradition from Jesus to the evangelists. We may call this approach a working hypothesis.

There are two facts we may not lose sight of:

1. That in the eyes of early Christianity Jesus was a unique and incomparable figure, King of kings and Lord of lords; and we may add: prophet of prophets, teacher of teachers, Messiah, Son of God, Lord: No one was considered his equal.

2. That it was not Jesus, the wisdom teacher, the prophet, or miracleworker, who was the center of early Christian convictions, but Jesus the crucified, the risen and living Lord, the exclusive Redeemer and Savior of the world.

Without forgetting these facts we may try to answer a few questions with the help of ordinary historical methods: from a purely technical view, how did Jesus operate when he preached and taught? How were his words received by his disciples and adherents? How were these words then handed down? How were a number of them provided with a narrative framework? And how did the narrative traditions originate? How did the larger "synthetic" collections come into being? And so forth.

That Jesus of Nazareth, despite his incomparable majesty, gave instruction is an item of information from the sources which we cannot dismiss as a secondary feature of the tradition.[35] By no means opposed to this is the fact that he also acted as a charismatic and a prophet. As many have noted, there are no clear boundaries between the teacher and the prophet. Both gathered around them disciples who preserved their pronouncements as well as the memory of their acts and fortunes.[36]

True, Jesus' high self-consciousness, and the exalted image which early Christianity had of him, conferred, in the eyes of his adherents, a special personal value on his words and the stories of his deeds. His words and the narratives of episodes in his life must have seemed extraordinarily weighty, even indispensable, so that they were preserved, studied, and examined for their own sake, not only for a variety of practical reasons. Of Jesus' words it was said they were "spirit and life" (John 6:63), that they would never pass away (Matt. 24:35), that it was a matter of life "to hear and to do them" (Matt. 7:24-27 and par.), etc. In

---

35. Cf. esp. Riesner, *Jesus als Lehrer* (n. 8).

36. I do not believe that the difference between M. Hengel's and my view of the teacher-charismatic relationship is as great as one would expect from reading Hengel's *The Charismatic Leader and His Followers,* 1981. Cf. idem, "Jesus als messianischer Lehrer der Weisheit und die Anfänge der Christologie," in *Sagesse et religion,* 1979, 147-88. Cf. also the essay "Gospels Criticism: A Perspective on the State of the Art" by E. E. Ellis in the present volume.

general I cannot picture an early Christian leader or teacher who would have
been content with a purely mythical picture of Christ. One imagines that this
possibility exists only in the fantasies of many modern exegetes. R. Riesner puts
it very well when he says that Jesus' understanding of himself and the interpretation of Jesus in early Christianity must have been an "extraordinary motive
for the transmission of the tradition."[37]

The early Christian sources show unequivocally that Jesus' adherents
were exclusively bound to *Jesus;* none of them was referred to another teacher
or prophet for supplementary studies. Jesus was the "only teacher" of early
Christianity in the sense that he possessed a unique and incomparable, a decisive
and permanent authority as representative of God and mediator of a definitive
revelation and a decisive work of redemption. The adherents of Jesus were to
regard him as the "one and only" teacher, as Matt. 23:8 expressly demanded—
regardless of whether the formulation is an interpretation or an authentic line in
this utterance of Jesus. This attitude comes out above all in the fact that, strictly
speaking, the concrete Jesus-tradition is only interested in Jesus: there is no other
teacher or prophet next to him. Nor did any of his followers receive the role of
"successor in office."[38] This is true of the entire period beginning with Jesus up
to the time of the evangelists. The concrete Jesus-tradition possessed a special
dignity and was something unique. And it belonged to the foundation which
every Christian church had to have. Already at their founding—ἐν πρώτοις—
the churches needed the Jesus-tradition as much as they needed certain holy
Scriptures of the Old Testament. In none of these instances do the sources inform
us how the required texts were passed on. We can only mention incidentally the
numerous things that are self-evident to us. For that reason it is a mere accident
when they are mentioned in a source (cf. e.g. II Tim. 4:13).

6.

For reasons of space I shall content myself with a simple distinction between a
tradition of words and a tradition of narratives. I assume the detailed divisions
are familiar enough.

With regard to the tradition of words, it is striking that Jesus' words—
logia as well as parables—are artful texts, composed with care and bearing all
the marks of poetic and narrative-technical skill.[39] Here we are not dealing with
ordinary everyday utterances, or simple descriptive and prescriptive sentences.

---

37. Op. cit., 351f.
38. Cf. *Anfänge* (see n. 8), 34f.
39. Cf. Riesner, op. cit., 392-407.

Nor is it just we who view matters this way; the evangelists were also conscious of this. To Jesus' words—logia as well as parables—they give one appellation: παραβολαί, which corresponds to the Hebrew משלים.[40] A *mashal* is an artful utterance; by contrast with everyday speech it is an artistically formulated text.

What distinguishes this sort of statement from ordinary discourse is that not only the content but also the form or wording itself has intrinsic value. Not only does the speaker wish to communicate something to his hearers, but he objectivizes it, creates an object which he "passes on" to them: the text. This object or text is not conceived as worthless wrapping paper that can immediately be disposed of. It is intended to be preserved.

It is true of many logia and parables of Jesus that they are not intended simply to give information or to prescribe something but *to open the eyes of the listeners;* their purpose is to lead the listeners to see something and to assent to it. But the text is also given to be kept and so to enable people to preserve, renew, broaden, and deepen the insight and, not least of all, to enable them to pass it on. To receive a *mashal* is to acquire not only an insight but also the medium by which one can preserve and spread the insight.

To a great extent this observation proves to be true both with regard to the parables and to the short logia which Riesner calls "teaching summaries."[41] After all, as a rule there is less room for variation in the wording of a short logion than in a narrative parable. In the case of the latter one is tempted to make it either as "literary" as possible or to change it at certain points to indicate discoveries one believes he has made in the parable. This we notice when we compare the synoptic parallels. One can also tell this from the way it is clothed in Greek. As a rule the logia are closer to the Aramaic than are the parables.[42]

For the form critics it was quite natural to think that numerous Jewish wisdom utterances and early Christian words of prophecy were, as the tradition was transmitted, put on the lips of Jesus. I reckon with the possibility that this may have happened—in good faith—but hardly without further ado or frequently. The attitude toward the Jesus-texts, and the fact that they are not all that numerous,[43] have helped to make it easy to distinguish them. This is surely

40. Cf. J. Jeremias, *The Parables of Jesus,* ET 1954, 17. Riesner (op. cit.) calls only the parables *mᵉšalîm* and refers to the logia as "teaching summaries," a term I do not consider appropriate. In the Gospels both parables and logia are called παραβολαί—in keeping with the Hebrew and Aramaic usage which underlies the word.

41. See previous note or the distinctions between parables and logia in Riesner's understanding, op. cit., 292-404.

42. Cf. M. Black, *An Aramaic Approach to the Gospels and Acts,* ³1967, 274-77.

43. We usually postulate that the evangelists made a scant selection from a full stream of Jesus-tradition. One must remember, however, that the extant extracanonical tradition does not support this postulate. Cf. the essay "Unknown Sayings of Jesus" by O. Hofius in the present volume.

the reason people take notice when a hitherto unknown saying of Jesus surfaces. F. Neugebauer, D. Hill, and J. D. G. Dunn have raised weighty objections against the opinion of the form critics that Jewish wisdom sayings and especially early Christian words of prophecy were simply put on the lips of the earthly Jesus.[44] I believe that this could happen from time to time but then in good faith and not without examination.[45]

It is also clear that sayings of Jesus have changed on their way from Jesus to the evangelists. Our texts reveal errors in memory, variations in translation, interpretative adaptations, and the like. Formulations are omitted, added, changed, etc. Occasionally this may have happened in a more charismatic-prophetic way, and at other times in a more rational-didactic manner, the latter being the more frequent. By this process later, postresurrection issues, ideas, and perspectives were embedded in the sayings of Jesus. One must remember, however, that as a rule this occurred only to a limited extent. When, for example, we consider the sayings of Jesus in the so-called Q material, we are struck by how little they have been influenced by the passion and resurrection stories of early Christianity or even by post-Easter christology, soteriology, pneumatology, and eschatology. It is hard to believe, however, that there was even a single early Christian church which was not interested in Jesus' death and resurrection or the redemptive-historical significance of these events. The Q material can never have expressed the whole truth, all that the circle behind it believed, thought, and taught about Jesus. I believe, however— partly in agreement with A. Polag—that the "archaic" character of the sayings of Jesus is most easily explained as a pointer to the circumstance that they were transmitted in fixed wording and with minimal editing from the time before Easter onward.[46] Nor is it only in the Q material that we can see how little the christology of the Church was allowed to change the sayings of Jesus. There are of course exceptions, especially interpretative additions.[47]

---

44. F. Neugebaur, "Geistsprüche und Jesuslogien," ZNW 53, 1962, 218-28; D. Hill, "On the Evidence for the Creative Role of Christian Prophets," NTS 20, 1973-74, 262-74; J. D. G. Dunn, "Prophetic 'I'-sayings and the Jesus-tradition: The Importance of Testing Prophetic Utterances within Early Christianity," NTS 24, 1977-78, 175-98. The problem is further discussed in M. E. Boring, Sayings of the Risen Jesus: Christian Prophecy and the Synoptic Tradition, 1982.

45. Cf. the reference in n. 10 above.

46. A. Polag, Die Christologie der Logienquelle, WMANT 45, 1977, 143. Cf. his essay in the present volume.

47. Cf. A. Polag, Christologie, passim.

7.

As far as the narrative traditions are concerned, these, as we all know, have certain peculiarities. Dibelius was forced to say that the tradition of narrative and the tradition of sayings are not subject to the same law.[48]

The principal difference between the tradition of words and the tradition of narrative actually consists in the fact that *from the beginning* the sayings have a spoken form, the form they had when first spoken. The tradition of narrative must have been formulated by someone who either saw or heard of what happened; hence the text originates at some remove from the main person.

But of the narrative traditions we also know that the sayings of Jesus in them have been subjected to less editing than the narrative elements in these texts. Here, too, respect for the exact wording of the sayings asserts itself. Greater freedom to edit the narrative elements and so to restructure the tradition of narrative as a whole or to rebuild the whole narrative in a new way has brought with it that it could be more easily influenced by the kerygma and the post-Easter outlook of early Christianity than the sayings themselves.

I do not believe, however, that this must be understood as though the narrative elements or traditions had a fluid wording. Once a narrative text was formulated, it, too, was handed down in memorized form, possibly with written notes for support. We must in the first place reckon with the fact that the changes we discover were *deliberate*, changes introduced by authoritative teachers or "authors" for the purpose of making clear a certain meaning.

It is not necessary in this brief sketch to discuss all the types of narrative text we can distinguish in the synoptic material. For that matter, it is not too important to distinguish them when one considers them only as different literary models one can reach for without being situated in a specific "Sitz im Leben." There is no reason, as we said, to reckon with the fact that the narrative Jesus-traditions originated *as texts* in various "situations and modes of conduct." They were certainly formulated on the basis of conscious editorial work. Apart from a category of vigorously inspired texts, a text was normally formulated *deliberately* and that by an individual person.[49] This person may perform the task in a private context or in a study group assembled for this purpose, regardless of the text model he has chosen.

In this connection the group certainly played a role as a stimulating organ—asking questions and answering them, wondering and talking—but

---

48. *From Tradition to Gospel*, 28.
49. Among the various forms of text production in the nations of the world (cf. n. 56) there are of course also examples of how a text comes into being as different listeners influence, with their own verbal participation, the forward movement of a storyteller; see e.g. B. af Klintberg (ed.), *Tro, sanning, sägen, Tre bidrag till en folkloristisk metodik*, 1973, 95-101.

also as organ of social control. One must assume that without the consent of this organ no new text or version of a text could be accepted and spread.

In the formulation of certain types of text—I have in mind particularly the so-called "pronouncement stories"[50]—the framework may have been formed rather freely. I believe, however, that even these kinds of text were normally formed on the basis of transmitted sayings of Jesus. Also the texts conveying didactic or polemical dialogues may well have a forceful saying as their historical nucleus. And there is no reason why the framework narrative, in all its brevity, should not also proceed from a factual event.[51]

As far as the passion stories are concerned, we there encounter the peculiar circumstance that though they consist of small self-contained units they are more firmly connected with each other and refer to each other to a greater extent than do the pericopes in general. From this circumstance the form critics derived the insight that the passion story in its fundamental form emerged early as a coherent whole.[52] R. Pesch believes that the narrative sequence in Mark 8–16 concerning Jesus' journey through Caesarea Philippi to Jerusalem and the events which occurred there, at a very early stage (before AD 37) formed a primitive gospel, and that in the infant church in Jerusalem.[53] I am fairly receptive to Pesch's proposals for reconstruction even though many of the details will have to remain uncertain.

8.

Before I conclude I wish briefly, in part as a summary and in part as an expansion, to list and comment on ten assumptions which were critical for the early stages of classical form criticism:

1. *The distinction between "Palestinian" and "Hellenistic."* In the face of what we today know about Hellenistic influence in Palestine we can use this distinction for making historical judgments only in exceptional cases. An important instrument of differentiation in the arsenal of the form critics has therefore come to nothing.

---

50. Cf., finally, *Semeia 20: Pronouncement Stories,* ed. R. C. Tannehill, 1981. The fact that these kinds of text were of Hellenistic origin is no hindrance to their being a familiar literary model in Palestine before the beginning of the Christian era.

51. To the extent that one may take account of the fact that the tradition was subject to "control," the narrative frameworks gain an a priori higher value as sources.

52. Dibelius, *From Tradition to Gospel,* 178-217; Bultmann, *History of the Synoptic Tradition,* 275. On this cf. Blank, *Analyse und Kritik* (n. 14), 52-55, 151-56.

53. R. Pesch, *Das Evangelium der Urgemeinde. Wieder hergestellt und erläutert,* Herder-bücherei 748, 1979; for the details, see Pesch's large commentary on Mark. Cf. further his response to criticism in his essay in the present volume.

2. *The idea that a synoptic genre should be viewed as "a sociological fact."* Even before the time of Jesus and early Christianity, these genres existed as literary models which were utilized side by side in the same context. There is no necessary connection between a conventional textual model and a certain situation or activity.

3. *The link between genre and Sitz im Leben.* If one should ask where a given synoptic text took shape the correct answer is not: in the *Sitz im Leben* where it was most urgently needed. The text was certainly formulated in the course of deliberate textual labor. In light of this an additional aid has become useless.

4. *The search for the pure form.* The fact that there are so few texts in the synoptic Gospels which meet the requirements of "pure form," in conjunction with the fact that "mixed" textual types were already current in pre-Christian materials, makes this search redundant. It only tempts us to make unhistorical generalizations.

5. *"Unliterary" and "literary."* Neither Jesus nor the Twelve nor other influential teachers of early Christianity were "unliterary" people, to whom texts, the oral transmission of fixed forms, or copying were foreign. From ancient times on, such matters were well known in Israel, indeed everyday actions in the life of society. Prophets appeared on the scene and passed their words down to their disciples who received them, transmitted them by word of mouth, or wrote them down. In the course of time books of prophecy were compiled. Wisdom teachers appeared and their disciples acted in the same way. In the course of time books of wisdom were compiled. Neither Jesus nor early Christianity needed to invent such skills or introduce them as innovations. The direct textual labor which the evangelists performed was no more than a refined form of the deliberate textual labor which was customary among Jesus' followers from the time of Jesus' activity on earth, and which Jesus himself also practiced in his own way when he carefully formulated his logia and parables.

6. *The relation between tradition and redaction.* When one remembers that throughout the whole period the concrete Jesus-tradition consisted essentially of *texts* that were memorized, interpreted, compiled, grouped, and re-grouped and on which authoritative teachers could undertake certain redactional operations (particularly in binding statements but also in the text of the traditions), then another picture emerges, one that differs from the scheme "first tradition—then redaction." The situation was rather one of continual interplay between transmission and "redaction." As far as "redactional operations" are concerned, they need not have been totally unhistorical. Such changes could also be made with awareness of historical relationships.

7. *The independence of individual traditions.* In all likelihood the sayings of Jesus were originally independent of each other as texts which were to a

limited extent reworked and adapted to the rest of the material.[54] However, concerning the narrative traditions one must assume that both the person who first formulated such a text and also those who later worked on it had a total image of Jesus which influenced their formulations. Hence the individual narrative tradition must not be regarded as a completely independent text to the same degree as the logia and the parables.

8. *The traditioners.* On the basis of their view as to how popular tradition came into being the form critics were hardly interested in the *persons* behind the synoptic texts. But in several respects the matter is important. Where tradition is "practiced," the bearers are important. In all likelihood the early Church arose around the circle of Jesus' closest disciples and it is equally likely that from the beginning they had learned the logia and parables by heart. Besides, Jesus' works and fate were still fresh in their minds. The gospel tradition, therefore, begins with certain traditioners who were familiar with the history of Jesus; and from the beginning it consists of a large number of loose logia and parables from the lips of Jesus as well as of memories of weighty episodes in his work—memories which had not yet crystallized into texts.

9. *The relationship between oral and written tradition: Before Matthew and Luke the gospel traditions were not available in a published (book) form.* It is hardly to be believed that the Gospel of Mark was thought of as a written summary of the entire Jesus-tradition. Written records of varying length, like notes and memory aids (ὑπομνήματα),[55] were surely in circulation at an early stage. It is not impossible, though perhaps not likely, that such records were already kept by the disciples in the period of Jesus' activity. In any case, they may well have come into use rather rapidly in the early Church, especially in predominantly Hellenistic congregations. I, for my part, believe that such records were only intended to be used as memory aids since the synoptic texts were in principle *oral* texts. It is, at any rate, hard to tell from looking at a text whether it was formulated to serve the memory or to be recorded on a sheet of papyrus. I know of no one who has provided us with stable criteria for judging this. Written texts may be firmly fixed; they may also be changeable. Oral texts may be changeable but also stable—extraordinarily stable even. It is not at all easy to attain certainty at this point: penetrating research and discussion are still needed.[56]

---

54. It seems to me that in the present situation it is difficult to decide the extent to which the larger models ("midrashic patterns"), which we find present in the discourses of the gospel, could possibly go back to Jesus himself (cf. Ellis, *New Directions* [n. 25], 309-15, and his essay in the present volume (esp. pp. 42f.). We still know too little of the different forms of "laboring with the word" in early Christianity.

55. Cf. the literature in n. 25.

56. If one remembers that even within a single culture oral tradition can be very diverse, and that it is inexhaustibly diverse when one includes all cultures in one's purview, it seems important to try to establish which analogies to the Jesus-tradition seem *nearest* to it. It is not clear to me, for

10. *Mark's achievement.* If Mark wrote the first of the Gospels preserved for us,[57] this hardly constituted a radically new beginning. Even before him direct textual work was done in the Church and compilations of varying lengths of the Jesus-tradition had been made. The rough plan which Mark followed in part came about quite naturally: a simple geographic-chronological sketch (starting with John the Baptist, followed by the main ministry in Galilee, concluding with the final journey to Jerusalem, with the events there recorded in a natural order), united with the knowledge that Jesus busied himself in the main with preaching, teaching, driving out demons, and healing the sick. The integrative identification of Jesus and the consideration of his work as a whole that Mark offers are found not only in the kerygma but also in the comprehensive surveys of Jesus' works as we find them, for instance, in the speeches in Acts and the formalized christological material.

9.

When the scattered New Testament writings were assembled it seemed natural to distinguish between εὐαγγέλιον (writings containing concrete Jesus-material) and ἀπόστολος (writings containing free apostolic instruction). However, these designations themselves might occasion misunderstanding: the apostles had had to deal with the material of the Gospels, and their own free instruction contained the good news about Jesus Christ. But, viewed objectively, there is justification for the division (with a certain reservation, of course, as it pertains to John's Gospel). There is also justification for placing the εὐαγγέλιον first and to treat these texts as basic. This does not have to eclipse the kerygma.

What the form critics did was to incorporate the εὐαγγέλιον in the ἀπόστολος. According to them the Gospels and the tradition underlying them should in principle be viewed as post-Easter Church-proclamation concerning Christ. In consequence, on the question of historicity, the criteria have been reversed: the burden of proof no longer rests with the person who regards a given Jesus-tradition unauthentic but with the person who asserts its authenticity.

It cannot be correct for us as historians to accept this point of view. Historians have to take seriously the clear distinction that the early Christian

---

instance, why we should elevate the type which A. B. Lord investigated in Yugoslavia to the status of standard model for "orality" or "oral tradition" or "oral composition" or "oral literature" or the like, when after all the world is full of alternatives. Cf. the discussion of Lord's theories in *The Relationships Among the Gospels* (see n. 25), 31-122. Also the phenomenon "written tradition" is a rather motley entity.

57. So far the arguments which have recently been adduced against the priority of Mark's Gospel have not convinced me.

sources make—with the exception of John's Gospel. Our *starting point* has to be the assertion of the source-documents that Jesus said and did what they say he said and did. I say this has to be our point of departure. Naturally, as scholarly investigators pursuing the historical-critical method we must test the isolated units as well as the larger complexes in terms of these questions: Can this or that really have been said or done by Jesus? Can this really have happened to him? Does this text in its present form or in some earlier form yield reliable information? Hence the burden of proof must lie on our shoulders when we doubt the assertions of the sources and eliminate secondary material. A *practical* argument has been furnished us by the debates about the question of criteria: to all appearances it hardly leads to a single undisputed result.[58]

Our criticism is necessary because we know—better than the Church before us knew—that the Jesus-traditions have been edited before they were written down. From that perspective it is necessary to examine what are probably post-Easter interpretations, changes, additions, or secondary creations. A number of texts in the Gospels are obviously rather free creations. Here I have in mind above all the prologues: the prehistories in Matthew and Luke as well as the histories of the baptism and temptation. But here, too, I believe that early Christianity took its starting point in something handed down, and, in the final analysis, something historical. Briefly expressed: *it only gave an interpretation where there was something to be interpreted.* This rule of thumb may also be applied in the evaluation of John's Gospel.

In short, I would by no means plead for a narrow-minded biblicism or a general credulity with regard to the assertions of the New Testament documents. In his or her analysis the investigator must be keen, precise, and unbiased; in the search for truth relentless criticism is indispensable. But one must have a sound starting point.

58. For a balanced discussion of the various criteria, cf. R. H. Stein, "The Criteria for Authenticity," in *Gospel Perspectives* I (see n. 29), 225-63.

The Theological Center
of the Sayings Source

Athanasius Polag

1. The Existence of Q

The problem of the sayings source does not lie in the question of its existence.
One might perhaps think that, given the insight that the two-source hypothesis
offers an oversimplified picture of the genesis of the Gospels, Q is thereby also
rendered invalid. However, in this case the child is hardier than the parent. By
a few strong arguments it is protected from the storm which its opponents have
unleashed.

The main argument for Q is still the agreement between Matthew and
Luke in particulars of language, and that not just in pithy wisdom sayings but
also in large syntactical units.[1] Of course, the texts of Q as a collection of
dominical sayings have a longer history of transmission. However, for the
compositional stage which is accessible to us by way of a comparison between
Matthew and Luke, one has to say on the basis of a high degree of agreement
that *these dominical sayings were present in the Greek language and in written
form.* That is more likely than that the measure of agreement can be traced back
solely to the stability of the oral tradition. Of course one has to reckon with the
constant influence of oral tradition, for in the early Church there was no
fundamental separation between oral and written tradition. Besides, within the
domain of written documents one also has to take account of a number of
variations we know from the textual witnesses which have come down to us.

A further argument for Q is the doublets. Opponents of Q have a very hard

---

1. E.g. Matt. 12:43-45; 23:37-39 and the Lucan parallels. Of decisive importance is the
agreement in position of the particles and possessive pronouns, which varies in oral tradition; cf.
Matt. 7:3-5 and the Lucan parallel.

time explaining the rise of the doublets, at least in Luke.[2] In such a case the historian will proceed from the hypothesis which can explain the largest number of phenomena and cause the least number of difficulties.

Explanations which avoid a written Q common to both evangelists and assume Luke's direct dependence on Matthew have so far not been able to make convincingly clear why Luke broke up the speech cycles of Matthew and why in numerous instances he offers the older wording of the text. It is revealing in this context that, despite his criticism of the two-source hypothesis, M.-É. Boismard admits the existence of Q as an independent collection of dominical sayings.[3]

E. E. Ellis, in his essay in the present volume, responds to this criticism of Q in some detail.[4] This criticism, however, does not seem to me as successful as one might conclude from his paper. What is said about Q is not as wildly hypothetical as S. Petrie, for example, suggests. Certainly, only very few of the critics cited by E. E. Ellis make the effort of going through the material word for word and of testing the different arguments in individual cases.

True, with the source material presently available we are not able to establish the precise extent of the sayings source. Omissions made by the Matthean or Lucan redactor(s), like those evidently made in processing the Marcan tradition, can only be suspected. Nor has it yet been established that entire texts which, on account of the agreement between Matthew and Luke, have been claimed for Q belong to a single collection. We do, however, have a sound argument for the position that extensive material belongs to a larger collection. And that argument is based on the agreement between Matthew and Luke in the sequence of sayings which constitutes an important component of the double traditions (at the very least the texts of Luke 3–11 and 17).[5] In this connection it is also clear that what is at stake here is a collection of sayings which divided the smaller cycles of sayings into different themes. That is an important fact.

The difficulty of proving that they belong to the source concerns especially the introductory pericopes (Matt. 3:7-12; 4:1-11; Lucan par.), which in genre and in the details of diction stand out from the major part of the double tradition. There are, to be sure, several connections to sayings in other cycles, e.g. the γέγραπται plus scriptural citation which appears, apart from the temptation pericope, in the double tradition only in Matt. 11:10. But one can also see this as accidental agreement. Hence no one can be denied the right to regard the material underlying the pericopes concerning the words of John the Baptist and

---

2. E.g. Luke 9:1-6/10:4-12; Luke 9:26/12:8, 9 as compared with Matt. 16:27/10:32, 33.

3. M.-É. Boismard and A. Lamouille, *Aus der Werkstatt der Evangelisten*, 1980, 15f.

4. E. E. Ellis, "Gospels Criticism: A Perspective on the State of the Art," pp. 26ff. in the present volume.

5. The observations of Vincent Taylor, "The Original Order of Q," in *New Testament Essays*, 1959, 246-69, are so far not out of date.

the temptation of Jesus as an independent unit of tradition, especially when he includes the baptism of Jesus as the centerpiece.

Since the tradents have barely edited the texts, linguistic evidence showing that the entire tradition belonged to a single collection are lacking. There may be certain indications that it did, but their cogency is limited.[6] For exegesis it does not seem to me to be very significant whether the entire double tradition goes back to a single collection or whether in addition to a large collection there are also three or four smaller cycles discernible in the double tradition which played the same role in the origination of Matthew and Luke as a source of the tradition of sayings of Jesus. In other contexts the historian must also work with fragments. What is important is that we can reckon with a larger collection, hence with a representative of a special tradition of dominical sayings.

2. The History of Q

Criticism of Q is predominantly directed toward the way in which this collection of dominical sayings is fitted by the representatives of source and form criticism into the process by which the Gospels arose. Involved here are the historical hypotheses concerning the life and work of the early Church and the description of their relationship to the activity of Jesus. In fact, a great deal of what has been said on this point in the context of literary-critical and form-critical studies must be revised. It is of great importance that at this point research has scored an advance, as P. Stuhlmacher has shown.[7] However, this does not derogate from the significance of a collection of dominical sayings like Q; it rather accentuates than lessens it.

Q is not a great literary achievement. It can only be understood as part of a multi-staged process of transmission. The texts of Q have a long history: in the majority of cases the wording of the sayings can be understood as a translation from Aramaic. But this history does pose serious difficulties. We have too little comparative material and know too little about the early Church. Even if the diction of the sayings was not subjected to constant editing, it is nevertheless certain that any collection of sayings was exposed in the process of transmission to constant change, at least by addition or omission. For that reason it is very likely that in the process by which Q was worked into Matthew or Luke a variety of versions of this collection was utilized. The extent to which creative Church additions (*Gemeindebildungen*)

---

6. Thus, for example, the expression ἡ γενεὰ αὕτη establishes a connection between Matt. 11:16-19; 12:38-42; and 23:23, 34-36 par. Luke; but one cannot be altogether certain since the formulation also occurs three times in Mark and at least once in the Matthaean and Lucan redactions.

7. P. Stuhlmacher, "The Theme: The Gospel and the Gospels," pp. 1ff. in the present volume.

were incorporated is a special problem. But its significance is relativized by
the fact that the additions had to be adjusted to the form and content of that
which had been transmitted before. One can hardly believe, therefore, that
the core of the traditional material would have been overwhelmed, in the
course of transmission, by secondary influences.

Since at first blush one can ascertain in Q the presence of groups of
sayings, the redaction-historical approach is challenged. But there one encounters grave difficulties. Basically, the extent of a given redaction can be reliably
determined only when one can compare a text with the earlier redactional
models, and in the case of Q that is unfortunately not possible. Add to this that,
in the case of Q, consistently preferred and uniformly used concepts, phrases,
and syntactic forms are very infrequent. So in the main one is dependent on the
catchword connections of the composition. But if one uses the criteria taken
from the contents and applies them in the evaluation of a redaction, one has to
acquire them from an evaluation of the theological history of the Church and
everything then depends on the correctness of this evaluation.

However, one can, with a high degree of probability, make two determi-
nations about the redaction. When the introductory pericopes belonged to Q
they were placed at the beginning of an already existing collection. They display
a christological interest not characteristic of the other cycles.

In the second place, an analysis of individual terms (e.g. ὁ υἱὸς τοῦ
ἀνθρωπου,[8] ἡ σοφία) shows—amid all the uncertainty—that the confessional
stance of the tradents belongs to another level of theological reflection than the
primary formation of the majority of the sayings. From this one can draw the
conclusion: when, despite the developed theology of the tradents, the wording
of the sayings is hardly changed, this wording must be valued very highly and
thus protected. Hence the textual transmission of the material adopted is highly
reliable. And one can further conclude that the sayings have been transmitted
in a context of competent interpretation.

Even if with regard to the scope and the history of Q there are many
unanswerable questions we may nevertheless assume further that in the Q
collection we have a bridge to that domain in which Jesus' preaching was
primarily received. The sayings source gives us words of Jesus with the least
amount of editing in comparison with other strands of tradition. There may, in

---

8. It seems to me that no convincing argument has until now been adduced against the
position that the Aramaic equivalent for ὁ υἱὸς τοῦ ἀνθρώπου, as it occurs in the authentic words of
Jesus, is employed neither as a title, in accordance with Daniel 7, nor in the generic sense of
"universal man," but in the special sense of "the man" as an accentuated paraphrase in place of a
pronoun. According to this view, this expression only became a christological title in the sense of
Daniel 7 in the tradition of the Church and as such was translated into Greek. In the discussion of
this phrase it is again clear that the arguments do not become true simply because they are repeated
so often.

addition, be many an authentic individual tradition but in Q we have access to the transmission process itself.

3. The Theological Center of Q

The real problem of the sayings source is its theology. The issue is not the content of the individual sayings but what it is that unites the texts.

In the context of literary-critical and form-critical study this question has never been in the foreground. Instead, the style and form of the sayings has received special attention. In this regard one can in fact gain a unified impression of the collection, provided one ignores the introductory pericopes. In most texts one finds short sayings which still often betray the rhythmic composition and structure of the Aramaic text. Wisdom sayings and prophetic utterance are predominant. Only two healings are reported (Matt. 8:5-10, 13; Luke 11:14); Jesus' activity, though in the wording of the sayings it is again and again presupposed, recedes almost entirely into the background. The phenomenon of a collection of short utterances of Jesus with no reports of his activity or mention of his cross and resurrection seems to have exerted a peculiar fascination upon the generation of the older literary criticism. The reason for this was probably that here they believed they had at their disposal a layer of the Jesus-tradition still uninfluenced by Paulinism, the effects of which they observed already in the earliest Gospel, the Gospel of Mark.[9] To be sure, in the course of time the form-critical view of the materials of Q corrected this impression of uniformity and the category of the sayings collection lost the character of something extraordinary. The question thus remains what it is that unites this comparatively large collection, the question, namely, whether there is something like a theological center.

Again and again reference is made to the peculiar fact that in Q there is no traditional material which is explicitly related to the suffering and resurrection of Jesus. Appertaining to this is the much-discussed circumstance that though the expression ὁ υἱὸς τοῦ ἀνθρώπου is used for the Jesus who works in the present and is involved in future judgment, it is not used for the Jesus who suffers, as in Mark. It is at this point that statements about the theology that integrates the collection often begin. But with this point of departure, the danger of overinterpretation begins to assert itself. For according to everything we have so far come to know about the life of the early Church it must be considered highly improbable that within the milieu of the disciples of Jesus there was ever a community for which the resurrection of Jesus was not the central content of

9. A. von Harnack, *Sprüche und Reden Jesu,* 1907, 171.

confession and the pivotal point of the teaching. To that extent the content of Q within the field of christology can never have been solely representative for the teaching of a church. The simplest explanation for the limits of Q is that the core of the collection, that which determines its character, goes back to the pre-Easter circle of disciples and hence that the genesis of the collection lies in the teaching activity of Jesus. This view is but seldom represented, however, because it is incompatible with the exegetical dogma of the Easter grave. In any case, in the interpretation of Q one may never lose sight of the fact that the Q tradition can only have been a complementary element in the life of any church. As such Q needed continually upgraded interpretation.

Formal criteria are not much more helpful in mediating an integrating center of Q. The composition is to a large extent controlled by catchword connections. From that perspective there is hardly a text which has redactionally been made so prominent that with it as paradigm one can discern a central confession around which the other traditions have been arranged. To underscore the crucial points was clearly, as in all such collections of sayings, a matter of interpretation.

Hence one must make a modest beginning: that which unites the collection is at bottom nothing other than the person of Jesus. However, one cannot rest content with this general observation. It is, generally speaking, not self-evident that for the Church this sayings material, both as regards the basileia sayings and as regards the words of threat and coming misfortune, was worth transmitting as a whole. To that end a certain view of the person of Jesus has to be assumed, one that can be formulated as follows: By the resurrection of Christ his importance for the history of the kingdom in its manifestation in Israel has not only been confirmed by God; rather, a renewed possibility of deciding for or against Jesus and his mission has been opened up; Jesus now lives with God and is nevertheless present in his Church in such a way that in this Church of disciples there is a possibility of meeting him in another form. From now on, until Jesus returns and is visible to every eye in the events of judgment, the offer of access to salvation stands. Accordingly, the message of the resurrection of Jesus is not simply a communication concerning the saving action of God but confronts people with the need to make a decision. Hence Jesus' words acquire their central meaning from the challenging events which occurred before Easter. At stake, precisely in the Church, is not only the issue of the risen one and the one expected to come in judgment but also that of him who leads people into new forms of activity. This mental outlook takes fully into account that which we know of the significance of the experience of the operation of the Spirit in the early Church.

The renewed offer, calling people to decision, gives to the words of Jesus a fresh relevance. In this connection one observation has to be made in particular. Of the sayings which Q transmits only a part relates directly to the conduct of people in response to the action of God and can in a general sense be described as parenetic, as for example the promise of salvation to the poor, the words concerning compassion and the willingness to forgive, the mission mandate to the disciples, and the words about prayer. This part is clearly outweighed in scope by the words of consolation and warning addressed to the disciples in view of the impending situation of temptation, words of judgment and of coming suffering.[10] This emphasis is also ascertainable in the arrangement, e.g. added to the beatitude for the poor is the beatitude for the persecuted (Luke 6:20-23). Accordingly, the Q collection is concerned not only with a decision but also with the consequences of this decision, the need for perseverance in the path chosen. A saying which stands out in the tradition illustrates this point by way of example: the image of the returning demon (Matt. 12:43-45). Q's concern is to avoid an emptiness after deliverance or the ending of the encounter with Jesus in collapse (Matt. 7:24-27). This permits an inference about the way in which, according to the conviction which underlies Q, the decision for Christ is viewed: this decision opens up a history.

This view to which we have come with regard to the tradents of Q is of course open to many questions. The most important one perhaps is why the renewal of the situation of decision for the Church was not just brought out by a newly formulated kerygma but also by the transmission of the words of Jesus. Is the basis for this simply that there already was a pre-Easter practice of preserving Jesus' sayings in the circle of the disciples, as this was self-evident for the disciples of a rabbi? Or was the conviction of the permanent significance of a teacher always, in a Jewish milieu, linked with a sayings tradition? In other words, was it only factors in the cultural environment which determined the practice of handing down the sayings of Jesus? If this is not considered plausible, one must assume that the existence of this sort of tradition was bound up with a view of Jesus' sayings that attributed a special worth to them.

If the sayings of Jesus were not valuable simply because he uttered them, their worth could only lie in the experience which the disciples had had with them: They had experienced how the sayings had elicited a decision and had led to new conduct. Accordingly, the tradents did not in the first place transmit the sayings of Jesus because of their feelings of devotion to him, in order to keep them from being lost, or because of their historical interest, but because the sayings had proven their power in bringing people to the point of opening themselves up to the new action of God and of what follows from it. It was this experience which gave to the handed-down sayings of Jesus priority over the Spirit-inspired words of the exalted Lord mediated by prophets and led to their

10. If one divides the double tradition into 75 units, there are 56 of them.

formal assimilation. If this view is correct, the text transmitted against the background of the experience of the tradents acquires its full weight; it was transmitted because they had experienced something with it and hoped for the renewal of such an experience. For that reason the transmission of the sayings of Jesus cannot be purely understood as an intellectual process—despite the great intellectual achievement that was bound up with it; it belongs in the context of religious experience.

That which imparts coherence to the Q collection is therefore its theological underpinning: the conviction of the tradents that for people who meet him Jesus opens up the possibility of committing themselves to God and his rule and of living out this commitment in a history. In this process his own word is a power that works.

4. The Gospel in Q

The central significance of the person of Jesus for the Q collection also comes out in connection with the theme of the εὐαγγέλιον.

The most important evidence for this is the pericope concerning John the Baptist's question (Matt. 11:2-6). It is the sole passage in Q which expressly deals with the question concerning the person of Jesus. The preaching of the gospel to the poor, πτωχοὶ εὐαγγελίζονται, is an element in the characterization of Jesus' ministry. The reference is, without question, to Isaiah 61. This implies that Jesus ushers in the year of the Lord's favor, the great release from debt and the liberation of the captives. Out of the hardening of his inner and outer relationships man is called into a new relationship with God, a relationship that is eschatologically new; it sustains the ultimate meaning of his life. True, this is an unconditional grant from the side of God but tied in with a decision. The concluding sentence: "Blessed is he who takes no offense at me" (Matt. 11:6) may not be isolated from the message. The good news, according to Q, is the word of the messenger of Isaiah 61 which enables people to make a decision. The concluding sentence demonstrates the close connection between the message of salvation and the relationship to Jesus—between reception of the word and personal experience.

It is true that in the passages in which the poor are explicitly named the messenger recedes into the background. We are referring to the beatitude (Luke 6:20, 21), the promise of participation in the kingdom of God, and to the Lord's prayer (Luke 11:2-4), the affirmation of God as Father of the poor[11] in the attitude of prayer and surrender. However, this discrepancy is only external; a

11. The petition for one's daily bread qualifies the disciple as poor.

large number of sayings show that the indissoluble link between message and messenger is constantly assumed. That is particularly clear in two instances which also belong to the interpretive horizon of Isaiah 61: concerning opening of the prison to those who are bound, Luke 11:20; the gathering of the people, Luke 11:23. This is augmented by Luke 11:31, 32; 12:8, 9; 14:27.[12]

Accordingly, in Q the gospel to the poor implies the person of the messenger. Herein lies the originating impulse for the fact that as theological reflection about the significance of Jesus progressed, the form of the tradition was changed. This development is already evident in the prefatory positioning of the introductory pericopes of Q. A collection of sayings in the real sense of the word no longer sufficed as an encompassing Gattung in non-Gnostic Christianity.

When the churches structured their Jesus-tradition in a way resembling the sketch of Acts 10:36-43, the texts of Q were then coordinated with other traditions which had a more comprehensive view of the work of God in Jesus. This was consistent because these texts had for a long time already been transmitted with a view toward a personal relationship to Jesus.

5. Conclusions

The value of the sayings source is not limited to the fact that it has transmitted to us the words of Jesus in their oldest form. In this collection we have access to the process by which the sayings of Jesus were transmitted and we encounter a view of the person of Jesus in the close linkage of salvation, message, and messenger on which the tradition rests. Q displays the connection between receiving the message of the kingdom of God and confessing Jesus.

The tradition of the words of Jesus is concerned not only with proclamation and utterance but also with decision and history. There was a unity of experience between the early Church and the disciples of Jesus. This unity of experience was decisive for the Church's association with the sayings of Jesus as we see them in Q. Scholarly exegesis, too, must constantly take account of the fact that these texts were not transmitted for the purpose of conveying information but in order to make personal experience possible.

---

12. The message is most emphatically linked with the person of the cry of jubilation in Matt. 11:25-27, but presumably this text belongs to the redactional context of the introductory pericopes.

The Gospel in Jerusalem:
Mark 14:12-26 as the Oldest Tradition
of the Early Church

Rudolph Pesch

That the early church formed in Jerusalem by the Galilean adherents of Jesus (cf. Acts 1:11; 2:7), first of all the "eleven" (cf. Matt. 28:16; Luke 24:9, 33; Acts 1:26; also Mark 16:14) and the "women" (cf. Acts 1:14; Mark 15:40f. par.; Luke 8:2, 3), was responsible for the initial (recollecting) collection and the (interpretive) formation of the Jesus-tradition, of "all that Jesus began to do and teach" (Acts 1:1), is undoubtable, regardless of whether one has to reckon with an antecedent formation of the tradition during Jesus' lifetime in the circle of his disciples (which is the more likely) or not.

Whether the "initial" tradition, gathered and formed within the framework of the Gospels, above all in that of the oldest Gospel, the Gospel of Mark, is still available to us, is a question, on the one hand, about the constancy of the subsequent tradition, but also a question about the formation (constitutive for the oral tradition) of the material to be transmitted in categories (imprintable upon the memory of the tradents) of (independent) individual traditions and in (non-independent) fragments of tradition which together combine in complexes of a comprehensive kind (which at an early stage must have exerted pressure toward written fixation).

The (formed) sayings of Jesus could, from the beginning (already in his lifetime), be transmitted by mere repetition (memorization), the modern technical analogy to tape recording. It is self-evident that its recitation in missionary preaching and catechesis in churches required comment (also in narrative form) in order to insure that the intent and meaning of the sayings transmitted would remain intelligible and accessible. The construction of sayings collections therefore has an "instrumental" character (for use in mission and catechesis). The acts of Jesus (as historical events which could not simply be repeated) required, from the beginning, narrative representation, in which certain features were emphasized through selection and perspective. Here the modern technical analogy is the camera. Narration is not only dependent (as is the repetition of sayings) on the memory of the narrator but also on his ability to capture and interpret the essentials of an event—on his horizon of understanding as it relates to events. The re-presentation of the works of Jesus constitutes a commentary on these works themselves and in no way depends on the precise reproduction of uninterpreted and indubitable "acts," but, just as constitutively, on the properly interpreted effect of these works, the properly conceived context or horizon (which has been opened by the works themselves and/or in which understanding is realized).

With respect to their being realized the saying and narrative traditions were fundamentally distinguished by pure recitation in the one case and by selective and perspectival re-presentation in the other, and particularly in the search for the historical Jesus, in establishing what he actually (and recognizably—with the means of historical criticism) "taught and did," is this distinction required. Hence, diverse criteria of research must be methodically employed. Nevertheless these traditions are bound up in the same process of transmission, a process that begins with the eyewitnesses who became ministers of the word (Luke 1:2) and leads down to the Gospels—in the *tradition* in which the *understanding* of the material transmitted does not automatically come with the act of repeating the sayings and narrating the stories (cf. Mark 4:10-12). Hence, from the beginning, interpretation, in whatever form it was practiced, was part of the tradition; and to the degree that Jesus' sayings and deeds had an impact in the early Church (also in the suspension of self-hardening, unbelief, and weakness as the real barriers to understanding) they were more accurately and deeply understood. In this process it did not just make sense, but it was even virtually mandatory and necessary, to restate and reshape the sayings of Jesus that were transmitted and to form anew (by the renewed selection of and by gaining new perspectives on the materials) the stories of his deeds and of his history. That in this process respect for the sayings of Jesus was greater than the respect accorded to the stories of the first narrators who reported on his history can be clearly seen in the Gospels and is (if one takes the distinction between saying and narrative tradition seriously) self-evident. As important and even decisive as the literalness of a given tradition (e.g. I Cor. 15:2) may be, the issue at stake is not completely this literalness itself, for the letter can kill but the Spirit makes alive. But it is the lifegiving Spirit, the Spirit of the Logos, who transmits himself in the tradition and inspired it; and the tradents receive their inspiration from him for as long as they remain "ministers of the word" (and do not permit "the masters of their own spirit" to rule). Also, from the beginning the discernment of spirits belonged to the tradition. To some extent it is the "third dimension" of tradition, its theological depth-dimension.

The search for the oldest tradition of the early Church cannot only be focused on conserved sayings and stories; it must itself be integrated in the "third dimension," the discernment of spirits. The history of Jesus and the story of its effects are to be understood historically, but then as history made accessible and opened up to us by the tradition. The manner in which it is made accessible and opened up to us is a question which engages the historical and theological dimensions of understanding equally. The precision of one's critical and historical judgment and the thoroughness of one's theological competence are equally under challenge, equally exposed to controversy and discussion. The clouding over of the discovery of truth threatens from two directions, and the "soundness" of knowledge likewise has double effect. Prejudices are worthless where history asserts its rights and where tradition seeks to be appropriately dealt with.

In those places that one's view of history is befogged, a great expenditure of energy, effort, and also acuteness are needed if one is to thrust one's way through the fog and recover clarity of vision.

That the *passion of Jesus*—setting aside for the moment the formalized kerygmatic tradition in its concentration on the redemptive significance of the death of Jesus or the contrast between death and resurrection—had to be transmitted in narrative form, not by the presentation of individual episodes (e.g. the arrest, the trial, the crucifixion, the burial) but of the entire complex of connected events, should really be a priori obvious; but the assumption that it was actually handed down in a more extensive narrative complex of course calls a posteriori for historical-critical demonstration. Whether this demonstration has been given would seem to be disputed. And, certainly, the scholarly battle over the result can only be fought out as a battle over the method which yielded the result.

1. The Pre-Marcan Passion Narrative as the Oldest Tradition in the Early Church of Jerusalem

On the basis of long and numerous preliminary studies I have, in the second volume of my commentary on Mark (no. 7 in the list below, thereafter *Mark2*) and in the publication (which was written for a wider circle of readers and which presented a more extensive account of the reconstruction process in question) entitled *Das Evangelium der Urgemeinde* (no. 8 in the list below), delimited the scope of the pre-Marcan passion narrative as Mark 8:27-33; 9:2-13, 30-35; 10:1, 32-34, 46-52; 11:1-23, 27-33; 12:1-12, 13-17, 34c, 35-37, 41-44; 13:1-2;

14:1–16:8 and demonstrated its origin in the early Jerusalem Church and determined that it dates back to the year AD 37 as *terminus ante quem.*

This process of reconstruction and the determination of the provenance and age of the pre-Marcan passion narrative may be seen and tested on the basis of the following published works of mine:

1. "Die Salbung Jesu in Bethanien (Mk 14,3-9). Eine Studie zur Passionsgeschichte," in *Orientierung an Jesus,* Festschrift J. Schmid, 1973, 267-85.

2. "Das Messiasbekenntnis des Petrus (Mk 8,27-30). Neuverhandlung einer alten Frage," *BZ* NF 17, 1973, 178-95; 18, 1974, 20-31.

3. "Die Verleugnung des Petrus. Eine Studie zu Mk 14,54.66-72 (und Mk 14,26-31)," in *Neues Testament und Kirche,* Festschrift R. Schnackenburg, 1974, 43-62.

4. "Der Schluß der vormarkinischen Passionsgeschichte und des Markusevangeliums: Mk 15,42–16,8," in M. Sabbe (ed.), *L'évangile selon Marc,* BETL 34, 1974, 435-70.

5. "Die Überlieferung der Passion Jesu," in K. Kertelge, *Rückfrage nach Jesus,* QD 63, 1974, 148-73.

6. "Die Passion des Menschensohnes. Eine Studie zu den Menschensohnworten der vormk Passionsgeschichte," in *Jesus und der Menschensohn,* Festschrift A. Vögtle, 1975, 166-95.

7. *Das Markusevangelium.* II: *Kommentar zu Kap. 8,27–16,20,* HTK II/2, [2]1980 (hereafter *Mark2*), 1-27. For detailed analyses and argumentation, see 27-36, 47-56, 69-82, 98-101, 102-5, 119-21, 147-52, 167-75, 176-206, 208-29, 236f., 249-57, 260-64, 268-73, 319-541.

8. *Das Evangelium der Urgemeinde. Wiederhergestellt und erläutert,* Herderbücherei 748, 1979, [2]1982.

9. With R. Kratz, *So liest man synoptisch.* VI-VII *(Passionsgeschichte),* 1979/1980.

(a) Criticism of My Proposed Reconstruction of the Pre-Marcan Passion Narrative

Shorter or longer critical reactions to this proposed determination of the scope, origin, and date of the pre-Marcan passion narrative have meanwhile appeared in considerable numbers:

E. Schweizer, *TR* 71, 1975, 21f.

J. Ernst, *ThGl* 66, 1976, 343f.

Idem, "Noch einmal: die Verleugnung Jesu durch Petrus," in A. Brandenburg and H. J. Urban, *Petrus und Papst,* 1977, 43-62.

G. Dautzenberg, "Die Zeit des Evangeliums. Mk 1,1-15 und die Komposition des Markusevangeliums," *BZ* NF 21, 1977, 219-34.

D. Dormeyer, *Der Sinn des Leidens Jesu. Historisch-kritische und textpragmatische Analysen zur Markuspassion,* SBS 96, 1979.

J. Gnilka, *Das Evangelium nach Markus*, EKK II/2, 1979, 348-50.

F. Neirynck, *L'évangile de Marc. À propos du commentaire de R. Pesch*, ALBO V/42, 1979.

D. Zeller, "Die Handlungsstruktur der Markuspassion," *ThQ* 159, 1979, 212-27.

J. Ernst, "Die Passionserzählung des Markus und die Aporien der Forschung," *ThGl* 70, 1980, 160-81.

J. Ernst, *Das Evangelium nach Markus*, RNT, 1981, 394-97.

M. Limbeck (ed.), *Redaktion und Theologie des Passionsberichtes nach den Synoptikern*, WdF 481, 1981.

Also in reviews of *Mark2*:

H. Conzelmann, *TR* 43, 1978, 321-24.

J. Ernst, *ThGl* 68, 1978, 454f.

A. Vögtle, *CiG* 30, 1978, 101f.

J. Hainz, *Theol. Lit. Dienst*, 1979, 51f.

X. Jacques, *Nouvelle revue théologique* 101, 1979, 584-86.

G. Lindeskog, *Zeitschrift für Religions- und Geistesgeschichte* 31, 1979, 218-20.

E. Ruckstuhl, *Schweizerische Kirchenzeitung* 47, 1979, 725-30.

A. Stöger, *Theologisch-praktische Quartalschrift* 127, 1979, 290f.

H. Räisänen, *ThLZ* 105, 1980, 428-30.

Also in reviews of both volumes of the commentary:

J. Blank, *BZ* NF 23, 1979, 129-35.

W. Schenk, *Die Zeichen der Zeit* 33, 1979, 395f.

U. Luz, *ThLZ* 105, 1980, 641-55.

F. Neirynck, *Ephemerides theologicae Lovanienses* 56, 1980, 442-45.

E. Trocmé, *RHPR* 60, 1980, 235f.

W. G. Kümmel, *TR* 45, 1980, 323-25.

Reviews of *Das Evangelium der Urgemeinde:*

T. Holz, *ThLZ* 105, 1980, 751.

G. G. Gamba, *Salesianum* 42, 1980, 940.

H. Rusche, *Franziskanische Studien* 62, 1980, 338.

S. Stahr, *Theologisch-praktische Quartalschrift* 128, 1980, 190.

L. Geysels, *De Nieuwe Boodschap* 107, 1980, 93f.

I. Maisch, *Die Welt der Bücher* 6, 1981, 194.

Already in his first comment (on "Die Überlieferung der Passion Jesu" [no. 5]) E. Schweizer remarked: "the hypothesis of a passion narrative going back to the Aramaic or Greek-speaking church at Jerusalem in the early period" is a challenge to "the whole of current scholarship" (22). Despite the many reactions, however, it cannot be said that this challenge has really been accepted by taking notice of the many-sided argumentation supporting the hypothesis. To be sure, Schweizer does concede: "It is doubtless correct that many of these segments are not possible apart from the context of the passion narrative, and it is important to point this out"; but he nevertheless believes: "Only this does not yet prove the existence of a real source." Still he grants: "I have allowed myself to be persuaded to the extent that I do consider it possible that the pre-Marcan passion narrative started at 11:1"—but he then restricts himself when he says that "he would certainly remove the brackets from, for example, 12:1-12; 14:3-9, 12-16, 22-25" (ibid.). On 14:3-9 Schweizer could have at the time—before the appearance of *Mark2* and of *Das Evangelium der Urgemeinde*—consulted the essay listed as no. 1.

In one of the most recent reactions W. G. Kümmel expressed himself in a similar vein: "There is, in fact, much evidence for an old coherent report concerning Jesus' suffering (Pesch rightly opposes breaking up the passion tradition as in recent scholarship), but I doubt that this passion narrative can be traced back as far as Mark 8:26 and that it can with precision be isolated as a whole" (325). Kümmel adds: "I have to consider fanciful Pesch's proofs for the origination of this passion narrative before 37 AD" (ibid.). Kümmel distinguishes himself from Schweizer in that he discusses no criterion and therefore does not allow for counter-criticism. Schweizer, for his part, discussed *inter alia* the criterion of "frequent use of place names and personal names" but seems to me unwarrantedly to isolate this criterion in the process.

The reactions of these two masters of New Testament studies is typical; for the others as well criticism swings between wholesale rejection of my hypothesis and relativization of it on the basis of partial criticism.

Schweizer's criticism is also typical inasmuch as, in addition to 14:12-16 and other segments, he wants to remove especially 14:22-25 from the pre-Marcan passion narrative: "Of course, the liturgy of the Lord's Supper (14:22-25) presupposes the context of the passion of Jesus in the Church; however, it was initially transmitted by itself, precisely at the celebration of the meal" (p. 22). In part 2 of this essay we will return to this special question.

To begin with, it seems fitting to analyze the criticism so far expressed—insofar as it does not consist in blanket rejection and can thus be appropriately ignored—in accordance with the three main dimensions of the hypothesis of an old pre-Marcan passion narrative rooted in the Jerusalem church: (i) criticism of the determination of scope, (ii) criticism of the determination of provenance, and (iii) criticism of the determination of age.

(i) Criticism of the determination of scope

Let us begin with an affirmative judgment of a colleague who—as is evident from the list of typographical errors he submitted—read the whole of *Mark2*. E. Ruckstuhl writes (726):

> Not only in the passion narrative in a restricted sense but in a long series of narratives from Mark 8:27 to 16:8, Pesch has demonstrated, section by

section and in detail, that they do not represent narrative units which originally existed independently of each other. On the contrary, they appear in many ways to be interrelated and are therefore to be understood as a meaningful, planned narrative whole. This coherent whole must be considered original in the sense that nowhere can individual units be shown that are held together only by a redactional framework. This does not in any way mean that there were no distinct memories and traditions concerning Jesus' passion and his pre-history which flowed together here; however, at an early date they were worked into a whole in such a way that an original diversity is not demonstrable. The spacious narrative framework which, according to Pesch, holds the second half of Mark's Gospel together and structures it presents a literary text which goes back to a time before 37 AD and must have originated in the early church of Jerusalem.

H. Conzelmann only gets a short distance beyond blanket criticism: he correctly sees that the substantiation of the hypothesis is "cumulative," but remains sceptical toward the arguments with their "inevitable statistics of terms and analysis of style." In his opinion, it is better not to argue "on the basis of the structure of the supposed pre-Marcan document" (15ff.). "An outline in thirteen parts each consisting of three subsections is imposed on the text. This was sketched on the drawing board and can at best be discovered in the text with a special pair of glasses" (322). Along with Conzelmann, H. Räisänen questions whether 8:27 is a narrative beginning: "8:27 hardly looks like the beginning of a long narrative (why, for instance, the verb *exelthen*, without any mention of the place from which Jesus 'went out'?" (429).

Against Conzelmann's assumption of a "special pair of glasses," my sharpest critic F. Neirynck comes to my assistance. He devotes an entire section of his critique of *Mark2* to the so-called "triads" in Mark's Gospel (65-72) and refers (as I do) to T. A. Burkill, E. Lohmeyer, M. Albertz, and G. Schneider, and beyond them to P. Alfaric. For the rest, Neirynck's critique only has in view "the stylistic argument" (38-57), which according to *Mark2*, 7 played only a subsidiary role in the reconstruction: "In the reconstruction of tradition complexes the Gattung-critical arguments which have literary-critical relevance become the more weighty, a judgment which applies, above all, to *the distinction between independent and non-independent text units.*" With a view to the "uniformity" of Mark's Gospel assumed by him, Neirynck attempts to relativize all the arguments which relate to style and vocabulary in the material of the pre-Marcan passion narrative. On the question whether Mark 8:27 is intelligible as "narrative beginning," cf. *Das Evangelium der Urgemeinde,* 56f., 73. In this connection one might also, like Räisänen, consider whether "Mark could not at the outset have reformulated an older narrative when he incorporated it into his work" (429), hence whether he changed ἦλθεν to ἐξῆλθεν (with a view to 8:22-26).

With that we have already come to the fourth and last author who went beyond a merely blanket criticism and offered a detailed critique: U. Luz. In view of the genre and form-critical information and discussion given to each pericope in section II of *Mark2*, of the judgment cited above from *Mark2*, 7, and of the enumeration of "non-independent units" in *Mark2*, 11—a judgment based on "genre and form critical criteria" (ibid.)—Luz's view of "the decided insignificance of form criticism in comparison with literary criticism" (643) remains unintelligible to me. Remarkable also is Luz's verdict concerning "Pesch's invalidation of tradition criticism in the domain of the pre-Marcan passion narrative" (645), which is further burdened by the obvious confusion of literary with tradition criticism. "Breaks, tensions, repetitions, roughnesses, etc." (645), suggests the diagnosis of literary criticism! And supposedly, that which in Pesch "is left" is literary criticism (643)! If Luz had read the commentary on individual pericopes, he could not have missed the tradition-critical and tradition-historical analyses and judgments (to be found, generally, in section IV of the commentary): e.g., *Mark2*, 55, 61, 63f., 64f., 66f., etc., etc. Luz's "critical inquiries" (644), which concern the scope of the pre-Marcan passion narrative, are focused on "the stylistic arguments" and the "problem of redactional language." If Luz finds fault with the fact that "neither the varying lengths of the pericopes, nor the Gattung-related distinctions which have important consequences for the style, have been considered" (644), he should have taken account of *Mark2*, 6: "This distribution must, to be sure, be spelled out in greater detail just as the phenomena must be differentiated according to the arrangement of materials." In making the assertion "that Mark recognizably has his favorite vocabulary," Luz should not have appealed to E. J. Pryke, *Redactional Style in the Marcan Gospel*, SNTSMS 33, 1978, because that work is neither independent nor trustworthy (cf. my review in *ThRev* 77, 1981, 198f.; also E. Best, *JSNT* 4, 1979, 69-76).

Luz asks: "Why should 10:1 belong to the passion narrative while 7:24a is in part redaction [so volume 1 of the commentary, 387]? Why should 11:18 have another literary origin than the closely related texts 3:6 (tradition) and 1:22 (redaction? [cf. 1, 117])?" (644). The argumentation for the assignment of 10:1 has been given at length in *Mark2*, 119, 121; that the phrase ἐκεῖθεν δὲ ἀναστάς in 7:24 is called redactional results from the judgment that the pericope so introduced is independent in terms of context (cf. also the third edition of the first volume of the commentary, 465). How 11:18 and 1:22 (where comparison suggests that there is a relationship between 11:18c and 1:22a) are closely related to 3:6 (which at most is true of 11:18b) is hard to see. For "the admiration-terminology in Mark's Gospel" Luz could have looked at the excursus in *Mark2*, 150-52 which supports the concise judgment about 11:18 on 199 (cf. the reference there to the excursus!).

For Luz "the scope and delimitation of the passion narrative" remain "problematic" (644). In his opinion, "the delimitation within the sphere of ch. 12 [is] arbitrary" (ibid.). Whether the verdict "arbitrary" is applicable to the substantiating arguments in *Mark2*, 213, 223, 224f., 228, 249f., 255f., 260, and 263 may be settled after reading and evaluating those sections. Luz next asks: "Why does the miracle story of 10:46-52 belong to it (it is localized in Jericho but, as is known, several other Marcan miracle stories have been traditionally localized as well!) but not 9:14-29?" (ibid.).

With regard to 10:46-52 the substantiation in *Mark2*, 167-74 has been offered at great length since this miracle story is one of the cornerstones of my reconstruction of the pre-Marcan passion narrative (beyond 11:1f.); cf. also *Das Evangelium der Urgemeinde*, 53. The reason that 9:14-29 cannot be considered a part of the pre-Marcan passion narrative can be read in *Mark2*, 84f.; this miracle story has nothing to do with Jesus' journey to Jerusalem, unlike 10:46-52 (where the en route motif is not just part of the framework!). Hence, it is unfortunately necessary to state that in his review U. Luz poses questions, the answers to which he could have read in the commentary. If these answers did not satisfy him, he could have shown this with the help of a different set of questions. Since Luz himself, despite the length of his review, does not enter into the argument, his frequent use of the word "arbitrary" (644 with n. 17: three times) in making his judgments is striking.

(ii) Criticism of the determination of provenance

On this point, apart from the agreement of E. Ruckstuhl (726), there is nothing to report. Presumably the opinion that the passion materials stem from the early church in Jerusalem may be the first to secure agreement. Still, from the silence of the critics one can hardly infer their consent.

(iii) Criticism of the determination of age

On this point, too, only U. Luz has expressed himself at length. "The determination of the date of the passion narrative [origin in Jerusalem before AD 37: *Mark2*, 21] is not obvious" (644). Perhaps the more extensive substantiation (with the additional argument: the treatment of Pilate who is only referred to by name and not in his official capacity as ἡγεμών as in Matthew and Luke) in *Das Evangelium der Urgemeinde*, 84-86 is more persuasive.

Luz objects (644f.): "I Cor. 11:23 presupposes knowledge of the Lord's Supper tradition in the context of the passion narrative, but not the pre-Marcan passion narrative"—was there then another?—and: "For instance, does the sentence 'Pope Paul VI visited the patriarch of Constantinople' assume that it was written during the lifetime of the patriarch?" (But compare my [modern] analogy in *Mark2*, 21.) I say, in response to these objections, that until my hypothesis has been refuted, I will hold that: "The evidence concerning age and provenance together unequivocally suggest an early date for the origination of the pre-Marcan passion narrative in the Aramaic-speaking early church in Jerusalem" (*Mark2*, 21).

(b) Implications of the Criticism

U. Luz correctly notes that the attribution of an early date to the pre-Marcan passion narrative by itself by no means justifies wholesale verdicts concerning the quality of the transmission of the individual materials. Such judgments can only be tradition-critical judgments of parts, which nevertheless concern the context as a whole. The fact that such judgments of parts seriously disturb the existing "consensus" is something Luz clearly indicates in the formulation of his comment: "The conclusions drawn for historical judgments from the early dating are therefore not always uniform" (645)—as if such conclusions can be easily drawn.

"Besides that, the dating before 37 leads Pesch into a peculiar situation of constraint with regard to judgments of historicity" (645). How is that? "Not only that he considers historical the Marcan tradition of the Lord's Supper, the Marcan passion chronology, and almost all indications concerning Jesus' trial" (645)—as though, given a later date for the passion narrative, this were not possible as well and as though the corresponding judgments had not been arrived at independently in the course of extensive tradition-critical analysis (cf. on this, the detailed commentary in three excurses in *Mark2*, 323-28, 364-77, 404-24); no, "many a time, to save his passion narrative, he has to take massive rationalisms, in the style of the eighteenth century, into the bargain: thus in 14:12-16 a preceding arrangement between Jesus and the householder is intended [*Mark 2*, 343-45]"— as though this interpretation were directly determined by the early dating and as though the conventional interpretation of 14:12-16 as a legend of miraculous finding spoke against an early date! It would seem that in New Testament scholarship there hardly exists any "consensus" about how early legends can arise and how late historically precise tradition can still be recorded.

Luz himself affirms that it is inappropriate to speak of "a situation of constraint with regard to judgments of historicity" by his reference to the tradition of Mark 16:1-8, which I regard as legend, and to the transfiguration narrative, described as a christological midrash (Mark 9:2-13). Certainly, when Luz finds "only two notable exceptions" in "the overall confidence in the historical tradition"—as he calls it, as though he had read none of the extended tradition-critical arguments (section IV of *Mark2*)—one must ask whether he has taken any notice of the judgments made with respect to Mark 8:31-33; 10:32-34; 14:1-2, 10-11, 18, 21, 26-31.

But in that Luz orients himself to the "offensive" outcome rather than to the method which—conveniently or inconveniently—leads to this outcome, he does not stand alone. H. Conzelmann, too, is annoyed by the statement: "Since the document arose at such an early stage it rests upon direct memory and has great historical value" (*Mark2*, 323). And J. Hainz is even more clear: "But this determination of the scope remains as incredible as the assertion that this pre-Marcan passion narrative stems from the first years of the primitive church at Jerusalem and is therefore invaluable in the search for the historical Jesus and for the theology of the earliest Church" (52). Incredible? Because what should not be true cannot be true? In the situation of challenge arising from my hypothesis the profoundly disturbed relationship of New Testament scholarship to history becomes, in my opinion, as clear as day.

The linkage of theology to history—in subordination to the biblical witness of the canon—is the linkage to the faith-interpreted history of God with his people. In the inquiry into the events of this history and in the attempt to understand their meaning, the "proof of age," which can be given with respect to the documents, counts as such for little; but one can as little forego the attempt to date the traditional materials carefully if one is to gain insight into the history of the tradition into which the meaning of that history is distilled. The stubbornly factual character of that history and of the concrete speech of the word of God resists the arbitrariness of our willful arrangements—even in the language of legend, which by no means lacks a relationship to history simply because it is not interested in the historical accuracy of the course of events portrayed in the world of the narrative but is very interested in the meaning of the history as faith understands it. For theologians there is no "situation of constraint with regard to judgments of historicity"; but for historical theology there does exist a necessity to encounter the tradition with a freely critical eye and to correct the "disarrangements" of the history of research.

(c) Mark 14:12-16 as Test Case

Whereas E. Schweizer wanted to separate 14:12-16, 22-25 from the pre-Marcan passion narrative and U. Luz was annoyed by the interpretation of 14:12-16 and the tradition-critical judgment concerning 14:22-25, J. Hainz stated in conclusion: "The tradition of the Last Supper may serve as a particularly explosive test case for Pesch's thesis that Mark was close to the historical Jesus. Pesch has come to grips with this decisive issue, not only in a special excursus in his commentary [*Mark2*, 364-77] but in the meantime also in a separate study [*Das Abendmahl und Jesu Todesverständnis*, no. 12 below]" (52).

Since, then, Mark 14:12-26 has become a focal point in the criticism of my hypothesis concerning the pre-Marcan passion narrative, there is good reason—the more so since further work and detailed criticism are already available—to undertake the analysis of the narrative section as the oldest tradition in the early Church.

2. Mark 14:12-26 as Oldest Tradition in the Early Church

According to my hypothesis, the narrative unit of 14:12-26 belongs to the pre-Marcan passion narrative which is datable before AD 37 and which stems from the early church at Jerusalem. It deals with the Passover meal that Jesus held with the Twelve in the night before his arrest and execution, and, in 14:22-25, contains the Marcan tradition of the Last Supper, a "particularly explosive test case for Pesch's thesis that Mark was close to the historical Jesus" (J. Hainz).

My work on the three related narrative sections (14:12-16; 17-21; 22-25, plus the transitional verse 14:26] can be found in publications 3, 6, and 7 [and 8 and 9] listed in section 1 of the present essay. Also relevant are *Mark2*, 340-72, the excursus "Die Abendmahlsüberlieferung," 364-77 in the same volume, and the following publications of mine:

10. "Das Abendmahl und Jesu Todesverstandnis," in K. Kertelge (ed.), *Der Tod Jesu,* QD 74, 1976, [2]1981, 137-87.

11. *Wie Jesus das Abendmahl hielt,* 1977, [3]1980.

12. *Das Abendmahl und Jesu Todesverständnis,* QD 80, 1978.

(a) Criticism of My Proposed View of Mark 14:12-26 as the Early Church's Oldest Tradition

Shorter or longer critical reactions to my proposed view of Mark 14:12-26 have been published both in thematic treatises and numerous reviews:

K. Kertelge, "Das Abendmahl im Markusevangelium," in *Begegnung mit dem Wort,* Festschrift H. Zimmermann, BBB 53, 1980, 67-80.
I. H. Marshall, *Last Supper and Lord's Supper,* 1980.
L. Oberlinner, *Todeserwartung und Todesgewissheit Jesu,* SBB 10, 1980, 130-34.
H. Schürmann, "Jesu Todesverständnis im Verstehenshorizont seiner Umwelt," *ThGl* 70, 1980, 141-60.
idem, "Jesu ureigenes Todesverständnis. Bemerkungen zur impliziten Soteriologie Jesu," in *Begegnung mit dem Wort,* Festschrift H. Zimmermann, BBB 53, 1980, 273-309.
J. Blank, "Der 'eschatologische Ausblick' Mk 14,25 und seine Bedeutung," in *Kontinuität und Einheit,* Festschrift F. Mußner, 1981, 508-18.

E. Ruckstuhl, "Neue und alte Überlegungen zu den Abendmahlsworten Jesu," in *Studien zum Neuen Testament und seiner Umwelt* A5, 1981, 79-106.

X. Leon-Dufour, "Prenez! Ceci est mon corps pour vous," *Nouvelle revue théologique* 114, 1982, 223-40.

P. Fiedler, "Probleme der Abendmahlsforschung," *Archiv für Liturgiewissenschaft* 24, 1982, 190-223.

H.-J. Klauck, *Herrenmahl und hellenistischer Kult,* NTA NF 15, 1982.

On "Das Abendmahl und Jesu Todesverständnis" (no. 10 above):

W. G. Kümmel, *TR* 43, 1978, 262-64.

J. P. Galvin, "Jesus' Approach to Death: An Examination of Some Recent Studies," *Theological Studies* 41, 1980, 713-44.

Reviews of *Wie Jesus das Abendmahl hielt:*

W. Bracht, *Theol. Lit. Dienst,* 1977, 41f.

H. Giesen, *OrdKorr* 18, 1977, 356.

H. Weder, *Kirchenblatt für die reformierte Schweiz,* June 8, 1978, 187f.

J. Imbach, *Laurentianum* 20, 1979, 191f.

W. G. Kümmel, *TR* 45, 1980, 332f.

Reviews of *Das Abendmahl und Jesu Todesverständnis:*

J. Imbach, *Miscellanea francescana* 79, 1979, 232f.

D. Nestle, *Deutsches Pfarrerblatt,* May, 1979.

E. Ruckstuhl, *Schweizerische Kirchenzeitung* 47, 1979, 725-30.

J. H. Emminghaus, *Bibel und Liturgie* 53, 1980, 36f.

H. Giesen, *Theologie der Gegenwart* 23, 1980, 59.

F. Hahn, *ThRev* 76, 1980, 265-72.

L. Visschers, *Tijdschrift voor Theologie* 19, 1979, 418.

R. J. Daly, *CBQ* 43, 1981, 308-10.

T. Holtz, *ThLZ* 106, 1981, 812f.

J. Kremer, *Theologisch-praktische Quartalschrift* 129, 1981, 188.

H. Weder, *Kirchenblatt für die reformierte Schweiz,* January 29, 1981.

W. G. Kümmel, *TR* 47, 1982, 159f.

Finally and at great length: R. J. Daly, "The Eucharist and Redemption: The Last Supper and Jesus' Understanding of His Death," *Biblical Theology Bulletin* 11, 1981, 21-27.

(i) Criticism of the evaluation of Mark 14:12-25(26) as a unified segment belonging to the pre-Marcan passion narrative

While W. G. Kümmel concedes that "It is indisputable that the Marcan text of the report of the Lord's Supper has been interpolated into the context of a Passover meal," he apparently wants to retain the notion of a secondary interpolation when he continues: ". . . it seems to me equally indisputable that the report itself bears no trace of the paschal character of this meal; for that reason the interpretation of the interpretive sayings [the bread-saying and the cup-saying] in terms of this paschal context is by no means convincing" (*TR* 43, 263f.). Kümmel later wrote: "In my opinion it is questionable whether one may *assume* the qualification of the Last Supper by the idea of the Passover (it is after all not mentioned!)" (*TR* 45, 332), and later still he appealed to F. Hahn for the opinion that "the thesis that Mark 14:22-25 fits without any difficulty into the course of a Passover meal remains unproven" (*TR* 47, 160). H. Giesen at one point also wanted to "explain part of the Marcan report from the circumstance that it has been interpolated into the present context" (*OrdKorr* 18, 356), but later found "Pesch's mode of argumentation quite convincing" (*Theologie der Gegenwart* 23, 59). T. Holtz even regards "the unity of the narrative unit (Mark 14:22-25) as well as its inseparable coinherence in the context" as *proven* (*ThLZ* 106, 813); see also I. H. Marshall, *Last Supper and Lord's Supper,* 35, 40f., and his emphatic agreement with my judgment; E. Ruckstuhl, *Schweizerische Kirchenzeitung* 47, 85.

Besides Kümmel, who advanced no arguments at all, F. Hahn disputed the original integration of 14:22-25 in the context of the Passover narrative of 14:12-26. In his elaboration he stated (*ThRev* 76, 268) that

> though Mark 14:22-24, 25 has no explicit introduction like I Cor. 11:23b, it does have an opening phrase which is not only conceivable at the beginning of an independent unit but which as such is clearly distinguishable from the context in which reference has already been made (14:18) to the common meal. Given this assumption, Mark 14:22a does not refer to the Passover meal presupposed in 14:12-17, 18-21 but, like the phrase μετὰ τὸ δειπνῆσαι, to the proper meal belonging to the Lord's Supper.

Hahn says nothing about the fact that in 14:26, i.e., in the following context, the Passover meal is presupposed by the hymn, nor does he in any way refer to my lengthy discussion of 14:22a (cf. *Das Abendmahl* [no. 12], 70-72) or to the long demonstration (ibid., 76-81) that 14:22-25 is not an independent narrative segment. Ignoring this for now, we must still ask at this point how it is that Mark 14:22a (καὶ ἐσθιόντων αὐτῶν) should refer, not to the immediate context, but to one deduced from I Cor. 11:25a (although in the narrative framework of I Cor. 11:23b-25 no participants in the meal are mentioned). How it is that Hahn, despite my contrary proof, should cling to the assertion that Mark 14:22-25 is an "independent unit" is almost inconceivable if one is not to deny him methodological familiarity with the distinction between independent and non-independent textual units.

For the relevant methodology cf. for example:

E. Zenger, "Ein Beispiel exegetischer Methoden aus dem Alten Testament," in J. Schreiner, *Einführung in die Methoden der biblischen Exegese,* 1971, 97-148, esp. 120.

W. Richter, *Exegese als Literaturwissenschaft,* 1971, 117f.
G. Fohrer, et al., *Exegese des Alten Testament,* UTB, 267, 1973, 80ff.
K. Berger, *Exegese des Neuen Testament,* UTB 658, 1977, 12ff.

In the third section of this essay we will return to this topic; cf. esp. n. 12.

At this point I must unfortunately disclose how carelessly Hahn has written his review. He asserts that my analysis of 14:22-25 is based *inter alia* "on the attempted demonstration that v. 22a deals with an element in the total narrative, *not however with an element indicating a new situation* (70f.)" (269). But anyone reading *Das Abendmahl,* 70f., immediately encounters the contrary judgment: "The opening phrase in vs. 22a, which is formulated differently and agrees with v. 18a only in part, refers to a new situation in the course of the Passover meal" (71).

In conclusion, it remains to be said that Hahn suggests to the reader of his review that "critical reflections" are at stake when he writes (267f.):

> It is surprising that in the treatment of the Matthean and Lucan text the author, with complete one-sidedness, proceeds redaction-historically; conversely, in Mark, despite his recognition of redactional details, he is especially interested in the material of the tradition, a "Gospel of the primitive Church" whose existence he already assumes (see the title of his latest publication based on the results of his commentary on Mark).

If the idea is to clarify "the basis of a historical inquiry into Jesus' understanding of his death" (*Das Abendmahl,* 21), one can, in the first place, only ask for the oldest source and that means redaction-critical investigation of whether Matthew and Luke are dependent on Mark and/or some additional tradition, plus literary-critical examination of the unity of the Marcan text and the question to what sources it belongs. In this matter also, one which he himself calls "critical," Hahn fails to display awareness of a carefully thought out methodology. And that in a review in which, with a lofty air, he warns systematic and practical theologians against "the premature notion that here they have at their disposal a new and presumably assured exegetical basis" (272).

Moreover, this talk of an "assured exegetical basis" presupposes a model of theology in which its individual disciplines tend to run independently alongside each other instead of being united with each other (in common devotion to the one "cause"). Such a model is the product of a deficit in terms of a common contemporary experience of the history of faith, for whose interpretation the canon (together with the tradition of the Church) remains the standard. An "*assured* exegetical basis" is always at the same time one that is justified from the perspective of systematic and practical theology.

This connection becomes exceptionally clear (*e contrario*) in the opinions of P. Fiedler ("Probleme der Abendmahlsforschung"), who—proceeding from the systematic (but erroneous) opinion that Jesus' own understanding of his death as propitiatory embraces "certain quite negative consequences—in the sense of a distancing and even a disclaiming—for his public proclamation of salvation" (191)—tries with all the (heedlessly used) means of the polemical arts to show that Mark 14:22-25 does not belong to the pre-Marcan passion narrative (and anticipating iii below let it be said here: is not the oldest Lord's Supper tradition; anticipating v: does not present a tradition from the history of Jesus). Fiedler's essay is marked by an accumulation of negative words like "supposed," "highly questionable," "arbitrary" (195), "spectacular" (196), "more than bold" (197), "troubled," "unconvincing," "questionable" (198), "supposed," "reading between the lines" (199), "even more questionable" (201), "ending in a dead end" (208), "of a cosmetic nature," "a surmise which masks," "maintains" (209), "fails" (210), "macabre," "massive step backward" (211), "exegetical leapfrog" (212), "deficiency" (213), and so forth. It is an essay which, in a publication for *practical* theology, demands from the reader the *systematic* judgment that "the redemptive death of Jesus contains a manner of acquiring redemption which is fundamentally distinct from that which Jesus had preached to the Jewish public" (191), and hence maintains, as *exegetical basis*, the assertion that "in Jesus' mouth there were no interpretive sayings, and in all probability there could not have been any" (196; see n. 31 on the same page, where Hahn's warning is cited) Fiedler maintains no less than the conviction that for the God of Jesus it is impossible to demand "the (self-)offering of a human life in death," and from this he infers "reservations against a mediatorial understanding of death, reservations which existed beyond good Friday" (211).

(ii) Criticism of the literary-critical evaluation of Mark 14:22-25 as an originally unified narrative segment

T. Holtz considers the unity of the narrative segment of Mark 14:22-25 a proven fact (813). F. Hahn, by writing "Mark 14:22-24, 25" (266), suggests he thinks the text is a synthesis. For the rest, the question of the unity of this segment (14:22-25) has not been touched in the reviews. J. Gnilka (*Das Evangelium nach Markus* 2, 239) starts with the thesis that 14:22-26 is a unity, which he provides with commentary; he considers the linkage in v. 22a "secondary" (240), similarly "the narrative comments in 23b and 26" (243), the Amen-opening in 14:25a, as also 14:25b (243). J. Ernst (*Das Evangelium nach Markus,* 413) also regards 14:22-26 as a distinct segment and thinks that "redactional interventions are to be suspected at the outset in the reference to eating (v. 22a) and at the end in the word 'hymn' " (v. 26a; 413). He also views the text as a combination of 14:22-24 and 14:25 (the rudiment of the depiction of a Passover meal; 415); similarly K. Kertelge ("Das Abendmahl im Markusevangelium," 71, 78).

These authors do reckon of course with a pre-Marcan redactional text layer, which can only be assumed to exist on the supposition that Mark 14:22b-24, 25 was an independent tradition and did not exist from the beginning as part of a context—and this, as the reader sees, is construed differently each time, depending on the author.

The question concerning the unity of a nonindependent context-bound narrative segment requires of course that consideration be given to the context in question if mistaken judgments are to be avoided. Since in the aforementioned authors I can find no new arguments, I can stay with my (extensively argued) judgment (*Das Abendmahl,* 71) that "the narrative unit of Mark 14:22-25 offers neither any clues for a literary-critical decomposition nor indices for a subsequent interpolation into the whole of the context."

It is self-evident that a textual demarcation in terms of 14:22-26—which would obviously favor the hypothesis of a secondary contextual interpolation— cannot be justified if one stays with the methodological criteria for determining the beginning and end of a text unit. On method, cf. esp. G. Fohrer, op. cit., 47f.

Mark 14:27 is not an opening for a text but presuppposes the opening in 14:26, which is defined by the movement of the actors from one location to another. Only the participle ὑμνήσαντες (to be interpreted as temporally prior to ἐξῆλθον) has the character of a transition, one that rounds off 14:22-25. As coordinating participle it belongs, however, to the beginning of a new narrative segment in a more comprehensive, scenically constructed, and consecutive narrative complex. Like the scene pictured in 14:17-21, so the following one (14:22-25) and the later one (14:32-42) end with statements by Jesus before the next scene is introduced (and the preceding scene is implicitly concluded) with new indications of the spatial-temporal framework.

(iii) Criticism of the tradition-historical evaluation of Mark 14:22-25 as the oldest tradition of the Lord's Supper

W. G. Kümmel wrote: "The notion that throughout, also in the case of the cup saying, the tradition of Mark is to be favored is one which, on several grounds, I do not consider convincingly demonstrated" (*TR* 43, 263)—but he still does not mention a single ground. Nor does he provide his reasons in his later reviews of 1980 and 1982. T. Holz, however, is able to follow me "in the evaluation of Mark's text as being older and more original than Paul's" (*ThLZ* 106, 812). On the other hand F. Hahn believes that prevailing scholarship has been "well-advised" to reckon "first of all both in the Marcan and the Pauline text with earlier as well as with later elements," in order then "to inquire what, on the basis of tradition-historical analysis, emerges as the older and therefore the oldest form of Jesus' farewell meal" (*ThRev* 76, 268). By saying that, he suggests to the reader of his review that I fundamentally did not take account of that possibility and arrived at my own result (Paul's tradition is derivable from the tradition in the pre-Marcan passion narrative: *Das Abendmahl,* 51), without having compared the narrative framework and the interpretive sayings line by line (cf. 38-51). Besides, though before (266) and after (269) he deals with tradition-historical concerns, Hahn attributes to me the production of a treatise "on a purely literary level . . . without in general paying attention to the more advanced (albeit sometimes one-sidedly applied) insights of form and tradition criticism with regard to a vital cultic tradition"; in addition, it is my intent, he says, "to eliminate the influence of the oral tradition from the outset" (268) Why does Hahn pass over in silence the fact that I have come to grips with the hypothesis of a cultic styling of the Last Supper tradition in the Matthean church (*Das Abendmahl,* 24), that on Luke 22:20 I remarked, to cite an example, that "the possibility that the liturgical tradition of Luke as distinct from Paul still read αἵματί μου must certainly remain open" (33), and that I myself wrote a section (Appendix 3, 66-69: Zur Vorstellung von der urchristlichen Eucharistiefeier") in which the data of cultic tradition were discussed? For the rest, cf. also the section on "Herkunft und Sinn der Paradosis 1 Kor 11,23b-25" (53-60).

That tradition-historical concern for possibly older forms of the sayings of the Last Supper than are present in the Marcan and Lucan/Pauline tradition cannot from the outset be rejected requires no discussion. In the same way it should not be seriously contested that an existing literary form may be (not has to be) the oldest. An inquiry behind the oldest text is only indicated when plausible tradition-historical considerations occasion or require this. I have attempted at some length to make clear (cf. e.g. *Das Abendmahl,* 72-76) that this is not the case.

Here, too, we must in the first place refer to the problem of tradition-historical methods which—as the relevant handbooks show—are least well-developed with respect to an acceptable criteriology (and therefore leave too much room for conjecture and even arbitrariness). G. Fohrer, op. cit., 99-136, again offers the most instruction.

For traditional-critical inquiries into Mark 14:22-25 we have available for comparison meal traditions, interpretive sayings, death prophecies, and individual motifs (blood of the covenant, new covenant, the motif of propitiation) and in the Pauline tradition of the Last Supper also the imperatives of institution (cf. *Das Abendmahl,* 76-81). The comparison with other meal traditions, interpretive sayings, and death prophecies does not permit the inference of a tradition-historical layering of the text, which in this respect, as far as I know, has not been claimed by anyone. It is, however, disputed whether tradition-historically an older form of the interpretive saying (with the motifs of covenant blood, the new covenant, and substitutionary atonement) is attainable. Even given the supposition that Paul's version of the tradition is derivable from Mark, a tradition-historical inquiry with respect to the possibility of comparing versions is not a priori to be rejected. But this becomes superfluous if in tradition-historical perspective also the form of the text as Mark transmits it is recognizable as the oldest.

One can demonstrate the possibilities of a tradition-critical reconstruction of a possibly older version by listing the possible combinations of the elements of the interpretive sayings that have come down to us (and thus avoid speculation beyond the boundaries of tradition).

On the bread-saying:

Τοῦτό ἐστιν: all versions
τὸ σῶμά μου: Mark/Matthew/Luke
μου τὸ σῶμα: Paul, hellenized, not original.

In any case, and incontrovertibly, one can accept as basic:

I. Τοῦτό ἐστιν τὸ σῶμά μου.

The following are clearly expansions:

τὸ ὑπὲρ ὑμῶν: Paul
τὸ ὑπὲρ ὑμῶν διδόμενον: Luke.

Insofar as διδόμενον is a Lucan expansion, a possible reconstruction of an older version could only read:

II. Τοῦτό ἐστιν τὸ σῶμα τὸ ὑπὲρ ὑμῶν.

A possible expansion by way of falling back on the phrase ὑπὲρ πολλῶν in the cup-saying (Mark; Matthew: περὶ πολλῶν) reads:

III. Τοῦτό ἐστιν τὸ σῶμά μου τὸ ὑπὲρ πολλῶν.

If one considers διδόμενον original, one can add it to versions II and III.

Versions I, II, and III are all being upheld (sometimes with διδόμενον) in scholarly research as the original version of the bread-saying. Version I is an actually existing one (Mark); version II is a combination of Mark and Paul; version III is a combination of Mark/Paul plus the Marcan cup-saying. Since version I can be shown to be the oldest of the actually existing ones (Mark/Matthew, Luke, Paul; cf. *Das Abendmahl,* 33, 46f.), versions II and III are developed versions whose precedence over version I would have to be substantiated by arguments to which in any case no cogency could be attributed.

What are these arguments and how is their credibility to be evaluated? Let us just take two recent examples:

H. Merklein, in "Erwägungen zur Überlieferungsgeschichte der neutestamentlichen Abendmahlstraditionen," *BZ* NF 21, 1977, 88-101, 235-44, proposes as the original version of the bread-saying a combination of Mark and Luke: Τοῦτό ἐστιν τὸ σῶμά μου τὸ ὑπὲρ πολλῶν διδόμενον, where he pulls in πολλῶν, in distinction from ὑμῶν, from the Marcan cup-saying (97f.). The argument is: "In the original form of the Last Supper celebration a bread-saying without any further explanation would hardly have been intelligible" (97). Merklein thus presupposes that Mark 14:22-25 is a cult-etiological text and that understanding of the saying derives from the framework of the Last Supper observance. Over against this, cf. my determination of the Gattung in *Das Abendmahl*, 35-51 (and on Merklein also 72f.).

E. Ruckstuhl suggests as the original form: Τοῦτό ἐστιν τὸ σῶμά μου τὸ ὑπὲρ πολλῶν (*Schweizerische Kirchenzeitung* 47, 729). His argument is this: The "preponderant probability" is that "at the start of the main meal Jesus interpreted the bread in the framework of the Passover celebration and at its conclusion linked the interpretation of the wine to the prayer of thanksgiving spoken over the third cup"; it therefore "makes sense to clarify soteriologically the bread-saying which had been spoken considerably earlier; for without an appropriate addition it was doubtless hard, if not impossible, for the disciples to understand it" (729). On the possibility of their understanding it, cf. *Das Abendmahl*, 90-93.

Neither of these arguments is very plausible since the argument of "unintelligibility" would much more speak *against* a subsequent abbreviation of the bread-saying (in Mark/Matthew), and much more in favor of a subsequent expansion.

In "Neue und alte Überlegungen zu den Abendmahlsworten Jesu" Ruckstuhl offers more precise grounds for his reconstruction. He proceeds from the idea that the tradition that stems from the Passover meal and goes back to Jesus himself soon branched out in the narrative report (Mark) and the cult-etiology (Paul), so that it makes sense to ask where the soteriological addition ὑπὲρ πολλῶν, which is more original than ὑπέρ ὑμῶν, had its origin, whether in the bread-saying or the cup-saying. As a new argument for the position that it belonged originally to the bread-saying Ruckstuhl now also makes the point that the earliest form of the cup-saying accepted by him (τοῦτο τὸ ποτήριον τὸ αἷμά μου τῆς διαθήκης) requires no addition and that the addition τὸ ἐκχυννόμενον ὑπὲρ πολλῶν is only "a technical development of the preceding sayings" (100). Ruckstuhl documents the grammatical possibility of the addition τὸ ὑπὲρ πολλῶν with the words ὑπὲρ ἡμῶν in Mark 9:40—which does not really seem conclusive. Since Ruckstuhl considers the short form of the cup-saying original and does not want to deny to Jesus the soteriological addition τὸ ὑπὲρ πολλῶν, his reconstruction is consistent. But the main argument remains this: "One may ask whether Jesus' bread-saying does not already have to contain a reference to the death which approached him and which he expected" (89) and "It is also more needed there than in the cup-saying since otherwise the bread-saying was hardly intelligible to the disciples" (101).

As eager as some are to seize the notion of a ramification of the tradition before the fixation of the passion narrative (Ruckstuhl rightly points out that the cult-etiology requires the earliest fixation), they are no less reluctant to continue to accept that for the narrative report there were comparable grounds for the reformulation of the original sayings of Jesus to those which may be assumed for the cult-etiology (which was detached from the unique situation of the original Passover meal with Jesus and prepared for the repeatable celebration of the Eucharist). There is no real ground not to regard the oldest *report* as a literal, word-for-word report (though the understanding of Jesus' interpretation of his death depends but little on the details of one version or another of his sayings as long as the traditional motifs remain present in them).

Let us take a closer look (in anticipation of the following section) at Ruckstuhl's reconstruction of the cup-saying which, based on a combination of Paul and Mark, is especially noteworthy. An abbreviation of τοῦτο τὸ ποτήριον to τοῦτο (Mark) is, as Ruckstuhl shows (102f.), entirely conceivable; but one is not compelled to postulate this, since Jesus himself, like an epitomist, could tie the cup-saying "as closely as possible to the wording of Ex. 24:8b" (103). In any case, since the "cup" refers to the contents of the cup, this is not decisive for the understanding of the saying. More interesting is the question whether nevertheless the shortened version (as compared with Mark's tradition) is original. Ruckstuhl correctly states: "Since the two main branches of the Last Supper tradition speak at the same place—in the cup-saying—of the covenant, one will have to regard the covenant motif as belonging to the original form of the cup-saying of Jesus" (96). Still, the phrase τὸ αἷμά μου τῆς διαθήκης does not by itself, as Ruckstuhl believes, refer to "the violent death toward which Jesus is proceeding" (96), nor does it by itself—despite the expiatory interpretation of the covenant blood of Ex. 24:8 in Palestinian Judaism (Targum)—refer to the fact that God intended Jesus' blood "for the atonement of the people" (97; cf. 99). These ideas are contained in the phrase τὸ ἐκχυννόμενον ὑπὲρ πολλῶν, which cannot be removed as dispensable or regarded as a later addition or "clarification" (p. 99).

On the cup-saying:

To be counted as belonging to the basic stock of the saying are, in the first place, the words which are common to all the versions:

> Τοῦτο
> ἐστιν (lacking in Luke)
> τὸ αἷμά μου (ἐμόν in Paul)
> ἡ διαθήκη.

From this common stock only a part of the Mark/Matthew version can be constructed and not a part of the Luke/Paul version:

> Τοῦτό ἐστιν τὸ αἷμά μου τῆς διαθήκης (Mark).

For this part the Luke/Paul version has two further elements:

> τὸ ποτήριον
> καινή.

Their inclusion in the basic stock brings it (since ἐμός in Paul is secondary) into proximity with the Luke version, which, being pre-Pauline, must be regarded as more original.

> Τοῦτο τὸ ποτήριόν (ἐστιν) ἡ καινὴ διαθήκη ἐν τῷ αἵματί μου.

Possible combinations result from abbreviations of the basic stock and from expansions made with the actually attested elements. Since the Matthean version is secondary (cf. *Das Abendmahl,* 25), a combination utilizing its second half can be omitted.

If we proceed from Mark's basic stock the following (meaningful) possibilities result:

> Τοῦτό ἐστιν τὸ αἷμά μου τῆς διαθήκης
>   + τὸ ἐκχυννόμενον ὑπὲρ πολλῶν (= Mark)
>   or + τὸ ὑπὲρ ὑμῶν ἐκχυννόμενον (= Luke)

or + τὸ ἐκχυννόμενον
or + τὸ ὑπὲρ πολλῶν
or + τὸ ὑπὲρ ὑμῶν.

A series of further possibilities would result if one were to strike τῆς διαθήκης from the common stock which, since ἡ διαθήκη occurs in all versions, is not advisable (on this see at length *Das Abendmahl,* 72-76).

If one surveys the versions listed, only one of them, the first (= Mark), is actually existent and unites all the motifs: covenant blood (Ex. 24:8), a "new" covenant (implicit) (Jer. 31:31), substitutionary atonement (Isa. 53), and a violent death ("shed blood"). By contrast, all the combined versions are deficient (and since no isolated transmission of the interpretive sayings is conceivable they are also incongruent with the context in the assumed framework of the pre-Marcan narrative tradition): they only raise unanswered questions.[1]

1. The possible combinations (and the corresponding possible understandings) for the cup-saying, set out completely, are as follows:

A, proceeding from the Marcan version: Τοῦτό ἐστιν:

1) τὸ αἷμα
2) τὸ αἷμά μου
3) τὸ αἷμα τῆς διαθήκης
4) τὸ αἷμά μου τῆς διαθήκης
5) τὸ αἷμα τὸ ἐκχυννόμενον
6) τὸ αἷμά μου τὸ ἐκχυννόμενον
7) τὸ αἷμα τῆς διαθήκης τὸ ἐκχυννόμεν
8) τὸ αἷμά μου τῆς διαθήκης τὸ ἐκχυννόμενον
9) τὸ αἷμα τὸ ὑπὲρ πολλῶν
10) τὸ αἷμά μου τὸ ὑπὲρ πολλῶν
11) τὸ αἷμα τὸ ὑπὲρ ὑμῶν
12) τὸ αἷμά μου τὸ ὑπὲρ ὑμῶν
13) τὸ αἷμα τῆς διαθήκης τὸ ὑπὲρ πολλῶν
14) τὸ αἷμά μου τῆς διαθήκης τὸ ὑπὲρ πολλῶν
15) τὸ αἷμα τῆς διαθήκης τὸ ὑπὲρ ὑμῶν
16) τὸ αἷμά μου τῆς διαθήκης τὸ ὑπὲρ ὑμῶν
17) τὸ αἷμα τὸ ἐκχυννόμενον ὑπὲρ πολλῶν
18) τὸ αἷμά μου τὸ ἐκχυννόμενον ὑπὲρ πολλῶν
19) τὸ αἷμα τὸ ἐκχυννόμενον ὑπὲρ ὑμῶν
20) τὸ αἷμά μου τὸ ἐκχυννόμενον ὑπὲρ ὑμῶν
21) τὸ αἷμα τῆς διαθήκης τὸ ἐκχυννόμενον ὑπὲρ πολλῶν
22) τὸ αἷμά μου τῆς διαθήκης τὸ ἐκχυννόμενον ὑπὲρ πολλῶν
23) τὸ αἷμα τῆς διαθήκης τὸ ἐκχυννόμενον ὑπὲρ ὑμῶν
24) τὸ αἷμά μου τῆς διαθήκης τὸ ἐκχυννόμενον ὑπὲρ ὑμῶν

B, proceeding from the Lucan/Pauline version: Τοῦτο τὸ ποτήριόν (ἐστιν):

25) ἡ διαθήκη
26) ἡ καινὴ διαθήκη
27) ἡ διαθήκη ἐν τῷ αἵματι
28) ἡ καινὴ διαθήκη ἐν τῷ αἵματι
29) ἡ διαθήκη ἐν τῷ αἵματί μου
30) ἡ καινὴ διαθήκη ἐν τῷ αἵματί μου

A decomposition of the Marcan version, like a combination of its basic stock (common to all versions) with elements of other versions, leads to no version that can on good grounds be defended as tradition-historically older.

---

31) ἡ διαθήκη ἐν τῷ αἵματι τὸ ὑπὲρ ὑμῶν ἐκχυννόμενον

32) ἡ διαθήκη ἐν τῷ αἵματί μου τὸ ὑπὲρ ὑμῶν ἐκχυννόμενον

33) ἡ διαθήκη ἐν τῷ αἵματι τὸ ὑπὲρ πολλῶν ἐκχυννόμενον

34) ἡ διαθήκη ἐν τῷ αἵματί μου τὸ ὑπὲρ πολλῶν ἐκχυννόμενον

35) ἡ καινὴ διαθήκη ἐν τῷ αἵματι τὸ ὑπὲρ ὑμῶν ἐκχυννόμενον

36) ἡ καινὴ διαθήκη ἐν τῷ αἵματί μου τὸ ὑπὲρ ὑμῶν ἐκχυννόμενον

37) ἡ καινὴ διαθήκη ἐν τῷ αἵματι τὸ ὑπὲρ πολλῶν ἐκχυννόμενον

38) ἡ καινὴ διαθήκη ἐν τῷ αἵματί μου τὸ ὑπὲρ πολλῶν ἐκχυννόμενον

39) ἡ διαθήκη ἐν τῷ αἵματι τὸ ὑπὲρ ὑμῶν

40) ἡ διαθήκη ἐν τῷ αἵματί μου τὸ ὑπὲρ ὑμῶν

41) ἡ καινὴ διαθήκη ἐν τῷ αἵματι τὸ ὑπὲρ ὑμῶν

42) ἡ καινὴ διαθήκη ἐν τῷ αἵματί μου τὸ ὑπὲρ ὑμῶν

43) ἡ καινὴ διαθήκη ἐν τῷ αἵματι τὸ ὑπὲρ πολλῶν

44) ἡ καινὴ διαθήκη ἐν τῷ αἵματί μου τὸ ὑπὲρ πολλῶν

45) ἡ διαθήκη ἐν τῷ αἵματι τὸ ὑπὲρ πολλῶν

46) ἡ διαθήκη ἐν τῷ αἵματί μου τὸ ὑπὲρ πολλῶν

A survey of the 46 possibilities (which can be doubled by the reversal of the introductions τοῦτο and τοῦτο τὸ ποτήριον—cf. e.g. Ruckstuhl, "Neue und alte Überlegungen," who combines number 4 with the Lucan/Pauline introduction) in the series A and B readily shows that, by contrast with the actually occurring versions (A22, B36, B30 = Paul except that he has ἐμῷ in place of μου), the sharply abbreviated versions do not seem very meaningful (A1, 2, 5, 6, 9-12, B25-27); this is also true of all the versions without the possessive pronoun μου (A1, 3, 5, 7, 9, 11, 13, 15, 17, 19, 21, 23, B25-28, 31, 33, 35, 37, 39, 41, 43, 45). In other words: every possible version which fails to utilize the *entire* basic stock of words common to the actually occurring versions will prove to have no chance of being considered original.

Of course, with regard to series A this generalization must be tested with reference to the element ἡ διαθήκη, which is missing in numbers 1, 2, 5, 6, 9-12, and 17-20. After taking account of what has been said before, we are left with numbers 18 and 20 to be tested. Number 18 is defended as original, for example, by E. Kutsch. Before we make a judgment about it, we must first deal with the remaining versions which remain to be tested next to the Marcan version (= 22), i.e., numbers 4, 8, 14, 16, and 24. Number 4 raises the question "which covenant?" which, without the substitution and atonement motifs, remains unanswered; number 4 is therefore not to be recommended. The same is true of number 8. Numbers 14, 16, 20, and 24, having ὑμῶν in place of πολλῶν, can only be considered more original if the version in question (and thus the cult-etiological framework) can be viewed as original. This circumstance points to the fact that the question concerning the original version cannot, in general, be answered without regard to the context (narrative report or cult-etiology). The decision between numbers 18 and 22 will also have to take account of this fact.

But first let us go back to series B. If one disregards the versions with πολλῶν (in distinction from ὑμῶν; for the same reasons as in series A, ὑμῶν fits the cult-etiological framework), initially numbers 29, 30, 32, 40, and 42 remain alongside the actually existing number 36. The question whether the versions with or without καινή can be considered more original is also one that cannot be settled without reference to the context. If the original locus of tradition is the cult-etiology, then the versions having the reference to the "new covenant" deserve priority (30 = Paul, except for μου; 36, 42). Since, however, all versions merely having τὸ ὑπὲρ ὑμῶν without ἐκχυννόμενον are grammatically difficult and not very meaningful, only numbers 30 and 36 remain. Number 30 fits very well in the cult-etiological framework of the pre-Pauline paradosis, but 36 does not, since the participle ἐκχυννόμενον, which looks toward the future (and is at the same time historicizing), only belongs in the narrative context of the Lucan farewell meal.

In short, what emerges is that each existing version can be considered the oldest in its

If we proceed from the basic stock of the Pauline/Lucan material, we get the following (plausible) possibilities:

Τοῦτο τὸ ποτήριον ἡ διαθήκη ἐν τῷ αἵματί μου
+ τὸ ὑπὲρ ὑμῶν ἐκχυννόμενον (= Luke)
+ τὸ ἐκχυννόμενον ὑπὲρ πολλῶν (= Mark).

Actually available are the basic stock (Paul) and the first expansion (Luke), versions meaningful only in their respective contexts (ἐκχυννόμενον: present participle with future meaning only in the situation before Jesus' death in the Lucan context). Since the Lucan version is, however, recognizably secondary (cf. *Das Abendmahl,* 33), a sensible tradition-historical reconstruction that goes beyond the basic stock (and, apart from ἐμός, = the Pauline version) slips from our grasp.

Like that of Mark, the Pauline version (in its own way) unites all the motifs: new covenant (Jer. 31:31), blood of the covenant (Ex. 24:8), the idea of substitution ("by my blood")—except for the motif of a violent death (which is connected with the liturgical context of the paradosis); cf. the betrayal saying in the introductory framework (I Cor. 11:23), about which H.-J. Klauck (*Herrenmahl und hellenistischer Kult,* 303) correctly remarks: "As an isolated cult formula the concise introduction with the mention of Jesus' name is better suited than the tradition of the Synoptics."

Since the linking of the aforementioned motifs in the Marcan as well as in the Pauline version displays, not tradition-historical development in layers, but their original combination, as I have shown at some length (cf. *Das Abendmahl,* 72-76, 93-101), there is no support for the attempt by abbreviation or combination to reconstruct an earlier version in opposition to these two oldest versions. What remains is the possibility to test by comparison whether one of

---

respective context (Mark's version in the narrative report; Paul's version in the cult-etiology). The question concerning the oldest version, therefore, coincides with that of the oldest context. And inasmuch as the narrative report is older, as I am convinced I have demonstrated, the question concerning the oldest version, inasmuch as the oldest record stands the test of tradition-critical examination, must also be stated as the question concerning the utterance of Jesus himself. Inasmuch as the oldest version (A22) remains intelligible as an utterance of Jesus (and as such proves to be superior to the remaining versions; cf. *Das Abendmahl und Jesu Todesverständnis* [12], 72-75, 93-101), it is inappropriate to propose reconstructions of a purely hypothetical nature in opposition to the oldest tradition (and the basic stock common to all the versions, see above). Hence version 18, considered as a possibility by E. Kutsch, must also be rejected as nonoriginal.

Thus, what we may learn from an examination of the possible combinations, which could of course be offered in greater detail, is this:

1. The question concerning the oldest version of the Last Supper sayings (also of the bread-saying, where the possibilities could be similarly tested) may not be posed without reference to the context of transmission: Can one regard it as an original utterance of Jesus by which he interpreted his death, or must one view it as only an original "cultic" utterance attributed to Jesus? The weakness of most attempts at reconstruction consists in the fact that the distinction (which I have deliberately pointed up) is not applied or observed.

2. A reconstruction that does not take into account the entire basic stock of elements common to the actually existing versions does not commend itself. In my opinion, one reason is that the Pauline version is traceable to the Marcan version and was reconstructed as a version of cult-etiology from the sayings of Jesus transmitted in the narrative report.

the two versions can be "derived" from the other. That the Pauline version is derivable and in all probability actually did derive from the Marcan version is a position I have undertaken to substantiate at length (*Das Abendmahl*, 46-51, 53-60).

Hence "the question whether motif- and tradition-historical considerations provide compelling literary-critical arguments for the nonhomogeneous (= synthetic) character" (*Das Abendmahl*, 72) of Mark 14:22-25 can therefore be answered in the negative and the search for an older wording of the Last Supper sayings behind Mark 14:22b, 24b can be ended as unwarranted.

(iv) Criticism of the Gattung- and form-critical evaluation of Mark 14:22-25

T. Holtz seems to agree with my analysis when he states: "Also the Pauline text turns out, especially as a result of a Gattung- and form-critical analysis, to be secondary over against Mark. Mark's version offers a narrative report which does not exceed the historical situation presented; Paul, on the other hand, offers a cult-etiology" (*ThLZ* 106, 812); similarly H. Giesen (*Theologie der Gegenwart* 23, 59). R. J. Daly, on the other hand (*CBQ* 43, 310), is not convinced (though he gives no argument).

J. Kremer inquires: "Is not the base of Mark 14:22-25 too limited to conclude from it that in terms of Gattung we are dealing here with a 'narrative report' in distinction from a 'cult-etiology' as found in I Cor. 11:23b-25, since these two kinds of text do not exclude each other?" (*Theologisch-praktische Quartalschrift* 129, 188). In response one must say that the reportorial character of Mark 14:22-25 is underscored by its context as much as the cult-etiological in I Cor. 11:23b-25 is by its context. Fundamentally, each text offers the base for the determination of its Gattung, to be sure, and the fact that the different kinds of text do not exclude each other, but only distinguish themselves from each other, is self-evident.

F. Hahn also seems to assent to my Gattung- and form-critical evaluation; only he thinks I would "unjustifiably accuse prevailing scholarship for not having carried out a 'Gattung-critical comparison'" (*ThRev* 76, 267). Unfortunately, a reference to the location of such a comparison is missing—I cannot find one in F. Hahn's works.

I note with special interest this agreement with Gattung- and form-critical analysis for a reason: for a tradition-critical analysis much depends on such an analysis! This is especially confirmed also by I. H. Marshall (*Last Supper*, 35).

(v) Criticism of my tradition-critical evaluation of Mark 14:22-25

W. G. Kümmel (supported by F. Hahn) cannot "get around the judgment that the interpretation of the last Supper sayings of Jesus, and hence of Jesus' understanding of his death, offered with much erudition but equally with great assurance by Pesch, has not been substantiated any more convincingly by this new argumentation" (*TR* 47, 160). A few critical remarks—and that is all that is needed to render a judgment! And the one who is being judged has no opportunity to come to terms with the grounds for the judgment (and possibly learn from them).

For F. Hahn it is "surprising how self-evidently Rudolf Pesch regards the Marcan text as the oldest tradition and at the same time as an authentic historical tradition" (*ThRev* 76, 270). Why "self-evidently"? Cf. the pains I have taken in *Das Abendmahl,* 69-90!

By contrast, according to T. Holtz, "Pesch demonstrates the historical reliability of the report" (p. 813).

Hahn calls the tradition-critical judgment in question with the statement: "The thesis that Mark 14:22-25 fits without any difficulty in the course of a Passover meal remains unproven" (269). If he were right, his doubts would also be justified. A nonindependent narrative like Mark 14:22-25 requires tradition-critical examination with careful scrutiny of the context (cf. *Das Abendmahl,* 81-83: "3. Mark 14:22-25 in the context of the pre-Marcan passion narrative"). Hence, with reference to *Mark2,* I had expressly stated: "Of special interest are the two scenes which precede 14:22-25, the Gattung, form, and historical worth of which are often falsely assessed," and for that reason I made brief reference to 14:12-16 and 14:17-21, which F. Hahn neither mentions nor discusses.

In the first place, a few remarks about the method of the tradition-critical examination of narrative texts are in order. An essential condition for tradition-critical judgment is Gattung- and form-analysis. Inasmuch as the Gattung of 14:12-25 is accurately described as a "reporting narrative," a label which also describes the intention of the narrator to report something that happened (which has not been openly doubted, cf. [iv] above), the attempt must be made to understand the narrative as a report of something that actually happened, and precisely to examine whether and in how far historical events form the presuppositions of the narrative report which—as stated at the beginning—always underlies the selective interpretation of the narrator according to his own perspective.

How does such an examination occur? Since U. Luz (see above) also called in question the judgment about 14:12-16, allow me to illustrate the method (partly anticipating the third main section of the present essay) with reference to this narrative segment. The basic question must, first of all, be: What is the theme of the narrative? The answer can only be: The preparation by two disciples of the Passover meal for Jesus and his disciples. Obviously the narrative concerning this theme or event will be reportorial.

Now, the possibility cannot be excluded a priori that the narrator freely staged the theme without fidelity to the factual event—whether experienced by him or transmitted to him; but if his narrative report is to be credible he must in any case be somewhat at home with the "properties" of the theme.

The narrative report of the preparation of the Passover meal must—if any narrative, be it ever so short, is to result— provide an outline possessing the "necessary features" that can then be colorfully enriched with some additional nonnecessary features. In any existing text both the necessary and the nonnecessary features can be distinguished with great certainty.

As a rule, to make a tradition-critical judgment *the necessary features* are irrelevant, since the narrator has to utilize them if he is to tell his story, whether or not he tells it with close adherence to the events he sets out to report. Exceptions are only those necessary features which unambiguously exhibit legendary or obviously concrete characteristics.

The nonnecessary features, on the other hand, are usually relevant for making tradition-critical judgments since the narrator does not have to utilize them to relate his theme, and since at these points his unfettered imagination, his orientation to certain legendary motifs, his kerygmatic interests, or his commitment to events experienced by him or transmitted to him, come most readily to expression.

Mark 14:12-16 is a reportorial narrative which consists of segments of *narrative* and segments of *discourse,* segments which must be distinguished from each other and can be analyzed by themselves and in relation to each other, especially with a view to the distinction between the necessary and the nonnecessary features. It is clear in advance that in a given narrative the necessary features are to be found first of all in the narrative parts which provide the backbone of the story. But in the narrative before us, one that is fundamentally informed by the correspondence between instruction and its execution, the segments of discourse also have special significance for the composition of the narrative.

In order quickly to gain clarity concerning the details of a narrative text, it is best to use *a simple scheme of text-normality* by means of which one grasps in succession the segments of narrative and the segments of discourse.

For the text at hand a relatively simple scheme is adequate (see pp. 134f.).

Jesus' discourse (vv. 13c, d, e, 14-15b) answers the question of the disciples by way of instructions (directed acts: the imperatives ὑπάγετε,[2] ἀκολουθήσατε, εἴπατε, ἑτοιμάσατε) and predictions (the futures ἀπαντήσει,

---

2. The first imperative, which is intended to set the action of the disciples in motion, has a semitizing conditional sense: imperative + καί + future = "If you go into the city, a man will meet you."

δείξει). The instructions match exactly the problem "where?" in that they are all locally oriented: the disciples must "go into the city," "follow" the man carrying a jar of water into the house that he "enters," ask the householder with a statement from the teacher "where" the guest room is "where" Jesus can eat the Passover with his disciples, and "there," in the large upper room, they will prepare the Passover.

The *predictions* serve the purpose of enabling the disciples to carry out their instructions: the water carrier who *will meet* them and whom they *must* follow will lead them into the house in which they will address to the householder Jesus' question concerning the room where they *must* make ready the Passover meal. The householder *will show* them the large upper room where they *must* prepare the meal.

The disciples' question concerning the "where" of the preparations for the Passover is answered only indirectly by Jesus with a peculiar mixture of indefiniteness (e.g. "a man," "wherever he enters") and concreteness (e.g. "carrying a water jar," "a large upper room furnished and ready")—in such a way that the place can only be found in accordance with Jesus' word (v. 16c, d) if the disciples carry out the instructions bound up with the predictions.

It is especially remarkable that the narrator, who in v. 14c, d, uses two-layered discourse, assumes that the householder will know who "the teacher" is who asks the two disciples to convey to him the question where the guest room is where the teacher can eat the Passover with his disciples. These assumptions exceed the horizon of the legendary miraculous foreknowledge of Jesus usually attributed to the narrative—exceed it unambiguously inasmuch as it—given the accepted attribution—forces a person to ascribe a corresponding miraculous knowledge to the householder. However, the narrator does not indicate his wish to insinuate this and immediately steers the understanding of his narrative clearly in another direction.

Jesus' discourse concerns the method by which the place for the preparation of the Passover can be found without naming it in advance. Hence, in an important additional respect, it corresponds to the discourse of the disciples; in this regard, namely, that the place was and remains a secret to the questioners (= all the disciples apart from the two mandated disciples who find it in the course of carrying out their mandate), hence in the motif of secrecy.

Let us summarize: the function of the discourse of the disciples, like that of Jesus' discourse, has something very important to do with keeping the place secret, and this in turn also clarifies the function of the nonnecessary features in the narrative part of our text. The double temporal reference in v. 12a, b is a signal that it is already very late for the preparation of the Passover meal, since it was customary for the lambs to be killed in the temple the afternoon of the fourteenth

1. Narrative in Mark 14:12-16:

Verse	Conjunction	Actor	Act (finite verb or participle)	Object	Circumstances place or time
12a	Καί		ἔθυον	τὸ πάσχα	τῇ πρώτῃ ἡμέρᾳ τῶν ἀζύμων
b	ὅτε				
c		οἱ μαθηταὶ αὐτοῦ	λέγουσιν	αὐτῷ	
13a	Καί		ἀποστέλλει	δύο τῶν μαθητῶν αὐτοῦ	
b	καί		λέγει	αὐτοῖς	
16a	Καί	οἱ μαθηταί	ἐξῆλθον		
b	καί		ἦλθον		εἰς τὴν πόλιν
c	καί		εὗρον		
d	καθὼς		εἶπεν	αὐτοῖς	
e	καί		ἡτοίμασαν	τὸ πάσχα	

The series of main clauses introduced by καί all contain information necessary for narration of the theme "preparation of the Passover meal." If one were to remove vv. 12c, 13b, and 16c-d from the text and add to v. 13a a final clause (e.g. "in order that they might prepare the Passover meal") in place of the direct speech, then a complete "short story" would result (adequate as an introduction to 14:17-21). The doubling in the introduction with the temporal notation (v. 12a) and the temporal dependent clause (v. 12b) is also not necessary. Consequently, the necessary features can perhaps be seen in vv. 12a, 13a, and 16a, b, e—and 16b appears necessary only on the assumption that Jesus (who is not mentioned!) is outside the city (Jerusalem).

The nonnecessary features refer especially to the time and place of the events (vv. 12a, b, 16c), to the speech of the disciples in which they initiate the action (v. 12c), and to the instructions and predictions of Jesus and their realization (vv. 13b, 16c, d). These nonnecessary features must be studied with a view to the questions of what function they possess and whether they show where the narrator received them.

2. Discourse in Mark 14:12-16:

Verse	Conjunction	Actor	Act — Actual	Act — Directed	Object(s)	Circumstances — Situation	Circumstances — Place
12d	[ποῦ]		θέλεις				ποῦ
12e	ἵνα		φάγῃς	ἀπελθόντες ἑτοιμάσωμεν	τὸ πάσχα.		
13c				ὑπάγετε	ὑμῖν		εἰς τὴν πόλιν
d	καί	ἄνθρωπος	ἀπαντήσει			κεράμιον ὕδατος βαστάζων	
e	καὶ [ὅπου ἐάν]		[βαστάζων]	ἀκολουθήσατε	[κεράμιον ὕδατος]		ὅπου ἐάν
14a			εἰσέλθῃ		αὐτῷ		
b	ὅτι			εἴπατε	τῷ οἰκοδεσπότῃ		
c	[ποῦ]	ὁ διδάσκαλος κατάλυμά μου	λέγει				
d	[ὅπου]					ἐστιν	ποῦ
e	καί			φάγω	τὸ πάσχα ὑμῖν	μετὰ τῶν μαθητῶν μου ὅπου	
15a		αὐτός	δείξει		ἀνάγαιον μέγα ἐστρωμένον ἕτοιμον		
b	καί		ἑτοιμάσατε		ὑμῖν		ἐκεῖ

The speech of the disciples (vv. 12d, e) asks—strikingly in light of the theme—not only what Jesus wants in relation to the preparation of the Passover, but above all "where" the disciples are to "go." A story is thus set up because the disciples must first learn *where* the preparation, according to Jesus, must take place. The required actions seem clear: they must "proceed" (as in the narrative framework a stay outside Jerusalem is presupposed) to "prepare." It is clear that Jesus wishes to eat the Passover; what is unclear is "where" (more precisely, where in the city) the necessary Passover (v. 12c) is to be prepared. Hence the discourse of the disciples concerns this problem of "where." Corresponding to this exposition of the problem is the accumulation of local references in Jesus' reply (the final column above and the reference to the ἀνάγαιον μέγα in v. 15a).

Hence the nonnecessary feature, the discourse in v. 12d, e, is to be studied in terms of its function. Why does the narrator introduce the problem of the location of the Passover and, above all, of its preparation?

of Nisan.³ Throughout the narrative the issue is the "place," and this is clearly because—in any case, according to the notions of the world of the narrative—to the end, i.e., until their arrival in the evening (v. 17), the place remains unknown to the disciples. The instructions and prediction of Jesus, as well as their implementation, are accentuated in the narrative because only so could the upper room be found by the two disciples under orders and according to v. 16c, d was indeed found. If one now also looks at the context of the narrative segment, the formulation of v. 17 immediately acquires sharp relief. In the evening Jesus comes (sing.) "with the Twelve," whom he leads since only he, not they, knows their destination. And if one glances at vv. 10f. the motif of secrecy becomes clear: Judas had been to see the chief priests in Jerusalem in order to come to an agreement with them concerning the arrest of Jesus at a favorable time—away from the pilgrim crowds (v. 2). Such a time arrived in the night of the Passover.

Hence the function of the nonnecessary features in vv. 12-16 is to present the complex of events entailed in the preparation of the Passover meal whose location had to be kept a secret. Its aim is not to attribute miraculous knowledge to Jesus and thereby to construct a legendary narrative.

The probable answer to the question from what source the narrator obtained the nonnecessary features which make his narrative so complex can (particularly with regard to the narrative that connects the segment with the context: the stay in Bethany [v. 3]; the betrayal by Judas [vv. 10f.]; the agreement between the temporal notations [vv. 1, 12]; Jesus guiding the Twelve to the place [v. 17]) only be this: the narrator relates the story as he relates it because he knows himself bound to events experienced by him or transmitted to him.⁴ The fact that, given this likely assumption, an explanation of this narrative segment can make each individual reference precisely intelligible is the best confirmation of this assumption. Cf. on this, *Mark2*, 340-45.

Consequently, the tradition-critical verdict can only be: On the basis of information concerning actual events Mark 14:12-16 tells the story of the preparation of the Passover meal, a preparation which was bound up with secrecy measures initiated by Jesus!

The *control test*, the critique of the legend-hypothesis, also confirms this hypothesis. For the critique of the attribution of the passage to the Gattung of "prophetic prediction" (I Sam. 10:1-10; I Kgs. 17:8-16; 2 Kgs. 1) cf. *Mark2*, 341, also 176-89 on Mark 11:1-11. The commentators who follow this hypothe-

---

3. Cf. Jub. 49:1: ". . . that you should kill it before it is evening"; 11QTemple 17:7: "and they shall sacrifice before the evening"; Jub. 49:12: "And it is not permissible to slay it during any period of the light, but during the period bordering on the evening"; 49:19: ". . . slay the Passover in the evening."

4. This does not mean that he tells the story with meticulous precision. It means that he represents the actual events (or the events as transmitted to him) selectively and according to his own perspective.

sis (cf. e.g. J. Gnilka, *Das Evangelium nach Markus* 2, ad loc.; J. Ernst, *Das Evangelium nach Markus,* ad loc.) sidestep the difficulties of vv. 14ff., according to which an unknown householder is said to make available a free, well-furnished upper room in response to the request passed on to him by unknown messengers of an unknown teacher shortly before the evening beginning the Passover celebration (in an overcrowded city). Even if the narrator had intended to attribute this much miraculous foreknowledge to the householder, the thrust of his tale would no longer be obvious to a public familiar with the circumstances (as is always presupposed in the pre-Marcan passion narrative). For example, when Gnilka states (and this is repeated by Ernst): "Water carriers who had drawn water from the spring of Gihon could certainly be encountered in Jerusalem at any time" (233) he not only overlooks the fact that a man with a jug of water (usually carried only by women) instead of a water skin (which men dragged) is precisely not an "everyday event" but that which marks the encounter with a water carrier as an unusual incident; in the legendary view of the narrator, the disciples would also have had to meet, of all people, a water carrier whose householder still had available a free and fully furnished upper room, etc. (see above). How then could one still hold that this is "not a fairytale motif" (Gnilka, 232)? And J. Ernst shows us to what pseudo-theological exegesis the legend hypothesis (as against the historical reality of the life of Jesus who does *not* simply turn himself over to his betrayer and in Gethsemane still prays to be *spared* the cup of suffering) leads when he comments (408, on vv. 13, 14):

> The course of events is transparent: everything, piece by piece, falls into place; that which now comes at Jesus proceeds according to a preconceived divine plan. However, he himself, the teacher, is not a mere object and sacrificial lamb without a will of his own but one who knows and consents. He himself gives the directions. . . . Beyond the prophetic element Mark also sketches the image of the Son who goes his own way and in his freedom is neither led or directed by any human agent. Jesus is not the "divine man" who by way of miraculous events exhibits himself, but the obedient man who surrenders himself, who affirms his mandate as one who knows, wills, and works. The supposedly "legendary" features in reality have a deep kerygmatic meaning: Jesus is not overtaken by events; the case is rather that he goes out to meet them.

Such comments offer paradigmatic proof how the lack of interest in the real history of Jesus opens all the doors to "edifying" speculation which silences the text itself and, from the materials of the history of revelation, creates a devotional icon.[5] Jesus' consent to his course of suffering (as it becomes clear

---

5. For the purpose of comparison, I will cite my own interpretation from *Das Evangelium der Urgemeinde,* 166f.:

in the Last Supper tradition) is not at all understood in its actuality, for Jesus did not seek a martyrdom but took a position in the face of history, which he did not view as his fate. The legend hypothesis also suffers from a failure to understand legend as a speech-form of faith which interprets historical reality. In this way, too, the disturbed relationship of New Testament scholarship to history is evident.

Back to Mark 14:22-25. As a component of the overall narrative of 14:12-26 this segment directly participates in the good tradition-critical reputation and credit deserved by the remaining segments. On vv. 17-21, cf. *Mark2*, 345-53.

(b) Implications of the Criticism

Striking in the criticism is how little attention was given the question of the Last Supper tradition as a component of the passion tradition and thus as a component of the oldest Jerusalem tradition, the "Gospel in Jerusalem." What is the explanation for this? The explanation is presumably the lasting effect of "the idea cherished by form critics for decades, of individual traditions completely detached and in 'free circulation' as isolated units" (Martin Hengel, *Acts and the History of Earliest Christianity,* 1979, 25). For J. Ernst, *Das Evangelium nach Markus,* 396, as for J. Gnilka, *Das Evangelium nach Markus* 2, 350, the narrative segments Mark 14:12-16, 17-21, and 22-25 are originally independent individual traditions, and with this verdict the most recent commentators only represent the *communis opinio* which the older form critics created.

To me, therefore, it seems fitting once more to demonstrate at some length that we have before us in Mark 14:22-26 a segment of the passion narrative which arose in Jerusalem at an early time, a segment which supports P. Stuhlmacher's opinions expressed in the first essay in the present volume:

> Since the leadership circle of the primitive Church in Jerusalem derived from the circle of Jesus' disciples and his family, one must, with regard

---

The passion narrative does not portray a naively other-worldly Jesus who blindly runs into the traps set for him by his enemies. Just as during the treacherous interrogations on the temple square Jesus thinks and reacts quick-wittedly, so now he acts with poise, intelligence, and prudence. Since on the evening of Passover the pilgrim crowds scattered into small groups for table fellowship, Jesus cannot at this time be certain with regard to the hostile attitude of the Jersualem authorities. He therefore takes precautionary measures related to the secrecy of his place of abode. Where the paschal meal is celebrated is not something that Judas can reveal to the high priest.

That the preparation for the Passover is related at all is certainly connected with the meaning that the events at the meal had for the community in which the story circulated, i.e., for the early Church. But beyond that one may consider whether Jesus attributed special significance to the Passover meal with his disciples because he planned to make it an occasion for interpreting his death.

to the gospel tradition, reckon with a continuum which was not a fortuitous coincidence but deliberately cultivated, a continuum which leads from the time of Jesus to the post-Easter Church. . . . On balance, a much larger part of the gospel tradition could represent historically trustworthy material than has been originally assumed by classic form criticism.

3. Once Again: Mark 14:12-26 as Component of the Pre-Marcan Passion Narrative and Oldest Tradition of the Early Church

Mark 14:12-26 consists of three narrative segments (vv. 12-16; 17-21; 22-25) and the beginning of a fourth (v. 26) with which at the same time a sequence of events, represented in three scenes, is concluded.[6] The interconnectedness of the events is mainly constituted by the theme of "Passover," the conclusion of which is signalled in v. 26 with "a hymn" (ὑμνήσαντες) of the hallel-psalms and the change of location of the persons involved (ἐξῆλθον). The three preceding scenes concern (1) the preparation of the Passover meal (vv. 12-16); (2) the announcement of betrayal during the preliminary part of the meal (vv. 17-21); and (3) Jesus' interpretation of his death in the course of the main Passover meal (vv. 22-25). The theme of "Passover" (with the action of eating *and* drinking), which constitutes the *interconnectedness* of the events, is in evidence from the opening temporal notation in v. 12 (τῇ πρώτῃ ἡμέρᾳ τῶν ἀζύμων, ὅτε τὸ πάσχα ἔθυον) up to and including the concluding and transitional notice in v. 26 (ὑμνήσαντες ἐξῆλθον), and is present in the narrative framework as well as in the discourse parts set within the framework, both in the narrated world of the text and in the world to which the text refers. A broad semantic field gives coherence to the whole of the text:

12b: τὸ πάσχα
12e: φάγῃς τὸ πάσχα
14d: τὸ πάσχα . . . φάγω
16e: ἡτοίμασαν τὸ πάσχα
18: φανακειμένων αὐτῶν καὶ ἐσθιόντων
18b: ὁ ἐσθίων μετ᾽ ἐμοῦ

A person devoted to the cause of God cannot be naive or rash, and cannot act without regard to his surroundings, to time and the historical hour: In his parables Jesus over and over presented to his listeners the need for appropriate and intelligent action by persons in the world. The "revelation" of God is bound to concrete "worldly" reality, to everyday as well as special events. False "idealizations" of a world-avoiding character do not do justice to its claim.

6. For the detailed proofs, cf. *Mark*2 ad loc. or *Das Abendmahl*. For Mark 14:12-26, cf. also the analysis in n. 1 above! For the analysis of the arrangement in scenes, cf. K. Berger, op. cit., 17.

20b: ὁ ἐμβαπτόμενος μετ᾽ ἐμοῦ εἰς τὸ τρύβλιον
22a: ἐσθιόντων αὐτῶν
        λαβὼν ἄρτον
23a: λαβὼν ποτήριον
23b: ἔπιον
25: οὐ μὴ πίω ἐκ τοῦ γενήματος τῆς ἀμπέλου
25b: ὅταν αὐτὸ πίνω καινόν.

In the *first* scene (vv. 12-16) the subject is the preparation of the Passover meal on the fourteenth of Nisan (v. 12a, b):

12d: ἑτοιμάσωμεν
15b: ἑτοιμάσατε
16b: ἡτοίμασαν.

Although in the second and third scenes (vv. 17-21, 22-25) the key word πάσχα, which occurs four times in the first scene (vv. 12b, e, 14d, 16b), is not used again—*there being no further occasion to use it*—it is clear, from the entire sequence of events and specific narrative givens, that here certain special events occurring in the course of the Passover meal are being reported.

In the *second* scene (vv. 17-21), the beginning of the Passover meal is situated correctly (in time) in the evening (v. 17: ὀφίας γενομένης) and (in place) in the city = Jerusalem (cf. vv. 13b, 16: εἰς τὴν πόλιν; v. 17: ἔρχεται) where the Passover is to be celebrated. The beginning of the meal is summarily indicated by two things: the participants, as was prescribed for Passover meals, reclined at the table (ἀνακειμένων αὐτῶν) and ate (καὶ ἐσθιόντων). That the scene has the preliminary part of the meal in view is clear from time to time in the discourses of Jesus: The allusion to the abbreviated quotation from Ps. 41:10 in v. 18b avoids the key word "bread" simply because during the preliminary part of the meal no bread was eaten; the dish mentioned in v. 21b, in which the betrayer dips (the herbs) with Jesus, has in view the mashed fruit dish which was part of the preliminary course and in which the participants dipped the bitter herbs.

The *third* scene (vv. 22-25) leads to the main Passover meal with the (apparent) repetition καὶ ἐσθιόντων αὐτῶν (v. 22, cf. v. 18a: καὶ ἀνακειμένων αὐτῶν καὶ ἐσθιόντων), which is a transitional scenic "separator." During the main meal the unleavened "bread" (v. 22) was eaten, and the main meal was concluded by singing a hymn (v. 26). Also the expression "the fruit of the vine" (τὸ γένημα τῆς ἀμπέλου, v. 25) *may* refer to the Passover. In conclusion, Jesus' journey with his disciples to the Mount of Olives (v. 26)—instead of to Bethany as in 11:11, 19; cf. 14:3—presupposes the night of the Passover during which the pilgrims had to remain within the city limits.

Hence Mark 14:12-26 represents a coherent sequence of events mainly constituted by the theme "Passover meal." But beyond that all three scenes of this narrative are linked by the theme "arrest and death of Jesus" which is discussed, or rather presupposed, in the discourses of Jesus. The special event which occurs during the preliminary part of the Passover (vv. 17-21) is *Jesus' prediction* (and the disciples' dismayed discussion of it) *that he will be betrayed*:

18b: εἷς ἐξ ὑμῶν παραδώσει με
20a: εἷς τῶν δώδεκα . . .
21b: ὁ υἱὸς τοῦ ἀνθρώπου παραδίδοται.

And this betrayal leads to his death:

21a: ὁ μὲν υἱὸς τοῦ ἀνθρώπου ὑπάγει καθὼς γέγραπται περὶ αὐτοῦ.

The special event which occurs during the main Passover meal (vv. 22-25) consists in the gestures and words by which Jesus interprets his death, which is clearly discussed in v. 24 (τὸ αἷμά μου . . . τὸ ἐκχυννόμενον), and his prophecy of death in the Amen-saying (v. 25). The journey to the Mount of Olives (v. 26) is made up of the walk to the place where in great anguish (v. 34) Jesus prays to have the cup of suffering removed from him (v. 36) and again announces his arrest (vv. 41f.), the place also where he is then betrayed and taken captive (vv. 43-52). And on the way there his death is again discussed in advance (vv. 27, 31).

But the theme of the betrayal which threatened Jesus (and of his death) is also presupposed and present in the first scene (vv. 12-16) inasmuch as the preparation of the Passover took place, under remarkable precautions of secrecy, in the "city" (vv. 13, 16), in a certain house (v. 14), in a room (v. 14) later specifically described as "upper room" (v. 15). The place where Jesus can observe the Passover with his disciples (cf. ποῦ in vv. 12, 14; ὅπου and ἐκεῖ in vv. 14, 15) appears to be questionable because in the city Jesus is in danger. Reference to this danger is clearly made in the following context (second and third scene) but also in the preceding context (vv. 1-11), to which our narrative segment, which is not conceived as an independent narrative, originally belonged. The linking of vv. 12-25 to the following context is clearly shown by v. 26.

But the link with the preceding context is also evident. The opening temporal notation (v. 12a, b) refers back to the temporal notation in v. 1a and thus to the events narrated from vv. 1ff. The mention of "his" (αὐτοῦ) disciples who spoke to "him," hence the reference to Jesus (whose name does not occur until v. 17 [and again in v. 27] and is used only once therefore in the large segment of vv. 12-26) with the personal pronoun[7] presupposes the preceding context in which Jesus was mentioned by name (in v. 6 for the last time). The act of sending the two disciples "into the city" (= Jerusalem; v. 13b) presupposes Jesus' stay outside of the city, in Bethany (vv. 3-9); from there the disciples had

7. On the creation of coherence by the use of "pro-forms," cf. K. Berger, op. cit., 15.

to "go" (v. 12d) or "set out" (v. 16a) in order to come into the city (v. 16b). Accordingly, in the evening, Jesus comes (v. 17) with the Twelve.

Whereas vv. 12-16 presuppose the entire context narrated before (vv. 1-11), they presuppose in particular the fact related in vv. 10f., that the day before, when Jesus attended a dinner in Bethany, Judas Iscariot had gone from there to the high priests in Jerusalem to agree on a favorable moment for the arrest. That the night of the Passover, in Jerusalem, during which the pilgrims and therefore also the supporters of Jesus who had long protected him (cf. 11:18; 12:12; 14:2) were scattered in smaller communities of celebrations, was a particularly suitable moment for a possible arrest of Jesus is clear from the outset to any hearer/reader familiar with the relevant local and liturgical circumstances. As a result he is also in a position to understand the remarkable directions Jesus gave (14:13-15) as steps taken to keep his whereabouts secret.

The literary-critical unity of the narrative segment 14:12-25 has already been demonstrated by the "themes" which hold it together. It can be made still more clear by reference to the stylistic unity and the absence of disturbing repetitions, tensions, etc.[8]

The *narrative skeleton of the first scene* (vv. 12-16) in vv. 12a, b, c, 13a, b, 16, with the exception of the temporal clause (introduced by ὅτε) in v. 12b and the modal clause καθὼς εἶπεν in v. 16d, has been provided throughout by paratactically arranged sentences linked by καί (a sevenfold καί arrangement). The tense of the narrative is the threefold historical present (vv. 12c, 13a, b) (except for the imperfect ἔθυον in v. 12b) in the beginning, twice to introduce discourse (λέγουσιν, λέγει), and the fivefold aorist at the end (v. 16).[9] In addition to the indefinite subject of the temporal clause in v. 12b, only Jesus (unnamed) and his disciples occur as actors. What is narrated is a dialogue and the sending out of two disciples "on the first day of Unleavened Bread" (circumstance of time) "into the city" (circumstance of place) to prepare the Passover meal.

The discourse parts of the first scene, the question of the disciples (v. 12d, e) and the instructions of Jesus (vv. 13c-15), serve to articulate the preparation of the Passover meal and are to that extent in complete agreement with the narrative framework (whose last part in v. 16 consists of a depiction of what the disciples did to carry out Jesus' orders and refers to the realization of his prediction).

The issue in the question of the disciples is the action Jesus willed (eat the Passover) and the action the disciples were obligated to perform (prepare the Passover)—more precisely the "where" of both. In all of its parts Jesus' answer

---

8. Basic to a responsible literary criticism is that a distinction be made between the enumeration of the phenomena and their valuation. Cf. G. Fohrer, op. cit., 48: "One can describe a text unit as unified when one cannot discern in it any *unresolvable* tension and/or *disturbing* repetitions" (italics added).

9. Cf. similarly Mark 11:1ff.

is oriented to the question of "where" (cf. the local terms: εἰς τὴν πόλιν, ὅπου ἐάν, ποῦ, ὅπου, ἐκεῖ). The disciples are directed by imperatives to carry out certain specific actions (ὑπάγετε, ἀκολουθήσατε, εἴπατε, ἑτοιμάσατε); predictions concerning the water carrier and the householder are made in future tense verbs (ἀπαντήσει, δείξει). One instruction to the two disciples is conditioned by the conduct of the water carrier (ὅπου ἐὰν εἰσέλθῃ), namely their message to the householder in which Jesus himself addresses the householder with the question *where* the room for the Passover meal is located.

At the end, the instruction of Jesus (ἐκεῖ ἑτοιμάσατε) corresponds to the question of the disciples (ποῦ . . . ἑτοιμάσωμεν). The "where" or "there" is clarified by the prediction concerning the conduct of the water carrier and the householder, or rather by the instructions given the disciples—but only for them as they carry out their instructions. For the rest the place remains a secret! (This is where the emphasis lies, not on some kind of legendary miraculous foreknowledge of Jesus.)

The narrative skeleton of the second scene (vv. 17-21) in vv. 17, 18a, 19a, 20, which provides the framework for a dialogue at the meal in the evening, consists of paratactic sentences (twofold καί arrangement at the beginning) which enclose the temporal genitive absolute construction, an asyndetic double sentence (internally linked by καί), plus a speech linked to the preceding by δέ. Asyndesis (v. 19a) and the δέ-connection (v. 20a) underscore the liveliness of the dialogue in which the topic is the explosive theme of the botrayal of Jesus. Again there is a change from the historical present at the beginning (v. 17) to an aorist for the main actions (which consist here, to be sure, of speech!). The genitive absolute constructions mark the moment of the beginning of the meal: When it was evening Jesus came *with the Twelve* to the place where the two disciples had prepared the Passover, reclined at table with them, and ate. For the rest, the framework for the dialogue around the table only underscores the bewilderment of the Twelve (v. 19: ἤρξαντο λυπεῖσθαι) and harmonizes with the context as well as with the discourse parts within the framework. In distinction from vv. 12c, 13a, 16a, the reference is now to the "Twelve" (v. 17) instead of to the "disciples," but this is not a disturbing tension (for literary critics to worry over) but a matter of precision necessary with a view to Jesus' speech (v. 18b: εἷς ἐξ ὑμῶν; v. 20b: εἷς τῶν δώδεκα).

The discourse parts of the second scene (vv. 18b, 19b, 20b, 21) are closely related, in v. 18b (ὁ ἐσθίων μετ᾿ ἐμοῦ without τὸν ἄρτον as would be expected in light of Ps. 41:9) and in v. 20b (ὁ ἐμβαπτόμενος μετ᾿ ἐμοῦ εἰς τὸ τρύβλιον), to the presupposed framework, the beginning of the preliminary part of the Passover. The discussion concerns the future betrayal of Jesus by someone sharing the meal, one of the Twelve eating "with him" (cf. μετ᾿ ἐμοῦ in vv. 18b, 20b). This betrayal will lead to the death of the Son of Man, according to the Scriptures, while the "woe"-saying strikes at the betrayer (v. 21).

Just as in the first scene the question concerning the locale is never cleared up for the listener/reader, so now the question concerning the betrayer is left unanswered (apart from the fact that he is one of the Twelve).

Also in the *narrative skeleton of the third scene* (vv. 22-25) Jesus and the Twelve remain the actors. After a "separator,"[10] a genitive absolute construction on the model of v. 18a though not identical, which again has temporal-modal sense and which indicates the progression from the preliminary part of the meal to the main meal, the story concerns the actions of Jesus (vv. 22a, 23a) and his disciples (v. 23b) and the interpretive sayings of Jesus. The sentences are paratactically arranged (sixfold ϰαί) and have coordinating participles. Since no preparatory actions are mentioned this time the historical present is absent (sixfold aorist). The hysteron proteron in v. 23b, the emphatic report of the drinking of the Twelve, is not a sign of the layering of the text; it is determined by the linkage of the Amen-saying (v. 25) to the cup-saying (v. 24b), since the prophecy of the coming death is clearly intended to conclude the scene (analogously to v. 21). The narrative skeleton is in harmony with the context and is intrinsically tension-free.

The discourse parts of the third scene, the interpretive sayings (vv. 22b, 24b) as well as the death prophecy, the concluding Amen-saying of Jesus (v. 25), are formulated with a view to the situation and together discuss Jesus' (future) death—which also fits the context. The gifts—the bread and the cup—are interpreted; the actions of the disciples (they *must* "take" the bread) and of Jesus (he drinks no more but will drink anew) are discussed.

To postulate a secondary interpolation of vv. 22-25 into the sequence of events presented in vv. 22-26 on the basis of the alleged *repetition* (in reality it is repetition with a difference) is purely arbitrary;[11] one could by the same reasoning eliminate vv. 17-21 from the narrative sequence, because this segment has in view the preparation of the Passover meal, a special incident during the preliminary part of the meal *and* a special event during the main part of the meal before it mentions the end (v. 26).

A look at the whole of vv. 12-26 yields the result that all action verbs (and participles; except for λυπεῖσθαι in v. 19!) relate to the Passover, as do all the objects of action, and finally all the local and temporal circumstances! Hence the most natural and highly probably assumption is that the "separator" in v. 22a has no other function than to indicate the progression at the Passover from the preliminary course to the main meal (in agreement with the presuppositions registered in the scenes themselves).

10. Cf. G. Fohrer, op. cit., 90; also *Das Abendmahl,* 71 with n. 167!
11. Cf. K. Berger, op. cit., 13f. on the function of repetitions when texts are intertwined for the sake of coherence: Repetition shows "the picking up of certain strands of action." Also cf. G. Fohrer, op. cit., 50: "Of course the question arises when a repetition is disturbing and when it is not; this is not something which may be left to the subjective feeling of the individual."

Another circumstance which militates against the position that vv. 22-25 are a secondary interpolation is that vv. 22-25 is not an independent narrative unit.[12] This is already apparent from the fact that the actors are not mentioned by name but can only be inferred from the context. Apart from the context there is no description of the situation which makes the actions intelligible, particularly because the phrase καὶ ἐσθιόντων αὐτῶν only acquires its specific meaning from the context.

Elsewhere already (*Das Abendmahl,* 70-72) I have shown that the genitive absolute can reproduce the beginning of a Semitic nominal sentence (having the function of a "separator"). The fact that a "repetition" only indicates a text layering when it jars the textual structure (and does not, as in this case, give precision to the sequence presented) should really be self-evident for a responsible application of literary-critical method.

---

12. At this point the question of the distinction between independent and nonindependent text units (raised in section 2.a.i of the present essay) can be fundamentally and paradigmatically taken up. E. Zenger, op. cit., 120, defines as criterión: "According to whether or not the horizon of a unit points beyond itself, one is dealing with a unit which has been composed or transmitted as an independent or a nonindependent unit." For him the case is that "the horizon of a unit (its angle of vision, the scope of its interests) results, in each case, from the formulas and schemata of the unit, which can also be found in other biblical texts." Cf. similarly, G. Fohrer, op. cit., 80f.

For the overarching horizon and hence the nonindependent or context-bound character of Mark 14:22-25 the following data—certainly in their cumulative impact—are conclusive criteria:

1. The question of the place and time of the events narrated finds no answer within the narrative unit itself; it does, however, in the preceding context (14:12-21, esp. vv. 12 and 17 [time], 13-17 [place]).

2. Persons are not mentioned by name, but only referred to by pronouns (αὐτῶν, αὐτοῖς, also πάντες in v. 23) and in the the verb endings; for that reason the hearer/reader is referred to information already in hand. Who is referred to by αὐτῶν, αὐτοῖς, and πάντες (after v. 17 "the Twelve") is only clear from the context (although the omission of Jesus' name could be explained by oral tradition, in which the clarification that Jesus was meant came from the freely-formed framework).

3. The key word πάντες is a formulaic element (cf. 14:27, 28, 31, 50) that refers to the overarching horizon (the following context).

4. The terminology of the meal (ἐσθίειν, λαμβάνειν ἄρτον, εὐλογεῖν, κλᾶν, λαμβάνειν ποτήριον, εὐχαριστεῖν, πίνειν, τὸ γένημα τῆς ἀμπέλου) forms a semantic field coherent with that in 14:12-21, and the introduction in 14:22a in the genitive absolute (with its connecting repetition) points to the Passover meal presupposed in the context and hence clarifies the question not answered in the unit itself concerning the specifics of the presupposed situation of the meal. The Passover meal constitutes the overarching horizon of the unit.

5. The amen-introduction (ἀμὴν λέγω ὑμῖν) in the case of a context-related prophecy is a formulaic element (cf. for 14:25 the amen-sayings in 14:9, 18, 30) that also refers to an overarching horizon.

6. The tight linkage of 14:22-25 to 14:17-21 is also evidenced by the fact that following noun antecedents (v. 17: "the Twelve"; v. 18: "Jesus") one not only encounters pronouns but also no tense change (in distinction from the procedure followed in the depiction of the preparatory actions in 14:12, 13, 17; cf. the sequence: v. 18: ὁ Ἰησοῦς εἶπεν; 20: ὁ δὲ εἶπεν αὐτοῖς; 22: καὶ εἶπεν; 24: καὶ εἶπεν αὐτοῖς).

Unfortunately, since—to the shame of current New Testament scholarship—this is not self-evident and many a scholar is as much as ever inclined to make a rough judgment according to his own taste,[13] an exercise offered with reference to the genitive absolute constructions which occur in Mark's Gospel at the beginning of text units (without preceding time notations) would seem to be in order. We shall not consider here cases like 14:18 where the construction does not occur at the beginning of the unit; nor the linking of occurrences in 5:35 (the combination of the story of the woman with the issue of blood and that of Jairus).

The following instances can be listed:

1. 1:32:   ὀψίας δὲ γενομένης
2. 9:9:   καὶ καταβαινόντων αὐτῶν ἐκ τοῦ ὄρους
3. 10:17:   καὶ ἐκπορευομένου αὐτοῦ εἰς ὁδόν
4. 13:1:   καὶ ἐκπορευομένου αὐτοῦ ἐκ τοῦ ἱεροῦ
5. 13:3:   καὶ καθημένου αὐτοῦ εἰς τὸ ὄρος τῶν ἐλαιῶν
6. 14:3:   καὶ ὄντος αὐτοῦ ἐν Βηθανίᾳ
7. 14:17:   καὶ ὀψίας γενομένης
8. 14:22:   καὶ ἐσθιόντων αὐτῶν
9. 14:43:   καὶ εὐθὺς ἔτι αὐτοῦ λαλοῦντος
10. 14:66: καὶ ὄντος τοῦ Πέτρου κάτω ἐν τῇ αὐλῇ
11. 15:33: καὶ γενομένης ὥρας ἕκτης
12. 15:42: καὶ ἤδη ὀψίας γενομένης
13. 16:1:   καὶ διαγενομένου τοῦ σαββάτου.

Already at first glance one is struck by the highly unequal distribution of the phenomenon (the genitive absolute construction at the beginning of a text unit) in the two halves of the Gospel of Mark. This unequal distribution finds its explanation upon the supposition of my reconstruction of the pre-Marcan passion narrative. For of the 13 instances 10 belong (all but numbers 1, 3, and 5) to the pre-Marcan passion narrative, in which they serve in each case to link nonindependent narrative units to the context. Among the 10 instances there are 4 linkages with place (9:9; 13:1; 14:3; 14:66; outside of the passion narrative in 10:17; 13:3), 4 linkages with time (14:17; 15:33, 42; 16:1; outside of the passion narrative in 1:32) and 2 linkages with event (14:22, 43). All these linkages start with καί. When Jesus *and* the disciples are the subject presupposed in the linkage, the subject switches each time to Jesus (9:9; 14:22). The frequency of the stylistic phenomenon within the pre-Marcan passion narrative and the fact that all the instances may be considered traditionally pre-Marcan is an argument in favor of the thesis that in 14:22 as well the pre-Marcan nonindependent narrative unit began with καὶ ἐσθιόντων αὐτῶν. The peculiar nature of this beginning only consists in the fact that in v. 18, in the introduction to Jesus' discourse (not as a linkage to event here but as temporal-modal determination) καὶ ἀνακειμένων αὐτῶν καὶ ἐσθιόντων precedes, so that in v. 22 καὶ ἐσθιόντων (αὐτῶν) seems to be a repetition. But since in v. 18 καὶ ἀνακειμένων αὐτῶν refers to the beginning of the meal and the scene in vv. 17-21 is played out with reference to the preliminary course, the linkage to event in v. 22 clearly

---

13. Cf. K. Berger, op. cit., 30, who also judges that "literary criticism has manifestly been used far and wide in much too frivolous a way as a means to determine sources."

has a new function, namely to indicate the situation of the main Passover meal likewise presupposed with the bread rite.

Beyond the aforementioned references to the linking of 14:12-26 to the macro-context of the pre-Marcan passion narrative, one may wish to consider also the references given in *Mark2*, 13f.; 340, 344f., 351f. and in *Das Evangelium der Urgemeinde*, 64-78 (place and time notations, sequence of situation-related Amen-sayings, Son of Man prophecies, the theme of the suffering of the just, the phrase εἷς τῶν δώδεκα, etc.).

The point which must once more be stressed here is that Mark 14:22-26 is only intelligible in the context of the passion narrative which was transmitted in Jerusalem in the early Church and may, therefore, be regarded as the earliest traditional material of the early Church—paradigmatically it is the situation which applies to the entire pre-Marcan passion narrative.

Mark 14:22-26 presupposes that the hearer/reader has the following information already at his or her disposal:

1. That Jesus was staying with his disciples in Bethany (14:3), in the vicinity of Jerusalem (11:1);
2. that this stay occurred at the time of the Passover (14:1);
3. that the Passover meal had to be observed in Jerusalem ("the city": 14:13c, 16b) in the evening, as the Passover lamb had to be killed "before it is evening" (Jub. 49:1);
4. that, in keeping with prescribed custom, Jesus wanted to spend the Passover night on the Mount of Olives (14:26) within the city limits, which on this night included the Mount of Olives;
5. that "Judas Iscariot, one of the Twelve" (vv. 10, 20b) sought to betray him and in fact did betray him (v. 43);
6. that, coming from Bethany, one could encounter a water carrier at the Gihon-spring;
7. that the Passover meal consisted of a preliminary course and a main meal and that bread was eaten only during the latter (vv. 18, 22);
8. that the Passover was concluded with the singing of the hallel-psalms (v. 26); and
9. that with a view to the danger which threatened Jesus (11:18; 12:12; 14:1f., 10f.) it was well advised to keep the place of the Passover a secret.

As a rule, such an accumulation of concrete givens does not make for traditions which are independent, or late, or removed from the place where the relevant events occurred. For a scholar not to reckon with the probable provenance of such a tradition from the primary circle of tradents in Jerusalem (cf. above, the first page of the present essay) and its responsibly supervised (as well as interpreted) transmissions, would be biased—in the final analysis, unscholarly—and unwarranted scepticism which cannot do justice to the responsibility of the historian and the theologian to history and to the witnesses of tradition.

4. Concluding Remark: "Why Go to All This Trouble?"

Why this reply to the criticism and why this renewed argumentation to prove that Mark 14:12-26 (including the pre-Marcan passion narrative) is the oldest tradition of the early Church? It is so important to show that it is wrong, as stated by P. Stuhlmacher, in his essay earlier in the present volume,

> with reference to the gospel tradition, [to play] the historic and kerygmatic interests against each other; from an early stage, the history of the words, deeds, and fate of Jesus is narrated in the Jesus-tradition as redemptive and revelational, a sequence of events which forms the foundation for the present and future of the traditioners.

Indeed; I am convinced of it.[14] Inasmuch as discourse concerning the history of salvation and revelation, a history that is constitutive for the Christian faith and the Church, the "manifestation in the flesh" (I Tim. 3:16), must be seriously maintained and considered constitutive for the contemporary experience of faith and Church, God's present-day action on behalf of his people, like his past action from the time of Abraham and his eschatological action through Jesus and the founding of his *ekklesia* (precisely also in the mode of the *analogia fidei*), is not understandable if the unbreakable linkage between history and kerygma (between events and their theological interpretation as God's action, interpretation distilled in the tradition) is not adhered to and remembered in a theology that is historically oriented and turned toward that history in a historical-critical (but not a radically sceptical) way.

---

14. Cf. on this point my lecture of 1973—long before the supposed "shift" ascribed to me in recent years—"Christus dem Fleische nach kennen (2 Kor 5,16)? Zur theologischen Bedeutung der Frage nach dem historischen Jesus," in *Kontinuität in Jesus,* 1974, 9-34.

The Pauline Gospel

Peter Stuhlmacher

In the context of our symposium the Pauline use of the words εὐαγγέλιον and εὐαγγελίζεσθαι is of interest especially for two reasons. First of all, in Paul we are dealing with a highly polished and terminologically distinctive use of these words and, secondly, from Paul's letters one can develop inferences and perspectives which are of great significance in understanding the Christian history of these words.

Of the total of 76 instances of the noun εὐαγγέλιον in the New Testament 60 occur in the letters of Paul, 48 in the undisputed letters and 12 in the deutero-Pauline letters.[1] Hence εὐαγγέλιον is one of Paul's favorite words. One cannot say this with the same degree of certainty of the verb εὐαγγελίζειν/εὐαγγελίζεσθαι. Although it occurs 54 times in the New Testament, it is used only 21 times in the Pauline letters, 19 times in the undisputed letters and twice in the deutero-Pauline letters; the other New Testament books contain 33 instances. Hence, for the Pauline tradition the noun is of greater importance than the verb. Paul uses the noun with special predilection for the saving message of Jesus Christ revealed to him by God.[2] On this point there is agreement in the field of New Testament studies.

By contrast, the course of the Christian history of the word, to which Paul's usage belongs, is still in dispute. To his book *The Constitution and Law of the Church in the First Two Centuries* (1910) Adolf Harnack added an appendix on the history of the term "gospel" in the early Church.[3] In its conceptual clarity and tradition-historical lucidity it is even today unrivalled. Harnack distinguishes five stages in the history of the word:

---

1. The statistical information is taken from the "overviews" compiled under the direction of K. Aland in vol. I of the *Vollständige Konkordanz zum Griechischen Neuen Testament*, 1978.
2. For Pauline word usage see in detail my book: *Das paulinische Evangelium*. I: *Vorgeschichte*, 1968, 56-63. Hereafter abbreviated as *PaulEv*.
3. Op. cit., 275-331.

1. In connection with Jesus' message of the kingdom of God Harnack offers the reservation: "As Q is silent on the point, it is not quite certain whether Jesus himself used בשורה (εὐαγγέλιον) merely for the glad tidings that Isa. 61:1 . . . was now fulfilled, or whether he went beyond this and used it to sum up his preaching."[4]

2. The message of the early Church, for which Harnack also enlists Mark and Matthew: "The primitive community denoted the preaching of the coming of the kingdom as בשורה, and its Hellenistic members in Palestine substituted the word εὐαγγέλιον, although this word does not occur in the Septuagint (which writes ἡ ἀγγελία)."[5]

3. "Paul exalts the conception εὐαγγέλιον both in word and in deed to the central position in his preaching. He conceives it as the tidings of God's plan of salvation, proclaimed by the prophets and realized through the death and resurrection of Christ."[6] For the apostle "the message of Christ" and "the gospel" are the same, which according to Harnack was "a turning-point of vast importance"[7] in the history of the word. The opposition between gospel and law, says Harnack, is "nowhere found in Paul": "When he speaks of the gospel, he is not thinking of the law but of the fulfillment of the promise. . . . On the other hand he thinks of 'gospel' and 'salvation' (σωτηρία) as inseparably united and indeed salvation for men as individuals. . . . This is the second great turning-point! It is plainly foreshadowed in the proclamation of Jesus but it does not emerge from the preaching of the kingdom."[8]

4. Luke avoids the use of the word εὐαγγέλιον altogether and uses it only twice in Acts but makes very extensive use of the verb εὐαγγελίζεσθαι both in his Gospel and in Acts. "He makes Jesus consistently proclaim 'the kingdom' as the glad tidings while the apostles with similar consistency proclaim Jesus Christ. . . . Luke thus connects in the most deliberate way the older usage of Mark with that of Paul, while giving both their due. We may thus learn from him too that in the mission to the Gentiles at a very early period the gospel of the Kingdom was transformed into the gospel of Christ."[9]

5. Whereas the verb εὐαγγελίζεσθαι retains its general sense of "to proclaim," from the end of the first century the usage of εὐαγγέλιον branches off as follows: "(1) It remains a general expression for the

4. Ibid., 324.
5. Ibid., 324, 325.
6. Ibid., 325.
7. Ibid., 326.
8. Ibid., 326.
9. Ibid., 327.

Christian preaching; (2) it receives the meaning 'tidings of the Crucified and Risen Christ' because this preaching of Christ crucified is its heart and core (therefore according to the gospel in its strictest sense only the Christian who suffers martyrdom proves his right to the name); (3) it receives the meaning 'gospel history' (deeds and sayings of Jesus), or it denotes the history of Jesus recorded in a fourfold written work . . . or each individual part of this written work . . . ; (4) finally, 'gospel' denotes the nature and influence of the new religion as the religion of grace and freedom in distinction from the Old Testament stage of law and bondage. To the ancient Catholic Fathers this fourfold sense of the word 'gospel' is known and familiar."[10]

Over against Harnack a number of scholars, including G. Strecker, insist to this day that the missionary expression εὐαγγέλιον, which is not in the Septuagint, must be explained (in distinction from the verb) especially from Greek linguistic tradition and indeed above all from that pertaining to the imperial cult.[11] Thus Paul becomes a representative of a mission terminology which initially developed in the Hellenistic Church, and it is difficult, or even impossible, to reason from the letters of Paul back to the word usage which commonly prevailed in Jerusalem. My own attempt to widen the word-historical basis for a Christian understanding of εὐαγγέλιον by pointing out the parallelism and interchangeability of בשורה (– εὐαγγέλιον) and שמועה (= ἀκοή) for the message of angels and prophets in the targums and other Jewish texts, and so to undergird Harnack's derivation of the word from the Semitic-Palestinian usage, has been variously received.[12] Hence the pre-Pauline Christian use of the

---

10. Ibid., 327, 328.
11. G. Strecker is currently the chief representative of this view in Germany. Cf. his "Das Evangelium Jesu Christi," in *Jesus Christus in Historie und Theologie*, Festschrift H. Conzelmann, ed. G. Strecker, 1975, 503-48 (= idem, *Eschaton und Historie. Gesammelte Aufsätze*, 1979, 183-228); idem, εὐαγγέλιον, *EWNT* II, cols. 176-86. In the latter Strecker writes (179f.):

The primary tradition-historical base for New Testament use of εὐ[αγγέλιον] must be sought in the circle of Hellenistic emperor worship. From this source the term found its way into Christian vocabulary. If the New Testament does not expressly mark off the demarcation lines from the terminology of the Greek-Hellenistic veneration of the ruler or the Hellenistic-Roman emperor cult, nevertheless this is accomplished with regard to content since the singular εὐ[αγγέλιον] of the Christ-event is distinguished as a unique eschatological event from all the εὐαγγέλια of the surrounding non-Christian world.

Similarly G. Friedrich, *TDNT* II, 725.
12. E. Käsemann, *Commentary on Romans*, ET 1980, believes "the derivation and concrete meaning of the singular τὸ εὐαγγέλιον used absolutely have still not been satisfactorily explained." He stresses that "no direct analogy to the absolute use of the noun in Paul can be found in Palestinian usage" (6-8) and, agreeing with G. Bornkamm (*RGG*³ II, 749f.), he writes that "the missionary community on Hellenistic soil" made use of the Palestinian tradition and in its usage of the word recognized also "the etymology of the Greek word" (8).
G. Strecker considers the reference to the usage of the word in the Targums basically irrelevant

noun is still in dispute and with it the relationship of Paul's gospel to the Jesus-tradition and the message of the apostles in Jerusalem.

In view of this state of the research the special word usage in Paul and the roots of this usage that can be inferred from Paul are to us equally of great interest. Accordingly, this is where the points of gravity will lie in this paper.

1. Origin and Authority of the Pauline Gospel

In his confrontation with adversaries Paul repeatedly and emphatically points out that his gospel and mission have their origin in God's free election of grace and his revelation. This is particularly evident in the letter to the Galatians: Paul is an apostle "not from men nor through man, but through Jesus Christ and God the Father who raised him (= Christ) from the dead" (Gal. 1:1). The gospel he preaches "is not man's gospel. For I did not receive it from man, nor was I taught it, but it came through a revelation" (vv. 11f.). But when he "set me apart before I was born and had called me through his grace" it pleased God "to reveal his Son to me, in order that I might preach him among the Gentiles" (vv. 15f.). In this manner the origin and authority of Paul's gospel have been placed beyond all human reach. Like Jeremiah the prophet Paul sees himself entrusted with the preaching of the gospel for good or ill; if he were to give it up he would fall a victim to the curse of God (I Cor. 9:16; cf. Jer. 20:9). The gospel that Paul serves is a power of revelation (Rom. 1:16). It provides the apostle with the liturgy of his mission[13] and it is his office, through the performance of this liturgy, to present

---

and methodologically mistaken. He states first of all that in the Masoretic text and in the Septuagint there is no established theological use of בשורה/εὐαγγέλιον, then points to the absence of בשורה in the Qumran texts and to the use of the word for both good and bad news in the early Jewish texts. In a note he continues (Strecker, "Evangelium," 507, n. 20 = Eschaton und Historie, 187, n. 20):

> It is redundant to enter upon a discussion of further instances in post-Old Testament Jewish literature. That they largely occur in an exegetical context [the Targums!] denotes that they do not necessarily represent independent word usage. In addition, they are to be dated after the rise of the New Testament so that on this ground also a link with the New Testament (which was written in Greek) is not likely.

In his EWNT article (II, col. 180) Strecker declares the "primary link of the noun εὐαγγέλιον to the Greek-Hellenistic tradition" to be "evident. It was precisely because of this link that the newness of the Christian message was intelligibly articulated in its surroundings."

U. Wilckens, Der Brief an die Römer, EKK VI/1, 1978, on the other hand, follows the interpretive direction I have proposed and regards as the principal point of contact for the early Christian use of the word-group εὐαγγέλ- the application made of Isa. 61:1f. in the preaching of Jesus (cf. Matt. 11:5; Luke 7:22; 4:18f.; 6:20ff./Matt. 5:3ff.).

13. C. E. B. Cranfield, The Epistle to the Romans, ICC, II, 1977, 755, proposes that Rom. 15:15ff. be understood in the sense that in his priestly ministry to the gospel Paul serves Christ, the High Priest, like a Levite. On λειτουργεῖν/λειτουργία for the ministry of Levites cf. Ex. 38:21 (LXX 37:19); Num. 1:50; 3:6, 31 and many other passages.

to God the well-pleasing and holy sacrifice of the Gentiles converted to faith by the gospel (Rom. 15:16; cf. 11:13ff.). Paul received the gospel he preaches, without human intermediation, before the walls of Damascus and for him this gospel is far more than merely a form of missionary preaching or Christ-message; it is a power of God to which he as apostle owes obedience.

Since God is the One who reveals himself once for all in and through Jesus Christ, there are not several εὐαγγέλια for Paul but only the one gospel of Jesus Christ (Gal. 1:6ff.). In terms of its origin and authority the gospel is εὐαγγέλιον (τοῦ) θεοῦ (Rom. 1:1; 15:16; II Cor. 11:7; I Thess. 2:2, 8, 9); in terms of its content it is εὐαγγέλιον τοῦ Χριστοῦ (Rom. 15:19; I Cor. 9:12; II Cor. 2:12; 9:13; 10:14; Gal. 1:7; Phil. 1:27; I Thess. 3:2).[14] In the gospel Christ is manifest as Reconciler and Lord;[15] anyone who violates this gospel and ventures to preach another Christ than the messianic Son of God and Lord necessarily falls under an anathema (Gal. 1:9; cf. II Cor. 11:3f.).

This Pauline view of the gospel has found its classic summary in the prescript of the letter to the Romans (Rom. 1:1-7). Terminologically it appears in the singular-technical sense of τὸ εὐαγγέλιον = *the* gospel. In the main letters of Paul it occurs 25 times and in the deutero-Pauline letters 6 times.[16]

2. The Content of the Pauline Gospel

In his polemic with his Galatian opponents Paul declares that he received the gospel through God's revelation when he was called (before the city gates of Damascus)—that is, one must suppose, he was given the content of the gospel. For the understanding of Paul's gospel much depends on a correct comprehension of that statement. At first glance it stands in glaring contradiction to I Cor. 15:1ff., where Paul himself describes the gospel as the tradition he received and passed on, a tradition common to him and to the apostles called before him (I Cor. 15:11).

Another very weighty question, which depends on a correct understanding of Gal. 1:12, 16, is from what time and in what sense the Pauline gospel is the

14. For a long time the question whether the genitives τοῦ θεοῦ and τοῦ Χριστοῦ are to be interpreted as objective or subjective has been in dispute. With regard to this debate Strecker correctly comments ("Evangelium," 524f. = *Eschaton und Historie*, 204f.):

> Though Paul may have found the absolute noun τὸ εὐαγγέλιον in the genitive relationships εὐαγγέλιον τοῦ θεοῦ and εὐαγγέλιον τοῦ Χριστοῦ in the Hellenistic Christian tradition, he nevertheless does not really distinguish how the objective genitive and the subjective genitive could, in this combination, be separated in terms of content.

15. In Paul "preaching the gospel" and "preaching Christ" are characteristically used interchangeably: cf. e.g. I Cor. 1:17 with 1:23; I Cor. 15:1, 11 with 15:12; II Cor. 4:3f. with 4:4.

16. On the passages in particular cf. my *PaulEv.*, 57f.

salvation message of justification and reconciliation by Christ through faith apart from the works of law (Rom. 3:28). That Paul does not yet speak of justification in the first letter to the Thessalonians but only in Galatians, in I Corinthians 1 and 2, II Cor. 5:21, and then at length in Romans, seems to suggest the conclusion that Paul's gospel was not formulated and developed as gospel of justification until after the confrontation with the Judaizers in Galatia (and Rome).[17]

It seems to me that Gal. 1:13-16 and II Cor. 4:4ff. are decisive for an understanding of the Damascus revelation. In Gal. 1:13ff. Paul states tersely that it pleased God to reveal "his Son" to him, the persecutor of the Church of Christ and the zealot for the legal traditions of the Pharisaic fathers. Whether ἐν ἐμοί in v. 16 should be translated "in me" or "to me" is still in dispute; II Cor. 4:5f. shows that both are meant at the same time. In any case, what the description in Galatians clearly comes down to is this: as persecutor of the Church and zealot for the law Paul was overtaken by the Damascus revelation. Its essential content was the appearance of Jesus as "Son of God." On the basis of Rom. 1:3; I Cor. 9:1; and Phil. 2:9ff. one must understand that expression as follows: In his Damascus vision Paul saw Christ exalted to the right hand of God (in accordance with Ps. 110:1) and installed as Son of God in the position of "Lord." This vision turned the persecutor of the Church and champion of the law into an apostle and preacher of the gospel among the Gentiles. Hence the revelation of Christ before the walls of Damascus effected in Paul's life a turning away from his Pharisaic zeal for the law and a turning to the Christ who revealed himself. The knowledge implied in this revelation can be more precisely defined on the basis of II Cor. 4:4ff. II Cor. 4:1-6 was also written in a situation of confrontation with Jewish Christian opponents of Paul's preaching and relates to his call before the gates of Damascus. Given these circumstances, Gal. 1:13-16 and II Cor. 4:4ff. are comparable and interpret each other.

According to II Cor. 4:4, to those who are willing and able to listen the gospel gives φωτισμός, i.e., illuminating knowledge. It gives this knowledge as εὐαγγέλιον τῆς δόξης τοῦ Χριστοῦ, ὅς ἐστιν εἰκὼν τοῦ θεοῦ. The gospel confers the illuminating knowledge of the glory of Christ who—like wisdom in Old Testament and Jewish tradition—is the manifest and effective image of God to the world. According to II Cor. 3:7-11, the glory of Christ and his ministry by far exceeds in splendor the glory of the Torah and its ministry. II Cor. 4:5f. shows how Paul himself came to knowledge of the gospel: God, the creator of light, shone in Paul's heart and that through the illumination of the knowledge of the glory and power of God in the face of the living Christ. Hence, before the walls of Damascus, Paul saw and learned to see God's power and glory in the

---

17. Thus G. Strecker, "Evangelium," 525, 528f. (= *Eschaton und Historie,* 205, 208f.).

face of the risen and exalted Son of God. This knowledge of Christ made him an apostle to the Gentiles and servant of Jesus Christ, since in virtue of this knowledge he had been persuaded to cease his activities as a persecutor and as a champion of the law. Both forms of activity, as II Cor. 5:16 teaches, were motivated by a view of Christ which Paul, after his call at Damascus, recognized as mistaken and false—Paul writes: ". . . even though we once regarded Christ from a human point of view, we regard him thus no longer." As persecutor of the Church Paul may have viewed Christ as a messianic seducer of the people whose shameful death on the cross was fully deserved[18] and whom one could only in blasphemy acknowledge as risen Lord and Messiah—to say nothing of the fact that under the influence of this "Lord" one could (like Stephen and his friends) find reason for expressing criticism of the temple and the law! In a way Acts 6:13ff. is the key to the persecution of Christians and to Paul's polemical zeal for the law up until his Damascus experience. Then Paul experienced in person the gracious compassion of God toward the recalcitrant sinner: the risen Christ met him as Lord and Reconciler. In this encounter Paul was illumined by the knowledge that Christ was not a messianic seducer and false prophet but the Lord, by the will of God, and the "end" (τέλος) of the law as a way of salvation (Rom. 10:4).[19] The glory radiating from his face by far exceeds in splendor that of the Torah. In the grip of this knowledge Paul entered upon his mission and, on account of his preaching of Christ, which was critical of the Torah, promptly became involved in serious confrontations with the synagogues and Jewish courts (cf. II Cor. 11:24ff.).

The result of all this was that from the time of his Damascus call Paul had at his disposal the essential content of his gospel in the form of his Torah-critical knowledge of Christ and that from the beginning of his mission he articulated this knowledge. Paul's gospel is a Torah-critical gospel of atonement and justification from the time of his Damascus experience, not just after the Galatian troubles![20] Hence we may take the apostle at his word in Gal. 1:12, 16.

18. On this argument for Jewish condemnation of Jesus in Jerusalem cf. A. Strobel, *Die Stunde der Wahrheit,* 1980, 81ff.

19. U. Wilckens, *Der Brief an die Römer,* EKK VI/2, 1980, 217, 221f., in dealing with the disputed τέλος, opts for the Solomonic translation "terminal goal" ("Endziel"), but at the same time emphasizes that "Christ is the end of the law inasmuch as he ended the function of the law to curse sinners." I consider the translation "end" more appropriate to the context and recommend that the inquiry into the meaning of the law before and under Christ be approached not so much with the aid of Rom. 10:4 as in terms of Rom. 8:3ff. (see below).

20. G. Strecker himself ("Evangelium," 521 = *Eschaton und Historie,* 201) develops the position that "the linkage between the atoning death and resurrection of Jesus Christ as essential content of the pre-Pauline εὐαγγέλιον was part of the tradition." Under these circumstances one may not read I Thess. 1:10 without reflection on Paul's preaching of the gospel. Here Paul proclaims Christ as the Savior from the coming wrath of God in a way no different from that in Rom. 7:24f.; 8:31-39; 11:26. It seems to me to be asking too much from an "occasional" letter like I Thessalonians

However, the question how the statements of Gal. 1:12 relate to I Cor. 15:1ff. must for the time being remain open and can only be elucidated if we now address the relationship of the Pauline gospel to tradition.

3. The Relation of the Pauline Gospel to Tradition

In order to deal, with appropriate brevity and with reference to our special focus, with the complex question concerning the relation of Paul's gospel to tradition we must keep in mind the following facts: From Paul's letters and from Acts we know that immediately after his call Paul was baptized in Damascus and instructed in the Christian tradition of faith (I Cor. 12:13;[21] Acts 9:17ff.). Three years later he went to Jerusalem to visit Peter and to learn from him about the message and work of Jesus (Gal. 1:18f.).[22] After some further years of independent mission work in Syria and Cilicia (Gal. 1:21) Paul was brought to Antioch by Barnabas and from there, together with Barnabas, he did mission work among the Gentiles (Acts 11:19-26). Thus Paul also became a representative of the Antiochian traditions of faith and mission. At the Council in Jerusalem Paul and Barnabas succeeded in obtaining acknowledgment of the Antiochian concept of mission. The Jerusalem "pillars" recognized the gospel of the Antiochians and the noninsistence on circumcising the Gentile converts that went with this gospel (Gal. 2:6ff.; Acts 15:22-27). It was only after the Jerusalem Council that the "Antiochian incident," which was probably linked with the problems associated with the so-called apostolic decree (Gal. 2:11-14), occurred.[23] Paul was no longer able, with his (Torah-critical) point of view, to maintain his position in Antioch over against Peter, Barnabas, and the Jewish-Christian majority and therefore began to develop and pursue a truly independent concept of missions. The collection of Paul's letters preserved for us stems from the period of this independent mission work. Apart from the letter to Philemon all these letters mirror the confrontations in which Paul was involved for the sake of the gospel attacked by his opponents.

---

to expect from it an explicit discussion of the issue of justification, even though the inquiry from the church concerned the question of the resurrection treated in chs. 4f.

For the rest it is not of course my intent to dispute that in response to the hostilities of Judaizers in Galatia Paul was led to particularly effective and thoughtful formulations of his message of justification. In Galatians 1 and 2, as much as in II Corinthians 4 and Philippians 3, Paul discusses the experience of his call as he looks back upon an event that occurred decades earlier.

21. ἡμεῖς πάντες in I Cor. 12:13 includes the apostle.

22. On the purpose of the visit to Peter mentioned in Gal. 1:18, cf. (as finally convincing) J. D. G. Dunn, "The Relationship between Paul and Jerusalem according to Galatians 1 and 2," *NTS* 28, 1982 (461-78), 463-66 (= *Jesus, Paul, and the Law,* 1990 [108-25], 110-13).

23. On this linkage cf. D. Lührmann, "Abendmahlsgemeinschaft? Gal 2,11ff.," in *Kirche,* Festschrift G. Bornkamm, ed. D. Lührmann and G. Strecker, 1980, 271-86, esp. 279ff.; P. Stuhlmacher, *Weg, Stil und Konsequenzen urchristlicher Mission,* ThB 12, 1981, 107-35, esp. 120f.

Familiar as these matters are, equally well-known is it that in his letters
Paul frequently cites fragments of tradition (very clearly in I Cor. 11:23ff.;
15:1ff.; and Phil. 2:6-11) and everywhere alludes to traditions (e.g. in Rom. 6:17
and 16:17). Among the traditions Paul adduces, the Jesus-traditions do play a
certain role but are not conspicuous or predominant; in part Paul cites these
traditions, as also the others, directly (cf. I Cor. 7:10; 9:14; 11:23ff.); in part he
only assumes them and alludes to them in passing (e.g. I Thess. 5:2; I Cor. 13:2;
Rom. 12:14). However, the apostle not only serves as tradent but also acts as
the creator and teacher of traditions himself (e.g. I Thess. 4:1; I Cor. 4:17). It
was not without reason that his letters were intended to be read publicly in the
churches (cf. I Thess. 5:27; Col. 4:16). This explains their enormous effect.

Now, as regards the relation of Paul's gospel to tradition, it seems to me
to be of equally great importance that (1) Paul describes the gospel revealed to
him as being itself a gift of salvation entrusted to him in order that he may preach
it, that (2) in stating the gospel he expressly and willingly takes over old
Jewish-Christian traditions of doctrine, and that (3) he continues to measure
himself critically against those called to be apostles before him and compares
himself with them. In this context it is imperative (4) to venture a more detailed
discussion of Rom. 10:14-17 because in terms of this somewhat neglected text
some interesting tradition-historical lines can be drawn from Paul to the old
(Jerusalem?) points of view

On (1): When in Gal. 1:16 Paul mentions that he has received a revelation
of the Son of God "in order that I might preach him among the Gentiles" he is
referring to missionary labor that he could only accomplish with the aid of his
own, as well as traditional, formulations. His gospel, precisely as a power of
revelation, demands that it be communicated and forces the bearer of that
revelation, i.e., the apostle, to pass it on. Not just in the Pastoral letters but
already in Paul himself the gospel appears as a gift of salvation which is
entrusted to the apostle in order that he may proclaim it in its purity and pass it
on to others (cf. I Cor. 9:16-18; Gal. 1:11; 2:2, 7; I Thess. 2:4). Thus the gospel
revealed to Paul has a quite natural affinity with doctrine and tradition.

On (2): Paul is fully consistent when in his preaching of the gospel he at
no time boasts of originality in the modern sense of the word but adopts the
traditions of faith which come to him from the Church at Damascus, from
Jerusalem, and from Antioch. He adopts them to the extent that they accommodate his knowledge of Christ and aid him in preaching Christ in the way in which
God has instructed him and in which he has experienced Christ before the city
walls of Damascus. The old Jerusalem tradition of doctrine and confession[24]

---

24. In the face of the bilingualism in Jerusalem, which confronts us paradigmatically in the
person of Peter, I consider it misleading to say as G. Strecker does: "In the form in which Paul

cited by Paul in I Cor. 15:3ff. is for the apostle a valid expression of his gospel
because here the salvation-historical and soteriological meaning of the death
and resurrection of Jesus are predominant; it is no different with the Last Supper
tradition in I Cor. 11:23-26 or the christological fragments in Rom. 3:25f.; 4:25;
and 8:3. These texts show that the gospel message which proceeds from
Jerusalem and that preached by Paul agree completely in their christological
essence. Not until the relationship between the tradition of the sin offering and
the law comes up do the differences arise. The glory of Christ which the apostle
was permitted to see in a vision outside Damascus was to him (in light of his
pre-faith view of Christ) inseparable from Jesus' death on the cross; to Paul it
seemed to be the glorification and heavenly vindication of the Son of God who
was persecuted on earth and condemned to die an accursed death on the cross.[25]
From this perspective the Pauline message quite naturally focuses on the death
and resurrection of Jesus Christ as the decisive events of salvation. The atoning
death of Jesus became for him the central event by which God broke the power
of sin and antiquated the law as a way of salvation. The traditions of the atoning
death of Jesus which Paul cites or to which he alludes in passing (e.g. I Cor.
15:3; II Cor. 5:21; Rom. 3:25f.; 4:25; 8:3, etc.) are simultaneously the basis for
and the essence of his Torah-critical message of justification.[26] Hence the
quotation of I Cor. 15:1ff. in no way contradicts the Pauline statements of Gal.
1:12, 15f. but is in fact quite compatible with it.

Since I have already dealt with the problem of Paul's use of the Jesus-
traditions in my reflections on "The Theme: The Gospel and the Gospels" (earlier
in the present volume), I would like to point out here simply that these traditions,
like the christological fragments already mentioned, are integrated by Paul into
his gospel message. In this process concentration on the death and resurrection
of Jesus has the effect of subordinating the report of Jesus' life on earth, his words
and deeds, to the tradition of the passion. However, as far as the passion tradition
and its center, Jesus' atoning death on the cross, are concerned, as is evident from
Paul's introduction to the Last Supper tradition: "For I received from the Lord
what I also delivered to you, that the Lord Jesus on the night when he was betrayed
took bread . . ." (I Cor. 11:23), Paul put great weight on the fact that Jesus already
himself spoke of atonement in his substitutionary death. Here the continuity of
the tradition from Jesus to Paul is decisive for the Pauline gospel!

---

encountered it," the confession of vv. 3ff. "must be traced back not to the Palestinian but to the
Hellenistic Church" ("Evangelium," 520 = *Eschaton und Historie,* 200). Paul himself, according to
vv. 8ff., values the fact that he teaches and holds high the same tradition as the apostles in Jerusalem!

25. In this context the renowned hymn in the letter to the Philippians was a valid expression
of Pauline christology. For an analysis and interpretation of this hymn, cf. O. Hofius, *Der
Christushymnus Philipper 2,6-11,* 1976.

26. In my essays in *Reconciliation, Law, and Righteousness,* 1986, 50-93, I discuss in greater
depth the meaning of these texts for the Pauline view of righteousness.

In Phil. 1:27 Paul employs the expression "let your manner of life be worthy of the gospel of Christ" (ἀξίως τοῦ εὐαγγελίου τοῦ Χριστοῦ πολιτεύειν). This is meaningful only if the gospel Paul preaches also implies and embraces standards for the Christian life. Because in I Thess. 4:1 the apostle refers to the fact that in the course of his missionary work he had communicated to the Thessalonians the tradition τὸ πῶς δεῖ ὑμᾶς περιπατεῖν καὶ ἀρέσκειν θεῷ ("how you ought to live and to please God"), and because in all his letters ethical paraclesis plays a significant role and clearly comes to the fore in the decalogue tradition and Jesus-tradition (cf. Rom. 12:13ff.; 13:8ff.), it seems to me meaningful to consider paraclesis (parenesis) an essential component of Paul's gospel. Paul proclaims Jesus Christ as Reconciler and Lord; accordingly, for him faith in this Lord embraces both trustful confession and obedient discipleship.

On (3): It is precisely in the context of the gospel traditions that the confrontation with opponents of Paul's message, confrontation forced upon him in Thessalonica, Galatia, Corinth, Rome, and Philippi, appears in Paul with such weighty consequences.[27] His mostly Jewish Christian opponents took offense at Paul's message of justification and reconciliation and accused him of preaching "cheap grace" (Bonhoeffer), of accommodating himself in his message to the wishes of the Gentiles, and of being remiss in encouraging obedience toward the commandment of God and in pointing to the day of judgment. To Paul's opponents, who after the Antiochian incident had initiated a kind of "counter-mission" against him, the true gospel was not to be found in the newly converted apostate Paul, who had only obtained his traditions second- or third-hand, but in the original apostles of Jerusalem, especially James the Lord's brother, and Peter, who from the very beginning had accompanied Jesus in Galilee. For Paul this meant that he had to assert his equality and independence over against these apostles, precisely in the context of his apostolic mission and preaching.

This explains not only the style and argumentation of Galatians 1 and 2 but also the famous utterances in I Cor. 9:1-27 and 15:1-11. Without concealing his outsider's role among the apostles Paul here puts the revelation of Christ that he received outside Damascus on the level of the appearances of Christ to the original apostles of Jerusalem, in which they were called. He insists that he teaches and preaches no other gospel than they and still maintains that he preaches that gospel more freely and effectively than Peter and his associates. In I Cor. 9:13ff. he brings to the fore that, in accordance with Jesus' own instructions, the messengers of the gospel are entitled to material support by the churches. Peter, the other apostles, and the brother of the Lord are therefore right

---

27. More on this situation of confrontation is found in *Reconciliation, Law, and Righteousness* (see n. 26), 75ff.

when they claim this support and do not work with their own hands and even travel with their wives (9:5). For Paul, however, it is a point of honor not to ask this from the Corinthians but to preach the gospel in Corinth free of charge (cf. II Cor. 11:9f.). In the background there is perhaps a link with Jesus' instructions in Matt. 10:8: "You received without pay, give without pay."[28] The Pauline method of preaching the gospel free of charge is therefore at least as legitimate as that of Peter and the others. But on the score of effectiveness Paul is superior to all the other apostles: "But by the grace of God I am what I am, and his grace toward me was not in vain. On the contrary I worked harder than any of them. Though it was not I, but the grace of God which is with me" (I Cor. 15:10). Surfacing here is a certain rivalry between Paul, Peter, and the others in Jerusalem,[29] which is possibly a reason that in the application and citation of the Jesus-traditions Paul is more restrained than might be expected. Paul is loath to put himself in a situation where he would be staunchly citing words and stories that would only prove him to be an attentive listener to Peter and so provide grist for the mills of his opponents.

On (4): Not only I Corinthians 9 and 15:1-11 are very informative in this context, but also Rom. 10:14-17. These verses belong to the large mid-section of chs. 9–11 which deal with Israel's history and fate, and introduce a series of arguments extending from v. 14 to v. 21 that can be subsumed under the title: "Faith and Unbelief toward the Gospel." Central in the apostle's view is the unbelief of Israel, but our verses reach beyond this acute problem and are based on the traditions of gospel and apostolate which must not be overlooked: they concern the relationship of Isa. 52:7 (Nah. 2:1) and Isa. 53:1 to the apostolic message.

In the context (Rom. 10:9-13) Paul is primarily concerned about the Christian confession that in the sight of God leads to righteousness and salvation. Vv. 9-11 state that the person who in faith acknowledges Christ as Lord

---

28. On the links of I Cor. 9:14ff. with the synoptic tradition of the sending out of the disciples, cf. D. Dungan, *The Sayings of Jesus in the Churches of Paul*, 1971, 33ff., 69ff.; D. C. Allison, Jr., "The Pauline Epistles and the Synoptic Gospels: The Pattern of the Parallels," *NTS* 28, 1982 (1-32), 9f.

29. I deliberately speak only of a "certain rivalry" because also after the Antiochian incident Paul prudently steered clear of a definitive break between himself and Peter and James the Lord's brother. M. Hengel is right when against F. C. Baur he points out (*Acts and the History of Earliest Christianity*, 1979, 192) that Peter was not a nomist and

> therefore was not Paul's real opponent. He did not belong to the group of "Judaists"; according to all that we know he did not require Gentile Christians in principle to be circumcised and to observe the ritual law. . . . Indeed, at a slightly different time, he followed a similar course to the "Hellenists." This "tolerance" and indeed "liberalism" of the former Galilean fisherman probably derived from the fact that as a disciple he was particularly close to Jesus and at a later stage could not deny the memory of the freedom which he had seen embodied in the person of his master.

finds salvation in the form of righteousness; for such faith the promise of Isa. 28:16b applies, a promise over which unbelieving Israel stumbled up to now (cf. 9:33). According to v. 12, in the faith in the Christ of God the distinction between Jew and Greek is eliminated (cf. Gal. 3:27). In Christ God acts as the same gracious God for Jews and Christians alike. In the riches of his mercy and on the basis of the unconditional character of his acceptance of believers from among Jews and Gentiles God acts in accord with the pentecostal promise vouchsafed in Joel 3:5 (LXX) that everyone who calls upon the name of the Lord will be saved (v. 13). According to Phil. 2:11 and I Cor. 1:2, the ὄνομα κυρίου was borne and represented by Jesus Christ. In Rom. 10:13 Paul understands Joel 3:5 (EVV 2:32) just as christologically as does Peter's Pentecost sermon in Acts (2:17-21). In the verses which follow (Rom. 10:14-17), with the help of a chain of exegetical syllogisms, Paul links the ὄνομα κυρίου with the preaching of the apostles. The preachers of the gospel appear in v. 15 as "those who preach good news," i.e., salvation, as foretold in Isa. 52:7 (Nah. 2:1). Then in v. 16 Paul broaches the problem (which is so urgent to him in Rom. 9–11) of the rejection of the gospel by a part of Israel and states the reasons for this experience of rejection by way of reference to Isa. 53:1. For Paul the ἀκοή meant the saving announcement of the story of God's servant Jesus Christ (cf. Rom. 4:25). The "we" behind the cry of Isa. 53:1 are for him the apostolic evangelists of v. 15. V. 17 is not a redactional gloss inserted later[30] but an important (for Paul) doctrinal summary of the text: Hence faith (in the sense of the saving invocation of the ὄνομα κυρίου of v. 13) comes from the preaching of the apostle, whose preaching is based on, and authorized by, the ῥῆμα Χριστοῦ. The expression ῥῆμα Χριστοῦ probably suggested itself to Paul in v. 8 (= Deut. 30:13). He intends to say that Christ himself has authorized the apostolic message. Clearly the reference is to the mission and preaching mandate conferred upon the apostles by the risen Christ (cf. Acts 1:8; Matt. 28:18ff.; I Cor. 9:1ff.; 15:5ff.; Gal. 1:1, 11f., 15f.). Hence, according to Paul, faith, and therefore salvation and righteousness, only exist where the message of the apostle is preached (and taken to heart) in virtue of the mandate and authority of the exalted Christ. So much for the context, in which Paul speaks not only of himself but of all the apostles.

Now in the first place, as far as the traditions in this passage are concerned, the quotation from Isa. 53:1 (LXX) is noteworthy. Ἀκοή is the translation here of שמועה in the Masoretic text; in the Targum at this place one reads בשורה. Now בשורה is the common Hebrew or Aramaic equivalent

---

30. So R. Bultmann, "Glossen in Römerbrief" (1947), in *Exegetica,* ed. E. Dinkler, 1967 (278-84), 280. Opposed are E. Käsemann, *Romans,* 295; C. E. B. Cranfield, *Romans,* 536f.; and above all U. Wilckens, *An die Römer* II, 229.

for εὐαγγέλιον (or εὐαγγελία). Hence in our passage, both in the present context and on the basis of Aramaic or Hebraic usage, it is legitimate to equate ἀκοή with the gospel.[31] In I Cor. 15:3-5; Rom. 4:25; and other traditions we can tell that the interpretation of Jesus' death from within Isaiah 53 was already part of the pre-Pauline faith and tradition of the (Jerusalem) Church. On the basis of the Last Supper sayings and Mark 10:45 there even exists a possibility of tracing this interpretation back to Jesus himself. Rom. 10:16 therefore stands in a tradition with a long past and again shows that Paul's understanding of the gospel is throughout in continuity with the very oldest views held in Jerusalem. From this perspective the description of the paradosis of I Cor. 15:3ff. as εὐαγγέλιον (in v. 1) can thus be calmly appropriated for a pre-Pauline stage of the tradition as well!

Tradition-historical reflection on the quotation from Isa. 52:7 in Rom. 10:15 takes us into similar connections: In Isa. 52:7 (Nah. 2:1) there is mention, in the singular, of the messenger of glad tidings who will announce to Israel the arrival of the kingdom of God and hence salvation and redemption. Ancient Judaism gave a fourfold interpretation of these passages: (a) in 11QMelch 15ff. the reference is (probably) to the appearance of Melchizedek as heavenly Savior at the end of time;[32] (b) in other texts the reference is to the public ministry of the Messiah or (c) to Elijah as end-time forerunner of the Messiah and finally (d) to the ministry of a number of *mᵉbaśśrîm* who begin rejoicing at the advent of the rule of God.[33] In the last instance the text is interpreted in light of Isa. 52:8. Midrash Tehillim on Ps. 147:1 §2 reads:

> Isaiah has said: How lovely on the mountains are the feet of the מבשר [messengers of glad tidings]. When the Holy One . . . will be king, they will all be messengers bearing good news, as it is said, He who declares good things causes peace to be heard. . . . The Holy One . . . is king: it is fitting to praise him. Why? Because they are for the dominion of the Holy One. . . . In that hour they all rejoice and exult and praise, for they see that He is king. Hence it is written: "He who says to Zion, Thy God is King." And what follows? "The voices of thy watchmen, they lift up their voice and rejoice together" [Isa. 52:8].

31. Here it is clear how, from a tradition-historical point of view, it is disastrous for Strecker to hold (see n. 12) that the word usage of the Targums, because of its exegetical embeddedness, contributes nothing essential to the understanding of the theological use of εὐαγγέλιον in the New Testament! On the basis of the LXX ἀκοή is the common translation for שמועה (cf. e.g. Obad. 1; Jer. 10:22; 30:8; Ezek. 16:56) and is used by Paul of preaching (cf. I Thess. 2:13; Gal. 3:25).

32. Cf. J. A. Fitzmyer, "Further Light on Melchizedek from Qumran Cave 11," in idem, *Essays on the Semitic Background of the New Testament*, 1971 (245-67), 252ff. The interpretation I proposed in *PaulEv.*, 145, 149, of מבשר in 11QMelch as referring to a (or the) end-time prophet is much less probable.

33. Cf. *PaulEv.*, 148f.

A comparable understanding of the actions of several end-time εὐαγγελιζόμενοι occurs in the Targum of Isa. 40:9, and in Joel 3:5 (LXX) and in Ps. 68(67):12 (LXX).[34]

If on this basis we now look at the quotation in Paul we are struck by the fact that contrary to the Hebrew text and the Septuagint version of Isa. 52:7, Paul reads the plural: τῶν εὐαγγελιζομένων τὰ ἀγαθά. Hence Paul advocates the plural interpretation of Isa. 52:7 (Nah. 2:1) and relates it to the apostles of Jesus Christ! As was indicated just now, in Joel 3:5 the Septuagint (which differs from the Masoretic text), quoted in Rom. 10:13, likewise reads the plural εὐαγγελιζόμενοι. In Rom. 10:15, then, Paul links Joel 3:5 (LXX) with Isa. 52:7 in accordance with the typical rabbinical procedure of inference by analogy[35] and understands Isa. 52:7 in light of Joel 3:5 (LXX); and in the process both passages are interpreted christologically in light of the resurrection and the eschatological appearance of Christ (in Jerusalem): for Paul the εὐαγγελιζόμενοι of Joel are the apostolic messengers and evangelists of κύριος Ἰησοῦς Χριστός, who endows them with the Spirit and sends them out as messengers of the gospel of the beginning of his saving rule.

J. Schniewind and G. Friedrich have already showed that the view of the end-time ministry of a host of εὐαγγελιζόμενοι (attested by Jewish authors in the Targum of Isa. 40:9; Midrash Tehillim on Ps. 147:1 §2; Joel 3:5 [LXX]; and Ps. 68(67):12 [LXX] and by a Christian author, Paul, in Rom. 10:15) can be utilized for an understanding of the apostolate and for the word history of εὐαγγέλιον.[36] Following their suggestions one gets an interesting line of thought: Jesus understood himself as the messianic evangelist to the poor in accordance with Isa. 61:1 (cf. Matt. 11:2-6 and par.).[37] The messianic evange-

---

34. On these texts, cf. my *PaulEv.*, 147-49, 160-61: While Midrash Tehillim on Ps. 147:1 §2 has in view the situation of the end-time praise for the advent of the royal rule of God and the מבשרים in this sense announce God's royal rule, the reference in the Targum of Isa. 40:9 is to a group of end-time prophets whose task it is to proclaim the revelation of the royal rule of God in Israel. In the Septuagint version of Joel 3:5, the εὐαγγελιζόμενοι are the addressees called by God to Zion and the heralds of the end-time message of salvation. Also, in the Septuagint version of Ps. 68(67):12 (EVV 68:11) the εὐαγγελιζόμενοι would seem to be those authorized to be equipped with the ῥῆμα of God and thus to be proclaimers of God's victorious arrival on the mountain of God. The context of Psalm 68(67) offers a possibility of seeing the situation of ἀγαλλίασις to which Midrash Tehillim refers (cf. v. 5) together with the (prophetic) preacher's office of the εὐαγγελιζόμενοι of the Targum of Isa. 40:9 and of Joel 3:5 (LXX). One may even consider whether in his formulations in Rom. 10:14ff. Paul did not also have in mind Psalm 68(67). In any case it is clear that the tradition of the εὐαγγελιζόμενοι has a much wider Jewish base than only in the exegesis of Isa. 52:7 in the (late) Midrash Tehillim.

35. O. Hofius has in his response to the present essay correctly drawn attention to the fact that already Paul in Rom. 9:30 makes an (exegetical) argument with the help of g°zerâ šawâ, so that e.g. the ἐν Σιων of Isa. 28:16 in 9:33 can also be linked to Joel 3:5 (ἐν τῷ ὄρει Σιων) in 10:35.

36. *TDNT* II, 719.

37. In my *Reconciliation, Law, and Righteousness*, 37ff., following W. G. Kümmel ("Jesu Antwort an Johannes den Täufer. Ein Beispiel zum Methodenproblem in der Jesusforschung," in idem, *Heilsgeschehen und Geschichte* II, 1978, 177-200) I have tried to demonstrate on what

list to the poor is at the same time the herald of the kingdom of God (cf. Isa. 52:7). Hence already at an early stage, perhaps even by Jesus himself and his disciples, Jesus' message was called "the gospel (of the kingdom of God)" (Mark 1:15 [Semitism!])[38]; cf. also Matt. 4:23; 9:35; and 24:24[39]). Already in his lifetime Jesus had given his disciples a share in his preaching and had sent them out for a certain time to preach first to Israel and to heal the sick as he himself did (Matt. 10:1-6/Luke 9:1-6).[40] Luke 9:6 expressly puts it thus: And they departed and went through the villages, εὐαγγελιζόμενοι καὶ θεραπεύοντες πανταχοῦ. Already before Easter Jesus' disciples were provisionally evangelists of the kingdom and apostles.

As a result of the appearances and the pentecostal Spirit-endowment depicted in Acts 2 as the fulfillment of the promise of Joel 3:1-5 (2:28-32), the old mission was transformed for them into an eschatological mission and preaching mandate lasting until the parousia of their risen and exalted Lord. Like the מבשרים in Midrash Tehillim on Ps. 147:1 § 2, at their common meals they broke out in eschatological rejoicing at the exaltation of the crucified Jesus to messianic king (cf. Acts 2:46). Again, in Acts Luke depicts the preaching activity of the apostles with the keyword εὐαγγελίζεσθαι: . . . οὐκ ἐπαύοντο

---

grounds Matt. 11:2-6 can be traced back to Jesus himself and what novel and provocative messianic claim is embodied in the saying. In addition U. Wilckens (*An die Römer* I, 74f. [n. 12 above]) has pointed out correctly that Isa. 61:1f. is not only important for Jesus' message in Matt. 11:2-6 par. but also determines the structure of the beatitudes (Luke 6:20ff./Matt. 5:3ff.) and plays a decisive role in Luke 4:18f. In light of this one may venture to describe Jesus as "messianic evangelist to the poor." In distinction from Strecker, in the work cited in n. 12, I therefore consider it likely that Jesus arrived at his messianic self-understanding with an eye to the early Jewish exegetical tradition of Isa. 61:1f. J. A. Fitzmyer, *Further Light* (see n. 32), 246, 253, in my opinion very appropriately, points out that in 11QMelch 4ff. both Isa. 61:1f. and Isa. 52:7 must be related to the eschatological appearance of Melchizedek as heavenly redeemer. In part the rabbinate interpreted Isa. 61:1f. and Isa. 52:7 as referring to the sending of the Messiah (cf. Billerbeck II, 156). My brief summary of the Jewish exegesis of Isa. 61:1f. in *PaulEv.*, 150, is to be corrected in light of Fitzmyer.

38. The semitizing language of πιστεύειν ἐν τῷ εὐαγγελίῳ is reminiscent of the Targum of Isa. 53:1 (which already struck A. Schlatter, *Der Glaube im Neuen Testament,* [4]1927, 590); this can best be understood (see R. Schnackenburg, " 'Das Evangelium' im Verständnis des ältesten Evangelisten," in *Orientierung an Jesus. Zur Theologie der Synoptiker,* Festschrift J. Schmid, ed. P. Hoffmann, 1973 [309-24], 320f.) as a tradition which definitely could go back to Jesus himself (cf. R. Pesch, *Das Markusevangelium* I, 1976, 101f.). G. Strecker, "Literarkritische Überlegungen zum εὐαγγέλιον-Begriff im Markusevangelium," in *Eschaton und Historie* (76-89), 78ff., also refers to the traditional, semitizing character of the phrase; still he decides in favor of the Marcan authorship of the summary in Mark 1:14, 15. Only on that basis can he write in his work on the history of the word εὐαγγέλιον (see n. 12): "According to the evidence of the available texts the term εὐαγγέλιον or its Hebrew or Aramaic equivalent cannot have been a part of the message of the historical Jesus" ("Evangelium," 513 = *Eschaton und Historie,* 193). On the basis of the material adduced in n. 37 and this note I no longer, as I originally tended to do, hold this view as tenable.

39. Even if these three passages are redactional, the historical facts of Jesus' message of the kingdom are strikingly described in them.

40. Further information on the sending out of the disciples is found in my essay mentioned above in n. 23 (p. 111) and in R. Pesch, "Voraussetzungen und Anfänge der urchristlichen Mission," in *Mission im Neuen Testament,* ed. K. Kertelge, 1982 (11-70), 26ff.

διδάσκοντες καὶ εὐαγγελιζόμενοι τὸν Χριστὸν Ἰησοῦν (Acts 5:42). Once the universal character both of Jesus' atoning death for "the many" (Mark 10:45 par.; 14:24 par.) and of the resurrection rule of Jesus had been recognized, the circle of the Hellenists (Acts 6:1), Peter, and the other apostles ventured to move from Jewish mission to Gentile mission (cf. Acts 10:34ff.; 11:19ff.). Acts 1:8; Matt. 28:16ff.; and Rom. 10:17 all show that the mandate to conduct a Gentile mission was based on a ῥῆμα Χριστοῦ, i.e., on the instructions of the exalted Christ. The apostles who set out to do mission work among the Gentiles increasingly saw themselves as the eschatological evangelists who, according to the Jewish exegetical tradition of Isa. 40:9; 52:7 (Nah. 2:1); Joel 3:5; and Ps 67:12 (LXX), were to be expected at the coming of God's kingdom. It is likely that these apostles and missionaries already described their missionary message as "the gospel (of God)" in keeping with the usage among the disciples before Easter. In the light of Easter this gospel was for them simultaneously "the gospel of Jesus Christ": they proclaimed the earthly Jesus as the risen and coming Lord of the world. Mark 8:35 and 10:29, but also 13:10 (and 14:9) document their understanding of the message.

Paul took over this terminology from these apostles and missionaries and provided it with his own emphases. Hence in Rom. 10:14-17, as in I Cor. 9:1f. and 15:8ff., he articulates not only his own understanding of the apostolate but also that which linked him with the missionaries to the Gentiles, with Peter and others in Jerusalem. Under these circumstances the interweaving of the terminology of gospel and that of mission is already pre-Pauline. Hence it is easy to understand why everywhere, in his churches and according to Galatians 2 also in Jerusalem and Antioch, Paul can now take for granted an understanding of the word εὐαγγέλιον. What we are dealing with is mission terminology that proceeded from Jerusalem and was current in the early Church also apart from Paul.[41]

Of course what I have presented is only a tradition-historical reconstruction, but it does make intelligible the various textual and traditional data before us. To an astonishing degree it confirms the perspectives on the development

41. The early New Testament materials nowhere show any trace of a direct or an indirect connection of the εὐαγγέλιον with the emperor cult (on this, cf. *PaulEv.*, 196ff.). Of course for the Greek-speaking addressees of Gentile missions connotative associations with emperor worship cannot be excluded. But if the majority of the Gentile converts originally came from the circle of the "God-fearers" (cf. W. Schmithals, *Der Römerbrief als historisches Problem*, 1975, 69ff.), then for this group of people, whose pre-conditioning was Jewish, the intellectual relationship of εὐαγγέλιον/εὐαγγελίζεσθαι to the synagogal tradition of interpretation and to the Septuagint was closer than that to the emperor-cult. Harnack did not for nothing soon give up the derivation of the missionary use of εὐαγγέλιον from the emperor cult, which he initially advocated, and turn to the view of the history of the word sketched at the outset of the present essay (cf. *PaulEv.*, 11f., 22ff.). Strecker's renewal of the attempt at derivation that Harnack recognized as wrong (see n. 12) cannot be verified either in tradition-history or in the history of missions.

of tradition that were sketched by Harnack and elaborated by J. Schniewind and G. Friedrich in *TDNT*.[42]

4. The Distinctive Character of the Pauline Gospel

Both in I Cor. 15:1-11 and in Romans Paul is concerned to demonstrate the continuities between his own preaching and that of the original apostles. He does this without deviating from the message of Christ that was shaped for him by the Damascus revelation. In his confrontations with critics and opponents he even has occasion from time to time to speak of "our" or of "my" gospel. This word usage can be traced from I Thessalonians (1:5) through the letters to the Corinthians (cf. II Cor. 4:3) right into the letter to the Romans (2:16; 16:25) and from there into the deutero-Pauline letters (II Thess. 2:14; II Tim. 2:8). It points to the fact that the apostle absolutely sensed that his gospel-preaching had a specific cast of its own and was prepared to fight consciously for its legitimacy.

Already in I Thessalonians we recognize this struggle on behalf of "his" gospel and from the letter to the Galatians on we see it exhibited plainly. In the course of this struggle Paul did not sidestep the confrontation with Peter and accepted the break with his Antiochian friends in the bargain (Gal. 2:11ff.). After Galatians, the letter to the Romans also mirrors this struggle. The famous utterance of Rom. 1:16: "For I am not ashamed of the gospel . . ." is most easily explained in the situation of the letter if Paul himself knows of resistance to his gospel in Rome (cf. Rom. 3:8; 16:17f.) and from the beginning of his great apologetic letter wants to make clear that also in Rome he intends to confront his critics and has decided to stand by the power of the gospel as it has been

---

42. *TDNT* II, 707-37. The line of development I sketched above is historically more satisfying than the attempt I made some years ago in *PaulEv.*, 210ff. to look for the origins of the Christian use of εὐαγγέλιον and εὐαγγελίζειν/εὐαγγελίζεσθαι in Rev. 10:7; 14:6. Strecker, "Evangelium," 515ff. (= *Eschaton und Historie*, 195ff.), has rightly criticized this attempt. However, his assertion that the neutral meaning of εὐαγγελίζειν in the sense of "to proclaim" "definitely fits the Greek-Hellenistic tradition" ("Evangelium," 516 = *Eschaton und Historie*, 196) is philologically weak.

As evidence for such neutral usage Strecker (like Friedrich, *TDNT* II, 711) can only refer to a fictitious letter of the orator and sophist Alciphron of the second century AD (*Ep.* 2.9.2), in which one music lover writes to another that in the late afternoon his herd of goats listened attentively to his flute music. The letter closes by saying: ταῦτά σε οὖν εὐαγγελίζομαι, φίλον ἄνδρα συνειδέναι βουλόμενος ὅτι μοι μουσικόν ἐστι τὸ αἰπόλιον. A. R. Brenner and F. H. Fobes, in their critical edition (*The Letters of Alciphron, Aelian and Philostratus*, 1949, 101), purposely translate this sentence: "Now I am telling you this as a piece of good news, for I wish my friend also to know that my herd of goats loves music." This one rhetorically stylized instance in Alciphron is not sufficient, surely, to establish a general attrition of εὐαγγελίζεσθαι to a mere ἀγγέλλειν in Hellenistic Greek! Rev. 10:7 and 14:6 are couched in Jewish Greek and εὐαγγέλιον αἰώνιον in 14:6 is the eternally valid message of judgment. This is Jewish, not Greek, word usage.

revealed to him. In the light of this determination one also gets a clear meaning from the embattled text of 2:16. Paul has been charged with preaching a message of cheap grace and with rendering sin and judgment harmless. In reply he refers pointedly in 2:16 to the fact that precisely in his gospel there is mention of judgment, the final judgment of God through Jesus Christ (cf. 6:12-23; 8:31-39; 14:10-12).

Paul's letters, with their allusions to preaching schemes,[43] doctrinal instruction,[44] and constantly pressing Church problems,[45] only give a rough picture of his actual work as a preacher and missionary. Paul said and taught a great deal more than the letters document! Nevertheless, they do give clear information concerning the basic outline of his message.

From the beginning the Pauline gospel is concerned to proclaim Christ as the Son of God who by his atoning death liberated us from sin, calls us to the obedience of faith, and empowers us to hope for salvation from the coming judgment of the wrath of God. From his Damascus call on (see above) this christological center controls Paul's gospel and is demonstrably present throughout Paul's letters, beginning with I Thess. 1:9f. The Pauline gospel is the gospel of the Christ "whom God made our wisdom, our righteousness, and sanctification and redemption" (I Cor. 1:30). If one calls the Pauline gospel "the gospel of justification" one must proceed from this christological center or lose sight of the bond uniting Paul's letters (including the deutero-Pauline letters). The theme "justification through the atoning death of Jesus Christ the servant of God" was already given to Paul in the confessional and baptismal tradition handed down to him (cf. II Cor. 5:21; Rom. 3:25f.; 4:25). He seized upon this theme and gave unmistakable expression to it in the light of his experience of being called (Phil. 3:4-11).

To the degree that for Paul Christ is the promised Messiah and Son of God (cf. only II Cor. 1:19f.; Rom. 1:3f.; 9:5; 15:8)[46] and faith in him accords with God's will to save since Abraham (cf. Gal. 3:6ff.; Rom. 4:3ff.), εὐαγγέλιον and ἐπαγγελία are intrinsically related for Paul: the gospel of God was promised beforehand through God's prophets in the Scriptures (Rom. 1:2) and is now, through the preaching of the apostle, made public (1:5; 16:26).

How the law and Christ are related is a question with which Paul wrestled from the moment of his calling. Interestingly enough, however, one nowhere finds in his letters the antithetical pair of terms "law and gospel," which is so familiar

---

43. Cf. H. Conzelmann, *An Outline of the Theology of the New Testament,* 1969, 164ff.
44. Ibid., 164.
45. Cf. II Cor. 11:28.
46. On the Pauline use of Χριστός, cf. M. Hengel, "Erwägungen zum Sprachgebrauch von Χριστός bei Paulus und in der 'vorpaulinischen' Überlieferung," in *Paul and Paulinism,* Festschrift C. K. Barrett, ed. M. D. Hooker and S. G. Wilson, 1982, 135-59.

in theology. It is not until Marcion that anyone looking at Paul speaks of a *separatio legis et evangelii!*[47] In place of such a *separatio,* it is Paul's concern consistently to preach Christ as the end of the law (as way of salvation) and at the same time to pronounce an unrestricted Yes to the commandment of God proclaimed by Christ himself. Pauline reflection on the relationship between the law and Christ found its most mature and at the same time its boldest expression in the letter to the Romans, namely in Rom. 7:1–8:11. If I am right, Paul here teaches that Christians, in virtue of the atoning death of Jesus, have died to the law as a way of salvation. Precisely on that account they can (and must) in the power of the Spirit follow the good, holy, and righteous command of God, which Christ freed from the oppressive perversion of its intent that sin effected from the time of the Fall (Gen. 3) and which he thus at last made really effective as an aid to living. By his sacrificial death Christ broke the power of sin and thus liberated the sinner from guilt and the law from its encirclement by sin. It is for that reason that, for Paul, Christ is simultaneously the end of the law as a way of salvation and the preacher of the law as the way of love (cf. e.g. Gal. 5:13-26; 6:2; Rom. 12:14ff.; 13:8ff.)! The practice of the ancient Church—one that seems at first blush so odd—of speaking of the gospel as the καινὸς νόμος τοῦ κυρίου ἡμῶν Ἰησοῦ Χριστοῦ, ἄνευ ζυγοῦ ἀνάγκης ὤν (Barn. 2:6), though not simply Pauline, is explicable only if one does not just read Paul with Reformation eyes but allows him also, and first of all, to preach his own view of the law and the gospel of Christ.

To me it seems that Paul could not have arrived at his dialectical view of the law (which I have sketched briefly here) without knowledge of the Jesus-tradition. It is not accidental that in Gal. 6:2 and I Cor. 9:21 he speaks of the νόμος Χριστοῦ as the alternative to Jewish legalism and Gentile lawlessness. But let us not pursue this special question any further. It is enough to point out that Jesus' interpretation of the love commandment as love of one's enemies comes clearly to the fore precisely in the letter to the Romans (cf. Rom. 12:14ff.).

For the apostle there is both an ἀρχή and a τέλος to his gospel message: Christ is more than both. In Phil. 4:15, with reference to the beginnings of his mission in Philippi, Paul speaks of the ἀρχή. Rom. 10:17 has in view the calling and the sending out of the apostles, and Rom. 15:19 the missionary region Paul had to traverse. For Paul the origin of the gospel lay in the missionary mandate of the risen Christ, so that the gospel preaching of the apostles, including that of Paul, had its geographic beginning in Jerusalem.[48] The τέλος of the gospel

---

47. Cf. Harnack, *Constitution,* 321-24.
48. In light of Rom. 15:19 the significance of the Jerusalem Council for Paul is clear even beyond what we read in Galatians 2. "Behind Rom. 15:19 there is a redemptive-historical concept of mission. One may well ask whether this concept as such did not have its birth in the negotiations of the Apostolic Council (Gal. 2:9)—or in any case its first official definition—and from there gained its ecumenical force and validity" (Wilckens, *An die Römer* III, 1982, 120).

which Paul must preach will have been achieved when the πλήρωμα τῶν ἐθνῶν has found its way into the salvation community composed of Jews and Gentiles (Rom. 11:25). The same is meant when in Rom. 15:16 the apostle writes that he is the priestly servant of the gospel to present to God the acceptable offering of the Gentiles (προσφορὰ τῶν ἐθνῶν). After this has happened all Israel may receive salvation through the Christ who will come from Zion as messianic Savior (11:26f.).[49] This entire redemptive historical-apocalyptic concept strongly resembles the tradition attested in Mark 13:10 (par.) that before the parousia of the Son of Man the gospel must first be preached to all the Gentile nations. Paul did not live to see the day of the parousia for which he longed in all his letters. The time of his gospel reaches beyond the span of his life.

5. Aftereffects of the Pauline Gospel

The aftereffects of the Pauline gospel are quite clearly perceptible in the deutero-Pauline letters but also show their ripples in I Peter and in Ignatius.

Terminologically the word "gospel" in the deutero-Pauline letters is closely akin to the word usage in the undisputed letters and in part identical with it. In the late Pauline tradition, from Rom. 16:25f. on, the gospel is understood as the redemptive-historical μυστήριον that the apostle had to proclaim around the world. Its essence is redemption through Jesus Christ and participation in the kingdom of God in the heavens that comes with it (cf. Col. 1:5, 23; Eph. 6:19). This view is much less removed from Paul than some have occasionally thought. Repeatedly the apostle puts his gospel message on a line with the prophetic preaching of the Old Testament (Gal. 1:15f.; I Cor. 9:16; and with particular clarity Rom. 1:1-7); for him it is the prophetic message of salvation in and through Christ that was promised long before and has at last become publicly known. For Paul the gospel stands in an apocalyptic horizon of expectation and appears, in II Cor. 4:3ff., for instance, as a revelation still veiled in the word, to which only those can listen who have not been blinded by "the god of this world." Hence, in Rom. 16:25f., Col. 1:26, and Eph. 6:19 one finds explicitly formulated that which had already been thought and believed in Paul.

I Tim. 1:11 reads like a resumption of II Cor. 4:4; II Tim. 2:8 may refer back to the prescript in Romans and the Christ-formula employed there (Rom. 1:3f.); and the entire fragment of II Tim. 1:6-12, with its double reference to the gospel in vv. 8 and 10, is a testamentary summary of genuine Pauline utterances like Phil. 1:7, 27; Phlm. 9-13 and the basic tenets of the Pauline soteriology of

---

49. On Rom. 11:25ff., cf. the brilliant article by O. Hofius, "Das Evangelium und Israel. Erwägungen zu Röm 9–11," *ZTK* 83, 1986, 297-324.

justification. We have already clarified above the fact that in the Pastoral letters the strongly accentuated character of the gospel as "sound doctrine" (cf. I Tim. 1:10; II Tim. 4:3, etc.) and as "what has been entrusted" (= παραθήκη; cf. I Tim. 6:20; II Tim. 1:12, 14) picks up and reinforces genuine Pauline utterances.[50]

Since reference to the apostolic message of Christ as εὐαγγέλιον τοῦ θεοῦ is not initially of Pauline origin but may have been current in Jerusalem and Antioch before and independently of Paul, I Pet. 4:17 (cf. with 2:8) need not only be interpreted in terms of Paul. The book of Acts strikingly uses the missionary expression "gospel" (which appears only twice in Acts) not only for Paul's message (Acts 20:24) but also for that of Peter (Acts 15:7; cf. with 10:36-43)!

In the letters of Ignatius as well Pauline and extra-Pauline influences seem to mingle. For all its independence Philad. 9:2 runs parallel to the redemptive-historical approach of the (preached) gospel in Rom. 1:1-7 and in late Pauline traditions like Rom. 16:25ff. Philad. 5:1f. is probably to be understood similarly when it describes and emphasizes the gospel as the σάρξ Ἰησοῦ (the embodiment of Jesus' earthly manifestation) and states that the prophets already pointed to the gospel in their preaching. Although this way of speaking may derive support from both Rom. 1:3f. and I Cor. 15:1ff., it no longer sounds purely Pauline. In Philad. 8:2 the written Old Testament and the orally transmitted gospel of the cross of Jesus, his death and resurrection, seem at first blush to be juxtaposed, something that could well be explained on the basis of Paul. I do not think one should simply reject the idea that there is in the phrase ἐν τῷ εὐαγγελίῳ οὐ πιστεύω an allusion to Mark 1:15[51] and hence, by implication, early evidence of a written form of the gospel. As for the two remaining passages in which Ignatius speaks of "gospel," Smyrn. 5:1 and 7:2, Harnack already wondered whether "gospel" here had not already taken on the sense of the (written) history of Jesus.[52] J. A. Fisher, in his edition of the letters of Ignatius, also does not wish to exclude this possibility though he prefers the interpretation "the Church's message of Christ."[53] A glance at Ignatius's letters as a whole shows that Ignatius already assumes as sources Matthew, probably also Mark, Acts, the Gospel of John, and the letters of Paul.[54] His use of the word "gospel" therefore need not be explained only in terms of Paul's usage.

---

50. More on the understanding of the gospel in the Pastoral letters is found in P. Trummer, *Die Paulustradition der Pastoralbriefe*, 1978, 130; H. von Lips, *Glaube-Gemeinde-Amt*, 1979, 40ff.

51. Cf. W. Bauer, *Die Briefe des Ignatius von Antiochia und der Polykarpbrief*, 1920, 261.

52. Harnack, *Constitution*, 319f.

53. J. A. Fisher, *Die Apostolischen Väter* I, 1976, 201, n. 36 (cf. 209, n. 31, 211, n. 48).

54. Ibid., 122.

6. The Outlook

We have not been able to discover a direct relationship between Paul's use of the word "gospel" and the New Testament Gospels. The word occurs 8 times in Mark's Gospel (Mark 1:1, 14, 15; 8:35; 10:29; 13:10; 14:9; 16:15); it is quite characteristic therefore for Mark and his tradition! By comparison, Matthew only uses it 4 times (Matt. 4:23; 9:35; 24:14; 26:13), whereas Luke and John avoid it altogether. For Mark and his tradition the close connection of the history of Jesus with the later missionary expression εὐαγγέλιον is characteristic. One cannot explain this result merely in light of Paul's practice. Under these circumstances the question arises whether the formulations can be satisfactorily explained in some other way. But that question lies outside the scope of this paper. In the attempt to find an explanation I would only suggest that Jesus himself, the pre-Pauline and para-Pauline missionary message, and—particularly—Peter not be neglected. That Peter's missionary message in Acts 15:7 (with retrospective reference to 10:36-43) is also described as εὐαγγέλιον is, in my opinion, more than an accident, and not merely a tendentious Lucan way of speaking. In comparison with Paul, Peter's special distinction was his relationship to the earthly Jesus and his role as initial witness to the resurrection. His missionary message could therefore be directly based on Jesus in a way that was not possible for Paul. The situation to which we are referring is mirrored in Acts 10:36-43.

What we have before us in Acts 10:36-43 is in no way merely a paradigm of "preaching" created by Luke (and referring back to Luke's Gospel) but above all a tradition-saturated presentation of how on the mission field the story of Jesus was told and taught to Gentiles.[55] As far as the highly disputed opening sentence is concerned, H. Riesenfeld[56] has opened the way to a truly natural understanding: τὸν λόγον is to be linked with καταλαμβάνομαι in v. 34 and is to be understood in apposition with the ὅτι-sentence in vv. 34f. Riesenfeld translates: "Truly I realize that God does not show partiality, but in every nation anyone who fears him and does what is right is acceptable to him; (this is) the

---

55. U. Wilckens, in *Die Missionsreden der Apostelgeschichte*, 1961, 69, after having commented on Acts 10:37-43 that "here Luke transformed the pattern of missionary preaching into the formal scheme of the gospel as he himself understood it," pointed out later, in the preface to the third edition of his book (1974), that further work had to be done on the question (to which he had not been able till then to supply a satisfactory solution) of the pre-Lucan tradition and Lucan composition in the speeches of Acts. Unfortunately, in 1974 he did not have available to him G. N. Stanton's dissertation, *Jesus of Nazareth in New Testament Preaching*, 1974. J. Roloff, *Die Apostelgeschichte*, 1981, 168, writes on our text: "At the very least in its conception but also in some of its formulations the scheme followed in vv. 39-41 probably reproduces extant traditions." I. H. Marshall, *The Acts of the Apostles*, 1980, 190ff. and G. Schneider, *Die Apostelgeschichte* II, 1982, 63f., 74-79, work out the traditional elements of the text more clearly.

56. H. Riesenfeld, "The Text of Acts X. 36," in *Text and Interpretation*, Festschrift M. Black, ed. E. Best and R. McL. Wilson, 1979, 191-94.

word which he sent to the children of Israel, proclaiming good news of peace through Jesus Christ—he is Lord of all. You know what took place throughout all Judea, beginning from Galilee after baptism which John preaches. . . ."[57]

G. N. Stanton has called attention to the interesting exegetical background of Peter's speech in vv. 36-43.[58] In it the story of Jesus is presented purely on the basis of quotations from Scripture: in order to speak successively of Jesus' mission, baptism, and Spirit-anointing, his works of healing, his death on the cross, his resurrection and appearances,[59] a midrash-like concatenation of Ps. 107:20; Isa. 52:7 (Nah. 2:1 LXX); Isa. 61:1; Deut. 21:22 and Hos. 6:2 forms the main thread. This exegetical framework and narrative paradigm are certainly not in the first place Lucan but traditional. The presentation of the story of Jesus, in its outline, is strikingly similar to the Gospel of Mark and must, according to Acts 10:34, be especially linked with Peter. Especially of interest to us is the relation of Isa. 52:7 (Nah. 2:1) in v. 36 to God's own message of salvation and peace, which assumed historical form in the sending of Jesus Christ. In Rom. 10:15 Paul characteristically offered a different interpretation of Isa. 52:7 (Nah. 2:1 LXX). Here in Acts 10:36ff. the story of Jesus appears literally as the "gospel of God" and hence as fulfillment of the Scriptures. The connections with Mark 1:1, 14, 15 are obvious and must not be ignored in the story of the origin and intention of the use of "gospel" in Mark and the headings of the Gospels.

Stated positively: in Acts 10:36-43 (+ 15:7) we catch sight of the gospel (of Peter) which was just as much εὐαγγέλιον τοῦ θεοῦ as that of Paul; it has connections with Paul's gospel and nevertheless makes a different use of the narrative of Jesus' history than Paul does in his Torah-critical teaching and preaching, which focused on the cross and resurrection of Jesus. Our (Petrine?) scheme presents a much stronger incentive for writing Gospels than Paul's. The Church needs both forms of proclamation to preserve, and ever to regain afresh, its identity as Church of Jesus Christ.

57. Op. cit. (see n. 56), 193. Schneider, op. cit. (n. 55), 75f. also agrees with Riesenfeld's proposal.

58. Op. cit. (see n. 55), 67-85, esp. 75.

59. Acts 10:41-43 then clearly shows the Lucan redaction of tradition. Cf. with Luke 24:30ff., 43.

The Gospel Genre

Robert Guelich

1. The Question of Genre

Much confusion surrounds the discussion of the Gospels from the standpoint of literary genre. Some of the confusion is endemic to the broader discipline of literary criticism itself. Not only does one look in vain for a precise, universally acceptable definition of genre but the function of genre within literary criticism appears to be multiple.[1]

In the classical and neo-classical periods, genre had a *normative* function of setting the parameters within which one wrote and by which a text was critiqued. In modern literary criticism genre has a more *descriptive* than regulative function. For example, in the words of R. Warren and A. Wellek, the theory of genre offers a "principle of ordering" for classifying literature according to "specifically literary types of organization or structure."[2] This usage of genre provides a means of identification and classification of literary works and periods. But even more recently, the discussion has focused on genre in its *interpretive* role as the means by which one comprehends a work. For example, E. D. Hirsch defines an "intrinsic genre" (the one germane to the text) as ". . . that sense of the whole by means of which an interpreter can correctly understand any part of its determinancy,"[3] and F. Kermode more loosely describes a genre as ". . . a context of expectation, an 'internal probability system'" that helps one comprehend a sentence, book, or life.[4]

---

1. W. Doty, "The concept of Genre in Literary Analysis," in *Proceedings: Society of Biblical Literature,* 1972, II, 413-47.
2. R. Warren and A. Wellek, *Theory of Literature,* ³1977, 226. Further, "genre (is) a grouping of literary works based . . . upon outer form (specific meter or structure) and also upon inner form (attitude, tone, purpose . . .)" (231).
3. E. D. Hirsch, *Validity in Interpretation,* 1967, 86.
4. F. Kermode, *The Genesis of Secrecy: On the Interpretation of Narrative,* 1979, 162-63, n. 20.

Despite the many definitions of genre and seeking to avoid the pitfalls of the discussion, one can note certain features of genre relevant to the discussion of the Gospels that seem to reflect a consensus within literary criticism. First, genre has to do with a text as a whole, as a composite of specific traits or characteristics which are formal and material. In other words, the genre of a text consists of its literary structure and organization (the formal components) and of its content with various levels of possible meanings (the material components). Second, genre is a comparative or derivative concept. It has to do not only with the text in question but with other similar or dissimilar texts. As a category or classification (both *explicitly* for the critic who seeks to identify and classify and *implicitly* for the interpreter who reads a text in terms of the "sense of the whole") genre stems from one's conscious or unconscious observation of formally and materially similar or dissimilar texts. Therefore, a genre must consist of more than one text either as a category to which one assigns the text or as the "context of expectation" from which one interprets a text.

Within biblical criticism, not only does the quest of the Gospels' genre suffer from the lack of consensus within literary criticism about the nature and function of genre, but biblical criticism also adds its own terminological complications. At times, form criticism appears to use "form" and "genre" interchangeably.[5] It is not unusual to hear references to the "form" (= Gattung) of the Gospels as well as references to the "genre" (= Gattung) of parables. Are "form" and "genre" interchangeable terms? Even more confusing, however, is the contention by many that the Gospels are *sui generis.* But how exclusive is *sui generis*—especially in view of contemporary hermeneutics, which defines genre as the "context of expectation" or the "sense of the whole" by which the text becomes intelligible? Where and how does one gain a sense of the whole without literary counterparts?

For the purposes of this paper, we shall use "genre" as a broad category to mean the text of the Gospels seen as a whole, a composite of numerous parts or "forms."[6] Furthermore, genre refers to the work as a whole viewed in comparison with other literary works. To that extent, genre will function in this essay *descriptively* as the means of identifying and classifying the Gospels within their literary matrix. The natural consequence, however, of this descriptive task has definite *interpretative* implications, since a work's genre inherently qualifies its interpretation. Consequently, by classifying the Gospels according

5. K. Koch, *The Growth of the Biblical Tradition,* 1969, 3-6, who uses "Gattung" and "Form" interchangeably. The English translation does not use "genre" but alternates between "type" and "form" as the translation for *Gattung.* Cf. *Was ist Formgeschichte?* 1964, 3-6.

6. J. A. Baird, "Genre Analysis as a Method of Historical Criticism," in *Proceedings* (n. 1 above) II, 386-87, argues that since Gunkel, "Form" refers to the smaller, individual units of which a "genre" (Gattung), the work as a whole, is composed.

to genre, one qualifies their interpretation and in so doing uses genre in its more *normative* role which regulates what is appropriate and inappropriate to the genre (cf. the "gospels" of the Nag Hammadi codices).

But can one speak of a gospel genre? Four canonical Gospels, each with its own title as "The Gospel according to . . . ," five works in the Nag Hammadi codices bearing the name "gospel,"[7] and numerous apocryphal gospels from the second century[8] all suggest the possibility of a gospel genre. A closer examination, however, reveals the distinctive form and content of the four canonical Gospels. Some find that only two of these actually qualify as "gospels"—Mark and John.[9] And W. Marxsen has gone so far as to suggest that Mark alone qualifies as a gospel,[10] a situation that would make the designation of one Gospel a "genre"—a contradiction in terms.[11] Is it possible then, as has been suggested, that the Gospels do not represent a distinct genre but carry a special label as "gospels" while belonging to another literary genre(s)?

Stated simply, therefore, our question is twofold: To what literary genre do the Gospels belong? and What bearing does the genre have for our understanding and interpretation of the Gospels?

2. Review of the Discussion

Numerous answers have been given to the question about the Gospels' genre.[12] But the variety of answers ultimately fall into two categories—one analogical, the other derivational. On the one hand, some have sought the Gospels' genre by aligning one or more Gospels with other literary genres. In other words, the Gospels find their analogy in other literature and belong to that literary genre. On the other hand, some, convinced that the Gospels are unique, *sui generis,* have sought to explain this distinctive genre in terms of how the gospel genre came into being.

7. The Gospel of Truth, Gospel of Thomas, Gospel of Philip, Gospel of the Egyptians, and Gospel of Mary (*BGU* 8502, 1).

8. See E. Hennecke and W. Schneemelcher, *New Testament Apocrypha* I, ET 1963.

9. E.g. J. M. Robinson, "On the *Gattung* of Mark (and John)," in *Jesus and Man's Hope*, ed. D. Buttrick, 1970, I, 99-129; idem, "The Johannine Trajectory," in *Trajectories Through Early Christianity*, 1971, 166-68. Cf. H. Koester, "One Jesus and Four Primitive Gospels," in *Trajectories*, 161-62.

10. W. Marxsen, *Mark the Evangelist*, 1969, 150, n. 106; see N. Perrin, "The Literary Gattung 'Gospel'—Some Observations," *ExpT* 82, 1970-71, 7.

11. Noted by Marxsen, *Mark*, 109 and R. Gundry, "Recent Investigations into the Literary Genre 'Gospel,' " in *New Dimensions in New Testament Study*, ed. R. Longenecker and M. C. Tenney, 1974, 114, but apparently overlooked by Perrin, "Gattung," 7.

12. See reviews in R. Gundry, "Investigations," 97-114; H. C. Kee, *Community of the New Age: Studies in Mark's Gospel*, 1977, 17-30; W. S. Vorster, *Wat is'n Evangelie?* 1981; and P. L. Shuler, *A Genre for the Gospels: The Biographical Character of Matthew*, 1982, 1-23.

2.1 *Analogical:* Beginning with a review of the "analogical" approach, one may further divide these studies into three groupings. Some have found the gospel genre in (1) Semitic literature, others in (2) Hellenistic literature, and still others in the broader perspective of (3) literary criticism in general.[13]

2.1.1 Some recent treatments of Mark's Gospel, assumed to be the earliest Gospel in these cases, within the Semitic context have closely associated this work with *apocalyptic* thought and literature.[14] While affirming the literary uniqueness of Mark,[15] each has explained and interpreted Mark from an apocalyptic perspective. So much so that N. Perrin has actually stated that Mark is "essentially an apocalypse,"[16] and W. Kelber has referred to the Gospel as an "apocalyptic vision."[17] H. C. Kee, much more guarded,[18] attributes Mark's approach to Scripture and the resultant self-understanding of his community and its role in God's purpose[19] to the "eschatological exegesis" of Jewish prophetic-apocalyptic tradition. This background, with its concern for the eschatological "consummation of the divine purpose in history," the "confirmation of God's true agent through signs and wonders," and the "dogmatic conviction of apocalyptic literature that God's chosen agent must suffer" to bring about the New Age, helped Mark "shape the structure of the Gospel."[20]

Since Mark obviously lacks many of the essential formal[21] and material[22] characteristics of an apocalypse, one could hardly classify it under that literary genre. None of the above mentioned actually assigns Mark to such a genre. Yet since genre also refers hermeneutically to how one interprets the work as seen as a whole and not simply to formal literary categories and since each of these noted above has interpreted the whole of Mark from such a context, the

13. This review does not purpose to be exhaustive regarding either the options suggested or the proponents of each. It intends simply to be representative of trends and scholars.

14. E.g. E. Marxsen, *Mark;* N. Perrin, "Gattung," 4-7; idem, *A Modern Pilgrimage in New Testament Christology,* 1974, 107; W. Kelber, "The History of the Kingdom in Mark—Aspects of Markan Eschatology," in *Proceedings* (n. 1 above) I, 86; idem, *The Kingdom in Mark: A New Place and Time,* 1974; H. C. Kee, *Community,* 64-67, 106-44.

15. E.g. Perrin, "Gattung," 4; *Christology,* 106-7. H. C. Kee, "Aretalogy and Gospel," *JBL* 92, 1973, 422; idem, *Community,* 30, follows A. Wilder: "(The gospel) is the only wholly new genre created by the Church and the author of Mark receives credit for it" (*The Language of the Gospel: Early Christian Rhetoric,* 1964).

16. "Historical Criticism, Literary Criticism and Hermeneutics: The Interpretation of the Parables of Jesus and the Gospel of Mark Today," *JR* 52, 1972, 365-66, 472.

17. "History," 86.

18. But note his rather infelicitous statement: "Written in a hagiographical style, *like other apocalyptic writings,* the Gospel of Mark . . . ," *Community,* 76 (italics added).

19. *Community,* 49.

20. "Aretalogy," 422.

21. E.g. pseudonymity, bizarre use of vision and or symbols, farewell discourse, posture of narrating past events as though future prophecy, etc.

22. No evidence of sequential dualism between present evil age and future life to come, no accompanying pessimism or ethical passivity; rather a strong sense of the presence of the New Age in and through Jesus' ministry in the midst of the evil age.

avoidance of the generic label "apocalypse" becomes moot. They in actuality treat Mark as an apocalypse.[23] The validity of this interpretation, however, runs aground on the formal and material discontinuity of Mark with the apocalyptic genre.

Coming from an entirely different tack and disputing the apocalyptic reading of Mark's Gospel, D. Lührmann has suggested that Mark's Gospel depicts Jesus and his ministry in the genre of biography, but a particular form of biography, the "biography of a righteous person."[24] Aware of the negative reaction among biblical critics to the notion of biography, Lührmann, following K. Baltzer, distinguishes between an "ideal biography" and contemporary or Hellenistic biographies. The former, often seen in Jewish writings concerning the prophets,[25] accents the "typical" or representative aspects of the subject in contrast to the latter, which accent the specific distinguishing characteristics of the individual.[26] Lührmann, by noting the shift of the prophet or servant role in Isa. 42:1 to the role of the righteous one in Wis. 2:12-20 (cf. Mark 1:11) and by noting the application of the plight of the righteous, especially from the Psalms, to Jesus' passion, concludes that Mark has structured his tradition "biographically" as the "typical" or paradigmatic way of the righteous.[27] In so doing, Mark summons the reader to identify with Jesus portrayed as the exemplary, suffering righteous person.[28]

Despite the strength of this thesis in recognizing the application of motifs from the suffering righteous in the Old Testament and intertestamental literature to Jesus' work in Mark, the parallels to such a precise literary genre do break down. Lührmann gives few characteristics of this genre apart from the exemplary suffering of a righteous person. But Mark differs considerably from the references in the Psalms and Wisdom to such a "biography." Rather than an anonymous figure whose exemplary life encourages others and calls for imitation, Mark's Gospel opens with a clear declaration of the subject's identity (1:1). In fact, the concrete, episodic rather than abstract, idealized character of Mark's narrative from beginning to end conflicts fundamentally with an "ideal biography." Furthermore, would such a genre sufficiently account for the word and works of Jesus and the significant, though debated, role of the disciples throughout the Gospel? Rather than a genre from which to interpret the parts, we seem to have a constituent part that has been inappropriately defined as the genre of the whole.

23. So D. Via's critique in *Kerygma and Comedy in the New Testament*, 1975, 78-90.
24. "Biographie des Gerechten als Evangelium," *WuD*, 1977, 23-50.
25. Lührmann takes his lead from the work of K. Baltzer, *Die Biographie des Propheten*, 1975.
26. Lührmann, "Biographie," 37. Consequently, the anonymous Servant of God in Isaiah serves as an example of such an "ideal biography."
27. Ibid., 39.
28. Ibid., 43-44.

Somewhat related to Lührmann's suggestion, E. Schweizer noted, almost in passing, that the Old Testament *historical works,* Jonah in particular, seem to offer the closest parallel to Mark's genre.[29] Baltzer goes further and includes Mark in his discussion of the biographies of the prophets,[30] and R. Brown hints at an analogy between Mark's account and the Elisha story.[31] Yet none of these develops the analogy to the level of assigning Mark to a comparable Old Testament genre. By contrast, M. Kline[32] has found the model for Mark's Gospel in the Exodus account and J. W. Bowman in the Passover *haggadah.*[33] Both, however, fail to establish the generic character of the respective Markan counterpart as well as the direct correspondence of Mark to any such model.[34] Consequently, Mark stands without a convincing generic parallel in Jewish literature.

2.1.2. Since Justin referred to the Gospels as "memoirs of the Apostles,"[35] the Gospels have been variously associated with the *biographical literature* of the Graeco-Roman world. Indeed, a "biographical" reading of the Gospels seems most natural even today for those who initially discover the Gospels. Certainly this perception underlay the nineteenth-century quests for the historical Jesus. And at a time when such a view of the Gospels was coming under severe attack in biblical criticism, C. H. Votaw wrote an extensive article in 1915 called "The Gospels and Contemporary Biographies."[36]

Recognizing the diversity in the broader category of "biography" as a generic designation, Votaw distinguished between "popular biography" and "historical biography,"[37] concluding that the Gospels clearly fell short of the latter category. Rather they belonged to the "popular biographies," along with

29. *The Good News According to Mark,* n.d., 24.

30. *Biographie der Propheten,* 85-89.

31. "Jesus and Elisha," *Perspective* 12, 1971, 85-104.

32. M. G. Kline, "The Old Testament Origins of the Gospel Genre," *WTJ* 38, 1975, 1-27.

33. *The Gospel of Mark: The New Christian Jewish Passover Haggadah,* 1965.

34. Among other suggested "models" for the Gospels with roots in Jewish life and literature, one should note the calendrical approaches of P. Carrington, *The Primitive Christian Calendar: A Study in the Making of the Markan Gospel,* 1952, and more recently M. D. Goulder's work, *The Evangelist's Calendar: A Lectionary Explanation of the Development of Scripture,* 1974: see 199-201 for his brief excursus on Mark. These works are fraught with assumptions about Jewish-Christian relationships and the use of lectionaries and calendrical cycles, apart from the fact that they hardly offer a sufficient generic explanation for the Gospels of Mark and Matthew, not to mention John.

35. There have been numerous references to this designation in his *Dialogue with Trypho,* 99–107. T. Zahn, in particular, develops this memoir analogy in *Geschichte des Neutestamentlichen Kanons,* 1889, I, 463-76.

36. Originally published in *American Journal of Theology* 19, 1915, 45-73 and republished as *The Gospels and Contemporary Biographies in the Greco-Roman World,* 1970.

37. Popular biography consists of ". . . memorabilia of a man's life, disconnected incidents and sayings without adequate chronology and connection, without showing his genetic relation to and his influences upon his times." Historical biography ". . . presents a man's life with fair completeness, order, accuracy out of an adequate knowledge of the facts" (*Biographies,* 7).

such works as Arrian's *Discourses of Epictetus*, Philostratus's *Life of Apollonius of Tyana*, Plato's *Dialogues*, and Xenophon's *Memorabilia* with which Votaw compared the Gospels. For him the common motif was the "message of each man (which) was the primary interest and value, together with the personality of the man behind the message."[38]

Often overlooked in the references to Votaw's work is his clear description of the Gospels' special character in contrast to the very documents with which he was comparing them. He repeatedly labels the Gospels "religious tracts intended to promote the Christian movement,"[39] "propagandist media,"[40] "propagandist writings of the early Christian movement" that "contain historical reminiscences, or memorabilia, of Jesus' ministry";[41] and "evangelistic tracts" to commend Jesus as "Christ, Lord, Savior and Teacher to the Mediterranean world."[42] Only by so broadly defining biography as a work about persons and their message could one gather "propagandist writings," the *Discourses* of Epictetus, and Plato's early *Dialogues* under the same literary genre.

One does not need to rehearse the lasting critique of this position voiced by K. L. Schmidt[43] and echoed by R. Bultmann[44] and G. Bornkamm.[45] But C. H. Talbert has recently returned to Votaw's thesis and attempted to establish it.[46] Rather than using the results of contemporary classical philology and the developments in biblical criticism over the past fifty years, Talbert sought to demonstrate the biographical genre of the Gospels simply by refuting Bultmann's threefold argument against the possibility.[47] Unfortunately, Talbert falls into the trap of assuming that a refutation of Bultmann's arguments leads to the confirmation of the Gospels as biographies. Countering Bultmann's arguments, even if successfully done,[48] may simply say more about the weakness of Bultmann's critique than about the validity of the Gospels being biographies.

38. Ibid., 11.
39. Ibid., 1.
40. Ibid., 2.
41. Ibid., 3.
42. Ibid., 4.
43. K. L. Schmidt, "Die Stellung der Evangelien in der allgemeinen Literaturgeschichte," in *EYXAPIΣTHPION: Studien zur Religion und Literatur des Alten und Neuen Testaments*, Festschrift H. Gunkel, ed. H. Schmidt, 1923, 50-134.
44. *RGG*² II, 418-22, in English = *Twentieth-Century Theology in the Making*, 1971, I, 86-92; *History of the Synoptic Tradition*, 1963, 373-74.
45. *RGG*³ II, 750.
46. *What is a Gospel: The Genre of the Canonical Gospels*, 1977.
47. Simply stated by Talbert: "1) The gospels are mythical, the Graeco-Roman biographies are not; 2) the gospels are cultic, the Graeco-Roman biographies are not; 3) while the gospels emerge from a community with a world-negating outlook, the literary biographies are produced by and for a world-affirming people," *Gospel*, 2.
48. See D. Aune's critical review of Talbert's work: "The Problem of the Genre of the Gospels: A Critique of C. H. Talbert's *What is a Gospel?*" in *Gospel Perspectives: Studies of History and Tradition in the Four Gospels*, ed. R. T. France and D. Wenham, 1981, 9-60.

In other words, showing that ancient biographies were at times "mythical" and "cultic" and arguing the similarity of the Gospels' attitude toward this world to the attitude of Graeco-Roman biographies does little to define the genre of biography.

P. L. Shuler[49] has recently followed Talbert's lead in tracing the gospel genre to Graeco-Roman biography and has sought, in contrast to Talbert, to delineate that genre more precisely. Finding evidence for a particular "type of *bios* literature, the primary purpose of which was to praise," implicit in the discussion of "history" and "biography"[50] of Polybius (*Hist.* 10.21.8), Cicero (*Epist. ad Fam.* 5.12.3), Lucian (*How to Write History* 7), and Cornelius Nepos (*Pelopidas* 16.1.1), Shuler calls this literary type more generally a "laudatory biography."[51] He concludes that it relates more specifically to the rhetorical genre known as "encomium."[52] This genre, according to Shuler, serves a laudatory purpose by accentuating the person and emphasizing his or her character or merit through selective use of virtues, deeds, exploits, sayings, and/or teaching. Among the literary techniques used in this genre, "amplification" (or exaggeration) and "comparison" stand out as tools for portraying the subject. After briefly examining several examples of this genre,[53] Shuler then applies this genre to Matthew's Gospel.[54]

Matthew opens with a "literary procedure" common to the encomium genre. In 1:1–4:11, the evangelist defines Jesus' identity and gives signs of future greatness by including " . . . the illustrious lineage of Jesus through his earthly father, his miraculous birth, his upright earthly father, the time and place of his birth, his escape from death as an infant, and his home town—'topoi' . . . accented by dreams, stellar illumination, and the adoration of the child."[55] The evangelist concludes by accepting the importance of Jesus' death, his innocence, and the sinister behavior of his enemies and includes several supernatural events surrounding Jesus' death and resurrection.[56] Furthermore, the evangelist uses the techniques of "amplification" in the progressive revelation of Jesus' identity at the outset and the use of the supernatural events and dreams in both the birth and death narratives. The "comparison" technique comes into play especially with reference to the Baptist and in the contrast between Jesus and his opponents drawn throughout the Gospel.

Assuming that Shuler has successfully delineated a genre of "laudatory

---

49. *A Genre for the Gospels: The Biographical Character of Matthew,* 1982.
50. Ibid., 37.
51. Ibid., 45.
52. Ibid., 85.
53. Ibid., 58-87.
54. Ibid., 88-106.
55. Ibid., 94.
56. Ibid., 96-97.

biography" similar in character to the encomium,[57] he still encounters the problem of a "rose by any other name." To be sure, Matthew does open with a series of narratives filled with the miraculous that serves to identify Jesus, close with an account of Jesus' death and resurrection that underscores his innocence and the injustice of his accusers, and heightens the account with supernatural events and dreams. But does all this make the product an encomium—a "laudatory biography"? Did the evangelist intend[58] to write a "laudatory biography," as explicitly indicated by Isocrates, Xenophon, Philo, Lucian, and Philostratus in their respective works, as noted by Shuler?[59] If so, why then the anonymity of the Gospel, the absence of stated intention, and the stark contrast in the way it reads from any of the examples cited?[60] In short, does the evangelist view his task to write a "biography" or to set forth the Christian message about what God was doing in and through Jesus Messiah? Is the ultimate focus not on God rather than on Jesus, as seen by the evangelist's deliberate use of the fulfillment motif, the infancy narrative, the baptism and temptation accounts, the "will of God" set forth in the Sermon (chs. 5–7), the mission of the "Kingdom" (ch. 10), the message of the "kingdom" (ch. 13), the "supernatural" events surrounding the passion and resurrection, and the final commission that identifies the work of the Son with the Father (28:18-20)?

To the extent that the Gospels do center around a person, Jesus and his ministry, they share a "biographical" element with the broad category of "biographical" literature then and since. But the great diversity within this category of "biographical" literature both in antiquity and in modern times has precluded any genuine precision in using "biography" as a generic designation. Thus Shuler's attempt at precision by his use of encomium or laudatory biography is commendable though futile. While perhaps delineating a specific genre of "laudatory biography," he has not succeeded at demonstrating that Matthew or the Gospels fall under that genre.

One is still faced with the reality of the Gospels as anonymous documents composed of various traditional units and literary forms whose language and style, in the words of Votaw, were "of the people, by the people and for the

---

57. See, however, the article in the present volume by A. Dihle, "Die Evangelien und die griechische Biographie."

58. Shuler contends that "authorial intent" is "fundamental to genre identification" (*Genre*, 32-34).

59. Ibid., 58-87.

60. Whereas the examples from Isocrates, Xenophon, Philo, Lucian, and Philostratus cited by Shuler reflect considerable diversity among themselves, none stands apart from the rest to the extent that Matthew's Gospel does. Granting the flexible character of a genre, one must still question whether the first-century reader would have "understood" Matthew in terms of an "encomium biography." Furthermore, Aune's critique noted above (n. 48) applies as well to Shuler's work.

people"[61] in contrast to the "literature" of biography. Were they, after all, "evangelistic tracts" or "popular biography"?

Much more enthusiasm and perhaps potential for analogy has surrounded the suggestion that the Gospels belonged to the genre of *aretalogy,* a special form of Hellenistic biography.[62] M. Smith summarizes this alternative by noting that "many accounts of ancient 'divine men' are variants of a recognizable aretalogical form" and "the Gospels are more similar to these accounts than to any other ancient non-Christian works we know of."[63] Yet Smith himself concedes that no Gospel, as we know them, follows this "aretalogical form."[64] Mark, whose first half may represent the remnants of such an aretalogy with its miracles that follow Jesus' becoming God's Son at the baptism and culminating in the glorification at the transfiguration, has, according to Smith, expanded and given a Judaizing reinterpretation to this "primitive aretalogy."[65]

Others have more or less shared Smith's view in attributing at least part of Mark and John to such a genre and have interpreted Mark and John to have been written to counter the christological "heresy" of a θεῖος ἀνήρ type. Thus while Mark and John may not be aretalogies themselves, they are the direct result of such, having incorporated and reworked such a genre as a correction of a false christology. Consequently, the aretalogy becomes a formative factor in the development of the Gospel genre of Mark and John.[66]

One might be tempted to leave the matter with this conjecture, since none of the Gospels represents in final form an aretalogy. But one cannot leave the discussion without also noting the serious question that Kee has raised not only about the ambiguity of the term aretalogy, but even about the very existence of such a defined literary genre.[67] Furthermore, the presence of miracle stories or even a collection of miracle stories need not in itself indicate the presence of an aretalogy, unless one so dilutes the term as to mean merely a collection of

61. Votaw, *Biographies,* 2.

62. M. Hadas and M. Smith, *Heroes and Gods: Spiritual Biographies in Antiquity,* 1965; M. Smith, "Prolegomena to a Discussion of Aretalogies, Divine Men, the Gospels and Jesus," *JBL* 90, 1971, 74-99.

63. "Prolegomena," 196.

64. Ibid., 197.

65. Ibid., 198.

66. E.g. J. Robinson, "The Problem of History in Mark, Reconsidered," *USQR* 20, 1965, 136-37; idem, "The Johannine Trajectory," in *Trajectories,* 266-68; H. Koester, "One Jesus and Four Primitive Gospels," in *Trajectories,* 187-93; L. E. Keck, "Mark 3:7-12 and Mark's Christology," *JBL* 84, 1965, 341-58; P. Achtemeier, "Towards the Isolation of Pre-Markan Miracle Catenae," *JBL* 89, 1970, 265-91. Cf. S. Schulz's similar thesis about the "lives" of "divine men" behind the Gospels in TU 87, 1964. W. Schmithals, *Das Evangelium nach Markus,* 1979, I, 45-46, suggests that the narrator of the Grundschrift followed "die Gestalt einer biographischen Aretalogie." T. Weeden's thesis posits such a christology serving as a foil for Mark's Gospel in *Mark—Traditions in Conflict,* 1971, although he makes no explicit mention of an aretalogy.

67. *Community,* 17-18 and "Aretalogy," 402-22; so also D. Tiede, *The Charismatic Figure as Miracle Worker,* SBLDS 1, 1972.

miracle stories.[68] The Old Testament and rabbinic miracle stories give ample illustration of such collections. And the function of the Marcan and Johannine miracle stories is much too debated to conclude that they either reflect an aretalogy or a θεῖος ἀνήρ christology.[69] D. Tiede's study underscores the danger of indiscriminately grouping together miracle stories, aretalogies, and the "divine man" concepts of the ancient world[70] in view of the great variety within each category.

Other Graeco-Roman literary genres have been suggested as possible models for the Gospels, such as the *Socratic dialogues*,[71] *Greek tragedy*,[72] *chriae*,[73] and *apothegms*.[74] Yet none of these has proven an adequate explanation for either the form or content of the New Testament Gospels, and they have little consequence in determining the Gospels' genre. Thus one looks in vain to

68. So M. Smith, "Prolegomena," 176-77; Robinson, "Gattung," 103; Kee, "Aretalogy," 409.

69. See C. R. Holladay's work, *Theios Aner in Hellenistic Judaism*, 1974, where study of Josephus's, Philo's, and Artapanus's use of θεός, θεῖος, and θεῖος ἀνήρ reflects a great range of functions. Furthermore, Holladay concludes that the miracle stories in Hellenistic Judaism stand in the tradition of Old Testament salvation history, which attributed the special powers to God rather than any "miracle worker."

70. D. L. Tiede, *Charismatic Figure*.

71. E.g. D. L. Barr, *Toward a Definition of the Gospel Genre: A Generic Analysis and Comparison of the Synoptic Gospels and the Socratic Dialogues by Means of Aristotle's Theory of Tragedy*, dissertation, 1974, who concludes that the Gospels more closely approximate Plato's early dialogues, though not sufficiently to call them generically the same, than Greek tragedies.

72. E.g. E. W. Busch, "Tragic Action in the Second Gospel," *JR* 11, 1931, 346-58; C. Beach, *The Gospel of Mark*, 1959. Both back away from arguing that Mark used Greek tragedy as a genre because of differences in style and setting that precluded Mark's familiarity with such literature. G. Bilezikian, *The Liberated Gospel: A Comparison of the Gospel of Mark and Greek Tragedy*, 1977, however, disputes that view by showing how accessible Greek tragedy was to Mark's world (33-50). He argues for Mark's use of the genre by using Aristotle's six essential criteria for tragedy drawn from the *Poetics*, the very criteria that led Barr, *Definition*, to place the Gospels closer to Plato's *Dialogues*. In any event, such a genre reduces the Gospels to that of a "passion play" or, in more familiar terms, a passion narrative with an extended introduction.

73. This term refers to a technical form used in classical rhetoric whose meaning and usage were quite fluid. See Kürzinger, "Die Aussage des Papias von Hierapolis zur literarischen Form des Markusevangelium," *BZ* 21, 1977, 245-64; H. Fischel, "Story and History: Observations on Graeco-Roman Rhetoric and Pharisaism," *American Oriental Society: Middle West Branch Semi-Centennial Volume*, 1969, 59-88; idem, "Studies in Cynicism and the Ancient Near East: The Transformation of a Chria," in *Religions in Antiquity*, ed. J. Neusner, 1968, 372-411 (these articles cited by Kee in *Community*, 184, n. 62); and Kee, *Community*, 22-23. Kürzinger notes that the form may extend from a statement about a person or analogy focusing on a saying or action by the person to a more extended narrative consisting of a saying, action, or both ("Aussage," 256-57). To this extent it corresponds to such literary forms as an apothegm, apomneumoneuma, gnome, or aphorism. According to Kürzinger, Papias (Eusebius, *HE* 3.39.15-16) had such a rhetorical meaning in mind when he wrote that Peter gave the Lord's teachings πρὸς τὰς χρείας ("in the manner or form of chriae"). This form may apply, as Papias suggests, to the pericopes of Jesus' words and deeds but hardly suffices as a genre that includes the extended passion narrative.

74. J. A. Baird, "Genre Analysis" (n. 6 above), 399, suggests in passing an "extended apothegm." Fortunately, he does not attempt the impossible and explain how such a form could be "expanded" sufficiently to encompass the form and content of Mark's Gospel.

the Graeco-Roman as to the Jewish literary world for a comparable literary analogy to the Gospels.

2.1.3. Bridging between what might be called the classical literary world and the world of contemporary literary criticism, D. Via's assigning Mark to the genre of tragicomedy reflects the approach of *structuralism* to Gospel criticism[75] and a shift from a "contextual"—the historical, sociological, and literary context—to a structuralist-literary orientation. Via eschews all attempts at delineating the Gospels' genre from a socio-historical reconstruction of the Gospels' setting,[76] since texts are not generated by history.[77] Via takes issue with the approach that seeks the genre from the analysis of a text's form and content.

Genre, according to Via, has to do with "the (unconscious) structure that controlled the material in the first place,"[78] a "hidden logical structure."[79] In other words, genre takes on a different meaning. It is the "structure or grid of syntagms[80] and paradigms"[81] gained by "abstracting from several works a number of traits which they have in common . . . and are deemed to be more important than other traits which they do not have in common."[82] Thus genre is that "hidden" or "unconscious" structure of the whole that is "beyond the text from which the latter draws its meaning."[83]

After examining the variety of formulations of the kerygma in Paul's writings in terms of the comic genre,[84] Via turns to Mark's Gospel. He concludes that Mark was written because ". . . the/a kerygma proclaiming, and faith in, the death and resurrection of Jesus reverberated in the mind of Mark and activated the comic genre whose nucleus is also death and resurrection. . . . The story took the shape it did because the comic genre—deep generative structure of the human mind—generated the Gospel of Mark. . . ."[85] Thus, not unlike the kerygmatic theologians, Via starts with the early Christian kerygma as the catalyst for Mark's Gospel. But his explanation of how the kerygma served as this catalyst differs greatly from the evolutionary and constructive models often

75. *Kerygma and Comedy in the New Testament: A Structuralist Approach to Hermeneutic,* 1975.

76. Ibid., 2-7, 78-90.

77. Ibid., 28-31, 94-95.

78. Ibid., 29, cf. 31, ". . . the logical structure of a narrative is more determinative than its literary form."

79. Ibid., 31.

80. "The syntagm is a linear and irreversible succession or chain of words . . . spoken or written," ibid., 11. In other words, the text or the narrative.

81. The paradigm is a system ". . . composed of operations or elements from the different texts (narratives) which have something in common, some kind of correlation," ibid., 11.

82. Ibid., 15.

83. Ibid.

84. "Death/resurrection is the image which stands at the heart of the comic form," ibid., 49.

85. Ibid., 93.

posited by form criticism. For him, the comic genre underlying the kerygma generated Mark's Gospel, which Via then designates generically to be a tragicomedy.[86] He supports his choice by referring to K. Guthke's work,[87] which argues that all tragicomedy has at least two of seven "structural patterns." Mark has four of the seven.[88]

Many fundamental issues of literary criticism are involved here, not the least being the very nature and function of texts. In several ways, one has the distinct sense of *déjà vu* when following Via's quest for genre. The quest for a genre behind the text looks very much like the quest for the kerygma behind the myth. Demythologization becomes "decomposing and recomposing (a text) on 'a different plane.' "[89] Instead of a history-transcending existentialist grid drawn from the history of religions school by the new hermeneutic, Via has placed on the text a structuralist-existentialist grid drawn by the structuralist from literary criticism. To this extent he may be the next logical, consistent twist or "generic transformation" of the genre "kerygmatic theology." What better alternative can one offer the text shaken free from its authorial intent and historical context?

Recognizing the impasse at the starting point of the question of genre, one can only say that any genre that can include the literary "forms of dramatic history, a biography or autobiography, the history of a given epoch—a Gospel . . ."[90] still has not answered why Mark wrote in the literary "form" he used.[91] In what sense, one must ask, did the "story take the shape it did because (of) the comic genre?"[92] Apparently, the genre could have generated numerous shapes, so one is still left without an explanation for Mark's literary form or shape, what has generally been called the "genre."

2.2. *Derivational:* Having reviewed some of the analogical explanations and noted their inadequacy either to provide comparable literary parallels sufficient to offer an appropriate genre (e.g. biography, apocalypse, aretalogy) or to offer an aetiological basis for explaining the particular form and materials of the Gospels (e.g. narrative history, tragicomedy), one comes again to the

86. Why the *tragi*comic genre rather than simply comic genre, the latter being the "generative structure in the kerygma which lies behind Mark," goes unexplained, except by reference to Beach's work on the tragic character of Mark's Gospel. Can one genre (comic) generate a work of another genre (tragicomedy)?

87. *Modern Tragicomedy,* 1966.

88. 1) It contrasts a tragic character with a comic world; 2) it contrasts the illusory world of the protagonist and the real world known to the audience or other characters (in Mark this is reversed, so that the protagonist knows the real world); 3) the course of events victimizes the protagonist who ironically becomes the tragic hero; 4) there is internal conflict within the protagonist of appearance and reality, promise and fulfillment or self-image and reality. *Kerygma,* 100-101.

89. Ibid., 15.

90. Ibid., 97.

91. Via's own question in ch. 3: "Why was Mark written in the form in which it was written?" ibid., 71.

92. Ibid., 93.

possiblity that the Gospels stand apart, having no precise parallels within literary genres. This absence of suitable literary parallels raises at least the possibility that the Gospels represent a new literary genre. This conclusion has had its own advocates for much of this century.[93] But one still must account for this particular genre and give it some definition.

Three such explanations for the uniqueness of the gospel genre have emerged with slight variations from time to time. One attributes the Gospels to (1) an evolutionary process of early Christian tradition. Another and much later alternative disputes the first and assigns the gospel genre to (2) the creative genius of Mark who gave rise to a new literary product, the gospel, by combining traditional material into a framework. Finally, another alternative attributes the gospel genre to (3) the evangelist's writing down and explicating the traditional outline of the primitive Christian kerygma.

2.2.1. The *evolutionary* or *"constructive"* model has dominated much of German gospel studies for the past half century. Dibelius[94] offers one of the clearest statements of the developmental or "constructive" approach that persists to the present.[95] Accordingly, the Gospels represent simply the final phase in the evolution of the early Christian tradition[96] with the primitive Church's kerygma at its core. The final product, the Gospels, and the process itself were influenced especially for Dibelius by three factors: The primitive communities' eschatology, the Church's mission, and the kerygma of Jesus' death and resurrection.

Dibelius begins with the premise that the early Church lived with the expectation of the imminent parousia. This eschatological orientation qualified their literary intentions and qualified the content of the message. First, such a future anticipation left little "inclination for the production of books," especially among an "unlettered people" whose capacity for literary productivity was questionable.[97] Yet the Gospels did emerge in barely a generation as "literary" products of an author with literary analogies, but nonetheless as the end-product of a nonliterary, organic development of the tradition within the sociological matrix of the believing community.[98] Second, the futuristic eschatology led the Church to focus early on the cross and the development of the passion narrative,

---

93. Although the roots extend to the influential work done by two nineteenth-century scholars, F. Overbeck (e.g. "Über die Anfänge der patristischen Literatur," *HZ* 48, 1882, 417-72) and E. Norden (e.g. *Die antike Kunstprosa* II, 1898). Both had major impact on M. Dibelius and K. L. Schmidt.

94. *From Tradition to Gospel*, 1935; so R. Bultmann, *History of the Synoptic Tradition*, 1963; K. L. Schmidt, *Der Rahmen der Geschichte Jesu: Literarkritische Untersuchungen zur ältesten Jesusüberlieferung*, 1919; idem, "Stellung."

95. *Tradition*, 1-36; so P. Vielhauer, *Geschichte der urchristlichen Literatur*, 1975, 348-55.

96. E.g. Dibelius, *Tradition*, 3-4; esp. Bultmann, *History*, 321.

97. *Tradition*, 9.

98. Ibid., 10-11.

since the passion narrative dealt with the first act of the end of the world as then believed and hoped.[99] By contrast, the "deeds of Jesus" preserved in the community's memory had only "incidental and not essential significance." These events in Jesus' ministry did not constitute the "introduction of the approaching world changes,"[100] and thus were not at the core of the primitive kerygma.

Dibelius developed his "constructive" approach by which he sought to reconstruct the process from tradition to Gospel by following Gunkel's lead and tracing the various Sitze im Leben of the traditional components of the Gospels. The broader context was the Church's mission in the world,[101] which offered multiple contexts necessitating the reshaping and formation of the traditional units from the Church's preaching. Thus the "sermon," broadly defined,[102] offered both the context and the parameters of the traditional material. Contextually, the various functions of the "sermon" in the mission shaped the traditions according to the sermon's requirements.[103] But, according to Dibelius, the sermon formally controlled what could have been used without "disturbing the sequence of the sermon."[104] This meant the absence of any disruptive features like a "detailed description of isolated matters" or anything the size of the passion narrative which was "too large for such a purpose."[105]

The heart of the earliest mission kerygma and the heart of the Gospels was the cross and resurrection of Christ. Dibelius based this conclusion on an analysis of I Cor. 15:3-7 and the sermons in Acts.[106] Since this was the heart of the primitive kerygma and since this kerygma stems from "eyewitnesses and ministers of the word" (Luke 1:1-4), he concluded that the traditional materials concerning the passion were of primary significance for the Church. Here "salvation was visible. . . ."[107] Consequently the passion narrative takes on its fundamental character in the formation of the Gospels.

Since the other units of the Jesus-tradition serve as examples or illustrations in the sermon, in contrast to the passion narrative, "in itself a sermon by means of what the story contained. . . ,"[108] one can see why P. Vielhauer has concluded with

---

99. Ibid., 22.

100. Ibid., 24.

101. Ibid., 11.

102. Ibid., 15: ". . . all forms of Christian propaganda are included: mission preaching, preaching during worship, and catechumen instruction.

103. Ibid., 26.

104. Ibid., 24-25.

105. Ibid., 27. To fit Dibelius's "sermon" context, the passion narrative served as the "text" for the sermon (23), or as an extended illustration following upon the message properly so-called (27).

106. Ibid., 15-22.

107. Ibid., 22.

108. Ibid., 27.

others, first, that the Gospels bring nothing new[109] and, second, that the Gospel is formally and materially a passion narrative with an extended introduction.[110] In other words, the composition of the Gospels offers nothing new in principle. It merely completes what began with the earliest tradition. Mark, in short, is a "sermon" with the passion narrative as its core, and all that precedes serves as examples and illustrations that set the stage for the heart of the sermon. The Gospel brings together into one great "sermon" the various traditions arising from multiple contexts in the mission. These disparate traditions of Jesus' ministry are drawn together by the bond of Jesus' death and resurrection.

In this manner, one can account for the Gospel's formal distinctiveness and set its definition. The form evolved or "organically developed" from the traditional process, which always had the passion at its core. Since this traditional development had no "literary" concerns or inclinations from the outset—even disdained such intentions—and since the materials developed out of the requirements of the Church's mission, one should not be surprised that the end product, the Gospel, stands without literary parallel. Its "form" was endemic to its content. And since the content ultimately focused on the kerygma of the passion, a Gospel is essentially a "sermon" or the passion kerygma with an extended narrative.

2.2.2. This evolutionary accounting for the gospel "genre" has come under severe attack at several points, especially for the role or rather lack of any definitive role attributed to the evangelists in this process. Güttgemanns's work represents one of the recent criticisms of this approach. He has faulted the "constructive" method at its starting points.[111]

First, while form criticism has been exacting in its search for the Sitz im Leben of the Gospels' traditional components, it has failed to take into account the Sitz im Leben that gave rise to the written Gospels.[112] Furthermore, one cannot transfer directly the principles at work in isolated oral traditional units to that of a written document which has its given framework.[113] Redaction criticism has shown the Gospels to be much more than the final stage in the development of anonymous tradition. Thus the familiar designation, "Kleinliteratur,"[114] misleads when it results in classifying the Gospels as popular community "folklore" and propagandistic materials. Each Gospel reflects a careful, if not sophisticated, literary production by the respective writer.

---

109. *Geschichte,* 354, citing Bultmann, *History,* 321.
110. *Geschichte,* 354, echoing M. Kähler, *The So-Called Historical Jesus and the Historic, Biblical Christ,* ET 1964.
111. E. Güttgemanns, *Offene Fragen zur Formgeschichte des Evangeliums,* 1970.
112. Ibid., 82-86.
113. Ibid., 86-92.
114. Cf. K. L. Schmidt, "Stellung," 50-134.

Second, the assumption that the primitive Church's "apocalyptic" eschatology precluded any literary interests has been convincingly countered by the
presence of apocalyptic literature in general and the writings of Qumran in
particular.[115] One may even ask more fundamentally whether the early communities' futuristic orientation led them not only to disdain literary pursuits but to
find the core of their gospel in the passion narrative rather than also in the words
and deeds of Jesus.[116]

Third, Güttgemanns appropriately questions the adequacy of Dibelius's
"sermon" context and the generally accepted primitive kerygma of the cross to
account for the Gospel's shape and content.[117] Even should one be justified in
positing a unified kerygma reflected in the development of the passion narrative,
one still has not accounted for the shape of Mark's Gospel, not to mention
Matthew, Luke, or John. Labeling everything prior to the passion narrative an
"extended introduction" or arguing that the passion narrative had a determinative role in selecting and shaping the order of the tradition used in leading to the
passion narrative begs the question of the shape and content of the Gospel.

Thus, Güttgemanns has argued, in view of the inadequacies of the "form-
critical" explanation of the gospel genre and in view of contemporary linguistic
and literary scholarship, that the Gospel's (Mark's) uniqueness derives from its
"origin" as a literary creation of Mark. To use Güttgemanns's words, the Gospel
form is an "autosemantic language form" that gains its meaning in and through
itself.[118] By combining the material (tradition) with a framework (the evangelist's own), the writer has created a Gestalt, a form that has its own theological
significance that is greater than the sum of its parts.[119] Therefore, Mark, for
example, can no longer be explained and appropriately interpreted by an
analysis of its parts removed from the whole.

Yet Güttgemanns himself never defines this "Gestalt" created by Mark
nor does he indicate what apart from random choice guided the first evangelist
in writing his Gospel. After dismissing the kerygma as an hypothetical unity
lost forever in the "darkness" of the past, he offers neither a structural analysis
of Mark's "deep structure" (genre for the structuralists) nor any explanation of
why Mark structured his Gospel the way he chose (genre as used in other literary
contexts). Güttgemanns leaves this assignment for a future task.[120] Whereas the
evolutionary or constructive approach of form criticism assigned the literary
uniqueness to the tradition and its history of development, Güttgemanns is

---

115. Güttgemanns, *Fragen,* 97-100.
116. Ibid., 100-103, notes how little influence the imminent expectation had on Mark.
117. Ibid., 190-222.
118. Ibid., 197: ". . . Eine Sprachform, die in ihrem 'Sinn' nur durch und aus sich selbst
erklärt werden kann. . . ."
119. Ibid., 184-88.
120. Ibid., 251.

satisfied with attributing this uniqueness to the literary creativity of the evangelist.[121] Neither approach, however, accounts for the formal and material characteristics of the Gospel, in short, its genre.

H.-T. Wrege concurs with Güttgemanns's rejection of the form-critical
solution to the question[122] and his conviction that the Gospel is a Gestalt in
which the whole is greater than the sum of the parts.[123] Furthermore, Wrege
accepts the literary uniqueness of the gospel genre and traces it to the mutual
interaction of the form and content, the evangelist's framework and the traditional units, the writing process.[124] But he offers a "structural" analysis and
explanation of the Gospel by examining both the preliterary and literary stages,
where he finds underlying structures (*Vorstrukturen*) such as "deed-
consequence," "humiliation-exaltation," "Jew first-then Greek," "fathers-
murders of the prophets," "master-student," etc., that led to the collecting of the
disparate traditional units into larger units like the passion narrative.[125]

These *Vorstrukturen* also influenced the evangelist's selection and arrangement of the tradition. For example, Mark parlayed the *Vorstruktur* of
"unknowing-fulfillment" into the messianic secret motif. In doing so, he was
able to combine the earthly Jesus ("not knowing"—before Easter) and the
exalted Lord ("fulfillment"—after Easter) for the reader.[126] The evangelist used
"fathers-prophet murderers" or "Jew first-then Greek" to set Jesus' way of the
cross and the eventual message of the gospel for the Gentiles[127] and the
"master-student" to indicate the way of discipleship.[128] Matthew and Luke-Acts
modify Mark by adapting these *Vorstrukturen* to their own schemas.[129]

Doubtless the preliterary as well as literary combination of disparate
tradition followed an organizing thread, one of which certainly was thematic
(cf. Vorstrukturen). But do the *Vorstrukturen* adequately explain the evangelists' selection and arrangement of the tradition from the perspective of the
Gospel seen as a whole? Does the underlying structure(s) consciously or
subconsciously give shape to the gospel genre? Or was the gospel genre itself

---

121. W. Schmithals, *Markus* I, 44-46, appears to take the "creativity" of the author quite
seriously. Rather than assigning the gospel genre to the writer of Mark's Gospel as we know it (a
redactional combination of a *Grundschrift* and Q), he assigns the basic narrative, beginning with
the Baptist and ending with the passion narrative, including the miracle stories, apothegms, and
some sayings material, to the author of the Grundschrift. He denies any historical evidence for the
existence of this material as oral tradition (44-45).

122. *Die Gestalt des Evangeliums: Aufbau und Struktur der Synoptiker sowie die Apostelgeschichte*, BEvTh 11, 1978, 11-48.

123. Ibid., 173-75.

124. Ibid., 169-72.

125. Ibid., 58-89.

126. Ibid., 111-22, 171.

127. Ibid., 58-95.

128. Ibid., 91-110.

129. Ibid., 124-58, 171.

a given that existed in its traditional framework that guided the evangelist's selection and ordering of the materials?

2.2.3. C. H. Dodd, whose work has been highly influential on the Anglo-American scene, offered an explanation that accounted for the "scheme of Gospel-writing by Mark" which served as the model for the other canonical Gospels.[130] On the surface, Dodd's stress on the kerygma and on the early Church's eschatology as formative influences on the Gospels appears closely related to Dibelius and the evolutionary approach to the Gospels. But Dodd differs at significant points to the extent that one must justifiably refer to his explanation of the gospel as the *explication* rather than the evolution of the kerygma.[131]

After carefully distinguishing between kerygma, the "public proclamation of Christianity to the non-Christian world," and didache as parenetic, apologetic, and expositional instruction,[132] Dodd sought first to delineate the basic outline of the Christian kerygma.[133] He distilled this outline from allusions in Paul to his own preaching (e.g. I Cor. 1:23; 2:2-6; 3:10; 15:1-17; II Cor. 4:4; Gal. 3:1; 1:14; Rom. 10:8-9; 14:9-10), from traditional formulations in his letters (e.g. I Cor. 15:3-7; Rom. 10:9; 8:31-34; 1:3-4, etc.), and from an analysis of the sermons in Acts.[134] Dodd's results correspond roughly to the outline found in Mark 1:14-15 and Acts 10:34-43.[135]

Though Dibelius read the primitive kerygma in terms of the death and resurrection, Dodd found a more extended base by including above all the emphasis of fulfilled Scripture and the return of Christ. The latter element becomes significant because he combines the death, resurrection, and return of Christ as one "eschatological process," "inseparable parts of a single divine event."[136] In particular, the expectation of Christ's return was for Dodd the "impending verification of the Church's faith that the finished work of Christ has in itself eschatological value."[137] Consequently, whereas Dibelius and

---

130. *The Apostolic Preaching and its Developments,* 1936; idem, "The Framework of the Gospel Narrative," *ExpT* 43, 1931-32, 396 400.

131. Similar approaches could be ascribed to J. Schreiber, *Theologie des Vertrauens: Eine redaktionsgeschichtliche Untersuchung des Markusevangeliums,* 1967, who, like G. Schille, *Anfänge der Kirche: Erwägungen zur apostolischen Frühgeschichte,* 1966, finds the outline of Phil. 2:6-11 behind Mark. P. Vielhauer, "Erwägungen zur Christologie des Markusevangeliums," in *Aufsätze zum Neuen Testament,* ThB 31, 1965, 199-214, finds a comparative religion parallel in the coronation scheme behind I Tim. 3:16; Heb. 1:5-13; cf. Rev. 5.

132. *Preaching,* 7.

133. Dodd uses "kerygma" as a technical but general term to refer to the "message" rather than to any specific formulation of the message.

134. *Preaching,* 9-24.

135. This comes close to Dibelius's allusion to the "skeleton" character of Acts' sermons; cf. *Tradition,* 25.

136. *Preaching,* 42, 33.

137. Ibid., 42.

followers focused on a "futuristic eschatology," Dodd read the kerygma in terms of a "realized eschatology." This reading enabled him to combine the preaching of "Christ crucified" and the "gospel of the Kingdom," since both were ultimately eschatological statements of God's promised redemptive activity.

The extended delay in Christ's return led to two adaptations, according to Dodd, in the Church's thought.[138] The "authentic line of development . . . led to a concentration of attention upon the historical accounts of the ministry, death and resurrection of Jesus, exhibited in an eschatological setting which made clear their absolute and final quality as saving fact."[139] This development can be traced through Paul's writings and other epistles (cf. I Peter and Hebrews) and emerges most clearly in Mark.

Mark confronts the dilemma of the delay by focusing on the "deeds and words of Jesus" as a "valuation of the life of Jesus in eschatological terms."[140] Mark 1–8 does not offer simply the "introduction" for the passion narrative but the theme of the "kerygma as a whole,"[141] which finds its explicit statement at Caesarea Philippi. Jesus has come as the promised Messiah. The theme of the passion begins in 8:31 so that Mark's proportionate emphasis on the passion corresponds with the emphasis of the primitive Christian preaching as reported in Acts, Paul, and Hebrews.[142] But even this tragic narrative of suffering eventuates in glory, a motif that occurs repeatedly in Mark 8:31–16:8 (cf. the Transfiguration; Mark 13; rending of the veil; centurion's confession). Only a glorious account of the resurrection is missing, having been lost as the ending of Mark.[143] Therefore, Mark "conceived himself as writing a form of the kerygma," a "rendering of the apostolic Preaching."[144]

Dodd supports this conclusion by showing how Mark actually follows and fills out the content of the outline of the apostolic preaching, especially as seen in Acts 10:34-43. First, Mark opens with the fulfillment of the Old Testament promise (1:1-15) by interpreting John's and Jesus' coming in view of Isaiah (cf. Acts 10:37, 43). Second, he expands the section (1:16–8:30) dealing with Jesus' ministry in Galilee "doing good and healing all that were oppressed by the devil" (cf. Acts 10:39-40). Therefore, Mark represents a "commentary on the kerygma."[145] Rather than being the final phase of the evolution of the early

138. Dodd concedes that a futuristic element developed in the early Church in view of the delayed return of Christ. He traces this departure from the kerygma and a return to Jewish apocalyptic through II Thessalonians, Mark 13, and Matthew's Gospel to the dead end street of second-century millennialism.

139. *Preaching*, 42.
140. Ibid., 46.
141. Ibid., 47.
142. Ibid., 49.
143. Ibid., 51.
144. Ibid., 47.
145. Ibid., 48-49.

Christian preaching (Dibelius), Mark is the "literaturization"[146] of the kerygma as the message of the Church. This explains what Mark is, its literary distinctiveness, the primitive Christian kerygma, and its basic shape.

Furthermore, by accepting the passion narrative (Mark 14–16) as a given in the tradition and by recognizing the arrangement of 8:31–12:44 around the passion sayings and Mark 13 as an assuring prelude for the passion narrative, Dodd needed only to find an organizing principle for the materials in 1:1–8:30. This "outline" he found in the summaries scattered throughout Mark. When taken together these summaries give a "perspicuous outline of the Galilaean Ministry, forming a frame into which the separate pictures are set."[147]

In this manner, Mark's Gospel emerges as a written expression of the Christian message about what God was doing in history through Jesus Christ— the kerygma, which Mark calls the "gospel" in 1:1. Strictly speaking the shape and content do not reflect the literary creativity of Mark, since these were basically given by the traditional "outline" of the kerygma and the traditional materials of the Church's preaching. But as the written kerygma the form and content have no comparable literary parallel. Mark's Gospel is unique. Yet it becomes a model for three other "Gospels," with only John a close follower of the model. Matthew and Luke make their own adaptation and modification of the models and thus alter the direction of the kerygma.[148]

The weakness of Dodd's explanation has been scored on several accounts. Whereas Dibelius's category of the sermon was too broad, Dodd's distinction between kerygma and didache is too discreet. Much hinges on the disputed unity of the primitive Christian kerygma, particularly since Dodd has expanded the content from essentially the passion to include the Old Testament promise-fulfillment, Jesus' ministry, and his return in glory to judge. This "message" is supposedly common to Paul, Acts, and the Gospels. Further, Dodd's reading of the kerygma in terms of a "realized eschatology" stands in stark contrast to those who read it as a "futuristic eschatology." And especially questionable is whether the deeds and words of Jesus ever took the place of the second advent as the vindication of the validity of Jesus' ministry and thus led to the writing of Mark's Gospel and John.

Despite the serious questions to these integral elements in Dodd's explanation, his greatest vulnerability lies in the existence of a basic outline of the

146. D. Aune coins this expression in "The Problem of the Genre of the Gospels," in *Gospel Perspectives* II, 45.

147. "Framework," 399.

148. *Preaching,* 52-54: Matthew combines didache and kerygma and accents a "new, higher code of ethics" and a sharpened emphasis on futuristic eschatology. Luke gives a more "rationalized and humanitarian rendering of the Gospel. . . ." Naturally, for Dodd, John's realized eschatology comes closest to preserving the trend in Mark of accenting Jesus' earthly ministry as a vindication of the validity of that ministry.

kerygma that helped structure Mark's Gospel. The evidence is drawn from a supposedly common historical context and tradition underlying Acts, Paul, and the Gospels. Many have questioned this history of the tradition. Furthermore, Dodd's theory that the Marcan summaries provided the structure for the episodic narratives of 1:1–8:30 has gained few followers because of the dubious traditional character of these summaries, which he grouped together as an "outline of the whole ministry."[149]

3. Mark 1:1 and the Gospel Genre

The survey has indicated the inadequacy of the analogical approach to the genre question, and the derivational approach leaves unanswered, for the most part, the ultimate questions of the Gospel's form and content as well. Only Dodd seems to have accounted for the structure and material of the gospel genre while giving due recognition to the role of the tradition and the evangelist. Yet Dodd's fatal flaw lay in his shaky foundation. Can one find a more adequate basis in the tradition for answering the genre question?

3.1. Mark's Gospel itself provides the major clue to the search for a genre. The Gospel opens with the familiar "heading"—"The beginning of the gospel of Jesus Messiah, Son of God"—that has spawned endless debates over the meaning of each word. Yet an equally critical factor in understanding 1:1 has often been overlooked in the recent debates, namely, the relationship of 1:1 to 1:2-3. Many texts and commentators read 1:1 as though a unit in itself with 1:2 beginning a new section. This reading frees 1:1 to function independently of 1:2-3 and provides a greater range of possible interpretations otherwise excluded by a combination of 1:1 with 1:2-3. But the use of καθὼς γέγραπται and the comparable function of ἀρχή in other "headings" make the reading of 1:1 with 1:2-3 imperative.[150]

3.1.1. Despite the observation that καθώς may at times begin a sentence,[151] the phrase καθὼς γέγραπται simply does not begin a new thought in New Testament Greek. First, the phrase καθὼς γέγραπται serves as one of several semi-technical introductory formulas for citing Scripture with numerous parallels in Jewish literature.[152] Then as an introductory citation formula, καθώς

149. "Framework," 399-400; cf. W. Egger, *Frohbotschaft und Lehre: Die Sammelberichte des Wirkens Jesu im Markusevangelium,* 1976.

150. See the work by G. Arnold, "Mk 1,1 und Eröffnungswendungen in griechischen und lateinischen Schriften," *ZNW* 68, 1977, 121-27.

151. Contra V. Taylor, *The Gospel According to St. Mark,* ²1966, whose examples are inapplicable, since they do not include καθὼς γέγραπται.

152. See J. Fitzmyer, "The Use of Explicit Old Testament Quotations in Qumran Literature

γέγραπται invariably links what follows with what has immediately preceded in the context.[153] Consequently, the "Isaiah" citation in 1:2b-3 is linked directly to the opening statement in 1:1 by the καθὼς γέγραπται (1:2a). In other words, one has no grounds for separating 1:1 as a general heading for the Gospel and starting a new section with 1:2a by taking the formula syntactically with what follows in 1:4-8 (e.g. RSV, "As it was written . . . John the baptizer appeared . . .").

3.1.2. What then is the function of the rather clumsy statement in 1:1-3? A study of comparable uses of ἀρχή in extrabiblical literature[154] has shown that it pertains either to the immediate context[155] at the opening of a work or to the actual beginning of a work's main section that is set off from preliminary comments.[156] In no instance, however, does ἀρχή introduce an entire work as a whole.[157] Therefore, since 1:1 has no preliminary comments preceding it ἀρχή must refer to the immediate context or opening section of the work. Mark 1:1-3 serves then as the heading for the "beginning" section of the Gospel rather than for the work as a whole. The contents of this heading set the limits of the "beginning."

3.1.3. If ἀρχή refers to the "beginning" section of Mark's Gospel, then "gospel" in 1:1 cannot refer more generally to the "Christian message" whose "beginning" consists of Jesus' ministry as depicted by Mark in his Gospel (1:4–16:8).[158] And since "beginning" is not synonymous with the content of 1:4–16:8, the "gospel of Jesus Messiah" in 1:1 must include at least what follows in 1:4–16:8, the opening part of which the evangelist designates the "beginning of the gospel." In other words, the evangelist applies εὐαγγέλιον in 1:1 to his literary work portraying Jesus' ministry in Galilee that eventuates in his death and resurrection in Jerusalem.[159] The evangelist calls his literary work "the gospel," because it represents the gospel concerning Jesus Messiah.

3.1.4. What precisely is the "beginning" of this "gospel"? The heading (1:1-3) indicates that the "beginning" corresponds to Isaiah's promise of a "messenger," a "voice in the wilderness," who prepares "the way of the Lord"

---

and in the New Testament," in *Essays on the Semitic Background of the New Testament,* 1971, 3-58, esp. 7-10.

153. E.g. II Kgs. 14:6 (LXX); Luke 2:23; Acts 7:42; cf. 13:33; 15:15; Rom. 1:17; 2:24; 3:4, 10; 4:17; 8:36; 9:13, 33; 10:15; 11:8, 26; 15:3, 9, 21; I Cor. 1:31; 2:9; II Cor. 8:15; 9:9.

154. See Arnold, "Eröffnungswendungen," 121-27.

155. E.g. Polybius 1.5.1; Dionysius of Halicarnassus 1.8.4; Josephus, *BJ* 1.30.

156. E.g. Isocrates, *Phil.* 1; Philo, *De Sob.* 1; *De Spec. Leg.* 1; Tacitus, *Hist.* 1.1.

157. The commonly cited parallel in Hos. 1:2 (LXX) does not hold up, since 1:2 does not serve as the heading for the book.

158. So Taylor, *Mark,* 152; R. Pesch, *Das Markusevangelium,* HTKNT II/1, 1977, 74-76; J. Gnilka, *Das Evangelium nach Markus,* EKK II/1, 1978, 42-43.

159. Cf., as representative of the opposing viewpoint, G. Strecker, "Das Evangelium Jesu Christi," in *Jesus Christus in Historie und Geschichte,* Festschrift H. Conzelmann, ed. G. Strecker, 1975, 536, n. 134.

(1:2b-3). Thus, Isaiah's promise sets the parameters of the "beginning." The Baptist's appearance and ministry in 1:4-8 corresponds without doubt to this promise. But Isaiah's promise and consequently the "beginning" do not conclude simply with the Baptist's appearance. The "Coming One" also appears in light of Isaiah.[160] John's role as preparer of the way includes Jesus' baptism (1:9-11) where Jesus is recognized as the heralded Coming One (cf. 1:7-8) whose way the "voice in the wilderness" had proclaimed (cf. Isa. 40:3).

Furthermore, the coming of the Spirit and the voice from heaven identify Jesus as the Spirit-equipped servant of Isa. 42:1 (1:11)[161] and the Spirit-anointed messenger of the gospel of Isa. 61:1 (cf. 52:7; Mark 1:14-15).[162] One might even argue that Mark's temptation account contains Isaianic motifs of the Edenic age of salvation.[163] Certainly, the emergence of Jesus, after the Baptist had been "delivered up,"[164] to preach the "gospel of God" (1:4) echoes Isa. 61:1 and 52:7, as seen in the eschatological explication concerning God's rule in 1:15 and the fulfillment of time. Thus "the beginning" of the gospel includes the appearance of the Baptist as the voice preparing the way (1:4-9; cf. 14a) and the appearance of the Coming One who is announced and equipped for his task of proclaiming God's eschatological rule (1:9-15) in keeping with Isaiah's promise. This for the evangelist is the "beginning of the gospel of Jesus Messiah" which he proceeds to narrate.[165]

By explicitly identifying the "beginning of the gospel" with Isaiah, Mark connects the gospel to its Old Testament Jewish roots. The evangelist shows how the beginning events correspond to the Old Testament promise. At the same time, he depicts what follows as the "gospel of Jesus Messiah," the meaning of which has now been shaped by the Scriptural context in which it has been placed.[166] This is seen further by his introduction of Jesus as the one preaching the "gospel of God" (1:14-15), a correspondence to Isaiah's promise of the one who would herald the "gospel" (cf. Isa. 61:1; 52:7) that hardly appears to be coincidental. But how do the "gospel of Jesus Messiah" and the "gospel of God" relate to Isaiah's promise of the "bearer of the gospel"?

160. R. Guelich, " 'The Beginning of the Gospel'—Mark 1:1-15," *BR* 27, 1982, 8-10; Lührmann, "Biographie," 27-30.

161. Lührmann, "Biographie," 27-30. See I. H. Marshall, "Son of God or Servant of Yahweh?—A Reconsideration of Mark 1:11," *NTS* 15, 1968-69, 326-36.

162. Lührmann, "Biographie," 27-30.

163. Note Mark's emphasis on the "wilderness," Jesus' presence "with the wild animals," and the "angels ministering to him." All support a paradise motif commensurate with Isaiah's depiction of the age of salvation (e.g. 11:6-8; 65:25; cf. *Test. Naph.* 8:4-6; *Vita Adae et Evae* 32–38; *Apoc. Moses* 10–11).

164. See W. Popkes, *Christus Traditus, Eine Untersuchung zum Begriff der Dahingabe im Neuen Testament,* AThANT 49, 1967, 143-45, for discussion of this verb as an indicator of Jesus' way.

165. E.g. L. Keck, "The Introduction to Mark's Gospel," *NTS* 12, 1965-66, 352-70.

166. Cf. similar usage in 13:10; 14:9; quite possibly the same usage lies behind 8:35; 10:29, where "the gospel" refers to the message about Jesus, the message that Mark has put into writing.

3.2. The phrases "the gospel of Jesus Messiah" and the "gospel of God" have their setting in the early Church's "Hellenistic" mission.[167] Yet Mark uses these phrases in a way novel to the rest of the New Testament.[168] First, he employs "the gospel of Jesus Messiah" to designate the narrative of Jesus' earthly ministry, which begins with the Baptist's appearance and eventuates in Jesus' death and resurrection in Jerusalem (1:4–16:8). Then the evangelist uses the "gospel of God" to refer to the message about the eschatological fulfillment of time and God's coming rule (1:15), rather than to speak about the one true God who acted and will act in his Son, as found, for example, in the "Hellenistic" mission (e.g. Rom. 1:1-4; I Thess. 2:8; cf. 1:9-10).[169] Yet since the "gospel of God" preached by Jesus (1:14-15) finds its expression for the evangelist not only in Jesus' preaching but above all in his ministry[170] of teaching, exorcisms, healings, and table fellowship with the sinners, which show him to be the "Messiah" (8:29) whose way must lead to the cross and resurrection (e.g. 8:31), the "gospel of God" is at the same time the "gospel concerning Jesus Messiah."[171]

3.2.1. This shift in gospel terminology by Mark represents no mean accomplishment. First, to identify the "gospel of Jesus Messiah" with the narrative of Jesus' ministry as well as to his death and resurrection breaks rather dramatically not only in form (narrative) but in content from the conceptual preaching and teaching of the "Hellenistic" mission, where "gospel of Christ" involved at times the hope of his return (e.g. I Thess. 1:10), his atoning death and resurrection (I Cor. 15:3-5), and his appointment as Son of God in power at the resurrection (Rom. 1:3-4).[172] The mission focus appears to have been clearly on the death, resurrection, and return and not at all on Jesus' earthly ministry. Much the same has been said of Paul's use of the "gospel."

3.2.2. Second, to identify the "gospel of God" with the message of fulfillment of time and the coming of God's kingdom also breaks dramatically with the monotheistic overtones of the "Hellenistic" mission suggested by I Thess. 1:9, even assuming that a christological component was inherent in this "gospel of God," as implied by I Thess. 1:9-10 and Rom. 1:1-5. The fulfillment and kingdom language of Mark 1:15 has its roots deep in Jewish expectation, a

---

167. Strecker, "Evangelium," 523-24, who traces this to "Hellenistic" mission settings; P. Stuhlmacher, *Das paulinische Evangelium*. I: *Vorgeschichte,* FRLANT 95, 1968, 258-82, who traces these phrases to the "Hellenistic-Jewish" mission context.

168. The debate over whether 1:14-15 stems from pre-Marcan tradition or Mark's redaction is moot, since the evangelist has arranged the material in this context.

169. Stuhlmacher, *Evangelium,* 259-60.

170. E.g. K. G. Reploh, *Markus—Lehrer der Gemeinde,* SBM 9, 1969; A. M. Ambrozic, *The Hidden Kingdom: A Redaction-Critical Study of the References to the Kingdom of God in Mark's Gospel,* CBQMS 11, 1972; W. Kelber, *The Kingdom in Mark: A New Place and Time,* 1974.

171. This "gospel of God" expressed as the "gospel of Jesus Messiah" has its roots, according to Mark, in Isaiah's promise. Cf. Acts 10:36.

172. So Strecker, "Evangelium," 517-23.

context quite foreign, it would seem, to the "Hellenistic" mission. This message finds its most natural home in the earliest mission setting of the Church within Judaism. Finally, to identify the eschatological "gospel of God" with the narrative "gospel of Jesus Messiah" reflects an apparent break with all precedents. The assumption of this break by Mark with all precedents, especially his focus on Jesus' earthly ministry, has given rise to numerous explanations of Mark's Gospel.[173]

3.2.3. Yet the explanation of Mark's use of "gospel" may lie in the tradition rather than in the evangelist's creative genius. By common consensus I Cor. 15:3-5 and Rom. 1:3-4 represent traditions stemming from the early Church, and Acts 10:34-43, though more debated, most likely also represents a traditional underlay. Each tradition explicitly or implicitly uses the *Scriptures* to identify God's redemptive purposes at work in Jesus; each identifies Jesus as the *"Messiah,"* and each culminates in the *cross and resurrection* as the focal point of Jesus' ministry. In I Cor. 15:1 and Rom. 1:1 respectively, Paul calls the message he had received as tradition and for which he had been set apart "the gospel." Acts 10:36 refers to this event as the "preaching of the gospel of peace." Thus, one can correctly call this tradition the "gospel."

Furthermore, Mark's Gospel corresponds in broad outline with this tradition, especially christologically. Jesus is introduced in 1:1 as "Messiah, Son of God." This identity is then underscored by the voice from heaven at the baptism (1:11), at the Transfiguration (9:7), and ultimately by the centurion at the end (15:39), while Peter confesses Jesus to be the "Messiah" at the turning point, if not the climax, of the Gospel (8:29). The "Son" (Ps. 2:7), however, is qualified in 1:11 as the "servant" (Isa. 42:1), as the transfigured (exalted) one in 9:2-8, and as the crucified Son of God in 15:39. The "Messiah" is qualified as the suffering Son of Man in 8:31; 9:31; 10:33-34, whose true identity is recognized by the Roman centurion at the cross.

Therefore, Mark's Gospel corresponds with the christological anomaly found in the tradition noted above, namely, God's Son, the Messiah, accomplishes his work in the cross and resurrection. To this extent, Mark's Gospel, like the "gospel" in the tradition, is a passion narrative. But this correspondence fails to explain why Mark gives a narrative of Jesus' earthly ministry as the "gospel of Jesus Messiah" and how he can identify this with the "gospel of God" in its eschatological dimension. For the answer, one must look more closely at Acts 10:34-43.

3.3. There seems to be little doubt that Acts 10:34-43 shares the basic

---

173. Some eschatologically oriented: e.g. Marxsen, *Mark,* with a futuristic orientation, or Kelber, *Kingdom,* with a realized orientation; others christologically motivated: e.g. Weeden, *Traditions,* to correct a false θεῖος ἀνήρ christology, or Schreiber, *Vertrauen,* to depict the redeemer myth behind Phil. 2:6-11.

framework of the "gospel," as we know it in Mark.[174] But the question remains whether the framework results from Luke's reflected structuring of the material in 10:34-43 into a "mini-gospel"[175] or whether a pre-Lucan tradition underlay Acts 10:36-43 containing the framework to which the Gospels correspond. Much, therefore, depends on the status of Acts 10:34-43 in critical studies.

The evaluation of this passage has just about come full circle. Whereas Dibelius considered the material indicative of a pre-Lucan sermon "skeleton"[176] and Dodd found in it the outline of the primitive kerygma,[177] later appraisals of this and the other speeches in Acts attributed the form and much of the content to Luke's redactional creativity rather than to the tradition.[178] U. Wilckens, for example, concluded that Luke shaped this "sermon" in the form of a "gospel" appropriate to its more catechetical (cf. Luke 1:1-4) than evangelistic function in Acts 10 (cf. οἴδατε ὑμεῖς, 10:36). This setting accounts for Luke's addition of the rather extensive Jesus materials found at its core.[179] The trend now, however, appears to favor a broader pre-Lucan tradition adapted by Luke for his purposes in Acts 10.[180]

P. Stuhlmacher, in particular, has argued strongly for a pre-Lucan tradition on the basis of language, correspondence to the tradition in I Cor. 15:3-5, and the incongruity between Luke's own Gospel outline and the outline of the summary in 10:33-43.[181] More recently, G. Stanton has also argued for the pre-Lucan character of this material primarily on the basis of the unusual use of four Old Testament passages (Ps. 107:20; Isa. 52:7; 61:1; Deut. 21:22) to summarize Jesus' life and give it significance.[182] Stanton then lists several

174. E.g. Dodd, *Preaching;* U. Wilckens, *Die Missionsreden der Apostelgeschichte,* WMANT, [2]1963, 68-70; Stuhlmacher, *Evangelium,* 277, n. 2.

175. So Wilckens, *Missionsreden,* 68-70.

176. Dibelius, *Tradition,* 25. But see "Die Bekehrung des Cornelius," in *Aufsätze zur Apostelgeschichte,* FRLANT 42, 1961, 96-107, esp. 97-98, where he underscores Luke's redactional work in 10:34-43. Cf. K. Haacker, "Dibelius und Cornelius: Ein Beispiel formgeschichtlicher Überlieferungskritik," *BZ* 24, 1980, 234-51, esp. 244-46.

177. Dodd, *Preaching,* 46.

178. E.g. especially Wilckens, *Missionsreden,* 63-70; E. Haenchen, *The Acts of the Apostles,* ET 1971, 351-59.

179. Wilckens, *Missionsreden,* 68-70.

180. E.g. H. Conzelmann, *Acts of the Apostles,* Hermeneia, ET 1987, 80; O. Steck, *Israel und das gewaltsame Geschick der Propheten,* WMANT 23, 1967, 267-69; Stuhlmacher, *Evangelium,* 277, n. 2, 279, n. 1; E. Lohse, "Die Frage nach dem historischen Jesus in der gegenwärtigen Forschung," *ThLZ* 87, 1962, 161-64 = *Die Einheit des Neuen Testaments: Exegetische Studien des Neuen Testaments,* 1973, esp. 35-36; G. Stanton, *Jesus of Nazareth in New Testament Preaching,* SNTSMS 27, 1974, 70-81; J. Roloff, *Die Apostelgeschichte,* NTD V, 1981, 168.

181. *Evangelium,* 279, n. 1: a) The unusual use of εὐαγγελίζομαι in 10:36; the catechetical use of οἴδατε ὑμεῖς; cf. λόγον and Acts 13:26, 32. b) The titular use of Christ, 10:36; the resurrection on the "third day," 10:40; reference to Scriptural basis, 10:43, in place of the usual call to repentance in previous sermons in Acts, all correspond to I Cor. 15:3-5. c) Luke's Gospel begins with an infancy narrative (also Haenchen, *Acts,* 360f.; E. Lohse, *Einheit,* 35-36).

182. Stanton, *Jesus,* 70-78, suggests that Ps. 107:20 (and its context) provides the language that opens this material, τὸν λόγον ἀπέστειλεν (10:36). The context of Ps. 107:20 identifies the subject as God, and "the word" delivers God's people and "heals" them. This motif, according to Stanton, is

distinctive themes in 10:36-43 that either contrast with Luke's usage elsewhere or do not appear in Luke's writings.[183]

One might further support this argument for the traditional character of the material most in question, i.e. the "life of Jesus" summary in 10:37-38, by noting that it consists of expressions quite untypical of Luke's language,[184] such as: "Jesus, the one from Nazareth,"[185] "with the Holy Spirit and power,"[186] "doing good" (hapax legomenon), "healing those oppressed by the devil,"[187] and the observation, "God was with him."[188] When one adds the unusual references to "hang him on a tree," his being "raised on the third day," and ordained to judge "the living and the dead" at the end, and the unusual expression "preaching the gospel of peace through Jesus Christ" at the beginning, one must conclude that the evidence[189] strongly favors the existence of pre-Lucan material behind Luke's redaction in 10:34-43.[190]

---

carried through the summary in 10:37 where it is picked up in the Isa. 61:1 context. The "word" is then identified as that "proclaiming the good news of peace through Jesus Christ," which is drawn from Isa. 52:7, to explicate the first Old Testament allusion. This "good news" is then picked up in 10:38 by the reference to Jesus' baptism where he is "anointed" with the "Spirit" to proclaim the good news to the poor and to "heal" the afflicted, a clear reference to Isa. 61:1. Finally, another Old Testament reference, Deut. 21:22, expresses Jesus' death as "hanging on the tree." Since this weaving together of verses was typical of early Church exegesis as found throughout the New Testament, but not particularly typical of Luke's style, Stanton finds this passage to contain traditional material.

183. For example, *Jesus*, 78-79: 1) Why give the Baptist such prominence in 10:37, if otherwise the great redemptive-historical break between the Baptist and Jesus is Luke's theme? 2) Jesus is depicted as a miracle worker and prophet rather than as teacher, cf. Acts 1:1. 3) The devil in Luke is more "psychological" (so H. Conzelmann, *The Theology of Luke*, 1960, 157), whereas he is the oppressor in a Marcan sense in 10:38. 4) Acts 10:42 makes no reference to Gentile mission, a motif appropriate to the context and emphasized in Acts 1:8 and Luke 24:47.

184. Contra Conzelmann, *Apostelgeschichte*, 80. Stanton, *Jesus*, 78-79, notes that "peace through Jesus Christ" sounds more like Rom. 5:1 than Luke and "Judge of the living and the dead" has no parallel elsewhere in Luke.

185. Cf. Ἰησοῦς ὁ Ναζωραῖος in 2:22; 3:6; 4:10; 6:14; 22:8; 26:9.

186. Cf. Acts 1:8, but also Rom. 1:4; I Cor. 2:4; I Thess. 1:5.

187. "Healing," a rather common concept in Luke but never combined with "oppressed by the devil" (note Stanton's observation about Luke's use of the "devil" in n. 171).

188. Cf. John 3:2; 8:29.

189. The evidence may not be beyond question in part. For example, Luke's use of λόγος in Acts, especially in combination with the "gospel" (cf. 8:4; 15:7, 35), may suggest a Lucan adaptation in 10:36 rather than Ps. 107:20. (Note H. Riesenfeld, "The Text of Acts x.36," in *Text and Interpretation*, Festschrift M. Black, ed. E. Best and R. McL. Wilson, 1979, 191-94, who argues for the longer reading that would change the focus of λόγον.) Yet that would not ameliorate the force of Isa. 52:7; 61:1 and Deut. 21:22 and its usage in this passage. Stuhlmacher and Lohse's argument (see n. 170) based on the incongruity of Luke's Gospel and the outline of 10:32-42 loses weight when one observes that Luke does not begin Jesus' ministry until after the baptism, when John was removed from the scene (Luke 3:18-22). Furthermore, the absence of a call to repentance may stem from the context rather than being in compliance with a tradition comparable to I Cor. 15:3-5 (Steck, *Geschick*, 207, n. 3, attributes the call to repentance found in the other sermons of Acts to their peculiar setting in a Jewish mission). The reference to the "prophets" as scriptural basis for the message has its parallel in Luke 24:27, 42-44.

190. Luke's redaction appears most evident in 1) his temporal destinction between John's preaching of baptism and Jesus' "beginning." This bifurcation between the Baptist's ministry and

3.3.1. If one takes genre to consist of a work's form and material viewed as a whole, this tradition underlying Acts 10:34-43 anticipates the literary genre of gospel, since Mark's Gospel directly corresponds formally and materially with this tradition. *Formally,* Mark clearly follows a similar outline, as Dodd argued a generation ago. First, the evangelist specifically refers to the Baptist's appearance, the baptism of Jesus and his emergence "after John had been delivered up" to preach the "gospel of God" (1:14-15) as the "beginning" of the "gospel of Jesus Messiah." Second, the narrative of Jesus' ministry from Galilee to Jerusalem certainly corresponds to his going about "doing good" and "healing the oppressed" as seen by his ministry to those with various needs.[191] Finally, the passion narrative and the Easter appearances move the story to its concluding climax in Jesus' atoning death (10:45; 14:24) and the resurrection, motifs included and developed in the conclusion of Acts 10:39-43. Such an "outline" may seem most natural for a "gospel" until compared with the later writings bearing the designation "gospel" and even Q, which has at times been called a primitive gospel.

3.3.2. *Materially,* Acts 10:36 begins with a clear reference to the Old Testament context of Jesus' ministry by citing Isa. 52:7. Mark introduces his work as the "gospel of Jesus Messiah," which includes his preaching of the "gospel of God" (1:1, 14-15). Acts 10:36 refers to the events seen in Jesus' ministry, death, and resurrection as "God preaching the gospel of peace through Jesus Christ." In other words, both Mark 1:1 and Acts 10:36 characterize the message about Jesus Christ as the "gospel": Acts by using the verb form found in Isa. 52:7, Mark by using the noun form drawn from Christian preaching (1:1). The content of each is the same, namely, God's promised redemptive activity to bring salvation and wholeness, or, in other words, the establishment of God's sovereign rule, the "kingdom of God," in history (Isa. 52:7; 61:1) through Jesus' ministry, death, and resurrection. The "gospel of peace" in Acts 10:34-43 and the "gospel of Jesus Messiah" in Mark 1:4–16:8 are one and the same, and their roots lie in God's promise given by Isaiah, according to Mark 1:1-3 and the opening statement of Acts 10:36. Therefore, Mark's choice of terminology in 1:1, 14-15—"gospel of Jesus Messiah" and "gospel of God"—corresponds materially with the usage of Acts 10:36 and the content of Acts 10:36-43. This correspondence suggests a common "gospel" tradition in the Church.

If the basic *framework* of Mark's Gospel and the Scriptural context for

---

Jesus', especially apparent in Luke 16:16 (cf. 3:19-22), makes the reference to the "anointing" at Jesus' baptism which "begins" his ministry in 10:37-38 a bit awkward, since "beginning" precedes the reference to the Baptist's preaching of baptism. 2) The reference to the "witnesses" in 10:39a and 3) the common eating and drinking with Jesus sound very similar to Luke 24:41-43. Finally, 4) the reference to the prophets as the basis for what has transpired appears similar to Luke 24:27, 42-44.

191. Doubtless coincidental, but Mark opens Jesus' public ministry with the awkwardly introduced exorcism of 1:21-28.

his calling it the "gospel of Jesus Messiah" corresponds to what one finds in the tradition behind Acts 10:34-43, the traditional character of Mark's *material* used in writing the Gospel is even more apparent. Certainly the preliterary existence of the Gospel's material in oral traditional units is one of the "assured results" of form criticism, W. Schmithals notwithstanding.[192] Form criticism has also shown how much of this material has been shaped along familiar lines, so that the Gospels contain "forms" that correspond to those found in extrabiblical sources. But the very existence of these traditional units and even traditional blocks of units behind Mark's Gospel should make the existence of the "gospel" in narrative as well as conceptual or propositional form obvious.

While form critics have scrutinized each traditional unit for nearly two generations in search of its literary form and socio-religious Sitz im Leben, the research has too frequently forgotten that each traditional unit made its own "christological" as well as "ecclesiological" (and now "sociological") statement. To the extent that each unit bore witness in some manner to who Jesus was as the one in whom God was acting in keeping with his Word—a motif that formed all traditional levels of the Church's life from "Jerusalem" to "Rome," as the New Testament writings repeatedly indicate—to that extent each traditional unit functioned as an expression in part of the "gospel." Just as the "*conceptual* gospel" focused at times on the return of Christ (I Thess. 1:9-10), the atoning death and resurrection (I Cor. 15:3-5), or the exalted Son of God (Rom. 1:3-4), the "*narrative* gospel" found its expression at times in miracle stories, apothegms, sayings, parables, discourses, and even the passion narrative. These represent but various expressions of the gospel, the good news about what God was doing or had done in Jesus' ministry.

3.4. Mark's achievement, therefore, lies in selecting, arranging, and bringing together[193] the traditional narrative and saying units or blocks around the traditional framework of the gospel as seen behind Acts 10:36-43 and putting it in writing. To the extent that Mark first put the "gospel" in *written* form, he created a new *literary* genre, the gospel. But Mark did not create this genre *de novo*. The necessary formal and material components lay at hand in the tradition. In other words, the literary gospel ultimately represents the Church's gospel in narrative form.

---

192. Schmithals's assignment of the form and content to the creativity of the writer of the Grundschrift and his denial of any historical trace of underlying oral tradition (*Markus* I, 44-45) fly in the face of the results of form criticism and fail to account for the amazing stylistic similarity between the Grundschrift and similar narratives and sayings found in Matthew's and Luke's special traditions.

193. This is not to deny the special emphases or the redactional contribution made by the evangelist, such as his emphasis on discipleship and the "messianic secret." Yet the absence of any clear-cut "pattern," or for that matter any agreement among scholars even on an outline of Mark, suggests that his primary task was to write the "gospel of Jesus Messiah."

3.4.1. This literary gospel then became the model for at least Matthew and Luke and perhaps John. To be sure, none of the other Gospels followed Mark's lead in his use of εὐαγγέλιον,[194] and both Matthew and Luke made their respective modifications of the genre by their adaptation of it and other traditional materials to shape their own Gospels according to the evangelist's and/or his community's situation.[195] But the emphasis on the differences between each Gospel has tended to blur the basic similarity of all three synoptic Gospels. Jesus is consistently portrayed as the "Messiah" promised in the Scriptures who carries out God's redemptive purposes. Matthew and Luke underscore this by "beginning" their Gospels with infancy narratives whose function above all accents who Jesus is in light of the Scriptures. Furthermore, all three Gospels open Jesus' ministry in Galilee against the backdrop of Isa. 61:1, though each does so differently (Mark 1:14-15; Luke 4:16-21; Matt. 5:3-6[196]). This ministry consists of words and deeds that show him to be the one in whom God was redemptively at work inaugurating his *shalom,* his sovereign rule of justice.[197] Finally, Matthew and Luke conclude with a passion narrative that culminates in the Easter appearances to witnesses who are then commissioned to proclaim the message, an element much closer to Acts 10:36-43 than to Mark 16, as it now stands.

3.4.2. Even John's Gospel fits the same basic framework though differing greatly in the materials used. After a prologue that identifies Jesus in terms of God, creation, the Baptist, and Moses (N.B. the backdrop of Jewish Scriptures), the narrative moves from the Baptist, the "voice" of Isa. 40:3, through Jesus' signs and discourses to the cross and resurrection and concludes with the equipping and commissioning of the disciples by the resurrected Christ.

The relation of John, however, to the model, Mark, remains far from clear.[198] Whereas some trace John's outline back to Marcan influence and others to an independent tradition with common roots in the synoptic tradition, the issue is ultimately moot for this discussion. In either case, the fourth Gospel

194. Matthew focuses the term even more by defining it as the "gospel of the kingdom," a phrase certainly congruent with Mark's usage, if one takes kingdom of God in the sense used by Matthew as an expression of God's promised redemptive activity for his own. Luke may well follow Mark's lead by his redemptive-historical division of the "gospel" into Israel (Scripture), Jesus Christ (Gospel), and witnesses (Acts).

195. Yet to consider Matthew a "manual of discipline" fails to account for the significant differences between Matthew and such "manuals" as the Didache or the Qumran Manual of Discipline. To consider Luke a *bios* again fails to note the basic breakdown between Luke's Gospel and supposedly similar "lives."

196. R. Guelich, *The Sermon on the Mount: A Foundation for Understanding,* 1982, 112-18.

197. See P. Stuhlmacher, "The New Righteousness in the Proclamation of Jesus," in *Reconciliation, Law, and Righteousness,* ET 1986, 30-49.

198. For a thorough discussion of recent viewpoints, see R. Kysar, *The Fourth Evangelist and His Gospel: An Examination of Contemporary Scholarship,* 1975, 38-66 and his survey in *NovT* 15, 1973, 134-52.

attests the fundamental format of the Church's message about Jesus around which the literary Gospels were written. Should John indeed be independent from Mark,[199] then one has another basis for the traditional character of the gospel genre in the early Church's preaching and teaching. Acts 10:34-43, Mark, and then John would all share the same basic "genre" of the gospel.

3.4.3. But what about the so-called "gospels" emerging in the second century and later? How do they correspond to the genre of the four Gospels? The Church fathers do refer to a number of other works as "gospels," and several writings bearing the designation "gospel" have appeared in manuscript finds, most notably among the Nag Hammadi codices.[200] Yet many of these "gospels" come to us in name only, since their content exists only in scattered citations, if at all. Consequently, the literary evidence remains so fragmentary that one can hardly make adequate comparisons.

Two developments, however, can be traced. On the one hand, sufficient evidence exists to suggest that some of the "gospels" referred to by the fathers represent variations of the canonical Gospels.[201] These would have followed the Gospels in structure and material. On the other hand, a distinctive type of "gospel" emerges that radically differs in structure and material from the Gospels. Since these "gospels" often consist of discourses or dialogues of Jesus, some have placed them on a trajectory with Q as another form of "gospel."[202] To the extent that Q and these "gospels" represent to the hearer/reader the "gospel" = "good news by Jesus of God's redemptive activity," they would indeed be "gospels." But to the degree that they differ formally and materially from the gospel genre noted in the Gospels and in the tradition behind Acts 10:36-43, they do not belong to the gospel genre. The same conclusion would obtain for a collection of miracle stories, apothegms, parables, and even the passion narrative itself. Whereas these are constituent parts of the gospel genre, they are not the whole and do not represent the gospel genre.

Furthermore, one cannot speak of these later "gospels" generically, since

199. The apparent tendency in contemporary Johannine scholarship, as seen in the works of R. Schnackenburg, *The Gospel According to St. John* I, 1968, 68-72; R. Brown, *The Gospel According to John,* AB, 1966, I, xli-xlvii; B. Lindars, *The Gospel of John,* NCBC, 1972, 25-28; O. Cullmann, *The Johannine Circle,* 1976; E. Haenchen, *John,* Hermeneia, ET 1984, I, 75; S. Smalley, *John: Evangelist and Interpreter,* 1978, 102-19. Two notable exceptions are C. K. Barrett, *The Gospel According to John,* [2]1978, 15-22 and F. Neirynck, "John and the Synoptics," in *L'Evangile de Jean,* ed. M. de Jonge, 1977, 73-106.

200. For an extensive survey see R. Kraft and J. Timbie's review of *The Nag Hammadi Library in English,* 1977, in *RSR* 8, 1982, 32-52. For a collection of these and related materials, see R. Cameron, *The Other Gospels: Non-Canonical Gospel Texts,* 1982.

201. E.g. the Gospel of the Nazaraeans and the Gospel of the Ebionites both appear to be variants of Matthew's Gospel. The Secret Gospel of Mark clearly relates to Mark and the Gospel of the Hebrews may reflect influence from all four canonical Gospels.

202. So Robinson, *Trajectories,* 71-113, and Koester, *Trajectories,* 166-204.

they do not reflect any homogeneity in structure and/or content. For example, five of the works associated with Nag Hammadi bear the designation "gospel" either in the opening line or in an incipit.[203] Yet one, the Gospel of the Egyptians, deals with the life and redemptive activity of Seth; another, the Gospel of Philip, is a collection of teaching on the sacraments and ethics; another, the Gospel of Thomas, is a collection of teachings by the "living Jesus"; and another, the Gospel of Mary, is a revelation discourse of the resurrected Lord with his disciples. If one discounts the use of "gospel" with three of these,[204] two remain that consist of Jesus' secret teaching to one or more disciples (the Gospels of Thomas and Mary). This theme and content appears in six other works from Nag Hammadi and in the Epistle of the Apostles. But none of these carries the designation of "gospel."[205] Three even exist in the genre of an epistle.[206] Therefore, these later writings contribute little of significance for the discussion of the gospel genre. The most that one can say is that the term "gospel" continued to function in the Church as it always had with the broader meaning of the message of "good news" about Jesus as the one who brings salvation, even though salvation in these writings has been radically redefined in contrast to its meaning in the canonical Scriptures.

4. Summary and Conclusions ·

In light of the review and discussion of the gospel genre, several observations can be made to draw this material together in summary with some obvious conclusions.

4.1. The Gospels do stand without adequate parallel in form and content in the literary world. By comparison they share formally and materially more in common with each other than either or all shares with any other literary genre. Therefore, the Gospels do constitute a literary genre.

4.2. The Gospels constitute a literary genre, but not a "unique literary genre." The Gospels' collective distinctiveness lies in their forming a genre. By definition, genre connotes a certain formal and material uniqueness about a work or group of works. Therefore, "unique literary genre" is redundant, since by definition a genre is unique. By referring to the Gospels as *sui generis* one simply affirms that they constitute their own literary genre.

203. The Gospel of Truth, Gospel of the Egyptians, Gospel of Thomas, Gospel of Philip, and Gospel of Mary.
204. The Gospel of Truth, Gospel of the Egyptians, and Gospel of Philip; so Robinson, *Trajectories*, 76-78.
205. The First Apocalypse of James, the Apocalypse of Peter, the Apocryphon of James, the Book of Thomas the Contender, the Sophia of Jesus Christ, the Letter of Peter to Philip, and the Dialogue of the Savior.
206. The Apocryphon of James, the Letter of Peter to Philip, and the Epistle of the Apostles.

4.3. The representatives of this genre are limited in number (four canonical Gospels and fewer lost apocryphal Gospels) and in time (to the period of the emerging Church, a generation or so before and after the turn of the first century AD). Furthermore, three of the four canonical Gospels are so closely related as to suggest that one influenced the other two, if not also the fourth. The evidence even suggests that some of the apocryphal Gospels were dependent on these earlier Gospels. Nevertheless, one can still without hesitation speak of a gospel genre, since genre neither requires a set number of representatives nor total literary independence.

4.4. What then is this literary genre called a "gospel"? *Formally,* a gospel is a narrative account concerning the public life and teaching of a significant person that is composed of discreet traditional units placed in the context of the Scriptures. Mark, Acts 10:34-42, and John each set the narrative against the backdrop of the Scripture and focus, beginning with the Baptist's appearance to "prepare the way," on Jesus' ministry as it ranged from Galilee to Jerusalem where the narrative concludes with the death, resurrection, and appearances to the disciples. The infancy narratives in Matthew and Luke do not formally change this pattern, since they serve to identify Jesus particularly in light of the Scriptures rather than to signal the beginning of Jesus' ministry. They, like Mark's "beginning" (1:1-15) and John's "prologue," highlight the Scriptural context of the ensuing narrative. Furthermore, Mark's ending, as it presently exists, anticipates Jesus' appearances to his own, a fact obviously known to the reader. Thus, Mark could have concluded with this assumption of his reader's knowledge, or one can also argue for a "lost ending." Ultimately the issue is moot, since the resurrection and appearances of Jesus are not in doubt.

Formally, the framework or structure of this narrative existed in the Church's preaching and teaching. The evidence for this lies in the common framework underlying Acts 10:36-43, Mark's Gospel, and possibly John's Gospel. Yet this framework set only the general parameters, allowing for considerable flexibility in the arrangement of the materials within the framework, as a comparison of all four Gospels indicates.

Materially, the genre consists of the message that God was at work in Jesus' life, death, and resurrection, effecting his promises found in the Scriptures. In other words, the gospel genre made a statement about God, Jesus Christ, and his/their ministry. Set in the context of the Scriptures, the message makes clear that God is God, Yahweh, the Lord, who had spoken about his actions in history on behalf of his people and the nations. Jesus is identified as the one whom God had ordained and in whose life and death God was at work to accomplish his purposes. These purposes were the establishment of *shalom,* wholeness, the reestablishment of broken relationships between himself and his own, the defeat of evil, the forgiveness of sins, and the vindication of the poor.

The heralding of this message was called "preaching the gospel." Therefore, the message was indeed the "gospel of God" and simultaneously the "gospel of Jesus Christ."

Materially, the tone, language, content, and style to a great extent were found in the discreet traditional units used by the evangelists. This material had been formed, used, and preserved as oral tradition in the Church. Each unit had served to indicate what God was doing in Christ and its implications for the hearer. Some of the units had been combined into collections of stories and/or sayings. Some remained as independent units. The evangelists exhibit great freedom to take over *en bloc* or to combine and rearrange the materials for their own needs and purposes. Yet each reflects a care of and faithfulness to the tradition—even when their reworking is traceable. The message of each Gospel remains amazingly similar.

4.5. In view of the traditional character of the framework and the material, indicating that the contents were the common possession of the community, the evangelists had no cause for claiming their work to be "original" or "their" gospel. The Church's gospel was the message of "good news" to the hearer and so was the literary gospel for the reader. This message did not come from the evangelist but from Jesus Christ, and ultimately from God. Thus, the very nature of the message and its traditional roots necessitated that the Gospels be anonymous. It was the "gospel concerning Jesus Messiah" preached by Jesus and by his commissioned witnesses that the evangelists sought to capture in writing.

4.6. The evangelists' use of tradition, shaped at times in familiar forms analogous to other familiar forms such as miracle stories, apothegms, discourses, etc., means that the components of the gospel genre do at times have "literary" parallels. Yet the evangelists' use of the traditional framework and material inherent in the distinctive Christian gospel meant that the actual literary product, their Gospels, stood without parallel. The Gospels form a literary genre by virtue of the form and content of the tradition with which the evangelists were working. Therefore, while creating the "literary genre" of the gospel by placing the traditional message in writing, the evangelists did not create the form and content of this gospel. That was the "whole" from which the parts were understood in the Church's preaching and teaching.

4.7. Because the gospel was familiar to the Church, the written genre had its setting in a familiar context, a context from which to interpret the Gospels. This also means that the historical context within the early Church that made the gospel genre intelligible must be taken into consideration when interpreting the Gospels as literary works. Removed from the historical context of the Church's gospel, which gave rise to the literary gospel genre, the Gospels become like J. Swift's *Gulliver's Travels* set free from its sociopolitical context. Such works take on meaning from another genre (e.g. children's literature or fairy tale on the one hand; historical narrative, biography, comedy, or even apocalypse, on the other). Consequently, one misses or distorts the "authorial intent," an issue that is irrelevant for some literary critics, but quite germane if one takes seriously the gospel genre as delineated above.

4.8. Since the Gospels constitute a literary genre and since a genre gives the sense of the whole, the "context of expectation," for the parts, one must read and interpret each Gospel as a whole. The exegetical atomization of the Gospels leads to the distortion of the literary products just as the atomization of the tradition has led to the distortion of the Church's gospel.

4.9. What then are the Gospels? The Gospels are a literary genre whose form and content consist of, to use Mark's words, the "gospel of Jesus Messiah, Son of God."

Literary, Theological, and Historical Problems in the Gospel of Mark

Martin Hengel

1. A Disputed Gospel

No Gospel has occupied scholars so intensively over the last decade as that of Mark, and nowhere has the discussion been more heated than in connection with it. In Germany, four extensive commentaries have appeared one after the other in rapid succession, and the irreconcilable differences between them show up the dilemmas of research into Mark. The monumental two-volume commentary by Rudolf Pesch[1] regards Mark as the "conservative redactor"[2] who for the most part uses written sources—here Pesch parts company with the early form-critical approach—and works on his traditions sparingly and with restraint, refraining from ambitious literary and theological elaboration. Therefore for Pesch the Gospel of Mark is the main source for a reconstruction of the activity and passion of Jesus.

At the opposite extreme to this stands the radical "redaction-critical" commentary by Walter Schmithals.[3] He throws overboard the results of the form criticism of his own teacher R. Bultmann, which for long had hypnotized

---

1. R. Pesch, *Das Marcusevangelium,* HTK II/1, [3]1980; II/2, [2]1980. See the extended critical reviews by F. Neirynck, *Evangelica, Gospel Studies—Études d'évangeli,* BETL 60, 1982, 491-564.

2. Op. cit., 1, 2: "Because Mark is guided by catechetical and missionary interests, because the conservative redactor is compiling traditional material and is hardly producing literature. . . ."

3. W. Schmithals, *Das Evangelium nach Markus,* two vols., ÖTK II/1, 2, 1979, and here above all the Introduction, 1, 21-70. See the review by Neirynck (above n. 1, 613-17): "Malgré le caractère fantaisiste de certaines positions de S., son commentaire rendra certainement service à l'exégèse marcienne" (617). Quite certainly, the author shows all that can be done with Mark today. He has now put forward his imaginatively constructed theories in the article "Evangelien," *TRE* X, 1982, 570-626 (above all 600-612), as the summary of about two hundred years of critical study of the Gospels. Here he refers above all to the investigations made by Gustav Volkmar, of which he has had a study made in a dissertation: B. Wildemann, *Das Evangelium als Lehrpoesie. Leben und*

scholars,[4] and in a final, consistent development of the work of Wrede sees Mark as a poet and theologian creating his own composition; in his view, by using a minimum of tradition and under the influence of a non-Christian Galilean Jesus sect, Mark has produced something like a "Jesus romance" with a marked theological profile. Here he was the first to introduce into the earliest history of Christianity the problem of the narrative Jesus tradition. Having spoken of "Mark," though, I must correct myself: the evangelist was not this creative theological genius; that role was played by the unknown author of a basic document. Schmithals attributes all that is "fine and good" to the latter; the evangelist himself largely corrupted this unique outline by introducing the messianic secret and many other follies.

For all their basic differences, the authors of both commentaries do, though, agree on one thing: in their almost unlimited confidence in the possibilities of literary criticism in the Second Gospel, a confidence which again dominates wide areas of New Testament scholarship today. Here we find ourselves taken back almost to the heyday of dissection into literary sources, in the nineteenth century, when attempts were made to extract an earlier "Ur-Markus" or a number of sources from the present Gospel. Thus Schmithals makes a razor-sharp division between "light and darkness," the basic document and the additions by the "dumb fool" Mark; with no less confidence, Pesch extracts the many written sources of the evangelist, especially the pre-Marcan passion narrative, deriving from the Jerusalem community of the late thirties. This, he believes, begins as early as Mark 8:27ff. Here he feels that we are on rock-hard historical ground.

The third commentary by Joachim Gnilka and the fourth by Josef Ernst[5] attempt, each in its own way, to find a balance between the extremes, which is not always easy. One could describe them both with Ovid's words, *medio tutissimus ibis*— you are safest in the middle.[6]

Werk Gustav Volkmars, Berlin theological dissertation 1982. Here one is reminded of the scene between Faust and Wagner:

> Forgive, it is a great amusement
> to put oneself in the spirit of the times
> to see how a wise man thought before us
> and how we have then recently developed things so splendidly.

4. Cf. W. Schmithals, "Kritik der Formkritik," *ZTK* 77, 1980, 149-85.

5. J. Gnilka, *Das Evangelium nach Markus,* EKK II/1, 1978; II/2, 1979 (on this cf. the review by Neirynck, op. cit., 609-31) and J. Ernst, *Das Evangelium nach Markus,* RNT, 1981.

6. *Metamorphoses* 2.137.

2. A Collector or a Creative Theologian?

(a) Redaction Criticism and Form Criticism

All in all, we might say that the tendency of scholars, above all in the USA, but also in France and Germany, is toward a purely redaction-critical approach, sometimes supplemented by structuralism, which neglects traditio-historical and historical questions. Even more radically than in Bultmann's time, many scholars believe that it is impossible in practice and a sign of antiquated methodology to ask historical questions about the earthly Jesus. One might almost suppose that, in the case of the earliest Gospel, views take a similar direction to that which has long been prominent in the case of the Gospel of John: i.e., the concern is only with the theological "bias" of the author and perhaps still with the sources which he used. Insufficient attention is paid to the fact that the author is not writing a theological treatise or even a polemical work which seeks to contest belief in miracles or a *theologia gloriae*,[7] but is narrating history, or more exactly, that he is describing the activity of Jesus, from his call to his messianic office to the message of the resurrection given by the angel at the empty tomb—in a manner that can well be compared with a biography, which at that time could take many different forms.[8] Those who heard the

7. A typical example of such investigations is the article by T. J. Weeden, "The Heresy that Necessitated Mark's Gospel," *ZNW* 59, 1968, 145-58, and his subsequent study, *Mark: Traditions in Conflict*, 1971; cf. his preface to the 1979 paperback edition, viif.

8. A possible connection between the Gospels, and above all the earliest Gospel, and ancient biographies was resolutely challenged by the fathers of form criticism. Granted, R. Bultmann, *History of the Synoptic Tradition* (1931), ET [2]1968, 370, concedes the decisive fact that "it seems but natural that the tradition which had an historical person at its center should have been conceived in the form of a coherent, historical, biographical story" (it is certainly not that; we could also have had a fabricated myth with heavenly journeys and revelations in the style of Enoch or the Ascension of Isaiah, in which above all the risen and glorified Jesus was portrayed), and even says that Mark "was the first to try to write . . . *a presentation of the life of Jesus*" (348, my italics). Then, however, he largely withdraws these insights by rejecting "Hellenistic biography" as a possible "(analogy) for explaining the form of the Gospel" with the often-quoted statement (cf. e.g. R. Pesch, op. cit., 1, 2), "There is no historical and biographical interest in the Gospels; that is why they have nothing to say about Jesus' human personality, his appearance and character, his origin, education and development" (372). The work does not have "a biographical unity, but a unity based upon the myth of the kerygma" (371). Here Bultmann is not only concerned with a modern scientific understanding of the "historical-biographical interest" which he fails to find in Mark; he also misunderstands completely the literary variety of "Hellenistic biography," which is not always interested in "appearance, character, origin, education, and development" in the same way.

The amazing thing about ancient biography is its varied form. Not only the ancient biographies of Heracles, Achilles, Theseus, Romulus, and many other figures from the primal period but also those of Pythagoras, Alexander, and Augustus show that myth and biography are not exclusive (cf. C. H. Talbert, *What is a Gospel?* 1977, 25ff.). Plutarch wrote biographies both of heroes from the mythical period (Heracles—this has not survived—Theseus, and Romulus) and contemporaries (Otho, Galba). His forty-eight biographical portraits which have survived are very different in content, though they have the same basic tendency. Although they are divided from the Gospels by a great gulf in terms of aim and style, they do contain numerous parallels: delight in

Gospel of Mark and the subsequent Gospels simply understood them as unique "biographies" which bear witness to the career and teaching of the unique Messiah and Son of God, Jesus of Nazareth. No one in antiquity thought that the Gospels were a literary genre of a quite new and special kind. It was not the literary genre that was unique but the person described in it and his work of salvation.

This kind of "biographical" narrative, which is not connected with an ongoing chronology—that only emerges after the entry into Jerusalem (Mark 11:1ff.)—but consists of "small units," i.e., brief anecdotal scenes which are joined together by brief transitional passages and between which individual groups of logia are sometimes interspersed, certainly has parallels in antiquity, both in the "Jewish" and in the "Hellenistic" sphere. However, I cannot go into that question in more detail here.

In this connection it is crucial to note that the collection of material, which recalls the rabbinic collections of anecdotes (Aboth of R. Nathan) or some Old Testament narrative cycles (the Samson, David, Elijah, and Elisha stories), indicates that Mark is not presenting romantic fiction, freely composed, with a theological coloring, but is working with material from tradition. An expert in Semitic popular tradition like Julius Wellhausen demonstrated that clearly, well before the discovery of form criticism. In Mark, we look in vain for the "revelation discourses," so typical of the Fourth Gospel—even in Mark 13 he uses predominantly pre-existing tradition. This bond with earlier individual traditions distinguishes Mark quite fundamentally from later romantic apocry-

---

miracle and anecdote, the focal point in the "passion narrative" (e.g. in Cato Minor and Eumenes), the scant chronological interest, the lack of a deeper psychology and a real development, the characterization through "words and actions," and so on. In some of them, the youth and education of the subjects are narrated extremely briefly (e.g., Sertorius and Eumenes or Lucian's Demonax). I hope that I shall have the opportunity to develop this theme at more length. In literary terms, Mark and Matthew seem to me to be better and more "dramatically" arranged than many of Plutarch's *Lives;* see pp. 213-17.

For the problem see also A. Dihle's essay in the present volume; G. N. Stanton, *Jesus of Nazareth in New Testament Preaching,* SNTSMS 27, 1974, 117ff.; M.Hengel, *Acts and the History of Earliest Christianity,* ET 1979, 18ff. H. Cancik, "Die Gattung Evangelium. Markus im Rahmen der antiken Historiographie," and "Bios und Logos. Formen geschichtliche Untersuchungen in Lukians 'Leben des Demonax,'" in *Markus-Philologie,* WUNT 33, 1984, 85ff., 110ff.

Moreover, scholars tend to overlook the fact that we have a biographical tradition from the Old Testament and Judaism which extends from the patriarchal narratives in Genesis, through the life of Moses from Exodus to Deuteronomy (see pp. 248ff.), to Tobit, Judith, and Esther and which has links with "Hellenistic biography" in II Maccabees, Philo, and Josephus, and especially in Philo's *Vita Mosis.* Old Testament scholars have so far taken too little notice of these "biographical" features of the narrative texts, or of the prophetic books. There are the beginnings of this in K. Baltzer, *Die Biographie der Propheten,* 1975, cf. especially 38f. The salvation-historical narrative tradition about men of God must have had biographical features. The special character of the Gospel lies in the fact that here we have the narrative of a "biographical" saving event in Jesus of Nazareth the Son of God, culminating in his death, which is unique and valid for all.

phal testimonies like the Protevangelium of James, the Infancy Gospel of Thomas, or the so-called Acts of Pilate, and for that very reason a *radical* redaction-critical approach cannot do him justice. Here form criticism still has an important task. Mark does not simply want to invent something new; he wants to find an appropriate way of expressing the Jesus tradition, which is binding on him. Here Pesch is quite right; the question is simply in what form Mark had the tradition, whether in written sources which can still be reconstructed by literary criticism or in oral form, already shaped kerygmatically by worship. The "pre-Marcan collections" which people are nowadays fond of discovering in the Second Gospel—e.g. in Mark 2–4—cannot in any way go back to a written source by another author. What is supposed to be "critical" scholarship simply posits things here which cannot be proved. The fact that long after Mark there was still a wealth of oral traditions about Jesus, many of them, of course, with a dubious form, is shown not only by Papias's zeal as a collector, but even more by the hyperbolic remark in John 21:25. *Radical* redaction critics basically do not know what to make of this kind of account; on the contrary, it is striking how in their concern to dehistoricize Mark's narrative they have recently found themselves led into an unbounded allegorization of the material, as they have to attribute to it a deeper, unhistorical, symbolic-dogmatic significance.[9]

On the other hand, though, the form-critical approach which has long prevailed has misunderstood the theological and literary competence of the second evangelist. Because he wrote in such a simple unliterary style, and with often apparent artlessness strung together individual pericopes one after the other; because the literary framework of the Gospel, which demonstrably comes from him, was amazingly simple, he was seen even more than the authors of the First and Third Gospels, rooted more strongly in literary convention, as the "collector and redactor."[10] Rudolf Bultmann goes so far as to claim that: "Mark is not sufficiently master of his material to be able to venture on a systematic construction himself."[11]

(b) The Arrangement of a Dramatic Narrative

In fact more recent investigations have again disclosed how marvelously Mark has arranged his Gospel. This is not a completely new insight. Adolf Jülicher,

9. That is true both of the exposition by W. Schmithals and of the investigations by W. Schreiber, *Theologie des Vertrauens,* 1967; *Die Markuspassion,* 1969, and his article "Die Bestattung Jesu," *ZNW* 72, 1981, 141-77, which is quite untested by historical insights. For a criticism of this method cf. E. Grässer, "Text und Situation," *Gesammelte Aufsätze zum NT,* 1973, 15 n. 9, 29f. n. 91. In this way Mark simply becomes a cryptogram the key to which has to be guessed at. Here we are at the threshold of a new epoch of exegetical whim, and may expect a good deal more of it.

10. M. Dibelius, *From Tradition to Gospel,* ET reissued 1971, 3.

11. R. Bultmann, *History of the Synoptic Tradition,* 350.

who was relatively critical of form criticism, already came to the conclusion that "The arrangement of the whole is well considered and effective." Of course we cannot echo Jülicher's other remark just as it is—"for on the whole Jesus' life developed in the way in which Mark portrayed it."[12] We simply know too little about this life as a connected whole.

However, one may say that Mark constructed his work as a dramatic narrative in several "acts," which might almost be said to correspond to the laws of ancient tragedy as worked out by Aristotle in his *Poetics*. In the same way it has proved possible to rediscover in it the laws governing arrangement in ancient rhetoric. This markedly literary approach may seem to be alien to the material or even to amount to playing with the Gospel, but it does help us to a better understanding of the work, which has been misunderstood by radical form criticism.[13]

In this way a very clear construction has been discovered in Mark, full of inner tension and very consistent. I do not want to discuss here the numerous attempts at division, but largely follow the proposal put forward by F. G. Lang:[14]

The evangelist begins with a "salvation-historical" "prologue" (1:1-13), which contains the appearance of John the Baptist and Jesus' baptism and temptation. As the last representative of the old covenant, already with an eschatological stamp, John the Baptist provides the external stimulus to the calling of Jesus to his "messianic office."

There follows as the "first act" the account of the activity of Jesus in Galilee (1:14–3:6), before the appointment of the Twelve. At the beginning we find a rhetorical *propositio* comparable to the programmatic summary of the

---

12. A. Jülicher and E. Fascher, *Einleitung in das Neue Testament,* [7]1931, 297. Cf. his article "Marcus im NT," *RE*[3] XII, 1903, 288-97. The remarks by Jülicher on Mark are among the best that have been written on the Second Gospel. Cf. e.g. 294:

> He is a master of the "gospel" material; from the wealth of what has been handed down about Jesus Christ he selects and groups material as seems appropriate to win new faith and strengthen old faith in the Son of God despite his apparent defeat. He writes not as a historian but as a religious agitator, but perhaps his greatest achievement was the insight that the most effective way of carrying out this agitation was to write a history of Christ, a continuous narrative of the life of Jesus. He did not practice historical criticism on his material . . . but similarly, he was not a didactic poet, nor did he try to preserve another's work exactly even down to the wording.

Jülicher anticipated much of what I shall be going on to say.

13. See above all the extremely stimulating dissertation by B. H. M. G. M. Standaert, *L'évangile selon Marc. Composition et genre littéraire,* Nijmegen, 1978, and before him the article by F. G. Lang, "Kompositionsanalyse des Markusevangeliums," *ZTK* 74, 1977, 1-24, of which too little notice is still taken.

14. Op. cit., 18ff. For the different attempts at division see R. Pesch, op. cit. (n. 1), 1, 32ff.; idem, *Naherwartungen,* 1968, 50ff. Of course there is no "absolutely valid" solution here. We cannot reconstruct exactly the plan which Mark made for himself before writing the Gospel. Therefore the discussion of details will be endless.

proclamation of Jesus in 1:14, 15. This account comes to a dramatic conclusion in 3:6: the first resolve by the Herodians and Pharisees, as representatives of the spiritual and religious leaders, to kill Jesus, after a series of controversial discussions.

The "second act" depicts the climax of Jesus' activity, beginning with the gathering of the crowds (3:7f.), the appointment of the Twelve, and the great miracles. Here the chapter of parables, 4, signalizes the hardening of heart among the people which was produced by the preaching of Jesus. Mark 6:1-6, the outright rejection in Nazareth, is an important turning point; in this pericope Mark very skillfully introduces all the necessary biographical details about Jesus' profession and family which we did not have in the brief introduction of Jesus in 1:9. The "second act" comes to a climax—in contrast to the external success of Jesus, but in analogy to 3:5—with Jesus' reproach to the disciples that they completely misunderstand him, and indeed that their hearts are hardened (8:14-22) because they have not understood the significance of his authoritative teaching (1:22, 27) and actions. Not only the leaders of the people, who have been Jesus' opponents from the start (3:5f.), and the crowds, but also Jesus' relatives and neighbors, indeed even his disciples, refuse to believe in him. It is this *universal* disobedience which necessitates Jesus' course toward a representative expiatory death. A novelistic digression about the execution of John the Baptist (6:14-29) is framed by the sending out of the Twelve. It demonstrates that there is no stopping the message of conversion for the sake of the coming kingdom of God, and is at the same time a pointer to the passion as the goal of the whole dramatic narrative. The miracle stories also move clearly toward a climax. They begin with a simple exorcism (1:23ff.) in the synagogue and reach their peak in the twofold feeding of the five thousand and the four thousand (Mark 6:35-44; 8:1-9).

The Gospel achieves its *peripeteia* in the third act, which to some degree brings the *anagnorisis*,[15] the disclosure of the messianic secret, in Peter's confession. F. G. Lang comments on this:[16]

In stylistic terms, the erroneous views about Jesus are first reported (v. 28) and then Peter confesses Jesus' true identity (v. 29). This produces a new situation for the disciples: being in the know about Jesus, they have been sworn to silence (v. 30). This leads to a new tension which is only resolved

15. Cf. Aristotle, *Poetics* 11.5 = 1452a.32: καλλίστη δὲ ἀναγνώρισις, ὅταν ἄμα περιπέτεια γένηται.

16. Op. cit., 20f. Here Lang refers to H. Lausberg, *Handbuch der literarischen Rhetorik*, 1960, I, 585, sec. 1213: "A sudden piece of knowledge which introduces a change of direction (μεταβολή) in the action." It presupposes an error, "tension in information between the person who is not informed and reality" (586). For the basic role of "recognition" in Mark cf. also Standaert (n. 13), 89ff.

by Jesus' acknowledgment before the Sanhedrin of who he is (14:61f.).
Moreover, up to 8:21 Jesus has external success, visible in his mighty acts
and the advent of the crowd; 8:31ff. equally abruptly brings the *peripeteia*,[17] the sudden shift to "misfortune": in accordance with all the
artistic rules . . . the announcement of the passion contains the element of
necessity (v. 31) and at the same time the element of surprise, in that Peter
makes a protest against it (vv. 32f.).

The intrinsic necessity of the course of suffering is manifest at the end of the "third
act" in 10:45 (see below, n. 24); Peter's confession as *anagnorisis* is matched in
10:46-52 by the messianic cry for help from the blind beggar immediately before
the last stage on the way up to Jerusalem. It shows that the mysterious knowledge
of Jesus' messianic authority has spread despite the prohibition—and it is precisely
this that will be the cause of his doom in Jerusalem.

The *lusis* or *katastrophe*, the violent breaking of the knot that has been tied,[18]
takes place in Jerusalem; it is directly prepared for by the "fourth act" (11:1–13:37),
with the entry, the cleansing of the temple, the controversies with representatives
of different groups, and the final eschatological instruction of the disciples.

With 14:1, the final resolve of the leaders of the people to put Jesus to
death, the "fifth and last act" and the *pathos*[19] proper begin; in a paradoxical
way this ends with the confession of the Gentile centurion that the crucified man
is the Son of God (15:39).

The deposition in the tomb and the discovery of the empty tomb form the
"epilogue" (15:40–16:8); here the Galilean women, who hitherto had been
completely passed over, keep the action going and form the bridge between the
crucifixion and what happens at the tomb (15:40-42, 47; 16:1ff.). One might
almost be tempted to compare the appearance of the angel to the women at the
empty tomb with the *Deus ex machina*[20] of the tragedies of Euripides, who
ushers in the miraculous change that brings a happy ending.

Of course the division proposed here is not the only possible one; the
ancient theories are not themselves agreed over the form of a dramatic *fabula*.
One might think of only three "acts":[21] 1:14–8:26; 8:27–10:52; 11:1–15:39.

---

17. Aristotle, *Poetics* 11.1 = 1452a.22ff.: ἔστι δὲ περιπέτεια μὲν ἡ εἰς τὸ ἐναντίον τῶν
πραττομένων μεταβολή . . . καὶ τοῦτο δὲ . . . κατὰ τὸ εἰκὸς ἢ ἀναγκαῖον. Cf. H. Lausberg, op. cit., I,
584f., sec. 1212.

18. See H. Lausberg, op. cit., I, 568, sec. 1194, 3 quotes Scaliger: *catastrophe (est) conversio
negotii exagitati in tranquillitatem non expectatam*, cf. I, 569f., sec. 1197.

19. Cf. op. cit., I, 583, sec. 1207 and Aristotle, *Poetics* 11.10 = 1452b.9ff.: alongside
περιπέτεια and ἀναγνώρισις, πάθος is the third important ingredient of the dramatic narrative (μῦθος
= *fabula*): πάθος δέ ἐστι πρᾶξις φθαρτικὴ ἢ ὀδυνηρά, οἷον οἵ τε ἐν τῷ φανερῷ θάνατοι καὶ αἱ
περιωδυνίαι καὶ τρώσεις καὶ ὅσα τοιαῦτα.

20. Cf. Standaert, op. cit. (n. 13)., 99ff.

21. Cf. H. Lausberg, op. cit. (n. 16), I, 568ff. secs. 1193-97. Aristotle begins from three parts,

This, too, preserves the decisive points of the tying of the knot, the *peripeteia* and the *resolution,* connected with the theme of *anagnorisis.*

Be this as it may, in terms of extent, construction, and inner drama the Second Gospel remains a work which can be illuminated in an amazing way by the rules which Aristotle established in connection with the successful form of literary mimesis. The statement from his *Poetics,* τὸ γὰρ καλὸν ἐν μεγέθει καὶ τάξει ἐστί,[22] can directly be applied to this work, which displays a compact, recognizable, well-ordered, and thought-out form.

F. G. Lang and Standaert go one stage further and would even presuppose as the literary aim of the evangelist the well-known effect of φόβος καὶ ἔλεος, fear and pity, which according to Aristotle the tragedy should produce in the public.[23] However, in this work, which from the beginning was created for worship, and indeed in my view grew out of worship, we may not in principle presuppose any division between "theological" and "literary" aim. As a kerygmatic narrative the Gospel has only one aim: to evoke and strengthen faith; the literary aims of producing tension, exaltation, and deep emotion are completely subordinate to this.

All in all, the form of the Gospel, composed in such a magisterial way, along with analogies between it and the dramatic *fabula* and rhetoric, should not lead us to questionable conclusions about the origin, education, and intention of the author (see below, pp. 230ff.). The dramatic element in his work is essentially different from that of Greek tragedy, for all its contacts with Aristotle's poetic theory. It is not a matter here of the intertwining of guilt and destiny, but of the presence of salvation precisely in the suffering and death of the Son of God—though this is misunderstood time and again.

(c) Arrangement and Theological Reflection

Almost every pericope and every logion has its well-considered place and its paradigmatic character. One could, for example, suppose that the soteriological

---

Poetics 7.3 = 1450b.26f.; cf. 12.1 = 1452b.14-16: μέρη δὲ τραγῳδίας . . . τάδε ἐστίν, πρόλογος ἐπεισόδιον ἔξοδος. The χορικόν as a fourth part can be left out of account as far as the *fabula* is concerned. Horace, *De arte poetica* 189, strictly demands five acts for the *fabula* and adds (191): *nec deus intersit, nisi dignus vindice nodus/inciderit.* Standaert, op. cit. (n. 13), 50f., posits an underlying rhetorical scheme of (introduction), narration, argumentation, dénouement (conclusion): (1:1-13;) 1:14–6:13; 6:14–10:52; 11:1–15:47 (; 16:1-8); here in turn he divides the middle section into three units: 6:14–8:21; 8:22–9:29; 9:30–10:52 (148, 172, 298ff.). However, I cannot see such a decisive break in 6:13, as 6:30 is directly attached to it. All attempts at division are in danger of being exaggerated for the sake of the cohesion of the scheme.

22. *Poetics* 7.2 = 1450b.37f. Cf. already Jülicher, *Einleitung* (n. 12), 297: "Mark has the best τάξις of all the Gospels. "

23. F. G. Lang, op. cit. (n. 13), 21, even wants to understand the ἐφοβοῦντο γάρ at the end in this sense. Cf. also Standaert, op. cit., 102ff.

significance of the death of Jesus as a representative atoning death was not of central importance for Mark because in the whole of the Gospel it is mentioned only twice, at 10:45 and 14:24. However, if we look more closely, we discover that both passages are stressed by the context: 10:45 brings to an end the whole instruction of the disciples before the entry into Jerusalem, which from 8:31 stands under the shadow of the suffering Son of Man, and 14:24, the saying about the blood of the covenant which is shed for many, marks the climax of the Last Supper scene. In other words, the position of the two texts in the wider context of the Gospel as a whole shows how unjustified such a judgment would be.[24]

The fact that Jesus forgives sins is expressed clearly only once (2:5-10), yet this is particularly important for the understanding of Jesus in Mark; that is the very reason why Mark has made it the theme of the first controversy with the religious leaders of Israel who are thinking to themselves in terms of the accusation which brings down on Jesus the death sentence from the Sanhedrin: "He blasphemes God." The first and last conflicts with his opponents agree in this verdict (2:7; 14:64).

We can only understand the significance of this action, which is narrated just once, at the beginning of Jesus' activity, in connection with the two statements about atonement toward the end, if we investigate the description of the overwhelming power of sin in Mark, which Jesus encounters through his activity and death. It does not just affect his opponents or the mass of the people, but equally the disciples, including their spokesman Peter, and indeed even the

---

24. Cf. e.g. J. Wellhausen, *Das Evangelium Marci*, [2]1909, 84: "The ἀπολύτρωσις by the death of Jesus finds its way into the Gospel only here; immediately before this, he has not died *for* the others and in their place, but has died *before* them." This is to misunderstand the climactic significance of 10:45, and makes the death of Jesus meaningless. P. Vielhauer, *Aufsätze zum NT*, ThB 31, 1965, 200, is an example of the false verdicts one arrives at by failing to note Mark's arrangement of his material:

The conception of the atoning death of Jesus ... is not determinative for Mark's christology. It occurs only twice (Mark 10:45; 14:24), and is missing completely where one would most expect it, in the passion narrative proper and the announcements of the passion. The dominant thought here is of the divine δεῖ, the foreknowledge of Jesus and his readiness to accept suffering; that is determined by scriptural proof and the idea of the fulfilment of prophecy.

In reality Mark 10:45, as the conclusion and climax of all the instruction of the disciples from 8:31 onward, is the first passage to put the career of Jesus in the right light; here the negative contrast saying in 8:37 prepares for the decisive concluding saying (see pp. 215f. above). Similarly, 14:24 illuminates the whole of the subsequent passion narrative. The tearing of the curtain of the temple in 15:38 is similarly best understood in the light of Leviticus 16, the sacrifice on the Day of Atonement. Mark 14:21, 49, the concluding saying of Jesus at his arrest, ἀλλ᾽ ἵνα πληρωθῶσιν αἱ γραφαί, shows that the divine δεῖ is not to be understood as a contrast to "scriptural proof" and "the fulfillment of prophecy," but rather that the two belong indissolubly together. J. R. Donahue is right here, in W. H. Kelber (ed.), *The Passion in Mark*, 1976, 13: "The leitmotiv of his whole Gospel," and 77, "a saying (10.45) which summarizes the theology of 8.27–10.52." For the tradition history and originality see P. Stuhlmacher, "Vicariously giving His Life for Many, Mark 10:45 (Matt. 10:28)," *Reconciliation, Law, and Righteousness: Essays in Biblical Theology*, 1986, 16-29; and M. Hengel, *The Atonement*, 1981, 34ff., 42, 49ff., 71ff.

women who run from the empty tomb "in fear and trembling" and do not obey the word of the angel (16:8).[25] Here sin apparently has the last word, and yet is already overcome by the atoning death of Jesus.

Mark does not narrate events and traditions simply by chance: what he selects and describes has a deeper significance, as a "typical ideal," from the call of the disciples up to Gethsemane and the crucifixion of Jesus as king of the Jews. *However, this strictness in his overall plan does not simply dispense with historicity; Mark only reports history which has undergone the deliberate reflection of faith.*[26] Even apparent incidental remarks like 7:3f.; 13:10, 14b; 14:9 and so on are significant as theological reflection. He does not create new narratives and sayings of Jesus in order to develop his own christology and soteriology, but uses a very deliberate process of selecting and ordering material in which hardly anything is left to chance.

In complete contrast to the form-critical approach, which saw the synoptic Gospels—and here again Mark in particular—as a product of popular "minor literature" growing up unconsciously, Standaert, in his investigation which is so surprising at many points, has conjectured on the basis of the discovery of dramatic or even rhetorical artifices in this mysterious work that the author had had a thorough training in rhetoric and literature. Only by his simple style did he accommodate himself to the capacity of his hearers to understand.[27] However, an analysis of biographical narratives from the Jewish Old Testament tradition, like Esther, Susanna, Judith,[28] the David and Elijah narratives, and

---

25. For the flight of the women, which corresponds to that of the disciples in Gethsemane (14:50 and 16:8: ἔφυγον), see M. Hengel, "Maria Magdalena und die Frauen als Zeugen," in *Abraham unser Vater. Festschrift für Otto Michel zum 60. Geburtstag,* 1963, 253.

26. For the connection beween faith and history see the worthwhile comments by H. Weder, "Zum Problem einer 'christlichen Exegese,' " *NTS* 27, 1981, 64-82, and idem, *Das Kreuz Jesu bei Paulus,* FRLANT 125, 1981, 49-119: "At all events it is inadmissible simply on the basis of their [viz. the Gospels'] kerygmatic character to argue for their historical unreliability. Unreliability can only be established in individual instances and by means of a *documentary* argument" (59ff.). Here the concept of "historical unreliability" must primarily be measured against ancient standards and not by the lofty ideals of modern criticism.

27. Standaert, op. cit. (n. 13), 486-91, 619ff., "De façon générale on peut affirmer que Marc est, dans l'histoire de l'éloquence chrétienne, un des tout premiers témoins du *sermo humilis,* tel que l'a défini plus tard Augustin" (488). F. G. Lang, op. cit. (n. 13), 18, already came to the conclusion: "If it is demonstrated that Mark makes use of a developed technique of composition, then of course his Gospel comes close to 'high literature.' That then presupposes a degree of literary training in the author." He goes on to presume in 22 n. 48 that while Mark had not studied Aristotle's *Poetics,* he was familiar with the nature of the Hellenistic theatre. This was not impossible even in Jerusalem. As the exagoge from the Hellenistic Jewish poet Ezekiel shows, dramatic theatre was even performed in Jewish circles. But such a hypothesis is unnecessary for understanding Mark as a writer. Dramatic story-telling and writing could also be learned from Old Testament and haggadic writings and novels.

28. Standaert himself has produced a comparative analysis in the light of the Book of Judith, op. cit., 392ff. Certainly this dramatic novella from the time of the successful Maccabaean revolt reflects the influence of Hellenistic literary conventions. Nevertheless it would be basically wrong

especially the Joseph story, could show that the rules of the well-ordered *fabula* which Aristotle brought to light were also valid outside the Graeco-Roman world.[29] The art of narrative is older, and does not necessarily presuppose academic education in the sense of Hellenistic rhetoric. That does not exclude the possibility that the rhetorical presentation of teaching, the capacity for lively narrative and refined discourse, could be learned in the Greek-speaking synagogue and the earliest community for missionary purposes.[30]

---

to presuppose that the author had a thorough training in rhetoric, since in all probability the work derives from a Hebrew original. For this see A. M. Dubarle, *Judith,* AnBib 24, 1966, I, 80-110, and E. Zenger, *Das Buch Judit,* JSHRZ I/6, 1981, 430f. Cf. also there, 436ff., on Judith as a "Hellenistic romance."

29. The coincidence of the *peripeteia* of a narrative and a recognition scene can also be found in the Joseph novella, Gen. 45:1-15, cf. J. G. Williams, *JBL* 101, 1982, 435: " 'composite artistry' of a high order." The verdict by H. Donner, *Die literarische Gestalt der alttestamentlichen Josephsgeschichte,* SHAW.PH [2]1976, is similar, cf. especially 10ff., 36, on the principle of doubling in the composition. The Saul and David narratives up to the account of the latter's succession to the throne offer masterpieces of admirably arranged, dramatic narrative art, in which the moment of knowledge on each occasion forms the climax of the narrative (cf. e.g. I Sam. 9:16ff.; 20:25ff.; 28:15ff.; II Sam. 12:5ff.; 18:19-32). For the Elijah narrative in I Kings 17–19 see now R. L. Cohn, "The Literary Logic of I Kings 17–19," *JBL* 101, 1982, 333-50: "An excellent example of a carefully woven literary tissue . . . the richness of its structural and thematic texture. At the same time that the story develops linearly, it establishes three parallel episodic sequences" (333, 349). At the same time, these examples show that artistic arrangement, tense narrative, and historical account need not necessarily be fundamentally opposed.

30. Therefore we can hardly assume that the author of the Second Gospel was an avid theatergoer or had advanced rhetorical training in the Hellenistic school. In my view there is no evidence that his very simple style, which Matthew and Luke improve, is simply a matter of adaptation to the hearer and is not his natural way of speaking. For the language, marked with semitisms, see N. Turner, *Style* (J. H. Moulton, *A Grammar of New Testament Greek* IV), 1976, 11-29: "On the one hand, it is felt that Mark's style is unpretentious, verging on the vernacular; on the other, that it is rich in Aramaisms. The latter are so much in evidence that early in this century scholars were convinced that Aramaic sources had been translated" (11). However, all his Greek is simple: ". . . he is manipulating none too skilfully but with a curious overall effectiveness, a stereotyped variety of Greek, rather inflexible and schematized, adhering to simple and rigid rules" (28).

In addition there is the fact that we have no literary work in Greek which has as many Aramaic expressions and formulae as the Second Gospel. See H. P. Rüger, "Die lexikalischen Aramaismen im Markusevangelium," in H. Cancik (ed.), *Markus-Philologie,* WUNT 33, 1984, 73-84: "The large number of lexical Aramaisms in the Gospel of Mark and the relative uniformity of the way in which they are reproduced by means of the Greek alphabet suggest that Mark could cope with Aramaisms." M. Reiser, "Alexanderroman und Markusevangelium," *Markus-Philologie,* 131-63, refers to the parallels in style and narrative method in the popular Alexander romance from the end of the third century.

Only fragments have come down to us from what was certainly an abundant Jewish Hellenistic literature—apart from Philo and Josephus and some "apocryphal texts." The pseudo-Philonic sermons *De Jona* and *De Sampsone,* which have both been preserved in Armenian, give us some impression of synagogue preaching, cf. F. Siegert, *Drei hellenistisch-jüdische Predigten* I, 1980. It can hardly be doubted that Greek-speaking Judaism had its own schools for the study of Scripture, apologetics, and liturgical rhetoric. Evidence of this, even in Jerusalem, is the well-known Theodotus inscription, *CIJ* II, no. 1404; cf. M. Hengel, *Between Jesus and Paul,* 1983, 17f.: ῷκο/δόμησε τὴν συναγωγὴν εἰς ἀν[άγν]ω/σ[ιν] νόμου καὶ εἰς [δ]ιδαχ[ὴ]ν ἐντολῶν.

3. The Fidelity of the Dramatic Narrator to History

It is clear from what has been said so far that the extremely different assessments of the Second Gospel by scholars rest on the fact that this work—probably more than any other New Testament writing, at least for the modern reader—is concerned with a *coincidentia oppositorum* which combines what German theological scholarship for a long time saw as an irreconcilable opposition: on the one hand narrative with dramatic tension, a clear theological and kerygmatic profile worked out with great literary skill, and on the other what for the circumstances of antiquity was a very respectable fidelity to tradition and history. All this is presented in an outwardly simple form and barbaric style. Mark certainly does not deal with his material more freely than, say, Plutarch. He selects examples from the tradition and shapes it, and of course he has a theological bias, but he does not simply have to invent things out of thin air. In him the separation of "tradition" and "redaction" is very difficult—if we leave aside the simple frameworks and stereotyped introductions—since like most of the writers of antiquity he adapts the material from the source or the tradition to his own style.[31] Precisely in so doing, he wants what he presents to be the gospel of Jesus Christ, εὐαγγέλιον Ἰησοῦ Χριστοῦ, that brings together two apparently irreconcilable things:[32] the narrative historical and biographical account and the proclamation of salvation as an address. Indeed, even for Mark, salvation did not lie in the changing theological constructions relevant to a particular period, but in what God had achieved for all men through his Son, the "carpenter" Jesus of Nazareth (Mark 1:9; 6:3), from the Sea of Galilee to Golgotha and the tomb in the rock, in a relatively short space of time about forty years before he wrote.[33] This obliges the narrator *also* to report the event in the

---

31. See S. J. D. Cohen, *Josephus in Galilee and Rome: His Vita and Development as a Historian,* 1979, 24-47:

> On the whole Josephus was faithful to his sources: he neither invented new episodes nor distorted the essential content of those previously narrated. However, he did not confuse fidelity with slavish imitation. Like all ancient historians, he molded his material to suit his own tendentious and literary aims . . . the language of the source was not reproduced but was entirely recast [47].

32. Typical of this ominous false opposition which even now pervades the literature is W. Marxsen, *Mark the Evangelist,* ET 1969, 131:

> It is a gospel. From the outset that means that his work is to be read as proclamation, and as such is an address and not "a report about Jesus." From this aspect, it is almost accidental that something in the way of a report also appears. In any case, it is only raw material. Paul can largely disregard this raw material.

Here W. Schadewaldt, the famous classical scholar, in *Die Zuverlässigkeit der synoptischen Tradition,* ThBeitr 13, 1982, 201-23, takes quite a different view.

33. For criticism of the widespread docetic attitude which is hostile to history, see H. Weder, *NTS* 27, 1981, 74-78. As Weder rightly stresses, message of salvation and historical event are not

past as it is detached from the present—a present of which the evangelist is only too well aware.[34] The hearer is invited to turn aside, to spend some time with the preacher and miracle worker Jesus in distant, foreign Galilee, to stand beside him in the last battle in Jerusalem and take part in his passion, like the women, from afar. At that time, when the Son of God was delivered over to be ultimately forsaken by God, God himself founded the new covenant in his blood and sealed it through the resurrection of the dead.

In his account, which retells a past event, Mark expresses in detail what Paul seeks to express in extremely concentrated form, focused on a single point, through the aorists of his confessional formulas and the reference to the cross of Jesus—though that should not be wrongly understood as a mere theological cipher. He describes the action of God in his Christ which took place in the past once and for all, and which preceded all the re-action of believers.[35] We could regard the statement in Rom. 5:8, "God showed his love for us in that Christ died (ἀπέθανεν) for us while we were still sinners" as a heading for the whole of the Second Gospel. For this "passion narrative with extended introduction"[36] is from the beginning directed toward the death of Jesus, since that alone is the real foundation of the salvation of believers. Therefore particularly in Mark this can be said to be integral to the "lived life of Jesus."[37]

---

simply identical. The history of Jesus points beyond itself because faith recognizes in this Jesus that God has come in him to us men.

> If we bear in mind how the synoptic Gospels refer to the history of Jesus, it is striking that they are not simply concerned with telling the story of Jesus. Rather, they keep leaving the historical sphere by narrating the history of Jesus as the history of the coming of God into the world. . . . The fascinating thing here is that faith has nevertheless never left the historical behind [75f.].

Here it should be remembered that for earliest Christianity, as for Judaism, history embraces a wider area than it does for us today. The heavenly world participates in earthly history (Luke 15:7, 10), and earthly history is directly dependent on what happens in heaven and is related to it (Luke 10:18; Mark 14:62). Our—premature—division of immanence and transcendence is therefore not to be found here.

34. For being-present-with Jesus and historical distance see J. Roloff, *Das Kerygma und der irdische Jesus,* 1969, 110ff., 205ff.

35. In connection with the Pauline theology of the cross. On this see H. Weder, *Kreuz* (n. 26), 12 n. 1, 40ff., 123ff., 154f., 165 n. 164, 179f., 224ff.; idem, *NTS* 27, 1981, 76:

> Paul never limited himself to giving only historical expression to the death of Jesus—say as the martyrdom of a prophet. He understood the death of Jesus on the cross as the action of the love of God (cf. Rom. 5.8). However, for him the cross never became a mere theological cipher. Rather, it denotes the particular, specific death of Jesus, and this character is decisive (cf. e.g. Gal. 3.13).

See also M. Hengel, *Crucifixion,* 1977, 88ff.; *Atonement,* 1981, 33ff., 65ff.

36. Cf. H. Weder, *Kreuz* (n. 26), 56 n. 22.

37. E. Jüngel, *God as the Mystery of the World,* ET 1983, 302 (italics in the original):

> There is an hermeneutically persuasive reason that the eschatological event of the identification of God with the Crucified One became an integral part of the life of Jesus as it was

Here lies the fundamental difference from the logia tradition, which Mark knows in a very distinctive form and takes for granted as being familiar to his audience. That he is writing later than the collection of sayings of Jesus in the so-called logia source follows from the fact that where he is working with individual traditions and logia which also appear in Q, his version is always more developed and later. One might almost say that he is writing the theologically necessary complement to such a collection only of the sayings of Jesus, which has become inadequate from the standpoint of the post-Easter community because—as Q shows—it lacks the kerygma of the death and resurrection and also an explicit christology. In my view this is an indication of the age and originality of such collections; the basic material in them could go back to the Hellenists in Jerusalem and they are probably already presupposed by Paul. Quite apart from the passion narrative, Mark introduces predominantly what is lacking in the logia source: miracle stories, controversies, and teaching specifically directed toward the disciples.[38] The sayings tradition which Mark incorporates was, of course, substantially different from the so-called Q source which Matthew and Luke used; therefore it cannot simply be said that he knew Q in the form that we find in Matthew and Luke. However, he was familiar with the sayings tradition of Jesus, though he included only relatively little of it in his Gospel. Because Mark put what we miss in the sayings tradition, the kerygma of the passion and christology, at the center of his "story of Jesus," he could describe it not as λόγια κυρίου, i.e., "words of (the revelation of) the Lord," but with good reason as εὐαγγέλιον Ἰησοῦ Χριστοῦ (see below, pp. 244, 250f.).

---

lived and thus became a rich story which demanded explication. In that sense, no theology of the Crucified One can or may do without the narration of the life and suffering of Jesus, as a life in the *act of the word* which tells of God's humanity.

Cf. also 302f.

38. Mark 1:22, ἦν γὰρ διδάσκων αὐτοὺς ὡς ἐξουσίαν ἔχων, and 27, διδαχὴ καινὴ κατ' ἐξουσίαν, presuppose among the congregation hearing the Gospel read in the service the knowledge of such teaching by Jesus with messianic authority. Matt. 7:28 has with good reason related the formula in Mark 1:22 to the audience of the Sermon on the Mount. The Gospel of Mark, as a passion narrative with extended introduction, does not claim to cover the whole of the tradition of Jesus which was available to the community. To some degree it was concerned to supplement the traditional "Jesus halacha" with an account of the "Jesus haggadah," which narrated the saving event and was necessary for faith. For the difficulty of the problem see M. Devisch, "La relation entre l'évangile de Marc et le document Q," in *L'Évangile selon Marc*, ed. M. Sabbe, BETL 34, 1974, 59-91. The conclusions which W. Schenk, "Der Einfluss der Logienquelle auf das Markusevangelium," *ZNW* 70, 1979, 141-65, draws on the basis of very hypothetical literary and form-critical considerations, namely that "Pre-Mark is primary to Q" but that the "Mark redaction is secondary to Q" (see ibid., 161) are not convincing. The most thorough investigation by R. Laufen, *Die Doppelüberlieferung der Logienquelle und des Markusevangeliums*, BBB 54, 1980, 386f., comes to the conclusion that neither Q nor Mark is literally dependent on the other but that in the case of the nine parallel traditions investigated, Q seems earlier in four cases and Mark in two, whereas in three cases both Mark and Q show partially earlier features. However, his analyses have not convinced me where he claims a priority for Mark, e.g. 93ff. on Matt. 3:11/Luke 3:16 in comparison with Mark 1:7f. and 302ff. on Matt. 10:38/Luke 14:27 and Mark 8:34.

At the same time, however, that means that he is not writing his account of Jesus to captivate the reader, to satisfy a need for historical information, or to admonish and improve him morally—although according to the standards of antiquity he also does all this. Still less does he want to satisfy pious desires for sensation through narrating the miracles of Jesus, any more than he wants to counter an exaggerated desire for miracle. Jesus' actions are quite ambivalent; they provoke the accusation that he is in league with the devil, i.e., is a magician, and they do not produce permanent, constant faith even in the disciples. Against the background of the *dynameis* of Jesus, the hardness of heart which affects everyone without exception appears all the more terrifying. For the evangelist the miracles are a reference to the messianic *exousia* of Jesus and an expression of the eschatological fulfillment of prophetic promises. Both these things cannot be understood in terms of the worn-out catchphrase *theios anēr*.

Of course this is not to forget the reference to the present experience of his community, the direct address to his readers or hearers. The terrifying example of the disciples is at the same time a warning, and the invitation to self-denial, discipleship, and taking up the cross cannot escape any hearer. The fatal error in the interpretation of the Gospels in general and of Mark in particular has been that scholars have thought that they had to decide between preaching and historical narration, that here there could only be an either-or. In reality the "theological" contribution of the evangelist lies in the fact that he combines both these things inseparably: he preaches by narrating; he writes history and in so doing proclaims. This is to some degree the *theological* side of that *coincidentia oppositorum* which marks out his work. At this point he has the model of Old Testament historiography before him, where this unity of narration and proclamation is often visible.

The intermediate reference to the present becomes clear above all in Mark 13, the so-called synoptic apocalypse, which for Mark represents the testament, the eschatological farewell discourse of Jesus. In this way it contains something like an extremely abbreviated "Church history in a nutshell," which leads up to the time at which the author was writing, presumably shortly before the destruction of Jerusalem.[39] The last word of Jesus, "What I tell you"—i.e., the

---

39. The question is whether in view of the complete destruction of the temple by Titus, Mark 13:1f. could be a new construction by the evangelist. I think this improbable. The expectation of a possible destruction of the temple was earlier than this. Moreover, 13:14ff. does not refer to specific events in the Jewish war but to an early Antichrist tradition from Jewish-Christian apocalyptic. Those who fled into the "hill-country" of Judah before the Roman advance in AD 70 ran directly into the hands of the Romans or the fanatical Sicarii in and around Masada. The experience depicted in the account of the messianic woes in 13:14-18 basically goes back to the period of the religious distress under the Seleucids. There is no mention of the destruction of Jerusalem and the concrete events of the Jewish war in 13:14-18, in contrast to the Matthean and Lucan parallels (Matt. 24:15, ἑστὸς ἐν τόπῳ ἁγίῳ, cf. 22:7; Luke 21:20, cf. 17:31; 19:43f.). Elsewhere, too, Mark has no reference to the siege and conquest of Jerusalem by the Romans. See now "The Gospel of Mark: Time of Origin and Situation," *Studies in the Gospel of Mark,* 1985, 1-30. The Gospel was presumably written in Rome in 69.

four disciples who are standing around Jesus, seated (13:3) on the Mount of Olives, looking at the temple—"I say to all, 'Watch!' " (13:37; cf. 14:38), shows that in the time of the evangelist the saying of Jesus addressed to the disciples in the Gospel has become a saying for a persecuted and threatened Church which is eagerly awaiting the parousia of the Son of Man.

4. The Messianic Secret

Following William Wrede, scholars have been fond of describing the "messianic secret" as the key to understanding the Second Gospel. There is some degree of justification in this, but the perspective must not become too one-sided. Thus it can be said with a pinch of salt that the question of the messianic authority and mission of Jesus gives the whole work its unity and that the theme of hiddenness is an essential part of it. However, all this is not artificially foisted on recalcitrant material, but is bound up with the innermost nature of the event that is described. Moreover, the whole complex has far more layers and is much more complicated than has been long assumed. Thus the way of Jesus to the cross, his expiatory death for the many, and the disciples' taking up the cross are just as important for Mark as the deliberate veiling of Jesus' messianic claim before the people. Only in suffering does the Marcan Jesus manifest his messianic status in the full sense. Messianic status and representative suffering belong indissolubly together.

More recent research has long been at odds over the unity, extent, and significance of the so-called messianic secret precisely because of these complications in the matter.[40] In the strict sense it applies only to two direct statements

---

40. The basic study is now H. Räisänen, *Das "Messiasgeheimnis" im Markusevangelium,* 1976, 159 (as translated in C. Tuckett [ed.], *The Messianic Secret,* 1983, 132):

> Wrede's study brought to prominence the basic question of whether the theological viewpoint of Mark's Gospel is based on a *single* secrecy theology. After the analysis undertaken [by Räisänen], the answer must be in the *negative.* Indeed it is not enough to separate from the secrecy theology the "contradictions" which were also identified by Wrede. It has transpired that even the material assembled by Wrede does *not* have the homogeneous unity which he and most exegetes have thought.

Cf. also the excursus by R. Pesch, op. cit. (n. 1), 2, 36-47. I cannot, however, accept Pesch's view that Mark can reconcile a "christology with a variety of conceptions, expressed in different kinds of traditional material with a christology oriented on the different honorific titles; . . . indeed he does not have a christological conception of his own" (45). The question is what Pesch wants to understand by "a christological conception of his own." Our modern understanding of theological "originality" is alien to Mark. He simply wants to give expression to the work and status of Christ, Son of Man and Son of God, in a way which corresponds to the truth that has been handed down. But he does this in a deliberately reflective way and has a christology of suffering and exaltation with an independent stamp which has contacts partly with Paul and above all with I Peter. Individual themes of it are developed further in Hebrews.

by Jesus: the first command to the disciples to be silent, after Peter's confession (8:30) and before the first prediction of the passion, and the second, when they are coming down the mount of revelation (9:9), to those with him, that they are to "tell no one what they had seen until the Son of man had risen from the dead." For Mark these are the consequences of the tremendous fact that the Messiah and Son of God did not reveal himself immediately in "the glory of his Father with the holy angels" (8:38) but obediently trod the way of the cross. For contemporary Judaism, as for the ancient world generally, this was an unheard-of and thoroughly offensive idea, which the disciples could not understand because it contradicted the traditional messianic expectation of salvation.

It is significant that from 9:13 on, the theme of the "messianic secret" fades completely into the background, at least outwardly, and in essence has already been done away with from the time of Bartimaeus's confession in Jericho (10:48) of Jesus as "Son of David." This time the disciples want to prevent the public confession, while Jesus positively accepts the cry. The situation has changed. The question of authority (11:28) already indicates that the leaders of the people know of Jesus' claim and want to use it to lure him out into the open; the high priest's question (14:61) is no longer a surprise: it simply puts into words ideas which have long been in the air and could already have motivated the accusation connected with the saying about destroying and rebuilding the temple (14:58). The surprise was Jesus' clear, unsurpassable confession of his unique status. There is no support in the text for the disclosure romance which Schweitzer wove around the unveiling of the messianic secret, to the effect that Judas had betrayed it to the leaders of the people. Mark does not present the whole matter as mysteriously as that. Indeed, already from Mark 9:11 onward there is no longer any injunction to the disciples to keep silent.

The other ingredients of the so-called messianic secret that Wrede constructed do not form a real unity, so they no longer call for any questionable overall theory, which in any case cannot be worked out strictly; these elements first of all have to be explained on their own terms. It goes without saying that Jesus rejects the acclamation that comes from the supernatural knowledge of the demons; he is in a battle with them. Here one could refer to James 2:19: "the demons believe and tremble." But their special knowledge, expressed in the call of the Stronger One who conjures them out, is inappropriate, and therefore they must be put to silence. The powers of evil cannot be legitimate witnesses to Jesus' divine sonship.[41] At the same time, Mark wants to use this theme to demonstrate the contrast between the people and the disciples, who do not yet know Jesus' status, and the invisible world of the spirits, who from the beginning have recognized Jesus as their messianic conqueror.

---

41. Mark 1:24f.; 1:34; 3:11f.; 5:7.

The commands to keep silent after healings, which are not maintained consistently, are meant to make clear that as a miracle worker Jesus wants to remain hidden. He wards off the press of the masses, in contrast to the popular miracle workers and magicians of the Hellenistic and Roman period, who could often be encountered in the Jewish sphere as well.[42] Both the command to keep silent at exorcisms and the prohibition to those who are healed against proclaiming their healing aloud may thus go back to the behavior of Jesus himself.

As H. Räisänen has shown, the so-called theory of parables (4:10ff.), i.e., that Jesus speaks in riddles to harden the heart of the people, has even less direct connection with the messianic secret. It is meant to explain the fact—which later caused offense to the community—that despite the teaching and the miracles of Jesus, the people did not recognize him in true faith but rejected him. They could not believe, because they did not understand Jesus' proclamation in "riddles."[43]

The hardening of heart and misunderstanding among the disciples in connection with Jesus' way to his passion are also to be separated from the messianic secret proper: they correspond to the lack of illusion in the anthropology of the evangelist, who in his narrative, and without special terminology, brings out something that was also familiar to Paul. One could refer to Rom. 3:22ff. as a commentary on that: "for there is no difference" (in Mark between the disciples and the people),[44] "for they have all sinned and fallen short of the glory of God, and are without merit justified by his grace through redemption in Jesus Christ." As I have already said (given contemporary exegesis of Mark one cannot repeat this often enough), it is no coincidence that the instruction of the disciples ends with the logion about the service of the Son of Man—Servant of God for the many (10:45), and that at the heart of the Last Supper we have the saying about the blood of the covenant which is shed (14:24). Marcan soteriology is based on these two sayings. Even self-denial and the discipleship of the cross are only possible under this sign: the logion 8:37, "for what may a man give as ransom for his life?," which concludes the whole complex, indeed

---

42. Mark 1:44 (cf. already 1:35ff.); 5:43; 7:36; 8:30; cf. also 9:30. This will have historical roots. Jesus the miracle healer did not see any propaganda for his person in the healings, and at times he had to ward off the masses.

43. H. Räisänen, *Die Parabeltheorie im Markusevangelium*, Helsinki 1973. This is presumably a secondary construction which need not, of course, come from the evangelist himself. The saying about the hardening of Israel's heart in Isa. 6:9f. = Mark 4:12 was in fact circulated widely in earliest Christianity (see John 12:40; Acts 28:26ff.; Rom. 11:8; II Cor. 3:14).

44. All are affected by the hardening of heart. The leaders of the people (3:5): συλλυπούμενος ἐπὶ τῇ πωρώσει τῆς καρδίας αὐτῶν; the crowd (4:12); the disciples (6:52): ἀλλ' ἦν αὐτῶν ἡ καρδία πεπωρωμένη, (8:17): οὔπω νοεῖτε οὐδὲ συνίετε; πεπωρωμένην ἔχετε τὴν καρδίαν. This twofold stress on the hardening of the disciples' hearts gives the reason why the way of suffering revealed in 8:31 is necessary for Jesus. From 8:32 on, the rejection of Jesus' suffering is the expression of such hardening.

points to the necessity of the sacrifice of Christ, as does 10:27, the answer to the terrified question of the disciples, "then who can be saved?": "With man it is impossible but not with God."

Hardly anyone still puts forward in its original form Wrede's famous theory, taken over by Bultmann,[45] that Mark stressed the messianic secret so much because the evangelist (or the tradition with which he was working) wanted to conceal the fact that in reality Jesus had no messianic self-awareness. The "messianic secret" is usually no longer explained by an attempted historical reconstruction but as an expression of specifically Marcan theology, predominantly his *theologia crucis*. However, the Marcan theology of the passion does not need such secondary expedients.[46] Quite apart from that, there is the question whether one may simply attribute to the redactional work of the evangelist all the *very* different components which are combined under the handy formula of the messianic secret. They are too complex, indeed too disparate for this. Certainly all this can *also* be subsumed under the umbrella phrase "the mystery of Jesus and his way of suffering." But this "mystery of Jesus" is not a secondary theory imposed by Mark on the whole tradition; its real basis lies in the mystery of the earthly Jesus himself.

In my view the phenomena of the messianic secret—in contrast to Wrede's theories, reduced and disparate—are best explained in terms of the tradition with which Mark worked. This tradition was still aware of Jesus' messianic claim, the reality of which should not be doubted, since otherwise, historically and in terms of their content, the whole of his activity up to his passion, which is without parallel in the history of ancient religion, not to mention the development of the earliest christology after Easter, would be incomprehensible. We have no indication whatsoever from the history of tradition that the status of Messiah in Judaism was connected in any way with the resurrection of a righteous man or prophet from the dead. Therefore it is hard to derive the messianic status of Jesus simply from the resurrection appearances. Appearances of the dead in a transfigured form and messianic status are two completely different things. Christology cannot be derived solely from the resurrection event—no matter how it is interpreted. The root must be sought in Jesus' conduct and execution. Of course he did not express his messianic claim

45. R. Bultmann, *Theology of the New Testament* I, ET 1952, 26-32: "The attempt to understand the Messiah-secret not as a theory of the evangelist but as historical fact (Schniewind), falls to pieces against the fact that its literary location is in the editorial sentences of the evangelist, not in the body of the traditional units" (32). Precisely that view is no longer tenable. Redaction and "old tradition" cannot be separated so easily. Therefore there is a growing tendency today to see only "redaction" almost everywhere, and to make Mark a "theologizing romancer" or "didactic poet" so that he can then be interpreted allegorically. In this way Mark is handed over even more to the whim of exegetes (see above, pp. 211-13).

46. See the accounts of research in H. Räisänen, op. cit. (n. 40), 18-49.

in a public proclamation, as in the Gospel of John, but at particular points, and indirectly, above all in instructing the disciples.[47]

In the last resort, the messianic secret goes back to the mysterious messianic authority of Jesus. So it is no invention of the gospel of the pre-Marcan community, but an expression of the mystery of Jesus himself which presses forward to the question of the Messiah. Mark expresses it in 4:41 by the question, "Who is this, that wind and sea obey him?" The mystery of the messianic *exousia* of Jesus and the mystery of the kingdom in 4:11 are indissolubly connected in the historical person of Jesus himself.[48] The discrepancies in the individual statements go back to the disparateness of the traditions about Jesus with which Mark is working, and have their ultimate root there. With so unique a figure as Jesus, who bursts all historical frameworks, there could be no "one-dimensional tradition," without tensions and apparent contradictions. His person and activity cannot be forced into the confines of ready-made christological theories.

5. The Theological Background of the Author

(a) His Relation to Paul

The soteriological contacts of the Second Gospel with Paul, which have often been mentioned, should not lead us to make Mark directly dependent in his theology on the apostle to the Gentiles.[49] Where there are echoes, they go back to common "pre-Pauline" traditions. There is hardly any trace in the Gospel of a direct connection between the two. The basic difference consists in the fact that Mark develops his εὐαγγέλιον Ἰησοῦ Χριστοῦ as a biographical account of Jesus, whereas Paul in his letters only expresses Jesus-traditions very peripherally and formally. There is therefore no direct route from the Pauline gospel for

---

47. See J. Jeremias, *New Testament Theology: The Proclamation of Jesus*, ET 1971, 250-99. For the messiahship of Jesus in the trial see A. Strobel, *Die Stunde der Wahrheit*, WUNT 21, 1980; and O. Betz, "Probleme des Prozesses Jesu," in *ANRW* II, 25/1, 1982, 565-647; see now also, in the same volume, the contributions by R. Leivestad, "Jesus-Messias-Menschensohn," 220-64, and H. Bietenhard, "Der Menschensohn . . . ," 265-350.

48. J. Jeremias, op. cit., 120, 256f.

49. Here I cannot go beyond the basic insights of Martin Werner's investigation, *Der Einfluss paulinischer Theologie im Markusevangelium*, BZNW 1, 1923, even if he stresses the differences in rather too pointed a way. Cf. already P. Wernle, *Die synoptische Frage*, 1899, 199ff., and also G. Delling, *Der Kreuzestod Jesu in der urchristlichen Verkündigung*, 1972, 57: "When all is said and done, Mark is not a pupil of Paul, i.e., has no direct contact with Pauline theology." Cf. 57f.: "We meet Mark as a representative of a *theologia crucis* in the time after Paul and his community . . . , as the witness to a *theologia crucis* alongside Paul; since all in all the Marcan community can hardly have shaped its traditional material on its own, the developed interpretation of the cross which we find here points us back, at all events in its beginnings, to the time before Paul." Could we not replace the unknown "Marcan community" here with a "teacher of Mark"? K. Romaniuk, "Le Problème des Paulinismes dans l'évangile de Marc," *NTS* 23, 1977, 266-74, is relatively critical.

the Gentiles, which is proclaimed in the preaching of the justification of the sinner by Christ, to the history of Jesus in Mark, though the evangelist not only knows but has worked out in a sublime way (2:13-17) the theme of the turning of the Son of God to sinners.

However, it is significant that in connection with the theme of Jesus and the sinners he does not echo the theme of the mission to the Gentiles in any way. The Jewish publicans are not a simple parable for "the Gentile sinners" (Gal. 2:15). The ministry of Jesus the Messiah is directed first of all to Israel. Nor is it possible to build any direct bridge to the evangelist from pre-Pauline formulas like I Cor. 15:3f., which indeed the apostle explicitly terms *euaggelion,* for here nothing is said about the activity of Jesus before his death. In order to understand Mark better we must ultimately investigate his origin and his tradition.

(b) The Greek-Speaking Jewish Christian from Jerusalem

Mark was a Greek-speaking Jewish Christian who also understood Aramaic. That is evident from the correct Aramaic quotations in his Gospel. I do not know any other work in Greek which has as many Aramaic or Hebrew words and formulas in so narrow a space as does the Second Gospel. They are too numerous and too exact to be explained as the conventional barbarisms (ῥῆσις βαρβαρική) of the miracle worker and magician. This fact of itself makes it very improbable that the Gospel is to be derived from "Gentile Christianity" (cf. Mark 3:17-19; 5:41; 7:11; 8:34; 10:46; 11:9f.; 14:1, 32, 36, 45; 15:22, 34). Most of these foreign-sounding words are omitted by Matthew and Luke. Presumably Mark came from Jerusalem; while he was unfamiliar with Galilee, he does know Jerusalem and Palestinian Judaism.[50] His "deficient knowledge" of the geography of Galilee, which contemporary exegetes like to criticize, in fact simply shows up the latter's historical incomprehension: without a map it would be difficult even for a man of antiquity like Mark to establish his bearings in a strange area a good seventy miles from his home city, which he had presumably left long before he began to write his work,

---

50. K. Niederwimmer, "Johannes Markus und die Frage nach dem Verfasser des zweiten Evangeliums," *ZNW* 58, 1967, 172-88, wants to see the author as an unknown Gentile Christian, "to whom Judaism is basically alien" (185). However, one can only infer from Niederwimmer's arguments that Judaism in the time of Jesus (and the problems of geographical knowledge in antiquity and the reliability of polemical descriptions in ancient texts) are basically alien to him. S. Schulz, *Die Stunde der Botschaft,* 1967, 127f., 139, believes on the basis of the chronological detail in 14:12 "that as a Gentile Christian Mark was no longer familiar with the complicated passover regulations" (ibid., 127), cf. E. Lohse, *Die Geschichte des Lebens und Sterbens Jesu Christi,* 1964, 43. In reality, the author, who is writing for Gentile Christian readers, has adapted the Jewish calculation of the day, not at all easy to understand, in which the day begins at sunset, to what is presumably the Roman calculation of time, and has moved the beginning of the feast to dawn. A. Strobel, *Ursprung und Geschichte des frühchristlichen Osterkalenders,* TU 121, 1977, 49, sees here "clearly the coloring of Christian terminology."

a strange area which he evidently had never visited.[51] As for his accounts of Jewish customs and historical circumstances, which are said to be not above criticism, it must be remembered that Mark does not mean to provide a historically accurate account in the modern sense, but presents Jewish customs polemically and tendentiously, i.e., in a vague and exaggerated way.[52] Nevertheless, alongside Josephus and Luke he is the most important source for Palestinian Judaism at the time of the procurators, in AD 6-70, and this fact is confirmed at many points by Josephus. Josephus seeks recognition as a scholarly and trustworthy historian, yet his carelessness is often shameful.[53] Mark does not have this ambition, so in this respect we should not ask so much of him.

51. His alleged ignorance of the geography of Palestine serves in a stereotyped and uncritical way to justify the assertion that the author could not have been a Palestinian Jew. Thus Niederwimmer, op. cit., 178: "At some points the Gospel reveals conceptions of the geography of Palestine which could only be found in one who was a stranger to the country." In recent times only F. G. Lang, " 'Über Sidon mitten ins Gebiet der Dekapolis.' Geographie und Theologie in Markus 7,31," ZDPV 94, 1978, 145-60, has seen the problem in the right terms. Accordingly hardly anyone has taken account of his arguments. See also my study "Luke the Historian and the Geography of Palestine in the Acts of the Apostles," in Between Jesus and Paul, ET 1983, 97ff. In addition to the modern example which I quote at the end, here is an even more topical one: When I visited my distinguished colleague A. Kuschke (to whom I had dedicated the above article on his seventieth birthday) in Kusterdingen, southeast of Tübingen, we were able to admire Pfrondorf to the north, beyond the Neckar. A colleague who had lived for many years in Tübingen asked me, "Is that beyond Wankheim?" "No," I had to tell him, "it's in the opposite direction." Should we not forgive the author the doubtful sequence of Bethphage/Bethany in Mark 11·1 (see Niederwimmner, 181), especially as the Roman road ran directly only to Bethphage and left Bethany on the left, to the south? Mark introduces it to show its approximate position, as he mentions it often later (11:11f.; 14:3). Perhaps critical New Testament scholars, too, need to learn that a Gospel is neither a geographical handbook of Palestine nor an exact account of Jewish customs. As many and as few mistakes are made in the Gospels as in monographs on the New Testament.
52. Niederwimmer, op. cit., 185, wants to conclude from 7:3f. "a lack of familiarity with Judaism." In reply, my question would be: what is our more accurate knowledge of Palestinian and Diaspora Judaism on the basis of which we can level such charges at the author of the Second Gospel? For the "hand-washing" see my article "Mk 7,3 πυγμῇ: Geschichte einer exegetischen Aporie und ihrer Lösung," ZNW 60, 1969, 182-98. For 7:4 see Billerbeck I, 934ff. and 2:14; Pesch, op. cit. (n. 1), 1, 371. Presumably we should follow Nestle/Aland[26] in reading βαπτίσωνται and referring to the bath to restore levitical purity which could be infringed by dealings with Gentiles in the market. The whole insertion has the character of a typical polemical exaggeration for the information of Gentile Christians. It is meant to take the Pharisaic Jewish παράδοσις τῶν πρεσβυτέρων ad absurdum. However, J. Neusner, The Rabbinic Traditions about the Pharisees before 70, 1971, III, 304, shows how much for all its inexactitude it has a good historical background: "Approximately 67% of all legal pericopae deal with dietary laws: ritual purity for meals and agricultural rules governing the fitness of food for Pharisaic consumption." The Pharisaic paradosis before the catastrophe and the intrinsic transformation of Palestinian Judaism was not least concerned with ritual purity at mealtimes. Cf. also Mark 7:15 and Gal. 2:11f. Mark, who did not set out to be a scholar, should be excused this polemically exaggerated account, and we should not draw senseless conclusions from it. The absurd closing sentence by Niederwimmer shows that even New Testament scholars are not immune from such exaggerations (188): "If this supposition is correct, then it would mean that the note by Papias appears as a prime example of that dogmatic ideology with which the second-century [?!] Church sought to conceal its own origins and provide a secondary interpretation."
53. See S. J. D. Cohen (n. 31), index 276 s.v. "Josephus' exaggerations; inconsistency and sloppiness; corrupt transmission of names and numbers."

(c) The Papias Note

As information about the origin of Mark's work we have the note by Papias
dating from about AD 120-130, i.e., the time of Hadrian; it comes from his
"five-volume" *Interpretation of the Lord's Sayings* (Λογίων κυριακῶν ἐξη-
γήσεις). It is often misunderstood and indeed mishandled in more recent
scholarship, but in my view it must be taken very seriously.[54]

> This also the elder used to say. Mark, indeed, having been the interpreter
> of Peter, wrote accurately, howbeit not in order, all that he recalled of
> what was either said or done by the Lord. For he heard nothing of the
> Lord, nor was he a follower of his, but, at a later date (as I said) of Peter;
> who used to adapt his instructions to the needs [of the hearers], but not
> with a view to putting together the teachings of the Lord in orderly fashion:
> so that Mark did no wrong in thus writing some things as he recalled them.
> For he kept a single aim in view: not to omit anything of what he heard,
> nor to state anything therein falsely. (Eusebius, *HE* 3.39.15)

Papias presumably received this report from the presbyter John, from Asia
Minor,[55] the height of whose activity should be put roughly a generation earlier,

---

54. The dating of this work is disputed. A. von Harnack, *Geschichte der altchristlichen
Literatur bis Eusebius, II: Die Chronologie der altchristlichen Literatur bis Eusebius* I, 1897, 721,
cf. 356ff., puts it in the period between 145 (140) and 160, though the year in which Papias was
born was "hardly later than 80" (ibid., 358). He is followed rather more cautiously by P. Vielhauer,
Geschichte der urchristlichen Literatur, 1975, 759: toward the end of or after the reign of Hadrian
(10.7.138); he wants to regard him as a contemporary of Justin, 785, cf. 254: "about the middle of
the second century . . . his contemporary and compatriot Justin." In reality a gulf separates the two.
Justin is hardly interested in oral tradition any more and keeps to the *written* "recollections of the
apostles," even if he quotes them relatively freely. See also L. Abramowski, essay in the present
volume. On the other hand, the new investigation by U. H. J. Körtner, *Papias von Hierapolis. Ein
Beitrag zur Geschichte des frühen Christentums,* FRLANT 133, 1983, 88-94, 225f., has produced
good arguments for an early date ca. 110. However, I cannot go back further in this connection than
Fragment XI of the Church History of Philip of Side (Funk/Bihlmeyer, *Apostolische Väter,* 1924,
138f.), which explicitly refers to the time of Hadrian (117-38).

In accordance with the title Papias interpreted what he regarded as the authoritative "Sayings
of the Lord"—in the widest sense. In contemporary literature λόγιον almost always means a divine
saying; see BAGD s.v., or Plutarch, *Theseus* 32.4; *Romulus* 14.1; *Numa* 9.3; *Aristides* 9.2; 15.3;
Camillus 4.1.3 and so on. Cf. also the fixed terminology of λόγια θεοῦ or κυρίου in the LXX Psalter;
Rom. 3:2; Acts 7:78; Heb. 5:12; I Pet. 4:11; Polycarp 7.1; Justin, *Dial.* 18.1; Irenaeus, *Adv. Haer.*
1 preface; 8.1, etc. Here for Papias it can refer also to anecdotes and brief narratives. He has a higher
estimation of oral tradition (see n. 61 below). The attempt by U. H. J. Körtner, op. cit., 143ff., to
define these λόγια by genre is mistaken. Papias is concerned with the religious sound of the term
λόγιον as opposed to the everyday word λόγος. See now also the collection of articles and fragments
with extended bibliography by J. Kürzinger, *Papias von Hierapolis und die Evangelien des Neuen
Testaments,* Eichstätter Materialien 4, 1983. However, I cannot agree with his interpretation of the
fragments about Mark and Matthew.

55. This important fact (καὶ τοῦθ' ὁ πρεσβύτερος ἔλεγεν) is overlooked or unreasonably
questioned in the "critical" literature, cf. e.g. Niederwimmer, op. cit., 185f.: "his alleged informant."
In connection with the proemium Eusebius reports (*HE* 3.39.7) of the presbyter: "But Papias says
that he himself heard Aristion and the presbyter John. Therefore he often mentions them by name

about 70-100. In more recent times scholars have tended to dismiss this much discussed and much maltreated note as a secondary, apologetic vindication of the apostolic origin of the Second Gospel. In reality it represents the markedly *critical comments* of an author who rated oral tradition even higher than written works. The connection between Peter and Mark, which in fact goes back to the first century and is attested independently of the presbyter in I Pet. 5:13,[56] cannot be a later invention in order to secure "apostolic" authority for the Gospel. Moreover, the main objection against the note in Papias, advanced by the representatives of the form-critical school, namely that the Second Gospel is not a literary work but a conglomerate of anonymous, popular, and collective Jesus-tradition, has now proved invalid.[57] But in that case, what are the reasons

---

and reproduces their traditions in his writing." Cf. 14, immediately before the Mark tradition: "He reports still other things in his writing from the interpretations of the Lord's sayings by the above-mentioned Aristion and the traditions of the presbyter John. After we have pointed this out to the curious, we think it necessary to add to his remarks made so far a tradition which he has handed down about Mark, the author of the Gospel." Here Papias is not advancing something that he has made up himself, but an old tradition guaranteed by the presbyter, which goes back to a time toward the end of the first century.

56. The claim that Papias invented the link between Mark the evangelist and Peter on the basis of his reading of I Pet. 5:13, which has proved particularly popular, is nonsense. J. Regul, *Die Antimarcionitischen Evangelienprologe,* 1969, who discusses the notes by Papias in detail on pp. 113-60, but in part with pettifogging arguments which lead him astray, and without historical understanding, claims without any justification (96) that Papias' testimony about Mark was "spun out of I Pet. 5:13, the key passage for connecting Mark and the Gospel attributed to him with the apostle Peter." Papias certainly knows I Peter (and I John, *HE* 3.39.17), but the date of his tradent is synchronous with the origin of I Peter under Domitian (81-96) or soon after him. Both traditions are independent and provide reciprocal confirmation. It is also an unprovable assertion that only the first clause of the quotation is the tradition of the presbyter and that the rest is only interpretation of Papias. Papias reproduces this tradition in his own words and the exact wording can no longer be reconstructed. Cf. already A. Jülicher, *RE* XII, 291:

> In no way does Papias provide here a literal protocol about a communication from his main authority the presbyter [John] . . . and it is no less arbitrary to seek to distinguish Papias' additions from what the presbyter says. Rather, Papias is completely responsible for the wording; in fact he is convinced that he is merely handing on what he received from a well-informed personality of the previous generation. As we have no reason to mistrust Papias, we note his judgment as that of a respected figure from the Church in Asia Minor between about 90 and 130.

My colleague Frau Abramowski, in her essay in the present volume (pp. 331f., n. 35), appeals for support for her view that the notes by Papias are unreliable to the judgment by E. Schwartz, op. cit. (see n. 59), 76f., and to his indication that even in the case of Origen, and far more elsewhere in his literary history, Eusebius had only written sources at his disposal. However, one can hardly compare Eusebius, a man of letters with a giant library at his disposal, with Papias, a collector of predominantly oral tradition. The nearest parallels to the Papias traditions, which also have a marked Jewish Christian stamp, are to be found in rabbinical sources. They have a bizarre hyperbolical character in common with these (cf. fragments I, III, and XI in Funk/Bihlmeyer).

57. Cf. e.g. K. L. Schmidt, "Die Stellung der Evangelien in der allgemeinen Literaturgeschichte," *EYXAPIΣTHPION* . FS H. Gunkel, II, 1923, 57f. = *Neues Testament—Judentum— Kirche,* ThB 69, 1981, 46f., on Papias, arguing with E. Meyer: "Mark is presented as the first proclaimer and literary author of the story of Jesus, but the literary character of the Gospel of Mark

which compel us to deny this extremely distinctive note any historical value? Do not the numerous so-called critical judgments (which in fact are often radically uncritical) express a basically ahistorical zeal which has ceased to be concerned with what this mysterious text really says?

The second note, about the Gospel of Matthew, in fact plays down the authority of the First Gospel, written in Greek ("So then, Matthew compiled the sayings [of the Lord] in the Hebrew language; but everyone translated them (or interpreted them) as he was able" (Eusebius, *HE* 3.39.16). It indicates that the First Gospel was not the original work of the apostle, but a secondary rendering of a basic Hebrew document. Therefore Pesch is wrong in his interpretation of the quotations from Papias when he supposes that Papias is providing an apologetic defense of the apostolicity of the Gospel of Mark and at the same time judging it by the better order of Matthew.[58] There is no indication that Matthew is arranged better, especially as in fact he followed the τάξις of Mark, which Papias found inadequate.

Moreover, the complaint about inadequate "order" does not in fact relate to the literary arrangement, which in the Second Gospel is faultless, but to the historical and chronological arrangement of the material. Therefore we might assume that Papias had in mind the quite different chronology and order of the Fourth Gospel: he quotes Revelation and I John, and in the second book of his work reports a tradition of the killing of John and James, the sons of Zebedee, by the Jews; in addition there is much to suggest that he knew the Fourth Gospel.[59] Thus his sequence of disciples, Andrew, Peter, and Philip, is matched

---

excludes so individual an origin." Here on the one hand Papias is interpreted wrongly, and on the other this presupposition has become questionable. E. Meyer, *Ursprung und Anfänge des Christentums*, I, *Die Evangelien*, [4-5]1924, reprinted 1962, 157ff., 245ff., had some correct insights which were buried under the form-critical wave; see the reviews by K. L. Schmidt, *CW* 35, 1921, 114-20, and M. Dibelius, *DLZ* 42, 1921, 225-35, which in my view are excessively sharp in their abrupt criticism and therefore are again in turn partly misleading.

58. Op. cit. (n. 1), 1, 5f. Pesch also speaks of an "apologetic commentary on the remark by the presbyter" (6) and wants to see I Pet. 5:13 as "the bridge toward an identification" (7f.). Cf. also R. Pesch, "Die Zuschreibung der Evangelien an apostolische Verfasser," *ZTK* 97, 1975, 56-71. By contrast, W. Bauer, *Orthodoxy and Heresy in Earliest Christianity*, ET 1972, 107, is right here: "Both personalities [i.e., Peter and Mark] appear to be so closely associated in Rome already in the first century [I Pet. 5:13] that I can hardly doubt that it was here that the origin of Mark's gospel was first attributed to the influence of Peter and that the 'elder' derived from this source what he passed on to Papias." The question is whether this oral "source" was reliable. I would say that it was. For the Mark-Peter tradition see also U. H. J. Körtner, "Markus der Mitarbeiter des Petrus," *ZNW* 71, 1980, 160-73, with very worthwhile considerations. However, because he puts too much confidence in the untenable theories of Niederwimmer (171 n. 54a), he arrives at a false conclusion.

59. Thus already with good reasons J. B. Lightfoot, *Biblical Essays*, [2]1904 (1893), 63-70, and E. Schwartz, "Über den Tod der Söhne Zebedaei," in *Gesammelte Schriften*, V, *Zum Neuen Testament und zum frühen Christentum*, 1963, 78ff. = AGG NF VII, 5, 1904, 23ff. Cf. also A. Jülicher and E. Fascher, *Einleitung in das NT*, [7]1931, 284f.; H. Merkel, *Widersprüche zwischen den Evangelien*, WUNT 13, 1971, 46ff.: "So Papias seems to have known the differences between the chronology of John and that of Mark and opted undisguisedly for John" (48f.). Cf. now

by the call of the disciples according to John 1:40ff.; furthermore, in the preface there is also an absolute use of the term "truth" which comes close to the Fourth Gospel (3.39.3 end): "the commandments given by the Lord to faith, and reaching us from the truth itself" (τὰς παρὰ τοῦ κυρίου τῇ πίστει δεδομένας ἐντολὰς καὶ ἀπ' αὐτῆς παραγινομένας τῆς ἀληθείας). Moreover, John in particular speaks of ἐντολαί of Jesus and the ἐντολὰς (or -ῆς) διδόναι (John 11:57; 12:49; 14:15, 21, 31; 15:10; I John 2:3f.; 3:22, 23, 24; 5:2f.);[60] the avoidance of the term apostle in the extant fragments and his predilection for "disciples of the Lord" could also be connected with John. Moreover, it is difficult to attribute apologetic intentions to Papias about 120 or 130 (or even ca. 110?): who would have doubted the authenticity of Mark or Matthew in his day? Gnostics like Basilides or Valentinus were keen to quote the Church's Gospels, and according to Irenaeus docetic Gnostics even had a preference for Mark.[61] By contrast

F. Siegert, "Unbeachtete Papiaszitate bei armenischen Schriftstellern," *NTS* 27, 1981, 605-14. For the argument whether Papias knew the Gospel of John see in detail J. Regul (op. cit., n. 56 above), 143ff., who challenges this view bitterly, but not very convincingly. His main argument, that Eusebius would have mentioned such an acquaintance, is wrong because Eusebius tendentiously and notoriously unreliably also says nothing of the use of Revelation by Papias, which is clearly established by the fragment of Andrew of Caesarea (F IV). In addition one can assume with W. Heitmüller, *ZNW* 15, 1914, 200, that Papias said things about the Gospel of John and Revelation which did not please Eusebius. I believe that the Fourth Gospel was adopted by the Great Church in Asia Minor precisely at the time of the presbyter and Papias, somewhere between 90 and 120. Some decades later it played a very important role there, as is evident from the dispute over Easter and the Montanist movement. Regul leaves completely unexplained the origin of the many-layered tradition of John in Asia Minor. The fragment of an interpretation of the Prologue of John by Valentinus contained in Irenaeus, *Adv. Haer.* 1.8.5 (Harvey I, 75, 78), suggests that the Valentinians already described the author of the Fourth Gospel as Ἰωάννης ὁ μαθητὴς τοῦ κυρίου. The attribution of the Gospel to John is connected with its reception into the Church, which, as Harnack already conjectured, took place in Asia Minor.

60. Eusebius, *HE* 3.39.4: "What Andrew or what Peter said, or what Philip or what Thomas or what James or what Matthew or another of the Lord's disciples." Cf. J. B. Lightfoot, op. cit., 69, and A. Ehrhardt, "The Gospels in the Muratorian Fragment," in *The Framework of the New Testament Stories*, 1964, 11-36 (= *Ostkirchliche Studien* 2, 1953, 121-38); however, he goes on to refer to the special stress on Andrew in connection with the origin of the Gospel of John in the Muratorian Canon (13ff., 19ff.). Of the thirteen fragments printed in Funk/Bihlmeyer, nine mention John in some way. That may largely rest on secondary tradition, but it is impossible to overlook the connection between the Bishop of Hierapolis and the Johannine tradition. Cf. also the interpretation of the Gospel of John by the presbyter in Irenaeus, *Adv. Haer.* 2.22.5 (Harvey I, 331f.) = John 8:56, and 5.36.1 (Harvey II, 428) = John 14:2, which probably goes back to Papias.

61. The picture that W. Bauer, op. cit. (n. 58), 184ff., and index s.v. Papias, draws of the Phrygian bishop is completely misleading. As elsewhere, Bauer works too much with the questionable argument from silence. There is nothing in the little that has been handed down of Papias's work to give the impression that he is deliberately writing to combat heresy. His polemic in the Preface against "those who write much" which delights "the many" and against the "strange commandments" is largely literary convention. Luke already wrote the πολλοί in 1:1 with a sharp pen. The fact that Papias still prefers the living oral tradition to "books" in principle and not just verbally (see n. 65 below) distinguishes him from those who attack the heretics in literature from the middle of the second century onward. Anti-Gnostic polemic is nowhere to be seen in the fragments. There is no basis for the statement that "the criticism of Mark and Matthew has its basis in the controversy with heretics and the gospel writings they supported [which?]" (W. Bauer, op.

Marcion had not yet appeared. His separation from the community in Rome presumably only took place about 144,[62] and his wrath is directed less against the evangelists than against the original apostles like Peter and John himself.[63] Therefore Papias's work is quite unsuitable for offering a defense against Marcion. The Old Testament, the real point of dispute, plays no part in the fragments, and the observations about Mark and Matthew do not look like a convincing defense. This exceptional work must be earlier. In addition to a (hypothetical) predilection for the Fourth Gospel, we could also presuppose that Papias's criticism in essence stemmed from his predilection for the *viva vox* (ζῶσα φωνὴ καὶ μένουσα, *HE* 3.39.4), the living oral tradition in contrast to written documents, which in fact was already anachronistic. We also find this—though in a different way—throughout earlier Christianity among a number of Gnostic teachers and beyond, though of course in that case without any depreciation of the written tradition, which by then had become indispensable.[64] Evidently this avid collector of earlier tradition had information of

---

cit., 185). K. Niederwimmer, op. cit. (n. 50), 186, makes Bauer's conjecture even cruder in his distinctive way: "... that Papias' apologia in favor of the Gospel of Mark is aimed at Gnostic circles. He is concerned to defend the Gospel of Mark (and of Matthew, cf. Eusebius, *HE* 3.39.16) against the charges of the Gnostics and even perhaps against the *advantages* [author's italics] of the Gnostic Gospels." For a criticism of this theory of a clearly anti-Gnostic attitude on the part of Papias see U. H. J Körtner, op. cit. (n. 54), 154-59. He thinks, rather, of heretics like the mysterious Nicolaitans (Rev. 2:6, 15). For Irenaeus and the Gnostic predilection for Mark see *Adv. Haer.* 3.11.7: *Qui autem Jesum separant a Christo et impassibilem perseverasse Christum, passum vero Jesum dicunt, id quod secundum Marcum est praeferentes Evangelium.* Cf. 3.10.6.

62. Cf. A. von Harnack, *Marcion,* [2]1924 reprinted 1960, 26-70*.

63. H. F. von Campenhausen, *The Formation of the Christian Bible,* 1972, 156, makes perhaps an over-pointed comment: "So far as we know, he never polemised against particular gospels. Instead, what he is attacking in the Great Church is the teaching of the first, judaising apostles."

64. Scholars are fond of referring in this connection to Clement of Alexandria, *Strom.* 7.106.4: "... and only later, at the time of Emperor Hadrian, did the founders of heresies appear— and remained until the time of the older Antoninus, as is the case with Basilides, though he also claims as his teacher Glaucias, who, as they themselves boast, was the interpreter of Peter. They also affirm that Valentinus had listened to Theodas. Now this last had been a pupil of Paul." The decisive passage cannot be interpreted simply, since here there is a clear distinction between Basilides, who calls Glaucias his teacher (καθάπερ ὁ Βασιλείδης, κἂν Γλαυκίαν ἐπιγράφηται διδάσκαλον), and the plural of those who boast of Glaucias as Peter's interpreter (ὡς αὐχοῦσιν αὐτοί, τὸν Πέτρον ἑρμηνέα). Stählin therefore gives an interpretative translation of this: "who, as the supporters of Basilides themselves boast, was the interpreter of Peter." Of course the plural could also be a general reference to the heretics, cf. 7.108.1 on them: κἂν τὴν Ματθίου αὐχοῦσι προσάγεσθαι δόξαν: "Even if they claim to present the view of (the apostle) Matthias." However, on the basis of the break in wording we must take into account that the Basilidians were the first to claim that Glaucias was the interpreter of Peter. Therefore the historical circumstances are stood on their head, when E. Schwartz, op. cit. (n. 59), 74 = 20f., assumes that in his note on Mark (which in reality goes back to the presbyter John) Papias is dependent on Gnostic assertions, a view which P. Vielhauer, op. cit. (n. 54), 764 n. 11, quotes with approval. Rather, the opposite is the case, that the Gnostics imitated the old Mark-Peter tradition for their aims. In contrast to the Basilidians, Papias does not in fact claim any tradition which connects Peter with Mark as his own legitimation. Nor does he make any claim to secret tradition.

both oral and written provenance, which went back one or two generations,[65] i.e., right to the time of the origin of the Gospels: in the case of Matthew about 90 and in the case of Mark probably about 69. His main authorities were the presbyter John, who is connected with the Johannine corpus, and the presbyter Aristion, from whom perhaps the inauthentic ending to Mark derives.

Papias's criticism of Mark starts from two points:

1. He did not put the words and actions of the Lord in the right order, whether chronologically or in terms of subject matter (οὐ μέντοι τάξει); this basic criticism certainly goes back to the presbyter's tradition.

2. He was not an immediate disciple of the Lord, but only of Peter; in other words his sources are only secondhand.

The undertone of the criticism can also be seen in the explanations which follow: the lack of order in his work which is the object of criticism goes back to Peter's actions in shaping his oral teaching—understandably—to the needs of the hearers; in other words he presented the Jesus-tradition in a disordered way by literary and historical standards and was uninterested in a collection (σύνταξις) of "words of the Lord" with a good literary or chronological arrangement. Mark was not in error in writing down only some (ἔνια, as they had remained in his memory (ὡς ἀπεμνημόνευσεν).

The positive statements, that as far as Mark remembered the teaching of Peter he set this down on paper ἀκριβῶς, and that he *took trouble* not to leave out or falsify anything that he had heard,[66] are conventional in character: similar formulas appear almost as stereotypes in the prologues of historians.[67] Such a

---

65. With him it already has a "nostalgic" character. Here the fragments of the Jesus-tradition which have been preserved fall back before the Gospels. See also H. F. von Campenhausen, op. cit. (n. 63), 130 n. 109: the high estimation of the *viva vox* "is especially characteristic of early Christianity." Cf. also Irenaeus to Florinus in Eusebius, *HE* 5.20.6f. and *Adv. Haer.* 3.2.1: *non enim per literas traditam illam, sed per vivam vocem,* sc. the *traditio* of the Church, which alone guarantees the true use of Scripture which the heretics lack. Irenaeus could be dependent on Papias, whom he knew, for this formulation. His aim is essentially different from that in Papias (see n. 61 above). Aristides, *Apol.* 15.3 (Goodspeed): ἔχουσι τὰς ἐντολὰς αὐτοῦ τοῦ κυρίου Ἰησοῦ Χριστοῦ ἐν ταῖς καρδίαις κεχαραγμένας.... For personal oral tradition which goes back over several generations cf. Plutarch, *Mark Antony* 28.2-7 and 68.4f.; *Kimon* 1.2–2.5; see also Josephus, *Vita* 3f., and Dio Cassius (born ca. 160) 69.1.3 on the death of Trajan and the adoption of Hadrian in August 117.

66. In his mistaken attempt to make Papias an untrustworthy apologist, P. Vielhauer, op. cit. (n. 54), 260, interprets the statements far too positively, given their wording: "He cannot challenge these objections, of which the second—that Mark was not an eye-witness account of a disciple— was particularly painful for his point of view [how does the author know that?] but seeks all the more energetically [?] to rob them of their force by asserting that the book simply contains the accurate and complete account of the teaching of Peter." There can be no question of that. Mark only wrote some things down as he remembered them (ἔνια γράψας ὡς ἀπεμνημόνευσεν). The concluding clause only says that Mark took trouble (ἐποιήσατο πρόνοιαν) not to leave out or falsify anything that he had heard. However, that may be presupposed in any student's seminar paper.

67. See S. J. D. Cohen (n. 31), 24f., especially on the universal formula, "Adding nothing and leaving nothing out" (27f.), which originally derives from legal terminology but was at that time taken over by the historians. See already H. Cancik, *Mythische und historische Wahrheit,* SBS 48,

concession was a matter of course, which can be taken for granted in any reasonably well-organized historian. Had Papias said less this would have been a direct dismissal of Mark.

Another striking point is the twofold stress on remembering. It corresponds with the stress on the remembering by the disciples in the Fourth Gospel (2:17, 22; 12:16; 15:20; 16:4) and the concept of the ἀπομνημονεύματα τῶν ἀποστόλων which are later prominent in Justin; the difference is that Papias limits Mark's recollection to the subordinate proclamation of Peter: Mark is not a direct eye-witness. It should no longer be denied that the "recollection" of the authors (i.e., of their informants and those who handed material on to them) and not primarily the inventive creativity of anonymous early Christian prophets, communities, or even self-confident theological poets, played the normative role in the origin of the synoptic Gospels. The authors are above all responsible for the selection and ordering of the material and for the linguistic and stylistic form that it is given.

(d) Mark and Peter

The dependence of the author on Peter, which plays a very important role in establishing the priority of Mark, but which today is usually completely

---

1970, 24ff., 85ff., 99-103. For its frequency see e.g. also Plutarch, *Lycurgus* 6.4; 13.2; 25.4; Theopompus, FGrHist 115 T 31 = Photius bibl. 176 p. 121a 35; Dionysius of Halicarnassus, *Thuc.* 5 (LCL, Vol. 465, p. 472) and 8 (p. 478), on Thucydides: πλείστην ἐποιήσατο πρόνοιαν, οὔτε προστιθεὶς τοῖς πράγμασιν οὐδὲν ὃ μὴ δίκαιον οὔτε ἀφαιρῶν, οὐδὲ ἐνεξουσιάζων τῇ γραφῇ.

For the later Christian terminology see the anonymous author against the Montanists (Eusebius, *HE* 5.16.3) and Polycrates of Smyrna, ibid., 5.24.2. The decisive concepts and formulas which Papias uses appear in a slightly different form in Josephus, *Ant.* 1.17: τὰ μὲν οὖν ἀκριβῆ τῶν ἐν ταῖς ἀναγραφαῖς προϊὼν ὁ λόγος κατὰ τὴν οἰκείαν τάξιν σημανεῖ· τοῦτο γὰρ διὰ ταύτης ποιήσειν τῆς πραγματείας ἐπηγγειλάμην οὐδὲν προσθεὶς οὐδ' αὖ παραλιπών. Directly before this we have the affirmation of the credibility of Moses, which is commended to the reader for examination. As he is speaking about such a distant past, he "had a great freedom for lying falsifications" (1.16: πολλὴν εἶχεν ἄδειαν ψευδῶν πλασμάτων). The whole text "consists of historiographical commonplaces" (Cohen, op. cit., 28). For the selection of ἔνια see Lucian, *Demonax* 12: Βούλομαι δὲ ἔνια παραθέσθαι; for "recollection" see ibid. 67: ταῦτα ὀλίγα πάνυ ἐκ πολλῶν ἀπεμνημόνευσα.

By contrast, the lack of τάξις is a real criticism: the notion corresponds to the καθεξῆς of Luke 1:3. Both the Preface and the note on Mark show us that, after Luke, Papias was the second author known to us who was most familiar with Greek literary usages, as was already stressed by E. Schwartz, op. cit. (n. 59), 70 = 18, on the account of Mark: "... these statements betray an elegant literary style." The charge of deficient τάξις is also part of this literary jargon and is no light one. It automatically also indicates erroneous arrangement, see H. Lausberg, op. cit. (n. 16), 241 sec. 443, 507 sec. 1055; in our case, however, it is not a matter of literary but of historical arrangement. In the case of a "historian" who describes "the words and acts" of a historical figure (for the formulation cf. Polybius 2.56.10; Gellius, *Noct. Att.* 14.3.5), a false arrangement of chronology and subject matter is a basic error. For Lucian, therefore, part of the once-for-allness of historiography (*Quom. hist. conscr.* 6) is: καὶ τάξιν ἥντινα τοῖς ἔργοις ἐφαρμοστέον, cf. also Josephus, *Ant.* 1.17; *BJ* 1.15. For Papias and his informant it is a question of the right "historical" ordering of the material—oriented on John—which they cannot find in Mark.

ignored or even abruptly rejected, should be maintained: it makes a substantial contribution to our understanding of the Gospel.[68] It is also confirmed, independently of Papias, by Justin in his reference to Mark 3:16f. as supposed "recollections of Peter."[69] There are good historical reasons for what at first sounds an unusual piece of information, that Mark was Peter's interpreter. It is obvious that the Galilean fisherman Simon will never have learned Greek thoroughly enough to have been able to present his teaching fluently in unexceptionable Greek.[70] The Greek Palestinian John Mark, whose house Peter visited first in the legend of Acts 12.12ff. after his liberation from prison, was presumably later his companion and indeed interpreter where that was necessary.[71] Peter's Greek will hardly have been pleasing to the fastidious ear of the ancient listener. The critical, educated reader might like to see for himself whether he has an unexceptionable *literary* command of German or French, and whether he is not grateful to a translator for help in preparing a report in a foreign language. (Although I myself speak English passably, I am nevertheless very grateful to have a first-class English translator, not only for my books, but also for English papers I have to read.) Did Peter have a better linguistic training than we do?

Given its essentially smaller extent, the Gospel of Mark mentions Simon

68. P. Wernle, to whom we owe what is still the basic study, *Die Synoptische Frage,* 1899, devotes himself at length to the question of Mark and the Peter tradition (195-208). He comes to what sounds to modern ears to be a bold conclusion: "Rather, the Gospel of Mark is the most valuable source for the 'theology' of Peter" (ibid., 200). Similarly E. Meyer, *Ursprung und Anfänge des Christentums,* I. *Die Evangelien,* [4-5]1924, 147-60. I would not go as far as this, but one should no longer completely deny any connection between Peter and Mark.

69. *Dial.* 106.3, after the renaming of the apostle Peter: καὶ γεγράφθαι ἐν τοῖς ἀπομνη-μονεύμασιν αὐτοῦ (= Πέτρου) γεγενημένον καὶ τοῦτο, μετὰ τοῦ καὶ ἄλλους δύο ἀδελφούς, υἱοὺς Ζεβεδαίου ὄντας, ἐπωνομακέναι ὀνόματι τοῦ Βοανεργές, ὅ ἐστιν υἱοὶ βροντῆς. Cf. also 103.8: the reminiscences were composed by his apostles and their "successors" (cf. Papias on Mark as "Peter's successor": in both cases we have the verb παρακολουθεῖν, i.e., Mark and Luke). The concept of ἀπομνημονεύματα in Justin is usually—and rightly—derived from the ἀπομνημονεύματα Σωκράτους of Xenophon, which Justin knew (cf. *Apol.* 2.11.3). See also L. Abramowski's essay in the present volume. However, the term appears in contemporary literature, e.g. as a collection of gleanings from reading in five books by Favorinus (ca. 80-150) and in his friend Plutarch, whose ἀπομνημονεύματα have unfortunately not survived. Plutarch, *Cato Major* 9.7, uses it in the sense of "famous comments" by Cato.

70. For the difficulties of the "barbarians," who could not speak Greek unexceptionably, see M. Hengel, *Jews, Greek and Barbarians,* ET 1980, 76f.

71. The *inscriptiones* and *subscriptiones* of the Gospels are very old—as is evident from the fact that there is complete unanimity over them toward the end of the second century, from Egypt to Lyons and from Africa to Antioch. Thus H. F. von Campenhausen, rightly, against the view widespread today, op. cit. (n. 63), 173 n. 123: "But these ancient and presumably original titles were already long established, as Papias indicates and indeed Justin as well . . . , and could no longer be altered arbitrarily at a later stage." See my "The Titles of the Gospels," *Studies in the Gospel of Mark,* ET 1985, 64-84. In all probability the Mark mentioned in the New Testament (I Pet. 5:13; Phlm. 24; Col. 4:10; II Tim. 4:11) and John Mark (Acts 12:12, 25; 15:37; 15:39 [which has only Μάρκος], are identical. The Second Gospel was not written anonymously by just anyone, but by a theological teacher with authority, behind whom there was an even greater authority.

Peter more frequently than the other synoptic Gospels and also more frequently than John, if we leave out the chapter which is critical of Peter in the supplement, John 21. Simon Peter is mentioned 25 times in Mark.[72] Simon is the first disciple to be mentioned, in 1:16, directly after the *propositio* in 1:14, 15, and quite unusually his brother Andrew is described as "the brother of Simon" (on this cf. 15:21). At the beginning of Jesus' ministry, after the call of the first four disciples and the first exorcism in the synagogue of Capernaum, Jesus visits the house of the brothers—a report in the Gospel which falls outside its framework and seems very personal—and heals Simon's mother-in-law (1:29). In 1:36, unusually, the first group of disciples is described as Σίμων καὶ οἱ μετ' αὐτοῦ. Subsequently he stands at the head of all the lists of disciples, the Twelve and also the three and the four.[73] All this cannot simply be explained as mere convention; there must be profound historical reasons behind it. As the spokesmen of the Twelve Peter not only acknowledges the messiahship of Jesus but is also sharply rejected by him (8:29, 32f.); he is an embodiment of the disciples' lack of understanding and their failure.[74] He is the last disciple whom Jesus addresses personally in Gethsemane (14:37), the last who accompanies Jesus as far as the courtyard of the high priest's palace

72. A survey of the mentions of Peter in Mark shows that they occur more frequently at the key points of the Gospel: at the beginning, in the *peripeteia,* and then at the beginning of the passion narrative. This is hardly a coincidence, but is connected with the general arrangement:

Ch. 1	2	3	4	5	6	7	8
1:16 2×S		3:16 2×S+P		5:37 P			8:29 P
1:29 S							8:32 P
1:30 S							8:33 P
1:36 S							

Ch. 9	10	11	12	13	14	15	16
9:2 P	10:28 P	11:21 P		13:3 P	14:29 P		16:7 P
9:5 P					14:33 P		
					14:37 P+S		
					14:54 P		
					14:66 P		
					14:67 P		
					14:70 P		
					14:72 P		

A striking feature here is, moreover, the clear division between the original name Simon and the Peter which was added by Jesus. The first disciple is called Simon up to the list of names (3:16) and then again in the special, familiar address in Gethsemane (14:54). Here the other Gospels do not distinguish so exactly in the nomenclature. This reveals a greater proximity to the Petrine tradition. The tendency of Mark is continued most closely by Matthew. He builds on the Gospel of Mark and adds further, more legendary traditions about Peter (14:28ff.; 16:16ff.; 17:25ff.). For the whole question see the essay by Reinhard Feldmeier in the present volume.

73. Cf. Mark 3:16ff.; 5:37; 9:2; 13:3.

74. Cf. in addition 8:29; 9:5; 10:28; 11:21; 13:3; 14:29, 37.

(14:37), indeed, even more, the last to be mentioned in the Gospel. The extraordinary formulation of 16:7, the angel's command to the women, "Go and say to his disciples and to Peter . . ." (τοῖς μαθηταῖς αὐτοῦ καὶ τῷ Πέτρῳ), puts the name of the disciple who appears first in the Gospel at the end as well: this is an *inclusio,* through which the evangelist deliberately wants to stress this one disciple in a quite special way.[75] It can hardly be doubted that Mark is clearly stressing the unique significance of Peter, though without disguising his failure. Might this not be connected with the special origin of his tradition? On the other hand, some kind of later theological polemic against Peter or Jewish Christianity generally should not be read out of the Second Gospel, for—apart from the Fourth Gospel with its mysterious beloved disciple—we cannot see any other standpoint, whether of disciples or community, which would afford the authority for such polemic.[76] Matthew and Luke took over this stress on Peter from Mark and gave it rather more marked legendary elaborations (thus especially Matthew); the firm starting point is, however, to be sought in Mark, who is very close to Peter's martyrdom in Rome in 64 in both time and space. By contrast, John wants to limit the significance of Peter over against the unknown beloved disciple.

Certainly Simon Peter does not appear as a living individual, but as a type; however, that is part of the kerygmatic style of the narrator generally and affects all the people in the Gospel including Jesus himself; one can see how the material has been given kerygmatic form over a generation. That makes it all

---

75. Cf. P. Wernle, op. cit. (n. 68), 197:

He is the leading figure in the circle of disciples at all the important points from the beginning to the end of the narrative. He is the first to be called, the first in the catalogue of apostles, whom Jesus calls the rock when he chooses him, the first to confess Jesus as Messiah and to see his glory; despite the denial, the disciple who follows him longest, the first to be vouchsafed an appearance.

H.-H. Stoldt, *Geschichte und Kritik der Markushypothese,* 1977, 180f., has protested against this interpretation. He may be right that we cannot derive the protophany to Peter directly from 16:7—though it could at least be an indication there to the community which knows about it (cf. I Cor. 15:4; Luke 24:34)—but he cannot give an explanation for the concentrated stress on Peter in Mark. In the parallel, Matt. 28:7f., the reference to Peter is deleted. The hypothesis of Schmithals, *ZTK* 77, 1980, 164, that here Mark is giving "an outline of the exemplary disciple or Christian which was self-contained from the start and only understandable in such a context," is correct only with some essential qualifications. In the first place, Peter's conduct is very often anything but exemplary, and secondly, some scenes (1:29, cf. I Cor. 9:5; 8:32f. or 14:66ff.) are much too specific for an abstract construction of this kind. Mark is not working—as Schmithals would like—freely to create a romance, or in a theologically abstract way, but is shaping tradition about Peter which is obviously close to him. James and John, the sons of Zebedee, also to some degree take on a profile of their own, though of course it is much more limited: 1:19f.; 3:17; 10:35ff.

76. W. H. Kelber, *Mark's Story of Jesus,* 1979, 90, is somewhat off the mark: "In sum, Mark's combined critique of the Twelve, the Three, Peter, Jesus' family, and the Galilean women is directed against people who are identifiable as representative figures of the Jerusalem Church." Unbridled redaction criticism makes everything possible in this way.

the more astounding how, despite all the narrative abbreviations, Mark nevertheless brings his vivid style to bear.[77]

Finally, it is striking that for Mark and his successors, James the brother of the Lord and the family of Jesus fade right into the background. Their existence is noted only in 6:3. However, the explanation of this is that from the beginning of the forties (cf. Acts 12:17; Gal. 2:9) James had forced Peter out of his position of primacy in Jerusalem and that there were tensions here which were hardly less than those between Paul and his opponents.[78]

There are yet other reasons for supposing that Petrine authority stands behind the Gospel of Mark. First, Mark's work was used by the historian Luke and also by Matthew, so self-consciously a Christian scribe, in a quite natural way as a guideline. The fidelity with which Matthew reproduces the whole of his Marcan model is particularly striking. Furthermore, the best explanation of the fact that the Second Gospel lived on in the Church, although Matthew had taken over about ninety percent of the material in it, is that the work of Mark was from the beginning bound up with the authority of the name of Peter. Furthermore, the only Gospel which deviates from the Marcan order fundamentally is the Fourth; in it the mysterious beloved disciple (said to be the author, 21:24) is always closer to Jesus than Peter, the guarantor of the Marcan-Synoptic tradition.

The Second Gospel probably developed out of living oral teaching and was composed for solemn reading in worship. The short cola, often with a rhythmic shape, point to oral recitation in the assembled community. The Gospel was written for the audience to listen to, and therefore is anything but an artificial literary composition written at a desk, stuck together from obscure written sources, countless notes, and flysheets.[79] Here we should not simply

77. For the various Peter traditions see T. Smith, *Petrine Controversies in Early Christianity,* WUNT, 1985; see further R. Pesch, "Simon Petrus," *Päpste und Papsttum* 15, 1980, 138-49, and the unfortunately unsatisfactory joint study *Peter in the New Testament,* ed. R. E. Brown, K. P. Donfried, and J. Reumann, 1974, 54-129. For Peter in the four Gospels and the significance of Mark as the starting point see Reinhard Feldmeier's essay in the present volume.

78. On James, see my article "Jakobus, der Herrenbruder—der erste 'Papst'?" *Glaube und Eschatologie,* Festschrift W. G. Kümmel, ed. E. Grässer and O. Merk, 1985, 71-104.

79. J. G. Herder, *Vom Erlöser der Menschen, Sämtliche Werke,* ed. B. Suphan, XIX, 1880, has recognized the decisive features of Mark's work: "His Gospel is arranged to be read aloud; it ends and abbreviates the discourse for heart and ear" (216). "In short, the Gospel of Mark is a *Gospel of the Church* written from living narrative for public reading in the community" (217). So when Herder speaks of the Gospels as a *"sacred epic"* (199) and describes this more closely as "the presentation of the Gospels in composition and aim" (author's italics), this applies quite specifically to the Second Gospel. And when he calls the evangelists "rhapsodists" (214), of whom could that be said with more justification than of Mark, the "living rhapsodist of this history" (217)? In his little noted commentary, *The Gospel of Saint Mark,* 1936, by arranging the text into sense units, i.e., short *Cola et Commata,* the American Jesuit and classical philologist James A. Kleist gives the reader the impression of the way in which the Gospel was presented; here the evangelist's sense of rhythm and speech melody is particularly striking (91-127), cf. 125f. on Mark 4:2: "The very rhythm,

project our own extracts and notes, our relatively mechanical "scientific" ways of working, on to Mark. Behind this work there is neither a mere collector of amorphous popular "community tradition" which was "current" (how are we to imagine that?) somewhere in the Gentile Christian churches, nor an anonymous, poetically inspired, Gentile Christian man of letters, but a theological teacher who himself must have been a master of the word and an authority in early Christianity. A Mr. Nobody would hardly have undertaken the revolutionary innovation of writing a gospel. In my view the author was at the same time a disciple of the greatest apostolic authority in the earliest Church. That could explain the initial success of his work.

On the other hand we should certainly not also assume some *slavish* dependence on the Peter tradition. The work of the second evangelist again puts its own personal theological stamp on that. For all their dependence, the deutero-Pauline letters Ephesians and Colossians, which come from unknown pupils of Paul, have a mark of their own, as does I John in comparison with the Gospel—not to mention Paul's disciple Luke. Certainly, about five years after the death of Peter and in the confusion of the civil war after Nero, a written Gospel from the hand of a disciple of Peter to point the way forward was the demand of the hour.

Unfortunately we know hardly anything about the theology of Peter, the most influential teacher, even in the Gentile Christian churches, alongside Paul. It would be attractive to attempt to reconstruct certain basic features from the Second Gospel, but this would rightly meet with objections from the start as being too imaginative a hypothesis. Here we must leave the question open.[80]

---

even apart from the meaning of the words, puts the hearer in a solemn and attentive mood." See also the observations of G. Lüderitz on "poetic rhythm" in the Second Gospel, in H. Cancik, op. cit. (n. 39), 168ff.: "Kola und Rhythmik," 183: "The similarity in diction . . . with books which are read in worship, could be an indication that the Gospel was written for such a use." B. H. M. G. M. Standaert, op. cit. (n. 13), 496-618, conjectures that the original Sitz im Leben of the Gospel was liturgical usage at baptism and Christian Easter celebrations on Easter Day in Rome. This is certainly to restrict the use of the work too much. It is in no way limited to one day in the year. On the other hand no Gospel leads up to Easter morning so clearly as Mark, and the exceptional, abrupt conclusion in 16:8 makes a liturgical response in the confession of the community plausible. On this see now also E. Trocmé, *The Passion as Liturgy,* 1983.

80. The discussions by O. Cullmann, *Peter: Disciple, Apostle, Martyr,* ET 1962, 66-70, show how little we know. I would agree with Cullmann that Peter was presumably not *all that* remote theologically from Paul, and also that the interpretation of the death of Jesus as an expiatory death was particularly significant for him. The deutero-Petrine I Peter also indicates this. For Peter as the first Easter witness see R. Pesch, op. cit. (n. 77), 48ff.

6. Mark's Work as Gospel

(a) Terminology

Nevertheless, perhaps I may be allowed a concluding hypothesis. Mark uses the term gospel, εὐαγγέλιον, seven times. At the beginning of his Gospel the εὐαγγέλιον Ἰησοῦ Χριστοῦ as an objective genitive means the gospel *about* Jesus Christ, i.e., the saving events of the ministry and death of Jesus in the "biographical" work[81] that is now beginning.[82]

In the *propositio* in 1:14 Jesus appears in Galilee and proclaims the εὐαγγέλιον τοῦ θεοῦ. Here we have a *genitivus auctoris,* the good news from God, which is explained in v. 15: "The time is fulfilled and the kingdom of God is here.[83] Repent and believe in the gospel." The good news of God is identical with the proclamation of the dawn of God's rule as the embodiment of the proclamation and activity of Jesus in Galilee. By contrast the gospel of Jesus Christ in 1:1 has an even more comprehensive character; it contains the *whole* saving event which begins with the forerunner, John the Baptist, and culminates in the death of Jesus for many and his resurrection. This is not yet to be found in all its fullness in Jesus' public announcement of the dawn of the kingdom of God alone. I.e., in contrast to the presentation of the proclamation of Jesus in the Fourth Gospel, in Mark there is still some tension between the preaching of God which begins in Galilee and the christological saving event which comprises the whole gospel, including the suffering and resurrection, indeed the promise of the parousia, of the Son of Man (8:34; 9:1; ch. 13; 14:62).

Accordingly Mark does not use the term εὐαγγέλιον again in the first part of his account. On the other hand, it occurs twice in the instruction of the

---

81. See above, pp. 211ff. S. Schulz, "Die Bedeutung des Markus für die Theologiegeschichte des Urchristentums," in *Studia Evangelica* II, TU 87, 1964, 135-45, has rightly pointed out that the "Evangelium" at the same time represents a "*historia* between Galilee and Jerusalem" to which "constitutive elements," including "geographical connections, chronological sequences, and biographical details" (136) belong. However, his derivation of this "consecutive, integrated *historia Jesu*" "from the popular tradition of the θεῖος ἀνήρ lives, as for example those of Apollonius of Tyana, Alexander of Abonuteichos, and Peregrinus Proteus" (143), is unfortunate. Popular θεῖος ἀνήρ lives of this kind cannot be demonstrated as a specific genre, and the Gospels have little to do with the later high-literary and partly polemical works of Lucian and Philostratus about these "heroes."

82. 1:1 is to be understood as the introduction to the book. The "contents" are εὐαγγέλιον Ἰησοῦ Χριστοῦ. The content of the work is the whole εὐαγγέλιον Ἰησοῦ Χριστοῦ from the appearance of John the Baptist to the parousia (Mark 13). The ἀρχὴ τοῦ εὐαγγελίου ... relates to the appearance of John the Baptist and the baptism and temptation of Jesus (1:1-13), i.e., it comprises the event of the public activity of the Son of God. Only a semicolon should be put between vv. 1 and 2, but a full stop after v. 3. "The beginning of the gospel of Jesus Christ (happened) as it is written. . . ." The account of Jesus proper begins in 1:14.

83. The perfect ἤγγικεν is to be understood, like the Aramaic *mt',* as present: cf. Mark 14:42: ἰδοὺ ὁ παραδιδούς με ἤγγικεν, "Behold he who betrays me is here." Cf. also J. Jeremias, *The Parables of Jesus,* ET [3]1972, 230: "The hour of fulfilment is come."

disciples after Peter's confession and the announcement of the passion: in 8:35 in the summons to self-denial, "For whoever will lose his life for my sake and the gospel's will save it," and similarly in 10:29, "For no one has forsaken house (and family) . . . and fields for my sake and the gospel's who will not receive it again a hundred fold. . . ." The ἕνεκεν ἐμοῦ καὶ ἕνεκεν τοῦ εὐαγγελίου is a hendiadys: "for Jesus' sake" at the same time means "for the gospel's sake," and vice versa. Jesus is the content of the gospel. This refers back to the wider understanding in 1:1.

The last instances have an almost Pauline ring; 13:10 disrupts the connection between the little apocalypse and the announcement of persecution, "but first the gospel must be preached to all peoples." Here the gospel is the embodiment of worldwide missionary preaching.[84] In 14:9, at the beginning of the passion narrative proper, this Pauline-sounding traditional and kerygmatic understanding of εὐαγγέλιον is bound up with the narration of the story of Jesus, above all the passion narrative, so that such a narrative appears as an essential ingredient of mission preaching generally: "Truly I say to you, wherever the gospel is *preached* throughout the world, what she has done will be *narrated* in memory of her."[85]

---

84. Cf. R. Pesch, op. cit. (n. 1), 2, 285, and G. Schneider, "Der Missionsauftrag Jesu in der Darstellung der Evangelien," in *Mission im Neuen Testament,* ed. K. Kertelge, QD 93, 1982, 84f. The saying has been inserted "redactionally" by Mark, though in terms of content it is "traditional." In my view the formulation derives from Greek-speaking Jewish Christian circles which, parallel to Paul, advocated the idea of a worldwide mission before the parousia. This was a group to which Peter is to be added in his later period, after his departure from Jerusalem (cf. Acts 12:17b) or in the years after the Apostolic Council. Cf. M. Hengel, *Acts and the History of Earliest Christianity,* 92-98: "Peter and the Mission to the Gentiles." Peter was not the slave of the Law that Marcion and the Tübingen school wanted to make him. See n. 91 below. The mission charge in Matt. 28:18-20 takes this line further, but it is significant that there, in accordance with the understanding of the first evangelist, the place of the proclamation of the gospel is taken by the extension of discipleship among the Gentiles and the teaching of the commandments of Jesus.

85. Here the evangelist has changed the narrative to suit his purpose. In my view we can only reconstruct the original version of the logion very hypothetically. See R. Pesch, op. cit. (n. 1), 2, 34f., and J. Jeremias, *Abba,* 1966, 115-20. This text is the Marcan climax to the story of the anointing and stands at the beginning of the passion narrative proper (the fifth act), immediately before the betrayal by the disciple Judas—the contrast is made quite deliberately. As such it has a key position in the Gospel. It is understandable that on the basis of his presuppositions Schmithals has to take particular exception to it. His hostility reaches such a pitch that he claims that 14:3-9 is "an originally redactional unit" which the dumb fool Mark formed on "historical and biographical grounds" without any "specifically theological interest," in order to "make it possible to divide passion week into days" (cf. idem, 593 n. 3). The "theologically coherent original version of the narrative" is in Luke 7:36-47, and Mark's bungled effort is simply "a bad copy" (595). Here Schmithals refers to M. Goguel, *The Life of Jesus,* ET 1933, 458, whose judgment is, however, much more cautious. Behind Mark and Luke there is "a simpler archetype." Luke's account comes "closest" to this. Schmithals's verdict on 14:9 is similarly expressed with dogmatic zeal: "The theological lack of taste in turning attention away from Jesus at the climax of the story, though the service of the woman is directed towards him, is also to be attributed to the historicizing bias of the evangelist" (590). *De gustibus non disputandum.* In my view it is a sign of the theological greatness of the evangelist and the enthusiastic humanity of his Gospel that in this pericope, which is framed by the resolve to kill Jesus and Judas' betrayal, he ventures to report that Jesus looked on an unknown

This unique terminology, which connects the christological *kerygma* that we know from Paul indivisibly with the whole *story of Jesus* as the saving event, was certainly not the personal invention of Mark. Some examples like 1:1; 13:10; 14:9 may be his own redactional construction; in the other instances he probably went back to earlier tradition.[86] We should probably already presuppose this christological connection of a narrative about Jesus and proclamation with the term εὐαγγέλιον in a large number of communities even before the composition of Mark's work. We find it about a generation after Mark in a striking, well-molded form, for example in Ignatius or even in the Didache, where in both instances there is already a hint of the transition to the written gospel.[87] Without this earlier terminology in numerous communities the term "Gospel" would probably never have come into being as a designation for those four kerygmatic biographies that we find in the New Testament canon. Where does this nomenclature come from?

(b) Peter and the Term *Gospel*

In our earliest evidence, the letters of Paul, only one figure appears to us from the Twelve, the most intimate group of disciples, whose influence extended from Jerusalem, via Antioch and Corinth, to Rome. He was in a particular way the conversation-partner and missionary rival of the apostle to the Gentiles. Paul visited him for two weeks in Jerusalem, two or three years after his conversion, and attacked him sharply in Antioch (Gal. 1:18; 2:10ff.); he also caused difficulties for Paul in his own community in Corinth. He was a figure who more than any other could act as spokesman of the disciples in connection with the wealth of the Jesus tradition: Simon Peter. We will not go far wrong if we regard him—more than all the other disciples of Jesus—as the authoritative mediator of the Jesus-tradition in the mission churches from Antioch to Rome. His original close connection with the Master contributed to his unique authority, as did the fact that he was first to see the Risen Lord.

On the other hand, we may regard it as certain that the word εὐαγγέλιον, which Paul uses so often as the embodiment of the new message, did not have

---

woman, in order to connect the worldwide proclamation of the message of victory with a narrative remembrance of her loving action.

86. For the tradition history of εὐαγγέλιον in the "Hellenistic Jewish-Christian community" see the basic work by P. Stuhlmacher, *Das paulinische Evangelium*, FRLANT 95, 1968, 254-86, also his essay on "The Pauline Gospel" in the present volume. Cf. also M. Hengel, *Between Jesus and Paul*, ET 1983, 26.

87. Ignatius, *Philad.* 5.1f.; 8:2; 9:2: ἐξαίρετον δέ τι ἔχει τὸ εὐαγγέλιον, τὴν παρουσίαν (here in the sense of the advent of Jesus in the incarnation, cf. BAGD, s.v. 2b) τοῦ σωτῆρος . . . τὸ πάθος αὐτοῦ καὶ τὴν ἀνάστασιν; Smyrn. 5:1; 7:2. In the Didache, in accordance with a community ordinance, εὐαγγέλιον refers more markedly to the words and commands of Jesus, 8:2; 11:3; 15:3.

first to be discovered by the apostle to the Gentiles, but goes back to the earliest Greek-speaking community in Jerusalem. Possibly, even, an Aramaic term underlies it, as the Targum on Isa. 53:1 renders the Hebrew שמועה in the question "Who has believed our report?" with בסורתא, the Aramaic equivalent of εὐαγγέλιον, and the term is to be derived from the verb בשר = εὐαγγελίζεσθαι, which is used by Deutero-Isaiah to describe the proclamation of the message of victory in the dawn of the kingdom of God (40:9; 60:6; 61:1);[88] in connection with that it also plays a role in the proclamation of Jesus.[89] I Cor. 15:1ff., where Paul describes the stereotyped kerygma of passion and resurrection as εὐαγγέλιον, which he himself has received as paradosis, also refers back to a very early pre-Pauline use of the word. Finally, Gal. 2:1-10 suggests that the term εὐαγγέλιον or its Aramaic equivalent was also not unfamiliar to the Jerusalem authorities.[90] In 2:7 Paul stresses that his conversation partners had realized that "I was entrusted with my gospel for the Gentiles, as Peter was with the (gospel) for the Jews."[91]

In the light of this, we have good reason to suppose that this term was also significant for Peter, though we no longer have any access to his preaching and his theology. It can hardly be doubted that he exercised enormous influence, which was hardly less than that of Paul. Of course, in contrast to Peter's influence, that of Paul was prolonged and revived by the collection and circulation of his letters. In Peter's case, by contrast, the recollection remained bound up with his person, his special Jesus-tradition, and not so much with his own theology, which was probably simpler than that of Paul, the former scribe. Now if the term εὐαγγέλιον was also vital for Peter, then the Jesus-tradition or the story of Jesus will have played a much greater role in it than with Paul. Perhaps Peter's speech to Cornelius with its account of the activity of Jesus (Acts 10:36-43) preserves a slight trace of this. Why should Luke, who sought to give the best theological portrait of Paul that he could in Acts 13:38f.; 20:24-36, not also have had some tradition about Peter? Possibly he was still aware that the

---

88. Cf. also Joel 3:5; Nah. 2:1; Isa. 41:27; 52:7; 61:1; Ps. 86:12. The original meaning, "message of victory," appears above all in II Sam. 18:19-32, cf. also II Sam. 4:10; II Kings 7:9. For the event see also Plutarch, *Demetrius* 17, where at the end (17:5) εὐαγγέλιον appears with the meaning of reward for a message (for the message of victory).

89. Cf. Luke 7:22 = Matt. 11:5 Q. Also 4:18, from the Lucan special material, where the evangelist puts Isa. 61:1 on the lips of Jesus himself in a way which is completely appropriate. For the Targum of Isa. 53:1, cf. Otto Betz's essay in the present volume.

90. Cf. P. Stuhlmacher, op. cit. (n. 86), 266ff. Peter, the Twelve, James, and all the apostles agree with the traditional εὐαγγέλιον which is expressed in I Cor.15:3f., see v. 11.

91. Like Paul, Peter too is entrusted by God (divine passive) with "the gospel" (πεπίστευμαι τὸ εὐαγγέλιον), but he proclaims it to the Jews. This restriction to the Jews may still have applied for the Apostolic Council about 48. As the Peter party in Corinth shows, there is no longer mention of such a restriction about five years later. Now Peter can also become the apostolic authority for Gentile Christians.

word "gospel" was not a term that Jesus used, so that he consistently deletes it four times in all from his Marcan model.[92] It is all the more striking that in Acts 20:24 Luke puts the word on Paul's lips with the significant formula that he has received from the Lord the ministry διαμαρτύρασθαι τὸ εὐαγγέλιον τῆς χάριτος τοῦ θεοῦ.

We find the second instance in 15:7, on Peter's lips: in the Cornelius story God has determined διὰ τοῦ στόματός μου ἀκοῦσαι τὰ ἔθνη τὸν λόγον τοῦ εὐαγγελίου καὶ πιστεῦσαι. One might almost suppose that in his last speech Peter is deliberately dismissed by Luke as a missionary to the Gentiles.

The point of contact between the term gospel and the Jesus-tradition in Peter could explain why Mark uses this word in so evocative a way, which in part deviates from Paul, and secondly why in some communities εὐαγγέλιον was evidently used as a designation for the story and teaching of Jesus; also, finally, how the connection between the Jesus-tradition and the term is manifestly rejected by the "Pauline" Luke in his Gospel. The Johannine circle, as so often, went its own way in the terminology of its proclamation, and it can do without the newly-coined word as it can do without ἀπόστολος in the sense of "messenger of Jesus." We find it in I Pet. 4:17—a unique occurrence in the non-Pauline letters.

The special terminology which is becoming evident for the first time in Mark, and which involves the narrative Jesus-tradition, would then finally have established itself despite all the resistance because in the last resort it still had behind it the old authority of the Petrine tradition, a tradition for which the historical tradition about Jesus and the good news belonged indissolubly together.

(c) Mark and the Story of Moses

There is an even more profound reason why here in Mark—and to my mind in the Petrine tradition which underlies it—the story of Jesus, including the tradition of his words, is designated "gospel." *Judaism, too, knew a historical saving event: the exodus from Egypt under the leadership of Moses and the handing down of the Torah to Israel through Moses.* The Torah comprised not

---

92. Cf. Mark 1:14b and Luke 4:15; Mark 8:35 and Luke 9:24; Mark 13:10 and Luke 21:13f. Luke 18:30 is most striking; here Mark 10:29, ἕνεκεν ἐμοῦ καὶ ἕνεκεν τοῦ εὐαγγελίου, is replaced by ἕνεκεν τῆς βασιλείας τοῦ θεοῦ. By contrast, Luke uses the verb εὐαγγελίζεσθαι relatively frequently in his Gospel, presumably taking up the language of LXX, cf. 4:18 = Isa. 61:1; 1:19; 2:10; 8:1; 16:16; 20:1. Apart from 7:22 = Matt. 11:5 Q (καὶ πτωχοὶ εὐαγγελίζονται, cf. again Isa. 61:1), all the passages could be "redactional." Matthew takes over three examples from Mark: 4:23, which is identical with 9:35; 24:14; 26:13). In the first three passages he defines the word εὐαγγέλιον by the genitive attribute τῆς βασιλείας. The term is completely absent from the Johannine corpus as also from the logia source. In Rev. 14:6 it does not have the specific meaning "message of salvation."

only the 613 prohibitions and commands,[93] but from Exodus to Deuteronomy a "biography" of the man of God,[94] which among other things also contained the eschatological promise of a "prophet" like Moses (Deut. 18:19ff.), in Judaism very closely bound up with the expectation of Elijah.[95] As the first redeemer, Moses was a type of the second redeemer, and Elijah was the first manifestation of the *Moses redivivus*. As such, he was transported, and his return was expected. It is striking how deeply the Gospel of Mark is stamped with the Moses-Elijah typology. This begins with John the Baptist, who for Mark is the *Elia redivivus;* it is continued in the baptism and temptation of Jesus in the wilderness; and is evident in the parallel between Mark 1:15 and Ex. 14:31,[96] which for Jewish tradition is the first climax of the saving event of the exodus, and in the confession of the Song of Moses made manifest the faith of Israel and its acknowledgment of the kingly rule of Yahweh (15:18). This typology then emerges again clearly in some of the miracle stories, above all in their climax, the stories of the feedings, and reaches its real high point in the scene of the Transfiguration with the appearance of Moses and Elijah, though it is not to them, but to the beloved Son, that the disciples must listen (9:7). Finally, it takes on markedly antitypical features in the Passover meal with the sacrifice of the covenant, the judgment on the shepherds (14:27; cf. Num. 27:17), the condemnation of Jesus by the high priest, his crucifixion, and the cry of dereliction. Probably every Jew and Jewish Christian knew legends about the end of Moses,

---

93. For this enumeration, which can be demonstrated for the first time in the second century, see Billerbeck I, 900; III, 542; IV, 438, and Targ. Jerus. I on Gen. 1:27.

94. Above all in Greek-speaking Judaism the Pentateuch could also be understood as a *vita Mosis* prefixed by an "extended introduction" in Genesis. Plutarch's double lives of Lycurgus and Numa and of Solon show in turn that Greek biography could contain extended passages of laws or religious ritual. In addition, Moses was "the best-known personality in Jewish history" (I. Heinemann, *PRE* XVI/1 [1933], col. 361). For Philo, who wrote an extended biography of Moses, he is "the πάνσοφος and ἱεροφάντης" (col. 369), and as such "the perfect man par excellence" (col. 371). In Josephus, *Ant.* 2.201–4.331, we have a detailed life of Moses with a marked apologetic stamp; it ends with an encomium (4.327-31) which describes him as the most significant prophet, whose word was as good as the voice of God (329).

95. Before the well-known passage about Elijah, Malachi 3 (3–4 in EVV), another text which is essential for Mark (cf. Mal. 3:1; Ex. 23:20: Mark 1:2; Mal. 3:23f. [EVV 4:5f.]: Mark 9:11f.), has a reference to the revelation of the Torah on Horeb to Moses as a binding saving event; the "shift" ushered in by Elijah, which brings salvation from judgment, amounts to repentance and obedience to the Torah (3:22, EVV 4:4):

> Remember the law of my servant Moses, the statutes and ordinances that I commanded him at Horeb for all Israel. Behold, I will send you Elijah the prophet before the great and terrible day of the Lord comes. And he will turn the hearts of the fathers to their children and the hearts of children to their fathers, lest I come and smite the land with a curse. (3:22-24, EVV 4:4-6)

96. Ex. 14:31: וייראו העם את־יהוה ויאמינו ביהוה; Mark 1:15b: μετανοεῖτε καὶ πιστεύετε ἐν τῷ εὐαγγελίῳ (= τοῦ θεοῦ, v. 14). Cf. on this the old Tannaitic commentary Mekilta on Ex. 14:31 (ed. Lauterbach I, 252f.). The faith of Israel brings about the gift of the spirit and thus confession, in the Song of Moses, 15:1-18. The redemption from Egypt is simply the reward of this faith.

that either he was taken up into heaven without having to die or that God himself
took his soul from his body without any of the pains of death, "as with a kiss."
The contrast between the death of Jesus and that of the man of Sinai is evident.[97]
In other words, the story of Jesus as the eschatological saving event, as gospel,
stands in a relationship of tension with the story of Moses as "saving event" for
Israel, or with the Torah as "saving" message. Jesus as messianic teacher on the
one hand enforces the law even more strictly with the commandment to love
(Mark 12:29-34), so that a scribe who has in fact to preserve the heritage of
Moses (cf. Matt. 23:2) agrees with him; indeed, he bases the resurrection of the
dead on the Torah—in a completely Pharisaic sense (cf. Mark 12:28: ὅτι καλῶς
ἀπεκρίθη αὐτοῖς [12:18-27]). On the other hand, however, he appears as the Lord
over the Torah (2:28), who puts in question the sabbath commandment, the
commandments about purity (7:15) or the permission for divorce, and who never
again wants to pour the old wine into new skins (2:22). In other words, in the
Gospel of Mark, the Pauline and Johannine contrast between Moses and Christ
which the Prologue of John reduced to the impressive formula, "The law was
given by Moses, but grace and truth have come through Jesus Christ" (John
1:17), takes the form of the typological-antitypical contrast of two historical
accounts. Matthew developed this dialectical relationship quite deliberately,
stressing in particular Jesus as the messianic teacher. In his work it finds new
expression in the antitheses of the Sermon on the Mount. It is astonishing to see
how here one evangelist extends his hand to another as a theological teacher.

The liturgical consequence of what in the last resort is predominantly an
antithetical parallel between Moses and Jesus is that the reading (and exposition)
of the Gospels gradually takes the place of the reading (and interpretation) of
the Torah as the climax of the ministry of the word,[98] while the Old Testament

---

97. Cf. K. Haacker and P. Schafer, "Nachbiblische Traditionen vom Tod des Mose," in
Josephus Studien. Festschrift O. Michel, 1974, 146-74. Cf. Josephus's comment in *Ant.* 4.325, which
rejects the idea of transportation. In Ps.-Philo, *Lib. Ant.* 19:16, Moses dies *in gloria*. In AssMos
10.12, a *receptione* has found its way into the text, probably "as a variant to *morte*" (160). In the
Samaritan *Memar Marqa* God makes sleep come on Moses, who lay down in a cave on Gerizim,
"and his soul left him without pain, indeed without his noticing it" (163). In Targ. Jer. I on Deut.
34:5 the death of Moses עַל־פִּי יהוה is interpreted as a death "by a kiss of the Memra of God," as it
also is in some midrashim (169f.). For the transportation and return see 170ff. Here Moses can be
connected with Elijah.

98. Probably Mark and Matthew were from the beginning written for reading in worship
(see above, p. 242). The liturgical reading of the Old Testament as Scripture and preaching is already
presupposed in I Tim. 4:13. Rev. 1:3 contains the earliest clear reference to the reading of a Christian
"scripture of revelation" in worship. But cf. already I Thess. 5:27; Col. 4:16. There is then evidence
in Justin, *Apol.* 1.67.3 of the reading of the Gospels in worship as a custom which everyone can
understand: καὶ τὰ ἀπομνημονεύματα τῶν ἀποστόλων ἢ τὰ συγγράμματα τῶν προφητῶν ἀναγινώσκεται.
Here it is striking that reading the Gospels is put first. In my view, the reading of Scripture in
communities with an originally Jewish Christian stamp, who parted company with the synagogue,
say in Rome, Antioch, and perhaps also in Corinth, goes back to the beginning of these communities.
Without relatively regular reading of Scripture in worship, Paul could never have argued in his

is subsumed totally under the prophetic promise which prepared for the gospel. The partly typological and partly antitypical relationship was also at work in Hebrews and then, in the second century, in I Clement, Barnabas, Justin, Melito of Sardis, and Irenaeus. One of its roots may lie in the fact that in the Gospel of Mark the story of Jesus as gospel first becomes visible in a dialectical relationship to the story of Moses as the "saving message" of the Torah. The subject matter itself is earlier and in the last resort goes back to Jesus.[99] Moreover, the contrast between law and gospel does not seem to have been so exclusively Pauline. Incidentally, it is grounded in a community tradition which thought even more strongly than Paul in terms of salvation history and typology, and which referred to the Jesus tradition; again we may ask whether it was not originally connected with the proclamation of Peter.

In that case, the Jesus story as gospel, which has been told to us above all by the Synoptics, i.e., in the first instance by Mark and—in a derivative form—by Luke and Matthew, who are dependent on him, would then also be influenced to some degree by Petrine tradition, making it the third significant corpus in the New Testament alongside the Pauline corpus and the Johannine corpus. The designation εὐαγγέλιον would then *perhaps* go back to this Petrine understanding of the gospel.

---

letters with the help of the Old Testament. How otherwise would the newly-won Gentile Christians have been able to understand his often complicated Scriptural arguments? II Cor. 3:14 certainly presupposes that Moses was also read in Christian worship (as a prophet with other prophets), but that here for Christians "the veil was taken away" and the prophetic saying was understood, in accordance with the Spirit, as promise. For the significance of Scriptural reading see also my study "The Titles of the Gospels" (n. 71 above).

99. Cf. Luke 16:16 = Matt. 11:12 Q; Luke 7:26ff. = Matt. 11:9ff. Q; Luke 11:30ff. = Matt. 12:41f. Q, etc.

The Portrayal of Peter
in the Synoptic Gospels

Reinhard Feldmeier

Mark[1] mentions Simon/Peter 25 times,[2] Matthew also mentions him 25 times, and Luke 30 times.[3] With a total number of 11,078 words in Mark, 18,298 in Matthew, and 19,448 in Luke, that gives a frequency in Mark of 1:443, in Luke of 1:648, and in Matthew of 1:722.[4] Given the approximate equivalence of Luke and Matthew, Peter is therefore mentioned most often in Mark (Mark:Matthew = 1:1.63; Mark:Luke = 1:1.46).

In the first instance this inequality is caused by Q, in which Peter is not mentioned anywhere,[5] just as in Q the disciples do not ever appear in an active role.[6]

1. In the Gospel of Mark Peter occupies a prominent position among the disciples. He is the first to be called (1:16), he receives the name "Peter" as a mark of honor, and is mentioned first in the list of disciples, a clear indication of the importance attached to him. Next come the sons of Zebedee, and only

---

1. I have not taken into account the additions at the end of the Gospel of Mark, which in terms of textual criticism are to be judged secondary.

2. In Mark 1:16 the designation of Andrew as "brother of Simon" is counted as an independent naming, because here we have an unusual closer definition of Andrew in relation to his brother (and not—as is usual—in relation to his father, as in the case of the sons of Zebedee). On the other hand, the change of Peter's name to Simon is only counted once.

3. The double name Simon Peter is counted once (cf. Matt. 16:16; Luke 5:8), as are similar formulations (Matt. 4:18; 10:2: "Simon, who is called Peter").

4. The numbers are taken from R. Morgenthaler's *Statistische Synopse*, 1971, 89.

5. Only Matt. 18:21 is disputed; cf. A. Polag, *Fragmenta Q*, [2]1982, 76f. (where there is further bibliography).

6. μαθητής is used only once for the disciples of John the Baptist (Matt. 11:2 par. Luke 7:18) and once in a saying about the master-disciple relationship (Matt. 10:24 par. Luke 6:40). The saying Matt. 19:28 par. Luke 22:30 probably refers to the Twelve as disciples; here Jesus promises those who follow him that they will sit on twelve thrones and judge the twelve tribes of Israel. Otherwise the disciples are not mentioned either as a totality or as individuals.

then his brother Andrew (who was called when he was, 3:16ff.). His special position is also expressed in the phrase Σίμων καὶ οἱ μετ᾽ αὐτοῦ (1:36). Simon always belongs to the most intimate circle around Jesus (5:37; 9:2; 13:3; 14:33), and apart from Mark 9:38ff. and 10:35-40 is the only disciple to appear as an individual over against Jesus (8:29, 32f.; 9:5; 10:28; 11:21; 14:29ff.). His failure in Gethsemane is a particular cause of grief to Jesus: "Simon, are you asleep (as well)?" (14:37). Moreover, Peter is the only one to follow Jesus after his arrest (14:56, 66-72), and after the resurrection of Jesus the women receive the command to tell the news "to his disciples and to Peter" (16:7).

There has been no lack of attempts to interpret this special position of Peter as a post-Easter interpolation. However, the very fact that some scholars want to see this as a confirmation of the position of the later leader of the Church and others as a challenge to him shows the impossibility of explaining the position of prominence given to Peter in Mark on the basis of one particular aim. For Peter is a prominent counterpart to Jesus for good and for ill. His confession of Christ (8:29) is followed by his opposition to the way Jesus is to go and by Jesus' subsequent rebuke to him, "Get behind me, Satan" (8:32f.); his readiness for unconditional discipleship (14:26-31) is matched by his fall, which is all the greater (14:37, 66-72). A retrojection stemming from the later Peter would have had to depict him in a much more clearly positive or negative way—depending on attitudes toward him.

Another feature which tells against a subsequent interpolation is the fact that Peter has no leading position within the circle of the Twelve; this is partially already reflected in the picture of Peter in the synoptic parallels (with their strong post-Easter stamp).

Finally, it is impossible to explain why James the brother of the Lord, who was soon to play such a decisive role in Jerusalem, still has no significance in Mark.

While it is impossible to deny that Peter may have been typified as the spokesman of the disciples, the features in Mark's picture of Peter, some of which are very distinctive, may well in essence go back to historical reminiscence .

2. Matthew has omitted the name Peter/Simon 9 times as compared with the Marcan original (Mark 1:16b, 30, 36; 5:37; 11:21; 13:3; 14:37b, 67; 16:7); 3 times he has added it in clearly redactional passages (Matt. 15:15; 18:21; 26:37); and 6 times the name appears in special material where it is impossible to make a clear distinction between tradition and redaction (Matt. 14:28f.; 16:17f.; 17:24f.).

2.1. The omissions do not say very much. 3 times they are governed by stylistic considerations (Mark 1:16b, 29b; 14:67), 3 times the restriction of the participants in an event, a discourse, or a question is removed in favor of all the disciples or all those involved (Mark 5:37; 11:21; 13:3). Mark 1:35-38 is missing from Matthew for reasons connected with the structure of his Gospel.[7] The

---

7. After the call of the disciples Matthew first of all portrays the "Christ of the word" (chs. 5–7) and then the "Christ of action" (chs. 8f.). He has either omitted (Mark 1:23-28) or integrated into ch. 8 (Mark 1:29-31 par. Matt. 8:14f.; Mark 1:32-34 par. Matt. 8:16f.) the actions of Jesus

omission of the reproach in Mark 14:37b, which is addressed only to Peter, is probably meant to spare him and share the responsibility with all the disciples. Like Luke, Matthew felt the strikingly lame "and Peter" (Mark 16:7) to be disruptive.

2.2. In the additions, Peter is similarly shown as spokesman of the disciples (Matt. 15:15; 18:21; 26:35). Matt. 18:21 already has him putting a question—of particular importance to a community already in existence; in contrast to Q he is thus introduced as a later authority in matters of community discipline.

2.3. In the special material, the sinking Peter (Matt. 14:28ff.) is a legendary extension of Jesus' walking on the water (Mark 6:45-52). The picture of Peter painted here—with "willing spirit" and "weak flesh"—corresponds to the picture of Peter as it is painted by Mark and others in the passion narrative. The picture of Peter which has been taken over has at this point moved further in the direction of anecdote and legend.

The tradition history of Matt. 16:16b-19, in which Peter is praised for his messianic confession, and which contains the saying about the keys, is a matter of dispute. At all events, here the Marcan framework is abandoned with a view to the post-Easter position of Peter, as is especially clear from the term ἐκκλησία (which the promise indicates as being permanently established).

The basic material in the passage on the question about the tax in Matt. 17:24-27 certainly goes back to the time before the destruction of the temple; we can no longer discover what role Peter played in the original (if any at all).[8] The remarkable thing about the narrative in its present form is that those who want to know something about the "teacher" turn to Peter, whereas Jesus (who already knows Peter's answer without being asked) simply instructs him. Here too there is probably already a reflection of the leading position of Peter after Easter; while he is instructed by Jesus, he does give authoritative answers to questions.

So in Matthew Peter—in the view of the third generation and beyond Mark—has become the man of the Church. However, in the Gospel as a whole he has no greater importance than he does in Mark.

3. In comparison with Mark, Luke has omitted the name Simon/Peter 15 times (1:16a, 16b, 36; 8:32, 33; 11:21; 13:3; 14:29, 33, 37a, 37b, 66, 67, 70; 16:7); he has added it 10 times (Luke 8:45; 9:32; 12:41; 22:8, 34, 55, 58, 60, 61a, 61b); 9 times it occurs in his special material (Luke 5:3, 4, 5, 8, 10a, 10b; 22:31; 24:12, 34). However, in these numbers it should be noted that Luke

reported by Mark 1:21-34. The departure from Capernaum (Mark 1:35-38) and the subsequent search for Jesus had to develop from there.

8. Cf. J. Schniewind, *Das Evangelium nach Matthäus*, 195f.; E. Lohmeyer/W. Schmauch, *Das Evangelium nach Matthäus*, 275f.; R. Bultmann, *The History of the Synoptic Tradition*, ET [2]1968, 34f.; E. Schweizer, *Good News according to Matthew*, ET 1976, 355-60, etc.

5.1-11 is regarded as special material, although at the same time a relationship with Mark 1:16ff. is probable.

3.1. 3 times the omissions are a matter of stylistic reshaping (Mark 14:66, 67, 70). The lame "and to Peter" in Mark 16:7 may also have fallen victim to stylistic polishing. In Luke, the narrative of the attempt by "Peter and those with him" to restrain Jesus (Mark 1:35-38),[9] which in Mark is presumably meant to be critical of the disciples, serves to stress Jesus' success: now it is the masses who look for Jesus and want to stay with him. The narrative of the withered fig tree is completely absent from Luke, and therefore so is Peter's question about it (Mark 11:21). Like Matthew, Luke too has done away with the restriction of the audience of the eschatological discourse to the four disciples who were first to be called (Mark 13:3). The name of Peter from Mark 14:29 is indeed omitted, but it is introduced into the dialogue (Luke 22:34). A clear redactional intent underlies the omission of the saying about Satan directed against Peter in Mark 8:32f.: as elsewhere in the Gospel, this feature of the disciples' failure is toned down or deleted. This theme evidently also governs the rendering of the Lucan pericope about Gethsemane (Luke 22:39-46): Jesus finds all the disciples sleeping only once, and paradoxically ἀπὸ τῆς λύπης (Luke 22:45 end). Accordingly the reproach to Peter is also omitted (Mark 14:37ab).[10]

3.2. Of the additions, 3 are determined by stylistic considerations (Luke 22:55, 58, 60). Luke 22:61 (Jesus sees Peter after his denial) cannot be regarded as redactional, but it does represent a novelistic intensification of the event which is secondary in terms of the history of the tradition. In Luke 22:34, the name of Peter, which has been omitted, is supplied (see above). As the verbal agreements show, Peter's sleep at the Transfiguration (Luke 9:32) has probably been drawn from the Marcan Gethsemane scene, and in Luke has taken the place of the saying about Satan as a toned-down expression of his failure to understand. It can therefore be explained from Luke's tendency, already noted, to spare the disciples.[11] A deliberate stress on Peter and John indicates their identification with the two disciples who are anonymous in Mark (Luke 22:8); this is probably influenced by the later significance of the two apostles (cf. Acts 3:1, 3ff., 11; 4:13, 19; 8:14).[12]

9. J. Gnilka, *Das Evangelium nach Markus,* I, 88.

10. A further reason for the omission could be the incorporation of Luke 22:43ff., which on the basis of intrinsic criteria belongs to the original text (cf. G. Schneider, "Engel und Blutschweiss," *BZ* NF 20, 1976, 112-16) and the associated reworking of the text. That does not alter in any way the fact that here Luke has strongly toned down the failure of the disciples.

11. Cf. I. H. Marshall, *The Gospel of Luke,* 1978, 385.

12. It is particularly clear in the case of John that this stress is caused by the later significance of the apostles. On important occasions, in contrast to the Gospel of Mark, John is mentioned by Luke before his brother James, who was executed in 44 (cf. Luke 8:51 with Mark 5:37; Luke 9:28 with Mark 9:2).

3.3. Peter is mentioned 6 times in the narrative about the miraculous catch
of fishes, which belongs to the Lucan special material (Luke 5:3, 4, 5, 8, 10a,
10b). This legend[13] has taken the place of the two brief Marcan narratives of the
call (Mark 1:16-20). The concentration on Peter is striking; in contrast to the
Marcan model, the saying about fishers of men is only applied to him. Here
Peter is called in quite a special way as the later leader of the Church and is
given the missionary commission (this corresponds to his role as the decisive
pioneer of the Pauline mission to the Gentiles in Acts). In remarkable parallelism
to John (20:3), Luke 24:12 reports a journey of Peter to the tomb. The protophany of the risen Jesus to Peter (Luke 24:34) is confirmed in I Cor. 15:5.

Summary

It is a striking feature of the synoptic parallels that in their picture of Peter, on
the one hand they are largely dependent on their Marcan model; on the other
hand the contours of the image of Peter are smoothed down. Negative features
are often deleted or toned down, while the usually hagiographical character of
the additions already shows more or less clearly the later "rock of the Church."
Here, too, historical reminiscence cannot be completely excluded (cf. Matt.
16:16ff.; Luke 22:31f.); however, for the most part the Marcan picture of Peter
is simply retouched on the basis of the later significance of Peter. The notes in
Luke 24:12, 34 show that Luke was familiar with a tradition corresponding to
I Cor. 15:3ff. It is striking that this post-Easter role of Peter otherwise plays no
part in Matthew's and Luke's accounts of the resurrection appearances.

13. R. Bultmann, op. cit., 217f.

Matthew as a Creative Interpreter of the Sayings of Jesus

Graham Stanton

In the context of this symposium Matthew's Gospel raises one fundamental question. Has the evangelist retained, developed, modified, or distorted the *theological content* of the traditions at his disposal? Or, to put the same question another way: Does a quite distinctive new understanding of either the content or the genre of εὐαγγέλιον (or both) emerge in Matthew?

This major issue cannot be fully resolved by one essay. I shall approach it by examining one particular phenomenon to which insufficient attention has been given: the points at which the evangelist himself has *expanded* the traditions of the words of Jesus to which he has had access.

For many decades now the great literary and theological skill of Matthew has been recognized. He repeats key points several times; he abbreviates Mark's verbosity and improves his clumsy Greek style; he clarifies many of the Marcan theological enigmas—even if, in so doing, he creates a few new puzzles for his readers. He reshapes, rearranges, and often conflates his two main sources, Mark and Q; he supplements them with additional material from a variety of sources (whether oral or written), and thereby creates a masterpiece of careful design.[1] Even if there is still little scholarly agreement on some of the details of the distinctive themes of the evangelist, nearly four decades of redaction-critical studies have shown that Matthew has placed his own stamp firmly on the traditions he uses.

Matthew is often seen as a revised and enlarged edition of Mark. This may well be an oversimplification, but the evangelist has been influenced very strongly indeed by Mark.[2] Even more important, however, is Matthew's pre-

---

1. See G. N. Stanton, "The Origin and Purpose of Matthew's Gospel: Matthean Scholarship from 1945-1980," *ANRW* II, 25/3, 1983.
2. M. D. Goulder, *Midrash and Lection in Matthew,* 1974, claims that apart from a very small number of oral traditions Matthew depends on no source other than Mark; on his view Matthew

sentation of the *sayings* of Jesus, only a relatively small proportion of which are taken from Mark. On any view the five grand Matthean discourses in chs. 5–7, 10, 13, 18, and 24–25 (with, perhaps, 23 as part of the fifth discourse) are most impressive. These discourses (and, to a lesser extent, several shorter collections of the sayings of Jesus) have a greater thematic unity and a more carefully worked out structure than any similar collections in Mark, Q, or Luke.

It is often assumed that Matthew has retained with relatively few modifications the sayings of Jesus in Mark and in Q. The evangelist's creativity is seen to lie primarily in the *rearrangement* of the sayings of Jesus in his traditions. W. G. Kümmel, for example, claims that Matthew changes "almost nothing in the sayings of Jesus he has taken over from Mark."[3] Studies of the Q material often conclude that while the original order of the Q material is usually retained by Luke, it is Matthew who (on the whole) retains more carefully than Luke its original wording. D. E. Garland has recently insisted that

> Matthew's redaction of his material respected in most cases the formulation of an earlier time, but his rearrangement and his juxtaposition of independent units of tradition gave them a significance which they did not previously possess. The result reflects Matthew's theology and intention, for an insertion of traditional material into a different context overrides the original connotation of that material. . . . He thus imposed his own message on traditional material by arranging it into a montage and creating a new context.[4]

These observations bypass the phenomenon to which I wish to draw attention: Matthew's creativity lies not just in the modifications he makes to individual sayings and in his rearrangement of them into new contexts, but also in his own *expansion* of a number of sayings of Jesus. I hope to show that careful attention to this phenomenon sheds important light on the evangelist's methods and purposes and gives at least a partial answer to the question posed at the outset of this essay.

In a study of the ways Matthew expands the sayings of Jesus, there is an obvious difficulty which must be faced immediately. How can we tell whether the expansion (or, to use a more neutral expression, the addition) comes from the evangelist's own hand or from tradition to which he had access? Redaction criticism can come to our aid at this point. The evangelist's distinctive vocabulary and style can be detected fairly readily: where there is general scholarly

---

has used midrashic techniques in order to expand Mark very considerably and to create the discourse. While he has certainly exaggerated his case and has also failed to demolish the Q hypothesis, some of his observations on the extent to which Matthew has been influenced by Mark are valuable.

3. *Introduction to the New Testament,* ET [2]1975, 107.

4. *The Intention of Matthew 23,* 1979, 22f. Garland is referring primarily to the composition of ch. 23, but also by implication at least to the other discourses.

agreement that the logion or phrases under discussion come from Matthew himself, a detailed redaction-critical analysis will be superfluous.

1.

I shall consider first of all what I take to be some examples of Matthean expansions of sayings of Jesus in Mark. If a fairly consistent pattern emerges, it will then be possible to turn to the Q material with greater confidence; finally, two passages in which the evangelist is dependent neither on Mark nor on Q, but on traditions not found elsewhere in the Gospel will be examined.

(a) Matt. 9:13a, b (cf. Mark 2:17) and Matt. 12:7 (cf. Mark 2:26f.)

In these two passages the wording of the quotation from Hos. 6:6, ἔλεος θέλω καὶ οὐ θυσίαν, and of part of the introduction, τί ἐστιν, is identical. While the quotation is too short to determine whether it is more closely related to the LXX than to the MT[5] (and thus more probably comes from the evangelist), the emphasis on mercy is found in several other passages in Matthew and is certainly typical of the evangelist.[6]

In Matt. 9:12 the reply of Jesus to the trenchant criticism levelled at him for eating with tax collectors and sinners is taken from Mark 2:17. The comment added by Matthew in his next verse strengthens the reply of Jesus by appealing to Scripture: Jesus can associate freely with sinners because God is gracious and merciful.[7]

Matt. 12:1-8 is a more difficult pericope. While it is possible that vv. 5-7 may all stem from the evangelist, v. 7 is almost certainly part of the evangelist's own addition to and interpretation of Mark 2:23-28.[8] Matthew is stressing that God is merciful and that the sabbath commandment should be considered in the light of his kindness. The sabbath commandment is not abolished; it is subordinated to the kindness and mercy of God. In this way the conduct of the disciples is defended.[9]

---

5. So, for example, K. Stendahl, *The School of Matthew and its Use of the Old Testament*, [2]1968, 128; W. Rothfuchs, *Die Erfüllungszitate des Matthäus-Evangeliums*, 1969, 25.

6. See G. Bornkamm, G. Barth, and H. J. Held, *Tradition and Intepretation in Matthew*, ET 1963, 26, 257.

7. πορεύομαι appears 28 times in Matthew, none in Mark; μανθάνω is used only here, at 11:29 (in a phrase that I take to be a Matthean redactional addition—see below) and at 24:32 (= Mark 13:28, the only use in Mark).

8. It is surely significant that Matthew inserts the same quotation of Hos. 6:6 into two almost adjacent Marcan pericopae (Mark 2:13-17 and 2:23-28) even though he alters the Marcan order at this point.

9. So also G. Barth in G. Bornkamm, G. Barth, and H. J. Held, op. cit., 81ff.

This presentation in both passages of Jesus' attitude to the law and the use of the Old Testament is quite consistent with Matthean teaching elsewhere. In both passages the evangelist himself creates "new" words of Jesus as part of his elucidation and exposition of the Marcan pericopae. As in the other passages where the Old Testament is quoted, Matthew is not reinterpreting Scripture in the light of Jesus, but rather citing Scripture in order to interpret the actions and teaching of Jesus.

(b) Matt. 10:5-6 (cf. Mark 6:6bff.) and Matt. 15:24 (cf. Mark 7:24ff.)

These passages should be considered together. In the latter passage Jesus explains to his disciples his apparent rejection of the Canaanite woman, "I was sent only to the lost sheep of the house of Israel." The words τὰ πρόβατα τὰ ἀπολωλότα οἴκου Ἰσραήλ are also used as part of the instruction given by Jesus to his disciples, "Go nowhere among the Gentiles . . ." (Matt. 10:1).

The use of identical wording as part of an expansion of Marcan traditions and the way the evangelist underlines carefully (as elsewhere in the Gospel) that the disciples act (and teach) in the same way as Jesus himself may both be taken to point to the hand of the evangelist himself.

Many exegetes have taken a rather different view. R. Bultmann's claim that Matt. 15:24 arose from discussions in the Palestinian Church about the Gentile mission is often quoted.[10] R. Hummel takes Matt. 10:5f.; 15:24; and 5:18f. as Jewish Christian material which Matthew consciously inserts into his Gospel and reinterprets.[11]

But in Matt. 15:24 it is clear that Matthew is simply attempting to clarify the rather puzzling Marcan pericope. There is no suggestion in Matthew's interpretation of the incident that a strict "Jewish Christian" restriction of mission to Israel is modified.[12] Matthew is stating as clearly as he can what he believes (following Mark) was the attitude of Jesus to the "lost sheep" and to non-Jews. For Matthew, Israel's rejection of her Messiah at the end of the life of Jesus leads to acceptance of the Gentiles.[13]

In the introduction to his account of the sending out of the disciples Mark's reference in 6:34 to the crowds as "sheep who do not have a shepherd" is expanded with "they were harassed and helpless" (9:36). This Matthean addi-

---

10. R. Bultmann, *The History of the Synoptic Tradition*, ET 1963, 167.

11. R. Hummel, *Die Auseinandersetzung zwischen Kirche und Judentum im Matthäusevangelium*, [2]1966, 167. See also J. P. Meier, *Law and History in Matthew's Gospel*, 1976, 27.

12. If Matt. 5:18 represents a strict Jewish Christian attitude to the law, 5:17 and 5:18d (ἕως ἂν πάντα γένηται) make it clear that for the evangelist this view has been modified.

13. So also W. Trilling, *Das Wahre Israel*, [3]1964, 105. (Trilling also takes 15:24 as the creation of the evangelist.) Similarly, G. Strecker, *Der Weg der Gerechtigkeit*, [3]1971, 196, though he refers with approval to R. Bultmann's view of the origin of the saying.

tion is surely in line with τὰ πρόβατα τὰ ἀπολωλότα in 10:6 and 15:24: the "sheep" are "lost" because those responsible for guiding them have failed.[14]

In neither case do we need to assume use of a Jewish Christian tradition.[15] The evangelist is entirely consistent with his emphases elsewhere in the Gospel. Once again Matthew is expanding his Marcan traditions in order to expound them.

(c) Matt. 21:41c and 43 (cf. Mark 12:9 and 11f.)

The reason for the evangelist's additions in the two passages just considered becomes even clearer in the light of his modifications to the Marcan parable of the wicked husbandmen. Matt. 21:43 is now widely accepted as the evangelist's own conclusion to the parable.[16] This is perhaps the clearest indication in the Gospel that the Matthean community saw itself as a separate and quite distinct entity over against Judaism.[17]

In the light of 21:43 Matthew has made expansions of Mark earlier in the parable at vv. 34 and 41c. In v. 34 καιρός and καρπός are taken from Mark but linked together in the phrase ὁ καιρὸς τῶν καρπῶν; in v. 41c τοὺς καρποὺς ἐν τοῖς καιροῖς αὐτῶν is an important expansion of Mark 12:9. In these verses, as in 21:43, the evangelist is drawing out what he takes to be the point of the Marcan parable. Although 21:43 is a sharper and clearer statement of the rejection of Israel than is found in any part of Mark 12:1-12, it is intended by Matthew to be his elucidation of vv. 9-11, especially καὶ δώσει τὸν ἀμπελῶνα ἄλλοις and the citation of Ps. 118:22f.

(d) Matt. 24:10-12, 26 (cf. Mark 13:13 and 23)

Although Matthew abbreviates Mark's eschatological discourse at several points, there are some significant additions. At 24:24 the evangelist follows Mark 13:22 almost verbatim: "For false Christs and false prophets will arise and show great signs and wonders, so as to lead astray, if possible, even the elect." In three places Matthew develops the theme of this verse in his own insertions

14. See H. Frankemölle, *Jahwebund und Kirche Jesu*, 1974, 137f.

15. G. D. Kilpatrick, *The Origins of the Gospel according to St. Matthew*, 1946, 27, even refers to the evangelist's *written* source.

16. See the detailed discussion of the individual words and phrases in W. Trilling, op. cit., 58ff. Strecker (op. cit., 164, n. 4), however, is not convinced and insists that it is not possible to decide whether the evangelist has drawn on independent tradition or has composed the verse himself. Some of the evidence used by Trilling is not decisive, but in the light of the cumulative evidence for the evangelist's *expansion* of his sources given in the present essay, I am convinced that Matthew composed 21:43 himself.

17. See D. Hare, *The Theme of Jewish Persecution of Christians in the Gospel according to St Matthew*, 1967, 153. Hare rejects Trilling's view that Matthew's community sees itself as the "true" Israel: the transfer is from Israel to *another people*, "non-Israel."

into Marcan material. At 24:5 he makes Mark 13:6 refer more explicitly to false Christs. Matt. 24:11 has no direct parallel in Mark, but it is a repetition of part of 24:24. At 24:26 the "false Christs" theme is taken up again in a verse which the evangelist himself adds to Mark—but this verse is simply an expansion of 24:23 and 24.

There is little doubt that at 24:10-12 all three logia stem from the evangelist and have been inserted into the Marcan context by him:[18] almost every word of 24:10 is taken from Mark 13:9-13; 24:11 comes from Mark 13:22, and 24:12, while not linked to Marcan phraseology, is thoroughly in line with Matthean emphases elsewhere. The "false prophets" theme is of special concern to the evangelist, as his redactional additions at 7:15, 21-23 confirm.

These additions are not the only ones made by the evangelist in ch. 24, but they show clearly how in his additional sayings of Jesus he is often simply elaborating themes found already in his sources: very often those themes are underlined by the evangelist himself elsewhere in the Gospel.

(e) Matt. 26:52-54 (cf. Mark 14:47ff.)

These three verses of words of Jesus have also been inserted by the evangelist into a Marcan context. At several points Matthew expands phrases found in the immediate context in Mark. D. Senior has shown convincingly that there is a "homogeneous conception behind Matthew's redactional intervention"[19] in these verses: since their vocabulary and themes are thoroughly Matthean there is no need to consider use of a special source.

These passages all show that Matthew has creatively added "new" sayings of Jesus into Marcan traditions. But his redactional work is not arbitrary: in these passages his intention has been to expound and elaborate his traditions. These conclusions can also be supported by a study of Matthew's additions to Marcan *narratives*—see, for example, 14:28-31; 16:12; 17:6-7, 13.[20]

---

18. For a good detailed discussion see J. Lambrecht, "The Parousia Discourse: Composition and Content in Mt. XXIV-XXV," in *L'Évangile selon Matthieu,* ed. M. Didier, 1972, 320f., nn. 28-29.

19. D. Senior, *The Passion Narrative according to Matthew,* 1975, 148. Senior provides a detailed discussion of Matt. 26:52-54 on pp. 130-48.

20. Cf. H. J. Held's conclusions on the basis of his study of Matthew's use of Mark's miracle stories: ". . . the retelling is in many cases fashioned in the light of a saying of Jesus in the pericope and brings it firmly into prominence. Thus the guiding throught in the interpretative retelling is already in the tradition itself." G. Bornkamm, G. Barth, and H. J. Held, op. cit., 298. See also D. Senior, op. cit., 335f., ". . . in the Passion narrative Matthew is not an innovator but a creative redactor."

2.

There are a number of passages in Matthew where the evangelist seems to have expanded Q traditions of the sayings of Jesus. In some cases it is of course possible that Matthew had access to a fuller form of Q than Luke; in some cases the evangelist may have expanded a Q logion with an independent piece of tradition. But there do seem to be several passages which are entirely consistent with the way Matthew has expanded Marcan sayings of Jesus in order to underline his own emphases. If, in an apparently expanded Q tradition, the additional phrases (or a complete logion) seem to be designed to *expound* the tradition to which they are related, and if Matthean vocabulary or themes are in evidence, then we may be fairly confident that the evangelist himself is responsible for the "new" words of Jesus.

(a) Matt. 6:9-13 (cf. Luke 11:2-4)

The addition to the opening address and the two petitions which are found only in the Matthean version of the Lord's Prayer probably come from Matthew rather than earlier tradition. For Matthew the coming of God's kingdom should mean that his will is done on earth, a point the evangelist stresses in his own additions to a Q logion (cf. Luke 6:46) at 7:21.[21] The addition to the final petition (ἀλλὰ ῥῦσαι ἡμᾶς ἀπὸ τοῦ πονηροῦ) can readily be seen as a "filling out" of καὶ μὴ εἰσενέγκῃς ἡμᾶς εἰς πειρασμόν: it is certainly in line with the Matthean interpretation of the parable of the sower (where at 13:19 ὁ πονηρός replaces Mark's ὁ σατανᾶς) and the Matthean interpretation of the parable of the weeds (where οἱ υἱοὶ τοῦ πονηροῦ at 13:38 is almost certainly from the evangelist).

(b) Matt. 7:12, 15-20 (cf. Luke 6:31 and 43-45)

In the final sections of the Sermon on the Mount Matthew summarizes, repeats, and develops a number of themes from earlier parts of the Sermon. At 7:12 the Q version of the "Golden Rule" is introduced by the Matthean πάντα ὅσα (cf. 28:20) and the additional words οὗτος γάρ ἐστιν ὁ νόμος καὶ οἱ προφῆται are surely the evangelist's own composition, which recall 5:17, a strongly redacted logion.

7:13-20 contains excellent examples of Matthew's carefully balanced and easily memorable representation of Q logia. There are a number of expansions which sharpen the point of the original logia. At 7:19 an additional logion which

---

21. In several redactional passages the evangelist carefully "balances" heaven and earth: 6:19-20; 6:25, 28; 16:19; 18:18; 28:18. 5:5 may have been created by the evangelist to expand and "balance" 5:3.

repeats Matt. 3:10 (Q, cf. Luke 3:9) is inserted. The final verse, 7:20, is a typical Matthean concluding summary.

(c) Matt. 7:21 (cf. Luke 6:46)

Here the evangelist has expanded considerably a Q logion. The Matthean version recalls 5:20, which is a "bridge" verse composed by the evangelist as a summary of 5:17-19 and as an introduction to vv. 21-48. The final clause of 7:21 recalls, as we have seen, Matthew's own expansion of the Lord's Prayer.

But there is an even more important modification in this verse. Whereas Luke 6:46 ("Why do you call me Lord, Lord, and do not do what I say?") and 6:47ff. (the house built near a stream) both refer to carrying out the sayings of Jesus, Matthew reshapes Luke 6:46 and makes it refer to "doing the will of my Father in heaven." In so doing he makes it quite clear that to hear and obey the words of Jesus is to do the will of the heavenly Father. Precisely the same christological point is made at the end of the second major discourse: at 10:40 (Matthean redaction of Q, cf. Luke 10:16) the disciples are told, "he who receives me receives him who sent me"; the preceding context has made it clear that "receiving" (δέχεσθαι) means "accepting the teaching of" (cf. Matt. 10:14, where the phrase added by Matthew, τοὺς λόγους ὑμῶν, to Mark 6:11 makes this point).

(d) Matt. 10:1-42

There are several significant expansions of Q (and Marcan) traditions in Matthew's "mission" discourse. At 10:8 the Q reference to healing (cf. Luke 10:9) and the Marcan reference to healing and exorcisms (Mark 6:12f.) are expanded by Matthew with references to raising the dead and cleansing lepers (cf. Matt. 11:5, Q) in order to emphasize that the disciples act in exactly the same way as Jesus himself.

At 10:24-25 Matthew expands considerably a Q logion (cf. Luke 6:40). This passage is probably recalled at 23:34 where the fate of those sent is related to the crucifixion. The disciple is not above his master: if Jesus suffers crucifixion, it can also be expected by his disciples.[22]

The final three verses of ch. 10 reveal Matthew's literary and theological skill particularly clearly. 10:41 has been composed by the evangelist: his distinctive vocabulary is clearly in evidence. This additional logion is not an arbitrary creation, for it is an expansion and development of 10:40 and 42. This important passage paves the way for the grand conclusion to Matthew's fifth

22. So D. Garland, op. cit., 177.

discourse where, in the evangelist's interpretation of the "great assize," his community is told that acceptance or rejection of Christian missionaries by "all the nations" will be seen in the final judgment as acceptance or rejection of the Son of Man.[23] At the end of both the second and the fifth discourses the Matthean community is told that Jesus continues to be "with" them in the closest possible way—the very theme with which the evangelist concludes his Gospel at 28:20.

(e) Matt. 18:10a, 14 (cf. Luke 15:3-7)

In Luke the parable of the lost sheep is a response to the critical comments of the scribes and Pharisees who are outraged by the way that Jesus associates with tax collectors and sinners: God's acceptance of the "undeserving" is proclaimed. But in Matthew the parable is addressed explicitly to the disciples and it is used to exhort the community to seek out the straying Christian "lost sheep" of the evangelist's own day.

The Matthean interpretation results partly from the new setting but also partly from the words of Jesus added by the evangelist as an introduction and conclusion to the parable. 18:14 includes several examples of the evangelist's distinctive vocabulary, and it almost certainly comes from Matthew himself. At 18:35 there is a further example of a thoroughly Matthean logion which has been added by the evangelist as a concluding summary to a parable.

Matt. 18:10a is probably the evangelist's own introduction to the parable. The phrase ἕν τῶν μικρῶν τούτων is used by the evangelist four times: at 10:42 (which, as we have seen, is part of an important redactional passage); at 18:6 (where Mark 9:42 has been expanded in order to state explicitly that the "little ones" believe *in Jesus*—the only time such a phrase is used in the synoptic traditions);[24] and at 18:10, 14 where there are no parallels. The phrase, then, derives ultimately from Mark, but it has been developed considerably by Matthew: as in numerous other passages, the evangelist takes *tradition* as his starting point.[25]

The Matthean use "one of these little ones" is thoroughly in line with the observations we have made on the passages considered so far in this essay. But it can hardly be claimed that in his interpretation of the parable *as a whole* the evangelist is simply developing, elucidating, or expounding the Q tradition as it is found in Luke.

Do our observations on the methods used by the evangelist need to be

23. See the discussion of this passage below.

24. A number of manuscripts do have εἰς ἐμέ at Mark 9:42, but I take this reading to be a harmonization to the Matthean tradition.

25. The origin of Matt. 18:10b is more difficult to determine. This logion has no parallels elsewhere in Matthew, or in Mark or Luke.

modified considerably in the light of this passage? I do not think so. The Lucan setting may not be original. There is a characteristically Lucan conclusion to the parable (Luke 15:7), and the present introduction in 15:1-3 may well have been added to the parable either by Luke or at an earlier stage. It is probable that *both* evangelists have interpreted the parable by setting it in quite different contexts. By its very nature parabolic and metaphorical language lends itself readily to reinterpretation; a new context can easily alter the thrust of a particular tradition even if the original words are retained.

(f) Matt. 5:13a, 14a, 16 (cf. Mark 9:49-50, 4:21; Luke 14:34-35, 8:16 and 11:33)

This passage is a further example of Matthean expansion of metaphorical or parabolic traditions. For convenience we shall consider it at this point even though it contains Marcan as well as Q traditions. It is extremely difficult to reconstruct the history of these enigmatic traditions which the evangelist has developed, but there is general scholarly agreement that Matthew has provided the parallel introductions ὑμεῖς ἐστε τὸ ἅλας τῆς γῆς (5:13a) and ὑμεῖς ἐστε τὸ φῶς τοῦ κόσμου (5:14a) as well as the whole of 5:16. This latter logion can be compared with 18:14 and 35: in each case a Matthean οὕτως logion summarizes and applies the preceding parable (or metaphor) to the community. Matthew has interpreted his traditions partly by juxtaposing the "salt," "city set on a hill," and "lampstand" sayings and partly by adding his own introduction and conclusion.

In so doing the evangelist stresses themes prominent elsewhere in the Gospel.[26] G. Eichholz draws attention, surely appropriately, to Schlatter's observation: the task given to the disciples in this passage is quite simply, "Make disciples of all nations."[27] The ethical conduct of the disciples is stressed in 5:16: τὰ καλὰ ἔργα is almost synonymous with δικαιοσύνη at 5:20.

In this passage there is an example (which seems to have escaped notice) of a pattern found elsewhere in Matthew. The disciples follow after Jesus: his coming to "Galilee of the Gentiles" is a "great light" (4:23); they are to be the "light of the world" (5:14).

(g) Matt. 23:28, 32-34 (cf. Luke 11:44, 47f.)

It is extremely difficult to isolate the evangelist's sources in Matthew 23: at times he uses traditions not found elsewhere (the so-called M traditions); at

---

26. See G. Bornkamm, op. cit., 16.

27. G. Eichholz, *Auslegung der Bergpredigt,* [2]1970, 58f. See also the interesting (but not completely convincing) discussion of this passage by M. J. Suggs, *Wisdom, Christology and Law in Matthew's Gospel,* 1970, 123ff.

times he uses Q traditions, and in several places he seems to have composed logia himself. 23:28 is a good example of an expansion of Q traditions by the evangelist. Once again a οὕτως logion (cf. 5:16; 18:14, 35, discussed above) elucidates the preceding simile in the sixth woe; this verse may well be intended by the evangelist to summarize the previous woes.[28]

Matt. 23:32 also develops the Q tradition: this logion has probably been composed by the evangelist as a summary of the seventh woe and as a transition to the verses which follow.[29] V. 33 parallels very closely the Q tradition applied by Matthew to the Pharisees and Sadducees at Matt. 3:7. The phrase γεννήματα ἐχιδνῶν is also found at 12:34 in Matthew's reshaping of a Q tradition (cf. Luke 6:45). The evangelist has added this verse here on the basis of Q traditions and his own modifications of them elsewhere.

In v. 34, in addition to important modifications of a Q logion (cf. Luke 11:49), which cannot be discussed here, the second half of the logion, καὶ σταυρώσετε καὶ ἐξ αὐτῶν μαστιγώσετε ἐν ταῖς συναγωγαῖς ὑμῶν (καὶ διώξετε) ἀπὸ πόλεως εἰς πόλιν has been added by the evangelist.[30] But once again he repeats phrases used elsewhere in the Gospel.[31] These verses confirm our earlier observations. The evangelist has added "new" words of Jesus to his Q traditions, but his intention is to elucidate, apply, and summarize his traditions rather than to supplement them with sayings which he created *de novo*.

3.

There are a number of important sayings of Jesus and parables in Matthew which are not found elsewhere in the Gospels. Exegetes have often reached quite divergent conclusions: some have claimed that many of these passages have been composed by the evangelist, while others have appealed to the use of independent tradition. If the cumulative argument of this essay is sound, we may expect to find that the evangelist is closely dependent on his sources but that he has not hesitated to expand them in order to repeat or develop his own redactional themes. This view can, I think, be advanced as a plausible hypothesis. A full defense of it is not

28. So also D. Garland, op. cit., 158, n. 29; R. Bultmann, op. cit., 113.

29. D. Hare, op. cit., 87, notes that it cannot be demonstrated that the diction of this verse is particularly characteristic of the evangelist and leaves open the possibility that it has been composed by the evangelist. But since this logion functions in a similar way to other Matthean logia which expand and "sum up" a preceding piece of tradition used by the evangelist, we may be reasonably confident that the evangelist has supplied this verse.

30. καὶ διώξετε is found in Luke 11:49 (Q).

31. μαστιγόω is found as a Matthean redaction of Mark 13:9 at 10:17; in the same verse Matthew adds αὐτῶν to ἐν ταῖς συναγωγαῖς (cf. Matt. 4:23; 9:35 — the evangelist's own summaries); the phrase ἀπὸ πόλεως εἰς πόλιν recalls Matt. 10:23.

possible here, but a brief examination of two passages will confirm that the
evangelist has used and expanded at least some so-called M traditions of sayings
of Jesus in the same way that he has Marcan and Q sayings.

(a) Matt. 11:28-30

There is now general scholarly agreement that this passage has not been taken
from Q. In its present context it refers to the disciples, though the original
tradition may have had a much wider audience in mind. Many of the words in
these verses are not found elsewhere in the Gospel, but two clauses seem to me
to be Matthean additions: καὶ μάθετε ἀπ᾽ ἐμοῦ, ὅτι πραΰς εἰμι καὶ ταπεινὸς τῇ
καρδίᾳ. The original tradition which was expanded by the evangelist may have
been as follows:

a   δεῦτε πρός με πάντες οἱ κοπιῶντες καὶ πεφορτισμένοι,
b   κἀγὼ ἀναπαύσω ὑμᾶς.
a'   ἄρατε τὸν ζυγόν μου ἐφ᾽ ὑμᾶς,
b'   καὶ εὑρήσετε ἀνάπαυσιν ταῖς ψυχαῖς ὑμῶν.
c   ὁ γὰρ ζυγός μου χρηστὸς καὶ τὸ φορτίον μου ἐλαφρόν ἐστιν.

The first four lines are well balanced and are undergirded by the "reasoning" of the fifth and final line. The clauses which have the clearest Matthean
parallels (either in vocabulary or thought), καὶ μάθετε ἀπ᾽ ἐμοῦ, ὅτι πραΰς εἰμι
καὶ ταπεινὸς τῇ καρδίᾳ, break up the flow of the "argument" in this section and
seem to come from the evangelist's own hand.[32] This must now be demonstrated
briefly.

The words "learn from me" recall numerous passages in the Gospel where
Jesus (and not Moses or the scribes and Pharisees) is the *one* teacher *par
excellence.*[33] The disciples must learn from Jesus, for they are to teach all nations
all that Jesus has commanded them (28:20).

Jesus as the "meek and lowly one" is also a Matthean theme. In his account
of the entry of Jesus into Jerusalem the evangelist deliberately modifies Zech.
9:9 in order to allow the paradox of Jesus the *humble* one who is king to stand
at the very center of the fulfillment citation in 21:4ff.: "Behold your king is
coming to you, humble (πραΰς), and mounted on an ass. . . ."

This very theme is central in two further fulfillment citations. At 12:15ff.,

---

32. For a fuller discussion see G. N. Stanton, "Matthew 11:28-30: Comfortable Words?"
ExpT 94, 1982, 3-9. The analysis offered there differs slightly from that given above. I am grateful
to A. Dihle for the suggestion that καὶ μάθετε ἀπ᾽ ἐμοῦ may also have been a Matthean insertion.
R. Guelich has pointed out to me that F. Filson's article, "Broken Patterns in the Gospel of
Matthew," *JBL* 75, 1956, 227ff. is relevant at this point.
33. D. Garland, op. cit., 58, though he does not refer to 11:29.

the longest of all Matthew's citations from Scripture, he has again reshaped the text to suit his own purposes and has emphasized the role of Jesus as humble servant. "Here is my servant, whom I have chosen, *my beloved on whom my favor rests. . . .*" At this point the evangelist has modified Isa. 42:1ff. in order to bring the phraseology into line with his account of the heavenly voice at the baptism of Jesus (3:15) and at the Transfiguration (17:5). Clearly this "servant" citation from Isaiah 42 is a most important passage for the evangelist.

There is a further interpretative modification to be seen in this citation of Isaiah 42 in ch. 12. Matthew's phrase at the beginning of 12:19, οὐκ ἐρίσει, can be explained neither from the MT nor from the LXX, but it can readily be related to the evangelist's concerns. At the end of the immediately preceding account of the healing of the man with the withered arm, Jesus *withdraws* deliberately in the face of Pharisaic opposition. He is the one who "will not strive, who will not shout, nor will his voice be heard in the streets. . . ."

At Matt. 8:17 the healing ministry of Jesus, which Matthew emphasizes strongly, is seen as a fulfillment of another "servant" passage, Isa. 53:4: "He took away our illnesses and lifted our diseases from us."

So who is issuing the invitation in Matt. 11:28-30 as the passage now stands with the evangelist's additions? It is not so much Jesus as Sophia (a theme which the evangelist barely hints at in his Gospel), but Jesus as the humble Servant of God on whom God's Spirit rests, the Servant whose healing acts reveal his compassion for those in need.

I take "all who are weary and heavy laden" to refer primarily to the costly and demanding nature of discipleship. Several verses earlier in ch. 11, as well as many in ch. 10, have stressed that disciples are to expect opposition and rejection. By linking 11:28-30 to the preceding pericope Matthew makes the end of this important discourse in ch. 11 become a word of encouragement to hard-pressed disciples—the very theme he emphasizes at the end of the discourses in ch. 10 and in ch. 25.

(b) Matt. 25:31-46

This pericope is Matthew's grand climax to his presentation of the teaching of Jesus. As these verses now stand in the Gospel they pick up and develop themes Matthew has emphasized earlier in the Gospel. Judgment is associated with the Son of Man in two redactional passages, 19:28 and 24:30. Provision of hospitality is a mark of acceptance (10:11ff.). Those who reject the disciples will be judged and punished (10:15 and, implicitly, 10:42). The punishment is so severe that it is clear that persecution is in mind. Earlier in the final discourse, in a redactional addition, persecution by *Gentiles* is mentioned explicitly at 24:9: "People of all nations will hate you for your allegiance to me."

By now it will be clear how I interpret this much-disputed pericope.[34] The Matthean community is committed to evangelism among all nations. Rejection, opposition, and persecution have been experienced. Quite naturally Matthean Christians have asked, "Why does God allow his enemies to play havoc with the new people who do bear the proper fruit (cf. 21:43)?" The evangelist's answer is that at the end all people will be judged, rewarded, and punished on the basis of their acceptance or rejection of those who have taught all nations all that Jesus has commanded. This passage functions as a final note of consolation and encouragement to the Matthean community.

This very theme is prominent in Jewish apocalypses written about the same time as Matthew—about AD 90. Following the triumph of the Romans in 70 there was bound to be bewilderment and confusion, and this is reflected in 4 Ezra and Baruch. 4 Ezra 7:37 and Baruch 72:2 provide very instructive parallels to the interpretation I have proposed.

This approach to 25:31-46 depends heavily on taking πάντα τὰ ἔθνη in v. 32 in a Matthean sense as "all non-Christian nations" and on interpreting ἑνὶ τούτων τῶν ἀδελφῶν μου τῶν ἐλαχίστων in v. 40 (and in v. 45) as a Matthean phrase referring to members of the Christian community. These phrases are redactional Matthean additions elsewhere; they have almost certainly been added by the evangelist to this tradition here.[35]

On this interpretation Matt. 25:31-46 is a further example of a passage which Matthew has expanded and reinterpreted in the light of his own concerns elsewhere. Here the evangelist's reinterpretation is probably very considerable, for the original tradition may well have stated that judgment of *disciples* would be on the basis of their acceptance or rejection of all sorts and conditions of persons in need. The evangelist's reinterpretation is bold, but it should not be seen as completely arbitrary. Parabolic language, which lends itself readily to reinterpretation, has been set in a new context and applied, as so often in Matthew, to the needs of the evangelist's community.

4.

From a wide range of examples (which is by no means an exhaustive list) a consistent pattern has emerged. The evangelist has expanded (often consid-

---

34. For recent discussions see U. Wilckens, "Gottes geringste Brüder—zu Mt. 25,31-46," in *Jesus und Paulus*, Festschrift W. G. Kümmel, ed. E. E. Ellis and E. Grässer, 1975, 363-83; J. Friedrich, *Gott im Bruder? Eine methodenkritische Untersuchung von Redaktion, Überlieferung und Traditionen in Mt. 25,31-46,* 1977; D. R. Catchpole, "The Poor on Earth and the Son of Man in Heaven. A Re-appraisal of Matthew XXV.31-46," *BJRL* 61, 1979, 355-97.

35. See J. Friedrich, op. cit., 258-70 for details.

erably) sayings of Jesus in Mark, Q, and "M." There are a surprisingly large number of additions—and we have not considered sayings which Matthew has repeated. In the expansions we almost invariably find themes which the evangelist has himself emphasized elsewhere.

At the beginning of this essay I referred to D. Garland's use of the analogy of a montage to illustrate the evangelist's methods. This analogy helpfully underlines the extent to which Matthew's Gospel is both *more than* and *other than* the sum of the individual traditions incorporated. The evangelist has reinterpreted his traditions by reshaping and "tidying" them, and by setting them in new contexts—often by juxtaposition with originally unrelated traditions. For all of this, the analogy of a "montage" is appropriate. But this analogy does not do justice to the extent to which the evangelist has himself *expanded* individual narrative and sayings traditions. Again and again we have seen that Matthew is creative but not innovative: he is committed to the traditions at his disposal, but he endeavors to *elucidate* them for his own community.

The evangelist's interests are varied. In the sayings we have considered, discipleship and community themes are prominent, but so too are christological and eschatological concerns. It is a mistake to try to decide which of these themes is *primary* for the evangelist, for in the context of the whole Gospel they are intertwined and interdependent.

If these observations are valid, there are two implications which are of some importance in the context of this symposium. The interpretative methods used by Matthew can be traced (though less clearly and less extensively) at other stages in the transmission of gospel traditions.[36] I am convinced that at all stages greater development of the traditions took place by setting them in new contexts and by attempts to elucidate them than by the "creation" *de novo* of sayings of Jesus. On the whole the words of Jesus were transmitted with great care: various attempts to clarify the traditions and make them applicable to new circumstances were probably more creative than the communities which first transmitted the traditions. Discussions of the role of Christian prophets in the development of the synoptic tradition often overlook this point. The expansions we have observed are not the work of a Christian prophet, but of an "exegete."[37]

If the evangelist Matthew is as creative as has been suggested, is his work

---

36. See, for example, J. Wanke, " 'Kommentarworte,' Älteste Kommentierungen von Herrenworten," *BZ* 24, 1980, 208-33.

37. For a wide-ranging discussion of this point, see M. E. Boring, *Sayings of the Risen Jesus,* 1982. With the exception of Matt. 28:18-20, Boring is rightly cautious about claims that individual sayings found in Matthew originated as words of Christian prophets. I do not think that 28:18-20 is an exception. Even this passage should be seen as an expansion and summary (in a new context) of themes the evangelist has stressed earlier in the Gospel. These verses are not so much the "key" (so O. Michel) which unlocks the whole Gospel (i.e., a new *revelation*) as a *grand finale* in which the evangelist summarizes his main points.

still a "Gospel"? Two factors suggest that if Mark is a εὐαγγέλιον, so is Matthew. As we have seen, the evangelist is constantly attempting to draw out the significance of his *traditions,* so he is almost certainly not attempting to create a new *genre.*

I believe that Matthew would have accepted εὐαγγέλιον as a title for his writing.[38] He uses τὸ εὐαγγέλιον τῆς βασιλείας as a summary of the proclamation of Jesus at 4:23 and 9:35. In three redactional passages, 24:14 (τοῦτο τὸ εὐαγγέλιον τῆς βασιλείας), 26:13 (τὸ εὐαγγέλιον τοῦτο), and 13:19 (τὸν λογόν τῆς βασιλείας), he is clearly thinking of his account of the words and deeds of Jesus as εὐαγγέλιον. By using the same term εὐαγγέλιον both for the proclamation of Jesus and for that of the Church of his own day he underlines the *continuity* between them. Twice Matthew omits Mark's phrase καὶ τοῦ εὐαγγελίου (Mark 8:35; 10:29): the most plausible explanation is that he is suspicious of Mark's apparent distinction between Jesus and the gospel in his phrase ἕνεκεν ἐμοῦ καὶ τοῦ εὐαγγελίου. For Matthew Jesus is (almost) τὸ εὐαγγέλιον (or ὁ λόγος) τῆς βασιλείας, and for that reason (among others) the words of Jesus are to be treasured carefully; they are elucidated by the evangelist so that they can be appropriated by his community and used in its proclamation (28:20a).

---

38. For a rather different view, see H. Frankemölle, op. cit., who claims that Matthew is a literary work, a *Buch der Geschichte* modelled on Jewish history writing such as Deuteronomy and Chronicles. This is, I think, an exaggerated claim which does not do justice to the importance for Matthew of the Old Testament prophetic writings and of Mark.

Luke and His "Gospel"

I. Howard Marshall

Forasmuch as many have undertaken to compile an account of the things which have been accomplished by the author of Luke-Acts, just as they have been interpreted for us by scholars in recent times, it seemed good to me also, even though I have not followed closely all that has been written, to set out my thoughts in order for you, most gentle reader, so that you may check the reliability of that of which you have been informed.

During the last few years the writings of Luke have been the object of a remarkable amount of study. After the impetus given to a fresh approach by H. Conzelmann, E. Haenchen, and H. Schürmann, there has been a large number of monographs by younger scholars, and then most recently a number of major commentaries by J. A. Fitzmyer, J. Roloff, W. Schmithals, G. Schneider, and E. Schweizer. It is, however, remarkable that in these works one important question is treated only briefly and inadequately or not at all. This is the question of the purpose of the author. Since the writers of commentaries usually write their introductions after the completion of their exegesis, one would expect them to be in a good position to discuss this crucial question and to express a mature opinion, but none of the commentators whom I have mentioned tackles it seriously. It is true that G. Schneider has devoted an article to the subject, but this is concerned more with how to solve the problem than with actually solving it.[1] The situation has been changed by the appearance of a monograph by R. Maddox specifically devoted to *The Purpose of Luke-Acts,* but despite the thorough and excellent treatment offered in this book there is perhaps still room for further thinking about this topic which may then act as a context for understanding the character of Luke's Gospel.

1. G. Schneider, "Der Zweck des lukanischen Doppelwerkes," *BZ* 21, 1977, 45-66.

273

1. Defining the Objective

Part of the difficulty lies in establishing the precise object of inquiry. We may distinguish at least four aspects of it. First, there is the *conscious aim* of the author. What purpose, if any, did the author consciously have as he wrote the book? If he had been asked what he was trying to do, how would he have answered? Second, it is necessary to recognize that an author may have had one or more *principal* aims and one or more *secondary* aims. It is all too easy to look for *the* aim or to elevate aims that can have been only secondary to the level of primary aims. In this connection I would mention theories which see Luke as endeavoring to deal with questions of riches and poverty in his Church[2] or to defend or rehabilitate Paul;[3] such themes, which come to expression in some parts of Luke-Acts, may well have been aspects of Luke's concern, but surely cannot have been his main concern.

Third, we need to inquire whether any specific, *concrete occasion* gave rise to the composition and thus shaped the author's aim. In my earlier work on the writings of Luke I suggested a fairly broad aim, namely that Luke's main aim was simply to present salvation to his readers; "it was enough that he should compose his record as a means of evangelism."[4] This approach was subjected to friendly criticism in a comment by R. P. Martin who argued that my severely negative approach, in which I rejected such concrete suggestions as that Luke was motivated by the delay of the parousia or by the need to attack Gnostic heresy, was "a weakness since it is arguable that no other New Testament book lacks a definite purpose in its composition and publication."[5] I accept the criticism; even if Luke wrote, as I rather vaguely suggested, to present salvation, one must still ask why he felt the need to do so, and whether we can identify any concrete circumstances which led him to do so in the precise way in which he did write.

However, there is also a fourth element in the picture, namely the question of what *circumstances and unconscious motives* may have affected the author and determined the character of his work. For example, it is possible that the Church was beginning to become more institutionalized in Luke's time, and that when he wrote Acts he unconsciously presented and defended a view of the Church that was related positively or negatively to this ongoing trend. Again, if the delay of the parousia was a dominant factor in Luke's situation, a hypothesis which I find very dubious, then I should find it very doubtful that Luke consciously set himself to reshape the character of his theological account of the early

2. R. J. Karris, "Poor and Rich: The Lukan *Sitz im Leben*," in *Perspectives on Luke-Acts,* ed. C. H. Talbert, 1978, 112-25.

3. See R. Maddox, *The Purpose of Luke-Acts,* 1981, 20f., for reference.

4. I. H. Marshall, *Luke: Historian and Theologian,* [2]1979, 221.

5. R. P. Martin, *New Testament Foundations* I, 1975, 248f.

Church in such a way as to take account of this fact; if it affected him at all, it must have done so as an unconscious factor in his theological environment.

We ought to keep the differences between these different aspects of the purpose of Luke-Acts in view, although I recognize that in practice the different aspects may merge with one another.

2. Luke-Acts as a Unity

One important factor pointed out by Maddox seems to need further emphasis and restatement in determining our starting point for research. It has indeed come to be generally recognized not only that Luke and Acts are the work of a single author but also that in their finished form they are two parts of a single literary work. To be sure, scholars are not agreed about the precise nature of the unity of the work in terms of its composition. It can be argued that there was a sizable time gap between the composition of Luke and of Acts, and that it is not clear that when Luke commenced to write his Gospel he already had it in mind to write the sequel. Nor is it certain that Acts was submitted to final revision by its author. However, it seems more probable to me that from the beginning Luke intended to write a two-part work, even if, as some think, there was some interval between the composition of the two parts.[6] I want, therefore, to carry out my investigation on the assumption that Luke-Acts was planned as a unity.

If this assumption is correct, then it will be evident that the correct question is the one posed by Maddox, namely, what is the purpose of Luke-Acts as a whole?[7] The important point, to which I think insufficient attention has been given, is that the question regarding the purpose of Part One can be asked only within the framework of the question regarding the purpose of the whole. It is only when we appreciate the purpose of the whole work that we can attempt to understand fully what Luke was doing that may have been distinctive in relation to the work of the other evangelists. That is to say, redaction-critical studies of the Gospel tend to compare Matthew and Mark with Luke when in fact the comparison ought perhaps to be made not with Luke but with Luke-Acts as a whole.

3. Luke's Models

This means that it may be inaccurate to speak of Luke as a Gospel writer or as the third evangelist. In fact we may well ask whether this description is an apt

6. So E. Schweizer, *The Good News according to Luke,* ET 1984, 7.
7. R. Maddox, op. cit., 19.

one in respect of the other synoptic evangelists, however convenient it may be for us to think of them in this way.

I assume without further argument that Luke knew Mark. But what was it that Mark was writing, and how did his work appear to his contemporaries? Mark commences with the words: "The beginning of the gospel of Jesus Christ, the Son of God." This phrase can be taken as referring to the whole of the book that follows or merely to the prologue in the immediately following verses.

On the former view it can be paraphrased: "This is the story of the beginning of the good news. . . ." This word εὐαγγέλιον must then be understood to refer to the Church's proclamation of the good news of salvation; it is not yet a title for the whole book, no matter how early we may set the use of the word "gospel" to refer to the individual accounts of the ministry of Jesus. Mark would then see the beginning or foundation of the Church's message in the ministry of Jesus; he proceeds to relate that story, but of course the effect is that he thus proclaims the Church's message so that his account is indeed a presentation of the gospel. J. Gnilka is thus correct when he states that Mark 1:1 is not the title of the book, but rather a summary or indication of its contents.[8] If this is a fair account of the situation, then it follows that there is no evidence that Mark thought of himself as writing a work that fell into the literary genre of "gospel," or rather as self-consciously creating that new genre. Rather he thought of himself as recounting the *beginning* of the good news, and therefore his story was perhaps open in principle to further extension.

If we adopt the latter view, then the prologue is the beginning of the story about Jesus related in Mark's book.[9] Mark then regarded telling the story of Jesus as a means—perhaps *the* means—of proclaiming the good news. But this is not the same thing as saying that he was creating a new literary genre which later writers would have felt bound to follow. Since his was the pioneering effort, later writers could have felt free to present their material in other ways.

More controversially, I would add that, although I cannot offer any convincing argument for my view, I confess to an intuitive feeling that Mark 16:8 is not the original, intended end of the Gospel, and that it is not beyond the bounds of probability that the Gospel proceeded further or that Mark intended some kind of sequel. I should not, however, wish to rest any part of my case on such conjectures. The point which I think is established is that for Mark the story of Jesus was a form of the gospel, a story that was in principle open to continuation.

According to the commonly accepted hypothesis of synoptic relationships Luke was also acquainted with the sayings source Q. This document has not survived; we do not have sufficient evidence to reconstruct it in detail, and in

8. J. Gnilka, *Das Evangelium nach Markus,* 1978, I, 42f.
9. See R. A. Guelich's essay in the present volume.

particular to reconstruct its beginning and end, and therefore I should want to be extremely cautious about determining its character and extent. The best analogy to it still seems to be the Gospel of Thomas, which understands itself as a collection of sayings of Jesus. As such, it would be a complete document in the sense of gathering together the earthly teaching of Jesus. The important point is that neither Luke nor Matthew followed its pattern in the composition of their works. Both writers incorporated the Q material in a pattern that is based on Mark. This is true for Luke regardless of whether he directly inserted the Q material into the edited version of Mark, which formed the backbone of his Gospel, or whether some form of the proto-Luke hypothesis is true in envisaging some kind of uniting of Q material with Luke's special material before this was itself united with Marcan material.[10] Luke, that is to say, deliberately rejected the Q-type of composition for one that was broadly similar to that of Mark.

Finally, there is the question of Matthew. I regard it as extremely unlikely that Luke was familiar with Matthew. But, although Matthew in no way provided a pattern for Luke to follow, nevertheless his own procedure is of interest as showing how another Christian at approximately the same time regarded his own work. Matthew commences with the statement: "The book of the genealogy of Jesus Christ, the son of David, the son of Abraham." This statement is usually regarded as an introduction to the actual genealogy which immediately follows it.[11] Another view, however, is possible. γένεσις does not strictly mean a genealogy, and in Matt. 1:18 it means "birth." Nor again is βίβλος the most apt phrase for describing the first seventeen verses of the book. I am therefore strongly tempted by the view of D. Hill[12] that Matt. 1:1 is to be taken, like Mark 1:1, as referring to the whole book, although I find it difficult to follow him in believing that "of Jesus Christ" is to be understood as a subjective genitive. Rather it seems that Matt. 1:1 is a title which announces that the theme is the story of the coming of Jesus in a broad sense. Whichever view we take of the matter, Matthew does not use the word "gospel" to describe the character of his work, but only to refer to the message preached by Jesus and his followers. He writes a book about Jesus, and although the book is a complete whole, it nevertheless points forward to the apostolic task of making disciples of all nations and preaching the gospel to the whole world.

From these comments it emerges that there is nothing to suggest that there was a fixed category of "gospel" into which Luke had to fit his work.[13] When

10. This still seems to me to be the most defensible part of the proto-Luke hypothesis; see I. H. Marshall, op. cit., 62.

11. E. Schweizer, *The Good News according to Matthew,* ET 1975, 24.

12. D. Hill, *The Gospel of Matthew,* 1972, 74f.

13. See C. H. Talbert, *What is a Gospel: The Genre of the Canonical Gospels,* 1977; D. E. Aune, "The Problem of the Genre of the Gospels: A Critique of C. H. Talbert's *What is a Gospel?*"

Luke refers to the works of his predecessors, he describes them as "accounts" or "narratives" and as being of the same character as his own work. But whereas Mark and certainly Matthew saw their tasks as accomplished by telling the story of Jesus up to the resurrection and so laying down the beginning of the Church's message, Luke took the story on to the arrival of Paul with the good news in Rome. What he wrote was a unified story, but it was broken up into two parts for a number of reasons. First, the example of his predecessors showed that there was a natural historical break at the ascension of Jesus; the story of the earthly life of Jesus could be treated as a unit on its own. Second, there was a theological break in the story at the ascension of Jesus, but, as Luke's treatment shows, the ascension formed a bridge between the two parts; it terminates Part One of the story, but it also commences Part Two. Third, there was the eminently practical consideration, which must certainly be allowed its full weight, that Luke was limited by the maximum length of a roll of papyrus, which is usually said to have been about the size required for Luke or Acts.

The point which, I suggest, emerges from this is that we should not think of Luke writing a Gospel and then taking the unprecedented step of adding a sequel. He was not writing a book called a "Gospel" followed by a separate sequel. Indeed, C. H. Talbert suggests that we should think of Luke writing an account of the early Church to which he prefixed a Gospel.[14] Rather at this time the concept of a "Gospel" had scarcely been formalized, and Luke was not tied to a stereotyped pattern whose bounds he decided to burst. On the contrary, Luke saw that the concept of the beginning of the Church's message in the story of Jesus naturally led on to an account of the spread of the Church. Or, to repeat the point made earlier, in a sense the true counterpart of the Gospel of Mark is not the Gospel of Luke but Luke-Acts. For Luke what Mark recorded was, as Mark had said, only the beginning, and Luke desired to present the full story. Although Mark himself had not taken this step, what he did was in principle open to expansion.

4. A Prologue to the Whole of Luke-Acts

This view of the matter is, I submit, supported by a reexamination of the prologue to Luke. In v. 1 "the things which have been accomplished among us"

---

in *Gospel Perspectives* II, ed. R. T. France and D. Wenham, 1981, 9-60; and R. A. Guelich's essay in the present volume for discussion from various perspectives. I do not dispute Guelich's general conclusions, but wish to guard against the assumption that Mark set a precedent which his successors felt *bound* to follow, even though they did in fact adopt his pattern.

14. C. H. Talbert, *Literary Patterns, Theological Themes and the Genre of Luke-Acts*, 1974, 30.

should not be confined to the story of the earthly life of Jesus but can very well be extended to include what had happened in the early days of the Church; this view of the phrase gives a better sense to "among us" than confining the reference to the earthly life of Jesus.[15] If this is correct, then the reference to the "attempts" of previous writers, which does not need to be adversely critical of what they did but nevertheless allows that there is room for a further attempt, may be not so much to any alleged deficiencies in how they related the story of Jesus but rather to the fact that they told only half the story and thus did not achieve the purpose which Luke himself felt was necessary to achieve. The fact that Luke speaks of what had been "accomplished" or "fulfilled" will again fit in with his understanding of things, since one of the points which he makes is that the history of the early Church as well as the career of Jesus was in accordance with the fulfillment of prophecy. The reference to those who were eyewitnesses and ministers of the word can also very naturally cover those who passed on to Luke both the story of Jesus and the story of the early days of the Church.

A particular problem is posed by the word παρακολουθέω, which Luke uses to describe his own activity preparatory to drawing up his account of what had happened. In my commentary I took the verb to refer to historical investigation of events outside the author's own personal experience. Maddox, however, has reexamined the evidence originally adduced by H. J. Cadbury that the verb refers to keeping informed about contemporary events or participating in them, and has shown that this is the common meaning of the term.[16] However, this view still seems difficult to me in view of the use of ἀκριβῶς, "accurately," with the verb, and Cadbury is forced to take the verb as "to keep in touch with" in order to meet this problem; once this is granted, however, the point is in effect allowed that the meaning of the verb can be widened to refer to research, and this is confirmed by the usage in Josephus, c. Apion 1.218. Perhaps, then, the scope of the verb here should be widened somewhat so that it includes both those events in the past which Luke had investigated by examining the relevant evidence both written and oral and also those more recent events in which he himself had personally participated.[17] (Here I am assuming the identity of the author of the "we-sections" of Acts with the author of the whole work, which has been most recently affirmed by J. A. Fitzmyer.)[18] It is, therefore, possible that the scope of Luke's investigations in the prologue is the whole area covered by Luke-Acts.

---

15. Against this view it can be argued that the perfect participle implies that the events form a completed whole, but this may be to press the force of the participle unduly. Luke could see that a series of events had been "fulfilled" and yet be capable of continuation.

16. R. Maddox, op. cit., 4f. and n. 23.

17. Cf. J. A. Fitzmyer, The Gospel according to Luke I-IX, AB, 1981, 296f.

18. Ibid., 35-53.

A further important point leading in the same direction is to be seen in the comment on the things of which Theophilus had been informed. However formal or informal catechetical instruction was at this stage (and I incline to a belief in its relative informality), it is highly improbable that such instruction was confined to the story of the life of Jesus or that it covered the story of Jesus in detail. What we know of the early kerygma and of the ethical instruction reflected in the epistles points to a wider area of teaching. In particular it is surely inconceivable that the teaching given to Theophilus said nothing about the experience of the Holy Spirit. Moreover, as J. Jervell has shown, the kerygma may well have included accounts of how the gospel had been effective in the foundation of the various churches.[19] From all this it follows that when Luke desired to give Theophilus a reliable account of the things in which he had already been instructed this account cannot have been confined to the material in the Gospel. Thus the prologue has in view the whole of the two-part work right from the start[20] and is not designed simply to refer to the Gospel.[21] This is, of course, what should be expected in the light of other literary prefaces of the time, which were intended to introduce the work as a whole. It is also confirmed by the prologue to Acts, which sums up Part One as being concerned with what Jesus began to do and to teach. It is unfortunate that Luke has not specified more clearly what he was going on to do in Acts, but at least his verdict on what he had already done is quite clear; the first part presents merely the beginning.

We can now claim that Luke saw his composition as a unified whole, introduced by a prologue which covers both parts of it, so that we are justified in inquiring what purpose he had for it as a whole and can attempt to ascertain the place of Part One in relation to the total purpose.

5. Clues to Luke's Purpose

In seeking to understand Luke-Acts as a whole we can leave aside any views of its purpose which do not take both parts of the story into account. Clues to the purpose will lie rather in common themes which can be traced through both parts. In previous discussions of the topic I have suggested that Luke's concern is to present salvation to his readers. This concept is a determinative one in both parts of the work. The birth narratives bring it out especially clearly, and I believe that this is quite deliberate on the part of Luke. But can we be more specific?

First, there is much to be said for the view of W. C. van Unnik that Acts

19. J. Jervell, *Luke and the People of God,* 1972, 19-39.
20. R. Maddox, op. cit., 1-6; J. A. Fitzmyer, op. cit., 289.
21. *Pace* H. Schürmann, *Das Lukas-Evangelium,* [2]1982, 4; E. Schweizer, *Luke,* 11.

presents the confirmation of the gospel which is recorded in the first part of the work. It shows how the salvation brought by Jesus became a reality for people separated from him in time and space, both Jews and Gentiles. The broad correspondences between the Gospel and Acts are significant in showing that the same kind of activity is going on in the time of the apostles as in the time of Jesus. Luke shows that the gospel "works."[22]

Second, this basic insight has been developed by Maddox. He is led to postulate that Luke's readers were having doubts about the truth of the gospel and the reality of salvation because of the way in which the Jews were rejecting both them and the gospel: how could the gospel of Jesus as the Messiah be true if the Jews by and large had rejected Jesus? Luke, therefore, takes up two main issues according to Maddox. First, he emphasizes that what was taking place in effect fulfilled the promises made in the Old Testament and was a present reality. Second, he emphasizes that this fulfillment had taken place "among us," that is to say, in the Christian Church.

> He writes to reassure the Christians of his day that their faith in Jesus is no aberration, but the authentic goal towards which God's ancient dealings with Israel were driving. The full stream of God's saving action in history had not passed them by, but has flowed straight into their community-life, in Jesus and the Holy Spirit. If there are apostates and heretics who have cut themselves off from participation in the Kingdom of God, it is not the Christians to whom such terms apply. It is Jesus, their Lord, in whom the promises of the ancient scriptures are fulfilled; it is Jesus who sends the Holy Spirit, whose powerful influence the Christians actually experience; and it is Jesus alone through whose name salvation occurs.[23]

Alongside these two views must be placed a third one, which is not intended as a statement of the total purpose of Luke but is rather a study of an important Lucan theme. I refer to the work of G. Lohfink, *Die Sammlung Israels*.[24] In this work we see how Luke has used his work to record the story of how God has gathered together the new Israel composed of both Jews and Gentiles. Jesus announces the good news to all Israel in the Gospel, but it is not until we reach Acts that we hear of the response in the "gathering" of Israel. Those Jews who respond to the Gospel form the new Israel which arises out of continuity with the old, and the Gentiles who respond to the Gospel also enter into this new Israel, the Church, but the Jews who reject the message are no longer reckoned among Israel. It follows that the Church did not exist before

22. W. C. van Unnik, " 'The Book of Acts,' the Confirmation of the Gospel," *NovT* 4, 1960.
23. R. Maddox, op. cit., 187. See earlier F. Danker, *Jesus and the New Age,* 1972, xiii-xvii.
24. G. Lohfink, *Die Sammlung Israels,* 1975.

the ascension, and also that the day of Pentecost is not to be regarded as its day of birth; rather the Church is continuous with Israel and grows out of it through the work of God himself who is its real Founder. Seen in this way, Luke-Acts records the story of the gathering of the new people of God.

We have here the ingredients which may help us toward a comprehensive picture of the purpose of Luke.

6. Defining Luke's Main Purpose

1. The theme of Luke is at first sight Jesus himself, or what he did and preached. Acts 1:1 must be taken as Luke's intended summary of the Gospel, so that the things fulfilled among us regarding which Theophilus was to be given reliable information must be understood as the deeds and words of Jesus. The problem is whether the same can be said of Acts: is it an account of what Jesus continued to do and to preach? Luke does not say so. It is rather the account of the witnesses who testify to Jesus from Jerusalem outward, and this is confirmed by the last verse of Acts, which refers to the activity of Paul in preaching the kingdom of God and teaching about the Lord Jesus quite openly and unhindered. From this it emerges that Jesus Christ is the theme of both parts of Luke-Acts only in the sense that Part One describes what he himself did and taught and Part Two describes how his followers testified and taught about him; Part One is the content of the witness, and Part Two is the action of witness. While therefore it is tempting to read into Acts 1:1 a contrast between what Jesus *began* to do and preach and what Jesus *continued* to do and teach, it is doubtful whether this is the intended contrast; we may be nearer the mark in contrasting what *Jesus* began with what his *followers* continued to do at his command and by the power of the Spirit. The point of comparison will then lie in the common activity: Jesus preached the kingdom as the manifestation of salvation, but the followers preached the kingdom and "another king." Thus the common thread is "the things accomplished among us" rather than simply the person of Jesus, and it is significant that the thought is of what happened and of the deeds of Jesus (the words being added in the second place): it is historical events with which Luke is concerned, but historical events which bring salvation. Further, the historical events are those to which testimony is borne by witnesses. We must avoid the frequently erected dichotomy between a salvation-historical understanding of Luke as being concerned purely with saving events and an existential view of him as being concerned purely with the kerygma. Deed and word, event and witness belong together in Luke as well as in the rest of the New Testament. The saving events are made known by the witnesses, but the witness would be empty if it was not a testimony to real events.

To say that Luke's main theme is the deeds and words of Jesus as attested by the witnesses which leads to salvation is, however, a very general statement, and it needs to be filled out to indicate what is specifically Lucan.

2. Luke's purpose is not merely to narrate the deeds and words of Jesus but to show how these did in fact lead to the experience of salvation and to the formation of the community of the saved. It was, therefore, impossible for him to stop at the end of Part One with a situation in which the post-Easter and post-Pentecost experience had not yet been realized and the disciples had merely been commanded to go and proclaim salvation. His purpose was to describe how salvation had become a reality as the witnesses went out in obedience to the Lord's command. Although Jesus gathered disciples during his earthly ministry, the meaning of discipleship after Easter was inevitably somewhat different, and Luke was concerned to make clear the reality and nature of the experience for his readers. In this way Luke manages to overcome an obvious deficiency in the work of his predecessors: they had not shown sufficiently clearly how the ministry and teaching of Jesus linked up with the history of the early Church. Luke's aim was *to bind together what happened before and after Easter,* to tie the two parts of the story together so that the "gospel story" could indeed be seen as the content of the Church's message.

It should be observed at this point that Luke does not draw a line between the history of the early Church and his own time. There is some doubt as to how salvation-history should be divided up in line with the general thesis of H. Conzelmann,[25] which sees three periods in the process:

View 1:	View 2:
Old Testament Period	Old Testament Period
Ministry of Jesus	Ministry of Jesus *and* period of the early Church
Pentecost–parousia	End of Acts–parousia

Neither of these schemes does justice to Luke's conception. First, Luke undoubtedly thinks in terms of promise and fulfillment. M. Rese's attempt to play down the significance of this element in Luke's thinking has in my opinion been convincingly refuted in a thesis by D. Bock, who attempts a more refined analysis of Luke's use of the Old Testament and shows that Rese's view is inadequate.[26] Second, I can find no clear evidence that Luke separates off the "ideal" period of the early Church from the period of the continuing Church.

---

25. H. Conzelmann, *The Theology of St. Luke,* ET 1961; see C. H. Talbert, op. cit., 106.

26. M. Rese, *Alttestamentliche Motive in der Theologie des Lukas,* 1969; idem, "Die Funktion der alttestamentlichen Zitate und Anspielungen in den Reden der Apostelgeschichte," in *Les Actes des Apôtres: Tradition, rédaction, théologie,* ed. J. Kremer, 1979, 61-79; D. Bock, *Proclamation from Prophecy and Pattern: Lucan Old Testament Christology,* unpublished thesis, Aberdeen, 1982.

His purpose is to show that what happened in the early Church can and must still go on in the Church in his day. Third, Luke's aim is to tie together closely the ministry of Jesus and the witness of the Church. Thus the pattern is more like this:

View 3:

Old Testament period of promise (creation to end of Old Testament period)
New Testament period of fulfillment—ministry of Jesus *and* witness of Church (extending to parousia)

Fourth, it follows incidentally that Luke does not conceive of the ministry of Jesus as "the middle of time"; it is true that it could be seen as falling in between the two other periods, and one can understand how Conzelmann was tempted to make this the key to Luke's view of salvation-history, but undoubtedly for Luke the coming of Jesus is primarily the beginning of the new age of fulfillment. Fifth, Luke does not make sharp breaks between the periods: the infancy narratives partake of the character of the old and the new, and similarly the resurrection and ascension period spans the time between the ministry of Jesus and the Church so as to bind them closely together. Thus the unity of salvation-history is manifested.

3. Through various common themes Luke expresses the continuity between the story of Jesus and the preaching and mission of the Church.

(I) Luke makes it clear that *the teaching* of the early Church is a continuation of that of Jesus with appropriate changes to take account of the post-Easter situation. In his editing of Acts he shows that the kingdom of God continued to be a theme in the apostolic preaching (Acts 1:3; 8:12; 19:8; 20:25; 28:23, 31). Although to some extent Luke plays down the significance of the kingdom in the Gospel, choosing rather to emphasize fulfillment and salvation themes, nevertheless he correctly recognizes the central place of this theme in the teaching of Jesus (Luke 4:43; 8:1). In Acts he is right in showing that the kingdom was still a theme of apostolic instruction, although other themes overshadowed it; it is now the kingdom and *Jesus* that are the theme of preaching. Yet it does not seem likely that he has significantly edited the tradition to bring out this continuity. The Gospel does show that faith and repentance are important factors in response to the ministry of Jesus, and that the effect of hearing the gospel and responding to it is salvation, but in these respects Luke simply brings out more clearly what is already latent in the tradition. One may see this crystallized in Luke 8:11-15, where Luke has edited the explanation of the parable of the sower to make some of these points more explicit (see 8:12b, 13b), but in so doing he has not effected any fundamental shift in understanding the tradition.

(II) Luke's *christology* in the Gospel and Acts is fundamentally the same. An important point of continuity is the use of the term κύριος in narrative in the Gospel, which expresses the conviction that the Jesus who is described there is one with the Lord who is proclaimed in Acts. Opinions differ whether Luke has carefully preserved the pre- and post-Easter distinction in the status of Jesus in his use of this device. Jesus is also declared to be the Son of God at the outset of the Gospel (Luke 1:32), and this understanding controls the christology of the whole work in my view. It is also significant that Luke can use the term Son of Man once, but only once, in Acts (7:56). Luke lets Peter summarize the earthly ministry of Jesus as part of his preaching in the house of Cornelius, so that the content of the gospel is seen to be closely tied to the kerygma; I share the view that the tradition reproduced in this sermon is that which lies behind the Gospels and is not a Lucan construction on the basis of his Gospel.[27] This passage is meant to summarize for the reader what Luke has already related in the Gospel and to show how the Gospel is to be understood. It is precisely because the Gospel is there that Luke can be content with so brief a summary of it in Acts.

(III) The *eschatology* of both parts of Luke's work is fundamentally the same.[28] The same combination of present realization and future hope is to be found, although the future element is less conspicuous in Acts. In both parts the present working of God is seen in the signs and wonders which are performed. There is in fact a degree of parallelism here which is meant to indicate that the same activity is at work in the early Church as in the case of Jesus, and it is made clear that it is through Jesus that the mighty works continue to be performed. The way in which to some extent the ministries of Peter and Paul parallel that of Jesus underlines this point. The Spirit who leads and empowers the Church is the Spirit of Jesus.

(IV) In both parts of the work the task of *mission* is presented, but the historical differences are carefully preserved, with the mission in the Gospel being restricted essentially to the Jews. There is nothing surprising in this, since the career of Jesus is best summed up as mission and since the sending out of the disciples on mission belongs to a well-attested tradition. This motif is not a distinctively Lucan one. Along with mission should be mentioned suffering and persecution. As C. K. Barrett has shown afresh, the theology of Luke is indeed a *theologia crucis,* and this is seen in the parallel fates of Jesus and his followers.[29]

3. An important element in Luke's work is to demonstrate that the truth

27. See P. Stuhlmacher's essay, "The Theme: The Gospel and the Gospels" in the present volume.

28. R. Maddox, op. cit., ch. 5.

29. C. K. Barrett, "Theologia Crucis—in Acts," in *Theologia Crucis—Signum Crucis,* ed. C. Andresen and G. Klein, 1979, 73-84.

of the gospel can be seen by the correspondence between prophecy and its fulfillment. Perhaps that is not the best way to put the point, which is rather that Luke shows how the ministry of Jesus and the mission of the Church were both foretold in Scripture and thus formed part of the divine plan.[30] The new element here is the way in which the Church's mission and above all the inclusion of the Gentiles are seen to be in accordance with Scripture, so that the credentials of the Church are thereby established. The effect of the argument from prophecy is thus to legitimate the ministry of salvation. All this forms part of a cumulative argument or demonstration of the reality of salvation. This of course is not a new move on the part of Luke, since we can see it already in the writings of Paul, especially in Romans 9–11, but it is given a new emphasis compared with the other Gospels. Along with this use of prophecy we should include the way in which the mission of the Church is also foretold or commanded by Jesus himself, so that what happens in Acts forms part of the deliberate purpose of the risen Lord. Both the teaching of Scripture and the teaching of Jesus legitimate the mission and the assembling of the new people of God.

4. Within this framework special importance attaches to the theme of the conversion of individuals and *the creation of the Church* which functions both as the community of believers and as the instrument of mission. Luke, we may say, writes to tell the members of the Church in his day "how we got here" both in terms of individual faith and of corporate union in the people of God. He is particularly concerned with showing how the Church has come together as a company of believing Jews and Gentiles and how it is related to the Jewish roots from which it sprung. This leads to his interest in the question of the law and problem of fellowship between Jews and Gentiles which is taken up in what is probably intended as the central scene in Acts, the so-called Council of Jerusalem.

We should possibly regard this last theme as summing up most comprehensively what Luke is trying to do in his two-part work. It is to show "how we got here" in the sense of giving an account of Christian origins which will demonstrate how salvation was brought to the world by Jesus and the apostolic witnesses who testified to Jesus. The effect of reading this account will be to give assurance to people such as Theophilus that what they had been taught catechetically was sound and reliable.[31] It follows from this that the things in which Theophilus had been instructed were not identical with "the things

---

30. J. Dupont, *The Salvation of the Gentiles,* 1979.
31. So rightly J. A. Fitzmyer, op. cit., 301. I am less certain that Luke-Acts is primarily an evangelistic work (*pace* C. F. D. Moule, *The Phenomenon of the New Testament,* 1967, 103), although clearly it is admirably fitted for this secondary purpose: the dividing line between people on the fringe of the Church who have not yet made a full commitment to Christian faith and those who have done so is obviously hard to draw.

accomplished among us" of which others had already written reports. It is not that Theophilus knew in detail the contents of Mark or similar works, or that he had been fully instructed orally in the story of Jesus. What he had received was catechetical instruction in the kerygma, more detailed than the sermon outlines in Acts, but not so detailed as in the Gospels in their accounts of Jesus. What he needed was fuller instruction to show the reliable basis on which his instruction rested.

7. Luke's Motivation

The problem which now arises is: Why did Luke do what he did? If we have identified accurately the intentions of his work, we have still to ask whether a concrete occasion can be discovered.

We may find it easier to reject some views of the occasion of Luke-Acts than to frame a positive hypothesis. Thus we can safely rule out the view that *the delay of the parousia* was the motivating force. The only way one might defend this view would be by saying that once the Church gave up focusing its hope of salvation on the imminent return of the Lord it was necessary to produce a reformulation of the story of its origins to show that salvation was a present experience mediated by the risen Lord and the Spirit. But this theory is shattered by the simple fact that long before Luke-Acts was written the Church had already come to this realization.

Second, it is unlikely that Luke-Acts was written to provide *a reply to heresy,* Gnostic or otherwise, and it surprises me that J. Roloff still defends this point of view.[32] In particular, W. Schmithals's attempt to defend this view in a new form is not persuasive.[33] He postulates a situation of persecution in the early second century in which the author was attacking a pre-Montanist, ultra-Pauline group who wished to sunder all connections with Judaism and hence with the Old Testament. This theory ignores the fact that persecution was a fairly constant factor in the first-century Church; it assumes a Roman hostility to the Jews from which the Christians were trying to escape by asserting their separate existence and for which the evidence is uncertain (especially outside Palestine); and it constructs a picture of an ultra-Pauline group which is not found in other sources nor necessary to explain Acts. There simply is no sign of an opposing group which Luke was trying to convert and win over.

Third, despite the many valuable details in his book and his correct assessment of the centrality of salvation for Luke I am unhappy with Maddox's

32. J. Roloff, *Die Apostelgeschichte,* 1981, 36.
33. W. Schmithals, *Das Evangelium nach Lukas,* 1980.

precise formulation of the view that it was *the position of the Jews* vis-à-vis the Church which was causing Luke's readers to have doubts about the reality of their salvation and the legitimacy of their claim to be the people of God.[34] On Maddox's own premise that the work was composed in the 80s it would seem that the fall of Jerusalem and the destruction of the temple must have been sufficient to convince the Christians that the future did not lie with Judaism and that Judaism was no longer enjoying God's favor. If, as I am inclined to believe, Luke-Acts was written somewhat earlier, then one has to say that uncertainty caused by the opposition of the Jewish leaders does not seem to have caused a crisis of confidence elsewhere in the Christian Church. It is true that Maddox tries to find the problem reflected in Romans, but I do not find him convincing on this point.[35]

The question boils down to: why did Luke think that Theophilus needed to be given ἀσφάλεια regarding the contents of Christian catechesis?

Is it too simplistic to say that the obvious answer to the question is the right one? If Theophilus and other Christians received catechetical instruction in the kerygma which was of a fairly general character, then it would be important to fill out the story for them by giving an account of those events which lay behind the kerygma, both the life of Jesus and the story of the growth of the Church. This situation would arise as soon as the Christian mission moved out into the Hellenistic world and into a time when the original eyewitnesses and ministers of the word were no longer able to keep in touch with all the congregations, and when the Church needed written documents to put alongside the spoken word. This is an old and familiar explanation of the origins of the written Gospel, but it is a plausible one. The merit of Luke is that he saw that an account of the story of Jesus alone was inadequate to fulfill this purpose; he needed to tell the story of Christian beginnings more broadly. I confess to an inability to be any more specific than this in the lack of any positive indications in Luke-Acts which would enable one to be more precise. Suggestions about the rich/poor problem in Luke's Church may illuminate some of Luke's secondary motivation, but do not throw any light on his main purpose in writing his work.

8. The Consequent Shaping of Luke-Acts

Our final question is whether we can see any ways in which this purpose may have shaped Luke's work. First, it is clear that Luke wished to present the events

---

34. R. Maddox, op. cit., 180-87.

35. This is not to say that the early Church did not face problems caused by the general failure of Judaism to respond to the gospel; what I question is whether a precisely delineated crisis can be identified as *the* occasion of Luke's work.

in such a way that they would be seen to confirm the reliability of the catechesis. He is therefore concerned with their theological significance. At the same time, however, the point of his work is that an "account" of what happened will secure this end. Therefore his intention must have been basically to present the facts, admittedly as he saw them, rather than to create a semifictitious account which would not in fact substantiate them. Luke's concern for ἀσφάλεια must imply a concern for accuracy, and other terms in the prologue, ἀχριβῶς and καθεξῆς, confirm this. (This does not mean that Luke thought that Christian faith was faith *in* certain historical events which could be *proved* to have happened, but it does mean that faith, which is a trust in God who has acted in certain events, is impossible if those events did not happen.)

The working out of this can be seen in Luke's treatment of his sources. His treatment of Mark and of the Q material shows him to have been consistently faithful in reproducing the substance of his sources. A recent thesis by an Aberdeen student has demonstrated the same point with respect to some of Luke's special source material preserved in the parables peculiar to this Gospel.[36] M. Hengel has reaffirmed the case for the basic historicity of the material in Acts.[37]

We must of course remember that the reliability of a writer is very much dependent upon the reliability of his sources, but this is a question that lies outside our present concern. Plainly Luke thought that the information which he had received was reliable in view of its origin. He seems to have sought to reassure Theophilus by means of a reference to the source of the material rather than by any kind of historical analysis and testing of the actual accounts.

Further, we must distinguish between Luke's concern for historicity and his success in achieving it. These are two different questions, although the obvious fact must be noted that in general a writer whose declared aim is reliability is more likely to achieve it than one who has no concern for it or is deliberately writing a fictitious or semifictitious narrative.

Yet again, there is the problem of the nature of ancient historical writing. How much liberty did a writer feel that he possessed in including in a historical narrative material that we should describe as legendary, or in revising his sources in the interests of his own Tendenz, or in giving a shaping to the narrative that is based in unhistorical construction?

Certainly Luke has edited his material, but I should want to emphasize that a good deal of Lucan redaction is basically literary and is not meant to forward a fresh theological interpretation of the material; here I reject the view

---

36. C. L. Blomberg, *The Tradition of the Parables peculiar to Luke's Central Section,* unpublished thesis, Aberdeen, 1982.

37. M. Hengel, *Acts and the History of Earliest Christianity,* ET 1979.

propounded in the case of Matthew's Gospel by R. H. Gundry that the evangelist's alterations can *all* be seen to have a theological motivation.[38] For details on this point with respect to Luke I must be allowed to refer to my commentary.[39] Of course some theological shaping has taken place, reflected in the choice of material, the structure of the work, and the presentation of individual pericopes. Luke obviously has some different emphases from Mark. But if my view of the prologue is correct, then Luke did not need to drastically rewrite an unsatisfactory Gospel of Mark in order to convince Theophilus. It was not dissatisfaction with Mark that led to his new attempt, but rather the need to expand Mark by the inclusion of the new material and the placing of the story within the broader context of an account of early Christian witness. This suggests that in principle the attempt to detect elaborate theological motivation behind every piece of Lucan redaction is wrongheaded, and we should pay more attention perhaps to Luke as a literary stylist.

Gospel critics often seem to take up two opposed positions. At one side there is the belief that if a narrative can be shown to be theologically motivated, then it follows that it was not motivated by historical interest, and therefore it is its historicity which needs to be demonstrated rather than its unhistorical character. This principle is a false one, as has been frequently pointed out. The view that the historicity of the Gospels rather than their unhistoricity must be demonstrated deserves to be buried once and for all. However, those who take the opposite position may also express themselves rashly. They often claim that, just as in law a person is assumed to be innocent until proved to be guilty, so too a narrative must be assumed to be historical until the contrary is proved. But this principle assumes that guilty and theological are analogous terms and that both are pejorative. This may not be so. Theology is not necessarily a bad thing, and it is the merit of the New Testament writers to have recognized that the simple historical statement "Jesus died on the cross" needs to be interpreted theologically as "Christ died for our sins." The problem is whether the recognition and expression of theological significance necessitates some manipulation and falsification of the history. There is no simple rule of thumb for answering this question, and we may often have to be agnostic in trying to do so. The point is that surely the probabilities lie with the view that Luke was trying to be faithful to history in expressing its theological significance, and if we can study his writings in this light we may begin to do justice to them.

---

38. R. H. Gundry, *Matthew: A Commentary on His Literary and Theological Art*, 1982.
39. I. H. Marshall, *The Gospel of Luke*, 1978.

Conclusion

I have argued in this essay that:

1. We need to distinguish between Luke's principal conscious aim(s), his secondary aims, the concrete occasion of his writing, and the unconscious factors that may have shaped his work.

2. The unity of Luke-Acts must be taken seriously in attempting to determine the purpose of the Gospel as part of the whole work.

3. To think of Luke as a *Gospel* writer may be misleading. There was no fixed "gospel"-genre into which he had to fit his work as a whole. He regarded the works of his predecessors as "accounts," not as Gospels. He was not writing a "Gospel" to which he subsequently added a sequel, but a two-part work.

4. Luke 1:1-4 is a prologue to Luke-Acts. The "things that have been accomplished among us" include the growth of the Church. If Luke had any quarrel with his predecessors, it was not because what they wrote was faulty but because it was incomplete.

5. Clues to Luke's purpose will therefore be found in threads running through both books: his stress on salvation, on the "confirmation" of the gospel in Acts (W. C. van Unnik), on the reality of the fulfillment of God's promises to the Jews (R. Maddox), and on the gathering of Israel (G. Lohfink).

6. Against this background Luke's main purpose was to confirm the kerygma/catechetical instruction heard by people like Theophilus with a fuller account of the basis of the kerygma in the story of Jesus, as handed down by faithful witnesses, and in the continuing story of the way in which through the activity of the witnesses the Church, composed of Jews and Gentiles, came into existence. He showed how the Old Testament promises were fulfilled in Jesus and the Church's mission, so that history is divided into a period of promise and a still-continuing period of fulfillment. The continuity between the ministry of Jesus and the witness of the Church is seen in various common themes—teaching about salvation, christology, eschatology, and mission. Luke writes to tell the Church "how we got here." What Theophilus had been taught was not the content of the Gospels in detail but the broad outline of the kerygma (including the ministry, death, and resurrection of Jesus and the coming of the Spirit, Acts 10:34ff.), which is now confirmed by a trustworthy account of Jesus and the Church.

7. A concrete occasion for this task is hard to find, except in terms of the geographical expansion of the Church and the demise of the original witnesses, which made it necessary for new converts to be assured that what was taught to them rested on the testimony of the first followers of Jesus.

8. The implications for understanding the Gospel are that Luke's theological motivation primarily led him to write what he regarded as a historical

account. His treatment of his sources is conservative, and it was motivated by literary reasons as much as by theological ones. He has emphasized the association of Jesus' ministry with salvation and brought out the connections with the kerygma and witness of the Church, but this is a matter of emphasis rather than of revision of the gospel tradition.

Luke is certainly to be regarded as an evangelist and the first part of his work is certainly a presentation of the gospel, but his distinctive contribution to the New Testament is a two-part work that links together the story of Jesus and the story of the experience of salvation and the gathering of the Church as the confirmation of the gospel of salvation.[40]

---

40. R. J. Dillon, "Previewing Luke's Project from His Prologue (Luke 1:1-4)," *CBQ* 43, 1981, 205-27, unfortunately did not come to my notice until after the completion of this essay.

Let John Be John:
A Gospel for Its Time*

James D. G. Dunn

1.

There are several reasons that the fourth Gospel is distinctive, even unique, among the New Testament documents. One is that it is more difficult in the case of John than with any other New Testament writing to speak of an "author." With every other New Testament document we can talk confidently of an "author," of the one who was more or less exclusively responsible for the words and sentiments of our texts as they now stand. We can set the goal of exegesis as the uncovering of the *intention* of the author, and pursue that goal as a meaningful and viable objective. But with John the concept of a single author, or of a document written from start to finish over one short period, becomes problematic. It is not simply that the history of traditions and/or sources *behind* John is obscure (the fourth Gospel is not alone in this). It is rather that the stages of composition of the Gospel itself are difficult to recover, and the relative importance of each stage for the final product difficult to determine. To what extent have the theology and character of the fourth Gospel been decisively stamped on the material at an *earlier* stage in the process—whatever that "earlier stage" might be—traditions or sources utilized, or an earlier edition of our present Gospel? Or, putting the same question from the other end of the process: how much of the Gospel is properly to be defined as "redactional"? And if we must speak of a redactor, to what extent has he determined the character and theology of what we now have?[1] The still vigorous debate on such

---

*Also delivered in modified form as one of the Wilkinson lectures at Northern Baptist Theological Seminary, Lombard, Illinois, in November 1982.

1. Cf. H. Thyen, "Aus der Literatur zum Johannesevangelium," *TR* 39, 1974, 252: "A large

questions shows how difficult New Testament scholarship has found it to achieve a firm orientation toward the fourth Gospel.[2] In the present essay we shall speak of "the fourth evangelist" to denote whoever put the Gospel into its present form without prejudice to the question of what and how much is more appropriately described as "redactional."

Another distinctive feature of John's Gospel, which appears to be further from the concerns of this symposium but which is nevertheless of relevance, is the way in which, more than any other New Testament writing, John has served as a bridge between the beginnings of Christianity in Jesus, and the orthodox faith which achieved definition at Nicea and which has provided the dogmatic basis of Christianity ever since. John is written about Jesus, about his ministry of word and sign in Judea and Galilee, and its traditions are certainly rooted in greater or less degree in the earliest memories of that ministry. At the same time, John's Gospel brought together the key categories which dominated the subsequent developing debates on christology (Logos and Son of God), and the Gospel has provided a portrayal of Jesus which has served as probably the chief inspiration and textbook for centuries of Christ-centered apologetic and piety.

It is presumably these two elements of John's distinctiveness which have caused scholarship such difficulty in locating the fourth Gospel within early Christianity. By this I do not refer simply to the difficulty of placing the fourth Gospel within the time-scale of early Christianity and within the geography of the eastern Mediterranean—the problem of date and place of composition. I am referring to the larger *problem of setting John within its historical context*—the difficulty of illuminating the cultural and theological situation(s) which called for this complex document to be written, the difficulty of determining to what extent such cultural and theological influences have shaped the Gospel, whether at an earlier or later stage in composition.

I emphasize this for two reasons. First, in my view the task of clarifying the historical context as much as possible is crucial for exegesis: the more fully and sympathetically we can enter into the historical context of a writing, the more likely we are to understand that writing, its character and theology, to perceive the intention of the one(s) who determined that character and theology. So with

---

part of the scholarly controversies concerning the interpretation of the fourth Gospel depends on whether one understands its standpoint to be that of the basic document or of the redaction."

2. See the review of the debate in R. Kysar, *The Fourth Evangelist and his Gospel*, 1975, Part One; R. Schnackenburg, "Entwicklung und der Stand der johanneischen Forschung seit 1955," *L'Évangile de Jean: Sources, rédaction, théologie*, ed. M. de Jonge, BETL 44, 1975. See also R. A. Culpepper, *The Johannine School*, SBLDS 26, 1975. Worth pondering is the caution of R. E. Brown, *The Community of the Beloved Disciple*, 1979, 28: "The tendency among some scholars, especially in Germany, to see an opposition between the Johannine evangelist and his sources, and thus antithetical phases of community life in the pre-Gospel period, is in my judgment almost certainly wrong."

John in particular, only by uncovering its historical context can we hope to hear it as the first readers were intended to hear it, the allusions and nuances as well as the explicit teaching. Second, the task of clarifying the tradition-process behind John, of illuminating both the continuities and the discontinuities with the earliest forms of the gospel, depends to a considerable extent on our achieving such a successful exegesis of John. Only when we have learned to recognize what the concerns of the fourth evangelist were in writing his Gospel will we be in a position to recognize whether these concerns have influenced his use of pre-formed material. Only when we have a clear grasp of what is Johannine can we hope to distinguish what is pre-Johannine in any systematic way. Of course, it by no means follows that the categories "Johannine" and "pre-Johannine" are mutually exclusive, that distinctive Johannine motifs are the *creation* of the fourth evangelist. But if we find that some of the motifs have been formulated to address the particular historical situation in which and to which the Gospel was written, we will be in a better position to determine the extent to which these motifs have shaped or molded the material used.

Consequently *the task of setting John in its historical context must be given a place of priority* in any inquiry into the gospel and the fourth Gospel. Unfortunately it is a task which has often been ignored, or which has been pursued without sufficient care.[3] In both cases, because the historical context has not been clarified, John has been *mis*understood, the fourth Gospel has not been heard in its own terms, John has not been allowed to be John. Let me say a little more on this as a way of explaining my own approach to John and his Gospel.

2.

The task of contextualizing the fourth Gospel and its message has been seriously ignored and misconceived in two directions—by reading John as though it belonged either to a *later* context or to a very *early* context.

2.1. The interpretation of John in the light of later developments is actually the classic reading of John. The fact that the fourth Gospel played such a crucial role in the development of christological and trinitarian dogma up to and beyond Nicea has resulted in generations of scholarship reading John in the light of these subsequent debates.[4] In particular, it has been all too easy to assume that the Athanasian and post-Nicene concern to define the *relation* between the Father

3. Cf. K. Wengst, *Bedrängte Gemeinde und verherrlichter Christus*, 1981, 29-32.
4. T. E. Pollard begins his *Johannine Christology and the Early Church*, SNTSMS 13, 1970, by citing F. C. Conybeare: "If Athanasius had not had the Fourth Gospel to draw texts from, Arius would never have been confuted." But he goes on to note "that if Arius had not had the Fourth Gospel to draw texts from, he would not have needed confuting" (13).

and the Son was already the fourth evangelist's concern. How natural, with a Gospel which speaks so much about God as Father and Jesus as the Son, simply to take it for granted that the evangelist too was wrestling with the problem of how to conceptualize and define the relationship between the first two persons of the Godhead. But that is something exegesis cannot simply assume. The use of the fourth Gospel within subsequent dogmatics, quite legitimate within its own terms, is *not* the key to a historically contextualized exegesis. If exegesis has the task of hearing John speak in its own terms and in its own time, so far as that is possible, then we exegetes must be prepared to speak on John's behalf if we see his Gospel being "hijacked" forward in time. For only when we have let John be itself and heard its message as its first readers heard it, so far as that is possible, only then will we be in a position to evaluate also the way in which John was used in the subsequent debates. Here not least we must be prepared to let John be John, for the dogmatic use of John too must justify itself by at least some reference to the meaning intended by the fourth evangelist.

2.2. Somewhat surprisingly the classic religionsgeschichtliche treatments of the fourth Gospel cannot be exempted from the same criticism at this point. Although rightly motivated as attempts to understand John's Gospel against the religious context of its time, their pursuit of the phantom of the pre-Christian Gnostic redeemer myth threw their whole endeavor off course. What emerged in the event was John set against and interpreted within the context of Mandaism and the later Gnostic systems.[5] The same criticism applies, though with less force, to those who have attempted to sustain a different or modified version of the Bultmann thesis—to locate John some way along a "gnosticizing trajectory."[6] We cannot criticize those who see the fourth Gospel simply as a stepping stone toward Nicene orthodoxy without criticizing also those who see the fourth Gospel simply as a stepping stone toward Gnosticism. To show how John was *used* by different factions from the second century onward is no answer to the question, What was the message John was intended to convey to its *first* readers? The *"dogmatic"* or the *"heretical"* John may in the event tell us very little about what we might call the *"historical"* John. To postulate a vague "gnosticizing" context for John may make meaningful sense of some elements in John, but only at the expense of ignoring such firmer indications of a historical

5. See e.g. the criticisms of W. A. Meeks, "The Man from Heaven in Johannine Sectarianism," *JBL* 91, 1972, 45: "Bultmann's synthetic myth is heavily dependent on the terminology of the Fourth Gospel; there is hardly any single document other than John in which all the elements of the 'gnostic redeemer myth' listed by Bultmann in his 1923 article are integrally displayed."

6. See particularly J. M. Robinson, "The Johannine Trajectory" (1968), in J. M. Robinson and H. Koester, *Trajectories through Early Christianity,* 1971, 232-68; L. Schottroff, *Der Glaubende und die feindliche Welt,* 1970; S. Schulz, *Johannes,* NTD IV, 1972, e.g. 28, 211; W. Langbrandtner, *Weltferner Gott oder Gott der Liebe: Der Ketzerstreit in der johanneischen Kirche,* BBE 6, 1977.

context which makes better sense of the whole, as we shall see. Even Käsemann, who attempts manfully to elucidate the fourth Gospel from its own internal logic and who in fact succeeds in grasping much of John's central thrust,[7] cannot in the event escape from his early religionsgeschichtliche perspective, and ends by accusing John of "gnosticizing tendencies" and "naive docetism," which the Church declared "orthodox" in error.[8]

A methodological point of some importance emerges from all this. I mean that the New Testament exgete should never forget that it is possible to presume too *broad* a historical context for a New Testament document as well as too *narrow* a context. The twentieth-century student of first- and second-century religion in the eastern Mediterranean (or of third- and fourth-century patristic thought, for that matter) may be as much hindered as helped by the breadth of his or her historical knowledge. The context within which the student sets a document like the fourth Gospel, consciously or unconsciously, may be far too wide, both in time and in geographical extent. He or she may detect wide-ranging influences and tendencies which were not actually factors in the understanding of the writer(s) and the first readers. It is as important for an exegete to remember the *limited horizons* of particular documents, as it is to appreciate the much more diverse currents within the broader milieu. A bird's-eye view of the whole scene, desirable as it is, will not facilitate a close encounter with a particular author on the ground. To the extent then that German scholarship on the fourth Gospel has been dominated by the Bultmann-Käsemann debate on John 1:14,[9] to that extent it is vulnerable to the criticism of treating the fourth Gospel anachronistically, of asking the right questions, but against too broad a background. Here too we must attempt to let John be John.[10]

3.

If John has been read too quickly as though it belonged to a later context, an alternative tendency has been to read the fourth Gospel as far as possible within the context of Jesus' own ministry in the late 20s or early 30s.

---

7. See below, n. 94.

8. E. Käsemann, *The Testament of Jesus,* ET 1968.

9. According to Thyen (n. 1), 50: the "Interpretationsmodelle" of Bultmann and Käsemann "limit Johannine studies to a corner."

10. On this whole subject cf. particularly the wisely cautionary comments of W. A. Meeks, " 'Am I a Jew?'—Johannine Christianity and Judaism," *Christianity, Judaism and other Greco-Roman Cults: Studies for Morton Smith,* ed. J. Neusner, 1975, I, 163-85, and Wengst's concise critique of some of the above theses in *Bedrängte Gemeinde* (n. 3), 12-22. My own *Christology in the Making: an Inquiry into the Origins of the Doctrine of Incarnation,* 1980, is in fact an exposition of the very important "limited horizons" point.

3.1. Most serious here has been the attempt to argue that the fourth Gospel is more or less strictly historical from start to finish. Not simply particular elements (like geographical notes) and particular traditions (like those about the Baptist) are historical, but the narratives as such were intended as historical descriptions of actual events in Jesus' life. Not simply individual sayings within the Johannine discourses, but the discourses as a whole were intended to document what Jesus actually said during his life on earth. On this view, everything John presents Jesus as doing or saying, Jesus must actually have done, must actually have said in more or less the words reported. Only if exegesis proceeds on this presupposition can we be faithful to the intent and meaning of the document as Scripture. Such would be the thrust of conservative scholars who try to push the recognition of historical tradition in John to its fullest extent.[11]

We should pay heed to such attempts, for not only is their concern to emphasize the historical character of John's Gospel as of crucial importance in itself, but they also represent a substantial body of belief at the popular level. We need, for example, only recall the multitudinous ecumenical pronouncements which take their justification from the prayer of Jesus in John 17 ("that they may be one even as we are one"—v. 22)—apparently on the grounds that this was a dominical word. Probably no issue marks off the bulk of New Testament scholarship so sharply from the piety of the pews than the issue of how the fourth Gospel should be understood. A New Testament scholarship which is concerned to be heard also by "the ordinary believer"[12] cannot be unconcerned at the way in which the fourth Gospel is expounded in so many churches today. For if it is a mistake to assume that the discourses of John are more or less a transcript of what Jesus actually said during his ministry in Galilee and Judea, and if preaching on that basis is misleading the people, then those of us who are concerned to exercise a teaching ministry in the Church cannot escape the obligation of correcting that mistake. Despite the desire to be true to Scripture, such expositions are not being true to John. They are *imposing* a context and an intention *on* John, not allowing an exegesis which is mindful of historical context to elucidate the questions of intention and meaning. They are not letting John be John.

3.2. What of our own concern to trace the traditions behind the fourth

---

11. See e.g. L. Morris, *Studies in the Fourth Gospel,* 1969, ch. 2; idem, *The Gospel according to John,* NICNT, 1971, 40-49; D. A. Carson, "Historical Tradition in the Fourth Gospel: After Dodd, What?" *Gospel Perspectives* II, ed. R. T. France and D. Wenham, 1981, 83-145; G. Maier, "Johannes und Matthäus—Zwiespalt oder Viergestalt des Evangeliums," ibid., 267-91; cf. the older work of E. Stauffer, *Jesus and his Story,* ET 1960, 149-59.

12. I do not imply that scholars have neglected this concern; see e.g. E. E. Ellis, *The World of St. John,* 1965; A. M. Hunter, *According to John,* 1968; S. S. Smalley, *John: Evangelist and Interpreter,* 1978.

Gospel, the continuities of the gospel within and behind the fourth Gospel? It is a concern which I certainly share. If John's Gospel cannot be shown to have firm roots in the history of Jesus Messiah, the value of John *is* significantly diminished; not least its role as a bridge between the beginnings of Christianity and the subsequent christological dogmas is undermined at one end.

Moreover, I am confident that the fourth Gospel does draw on good tradition at many points. I think, for example, of the topographical notes (Aenon near Salim, the pools of Bethzatha and Siloam, a town called Ephraim, etc.), and the parallel traditions (particularly regarding John the Baptist, the calling of the disciples, the cleansing of the temple, the healing miracles and the feeding of the five thousand, and the passion narrative). At such points John can quite justifiably be said to supplement the synoptics, whether by design or simply because the traditions utilized by John were fuller at various points.[13] I think too of how particular verses central to the themes of various Johannine discourses can be paralleled by individual sayings in the Synoptic tradition (e.g. John 3:3, 5, another version of Matt. 18:3/Mark 10:15; John 5:19 and 10:15 possible variants of Matt. 11:27; John 6:53 drawing on the tradition of the Last Supper; John 10:1-5 a development of the parable of the lost sheep in Matt. 18:12-13; John 13:20 parallel to Matt. 10:40) and how even the striking "I am" formula in John can be paralleled to some extent by Mark 6:50 (cf. 14:62). In all this the definitive work of C. H. Dodd still stands as a landmark in Johannine study.[14] It has been and will be supplemented at individual points.[15] But it is hard to imagine its main findings being overthrown or their overall balance being much altered.

I also consider it highly probable, in the light of John 19:35; 20:2-9 and 21:24, that the source and validator of this earlier tradition was the historical individual described as "the beloved disciple"; though I am less certain of the extent to which the beloved disciple has been idealized.[16] So too it must be considered probable, in the light of John 4, that Samaritans were involved in the history of the Johannine community; though I am much less certain that we can

13. Despite recent restatements of the view that John knew and used one or more of the synoptics, I find the evidence not wholly persuasive. See e.g. the review of the discussion by Kysar (n. 2), 54-66. Since then note particularly F. Neirynck, "John and the Synoptics," *L'Évangile de Jean* (n. 2), 73-106; C. K. Barrett, *John,* ²1978, 15-18, 42-46; Mgr de Solages, *Jean et les Synoptiques,* 1979; D. M. Smith, "John and the Synoptics: Some Dimensions of the Problem," *NTS* 26, 1979-80, 425-44; J. Becker, "Aus der Literatur zum Johannesevangelium," *TR* 47, 1982, 289-94.

14. C. H. Dodd, *Historical Tradition in the Fourth Gospel,* 1963.

15. See particularly the sequence of studies by B. Lindars, *Behind the Fourth Gospel,* 1971; idem, *The Gospel of John,* NCBC, 1972, esp. 46-54; idem, "Traditions behind the Fourth Gospel," *L'Évangile de Jean* (n. 2), 107-24; idem, "John and the Synoptic Gospels: A Test Case," *NTS* 27, 1980-81, 287-94; idem, "Discourse and Tradition: The Use of the Sayings of Jesus in the Discourses of the Fourth Gospel," *JSNT* 13, 1981, 83-101.

16. See particularly H. Thyen, "Aus der Literatur zum Johannesevangelium," *TR* 42, 1977, 213-61; Brown (n. 2), 31-34; M. de Jonge, "The Beloved Disciple and the Date of the Gospel of John," *Text and Interpretation,* Festschrift M. Black, ed. E. Best and R. McL. Wilson, 1979, 99-114.

use the different *emphases* within the Gospel's christology as evidence of
different *stages* in the development of the same Johannine community.[17] All in
all, then, there are sufficient indications from within the Gospel itself that the
fourth evangelist's clearly implied concern to preserve and reproclaim the truth
of Jesus and the "testimony" of those who were with Christ "from the beginning"
(15:27; 16:13) is to be taken with all seriousness.

My point, however, is that it is difficult to advance the discussion about
such issues until the historical context of the fourth Gospel itself has been
clarified, until, in other words, we know whether we have to discount (for the
purposes of tracing historical tradition) certain emphases as belonging to the
latest stage of the tradition history. Not only so, but it is worth bearing in mind
that a tradition-historical investigation, precisely because it is more concerned
with the points of similarity and contact with the synoptic tradition, may well
pay too little attention to the Johannine *distinctives,* particularly the theological
features which give John its distinctive character.

If, in addition, the inquiry is directed toward demonstrating the historical
trustworthiness of the earlier tradition, that may detract still further from the
Gospel itself by strengthening the hidden assumption or implied inference that
John's Gospel is "authentic" or "authoritative" only in proportion as it draws
on historical tradition: the more we can show the fourth Gospel to have been
dependent on tradition which goes back to the 30s, the more we value it. For all
that a legitimate concern is involved here: What if John's Gospel was *not*
intended primarily as a supplement to one or more of the other three? What if
John's Gospel was not intended to serve as a source of *historical* information
about Jesus in his ministry on earth?[18] In that case an inquiry which sought to
vindicate John by demonstrating the historical roots of his tradition would in
fact be missing the point, *John's* point. Here too it may be more important even
for our present purposes to insist, Let John be John!

It will be clear by now that I wish to tackle the whole question of
Traditionsgeschichte with reference to John from the *other* end—by attempting
to understand the finished product of the fourth Gospel in its own terms, within
its own context. Where other approaches are more obvious and more attractive

17. See Brown (n. 2), 25-28, in discussion with alternative reconstructions particularly
of J. L. Martyn, "Glimpses into the History of the Johannine Community," *L'Évangile de Jean*
(n. 2), 149-75, reprinted in J. L. Martyn, *The Gospel of John in Christian History,* 1978, 90-121.
See also U. B. Müller, *Die Geschichte der Christologie in der johanneischen Gemeinde,* SBS 77,
1975; G. Richter, "Präsentische und futurische Eschatologie im 4. Evangelium" (1975), *Studien
zum Johannesevangelium,* ed. J. Hainz, 1977, 346-82, esp. 354-81; Langbrandtner (n. 6), esp.
117-20.

18. Cf. Lindars, "Discourse and Tradition" (n. 15), 83: "Although . . . the sayings tradition
is the only source of the discourses in the strict sense, the meaning and purpose of the discourses
are not dictated by the sayings, but relate closely to the conditions of Johannine Christianity at the
time when the evangelist is writing, probably late in the first century."

with regard to the other Gospels, by virtue of their high degree of similarity of form and content, with the fourth Gospel it is the *distinctiveness* of John which we must come to terms with in the first instance. The more we can clarify the Johannine distinctives, the reasons for any discontinuities and their theological significance, the better position we will be in to highlight the points of similarity and continuity. By hearing the Gospel according to *John* clearly we may hear the gospel according to all four evangelists more clearly too.

4.

Two observations provide our point of departure. Having achieved a preliminary "fix" on John we will then be able to "spiral in" to gain a closer look at the fourth Gospel within its historical context.

4.1. First, in attempting to let John be John, I make no apology for focusing on *John's christology*. For one thing, the stated *aim* of the Gospel as it now stands gives first place to christological claims: "these things are written that you may believe that Jesus is the Christ, the Son of God . . ." (20:31). We need not decide here whether this is an evangelistic aim for a Gospel written to nonbelievers, or, as is more probable, a didactic aim to strengthen the faith of those who have already believed, at least in some measure.[19] Either way the first objective of the evangelist is christological—so to present Jesus in his Gospel that his readers may believe the Christian claim expressed in the formulation, "Jesus is the Christ, the Son of God."

For another, it is abundantly apparent that most of the Johannine *distinctives* come to clearest expression in John's christology. Certainly we can find many synoptic-like traditions in the Johannine discourses; but it is the thoroughgoing portrayal of the Son sent from the Father, conscious of his preexistence, the descending-ascending Son of Man, making the profoundest claims in his "I am" assertions, which both *dominates* John's christology *and* distances it most strikingly from the synoptic tradition. Bultmann after all did have a point when he insisted that any attempt to solve the "Johannine puzzle" must begin with John's portrayal of Jesus as the descending-ascending redeemer[20]—a rock on which many a thesis regarding John has come to grief. If we can reach a clearer understanding of these Johannine distinctives, we will be in a better position both to distinguish the historical roots of John's tradition and to evaluate the Johannine elaboration of that tradition.

We can also learn the same lesson from what we might call *the points of*

---

19. See e.g. Wengst (n. 3), 33-36 and those cited by Meeks (n. 10), 180 n. 64.
20. See the references in Meeks (n. 5), 44.

sensitivity in the Gospel, the points at which an effort is evidently being made to clarify some confusion or to counter opposing views. These points obviously tell us something about the situation to which such polemic or apologetic is addressed—a subject to which we must return shortly. For the moment, all we need note is how consistently these points of sensitivity focus on the Christian claims concerning Christ—for example, the repeated contrast with John the Baptist in the first three chapters, with the Baptist being deliberately set over against the Christ as his inferior (1:6-9, 15, 20; 3:28-31);[21] the way in which older battles over the law and the sabbath have become christological battles (particularly chs. 5, 7, and 9);[22] the dramatic unfolding of the mounting *krisis* in the middle section of the Gospel, where the point of *krisis* particularly for the wavering crowd is consistently the status of Jesus (7:12-15, 25-27, 31, 40-44, 52; 8:12, 25, 48, 53; 9:16-17, 29-33; 10:19-21, 24, 33; 11:27; 12:34);[23] or the way in which the evangelist depicts the disciples' faith in the Christ going from initial confidence through crisis and clarification to the climactic confession of Thomas, "My Lord and my God" (1:41, 45, 49; 6:68-69; 14:5-11; 20:28).

The christological claim is at the heart of the fourth Gospel, including not least the distinctively Johannine elements of that claim. Clearly then it is the reason for and rationale of this christological claim which we must illuminate if we are to have any hope of understanding the good news as preached by John.

4.2. Second, in attempting to set John within its historical context, it is *the context of late first-century Judaism* which must have first claim on our attention. This view has been well argued several times and has won increasing support during the past twenty years, so that I need do little more than rehearse its main outline. The factors of greatest significance are John's references to "the Jews" and his use of the word ἀποσυνάγωγος (9:22; 12:42; 16:2).

"The Jews" feature regularly in the fourth Gospel as the opponents of Jesus. In this role they appear as a single coherent group. More important, in this role they are evidently the official representatives of Judaism, the religious authorities who determine matters of faith and polity for the people (1:19; 5:16; 9:18; 18:12; 19:31; even Jews fear "the Jews"—7:13; 9:22; 19:38; 20:19). In this role, in fact, "the Jews" are often more or less synonymous with the Pharisees (cf. 1:19 and 24; 7:1 and 32; 8:13 and 22; 9:13 and 18; 18:3 and 12), and, most striking of all, with "the world" in its hatred of Jesus (cf. particularly 8:21-47 with 15:18-25).[24] As for ἀποσυνάγωγος, the significance particularly of

---

21. W. Wink, *John the Baptist in the Gospel Tradition,* SNTSMS 7, 1968, ch. V.

22. See particularly S. Pancaro, *The Law in the Fourth Gospel, NovT* Supplements 42, 1975.

23. It was C. H. Dodd's masterly exposition of this theme in his *The Interpretation of the Fourth Gospel,* 1953, 345-89, which first stirred my interest in John as a work of theology in my student days.

24. See e.g. E. Grässer, "Die antijüdische Polemik im Johannesevangelium," *NTS* 11, 1964-65, 74-90; R. E. Brown, *John 1-12,* AB, 1966, lxxi; Wengst (n. 3), 37-44. That the fourth

9:22 is that it seems to presuppose a formal decision made by Jewish authorities to excommunicate Jews from the synagogue on the sole ground that they confessed Jesus to be the Messiah.[25]

The prominence and character of this tension between Jesus and "the Jews" point the exegete firmly toward a mainly Jewish context for the fourth Gospel, somewhere after the destruction of Jerusalem in AD 70. (1) The sharpness of the breach between Jesus and "the Jews" and the sustained vehemence of the polemic in the middle section of the Gospel is matched elsewhere in the New Testament only in part, even when we include Matthew 23. (2) The breach evidently centered on the Christian confession of Jesus as Messiah. And although Jesus was, of course, crucified as a messianic claimant,[26] there is *no* indication that in the intervening years the confession of Jesus as Messiah was regarded as a "make or break" issue between Jewish Christians and the leaders of Judaism.[27] There *were* issues which brought Jew and Christian to blows (particularly the temple and the law). But in Jerusalem itself, and probably also in areas of the Christian mission controlled from Jerusalem, Jews who believed Jesus to be the Messiah were apparently undisturbed (and even highly regarded) in the period prior to the Jewish revolt. (3) In particular, there is no clear evidence of an official policy of excluding Jews who believed in Jesus from the synagogue during the same period. Although Church and synagogue pulled apart in the Gentile mission, there is no indication of such a disruption within the Jewish mission (cf. Acts 21:20-21). Thus, when Josephus writes of Syria in the period prior to the Jewish war, he seems to know of no faction within the Jewish communities excluded from the synagogue. And even in the Gentile mission it is significant that (prior to the Neronian persecution at least) the Roman authorities thought of Jewish-Christian controversy as an internal Jewish affair (Acts 18:15; Suetonius, *Claudius* 25.4).[28] (4) The degree

---

evangelist also uses the phrase in a broader, less polemical way does not diminish the force of this point; see e.g. most recently, F. Hahn, " 'Die Juden' im Johannesevangelium," *Kontinuität und Einheit*, Festschrift F. Mussner, ed. P. G. Müller and W. Stenger, 1981, 430-38. On the irony of John 19:15 ("We have no king but Caesar") see particularly W. A. Meeks, *The Prophet-King: Moses Traditions and the Johannine Christology, NovT* Supplements 14, 1967, 76-78.

25. See particularly J. L. Martyn, *History and Theology in the Fourth Gospel*, 1968, ²1979, ch. 2, whose main thesis that the evangelist presents a two-level drama (an *einmaliges* event during Jesus' earthly lifetime, and the situation facing his own community) has been widely accepted.

26. In recent literature see particularly O. Betz, "Probleme des Prozesses Jesu," *ANRW* II, 25/1, 1982, 565-647, esp. 633-37; A. E. Harvey, *Jesus and the Constraints of History*, 1982, ch. 2.

27. See particularly Martyn (n. 25), 45-51; B. Lindars, "The Persecution of Christians in John 15,18–16,4a," in *Suffering and Martyrdom in the New Testament*, ed. W. Horbury and B. McNeil, 1981, (48-69) 49-51; against J. A. T. Robinson, *Redating the New Testament*, 1976, esp. 272-74, and Carson (n. 11), who pick at the evidence and do not succeed in producing an alternative historical context which fits all the elements of 9:22 so well.

28. The recognition that Christians were an entity distinct from the Jews is first attested by Tacitus (*Annals* 15.44.2-5), though it is significant that Tacitus accuses them of "hatred of the human

to which the Pharisees emerge in the fourth Gospel as the dominant force in Judaism, in contrast to the other Gospels (even "many of the rulers" fear "the Pharisees"—12:42),[29] is surely best explained as a reflection of the growing dominance of the rabbinic authorities within Judaism during the Jabnean period.

Finally (5) there is enough evidence to indicate that it was precisely during this period that rabbinic Judaism began to take deliberate steps to mark itself off from other claimants to the broader heritage of pre-70 Judaism. It should be noted that this last point does not depend on establishing a precise text and date for the twelfth Benediction, the *birkat-ha-minim,* or on postulating a specific reference to Christians in this malediction on heretics.[30] It is enough to note that rabbinic tradition traces the composition of the *birkat-ha-minim* back to the time of Gamaliel II (b. Ber. 28b)[31] and that it was probably aimed at those regarded by the rabbis as (Jewish) sectarians, including Jewish Christians.[32] The point then is that the independent evidence of Jewish tradition confirms what the internal evidence of the fourth Gospel made probable anyway (cf. also Justin, *Dial.* 16; 47; 96)—viz., that rabbinic Judaism began to take steps in the late first century and early second century to exclude various expressions of heterodoxy, which from the point of view of (newly) normative Judaism had come to be regarded as heresy—including Jewish Christian belief in Jesus as Messiah.

It is possible therefore to reach the fairly strong conclusion that the fourth Gospel itself reflects the situation confronting the Johannine author/school/ community in the late first century of our era—a situation where the Jewish Christians concerned saw themselves threatened by the world as represented particularly by the Jewish authorities where they were.[33] The fact that christology seems to have been the focal point of the confrontation between the fourth evangelist and "the

---

race," that is, the old charge regularly brought against the Jews—see M. Stern, *Greek and Latin Authors on Jews and Judaism* II, 1980, 93.

29. See e.g. Martyn (n. 25), 84-89; Lindars, *John* (n. 15), 37; H. F. Weiss, *TDNT* IX, 43-45.

30. Martyn (n. 25), 58, assumes too quickly that Christians (= Nazarenes) were explicitly mentioned in the Jabnean form; but see the fuller discussions listed in n. 32 below.

31. The period of Gamaliel II's ascendancy at Jabneh is usually reckoned from about 80 to 115. Most scholars accept a date for the *birkat-ha-minim* in the middle 80s, though note Martyn's (n. 25) increased caution and its reasons, discussed in his 1979 edition (nn. 69, 75).

32. See particularly W. Horbury, "The Benediction of the *Minim* and Early Jewish-Christian Controversy," *JTS* 33, 1982, 19-61, which includes discussion of the too cautious treatment by R. Kimelman, *"Birkat Ha-Minim* and the Lack of Evidence for an Anti-Christian Jewish Prayer in Late Antiquity," *Jewish and Christian Self-Definition:* II: *Aspects of Judaism in the Graeco-Roman Period,* ed. E. P. Sanders, 1981, 226-44, 391-403; see also A. F. Segal's note in the following essay (409f., n. 57) cited below (n. 62); earlier bibliography in Wengst (n. 3), notes to pp. 53ff.

33. Wengst (n. 3) thinks it possible to locate the Johannine community with some precision within the southern part of Agrippa II's kingdom, in the territory of Gaulanitis and Batanea (77-93); but it is enough for our purposes to note that there is at least one setting in the general area of the eastern Mediterranean which matches the probable historical context of the fourth Gospel so well. Cf. O. Cullmann, *The Johannine Circle,* ET 1976, 59f. On the "sectarian" consciousness of the Johannine community, see particularly Meeks (n. 5) and D. M. Smith, "Johannine Christianity: Some Reflections on its Character and Delineation," *NTS* 21, 1974-75, 222-48.

Jews" provides strong encouragement for us to investigate the issues involved more closely in the hope of shedding further light on the historical context of the Gospel and on the reasons for its distinctive christological emphases.

5.

The second stage of our inquiry is to question more closely why it was that the Christian confession of Jesus as Messiah provoked such confrontation between the Johannine Jewish-Christian "sect" and "the Jews." We can hope to shed some light on these questions both from the fourth Gospel itself and from what we know of Judaism between the revolts.

5.1. What were the particular issues at stake so far as "the Jews" were concerned in their confrontation with Jesus? It was not simply the assertion that Jesus was Messiah, which might well have remained largely unexceptionable or at least nonheretical in itself. What caused the trouble was the fact that the Messiah claim was itself a summary for a much fuller christology—all in fact that is expressed more adequately, so far as John is concerned at any rate, in the title *"Son of God."* To defend and win belief in Jesus as the Son of God is the evangelist's stated aim in 20:31, where "Son of God" is the necessary supplement to and explanation of the less provocative "Messiah" claim (similarly 11:27). And it is precisely on the grounds that Jesus "made himself Son of God" that "the Jews" denounce Jesus to Pilate (19:7).

When we unpack this claim and the reasons for its offensiveness to Jewish ears, it becomes clear that one of the main contentious points revolves around the question of Jesus' *origin:* Where has he come from?—from Bethlehem, from Galilee, from where? The Gospel reader, of course, knowing full well the evangelist's answer—"from his Father in heaven" (see particularly 6:41; 7:27-29, 42, 52; 8:23; 9:29; 19:9). Most disturbing of all to "the Jews" is the inference they draw that in claiming to be Son of God, Jesus has made himself "equal to God" (5:18), indeed has made himself *God* (10:33)[34]—a significance for "Son of God" which the evangelist, of course, wants to press home on his own account (1:1, 18; 20:28).

That it is the question of Jesus' heavenly origin and status which is mainly at issue in all this is confirmed by the most distinctive feature of the Johannine Son of Man sayings. The offense of Jesus' teaching is both heightened and (if it can be accepted) resolved by reference to the Son of Man's descent from heaven and ascent to heaven (3:12-13; 6:61-62).[35] Bound

---

34. 𝔭[66] reads τὸν θεόν.

35. "Wherever the [ascent/descent] motif occurs, it is in a context where the primary point of the story is the inability of the men of 'this world,' preeminently 'the Jews,' to understand and accept Jesus"—Meeks (n. 5), 58.

up with this is one of the most consistent emphases of the fourth Gospel, on Jesus as the bearer of divine revelation—the Son of God who makes known the heavenly mysteries with authority, precisely because he has been sent from heaven and speaks of what he has seen and heard with his Father (see particularly 1:17-18, 49-51; 3:10-13, 32; 7:16-18; 8:14, 28, 38; 12:49-50; 14:10; 15:15; 17:14).

It is clear then that what is at stake for the Johannine community is the full significance of the confession "Jesus is the Christ, the Son of God." And what is of particular importance for the evangelist, and particularly contentious to the Jews of his time, is the claim that this confession includes belief that Jesus came from heaven and speaks with the authority of God.[36]

5.2. When we set this fuller picture of John's christology into the context of post-70 Judaism, it quickly becomes apparent that there are some striking overlaps with the Johannine concerns. As has been more clearly perceived in the past few years, Judaism between the two revolts was not yet the massively uniform structure embodied in the Mishnah and Talmuds.[37] The disappearance of other parties (Sadducees, Zealots, Essenes) did not mean a disappearance of other facets of pre-70 Judaism. In particular, recent scholarship has reminded us of two other important strands of that broader Judaism which survived the destruction of the temple—the apocalyptic and merkabah mystical traditions.[38] Several points of relevance for our inquiry emerge here.

First, we should note the extent to which these two strands themselves overlap. Both apocalyptic and merkabah mysticism are characterized precisely by their claim to a direct knowledge of heavenly mysteries, either by means of a vision, or, more frequently, by means of an ascent to heaven.[39] Such ascents to heaven are attributed not only to Enoch (I Enoch 14:8ff.; 39:3ff.; 70–71; II Enoch 3ff.) and to Abraham (Test. Abr. 10ff.; Apoc. Abr. 15ff.; cf. also IV Ezra 3:14; II Bar. 4:4), but also to Adam (Life of Adam and Eve 25–29), to Levi (Test. Levi 2:5ff.), to Baruch (II Bar. 76; 3 Baruch) and to Isaiah (Asc. Isa. 7ff.; cf. Sir. 48:24-25)[40]—most of these reports are either roughly contemporary with or

---

36. The subsequent ascent through death and resurrection is, of course, also of crucial significance for John's christology, as I have myself noted elsewhere ("John 6—a Eucharistic Discourse?" NTS 17, 1970-71, 328-38; also Unity and Diversity in the New Testament, 1977, 301-2), but to include that aspect within the present essay would enlarge the discussion too much (though see below, section 9.2).

37. See now the welcome ET of G. Alon, The Jews in their Land in the Talmudic Age, 1980.

38. See particularly I. Gruenwald, Apocalyptic and Merkabah Mysticism, 1980; C. Rowland, The Open Heaven: a Study of Apocalyptic in Judaism and Early Christianity, 1982.

39. This overlap has been obscured by identifying apocalyptic too closely with eschatology. See particularly the important corrective by Rowland on this point (n. 38). D. J. Halperin, The Merkabah in Rabbinic Literature, 1980, does not take sufficient account of this overlap.

40. Note also the "final" ascents of Elijah (esp. II Kdms. 2:11; Sir. 48:9-10; 1 Enoch 90:31), Ezra (IV Ezra 14:9), and Abel (Test. Abel 11; Asc. Isa. 9:8).

predate the period in which we are interested.[41] So too the account of Moses' ascent of Mt. Sinai (Ex. 19:3; 24:18) evidently encouraged several circles within Judaism to view it as an ascent to heaven (Philo, *Mos.* 1.158; *Qu. Ex.* 2.29, 40, 46; Josephus, *Ant.* 3.96; II Bar. 4:2-7; *Lib. Ant.* 12:1; *Memar Marqah* 4:3, 7; 5:3; cf. Ezekiel the Tragedian in Eusebius, *Praep. Evang.* 9.29.5-6; IV Ezra 14:5; II Bar. 59).[42] Likewise the practice of merkabah mysticism, in which one sought by meditation, particularly on the chariot vision of Ezekiel 1 (but also passages like Isa. 6 and Dan. 7:9-10, as well as the story of creation in Gen. 1), to experience for oneself a mystical ascent to or revelation of the throne of God, seems to have been already well established in our period.[43] Such interest is evident already in I Enoch 14, is hinted at in Sir. 49:8, and is clearly attested in the so-called "angelic liturgy" of Qumran (4QSl [4QŠirŠabb] 40:24).[44] Not least relevant here are the appearance in some of these visions of a glorious being closely related in appearance to God (Ezek. 8:2 compared with 1:26-7; Dan. 7:13 LXX; 10:5-6; Apoc. Abr. 10; Apoc. Zeph. 9:12–10:9)[45] and the motif of the transformation into angel-like form of the one who ascends himself, notably Moses and Isaiah (see above), and most strikingly Enoch (I Enoch 71:11; II Enoch 22:8; Asc. Isa. 9:9), who is identified as the Son of Man in the Similitudes of Enoch (I Enoch 71:14) and subsequently as Metatron in III Enoch 3–16.[46]

Second, we should note also that *both* early Christianity *and* the Jabnean sages were not unaffected by such tendencies within Judaism. Paul's account of a visionary ascent to the third heaven (II Cor. 12:2-4) may well support the view that Paul himself was familiar with the practice of merkabah mysticism,[47]

41. For fuller detail see A. F. Segal, "Heavenly Ascent in Hellenistic Judaism, Early Christianity, and their Environment," *ANRW* II, 23/2, 1980, 1352-68.

42. See particularly Meeks (n. 24), 110-11, 120-25, 147-49, 156-59, 206-9, 241-44; idem, "Moses as God and King," *Religions in Antiquity: Essays in Memory of E. R. Goodenough*, ed. J. Neusner, 1968, 354-71.

43. Modern interest in merkabah mysticism as a feature of second temple Judaism derives chiefly from G. G. Scholem, *Major Trends in Jewish Mysticism,* 1941, reprint 1961, esp. 42-44.

44. J. Strugnell, "The Angelic Liturgy at Qumran," *Vetus Testamentum* Supplements 7, 1959, 318-45. See further C. Rowland, "The Visions of God in Apocalyptic Literature," *JSJ* 10, 1979, 137-54. In a paper delivered at the SNTS Conference in Leuven, Belgium, 1982, H. C. Kee argued that Joseph and Asenath stands within the merkabah mystical tradition of Judaism ("The Socio-Cultural Setting of Joseph and Asenath").

45. Rowland (n. 38), 94-103, though unfortunately he fails to ask whether similarities in such visionary appearances may be due simply to the seer having to draw on a common but inevitably limited stock of imagery deemed appropriate to describe glorious heavenly beings. See also R. Bauckham, "The Worship of Jesus in Apocalyptic Christianity," *NTS* 27, 1981 (322-41), 323-27.

46. See also J. A. Bühner, *Der Gesandte und sein Weg im 4. Evangelium,* 1977, 353-62. In his otherwise valuable exploration of the historical context of the fourth Gospel, Wengst (n. 3) unfortunately ignores this whole dimension almost entirely—taking note of Meeks only in passing and dismissing Bühner in a footnote (17, n. 24).

47. J. W. Bowker, " 'Merkabah' Visions and the Visions of Paul," *JSS* 16, 1971, 157-73: ". . . Paul practised *merkabah* contemplation as an ordinary consequence of his highly extended Pharisaic training" (172).

and the vision of John the seer (Rev. 1:13-16) has some striking points of contact with the earlier visions of Ezekiel 1 and of Daniel (Dan. 7; 10:5-6).[48] As for the rabbis, there is strong evidence that Johanan ben Zakkai, who played the leading role in initially reestablishing rabbinic Judaism at Jabneh, was himself greatly interested in the chariot chapter of Ezekiel 1 and probably practiced meditation on it (Tos. Hag. 2:1 and parallels).[49] More striking is the tradition about the four sages who "entered the garden *(pardes)*" (Tos. Hag. 2:3-4 and parallels). As most agree, the tradition probably refers in a veiled way to a vision of the chariot throne of God. This is confirmed by such fuller information as we have about these rabbis.[50] One of them, Elisha ben Abuyah, is remembered as an arch-heretic, because in his vision of heaven he mistook the glorious figure sitting on a great throne (Metatron) as a second power in heaven—thus denying the unity of God (b. Hag. 15a; III Enoch 16); one of the starting points for this "two powers" heresy seems to have been speculation on the plural thrones in Dan. 7:9.[51] There is also a tradition regarding another of the four, the famous rabbi Akiba, in which he is rebuked for his speculation as to the occupant of the second throne in Dan. 7:9 (b. Hag. 14a; b. Sanh. 38b).

Third, we know that there were already strong reactions against some of these tendencies in apocalyptic and merkabah speculation. Sir. 3:18-25 can be readily understood as an exhortation to refrain from speculations involving visionary experiences.[52] And IV Ezra 8:20f. seems to be directed against claims to be able to see and describe God's throne.[53] In specifically Christian circles we may recall the strong warnings against angel worship in Col. 2:18 and Hebrews 1–2,[54] and the early churches' hesitation over granting too much authority to the book of Revelation. Similarly, the rabbinic polemic against angelology probably goes back to our period,[55] there are explicit cautionary notes concerning the chariot chapter in the Mishnah (m. Hag. 2:1; m. Meg. 4:10), and the apostasy of Elisha ben Abuyah is a notorious fact elsewhere in rabbinic tradition.[56] We may also note how frequently subsequent rabbinic

48. C. Rowland, "The Vision of the Risen Christ in Rev 1,13ff.: The Debt of an Early Christology to an Aspect of Jewish Angelology," *JTS* 31, 1980, 1-11.

49. See J. Neusner, *A Life of Yohanan ben Zakkai,* [2]1970, 134-40; Gruenwald (n. 38), 75-86; Rowland (n. 38), 282-305. Halperin (n. 39), 107-40, is more skeptical.

50. Gruenwald (n. 38), 86-92; Rowland (n. 38), 306-40. Halperin (n. 39), 89-92, disputes the link to merkabah mysticism.

51. See A. F. Segal, *The Powers in Heaven: Early Rabbinic Reports about Christianity and Gnosticism,* 1977, particularly 33-67, 148-49.

52. Gruenwald (n. 38), 17-18.

53. Rowland (n. 38), 54-55.

54. See also Bauckham (n. 45).

55. P. S. Alexander, "The Targumim and Early Exegesis of 'Sons of God' in Gen 6," *JJS* 23, 1972, 60-71; see also J. Goldin, " 'Not by Means of an Angel and Not by Means of a Messenger,' " *Religions in Antiquity* (n. 42), 412-24.

56. See Rowland (n. 38), 331-39.

polemic against the *minim* consists in a defense of monotheism, the unity of God.[57]

5.3. All this evidence points strongly to a threefold conclusion. (1) There was evidently considerable interest in the possibility of gaining heavenly knowledge through visions and heavenly ascents in the period between the two Jewish revolts. (2) This interest is reflected in the fourth Gospel as well as in our other sources from this period. (3) There were various degrees of misgiving about and hostility to this interest as too speculative and dangerous among both Christians and the rabbis.

6.

The main question which remains for us therefore is: Does an awareness of *this* context, of these crosscurrents in Jewish and Christian thinking during the period in which the fourth Gospel was probably written, help us to make clearer sense of the Johannine distinctives? If we return again to the Gospel itself, we should now be in a better position to appreciate some of John's finer points as he seeks to promote faith in Jesus as the Christ, the Son of God, to hear more of the nuances which a first-century reader would have been expected to observe. We will have time to note only a few key examples.

6.1. The prologue ends with the highest claim for the revelatory significance of Jesus: "No one has ever seen God; the only Son/God . . . has made him known" (1:18). True knowledge of God comes through only one—Jesus, the incarnate Logos. The reader is probably intended to bear this blunt assertion in mind when he comes to the next climax of christological confession—the exchange with Nathanael (1:47-51).[58] The train of thought is at first puzzling, but it gains invaluable illumination from the background sketched out above. In mystical thought "Israel" is taken to mean "he that sees" or "he that sees God" (as often in Philo).[59] Nathanael is presented as "a genuine Israelite," who has begun to believe in Jesus ("rabbi, Son of God, King of Israel"—1:49). But Jesus replies that he will see more than that—a vision just like that of the first Israel (Jacob—Gen. 28:12), where the central feature will be the Son of Man mediating between heaven and earth (1:51).[60] For no one else has seen God—not

---

57. See the texts collected by R. T. Herford, *Christianity in Talmud and Midrash*, 1966, 291-307.

58. Cf. M. de Jonge, *Jesus: Stranger from Heaven and Son of God*, 1977, 83: "1,19-50 stands between 1,18 and 1,51, both dealing with the heavenly status of the One to whom all the designations in the intermediate section point in their own way."

59. See references in vol. X of the Loeb edition of *Philo*, p. 334, note; J. Z. Smith, "The Prayer of Joseph," *Religions in Antiquity* (n. 42), 265-68.

60. Cf. H. Odeberg, *The Fourth Gospel*, 1929, 33-40; Dodd (n. 23), 245-46; N. A. Dahl,

Moses (1:17; cf. Ex. 33:20; Deut. 4:12), and not even Israel. The true Israelite is thus encouraged to "see" that all God's self-revelation now comes to focus in and through Jesus (1:18, 51); God can only be seen to the extent that one sees him in and through (the revelation of) Christ.

John 1 links with John 3 in that another sympathetic Jew (3:2) needs similar instruction. Though "a teacher of Israel" (3:9), Nicodemus has no idea how one can "see the kingdom of God," how it is possible to "enter the heavenly realm" (3:3, 5).[61] Such knowledge cannot be attained by an ascent to heaven—"*no one* has ascended into heaven"(3:13). This sweeping assertion can hardly be other than a polemic against current beliefs in the possibility of such heavenly ascents, through contemplation on the divine chariot or otherwise.[62] Such knowledge of heavenly things is possible *only* for him who *de*scended from heaven, the Son of Man (3:12-13). Mention of Moses in the following verse and the return to the same theme in 3:31-36 ("he who comes from above is above all") effectively distances this Son of Man from any competing claims about the heavenly commissions of Moses and John the Baptist (cf. 1:6, 17). Not even Moses ascended to heaven, and the Baptist remains rootedly "of the earth."[63] True knowledge of heaven comes only from Christ, he who is from above and bears witness to what he (alone) has seen there.[64]

In John 6 the narrative moves with fine dramatic sense from the enthusiastic recognition of Jesus as "the prophet who is to come into the world" (6:14), the prophet like Moses who could be asked to repeat the miracle of manna (6:31), to the point where many of his own disciples take offense (6:60f., 66). What causes the offense is the way in which the category of prophet is transcended and left behind: to speak of Jesus as "him whom God sent" (6:29) is only adequate if by that phrase is meant "sent from heaven," without implication of any previous ascent; his subsequent ascent is to "where he was before," to his place of origin (6:62). Moses too is pushed to one side (6:32). The manna miracle

---

"The Johannine Church and History," in *Current Issues in New Testament Interpretation,* Festschrift O. A. Piper, ed. W. Klassen and G. F. Snyder, 1962, 136, notes that "in the Haggadah, Genesis 28,12, like other visionary texts, is often combined with Daniel 7 and Ezekiel 1"; P. Borgen, "God's Agent in the Fourth Gospel," *Religions in Antiquity* (n. 42), 145-46.

61. In John the kingdom of God = "the heavenly realm on high to which the divine envoy leads (cf. 14:3; 12:26; 17:24)"—R. Schnackenburg, *The Gospel according to St John,* I, 1968, 366f.

62. Odeberg (n. 60), 72-98; Meeks (n. 24), 295-301; F. J. Moloney, *The Johannine Son of Man,* 1976, ²1978, 54-57; A. F. Segal, "Ruler of this World: Attitudes about Mediator Figures and the Importance of Sociology for Self-Definition," *Jewish and Christian Self-Definition* (n. 32), 245-68, esp. 255f.

63. Cf. Targum Neofiti on Deut. 30:12, cited below in section 7.2.

64. Cf. Meeks (n. 5), 52-57, though to insist that "the one born from above/from the spirit" can *only* be the Son of Man, Jesus (53), is overscrupulous. See also J. H. Neyrey, "John III—a Debate over Johannine Epistemology and Christology," *NovT* 23, 1981, 115-27.

does not exalt Moses, as the Jews assumed;[65] that model of divine mediation (cf. Deut. 18:18) is inadequate to express the significance of Jesus. The direct communication from God promised by Isa. 54:13 is now a reality in Jesus (not the Torah); he is the yardstick by which all claims to knowledge from God must be tested, for only he has seen the Father (John 6:45-46).[66] Thus the experience which mediates eternal life is believing recognition that Jesus is himself from God, the living bread which came down from heaven, the life from God incarnate in Jesus (6:35-58).

Finally, we might note in chs. 7 and 12 some indication that John's constituents were aware of wider speculations within Judaism about the Messiah's origin and end. Some thought simply in terms of Davidic descent and birth at Bethlehem (7:42); others, who claim that no one knows where the Christ comes from (7:27), may thereby allude to the sort of speculation we find in the Similitudes of Enoch, in IV Ezra and II Baruch, about the hiddenness of the Messiah in the divine purpose (in heaven? I Enoch 48:6-7; 62:7; IV Ezra 7:28; 12:32; 13:26, 32, 52; II Bar. 29:3; 39:7).[67] So too the crowd's opinion "that the Christ remains forever" (John 12:34) may well reflect the sort of speculation that various heroes of the past had been translated or apotheosized to heaven, in some cases at least without tasting death (Enoch, Elijah, Abel?, Moses?, Ezra),[68] or (less likely) the targumic tradition which found in Isa. 9:5's phrase "everlasting Father" a reference to the eternal existence of the Messiah.[69] The fourth evangelist does not respond directly to such queries. He simply drives on single-mindedly toward the climax of each of these sections (8:48-59; 12:44-50), in which the emphasis on the continuity between the Father and the Son transcends all such speculations and leaves them behind.

These examples must suffice to show how central it is for John that *Jesus is from above,* and because he is from above, *he brings and embodies the truth,* the true knowledge of God and of heavenly things.

6.2. What is the fourth evangelist trying to do in all this? Clearly he is in touch with something at least of the range of theological reflection about God, about God's favored servants, about the means of gaining heavenly knowledge, particularly through ascending to heaven—the sort of speculation, in fact, which we know was current toward the end of the first century. Some of this reflection he merely acknowledges in passing; some he makes use of. He

---

65. Cf. particularly G. Vermes, " 'He is the Bread': Targum Neofiti Exodus 16,15," *Post-Biblical Jewish Studies,* 1975, 139-46.

66. See particularly P. Borgen, *Bread from Heaven, NovT* Supplements 10, 1965, esp. 150-54.

67. De Jonge (n. 58), 90-91.

68. See above, section 5.2 and n. 40; cf. Barrett (n. 13), 427.

69. See particularly B. McNeil, "The Quotation at John 12,34," *NovT* 19, 1977, 22-33.

maintains the Christian claim to the messiahship of Jesus without debating all the questions being discussed. The language of heavenly ascent and descent is taken over for his own purposes. One of his chief categories, Jesus as the one sent from God, is an elaboration of a familiar prophetic category—the prophet as the agent of God.[70] But clearly he also sees Jesus as transcending such categories as "prophet" and "king" and even "Messiah."[71] Clearly he wants to say more—much more. What precisely is this "more?" And why does it bring the wrath of "the Jews" upon the Christian believers?

The answer most probably is bound up with these points that John has taken such care to emphasize so much, those claims which prove so contentious to "the Jews." One is John's claim of a *heavenly origin* for Jesus the Messiah, a heavenly origin which goes back to the beginning of time. Jesus is not one whose claims on our attention derive from an ascent to heaven; they derive rather from the fact that he descended from heaven. The other is John's claim for *a closeness of continuity* between Father and Son which is more than simply identity of will or function: the Son is so like, so close to the Father, that we can even speak of some kind of identity of being (he makes himself God; he and the Father are one).

The importance of these points receives striking confirmation when we compare the findings of the two studies which, more than any other in recent years, have succeeded in setting the fourth Gospel's christology within the historical context of late first-century Judaism. In his ground-breaking investigation of the background to John's christology, W. A. Meeks recognized one major point of distinctiveness: the Johannine "pattern of *descent/ascent* of a heavenly messenger has no direct parallel in the Moses traditions (of Jewish and Samaritan theology)."[72] Subsequently Meeks also conceded de Jonge's criticism that "Jesus' kingship and his prophetic mission are both redefined in terms of the *unique relationship* between Son and Father, as portrayed in the fourth Gospel."[73]

The other most thorough recent investigation of the background of the fourth Gospel's christology, by J. A. Bühner, highlights—by failing to explain—precisely the same two points. He attempts to root the idea of the Son's preexistence in the *Berufungsvision* of the prophet, interpreted in the light of the fact that the same commissioning formula (God sent) is used also of angelic messengers.[74] But the idea of Jesus as a glorious angel, even an angel like the figure of Ezek. 8:2 or Jaoel in the Apocalypse of Abraham, is simply not present

---

70. See particularly Bühner (n. 46), part three.
71. See particularly the two essays on these three titles by de Jonge (n. 58), chs. III and IV.
72. Meeks (n. 24), 297.
73. De Jonge (n. 58), 52; Meeks (n. 10), 173.
74. Note also the important earlier study of the question from this aspect by Borgen (n. 60).

in John:[75] In 1:51 the Son of Man seems to be of a different order from "the angels of God"; and the polemic of 3:13 seems likewise intended precisely to distance Jesus, the Son of Man, from such visionary ascents.[76] The commissioning formula is too narrow a base to sustain such a thesis. John's language almost certainly grew out of this kind of talk of divine commissioning of the prophet, but his christology is neither contained in nor explained by it—particularly, once again, his emphasis on a *preexistence* that is precosmic (as in 8:25 and 17:5), or his emphasis on a *unity* between Father and Son (as in 1:18 and 10:30) which goes far beyond the identity of sender and sent on the *šālîaḥ* model.

The very fact that John moves beyond such background parallels at just these points strengthens the impression given by passages like those examined above (6:1), that it is precisely these two points which John wishes to emphasize. In presenting Jesus as the Messiah, the Son of God who is also the Son of Man, the fourth evangelist wants to persuade his readers of *a heavenly origin* for Jesus the Messiah which goes back to the beginning of time, and of *a closeness of continuity* between Father and Son which is more than simply identity of will or function. From where then does he derive these emphases? Our task remains incomplete unless we can clarify the source of these key Johannine distinctives.

In fact, the fourth evangelist himself probably gives us the decisive clue, in the prologue. The prologue seems to be intended to provide a category or model, that of Wisdom or Logos,[77] in terms of which the reader can (and should) understand the christology of the whole.[78] In the final stage of our attempt to illuminate the Johannine distinctives in the light of John's historical context we shall focus therefore on John's Wisdom christology.

---

75. Possible parallels like 11QMelch (?) and the Prayer of Joseph hardly provide encouragement for the thesis. Other examples of descending angels (collected by C. H. Talbert, "The Myth of a Descending-Ascending Redeemer in Mediterranean Antiquity," *NTS* 22, 1975-76, 422-26, and *What is a Gospel? The Genre of the Canonical Gospels*, 1977, 57-61) are only "short-term visitors."

76. According to 1:51 ascent precedes descent even in the case of the angels of God. Both Bühner (n. 46) and P. Borgen, "Some Exegetical Traditions as Background for the Son of Man Sayings in John's Gospel (John 3,13-14 and Context)," *L'Évangile de Jean* (n. 2), 243-58, argue that the fourth evangelist's language implies a *previous* ascent, to "become" the Son of Man, prior to his descent as Son of Man (in Borgen's case, an "ascent" in preexistence). But this forces too much upon the language, and throws the Johannine christology into confusion (the Logos "ascends" to become the Son of Man?!); cf. Barrett (n. 13), 213.

77. Wisdom and Logos are virtually synonymous so far as our present inquiry is concerned; see Dunn (n. 10), index under "Word and Wisdom."

78. I find it impossible to regard the prologue of John's Gospel as redactional (i.e., added after the fourth evangelist put the Gospel into its present form); the themes of the prologue are too closely integrated into the Gospel as a whole and are so clearly intended to introduce these themes that such a conclusion is rendered implausible.

7.

Does the Wisdom christology of the prologue explain these points of distinctiveness which our religionsgeschichtliche investigation has brought to the fore?

7.1. It is often assumed that the Wisdom/Logos motifs are more or less confined within the prologue, and so are without relevance to the rest of the Gospel. On the contrary, however, language and imagery fron the Wisdom/Logos tradition occur repeatedly in the fourth Gospel, as R. E. Brown in particular has shown.[79] These include, not least, the idea of being sent or descending from heaven, as in 3:13 (the nearest parallels are in Wisd. 9:16-17; Bar. 3:29; 1 Enoch 42—both descent and ascent),[80] and the "I am" statements, which can be paralleled both in first person singular speech (Prov. 8 and Sir. 24) and in content (e.g. light—Wisd. 7:26, 29; food and drink—Sir. 24:19-22; shepherd—Philo, *Agr.* 51; *Mut.* 116).[81] Most important of all, it is only in the Wisdom/Logos tradition of the Jewish background that we have anything really close to the synthesis of Johannine conceptuality—a Wisdom/Logos which is distinct from all other potential intermediaries, angelic or human, precisely by virtue of *its precosmic existence with God* (e.g. Prov. 8:27-30; Sir. 24:9; Wisd. 9:9), and precisely by virtue of *its close identity with God* (e.g. Ps. 33:6; Wisd. 7:25; Philo, *Opif.* 24; *Sac.* 64). The point of distinctiveness being that Wisdom/Logos is *not* a heavenly being over against God, but is *God himself, God in his self-manifestation,* God insofar as he may be known by the human mind.[82] It is precisely for this reason, because the Son is the incarnate *Logos,* God in his "knowability" and "visibility," that the *Son* can say, "He that has seen *me* has seen the *Father*" (12:45; 14:9). In a similar way, the working out of the "glory" motif of the prologue (1:14) includes the otherwise puzzling 12:41 ("Isaiah saw his glory and spoke of him"), where Isaiah's vision of the *Lord* sitting on his throne (Isa. 6) is interpreted as a vision of *Christ's* glory—presumably because for the fourth evangelist Christ is to be identified not with one of the seraphim,

---

79. Brown (n. 24), esp. cxxii-cxxv and index under "Wisdom."

80. To reject a Wisdom background at this point on the grounds that the language parallels are not close enough (the usual objection) is to refuse to allow the fourth evangelist any creativity of his own—an implausible evaluation, considering the distinctive character of the Gospel. Closer parallels, as in later Gnosticism, probably imply dependence—on John! Since the Gnostic Sophia myth is also dependent on the *Jewish* Wisdom tradition (G. W. Macrae, "The Jewish Background of the Gnostic Sophia Myth," *NovT* 12, 1970, 86-101), it is wiser to conclude that the descent/ascent motif in its Johannine form is a creation of the Johannine school itself, formed precisely by the conviction that the full significance of Jesus could be grasped only in terms of the identification of Christ as Wisdom.

81. Cf. particularly E. Schweizer, "Zum religionsgeschichtlichen Hintergrund der 'Sendungsformel' Gal 4,4f.; Röm 8,3f.; Joh 3,16f.; 1Joh 4,9," *Beiträge zur Theologie des Neuen Testaments,* 1970, 83-95. On 8:58 see esp. Lindars, "Discourse and Tradition" (n. 15), 96.

82. See my *Christology* (n. 10), 168-76, 217-30.

as in some later Christian thought, but as *the shekinah of God,* the visible presence of God himself.[83]

The key then to understanding the Johannine distinctives in his presentation of Jesus as Messiah, Son of God, and Son of Man, is to see these titles primarily as *an elaboration of the initial explicit identification of Jesus as the incarnate Wisdom/Logos*—an identification taken over certainly from earlier Christian tradition,[84] but expounded in John's own distinctive fashion. It is this which alone satisfactorily explains John's repeated emphasis on the direct continuity between this Jesus and God from the beginning of time. The revelation which Jesus brings seems to be so limited, precisely because what he reveals is not information but, quite simply, God, that he is God in his self-revelation.[85] *This* is what it means for the fourth evangelist to confess Jesus as the Messiah, the Son of God. It is this faith which he wants to win or sustain in his readers.

7.2. The coherence of this exegesis (on internal grounds) is confirmed by the fact that this understanding of John's claims regarding Christ provides an excellent explanation for the fierceness of the rabbinic opposition to the Jesus of the fourth Gospel. As we have already noted (section 5.2 above), the Jabnean rabbis were at least to some degree engaged in a similar interaction with these other (apocalyptic and mystical) strands of Judaism to that which we find in the fourth Gospel. And in a similar way they were both drawing *on* that broader tradition, *and,* over the period between the two Jewish revolts, beginning to distance themselves from unacceptable elements within it.

The difference was that while the Christians were focusing what they wanted to say on *Jesus,* the rabbis were focusing on the *law.* Clear hints of this fact, so abundantly obvious from rabbinic sources, occur at several points in John (7:49; 9:28-29; 12:34; 19:7). Already within the Wisdom tradition a firm equation between Wisdom and Torah had been established (Sir. 24:23, 25; Bar. 3:36–4:4). And the rabbis probably took up and developed this equation just as the Christians were developing the identification of Wisdom with Christ. One indication may lie in the fact that Deut. 30:12-14, which the Baruch passage just cited referred to Wisdom, was interpreted by Targum Neofiti with reference to Moses and the law: "The law is not in the heavens, that one should say: Would that we had one like Moses the prophet who would go up to heaven and fetch it for us. . . ." And certainly we can have little doubt that the allusions to "the

---

83. Cf. Dahl (n. 60), 131-32. On the shekinah as the immediate presence of God, see A. M. Goldberg, *Untersuchungen über die Vorstellung von der Schekhinah in der frühen rabbinischen Literatur,* 1969; E. E. Urbach, *The Sages: their Concepts and Beliefs,* [2]1979, ch. III.

84. See below, section 9.2.

85. Cf. E. Haenchen, " 'Der Vater, der mich gesandt hat,' " *NTS* 9, 1962-63, 208-16, reprinted in *Gott und Mensch,* 1965, 68-77, esp. 71-73; Wengst (n. 3), 101-4. My formulation alludes, of course, to Bultmann's famous comment: "Jesus as the revealer of God reveals nothing but that he is the revealer" (*Theology of the New Testament* II, ET 1955, 66).

gift of God" and "living water" in John 4:10 have in mind the rabbinic readiness to use such phrases of the Torah.[86] In effect, what the Christians were claiming for Christ, the rabbis were claiming for the law. And quite soon (we do not know how soon) they began to speak of the law as preexistent[87]— just as Christians had begun to speak of Christ in the same way.

More important still, what we see reflected in the fourth Gospel is the debate between Christian and rabbi at a crucial stage in these mutual developments. On the one hand, we see the fourth evangelist disputing the rabbinic exaltation of the law: the law is *not* the climax of God's revelation, *Christ* is the climax; the law bears witness to *him* (1:45; 5:39, 46). Beside the fullness of divine revelation in Christ, the law is defective (1:17). Compared with the climactic revelation of Christ, the revelation given through Moses, Sinai and the whole wilderness period is deficient (3:9-15; 5:37-47; 6:35-58; 7:14-24; 10:34-6).[88] The Wisdom of God is present in the Torah, but present in fullness only in Christ. Christ, *not* the Torah, is the embodiment of divine Wisdom, the incarnation of God's Word.

On the other hand, at one and the same time, we see reflected the *rabbinic* opposition to the *Christian* claim regarding Christ. As the fourth evangelist protests against the rabbinic exaltation of the law (and by implication, the rabbinic equation of Wisdom with the law), so the rabbis protest against the Christian identification of Wisdom as Christ. "The Jews" recognized that so to identify Christ with Wisdom/Logos, the self-expression of God, was to make Jesus equal with God (5:18), was to make him not simply an angel or heavenly figure (like Enoch), but *God* (10:33). The equation of Wisdom with the Torah was attractive as an alternative, presumably not least because it posed no such threat to Jewish monotheism. But "the Jews" could not understand John's christology except as a severe threat to the unity of God—just as John no doubt considered their over-exaltation of Moses and the law a threat to the claims of the revelation given in and through Christ. Evidently then, in rabbinic eyes, the fourth evangelist and his community/school belonged with those others within Judaism who were speculating too unguardedly (not least about the vision of Dan. 7), on the basis of revelation they claimed to have received, and who, in consequence, were endangering the primary axiom of Judaism—the oneness of God.

In short, what we see reflected in the fourth Gospel is a three- (or even

---

86. Barrett (n. 13), 233.

87. Texts are gathered in Billerbeck II, 353-55. See Dunn (n. 10), ch. VI, n. 43.

88. See particularly the richly seminal study of Dahl (n. 60), here p. 133; Meeks (n. 24), 287-91, 299-301; idem, "The Divine Agent and his Counterfeit in Philo and the Fourth Gospel," *Aspects of Religious Propaganda in Judaism and Early Christianity,* ed. E. Schüssler Fiorenza, 1976 (43-76), 56-58; de Jonge (n. 58), 56-58; and exposition with notes, section 6.1 above.

four-)way dialogue—the fourth evangelist in dialogue with broader strands of apocalyptic and mystical Judaism, with the rabbis of Jabneh, and possibly with other Christians too.[89] The fourth evangelist draws on this larger heritage, both Christian and Jewish, as the others do in their own way. And, under the inspiration of the Spirit of Jesus (14:26; 16:13-15), and in debate with these alternative theologies of revelation and salvation, he presents his own faith centered on Jesus the Christ, the Son of God.

8.

8.1. This essay has attempted to take the first step toward clarifying the Gospel of John in its relation to the gospel particularly as presented by the other three evangelists. As a first step it seemed necessary to try to understand John in its own terms, to seek to clarify the distinctive features of the fourth Gospel's presentation of Christ by situating it as far as possible within the context in which and in relation to which it was written. Over against those who have left out that first step and have sought to understand John's christology *too quickly* as an expression of later orthodoxy (or later heresy) or in relation to the historical Jesus *per se,* it is important for exegesis to insist that John must first be allowed to be itself before its relation to other expressions of the gospel can be properly and fully explored. Insofar as we have been able to fulfill even that modest aim within the scope of this essay, we can now attempt to draw out the most obvious and potentially important conclusions, before finally reflecting briefly on the next step, for which we have only been able to prepare.

8.2. One immediate result is in effect quite *a major shift in perspective.* The apparent dominance of the Son of God category over the initial Logos category is misleading. Rather, the fourth evangelist evidently intended what is in fact the much vaguer title (Son of God)[90] to serve as a vehicle for his basically Wisdom christology. The fourth evangelist really did intend his Gospel to be read through the window of the prologue. The *Son of God* reveals nothing other than that he is the *Wisdom of God,* God in his encounter with mankind. The late first-century Jewish desire for knowledge of heavenly things is met in Jesus, because he is the Logos of God, God insofar as he may be known and seen by mankind: whoever has seen the Son has seen the Father (12:45; 14:9).

To put it another way, by reading the Father-Son language in the light of the Wisdom/Logos prologue, the range of options possible in the title Son

---

89. Cf. Segal (n. 62), 256. On the intra-Christian dialogue see above, n. 17; also de Jonge (n. 58), 99.
90. Dunn (n. 10), 14-16.

of God is narrowed dramatically. Over against any who might be content with a prophet christology, or a merely Davidic Messiah christology, John insists unreservedly on a Wisdom christology. In modern terms, which echo John's to a significant degree, the fourth evangelist insists that a christology "from below" is inadequate (a christology of inspiration or mystical ascent or apotheosis). The meaning of Christ cannot be expressed except as a christology "from above." Over against any who might offer an alternative theology of revelation and redemption (through Torah or angel?) he insists that Christ alone is able to reveal God, to bring the true knowledge of God, to mediate the fullness of his grace (1:16-18). And that can only be because he is the Wisdom of God incarnate, the fullest possible embodiment in human flesh of God in his outreach to this world.

8.3. It follows that in a vitally important sense, for the fourth evangelist, *theo*logy (in the narrower sense) is more important than *christ*ology.[91] We only let John be John if we recognize that the primary debate the fourth evangelist engaged in with the rabbis was actually a debate about *monotheism.* The fourth Gospel belongs, in religionsgeschichtliche terms, to that diverse body of late first-century and early second-century Jewish piety and literature that explored the boundaries of earlier conceptualities of deity and revelation within a framework of monotheism. Set against that context, what we see is John in effect claiming that Christian revelation could not be expressed without understanding Jesus in full-blown Wisdom terms, without, in that sense, redefining the basic category of Jewish monotheism itself. The fourth evangelist had no intention of breaking or moving out from that category. Precisely because Wisdom/Logos rather than Son of God is his primary category, he remains a monotheist—for while "Son" is more fitted to express distinction and relation (as Athanasius realized), "Logos" by definition better expresses sameness and continuity.[92] But "the Jews" focused more on the talk of sonship and heard it as a blasphemy against the unity of God. At this point the fourth Gospel becomes a valuable witness not only to the development of early Christian theology, but also to the tensions within late first-century Judaism, important background for understanding the subsequent rabbinic rejection of the two-powers heresy.

This insight enables us to sharpen our initial criticisms both of subsequent Christian interpretation of John in relation to Nicene orthodoxy, and of the earlier religionsgeschichtliche interpretation of John (section 2 above). On the one hand, the fourth Gospel is not speaking to a trinitarian debate about the

---

91. Cf. C. K. Barrett, "Christocentric or Theocentric? Observations on the Theological Method of the Fourth Gospel" (1976), in idem, *Essays on John,* 1982, 1-18.

92. Hence the ambiguity between *lógos* = unuttered thought, and *logos* = uttered thought, for *logos* denotes precisely the continuity between the same thought in its unexpressed and expressed forms. Cf. the ambiguity of Philo, *Sac.* 80-83; *Ebr.* 157; *Som.* 1.102-14.

interior relationships within the Godhead. It is speaking to a discussion about monotheism, advocating the necessity of identifying Jesus with God insofar as God makes himself known to mankind. Thus, for example, to understand John's frequent talk of the Son's obedience to the Father as an assertion of the Son's *subordination* to the Father is anachronistic and not quite to the point.[93] It would be more accurate to say that the fourth evangelist's intention was to emphasize the *continuity* between Father and Son, the continuity of Wisdom/Logos: he is doing the same work as God (5:17); his hand and the Father's hand are one (10:28-29); he speaks with the authority of God (14:10).[94] The issue here is not so much one of *relation* between Father and Son, as of the validity of the Logos-Son's *revelation* of the Father.[95] If the fourth Gospel is interpreted primarily as an exposition of the relationship between the Father and the Son, it becomes difficult to avoid slipping over into a form of bitheism or tritheism— as popular treatments purporting to expound the orthodox trinitarian faith often demonstrate. Rather, the fourth evangelist's contribution to that subsequent stage of Christian reflection is that *by his presentation of the Logos-Son he established monotheism as the primary framework for further thought.* That presumably is why the next main stage in the intra-Christian discussion was debate concerning the modalist option. And, more important, that is why when "Logos" finally gave way to "Son" as the primary category of christology, Christian belief in the oneness of God was not threatened—because the earlier Logos christology pioneered by John had already secured the base of Christian monotheism. From John onward, to understand the Son other than as the Logos-Son is to misunderstand Christianity.[96]

On the other hand, by thus letting John be John we can recognize more clearly that both "sides" of the earlier religionsgeschichtliche investigation are partly right and partly wrong. Meeks, Borgen, Bühner, etc. are right in seeing late first-century Jewish thought as John's primary historical context; but they have not given enough weight to the significance of Wisdom/Logos as John's dominant leitmotif.[97] Bultmann and his followers were right insofar as they recognized that the "Wisdom myth" is the decisive extra factor in John's christology; but in interpreting this Wisdom tradition in the light of or as a precursor to the Gnostic

93. Cf. e.g. the "subordination" of the uttered *logos* to the expressed *logos* in Philo, *Abr.* 83.

94. Cf. Käsemann (n. 8), 25: "John's peculiarity is that he knows only one single dogma, the christological dogma of the unity of Jesus with the Father"; and Appold in n. 95 below.

95. Cf. particularly M. L. Appold, *The Oneness Motif in the Fourth Gospel,* WUNT 1, 1976, 18-34: "John's christology leaves no room for even incipient subordination" (22)! I would thus want to qualify Barrett's otherwise important counter-emphasis, " 'The Father is Greater than I' John 14,28. Subordinationist Christology in the New Testament" (1974), in *Essays* (n. 91), 19-36.

96. See my debate with Maurice Wiles in *Theology* 85, 1982, 92-98, 324-32, 360-61.

97. Bühner (n. 46) dismisses the possibility of Wisdom influence on John's christology in far too casual a manner (87-103, 411); but Borgen (n. 60), 146, and Meeks (n. 5), 59, 61, recognize its importance without giving it primary weight.

redeemer myth, they distorted the picture even more. The key is to recognize that
what John draws on is the Wisdom tradition *within* Judaism—where Wis-
dom/Logos is not understood as a divine being distinct from God, interpreted as
an "intermediary being" between God in his lofty transcendence and his world,[98]
but rather where Wisdom is understood precisely as the expression of God's
immanence.[99] It is precisely because the incarnate Logos has made God visible in
his immanence that the heavenly ascent or mystical vision is unnecessary,[100] just
as it is precisely because the immanent God has made himself known in the man
Jesus that the equation of Wisdom with Torah is inadequate.

In short, however we may think John's Logos-Son christology stretches
monotheism, it is only when we understand John as an expression of Christian
monotheism that we understand it aright.

9.

Finally, we must ask what light our findings throw on the larger questions of
this symposium. Now that we have come to a clearer understanding of John in
its own terms, what corollaries follow for our understanding of John's relation
to the other Gospels? If we now understand better the emphases and motivations
of the Johannine distinctives, what pointers do they provide for the next stage
of an inquiry into the continuities and discontinuities between John and the
earlier tradition on which John draws?

9.1. The most striking point to emerge from our study in this connection
must be *the extent to which the Johannine distinctives have been formulated out
of John's interaction with the other strands of late first-century Judaism.* In
terms of the tradition history of the material incorporated into the fourth Gospel,
it would appear that some of John's key emphases belong (in their Johannine
formulation at least) to the later stages of that tradition history—in particular,
the question of Jesus' origin, John's insistence that Jesus descended from
heaven, and the assertion of Jesus' precosmic existence with God and identity
as Son of God with the Father.

Equally striking, however, is the degree to which these Johannine distinctives mark John off *both* from earlier forms of the Jesus-tradition *and* from its
context within late first-century Judaism. It is *not* the case that John's differences

---

98. W. Bousset and H. Gressmann, *Die Religion des Judentums im späthellenistischen
Zeitalter,* HNT 21, [4]1966, 319.

99. See Dunn (n. 82 above); idem, "Was Christianity a Monotheistic Faith from the
Beginning?", *Scottish Journal of Theology* 35, 1982, 303-36.

100. Contrast Scholem (n. 43), 55: in merkabah mysticism "the idea of the Shekinah and of
God's immanence plays practically no part at all."

from the earliest Jesus-tradition can be explained simply by John's drawing ideas from the contemporary melting pot of religious reflection; John's emphases are distinctive also when set against the broader context of the late first century, and are better explained as John's development of the *earlier Christian tradition.* Nor is it the case, conversely, that John's differences from its historical context are to be explained simply as elements drawn from the earlier Jesus-tradition; the Johannine formulation presupposes too much of the issues and speculations which came to the fore in the late first century, so that if the Johannine distinctives *are* derived from the earlier Christian tradition, they have to be explained as a *development* of that tradition.

In short, if we are to do justice to the Johannine distinctives, we have to see them as a development of the Jesus-tradition designed to express the truth of Jesus as understood within the Johannine circle. It was a development which was actually part of the late first-century exploration of the conceptualities available and appropriate to talk of God's revelation and salvation, and which probably was in the vanguard of that exploration. It was a developing theology which was partly reacting against other strands of that exploration and partly stimulating reaction from others (the rabbis in particular), and which was in process of formulating a distinctive *Christian* theology which would be increasingly unacceptable for the rest of Judaism, being perceived as a denial of the unity of God.

9.2. Clearly, then, more study is required of what precisely is involved in this *development* of the earlier Christian traditions about Jesus. Does such clarification as we have achieved of the later stages of the tradition history of John's material throw any light on the earlier stages?

One thing can be said straightaway. Our findings do not require us to modify in any degree our earlier recognition of the many points of continuity between John and the earlier synoptic tradition (section 3.2 above). On the contrary, the recognition that what we have in John is development of the earlier Christian tradition underscores the importance of these points of continuity. Moreover, we can trace something of the course of the development even of John's distinctives, particularly his Wisdom christology and his emphasis on Christ's preexistence, in the Wisdom christology of Paul and of Hebrews (I Cor. 8:6; Col. 1:15-20; Heb. 1:3-4).[101] Even John's integration of a Wisdom christology (Jesus identified *as* Wisdom) into the Jesus-tradition is paralleled in some degree in the Matthean redaction of Q at three or four points (Matt. 11:19/Luke 7:35; Matt. 11:25-30/Luke 10:21f.; Matt. 23:34-36/Luke 11:49-51; Matt. 23:37-39/Luke 13:34f.).[102] It is not so much the *content* of the fourth evangelist's

101. See Dunn (n. 10), 176-96 and 206-9.
102. See Dunn (n. 10), 197-204. To my bibliography there add M. Hengel, "Jesus als messianischer Lehrer der Weisheit und die Anfänge der Christologie," in *Sagesse et Religion,* 1979 (148-88), 149-60.

distinctive christology which marks him out, then, as the *way* in which he formulates it, as the *degree of development* of the Jesus-tradition which distinguishes the fourth Gospel from the Synoptics—the style of elaborate discourse and self-testimony, with only minimal parallel in the synoptic form of the tradition.

Another striking fact is that the fourth evangelist obviously felt it necessary to retain the format of a *Gospel*. For all its differences from the Synoptics, John is far closer to them than to any other ancient writing (as this symposium has shown). Although it is the discourses of Jesus which are the most elaborated feature of John's Gospel, the evangelist did not elect to present a document consisting solely of the discourses or sayings of the redeemer (we may contrast Gnostic equivalents like the Gospel of Thomas, Thomas the Contender, and Pistis Sophia). Rather he chose, and chose deliberately, to retain the developed discourse material within the framework of a Gospel as laid down by Mark— traditions of Jesus' miracles and teaching building up all the while to the climax of the cross.[103]

All this highlights what in many ways is the most fascinating aspect of the fourth Gospel—the fact that the author(s) felt *both* free toward the Jesus-tradition (the degree of development) *and* bound to it and its Gospel framework at one and the same time. It is this interplay of freedom and constraint—greater freedom than we find in the Synoptics, greater restraint than we find in the Gnostic equivalents—which requires more detailed study. How could John think that such a degree of development was still being true to the word "from the beginning"? Did he exercise sufficient restraint?—the implication that some of the Johannine community went off into a docetic christology (I John 2:19) and I John's increased emphasis on continuity with the original word (I John 1:1; 2:7, 24; 3:11) serve only to sharpen the question.[104] Does the fourth Gospel provide an exemplary case study of how to reexpress the gospel in the different and constantly changing circumstances of a later era while remaining true to the earlier tradition of the gospel—or a cautionary tale? These are some of the issues at stake in a fuller investigation of the actual tradition-historical process, which began with the synoptic-like sayings from the earliest Jesus-tradition scattered throughout the fourth Gospel, and which ended with the elaborate discourses of the fourth Gospel, itself aimed at presenting the gospel to a later audience. Such an investigation would provide an agenda in itself for another symposium. Hopefully we have succeeded in letting John be John, but perhaps the greater challenge is to let John's Gospel be John's Gospel—both *gospel* and *John's* Gospel!

---

103. Cf. Dunn (n. 36), 287, 301f., 307.
104. See particularly Brown (n. 2), 109-23.

The "Memoirs of the Apostles" in Justin

Luise Abramowski

In the extant works of Justin the phrase ἀπομνημονεύματα τῶν ἀποστόλων occurs twice in the *First Apology* (66.3; 67.3) and thirteen times in the *Dialogue* with Trypho, which was written after the *Apology*. To this is to be added *Apol.* 33:5[1] as a verbal allusion.

In the *Apology* the *apomnemoneumata* are identified with the Gospels (66.3), but whether or not the identifying relative clause is a gloss in the text is disputed.[2] Here the *apomnemoneumata* are cited as the source for the Last Supper sayings: "For the apostles in the 'apomnemoneumata,' which they produced (γενομένοις) (and) *which are called Gospels*, have handed down what Jesus ordered them to do. . . ." The identifying relative clause does in fact have the typical form of a gloss—but this assessment is only decisive at first glance since we are, finally, dealing here with a piece of writing addressed to Gentiles. The Gentile, though familiar with the literary term, was not acquainted with the ecclesiastical expression, so there is reason seriously to consider the genuineness of the elucidation. Besides, one may wish to compare *Apol.* 65.1, τοὺς λεγομένους ἀδελφούς; 65.5, οἱ καλούμενοι παρ' ἡμῖν διάκονοι; and *Dial.* 10.2 (in the mouth of Trypho), ἐν τῷ λεγομένῳ εὐαγγελίῳ. The reference to the *apomnemoneumata* in *Apol.* 67.3 is part of the account of the regular worship service: we are told that the *apomnemoneumata* of the apostles or the συγγράμματα of the prophets are read in the gathering (συνέλευσις).

The term occurs in the *Dialogue* in one continuous section which fills only nine pages in Goodspeed's edition, namely in the christological interpretation

---

1. Also cited below.
2. Cf. E. F. Osborn, *Justin Martyr,* BhTH 47, 1973, 124, n. 29. Osborn's book does have a chapter on "the memoirs of the apostles," but about the meaning of this designation and its function in Justin it says very little (see 123 bottom). We read: "The use of this word may be understood from the principle that Justin is an apologist who is writing for Jews and Romans." Hyldahl's essay cited below is not used nor is it mentioned in the bibliography.

of Ps. 21 LXX (22):2-24. In *Dial.* 97.3f. Justin cites Ps. 21:17-19 (a passage he often quotes[3]) and uses the occasion to write out the entire first half of the psalm in the following section (ch. 98) and then to explain it piece by piece (up through ch. 106). Probably ch. 107 on the resurrection also belongs to this exposition; in any case in 107.1 *apomnemoneumata* is used one more time. Bousset, having made the same observations, drew from it the conclusion that Justin here "incorporated an already completed commentary on Ps. 21 into his Dialogue."[4] There is, indeed, no other recognizable formal reason which requires this formulation to indicate the source of the quotations in chs. 100–107 in distinction from the rest of the work. (The assumption of an author other than Justin himself is not necessary.)

Other formulas for New Testament quotations are, for example: *Dial.* 18.1: "short sayings of Jesus"; 18.3: "decree by our new Lawgiver"; and 85.7: "Jesus commanded us" (just before this a long passage from the Old Testament has been quoted as "Scripture"). The statement in *Dial.* 88.3 (referring to the dove at the baptism of Jesus) that "the apostles of this our Christ himself testify" comes close to the title "the memoirs of the apostles" and is an allusion to it. Recently it has again been postulated, for that matter, that Justin worked a self-contained literary unit (chs. 10–29 on the law) into the *Dialogue* (von Campenhausen following Prigent[5]).

If indeed the section on Ps. 21 (22) in the *Dialogue* is originally an independent small composition written by Justin, then of course the question of priority as it relates to the *Apology* and the *Dialogue* as literary wholes no longer applies, for this exegetical-christological treatise may in fact be older than the *Apology*. We are to maintain that Justin did not extend the literary-technical designation of the Gospels as used in the incorporated treatise to the work as a whole (except for the allusion in 88.3). Justin clearly did not deem this necessary for the intention of the whole. And that in turn has to do, perhaps, with the fact that the christological explanation of Ps. 21(22):2-24 in *Dial.* 98–107 was possibly addressed to people other than the Jews (the same applies to *Dial.* 10–29 on the law[6]).

In the short introduction (*Dial.* 98.1) which precedes the long text of the psalm, Justin offers several reasons why he quotes so much of it. The last of these is that Christ thereby "shows that he indeed (ἀληθῶς) became a man who was capable of suffering (ἀντιληπτικὸς παθῶν)." And following the quotation he writes

3. Osborn, op. cit., 102: ". . . Psalm xxii which Justin quotes twenty-six times."

4. W. Bousset, *Jüdisch-christlicher Schulbetrieb in Alexandria und Rome,* 1915, 292.

5. H. von Campenhausen, *The Formation of the Christian Bible,* 1972, 94, n. 174, referring to Prigent, *Justin,* 74f. Bousset postulated the existence of a considerable number of such treatises in the *Dialogue;* see his list, op. cit., 298f.

6. H. von Campenhausen, op. cit.: *Dial.* 10–29 "must originally have been aimed at gnostics and Marcionites."

that the whole psalm refers to Christ, in proof of which Justin now expounds it
(99.1). Jesus' prayer in Gethsemane makes clear that he had "really become a man
capable of suffering (ἀληθῶς παθητὸς ἄνθρωπος γεγένηται)" (99.2). The colon of
v. 3 of the psalm, καὶ οὐκ εἰς ἄνοιαν ἐμοί (Haeuser: "and I have known of it"; more
literally: "and not for lack of understanding in me"[7]), occasions the following train
of thought: it was not from lack of understanding that God asked Adam where he
was, and Cain where Abel was, but he asked these questions to convict each of
those two of what sort he was; and to provide us with knowledge (γνῶσιν) by
recording them. So Christ testified not to a lack of understanding on his part but
to a lack of understanding on the part of those who, refusing to believe that he was
the Christ, thought he would die and like anyone else remain in Hades (99.3). This
last clause seems, christologically, to point in a different direction[8] from the two
clauses about Jesus' capacity for suffering in 98.1 and 99.2. But 100.2 again picks
up the thread of argumentation followed in 98.1: Christ is the first-begotten of God
and before all creatures *and* the son of the patriarchs, since he, having become
incarnate by a virgin of their race, condescended to become a man without
comeliness[9] or honor and subject to suffering (παθητός). Not only is he truly
capable of suffering but he has in fact truly suffered: Jesus' agony (103.8) in
Gethsemane makes us understand that the Father wished his Son to endure these
severe sufferings for us in reality (καὶ ἐν τοιούτοις πάθεσιν ἀληθῶς γεγονέναι) and
prevents us from saying that as Son of God he could not feel (οὐκ ἀντελαμβάνετο)
what was done and inflicted on him. Haeuser already remarked about these
passages that they were directed against the docetism of the Gnostics.[10]

From what we have said so far it is clear that the exegesis of Ps. 21 (22)
in its independent form had an antidocetic tendency. The rejection of God's
supposed ignorance in the account of Paradise and in the story of Cain and Abel
takes us out of the sphere of the merely vaguely antidocetic and into that of the
anti-Gnostic. It is no accident that in the passage in question (100.3) the word
γνῶσις occurs—and knowledge of Scripture is in view; hence the key word is
enlisted in the service of the non-Gnostic interpretation of Scripture.

Over against the Jews Justin had to demonstrate in the *Dialogue* that the
Old Testament had predicted the coming of a Messiah who would *suffer*.
Accordingly, he could easily fit the brief exposition of Ps. 21 (22), which
strongly emphasizes the real suffering of Christ Jesus, hence of the Messiah who
came, into the larger writing with its different objective and front.

7. The RSV (cf. the Luther Bible), following the Hebrew, has "but find no rest."
    8. The clause sounds anti-Jewish and would then be a sign that the text had been worked
over for the purpose of the *Dialogue*. In the original anti-Gnostic form of the text the allusion here
was probably to the Gnostic distinction between Jesus and Christ.
    9. ἀειδής.
    10. *Bibliothek der Kirchenväter*, second series, 33, 170, n. 3.

Now it is worth noting that in this short anti-Gnostic exposition there is repeated reference to the *apomnemoneumata of the apostles,* whereas in the *Apology* the expression occurs only twice. One has to conclude, therefore, in contrast to widely held opinion, that this title was introduced not for apologetic reasons but from anti-Gnostic motives.

In his essay on Hegesippus's *Hypomnemata*[11] Niels Hyldahl presents a section on the term *apomnemoneumata.*[12] In that section he concludes[13] that, though *hypomnemata* and *apomnemoneumata* can both be translated "notes" or "records," they nevertheless refer to two distinct literary categories. In this connection Hyldahl mentions a series of examples of ancient *apomnemoneumata,* beginning with the most famous, Xenophon's *Memorabilia* of Socrates. "Besides, Justin Martyr, as is well known, applied this name to the Gospels. By this means he characterizes them from a literary point of view, since in his day the designation 'Gospel' was still used in hardly any other sense than 'good news,' hence in a non-literary sense."

To this must be added that in Justin the word εὐαγγέλιον occurs three times.

> In *Apol.* 66.3 the *apomnemoneumata* read in the worship services are identified with the Gospels; whether or not the reference comes from Justin, what is meant is clearly the Gospels as written.
> In *Dial.* 10.2 Trypho mentions "the precepts . . . which are marvelous and great" that he knows since he has taken the trouble to read "what you call your Gospel."[14]
> Finally, in the exposition of Ps. 21 (22), in *Dial.* 100.1, it is said of Jesus: ἐν τῷ εὐαγγελίῳ γέγραπται εἰπών, and then follows Matt. 11:27.

If anything, then, Justin is a witness for "Gospel" as book, and Hyldahl's explanation of why Justin speaks more freely of "apomnemoneumata" than of "Gospel" cannot be the correct one.

Hyldahl replied[15] in detail to the objections that were raised in 1954 by Richard Heard against the classification of Justin's *apomnemoneumata* in the literature of memoirs as a literary category. Heard sought, instead, to establish a connection with the verb ἀπομνημονεύω used by Papias. But according to Hyldahl, the verb occurs too frequently in the Christian literature of the second century for that purpose; he refers to the examples in Zahn.[16] Heard also "failed to recognize the unique position that Socrates occupies in the writings of Justin."

---

11. N. Hyldahl, "Hegesipps Hypomnemata," *ST* 14, 1960, 70-113.
12. Ibid., 77-83.
13. Ibid., 78.
14. Justin refers back to this later, *Dial.* 18.1.
15. Op. cit., 79.
16. T. Zahn, *Geschichte des neutestamentlichen Kanons* I/2, 1889, 471-76.

Hyldahl summarizes Zahn's results on memoirs as follows:[17]

It is to Zahn's credit that he treated the different *apomnemoneumata* as a distinct Gattung. Proceeding from the *Memorabilia* of Xenophon, he defines as a literary category that of the "memoirs" of a specific person. The narrator is an eyewitness. The persons in question are "not the heroes of the deed but masters of philosophy" (p. 473). That the narrator is an eyewitness also comes to expression in Justin: the Gospels he used were written by the apostles. *Apomnemoneumata* are neither notes for one's own recollection and use, nor collections of "memoirs" for those who come after—that would be *hypomnemata*—but "memories" of a significant person. This is the main point of departure. In individual instances there is a certain fluidity within this understanding of the category. Xenophon, for instance, also relates matters which not he himself but others experienced, and at one point Justin concedes that it was not just the apostles who wrote the Gospels but also those who followed them.[18] The *apomnemoneumata* of Favorinus, by comparison, occupied an exceptional position because Favorinus was not himself an eyewitness of the things he told about.[19]

Hyldahl had certain objections to the idea that being an eyewitness is an indispensable instrument for the determination of the Gattung. "One cannot simply assume that that which a person remembers was recorded by the same person who experienced them. The essential thing was that one had memories to record at all."[20] Among his literary references and collections of material on ὑπόμνημα and ἀπομνημόνευμα Hyldahl[21] also cites Martin Dibelius on the *apomnemoneumata* in Justin: "An apologetic tendency is operative which is lifting up Christendom into the region of culture. By means of the title 'Memoirs' the gospel books would be classified as literature proper"—a judgment also adopted by von Campenhausen.[22]

This can perhaps be stated in greater detail. In the first place one must remember that there is emphatic reference in general to the *written* character of the Gospels; in the second century this is still anything but self-evident. Secondly, it is surely no accident that Justin chose a literary classification which was otherwise used for "memoirs of a master philosopher." As Pierre Hadot reminds us from another perspective,[23]

17. Op. cit., 79f.
18. *Dial.* 103.8 (cited below).
19. But Favorinus also talks about famous philosophers.
20. This was underscored in the discussion of the present essay by A. Dihle; Xenophon also used literary sources.
21. Op. cit., 82.
22. Dibelius, *From Tradition to Gospel*, ET 1934, 40; von Campenhausen, 184; see also Osborn (n. 2 above).
23. P. Hadot, *Exercices spirituels et philosophie antique*, 1981, 61. See also the chapter on "the true philosophy" in Osborn, which deals with the presentation of biblical proof in Justin.

an entire strand in the Christian tradition [presented Christianity] as a *philosophy*. This assimilation started with the Christian authors of the second century who are called Apologists, particularly Justin. To contrast this philosophy, which in their view was Christianity, with Greek philosophy, they called it "our philosophy" or "barbaric philosophy."[24] Nevertheless they do not regard Christianity as one philosophy among others but as *the* philosophy. That which is scattered and fragmented in Greek philosophy is brought together and systematized in Christian philosophy. In their eyes the Greek philosophers had only particles of the Logos in their possession whereas Christians possessed the very Logos that had incarnated itself in Jesus Christ. If to philosophize means to live in accord with the law of reason, then Christians philosophize when they live in harmony with the law of the divine Logos.

The selection of the classification *apomnemoneumata* for the written Gospels, in my opinion, may well be related to the fact that they embody the thinking of the master of philosophy proper, namely that of Christ. For Justin the earthly Jesus is in fact in essence διδάσκαλος (and a component of Justin's teaching is the theology of the logos—in distinction from the New Testament).

The connection that Hyldahl establishes between the unique position of Socrates in the writings of Justin and the selection of a literary designation whose most ancient and famous example was the *Memorabilia* of Xenophon concerning Socrates is extraordinarily acute and plausible. Granted, in the texts at our disposal it is left to the education of the reader to pick up this connection, because Justin himself does not expressly make it. But we know that Justin knew Xenophon (*Second Apology* 11.2f.[25]); he also quotes Plato on Socrates (*Second Apology* 10.5). To Socrates he ascribed the ἀληθὴς λόγος (*Apol.* 5.3); Socrates had some (ἀπὸ μέρους) knowledge of Christ (*Second Apology* 10.8). In this last passage Christ is said to be the Logos who is eternal and who predicted things to come through the prophets, assumed our human nature, and taught us these doctrines. Socrates convinced no one and died; Christ, on the other hand, persuaded both philosophers and laypeople to the point where they despised death.

From this perspective one can then interpret the striking appearance of *apomnemoneumata* as title for the Gospels, surfacing as it did in the anti-Gnostic exposition of the psalm which speaks of Jesus' suffering. If the issue is that Christ must be acknowledged as the one who really suffered—and that as we showed earlier is the original intent of the treatise—then it is natural for Justin, who hints at the idea of Socrates as a forerunner of Jesus, to adopt a heading which applies especially to memories of one who was condemned to death for his convictions. The Gnostics were educated well enough to catch such allu-

---

24. So Tatian.
25. But he does not mention Xenophon's *Apomnemoneumata*!

sions; the philosophical cross-connections have been established for the great heads of the schools in the second century, for the Roman Gnostics opposed by Hippolytus, and for the writings of Nag Hammadi.

An objection of Heard[26] against Zahn's thesis relates to the different kinds of genitive with which the memoirs are grammatically connected in Justin and in the secular literature. In Justin the authors of the memoirs are referred to, and not the philosophical master to whom they are devoted. To this objection Hyldahl replied that the decisive criterion for the determination of Gattung would be the term *apomnemoneumata* itself. Still, one has to grant that Justin's form of the title is a hybrid. The special form of the title is more understandable, however, given an anti-Gnostic focus, than an apologetic one, where the genitive τοῦ Ἰησοῦ Χριστοῦ [τοῦ σωτῆρος ἡμῶν] would have suggested a more precise parallel to the memoirs of philosophers. Justin (at least according to the available sources) would be the first Christian author who appealed against Gnostic opponents to the apostles.

Fortunately Justin also provides a certain amount of explicit information about his intentions when speaking of *apomnemoneumata*. Most prominent here is the written character of these memoirs, the fact of their having been recorded and written down.[27] As noted earlier, in the second century this emphasis on the written character of the New Testament material is anything but self-evident. In his writing Papias simply declares the φωνὴ ζῶσα καὶ μένουσα to be more useful than books;[28] and Irenaeus has to go to great pains to justify the written character

---

26. Hyldahl, 79.
27. My colleague, O. Hofius, contributed the following reference for which I am indebted to him:

> The Apocryphon of James (Nag Hammadi Codex 1, 2) 2:7ff.: "Now the twelve disciples [were] sitting all together at [the same time] and, *remembering* what the Savior had said to each one of them, whether secretly or openly, they were *setting it down in books.*" In a commentary on the Apocryphon (*Epistula Jacobi Apocrypha,* ed. Malinine, etc., 39) there is a reference to the *apomnemoneumata* mentioned in Justin.

I agree with Hofius that the Apocryphon of James presupposes "written memoirs of the disciples." According to Hofius, the author has in mind "the recording of the pre-Easter sayings of the 'Savior,' hence writings like the Gospel of Thomas." Now F. E. Williams, in his introduction to the Apocryphon (*The Nag Hammadi Library,* ed. J. M. Robinson, [1]1981, 29, cf. [2]1988, 30), suspects that it was written in the third century, and so many cross-references to the synoptic Gospels can be established (the discussions of the kingdom of God clearly tie in with Acts 1:4) that it hardly seems necessary to think of the Gnostic gospels at all! Given such a late date of origin it is quite well possible that the author was familiar with Justin.

28. Eusebius, *HE* 3.39.4. In the Papias fragment the "disciples of the Lord" are mentioned twice; the second instance is clearly a gloss which should be deleted; the missing article in the Greek already indicates that something is wrong. The gloss declares also Aristion and the presbyter John to be disciples of the Lord. Jerome read *discipuli domini;* Rufinus read *ceterique discipuli,* either proposing an assimilation with line 19 or finding one there already. The Syriac translation, however, does not reproduce these words, hence did not read them in the text (I cannot accept the oral objection from my colleague M. Hengel that the Syriac translation is so free that this finding does not mean

of the Gospels vis-à-vis the Gnostics—the Gnostics favoring the *viva vox*.[29] Also in Justin himself the insistence on the written character of the material of the Gospels is exceptional. For that which is for him self-evidently "Scripture" or "Scriptures," the Old Testament, *speaks and talks,* as the citation formulas show. "For him Scripture is alive and active," Osborn correctly remarks;[30] "God is a God who speaks." As for the New Testament, Justin's quotations are

---

anything; the strict literalness of Syriac translation begins gradually with the christological conflicts, hence for dogmatic reasons; until then the text was rendered more into a paraphrase than a translation, but even under these conditions one can tell whether the actual words of the text were reproduced or not). The gloss must be very old if Jerome and Rufinus already knew it.

The best proof that "disciples of the Lord" as a phrase in apposition with Aristion and the presbyter John does not stem from Eusebius is Eusebius's own discussion of the two Johns in 3.39.5ff. There he speaks of "apostles" rather than "disciples of the Lord"; Papias counts one John among the apostles and in the following part of his discourse he mentions, as *outside the number of the apostles,* another John whom he "clearly" describes as "the elder." For Eusebius it is important that Papias is a witness to the existence of two people bearing the name John, who are clearly distinguished from each other. If in the Papias fragment Eusebius had found in the case of the elder John the apposition "disciple of the Lord" he would have mentioned this designation in his discussion; also he would not simply have equated "apostles" and "disciples" of the Lord if he had had to include Aristion and the elder John in this group.

I have subsequently learned that with this argument fashioned from the context in Eusebius, as with the rejection as spurious of the appositive phrase, I find myself, after all, in the distinguished company of T. Mommsen; and it was Prof. Hengel who kindly called my attention to Mommsen's article in *ZNW* 3, 1902, 156-59.

To support his point of view my esteemed colleague M. Hengel cited the letter of bishop Polycrates of Ephesus to the Roman bishop Victor, in which John is referred to as having died in Ephesus (Eusebius, *HE* 5.24.3): "Also there is John, who leaned back on the Lord's breast, and who became a . . . priest wearing the mitre, a martyr and a teacher; he too sleeps in Ephesus." Though this disciple is considered the disciple whom Jesus loved, he is not given the title of "elder." The time of Victor is fixed around 189-98; hence the letter of Polycrates was written decades after Papias. However, Polycrates's description of John is certainly not based on the Papias fragments which have been preserved but, I believe, on local traditions.

How are we to construe the relationship between the two Johns? (Dionysius of Alexandria, in the third century, even knew of two tombs, each reputed to be John's, which were shown in Ephesus [*HE* 7.25.16]; this is the source of Eusebius's mention of the two tombs at Ephesus in his material on Papias [3.39.6]). Irenaeus (*Adv. Haer.* 5.33.1), intentionally or unintentionally, suggests an identification of John the disciple of the Lord with John the man whom Papias heard (and who, according to *HE* 3.39.7, is the elder) when, introducing a supposed saying of the Lord, he says: *quemadmodum presbyteri meminerunt, qui Ioannem discipulum domini viderunt, audisse se ab eo . . . ,* and continues in 4: *Haec autem et Papias Ioannis auditor, Polycarpi autem contubernalis, vetus homo, per scripturam testimonium perhibet in quarto librorum suorum.* What Irenaeus says in 1 would correspond with the Papias quotation (lines 16-19) in *HE* 3.39.4. Irenaeus, who came from Asia Minor, is a contemporary of Polycrates. He is also the one who makes Bishop Polycarp of Smyrna, with whom he was personally acquainted, into a disciple of John, although the letter of Ignatius to Polycarp, the letter of Polycarp to Philippi, and the Martyrdom of Polycarp say nothing about this. In the face of these witnesses, the "traditions of Asia Minor" represented by Irenaeus, at least as they concern information about historic persons, must be utilized very critically.

Accordingly, I regard the gloss "disciples of the Lord" on Aristion and the elder John in Eusebius an "Irenaecizing" of the text in a very old manuscript of Eusebius's *Church History.*

29. *Adv. Haer.* 3.2.1. This insistence on the *viva vox* was not at all a hindrance to tireless literary production among the Gnostics. In this respect the reworking of available Scriptures plays a striking role.

30. Op. cit., 87.

"primarily concerned with the sayings of Jesus, and he thought of the sayings in this way and not as the record of a particular apostle. When he writes, the particular account of each apostle never becomes a factor."[31] This applies not only to Justin; von Campenhausen notes:[32] "In the first one and a half centuries of the church's history there is no single Gospel writing which is directly made known, named, or in any way given prominence by quotation. Written and oral traditions run side by side." "There is no indication of any sort of 'collection' of Jesus' words."[33] Alongside the synoptic sayings, words of Jesus are freely quoted which we, judging from their provenance and meaning, are compelled to describe as "apocryphal."[34]

So though Justin can generally introduce an Old Testament quotation with the words: "Another Scripture *says,*" in mentioning the *apomnemoneumata* he expressly states that what he has cited is *written* there. The two passages in the *Apology* similarly presuppose the written character of the material referred to: *Apol.* 67.3 states that in the worship services there was *reading* from the memoirs of the apostles; *Apol.* 66.3 mentions "the apostles in the memoirs which stem from (γενομένοις) them. . . ." In the *Dialogue* mention of the apostles is linked half the time to the exposition of Ps. 21 (22) (9 times out of 18); *Dial.* 88.3 ("as the apostles of this our Christ have written"), which has already been considered earlier as an allusion to the "memoirs," must be added to this.[35]

31. Ibid., 125f.
32. Op. cit., 121.
33. Ibid., n. 64.
34. Ibid., 121.
35. It is worth noting that the Revelation of John is "the only book of the New Testament to which Justin specifically refers" (Osborn, 137), both by author and title (*Dial.* 81.4). The reason is probably that the title and recipient and thus the literary author of the Apocalypse are all mentioned in the first verse of the first chapter. Here I shall allow myself a long quotation from an academic paper delivered in 1904 by E. Schwartz: "Über den Tod der Söhne Zebedaei. Ein Beitrag zur Geschichte des Johannesevangeliums" (= *Gesammelte Schriften* V, 1963, 48-123). Despite the wit and keenness of the author the paper is hard to read, . . . partly because of the enormous amount of material he has brought together. Even if one cannot accept every individual thesis or conclusion of Schwartz one must not overlook a literary observation like the following, which is based on his knowledge of the literature of antiquity as a whole, especially since it is helpful in cutting down to its fitting measure the weight of the Papias fragments concerning the authors of the Gospels (cf. also M. Hengel's contribution in this volume). Schwartz writes on 76f. (italics added):

> With regard to the recurrent inclination to pass off Papias's remarks about the first two Synoptists as "ancient information" and to utilize them in some fashion or other, a somewhat more general observation may not be out of place. The history of classical literature has gradually learned to work with the notions of the literary-historical legend, novella, or fabrication; after untold attempts at establishing the factuality of statements made it has discovered that *only in special cases does there exist a tradition about a given literary production independent of the self-witness of the literary production itself; and that the person who utilizes a literary-historical tradition must always first demonstrate its character as a historical document. General grounds of probability cannot take the place of this demonstration.* It is no different with Christian authors. In his literary history Eusebius has taken reasonable pains; as he says in the preface he had no other material at his disposal than

The chief function of the memoirs of the apostles in the exposition of the twenty-first psalm consists in the fact that they document as having *happened* that which is predicted in the psalm (thus *Dial.* 101.3; 102.5; 103.8; 104; 105.1; 106.1, 2, 4). Ch. 104 characteristically states that what was said in vv. 16-19 προαγγελία ἦν of the kind of death to which Jesus would be condemned, which also γέγραπται γενόμενον in the memoirs of the apostles. *Dial.* 107.1 refers to the resurrection, to which the memoirs testify, and with this to the story of Jonah as the Old Testament promise of this event. The outcome of all this is that the accentuation of the written character of the apostles' memories of events constitutes a marked expression of the scheme of promise and fulfillment. This special form was necessary in argumentation in which *proofs* had to be provided, in this case against Gnostics, for the reality of the suffering and death by crucifixion of Jesus as the Christ.

As is generally known, in the *Apology* the fulfillment of what was foretold by the prophets is proof for the truth of the Christian faith, a proof which should also be convincing to the Gentiles (thus, basically, *Apol.* 30). Against the possible objection that "he whom we call Christ" could acquire the title "Son of God" because he was such a great magician, Justin remarks: What convinces us is that ὄψει ὁρᾶν γενόμενα καὶ γινόμενα, events "that were predicted πρὶν ἢ γενέσθαι." Here it is natural to refer to the memoirs of the apostles for the notion of their being eyewitnesses. Justin refrains from doing this, though, shortly after, in 33.5, he alludes to this title, without however, interestingly enough, stressing the written character of the memoirs; there Justin cites Luke 1:31f. (the annunciation) with the following reference to the source: ὡς οἱ ἀπομνημονεύσαντες πάντα τὰ περὶ τοῦ σωτῆρος ἡμῶν Ἰησοῦ Χριστοῦ ἐδίδαξαν, οἷς ἐπιστεύσαμεν.

Instead of apostolic records he presents to the Gentiles a possibility of secular "official" instruction. In *Apol.* 34.1 he presents the prophecy of Micah concerning Bethlehem in Judah. Now, says Justin, "this [Bethlehem] is a certain village in the land of the Jews, thirty-five stadia from Jerusalem, where Jesus Christ was born, as you can learn ἐκ τῶν ἀπογραφῶν[36] τῶν γενομένων ἐπὶ

---

the self-witness of the books at hand. Not once was he able to say anything about the external history of the works of Origen, in which he was genuinely interested, apart from what he found in or among them. And if in the case of authors who as individuals and sometimes as well-known personalities stood in the glare of publicity there is so little information about their production, how much more is this not the situation in the case of the Gospels, whose authors intentionally or unintentionally adhered to the obscurity of the Church, since they neither would nor could be anything other than preachers of the one message, a message that was independent of their humanity? There is not even the shadow of a hope that there ever existed any trustworthy information about the way in which the Gospels came into being: the Christians of antiquity had other cares than to search out and preserve the history of the inscripturation of the Gospels, and when Gnosticism forced this concern upon them they filled the vacuum with inventions of their own as Gnosticism did before them.

36. Cf. Luke 2:1, 3: ἀπογράφεσθαι; 2:2: ἀπογραφή.

Κυρηνίου, your first procurator (ἐπίτροπος) in Judea." *Apol.* 35.5 cites from Ps. 21 the piercing of the sufferer's hands and feet and the casting of lots for his clothing; the following lines depict how all this occurred during the crucifixion of Jesus. Then 35.9 says: καὶ ταῦτα ὅτι γέγονε, δύνασθε μαθεῖν ἐκ τῶν ἐκ τῶν ἐπὶ Ποντίου Πιλάτου γενομένων ἄκτων. Later the reader is once again referred to the Acts "which originated under Pilate": *Apol.* 48.1: "Concerning the prophecy that our Christ should cure all diseases and raise the dead to life, hear what was spoken"; 48.2: "Here are the exact words of the prophecy: . . ." Goodspeed italicized the rest of the paragraph completely, designating it as a quotation. But the first three words, τῇ παρουσίᾳ αὐτοῦ, "at his coming," are not a quotation. What follows is a combination of Isa. 35:6 and Matt. 11:5 with rearrangements and abbreviations in both parts. The raising of the dead naturally belongs in the New Testament component of the "quotation." Then, in 48.3, analogously to *Apol.* 35.9, we read: "that Christ did perform such deeds you can learn ἐκ τῶν ἐπὶ Ποντίου Πιλάτου γενομένων ἄκτων." "The Acts of Pilate" of the fourth century probably took as their base this mention of "Acts originating under Pilate."[37] Osborn simply states:[38] "There are no reasons for believing that such a writing existed in Justin's time," without giving an opinion on what Justin could have intended in these passages.

The *function* of ἀπογραφή and ἄκτα in Justin's argument is clear: the Gentile reader was referred to records of measures taken by the Roman administration which were datable by the periods in which high officials were in power and thus demonstrated that the events in question occurred at ascertainable points in time. But is it possible that the tax-lists under Cyrenius and the official record of Pilate's verdict were available to Justin? I assume that he derived his knowledge of the census from Luke 2 and that by the "acts" he meant the passion narrative of the Gospels. He shows his hand in *Apol.* 48 (see above): the description of the earthly activity of Jesus as Savior is in fact Jesus' answer to the question of John the Baptist (Justin defines it even more "in accord with Scripture" than Matt. 11!) and the evidence for the events is the narrative of the Gospels—which means that in *Apol.* 48 "the acts under Pilate" are only another word for the Gospel or Gospels. In the case of the tax-lists and the "acts" of Jesus' trial and verdict Justin, had he been asked, would probably have answered: the tax-lists of the time of Cyrenius are mentioned in our books, as is the trial before the governor; hence one would be able to check out the information on Bethlehem in the tax-lists; the existence of an official Roman record concerning the trial of Jesus follows from the fact of the trial itself. But for the life of Jesus between his birth and his trial,

---

37. E. Bammel, "Pilatus," *RGG*[3] V, 383f., referring to *Apol.* 35 and 48, speaks of "reports concerning Pilate" "going back to the second century"; but such reports cannot be what *Justin* had in mind.

38. Op. cit., 133.

for which there must have existed official documents in Jesus' day, Justin could hardly have given such an answer.

If for the demonstration of the factual fulfillment of that which was promised Justin employed a terminology vis-à-vis the Gentiles different from that vis-à-vis the Gnostics but has the same Scriptures in view, then the conclusion seems natural that he formed the title "Memoirs of the Apostles" on anti-Gnostic grounds and did not, for example, take the term over from the Church's apologetic practice in its discussion with the Gnostics. Rather, conversely, in his apologetic writing he takes over the title already formed in that discussion but then in a descriptive section (*Apol.* 66 and 67) in the somewhat neutral application of the aspect of the "writtenness" of the Gospels.

For the sake of completeness I would still like to point out that the problem of the *literalness* (or rather the nonliteralness) of the New Testament quotations in Justin is to be distinguished from the subject of the "writtenness" of the apostles' memoirs. (Although the Old Testament is unquestionably "Scripture," the same problem exists there.) An extensive literature has existed for two centuries now on the matter of biblical, particularly Old Testament, quotations but I myself have not undertaken any inquiries into the question. After dealing with problems Osborn suggested in the end "that Justin used a harmony of the synoptic Gospels" (the main proof for this being the combined citations), "which was a teaching and apologetic anthology, but that this harmony was primarily transmitted in oral form."[39]

> In Justin we have to do with oral tradition; but it is not the kind of oral tradition which Koester postulates for the Apostolic Fathers. It is much more a secondary or tertiary growth. Between the original oral synoptic tradition and Justin's oral tradition stand the written Gospels. Oral tradition in Justin is largely the transmission in unwritten form of what had been written in the synoptic Gospels.[40]

One may be tempted to see in the memoirs such a harmony of the Gospels in book form. But the explicit identification of the memoirs with the Gospels (although the origin of the identification is not altogether certain) argues against this. Another argument against it is that Justin apparently knew Papias or someone comparable with information about individual Gospels and the authors of Gospels. In *Dial.* 103.8 Justin speaks of "memoirs of the apostles and their successors." In *Dial.* 106.3 there is mention, by way of exception, of ἀπομνημονεύματα αὐτοῦ. The αὐτός here, according to the context, can only be Peter, so that theoretically one could think of the Gospel of Peter.[41] But what Justin

---

39. Ibid., 121.
40. Ibid., 132.
41. See already Haeuser, op. cit., 173, n. 2; Haeuser also mentions the following possibility.

here employs in the course of his argument, the surnaming of the sons of Zebedee as "Boanerges, which means sons of thunder," has been taken from Mark 3:16f. Justin apparently knew the view that the Gospel of Mark was the record of the preaching of Peter. From that point of view also there is no ground for doubting that the memoirs of the apostles are our Gospels.

"Unknown Sayings of Jesus"

Otfried Hofius

1.

The first reference to "unknown" sayings of Jesus occurs in the third book of the *Church History* of Eusebius. According to the bishop of Caesarea, Papias, in his work *Explanation of the Sayings of the Lord* (ca. AD 130), reproduced from the "unwritten" tradition, *inter alia*, ξένας τινὰς παραβολὰς τοῦ σωτῆρος καὶ διδασ-καλίας αὐτοῦ[1]—"some unknown parables and teachings of the Savior,"[2] which are not recorded in the four canonical Gospels. It is to such sayings of Jesus, which we are accustomed to call "agrapha," that the following reflections are devoted. In the process I shall use the ambiguous term *agrapha* in a specifically defined sense: an *agraphon* is a saying attributed to the earthly Jesus which has not been transmitted in the oldest version of the four canonical Gospels.[3]

By this definition all those texts have been excluded from consideration which are presented as sayings of the preexistent Christ or of the risen or ascended Christ. The corresponding New Testament pronouncements[4] do not belong to the category of agrapha, any more, therefore, than for example the sayings of the preexistent Jesus in the Naasene hymn (Hippolytus, *Ref.* 5.10.2) or the numerous instructions to the disciples and revelational discourses put in

---

1. Eusebius, *HE* 3.39.11.
2. As translated in Eusebius, *The History of the Church from Christ to Constantine,* tr. G. A. Williamson, 1966, 151, 152.
3. Cf. L. Vaganay, "Agrapha," *DBS* I, 1928 (159-98), 160ff.; J. Jeremias, "Agrapha," *RGG*[3] I, 1957, 177f.; idem, *Unbekannte Jesusworte,* [3]1963 (= 1964, 1980), assisted by O. Hofius (cf. earlier ET, *Unknown Sayings of Jesus,* 1957); O. Hofius, "Agrapha," *TRE* II, 1978 (103-10), 103f.; further, S. Leanza, *I Detti extracanonici di Gesu',* 1977, 7f. In *Unbekannte Jesusworte* words of the risen Lord not recorded in the Gospels are considered agrapha (cf. the argument on p. 20). This decision, which I then supported, seemed to me later to be in need of revision (see my article in *TRE*).
4. Words of the preexistent Christ: Heb. 2:12f. (= Ps. 22:23; Isa. 8:17f.); 10:5ff. (= Ps. 40:7ff.). Words of the risen or exalted Christ: Acts 1:4f., 7f.; 9:4-6, 10-12, 15f.; 11:16; 18:9f.; 22:7f., 10, 18, 21; 23:11; 26:14-18; II Cor. 12:9; Rev. 1:11, 17-20; 2:1-3, 22; 16:15; 22:10-16, 20.

the mouth of the risen Christ in Christian and Christian Gnostic writings. As a rule[5] an agraphon is also not present when early Christian writings and the liturgical texts of the ancient Church cite a prophetic saying from the Old Testament or a New Testament word of the apostles as "a word of the Lord."[6] The attribution of such quotations to the Lord is based on the theological conviction that the preexistent Christ—as the κύριος attested in the Old Testament—spoke through the mouth of the prophets and the exalted Christ as the Lord present in the Church spoke through the mouth of the apostles.[7]

Finally, the above definition excludes still another group of texts from the list of agrapha. We are thinking of the countless cases in which a saying of Jesus preserved in the canonical Gospels is reproduced in a different form, or cited loosely, because of faulty memory or from indifference vis-à-vis the precise wording.[8] For example, when in the Syrian Church father Afrahat we read the logion: "If you have faith, even a mountain will move before you,"[9] this is not an agraphon but a free and condensed formulation of the saying in Matt. 17:20b (or Matt. 21:21). A free and compressed reproduction of the saying of Matt. 6:25ff. (par. Luke 12:22ff.) occurs in Oxyrhynchus Papyrus 655 (I, a, b).[10] Also the concluding sentence αὐτὸς δώσει ὑμῖν τὸ ἔνδυμα ὑμῖν is no agraphon therefore but a concise summary of Matt. 6:30 (par. Luke 12:28). Also to be excluded from the agrapha are, finally, those passages in the letters of Paul in which the apostle refers to a saying of Jesus that has come down in the synoptic Gospels.[11]

---

5. Some yet-to-be-mentioned mistaken transferences form an exception.

6. The saying of the "savior" in Clement of Alexandria, *Excerpta ex Theodoto* 2.2, σῷζου σὺ καὶ ἡ ψυχή σου, is no agraphon either. It is a free quotation from Gen. 19:17 LXX and is understood by Theodotus the Gnostic as a saying of the preexistent σωτήρ.

7. On this cf. the Syriac *Didascalia* 21 (CSCO 407, ed. A. Vööbus, 210, 3f.): introduction of Isa. 65:1 with the words: "as our Lord and Savior has said through the prophet Isaiah"; *Liber Graduum,* Serm. 10.5 (PS 13, ed. M. Kmosko, Rom. 257, 21ff.): introduction of Rom. 14:21 with the words: "this our Lord has commanded us . . . and spoken through Paul." Instructive is the prayer attributed to John Chrysostom and addressed to the Lord Jesus Christ from the Greek *Akoluthia of Confession* (Μικρὸν Εὐχολόγιον, ed. Panteleemon, 177f.). Here the following predications occur next to each other: "You who through Nathan the prophet forgave David his sin and told him: 'thus also the Lord has taken away your sins' (= II Sam. 12:13)"; "you who said to the woman: 'Woman, your sins are forgiven you' (= Luke 7:48)"; "you who said: 'Confess your sins to one another' (= Jas. 5:16a)."

8. Cf. W. Bauer, *Das Leben Jesu im Zeitalter der neutestamentlicher Apokryphen,* 1909 (reprinted 1967), 378 (e.g. n. 1).

9. Afrahat, *Demonstrationes* (PS 1/1, ed. J. Parisot) 1.17.

10. E. Klostermann, *Apocrypha* II: *Evangelien,* KlT 8, [3]1929, 23.

11. Rom. 14:14; Mark 7:15 (par. Matt. 15:11); I Cor. 7:10f.; Mark 10:11f. (par. Luke 16:18/Matt. 19:9; cf. 5:32); I Cor. 9:14; Mark 10:10 (par. Luke 10:7); I Cor. 11:24f.; Mark 14:22-24 (par.).

2.

If we now turn to the *sources* where the agrapha occur, we must mention the Acts of Luke as the oldest document. According to Acts 20:17-38 Paul concluded his farewell address to the elders of the church of Ephesus with the words (20:35): "Always I have shown you that by so laboring one must help the weak, remembering the words of the Lord Jesus, that he said, 'It is more blessed to give than to receive' (μακάριόν ἐστιν μᾶλλον διδόναι ἢ λαμβάνειν)."

If I consider this passage the oldest instance of a saying of Jesus outside the Gospels this is so because in my conviction there is *no* agraphon in I Thess. 4:15-17.[12] In these (exegetically highly controversial) verses Paul seeks to dispel the fear of the Thessalonians that the members of the church who have passed away will not experience the parousia of Christ. Over against this fear, the apostle has already stressed in v. 14 that God would also, through his returning Son, our Lord, lead the Christians who had fallen asleep to glory. The implied assertion that the Christians who had fallen asleep would not be at a disadvantage by comparison with the living is stated and validated in vv. 15ff.:

> (15) For this we say to you ἐν λόγῳ κυρίου, that we, the living, who remain until the coming of the Lord, will not precede those who have fallen asleep. (16) For the Lord himself—with a cry of command, with the archangel's call, and with the sound of the trumpet of God—will descend from heaven. And the dead in Christ will rise first. (17) Then we, the living, who remain, shall be caught up together with them in the clouds to meet the Lord in the air; and so we will always be with the Lord. (18) Therefore, comfort one another with these words.

Within the structure of the text the λόγοι of comfort embrace vv. 15b-17. The crucial core is the assertion that on the day of the parousia the dead in Christ will rise first and then the dead and the living will *together* meet the Lord as he comes down from heaven. The apostle communicates these words of comfort to the Thessalonians ἐν λόγῳ κυρίου.

G. Kittel counts the phrase ἐν λόγῳ κυρίου among the formulations by which Paul cites an independent dominical saying of the earthly Jesus.[13] If this were so v. 15a would have to be translated: ". . . this we say to you *with* a word of the Lord" (or "*in* a word of the Lord"). J. Jeremias appeals to Kittel when he says that "as the phrase ἐν λόγῳ κυρίου . . . shows, Paul . . . was convinced that

---

12. Contra Jeremias, *Unbekannte Jesusworte,* 77-79, who states that "the oldest of the sayings outside the Gospels is . . . this—I Thess. 4:16-17a" (77). On Jeremias's detailed argument see the (in my view, correct) criticisms of B. Henneken, *Verkündigung und Prophetie im Ersten Thessalonicherbrief. Ein Beitrag zur Theologie des Wortes Gottes,* SBS 29, 1969, 85ff.

13. G. Kittel, *TDNT* IV, 106, n. 145.

he was passing on a saying of the earthly Lord."[14] However, it is more than doubtful that in the phrase Paul uses we have a citation formula. Paul is not quoting material here but—as particularly the use of the first person plural in vv. 15b and 17 and the words αὐτὸς ὁ κύριος in v. 16a show—formulating on his own.[15] Add to this the difficulty of deciding precisely in which sentences the dominical saying is to be found.[16]

Particularly important is that the phrase ἐν λόγῳ κυρίου is altogether exceptional in the New Testament but does occur in a few passages in the Septuagint.[17] In light of these passages two possible solutions can be discussed:

1. According to the story in III Kdms. (I Kgs.) 12:33–13:34 a prophetic man of God comes ἐν λόγῳ κυρίου to Bethel (13:1) and there he cries out ἐν λόγῳ κυρίου a threat against the altar and its priests (ἐπεκάλεσεν, 13:2; ἐλάλησεν, 13:32; cf. also 13:5). In these passages the expression ἐν λόγῳ κυρίου means "on the basis of a word of the Lord that has come to a prophet."[18] It signifies the prophetic legitimation—based on having received a word from the Lord personally—of the man of God. The same meaning occurs in III Kdms. 21:35 (= I Kgs. 20:35)[19] and—related to a command from Moses[20]—in I Chr. 15:15 LXX.[21]

If one understands I Thess. 4:15a in this sense, Paul is appealing to a word of revelation he has personally received from the exalted Lord: "This I say to you on the basis of a word of the Lord (to me)."[22] That is, in I Thess. 4:15b-17

---

14. J. Jeremias, *Unbekannte Jesusworte*, 78.

15. Rom. 14:14; I Cor. 7:10f.; 9:14 are not literal citations either; in their linguistic structure, however, these passages are very different from I Thess. 4:15ff.

16. The various proposed solutions (15b-17, 16-17, 16-17a, 15b only, 17 only) in my opinion only show that the search for the "quotation" is wasted effort.

17. III Kdms. (I Kgs.) 13:1, 2, 5, 32; 21(MT 20):35; II Chr. 30:12; Sir. 48:3. Cf. further ἐν ῥήματι κυρίου, III Kdms. 13:18; ἐν λόγῳ θεοῦ, I Chr. 15:15; ἐν λόγῳ ὑψίστου, Sir. 48:5.

18. Cf. Henneken (n. 12), 92ff. With reference to the underlying Hebrew text בדבר יהוה M. Noth, *Könige I*, BK, 1968, 296, explains: "The ב may be taken instrumentally; accordingly, the expression can be translated: 'in virtue of the word of the Lord' "; Noth also translates it: "on instructions from the Lord" (288f.). E. Würthwein, *Das Erste Buch der Könige. Kapitel 1-16*, ATD, 1977, translates: "on command of the Lord" (166) and remarks: "The formula ... intends to express that the man of God does not take a single step without divine direction" (169). Cf. also W. Zimmerli, *Ezekiel*, ET Hermeneia, I, 93 (on Ezek. 3:4). For the phrase דבר בדבר יהוה Zimmerli suspects that the meaning is: "speaking Yahweh's word 'in a prophetic commission, officially.' "

19. Καὶ ἄνθρωπος εἷς ἐκ τῶν υἱῶν τῶν προφητῶν εἶπεν πρὸς τὸν πλησίον αὐτοῦ ἐν λόγῳ κυρίου = "And a certain man of the sons of the prophets spoke on the basis of a word of the Lord (that he had received) to his companion."

20. . . . ὡς ἐνετείλατο Μωυσῆς ἐν λόγῳ θεοῦ = "as Moses had commanded on the basis of the word of the Lord (which had come to him)" (cf. Num. 4:15; 7:9).

21. See finally the word of the prophet of Bethel in III Kdms. (I Kgs.) 13:18: ἄγγελος λελάληκεν πρός με ἐν ῥήματι κυρίου λέγων = "an angel spoke to me on the basis of a word of the Lord (which came to him)."

22. On the details see Henneken (n. 12), 73ff. See also E. von Dobschütz, *Die Thessalonicherbriefe*, KEK, [7]1909 (reprinted 1974), 193f.

Paul is saying in his own words what has been revealed to him in an ἀποκάλυψις.[23] This supposition finds support in I Cor. 15:51f., where in my opinion Paul refers to the same word of revelation,[24] and introduces his statement with the words: ἰδοὺ μυστήριον ὑμῖν λέγω. I Thess. 4:15b or I Cor. 15:51b, 52a is then a reference to this word of revelation while I Thess. 4:16f. and I Cor. 15:52b are to be regarded as an explication of it.

2. Sir. 48:3, 5 may suggest another interpretation of the phrase ἐν λόγῳ κυρίου. Of Elijah, whose word burned like a torch (v. 1), v. 3 says that he shut up the heavens ἐν λόγῳ κυρίου (= I Kgs. 17:1) and three times brought down fire (= I Kgs. 18:36-38; II Kgs. 1:10, 12), and v. 5, that ἐν λόγῳ ὑψίστου he raised a corpse from death (= I Kgs. 17:17ff.). Since according to the biblical narrative Elijah did not perform these deeds on the basis of a word of the Lord, ἐν λόγῳ κυρίου and ἐν λόγῳ ὑψίστου may, in a derivative sense, simply describe the power and characteristic divine authority given by God to the prophet.[25]

Accordingly, one could understand I Thess. 4:15a to mean that for the content of vv. 15b-17 Paul is appealing to the authority of the exalted Lord. In the formulation τοῦτο ὑμῖν λέγομεν ἐν λόγῳ κυρίου we would then have to recognize a parallel to those Pauline texts in which the apostle claims the authority of the exalted Lord for directives meant for the life of the churches or individual Christians, and thus makes clear that he is speaking with ultimate binding force.[26]

Somewhere between these two possibilities the explanation for I Thess. 4:15-17 must be found—with the first-mentioned proposal in my opinion deserving preference. On the other hand, the idea that Paul is citing a word of the earthly Lord cannot be convincingly demonstrated.[27] The situation is no

23. In II Cor. 12:9 Paul cites a word he received from the exalted κύριος, and in II Cor. 12:1ff. he speaks of ἀποκαλύψεις κυρίου (vv. 1 and 7). That he is thinking of *verbal* revelations is evident from v. 4. The ἄρρητα ῥήματα are not unintelligible words but, as Paul himself explains, words "which no human may utter"; that is, "they were unutterable in the sense that they conveyed divine secrets which were not to be communicated to men at large" (C. K. Barrett, *A Commentary on the Second Epistle to the Corinthians,* 1973, 311).

24. Cf. Henneken, op. cit., 95ff.

25. The son of Sirach could have read in the relevant texts themselves a reference to the power and authority of Elijah: see I Kgs. 17:1; 17:24; 18:36; II Kgs. 1:10, 12. However, with regard to (Hebrew) Sir. 48:3 one could ask perhaps whether the phrase בדבר אל was occasioned by בדבריך in I Kgs. 18:36.

26. I Thess. 4:1f.; Rom. 15:30; I Cor. 1:10; 14:37; also I Cor. 7:25 (on this see F. Hahn, *The Titles of Jesus in Christology,* ET 1969, 122, n. 143). On the thought that Christ himself spoke through the apostle, whose authority was thus the authority of Christ, see also II Cor. 13:3.

27. N. Hyldahl, "Auferstehung Christi–Auferstehung der Toten (1 Thess. 4,13-18)," in S. Pedersen, *Die Paulinische Literatur und Theologie,* 1980, 119-35, like other exegetes before him, links the "dominical saying" which is supposed to be in vv. 16ff. with the depiction of the parousia in Matt. 24:30f. (129ff.). This attempt to trace it to a logion corresponding with Matt. 24:30f. is not convincing, however, if for no other reason than that the statements essential to Paul (the resurrection of the Christians who have died and their equal status with the living) do not occur in this logion. One has to assume that Paul derived these utterances from the words καὶ ἐπισυνάξουσιν τοὺς ἐκλεκτοὺς αὐτοῦ κ.τ.λ (Matt. 24:31)—which I regard as quite unlikely.

better in the case of the thesis that the apostle is basing his statements on the saying of an early Christian prophet who has uttered it in the name of the exalted Lord,[28] an utterance which "has entered the tradition as a dominical saying."[29] The Old Testament passages we have cited argue against this thesis, for according to them he who speaks ἐν λόγῳ κυρίου has himself *directly* received the "word of the Lord" from God.

Whether, beside the saying of Acts 20:35, a second agraphon has been handed down to us in the New Testament itself requires a somewhat lengthier discussion. With regard to other sources a brief overview will have to suffice.[30] To be mentioned first is that some ancient Gospel manuscripts contain agrapha in secondary additions.[31] From this relatively slim body of material allow me to single out: the dominical saying in the story of Jesus in Luke 6:5 (Codex D); the three sayings of Jesus in the narrative of John 7:53–8:11 (8:7b, 10b, 11b), which originally was not a part of John's Gospel; and the utterance of Jesus in Luke 9:55b, 56a that was later inserted in the pericope of Luke 9:51-56. Agrapha occur also in the so-called apocrypha of the New Testament,[32] among which the fragments of lost gospels deserve special mention; further, in relatively large numbers, among the Christian authors from the second century on as in the Church orders and liturgies of the ancient Church.[33] Further material is provided by the Christian Gnostic literature. Of special importance is the Coptic Gospel of Thomas in Codex II of Nag Hammadi[34] since it is a

---

28. Thus G. Friedrich, *Der erste Brief an die Thessalonicher*, NTD VIII, [14]1976, 243.

29. So e.g., W. Marxsen, "Auslegung von I Thess 4,13-18," *ZTK* 66, 1969 (22-37), 36.

30. See for the specific sayings J. Jeremias, *Unbekannte Jesusworte*, 20ff., and my article (n. 3 above), 104f. Still indispensable are the large, though uncritical, compilation by A. Resch, *Agrapha. Außercanonische Schriftfragmente*, TU NF 15/3, 4, 1906 (a revision of *Agrapha. Außercanonische Evangelienfragmente*, TU 5/4, 1889); E. Klostermann, *Apocrypha III: Agrapha*, KlT 11, 1911.

31. I do not consign to this group the word of the cross of Luke 23:34a, which is missing in important textual witnesses but which in my opinion is to be assigned on intrinsic grounds to the original stock of the Gospel of Luke. Cf. G. Schneider, *Das Evangelium nach Lukas* II, ÖTK, 1977, 483; I. H. Marshall, *Commentary on Luke*, NIGTC, 1978, 867f.

32. From writings which are in a broader sense to be included here I will meanwhile note two additional agrapha: *Die Bücher der Einsetzung der Erzengel Michael und Gabriel*, CSCO 225, ed. C. D. G. Müller, 1962, 32:32–33:31; 76:17ff.

33. The material preserved in liturgical texts may be richer than hitherto existing collections (Resch [n. 30], 355ff.; F. Cabrol, *Agrapha*, DACL I, 1907, 979-84; Jeremias, *Unbekannte Jesusworte*, 28) have led us to think. J. Karawidopulos has called attention to a liturgical agraphon that had been overlooked before: "Ein Agraphon in einem liturgischen Text der griechischen Kirche," *ZNW* 62, 1971, 299f. His assumption (expressed on 299) "that there are still more agrapha, especially in later texts" is well-founded. There is a wealth of material, especially in the prayers and hymns of the West Syrian (Jacobite) Church, that needs to be collected and screened; cf. e.g. *The Book of Common Prayer of the Syrian Antiochian Church*, tr. B. Griffith, 1972, 30, 33, 62, 64, 77, 114f., 132, 140, 154, 188, 198, 242, 295, 305; H. Denzinger, *Ritus Orientalium Captorum Syrorum et Armenorum in administrandis Sacramentis* II, 1864 (reprinted 1961), 516f. See nn. 62 and 86 below for two long-neglected liturgical agrapha.

34. A. Guillaumont, et al., *Evangelium nach Thomas,* 1959; J. Leipoldt, *Das Evangelium nach Thomas,* TU 101, 1967.

collection of Jesus-logia presumably based on an older non-Gnostic collection of sayings.[35] Older collections of sayings may also have been incorporated[36] in the *Apocryphon of James* (Nag Hammadi Codex I, 2)[37] and in the *Dialogue of the Savior* (Nag Hammadi Codex III, 5).[38] Last to be mentioned as sources for the agrapha are the Manichean and Mandaean writings; the rabbinical literature, in which there is, strikingly enough, only one solitary agraphon to be noted,[39] and the Jewish *Toledot Jesu*;[40] the Koran as well as the writings of Islamic ascetics and mystics in which the number of sayings attributed to Jesus runs into the hundreds.

3.

The extensive material which can be assembled from the sources requires critical examination.[41] In this connection the main question cannot immediately be that concerning the authenticity of the sayings attributed to Jesus. As Jeremias has stated, our aim in this process must much rather be to single out those sayings "which can be compared with respect to content, form, and tradition history with those of the Synoptic Gospels."[42]

If one employs this criterion of selection, a considerable number of agrapha can be eliminated from the start. To this group belong utterances that are pure fabrications or have been secured through modifications of canonical

35. From the prologue of the Gnostic edition ("these are the secret words which the living Jesus spoke and Didymus Judas Thomas wrote") it cannot be inferred that the sayings are meant to be understood as revelation-sayings of the risen Lord; cf. E. Haenchen, *Die Botschaft des Thomas-Evangeliums,* ThBT 6, 1961, 35f. The epithet "living" (cf. Gospel of Thomas 59) refers to the divine being of Jesus (cf. Gospel of Truth [Nag Hammadi Codex I, 3] 20:29f.), just as God himself is called "the living Father" (Gospel of Thomas 3, 50) or "the Living One" (37). As is evident from indications of the situation in several logia (22, 60, 72, 79, 100) the Gospel of Thomas aims to be a collection of sayings by the *pre-Easter* Jesus, the secret sense of which is known only to Gnostics (prologue). Cf. with this character of the Gospel of Thomas the mention of the disciples' memoirs in the Apocryphon of James (see n. 37) 2:7-15.

36. Cf. H. Köster, "Dialog und Spruchüberlieferung in den gnostischen Texten von Nag Hammadi," *EvTh* 39, 1979, 532-56. I am not able to concur with Köster's judgment concerning the great antiquity of the collections of sayings.

37. M. Malinine, et al., *Epistula Iacobi Apocrypha,* 1968.

38. English translation in *The Nag Hammadi Library,* [1]1977, 229ff., [2]1988, 244ff.

39. b. Abodah Zarah 17a par. Qoheleth Rabbah 1 §24 on v. 8. Cf. J. Maier, *Jesus von Nazareth in der talmudischen Überlieferung,* 1978, 144ff.

40. G. Schlichting, *Ein jüdisches Leben Jesu,* WUNT 24, 1982, 78ff. passim.

41. Fundamental work has been done in this area especially by: J. H. Ropes, *Die Sprüche Jesu, die in den kanonischen Evangelien nicht überliefert sind. Eine kritische Bearbeitung des von D. Alfred Resch gesammelten Materials,* TU 14/2, 1896; idem, "Agrapha," *HDB* Extra Vol., 1904, 343-52; W. Bauer, *Das Leben Jesu* (n. 8), 351-60, 377-415; L. Vaganay, *Agrapha* (n. 3); J. Jeremias, in the three editions of *Unbekannte Jesusworte* (1948, 1951, 1963).

42. J. Jeremias, *Unbekannte Jesusworte,* 47 (cf. 44f.). Since Jeremias adds "and whose historical authenticity can be considered in all seriousness," this seems problematic to me.

dominical sayings that cause Jesus to make ascetic demands[43] or to utter heretical views.[44] Further to be mentioned here are the—equally fictitious—pronouncements which are put in Jesus' mouth in the context of legendary Jesus-stories and which one can therefore describe as haggadic agrapha. Lastly to be adduced are the wisdom sayings of diverse provenance which are attributed to Jesus by Islamic authors in virtue of their high esteem of him[45] and the sayings attributed to Jesus for polemical reasons in Mandaean texts and intended to unmask him as a false Messiah.[46]

As regards the remaining agrapha, though to a large extent they cannot be faulted for their content, the majority of them are questionable from a traditional-historical point of view. I shall adduce a number of examples of this kind, also citing some agrapha which have been given relatively large credence by Jeremias and toward which in the course of time I myself have become ever more skeptical. I shall sum up the agrapha in question in four groups:[47]

1. A first group embraces biblical and extrabiblical quotations that as a rule are attributed to Jesus by mistake, by accident, or on purpose. A case of deliberate transference doubtless occurs when the saying Paul cites in I Cor. 2:9 is presented in several sources as an utterance of Jesus.[48] The oldest instance occurs in the Coptic Gospel of Thomas (Gospel of Thomas 17):

> Jesus said: I will give you what eye has not seen and what ear has not heard and what hand has not touched and (what) has not arisen in the heart of man.

43. An example is the demand for sexual abstinence (adduced by Clement of Alexandria, *Strom.* 3.9.63, from the Gospel to the Egyptians): "I came to destroy the works of the female."

44. A number of such Gnostic inventions may be taken from the Coptic Gospel according to Thomas: "Blessed is he who was before he came into being" (19a); "If they say to you: 'From where have you originated?' say to them 'We have come from the Light, where the Light has originated through itself' " (50a); "Whoever has known the world has found a corpse, and whoever has found a corpse, of him the world is not worthy" (56); and "Whoever finds himself, of him the world is not worthy" (111b). Heretical polemic against the Old Testament (the prophets) is palpably present in the agraphon cited by Augustine in *Contra adversarium legis et prophetarum* 2.4.14: "dimisistis vivum qui ante vos est et de mortuis fabulamini" ("You have dismissed the Living [One] who is before you and you have spoken about the dead"). Augustine correctly emphasizes that this utterance (= Gospel of Thomas 52) is heretical.

45. Among them the famous agraphon: "This world is a bridge. Pass over it. But build not your dwelling there." Cf. J. Jeremias, "Zur Überlieferungsgeschichte des Agraphon 'Die Welt ist eine Brücke,' " *NAWG*, Phil.-hist. Kl., 1953, 95-103; idem, *Unbekannte Jesusworte*, 105ff.

46. See e.g. M. Lidzbarski, *Ginzā. Der Schatz oder Das große Buch der Mandäer*, 1925, 47, 16ff.

47. Beyond this, see in Jeremias, *Unbekannte Jesusworte*, 41-44, the texts listed under the rubric "Agrapha als kompositionstechnisches Hilfsmittel," which I will not discuss here.

48. Gospel of Thomas 17; Martyrium Petri 10 = *Actus Petri cum Simone* 39; *Liber Graduum*, Serm. 16.12 (ed. M. Kmosko, PS I/3, 412, 19ff.); Pseudo-Titus Epistle (in E. Hennecke and W. Schneemelcher, *New Testament Apocrypha* II, 1965, 141ff.); Turfan Fragment M 789.

The unknown provenance of the saying cited by Paul provided an occasion for attributing it to Jesus.

As another conscious formation one must consider the agraphon recorded by Clement of Alexandria which was doubtless formulated on the basis of Paul's discussion in I Cor. 7:1-9, 25-38:

> He who is married should not renounce his wife,
> and he who is unmarried should not marry.

> ὁ γήμας μὴ ἐκβαλλέτω
> καὶ ὁ μὴ γαμήσας μὴ γαμείτω.[49]

On the other hand, in logion 58 of the Gospel of Thomas we may well be dealing with a mistaken transference based on the two macarisms in Jas. 1:12 (μακάριος ἀνὴρ ὃς ὑπομένει πειρασμόν, ὅτι δόκιμος γενόμενος λήμψεται τὸν στέφανον τῆς ζωῆς) and I Pet. 3:14 (εἰ καὶ πάσχοιτε διὰ δικαιοσύνην, μακάριοι):

> Blessed is the man who has suffered;
> he has found the Life.[50]

In the case of the agraphon of Acts 20:35 ("It is more blessed to give than to receive"), we are dealing with a maxim that circulated in the Graeco-Roman world, as a wealth of evidence shows,[51] which is erroneously attributed to Jesus.

I also consider as erroneous transference two agrapha which Jeremias judges to be equal in worth to the synoptic tradition.[52] The agraphon first handed down by Justin,

> There will be schisms and heresies

> ἔσονται σχίσματα καὶ αἱρέσεις,[53]

originated, in my opinion, from I Cor. 11:18f., where Paul's comment, ἀκούω σχίσματα ἐν ὑμῖν ὑπάρχειν (v. 18), is linked with the observation δεῖ γὰρ καὶ αἱρέσεις ἐν ὑμῖν εἶναι (v. 19). Presumably synoptic sayings like Matt. 24:5, 11, 24f. were the occasion for attributing them to Jesus.[54]

---

49. Clement of Alexandria, *Strom.* 3.15.97. For the first line see esp. I Cor. 7:10f., 27a and for the second I Cor. 7:1, 7a, 8, 26, 32ff.

50. On account of the asyndetic parataxis (not unusual in Coptic) the translation "Blessed is the man who has suffered and found life" is also possible.

51. Cf. E. Haenchen, *The Acts of the Apostles,* ET 1971, 594f., n. 5. See also the material on Acts 20:35 recorded in J. J. Wettstein, *Novum Testamentum Graecum* II, 1752 (reprinted 1962), 600. H. Koester suspects that Acts 20:35 "was probably a Jewish logion" ("Die außerkanonischen Herrenworte als Produkte der christlichen Gemeinde," *ZNW* 48, 1957 [220-37], 228), but convincing proof is lacking.

52. *Unbekannte Jesusworte,* 74f. and 71-73 (see n. 55 below).

53. Justin, *Dial.* 35.3. The agraphon also occurs in Didymus, *De Trinitate* 3.22 and in the Syriac *Didascalia,* ch. 23 (ed. A. Vööbus, CSCO 407, 226, 2).

54. Cf. Justin, *Dial.* 51.2; Pseudo-Clement, *Hom.* 2.17.4; 16.21.4.

The agraphon cited by Tertullian:

No one can obtain the kingdom of heaven who has not passed through temptation.

Neminem intemptatum regna caelestia consecuturum.[55]

may be derived from Acts 14:22b, which appears in the Acts of John of pseudo-Prochorus as a statement of Jesus:[56] διὰ πολλῶν θλίψεων δεῖ ἡμᾶς εἰσελθεῖν εἰς τὴν βασιλείαν τοῦ θεοῦ. As Tertullian expressly mentions, the saying he cited had its place in the passion narrative just before the Gethsemane story. This reference suggests that Tertullian had in mind Luke 22:28f.: "You are those who have continued with me in my trials; as my Father appointed a kingdom for me, so do I appoint for you. . . ."

The agraphon from the Greek *akoluthia* for the anointing of the sick (particularly interesting for the history of theology), to which J. Karawidopulos calls attention in *ZNW* (1971), is also to be classified as belonging to the category of transferences.[57] Cited there in a prayer— each time introduced by σὺ εἶ ὁ εἰπών— are four Jesus-sayings: Luke 5:32; John 6:37b; Luke 15:7; and the agraphon:

ὁσάκις ἂν πέσῃς, ἔγειραι,
καὶ σωθήσῃ

As often as you fall, rise up,
and you will be saved.[58]

The agraphon was certainly not created by the author of the prayer. Karawidopulos believes it may stem "from an ancient tradition," perhaps even from "a lost document."[59] I myself have expressed the suspicion (*TRE* II, 106) that it is "a tendentious invention of the Great Church" and commented: "It may tie in with Prov. 24:16a; Jer. 8:4; Mic. 7:8, and owe its existence to a discussion of the question whether for the Christian who falls into sin after baptism there is the possibility of repentance." Whereas I have found evidence to confirm my judgment concerning the Sitz im Leben of the agraphon, I have to revise my classification of it as a free invention, since in my opinion light can be shed on the history of the saying. The prayer to which we owe our agraphon presents

---

55. Tertullian, *De Baptismo* 20.2. Jeremias leaves open the possibility that as a result of an error of memory a saying like Jas. 1:12 (cf. 13) was held to be a passion saying of Jesus (*Unbekannte Jesusworte*, 72).

56. On this, see Resch (n. 30), 89, agraphon no. 68b.

57. See n. 33.

58. *Μικρὸν Εὐχολόγιον* (n. 7), 146f. The agraphon also occurs in the corresponding prayer of the Coptic rite (Denzinger [n. 33] II, 491), but not, however, in the corresponding prayer of the West Syrian Jacobite rite (ibid., 509).

59. Karawidopulos (n. 33), 300 and 299, respectively.

Luke 15:7 in an abbreviated form which differs from the New Testament wording: χαρὰ γίνεται ἐν οὐρανῷ ἐπὶ ἑνὶ ἁμαρτωλῷ μετανοοῦντι. The same wording occurs in the *Apostolic Constitutions,*[60] and that in a context which requires the bishop to accept the fallen and repentant Christian.[61] The bishop is required to promise σωτηρία to such a person (2.13.5) since it is the will of God that the returning sinner have the ἐλπὶς σωτηρίας (2.12.3). In this context Ezek. 33:11 (also incorporated in the prayer referred to) is cited on the one hand (2.12.2); and on the other, it is recalled that through the prophet Jeremiah God himself emphatically urged μετάνοια (2.14.2): μὴ ὁ πίπτων οὐκ ἀνίσταται ἢ ὁ ἀποστρέφων οὐκ ἐπιστρέφει; . . . ἐπιστράφητε, υἱοὶ ἀφεστηκότες, καὶ ἐγὼ ἰάσομαι τὰ συντρίμματα ὑμῶν—"Does not he who falls stand up again and does not he who errs again return? . . . Return, you fallen sons, and I will heal your brokenness." Our agraphon goes back to this combination of words from Jer. 8:4f. and Jer. 3:22, since it can easily be understood as an interpretive summary of Old Testament utterances of God. If this summary were then given a status equal to that of the canonical sayings of Jesus and hence became an agraphon, the explanation is that the ancient Greek Church heard the voice of the incarnate God in the Old Testament oracle. A witness for this is the prayer which contains the agraphon—namely the wording of the address: ὁ θεὸς ὁ μέγας καὶ ὕψιστος . . . , ὁ διὰ τὴν τῶν ἁμαρτωλῶν σωτηρίαν ἐνανθρωπήσας θεὸς ὤν.

2. Belonging, as a second group, to the agrapha that cannot on tradition-historical grounds be treated the same as the synoptic tradition, are the pronouncements which bear the stamp of the vocabulary and theology of the Gospel of John. Thus dependence on the Johannine bread discourse (John 6) is manifest when according to the communion liturgy of the east Syrian (= Nestorian) Church Jesus said to his disciples "in secret," that is, at the institution of the Lord's Supper:

> I am the bread that came down from heaven.
> He who comes in love and receives it
> lives in me for ever, and inherits the kingdom.[62]

In the dominical saying which Eusebius drew from the Nazarene Gospel we are hardly dealing with a "preliminary stage in the development of John's Gospel"[63] but with an echo of the Johannine text:[64]

---

60. *Apostolic Constitutions* 2.13.5; see also 8.9.5; 47.52.

61. *Apostolic Constitutions* 2.12-18 (F. X. Funk, *Didascalia et Constitutiones Apostolorum* I, 1905, 49ff.).

62. *The Liturgy of the Holy Apostolic and Catholic Church of the East,* 1949, 30; cf. *The Liturgy of the Holy Apostles Adai and Mari,* 1893, 28. F. E. Brightman and C. E. Hammond, *Liturgies Eastern and Western* I: *Eastern Liturgies,* 1896, 290. The Syrian missal of the Syro-Malabar Church reads: ". . . and receives me (!). . . ." *Ṭaksā' d'Qudāšā',* 1960, 37f.

63. So Jeremias in the second edition of *Unbekannte Jesusworte,* 1951, 65.

64. For the attribution to the Nazarene Gospel, see P. Vielhauer, "Jewish-Christian Gospels," in E. Hennecke and W. Schneemelcher, *New Testament Apocrypha* I, ET 1963 (117-65), 122, 139f., 143f.

I choose for myself the worthy ones;
the worthy are they whom my Father in heaven gives me.[65]

The first line is indebted to passages like John 6:70; 13:18; 15:16, 19; the reference to the gift of the Father to passages like John 6:37, 39; 10:29; 17:2, 6, 9.

As a final example of dependence on John's Gospel allow me to adduce an agraphon from the apocryphal Acts of Peter, one that hardly compares with the logia of the synoptic tradition:[66]

They that are with me have not understood me.

Qui mecum sunt non me intellexerunt.[67]

A similar-sounding saying occurs in the Apocryphon of James: "I have been with you and you have not known me,"[68] and Gospel of Thomas 91 includes the statement: "and him who is before your face you have not known." Accordingly, for the agraphon of the Acts of Peter one may suspect a Gnostic bias.[69] Since the author of the Acts of Peter in fact knew and used the Gospel of John[70] it is natural to see behind this agraphon the question of Jesus addressed to Philip in John 14:9: "Have I been with you so long and yet you do not know me?"—where we must note that the Vulgate has the plural: *Tanto tempore vobiscum sum et non cognovistis me?*

3. Larger than the category of "Johannine" agrapha is the third group of Jesus-sayings, those which clearly betray their dependence on the synoptic tradition. A saying occurring in the Syriac *Liber Graduum* represents a simple expansion of Luke 10:16b:

He who despises you despises me
and he who honors you honors me.[71]

Also to be reckoned among the secondary expansions is the beautiful agraphon in Gospel of Thomas 25:

Love your brother as your soul,
guard him as the apple of your eye.

---

65. Eusebius, *Theophania* syr. 4.12 (ed. S. Lee, 1842, 234). For the understanding of the Syriac word *šappîrê* in the sense of Greek ἄξιοι cf. Jeremias, *Unbekannte Jesusworte*, 65, n. 1. See further also the saying of the Resurrected One to the disciples that Clement of Alexandria (*Strom.* 6.6.48) cites from the *Kerygma Petri:* ἐξελεξάμην ὑμᾶς δώδεκα μαθητὰς κρίνας ἀξίους ἐμοῦ.

66. *Unbekannte Jesusworte*, 86f.

67. *Actus Vercellenses* (= *Actus Petri cum Simone*), ch. 10 (R. A. Lipsius and M. Bonnet, *Acta Apostolorum Apocrypha* I, 1891, 58, 5f.).

68. Codex I, 12, 36f.; cf. ibid., 13, 38ff.; Gospel of Thomas 43.

69. So my view in *TRE* II, 107. Cf. already H. von Campenhausen, *Kirchliches Amt und geistliche Vollmacht in den ersten drei Jahrhunderten*, BhTh 14, 1953, 11, n. 3. Jeremias's objections to the idea of Gnostic bias (*Unbekannte Jesusworte*, 87) are not persuasive, in view of the sayings in the Apocryphon of James and the Gospel of Thomas.

70. See besides ch. 10 esp. chs. 7 and 20.

71. *Liber Graduum*, Serm. 17.1 (ed. M. Kmosko, PS I/3, 417, 1ff.).

The first line reproduces the love commandment (Lev. 19:18)[72] adopted by Jesus (Matt. 19:19b; Mark 12:31 par.), except that under the influence of Lev. 19:17a ("You shall not hate your brother in your heart") "neighbor" has been replaced by "brother."[73] The love commandment, then, has been broadened into a synonymous saying which employs a metaphor borrowed from the Old Testament (Deut. 32:10; Ps. 17:8; Prov. 7:2).

That synoptic sayings of Jesus are also expanded by interpretive additions is shown, for example, in the agraphon:

> Blessed are they who suffer
> on account of the destruction of those who do not believe.[74]

While here the addition (possibly formulated under the influence of Phil. 3:18f. or Rom. 9:2f.) to Matt. 5:4a is intended to be heard as a component of the dominical saying, in view of Justin, *Apol. I* 15.8, a certain judgment can hardly be rendered. Following Luke 5:32 ("I came not to call the righteous but sinners to repentance") we read there the sentence: "The Heavenly Father wishes the repentance of a sinner rather than his punishment." Many scholars count this addition among the agrapha.[75] It may, however, be an argument by Justin and hence not intended as a dominical saying.[76]

Not a few of the agrapha indebted to the synoptic tradition prove to be modifications of canonical sayings or blends of related canonical pronouncements. Gospel of Thomas 48, which is one of the most impressive aphorisms of this gospel, is a combination of both:

> If two live with each other in peace[77] in the same house,
> they will say to the mountain: "Be moved,"
> and it will be moved.

---

72. The formulation "as your soul" instead of "as yourself" (Lev. 19:18 MT, LXX; Matt. 19:19b; Mark 12:31 par.) corresponds to the text in the Syrian Bible.

73. Cf. on this also Jub. 36:4; Test. Gad 6:1 (variant reading). It is less likely that the influence of I John 2:10; 4:21 is present here.

74. Syr. *Didascalia*, ch. 21 (ed. A. Vööbus, CSCO 407, 209, 11f.).

75. Thus e.g. Resch (n. 30), 98f. (no. 73); Ropes, "Agrapha" (n. 41), 349 (no. 56).

76. Cf. E. Klostermann, "Zu den Agrapha," *ZNW* 6, 1905 (104-6), 105f.; idem, *Apocrypha* III (n. 30), 6 on no. 24; Vaganay (n. 3), 185f.

77. Coptic *^{e}r eirēnē* is often rendered by the translators of the Gospel of Thomas as "make peace" (so W. Till in Guillaumont, et al. [n. 34] 29; Haenchen, *Botschaft* [n. 35] 23; idem, *Synopsis Quattuor Evangeliorum*, ed. K. Aland [²1964] 523; B. M. Metzger, op. cit.; R. Haardt, *Die Gnosis. Wesen und Zeugnisse* [1967] 195; T. O. Lambdin, *The Nag Hammadi Library* [n. 38] 123). In my opinion "to live in peace" (so e.g. H. Quecke, "Das Thomasevangelium," W. C. van Unnik, *Evangelien aus den Nilsand* [1960] 161-173: 166; R. Kasser, *L'Évangile selon Thomas* [1967] 77; Leipoldt [n. 34] 39; H. Greeven, *Synopse der drei ersten Evangelien* [1981] 198) is the correct translation. I base this on the Sahidic translation of Mark 9:50; Rom. 12:18; I Thess. 5:13, where *^{e}r eirēnē* corresponds with εἰρηνεύειν. Particularly relevant to *^{e}r eirēnē m^{e}nnouerēu* in Gospel of Thomas 48 is the analogous formulation of Mark 9:50 *sa: ^{e}r eirēnē m^{e}nnouerēu* = εἰρηνεύετε ἐν ἀλλήλοις.

This agraphon owes its existence to a combination of Matt. 18:19 and Matt. 17:20.[78] That the apodosis of the Coptic saying corresponds to the apodosis of Matt. 17:20 (ἐρεῖτε τῷ ὄρει τούτῳ· μετάβα ἔνθεν ἐκεῖ, καὶ μεταβήσεται) goes without saying.[79] The protasis of the Coptic saying goes back to an abbreviated rendering of the protasis of Matt. 18:19, which read: ἐὰν δύο συμφωνήσωσιν ἐν τῷ αὐτῷ.[80] In this rendering the verb συμφωνεῖν, as in Matt. 18:19, had the meaning "to agree." Accordingly, the saying made up from Matt. 18:19 and Matt. 17:20 to which the Coptic agraphon goes back, read: "When two agree in the same (prayer) endeavor, they will say to the mountain "move," and it will move."[81] The development toward the Coptic wording which is different in the protasis is explained by the fact that συμφωνεῖν can also mean "to be of the same opinion," "to be in harmony," "to be of the same mind."[82] If συμφωνεῖν is understood in this sense, the resulting meaning of the prepositional phrase ἐν τῷ αὐτῷ is "at the same place," which the Coptic then renders "in the same house."

So far we have had to do with agrapha that came into being as a result of the expansion, interpretation, modification, and combination of synoptic Jesus-sayings, but we also occasionally run into agrapha that were created anew on the model of synoptic sayings. In a small collection of dominical sayings undertaken for catechetical and homiletical purposes, there appears, beside six sayings which have parallels in the synoptic Gospels, the analogously created logion, I Clem. 13:2:

As you prove yourself kind,
so you will experience kindness.

ὡς χρηστεύεσθε,
οὕτως χρηστευθήσεται ὑμῖν.[83]

The cry of woe in Gospel of Thomas 102 constitutes an analogous formation to Matt. 23:13 (par. Luke 11:52; cf. Gospel of Thomas 39a) and at the same time picks up a Greek proverb.[84] It reads:

78. Cf. W. Schrage, *Das Verhältnis des Thomas-Evangeliums zur synoptischen Tradition und zu den koptischen Evangelienübersetzungen,* BZNW 29, 1964, 116f.

79. The Coptic apodosis has the third person plural in distinction from Matt. 17:20, which is to be understood as a consequence of the Coptic protasis; cf. Schrage, op. cit., 117.

80. This abbreviated form of the protasis of Matt. 18:19 is instanced by the Latin text of the Syrian *Didascalia,* in which the combination of the two passages (Matt. 18:19; 21:21) dealing with prayer reads: *Duo si convenerint in unum et dixerint monti huic: tolle et mitte te in mare, fiet* (Funk [n. 61], 192, 23f.; the Syrian version is longer, see A. Vööbus, ed., CSCO 407, 161, 19ff.).

81. Cf. Haenchen, *Botschaft* (n. 35), 38f., n. 11.

82. Cf. BAGD, s.v. 2.a, which refers to *Herm. Vis.* 3.5.1, where it is said of the apostles, teachers, and deacons of the earliest period that: πάντοτε ἑαυτοῖς συνεφώνησαν καὶ ἐν ἑαυτοῖς εἰρήνην ἔσχαν, "always they were in agreement and kept the peace among themselves."

83. Cf. H. Koester, *Synoptische Überlieferung bei den Apostolischen Vätern,* TU 65, 1957, 12ff.

84. On this, see the material in J. B. Bauer, "Echte Jesusworte?" in van Unnik (n. 77) (108-50), 149, n. 80.

> Woe to the Pharisees, for they are like a dog sleeping in the oxen's manger, which neither eats nor allows the oxen to eat.

That more than one synoptic saying may be involved in the formation of a new dominical saying is evident from the logion secondarily inserted into the pericope Luke 9:51-56:

> Do you not know of what manner of spirit you are? The Son of man came not to destroy people's lives but to save them" (. . . οὐκ ἦλθεν ψυχὰς ἀνθρώπων ἀπολέσαι ἀλλὰ σῶσαι).

These words, introduced by καὶ εἶπεν, were added to the sentence στραφεὶς δὲ ἐπετίμησεν αὐτοῖς (v. 55) because a copyist had the (somewhat justified) impression that upon this notation a word from Jesus had to follow. This splendid agraphon is doubtless a new formation, but based, it seems to me, on the two Jesus-sayings in Luke 6:9 (ἔξεστιν . . . ψυχὴν σῶσαι ἢ ἀπολέσαι) and Luke 19:10.[85] The spirit which animated the disciples of Jesus can, in the opinion of the interpolator, only be the spirit of their Lord—and that means: the spirit of him who as the Son of Man came to seek and to save the lost (Luke 19:10) decided with his very existence the question whether one should "save lives or destroy them" (Luke 6:9).

4. A fourth and final group of agrapha, the origin of which can be localized in the process of transmission, are logia which came into being where a narrative notation from the canonical Gospels was converted into a direct saying of Jesus. This group is represented by an agraphon formulated in light of Luke 18:1 and transmitted by Afrahat:

> Pray and do not lose heart.[86]

In view of Luke's fidelity to the tradition of dominical sayings[87] that came down to him, it is virtually excluded that in Luke 18:1 he changed a saying of Jesus from direct into indirect speech.[88]

---

85. Another possibility is John 3:17 (so Marshall, *Luke* [n. 31], 407). For instance, in the narrative of John 7:53–8:11 one can trace the memory of synoptic *and* Johannine sayings of Jesus (8:7b cf. Matt. 7:1-5; 8:11b cf. John 3:17; 8:15b cf. John 5:14). The same applies to the sayings of Jesus in Papyrus Egerton 2 (H. I. Bell and T. C. Skeat, *The New Gospel Fragments,* 1935). The author of this unknown gospel knew the four canonical Gospels—thus, correctly, J. Jeremias, "An Unknown Gospel with Johannine Elements (Pap. Egerton 2)," in Hennecke/Schneemelcher I (n. 64) (94-97), 95; idem, *Unbekannte Jesusworte,* 42ff. Of a different view but not convincing is Köster, *Dialog und Spruchüberlieferung* (n. 38), 554f.

86. Afrahat, *Demonstrationes* 4.16 (ed. J. Parisot, PS I/1, 173, 26). An analogous example occurs in a prayer from the Greek and Coptic *akoluthia* for the anointing of the sick (*Μικρὸν Εὐχολόγιον* [n. 7], 171; Denzinger [n. 33] II, 498): conversion of Matt. 10:1 into a saying of Jesus.

87. On this see J. Jeremias, *Die Sprache des Lukasevangeliums,* 1980, 9.

88. So Resch (n. 30), 138.

4.

This critical process of elimination, illustrated by means of a few examples, melts the number of agrapha down to a minimum. Among the "rest which remain" of those sayings "which neither with respect to their content nor their transmission give rise to objections of weight but which fit into the framework of the tradition recorded in our four Gospels"[89] Jeremias, in the latest edition of *Unbekannte Jesusworte,* counted eighteen agrapha to which he devoted a careful exposition.[90] However, as I found through continued study of the agrapha, this number is decidedly too high. It must—especially on tradition-historical grounds—again be reduced by a half.[91]

As far as the nine remaining agrapha are concerned, if one applies a very critical standard, then even here in five cases tradition-historical objections cannot be totally eliminated.

1. A leaf of parchment from a miniature book of the Gospels probably designed for use as an amulet, Oxyrhynchus Papyrus 840, contains a lengthy narrative about a clash between Jesus and a Pharisaic chief priest named Levi in the outer court of the temple.[92] In this narrative Jesus speaks twice. To the chief priest, who charges him and his disciples with ritual impurity, Jesus addresses the question:

> How is it then with you? For you are here in the temple. Are you then clean?

And when Levi affirms that he is clean because he has performed the rites of purity Jesus answers him:

> Woe to you blind who see not! You have washed yourself in water that is poured forth, in which dogs and swine lie night and day, and washed and scoured your outer skin, which harlots and flute girls also anoint, bathe, scour, and beautify to arouse desire in men, but inwardly they are filled with scorpions and with [all manner of ev]il. But I and [my disciples], of whom you say that we have not [bathed, have bath]ed ourselves in the liv[ing and clean] water, which comes down from [the Father in heaven].

Jeremias has advanced substantial arguments in favor of the historicity of the narrative and the authenticity of the sayings of Jesus preserved in it.[93] The

---

89. Jeremias, *Unbekannte Jesusworte,* 44f.

90. Ibid., 47-99. With regard to the eighteen texts Jeremias did emphasize that in many cases one can argue about whether an agraphon has a claim to authenticity as high as the sayings in the synoptic Gospels (45). Cf. also idem, "Isolated Sayings of the Lord," in Hennecke/Schneemelcher I (n. 64) (85-90), 86f.

91. On this point see my brief reflections in *TRE* II, 107f.

92. Cf. text and translation in Jeremias, *Unbekannte Jesusworte,* 50ff.

93. Cf. ibid.; idem, "Der Zusammenstoß Jesu mit dem pharisäischen Oberpriester auf dem Tempelplatz," in FS Anton Fridrichsen (CB.NT 11, 1947) 97-108; idem, "An Unknown Gospel of Synoptic Type (Pap. Ox. 840)," in Hennecke/Schneemelcher I (n. 64), 92-94. Cf. also W. Bieder, *Die Verheißung der Taufe im Neuen Testament,* 1966, 95-101.

questions remain whether the contrast between external purity and internal impurity expressed here was not modeled on the cry of woe in Matt. 23:27f. and whether the reference to cleansing in "living" water was not oriented to statements in John's Gospel (4:10ff.; 7:37; 3:5; 13:10f.; 15:3).[94]

2. The Syriac *Liber Graduum* repeatedly presents this agraphon:

As you were found
so will you be taken away.[95]

This is a reference to the sifting (which excludes every possibility of conversion) which the angels of God will carry out on the day of judgment when it suddenly dawns. One must take into consideration that the agraphon only tersely summarizes what is depicted at length in synoptic sayings like Matt. 24:27, 40f. and Luke 17:24, 26-30, 34f.

3. Among the parables preserved in the Coptic Gospel of Thomas which have no parallel in the synoptic Gospels[96] the parable of the great fish stands out both in form and in content (Gospel of Thomas 8):

The kingdom is like a wise fisherman[97] who cast his net into the sea; he drew it up from the sea full of small fish; among them he found a large (and) good[98] fish; that wise fisherman threw all the small fish down into the sea; he chose the large fish without regret.

94. Also Jeremias, *Unbekannte Jesusworte,* 58, sees a "later stylization" in the concluding lines (lines 41-45). Concerning the woe pronouncement over the "blind," cf. also Matt. 23:16f., 19, 24, 26 (15:14) and the mention of "dogs and swine" in Matt. 7:6.

95. *Liber Graduum,* Serm. 3.3 (ed. M. Kmosko, PS I/3, 49, 26f.); 3.3 (52, 7f.); 15.4 (344, 15f.); similarly 24.2 (720, 13). I regard the extracanonical dominical saying in Justin, *Dial.* 47.5 (ἐν οἷς ἄν ὑμᾶς καταλάβω, ἐν τούτοις καὶ κρίνω) as a secondary reshaping of an agraphon (possibly influenced by Ezek. 33:20). See thereon and on the numerous parallels my comments in Jeremias, *Unbekannte Jesusworte,* 30-84. For further material see A. Baker, "Justin's Agraphon in the Dialogue with Trypho," *JBL* 87 (1968) 277-287.

96. Apart from Gospel of Thomas 8 we are speaking of the parables of the little children in the field (21a), the inattentive woman (97), and the criminal (98). I view logia 21a and 97 as Gnostic creations and 98 as a secondary and unimaginative analogue to Luke 14:28-32. C.-H. Hunzinger, "Unbekannte Gleichnisse Jesu aus dem Thomas-Evangelium," in *Judentum—Urchristentum—Kirche,* Festschrift J. Jeremias, BZNW 26, [2]1964 (209-20), 211ff., pleads for the authenticity of 98 (cf. J. Jeremias, *The Parables of Jesus,* ET [2]1972, 196f.). I cannot believe that Jesus, who on the evidence of the synoptic Gospels was a master story-teller, would have invented such an utterly artificial and unrealistic scene.

97. The Coptic text reads: "The Man is like a wise fisherman." In place of Coptic *rōme* (man) the reading *m*ᶜ*ntero* (= βασιλεία) must have been original; see on this emendation, J. Jeremias, *Unbekannte Jesusworte,* 85; P. Nagel, "Die Parabel vom klugen Fischer in Thomasevangelium von Nag Hammadi," in *Beiträge zur Alten Geschichte und deren Nachleben,* Festschrift F. Altheim, I, 1969, 518-24. For the translation of the beginning of the parable cf. Jeremias, *Parables* (n. 96), 102, n. 56.

98. The Coptic word *nouf* may be a rendering of καλός (cf. Greeven [n. 77] 96), but not of ἀγαθός (so Kasser [n. 77] 40). In favor of this assumption is Clement of Alexandria, *Strom.* 1.16.3 (ἐν πολλῇ τῇ τῶν ἰχθύων ἄγρα ὁ καλλιχθύς), which does admittedly refer to our parable (cf. Hunzinger [n. 96] 217f., n. 37). In the Sahidic translation of the New Testament *nouf* is the translation of καλός 92 times, and of ἀγαθός 32 times. Cf. also the translation by T. O. Lambdin in *The Nag Hammadi Library,* [2]1988, 127: "a fine large fish."

Though in the context of the Gospel of Thomas this parable doubtless also has a Gnostic meaning,[99] in no way does it permit itself to be understood as a partially Gnostic secondary form of the parable of the fishnet (Matt. 13:47f.).[100] What we have here is rather an independent and original but definitely non-Gnostic parable that in structure and meaning bears a close relationship to the parable of the pearl of great value (Matt. 13:45f.) and also has some affinity with the parable of the treasure hidden in the field (Matt. 13:44). In addition, with the two Matthean parables it also shares the feature that it utilizes a traditional narrative motif.[101] When the fisherman catches a "large" and "good" fish and then does something unusual (choosing just the one fish), this is very reminiscent of a passage in the story (told by Herodotus) of the ring of Polycrates.[102] There a fisherman catches "a large and beautiful fish" (ἀνὴρ ἁλιεὺς λαβὼν ἰχθὺν μέγαν τε καὶ καλόν), which, with a florid speech, he then presents to the king as a gift. The motif, widespread in antiquity, of the catch of a large and beautiful fish may also have been used in the parable. That the story of the ring of Polycrates was known in Palestine is evident from Matt. 17:27 and rabbinical narratives.[103]

Now as far as the tradition-historical assessment of the parable of the great fish is concerned, there are two conceivable possibilities. Since the parable is marked by Palestinian local coloring[104] and displays a very close affinity with the two parables in Matthew (13:44, 45f.), there is the possibility, on the one hand, that we are dealing with an old independent tradition which may have as high a claim to authenticity as the Matthean parables. On the other hand, however, there is also the possibility that we are dealing here with a secondary reproduction formed on the model of the parable of the pearl of great value—and that in the form in which the Gospel of Thomas gives it in logion 76: "The Kingdom of the Father is like a man, a merchant, who possessed merchandise (and) found a pearl. That merchant was prudent. He sold the merchandise and bought the one pearl for himself."

4. Clement of Alexandria, Origen, and Eusebius all cite as a saying of Jesus this prayer directive:

Ask for the great things
and God will add to you the little things.

---

99. Cf. Schrage (n. 78), 37ff.
100. Contra Schrage.
101. On Matt. 13:44, 45f., see Jeremias, *Parables* (n. 96), 198-201, and for the rabbinical material see Billerbeck I, 614, 674f.
102. Herodotus, *Hist.* 3.40-43; here 42.1f.
103. b. Shabb. 119a; Gen. Rabbah 11:5 on 2:3 par. Pesiqtah Rabbati 23:6; Qoheleth Rabbah 11:3 on v. 1.
104. Cf. Jeremias, *Unbekannte Jesusworte,* 85f.

αἰτεῖσθε τὰ μεγάλα,
καὶ τὰ μικρὰ ὑμῖν προστεθήσεται.[105]

This prayer directive is both formally and materially related to Matt. 6:33 par. Luke 12:31 (ζητεῖτε . . . πρῶτον τὴν βασιλείαν [τοῦ θεοῦ] καὶ τὴν δικαιοσύνην αὐτοῦ, καὶ ταῦτα πάντα προστεθήσεται ὑμῖν / ζητεῖτε τὴν βασιλείαν αὐτοῦ, καὶ ταῦτα προστεθήσεται ὑμῖν). Hence this agraphon could be an application of the synoptic maxim to the subject of prayer, an application made perhaps in the catechetical instruction of the Church.[106] However, the alternative possibility that it is an independent dominical saying, definitely remains worth considering.[107]

5. In early Christian writings a saying occurs with extreme frequency which calls the followers of Jesus to exercise sober evaluation and to discern spirits.

Be approved money changers.

γίνεσθε τραπεζῖται δόκιμοι.[108]

Origen and other authors expressly designate the maxim as a saying of Jesus,[109] and it is definitely conceivable that the maxim was already passed down in the earliest Church as a pronouncement from Jesus.

A reason for not adopting this assumption, however, may be the circumstance that in the earliest authors this agraphon is linked with an allusion to I Thess. 5:21f. (πάντα δοκιμάζετε, τὸ καλὸν κατέχετε ἀπὸ παντὸς εἴδους πονηροῦ ἀπέχεσθε) or with a direct quotation of this Pauline statement.[110] These early Christian authors clearly understood the word εἶδος—against the meaning found in Paul's writings—in the sense of "piece of money"[111] and accordingly found in I Thess. 5:21f. the directive to test critically the spirits (vv. 19f.), just as a skillful money changer tests coins. In light of this, one cannot rule out the possibility that the agraphon originated from this statement of Paul, thus interpreted, and therefore that, as W. Bauer suspected, it is "but an epexegesis of I Thess. 5:21."[112] That Dionysius

---

105. Clement of Alexandria, *Strom.* 1.24.158; Origen, *In Ps.* 4.4; *De orat.* 2.2; 14.1; Eusebius, *In Ps.* 16.2. Origen and Eusebius write αἰτεῖτε; προστεθήσεται is divine passive.

106. Koester is a bit too certain that the agraphon is "doubtless" a newly-formed analogue modeled on Matt. 6:33 (cf. *Die außerkanonischen Herrenworte* [n. 51], 226).

107. Cf. Jeremias, *Unbekannte Jesusworte,* 93ff.

108. The material is in Resch (n. 30), 112ff. In addition there is G. W. H. Lampe, *A Patristic Greek Lexicon,* ⁵1978, 1400, s.v. τραπεζίτης. On the imagery cf. Philo, *De Spec. Leg.* 4.77: "Let him who prepares himself to sit in judgment isolate and separate things according to their nature like a good money changer (καθάπερ ἀργυραμοιβὸς ἀγαθός) to avoid bringing together and confusing the genuine and the spurious."

109. Origen, *In Joh.* 19.7; Pistis Sophia, ch. 134; *Ps.-Clem. Hom.* 2.51.1; 3.50.2; 18.20.4; John Chrysostom, *Hom. in princ. Act. Apost.* 4.2; Jerome, *Ep.* 99.11.2; Socrates, *HE* 3.16; *Vita St. Syncleticae* 100.

110. So already the oldest witness, Clement of Alexandria, who adduces the saying as a word of Scripture: γίνεσθε δὲ δόκιμοι τραπεζῖται, τὰ μὲν ἀποδοκιμάζοντες, τὸ δὲ καλὸν κατέχοντες (*Strom.* 1.28.177).

111. Cf. J. Jeremias, *Unbekannte Jesusworte,* 97f.

112. W. Bauer, *Das Leben Jesu* (n. 8), 400.

of Alexandria, a contemporary of Origen, commented on the saying as ἀποστολικὴ φωνή[113] deserves consideration in this connection.

While these five agrapha thus elude unambiguous tradition-historical appraisal, there are no well-founded objections against the four remaining ones.[114] With these four, dependence on the synoptic tradition or development from an Old Testament or apostolic saying can neither be demonstrated nor even suspected on arguable grounds:

1. In Codex Bezae Cantabrigiensis (D) there occurs, in place of Luke 6:5, a short narrative at the center of which is a dominical warning against a frivolous transgression of the sabbath commandment:

> On the same day he saw a man working on the sabbath. Then said he unto him: *"Man, if thou knowest what you are doing, you are blessed. But if you do not know, you are cursed and a transgressor of the law."* (ἄνθρωπε, εἰ μὲν οἶδας τί ποιεῖς, μακάριος εἶ, εἰ δὲ μὴ οἶδας, ἐπικατάρατος καὶ παραβάτης εἶ τοῦ νόμου.)

A New Testament pronouncement comparable to this agraphon can nowhere be specified. Jeremias has persuasively shown that the language of this antithetical sentence definitely suggests that the most likely provenance is Palestine.[115]

2. A Coptic agraphon (Gospel of Thomas 82), which was also familiar to Origen and Didymus of Alexandria and may have been drawn by both from a Greek version of the Gospel of Thomas, speaks of the seriousness and promise of discipleship:[116]

> Whoever is near me
> is near the fire;
> whoever is far from me
> is far from the kingdom.

> ὁ ἐγγύς μου,
> ἐγγὺς τοῦ πυρός.
> ὁ δὲ μακρὰν ἀπ' ἐμοῦ,
> μακρὰν ἀπὸ τῆς βασιλείας.

C. Burchard has called attention to the similarity in formal structure between this agraphon and the statement in b. Qid. 66b par. b. Zeb. 13a: "Ahiba, he that

---

113. Eusebius, *HE* 7.7.3. Cyril of Alexandria ascribes the saying to Paul (see Resch [n. 30] 116, no. 34-36).

114. For these agrapha see Jeremias, *Unbekannte Jesusworte*, 61-64, 64-73, 88f., 91f.

115. Ibid., 61, 62. Against Dalman's argument that the vocative ἄνθρωπε is a Grecism, Jeremias remarks that "the address 'Man' is attested in Hebrew (Mic. 6:8; Ezek. 2:1ff.; Dan. 8:17) and in Arabic, but, as far as we know, however, not in Aramaic." As an *Aramaic* instance I would cite Midrash Ps. 103.10 on v. 7: "O man (וההי בר נש), when your deeds are merciful, you will receive mercy (from God)." For Hebrew examples in the rabbinic literature, see Lev. R. 2.6 on 1:2; Eccl. R. 1 § 4 on v. 3.

116. Origen, *In Jerem. Hom. lat.* 3.3; Didymus, *In Ps.* 88.8. On this agraphon and on the tradition, independent of the Gospel of Thomas, of the agraphon surviving in an Armenian "Explanation of the Gospel" ascribed to Ephraem Syrus, see Jeremias, *Unbekannte Jesusworte*, 64ff.

separates himself from you separates himself from life."[117] In content this agraphon, like the logion in Luke 12:49 (cf. Mark 9:49) brings to expression that the eschatological fire of tribulation and eschatological salvation (βασιλεία) appeared with the coming of Jesus and that the issue of fellowship with God or distance from God hinges on one's attitude to Jesus.[118] The echoes of Luke 12:49 and Mark 9:49 do not, however, allow us to view the agraphon as a new formation developed from the synoptic sayings.

3. From the Gospel to the Hebrews Jerome adduces a teaching of Jesus to the disciples which—in light of the Aramaic wording underlying it—is to be translated:

> And never be joyful,
> save when you look upon your brother in love.
>
> Et numquam (inquit) laeti sitis,
> nisi cum fratrem vestrum videritis in caritate.[119]

While Gospel of Thomas 25, discussed above, can clearly be regarded as an expansion of the love-commandment (Lev. 19:18 = Matt. 19:19b; Mark 12:31 par.), the agraphon from the Gospel to the Hebrews can hardly be understood as a "variation" on that commandment.[120]

4. In the fragmentarily preserved Oxyrhynchus Papyrus 1224,[121] which is probably from an apocryphal gospel, we read this statement of Jesus:

> And pray for your [ene]mies (cf. Matt. 5:44),
> For he who is not [against yo]u is for you (cf. Luke 9:50).
> [He that] stands far off [today] will tomorrow be [near you].

The first clause, a version of the command to love one's enemies modified to relate to intercession (Matt. 5:44; Luke 6:27), occurs also in the Didache, in Justin, and in the Syriac *Didascalia*.[122] The second is an almost word-for-word reproduction of Luke 9:50b. Linked with the two familiar logia is an agraphon which cannot be explained as an adaptation of a canonical dominical saying:

> [ὁ σήμερον ὢ]ν μακρὰν αὔριον [ἐγγὺς ὑμῶν γ]ενήσεται.

This agraphon may have been familiar to the author of the *Liber Graduum*. Serm. 20.13 explains that the Lord also became an example to Christians of how to relate to their enemies: "Vos, inquit, patienter *orate pro eis,* ut salventur. Si

117. C. Burchard, "Das doppelte Liebesgebot in der frühen christlichen Überlieferung," in *Der Ruf Jesu und die Antwort der Gemeinde,* Festschrift J. Jeremias, 1970 (39-62), 57, n. 80.

118. Cf. F. Lang, TDNT VI, 943f., n. 84; Jeremias, *Unbekannte Jesusworte,* 70f.

119. Jerome, *In Eph.* 5.4. On the language cf. Jeremias, *Unbekannte Jesusworte,* 88f.

120. Against Köster, *Die außerkanonischen Herrenworte* (n. 51), 227.

121. Klostermann (n. 10), 26.

122. Did. 1:3; Justin, *Apol. I* 15.9; Syr. *Didascalia,* ch. 21 (ed. A. Vööbus, CSCO 407, 209, 10). Cf. A. Vööbus, *Studies in the History of the Gospel Text in Syriac,* CSCO 128, 1951, 137f.

paenitentiam, inquit, egerint, ecce eos ipsos pudebit delictorum suorum *et adibunt vos* (Syriac: *w'tjn l'pjkwn*) et vivent. . . . Vos autem, ait, . . . *orate pro eis,* ut surgant."[123]

If, looking back, we now summarize the results of our examination, we have to say: Of the immense quantity of agrapha only nine texts remain which can be put, with some reservations, on a level with the sayings of Jesus in the synoptic Gospels. That for these nine agrapha this does not settle the issue of *authenticity,* but only raises it, is self-evident. At this point I do not wish to enter upon a discussion of this question except to say that I consider the historicity of the scene pictured in Luke 6:5 D and the authenticity of the directive "Be approved money changers" quite improbable,[124] and that, in my opinion, neither the authenticity nor the nonauthenticity of the remaining seven can be stringently proven.

5.

A brief sketch of a number of observations resulting from our study of the agrapha must now close our reflections:

1. The number of agrapha which can be put on a level with the sayings of Jesus in the synoptic Gospels is strikingly small: nine sayings, if one includes the texts which are doubtful from a tradition-historical point of view, and only four if one excludes them. This finding, in my opinion, constitutes an argument against the assumption that the Jesus-logia incorporated in the synoptic Gospels represent a much larger pre-synoptic stock of traditional material and that the body of material presented in the synoptic Gospels must be regarded as the result of a deliberate process of selection and elimination. On the contrary—also taking the Gospel of John into our purview—one may say: "Our four canonical Gospels embrace with great completeness almost all the early Church knew of the sayings and deeds of Jesus in the second half of the first century."[125] If at the end of the first century there had been in existence, in addition to the synoptic Gospels, still another rich—oral or even written—deposit of logia, then why

123. Tr. by M. Kmosko, PS I/3, 563, 13ff. Also cf. Did. 1:3: ὑμεῖς δὲ φιλεῖτε τοὺς μισοῦντας ὑμᾶς, καὶ οὐχ ἕξετε ἐχθρόν; Syr. *Didascalia* lat. (Funk [n. 61], 8, 3f.): "diligite odientes vos et orate pro maledicentibus vos, et inimicum nullum habebitis" (= Syr., ch. 1 [ed. A. Vööbus, CSCO 401, 14, 3f.]).

124. For Luke 6:5 D I refer to E. Lohse, *TDNT* VII, 23f.; H. Schürmann, *Das Lukasevangelium,* HTK I, 1969, 304, n. 29; J. Roloff, *Das Kerygma und der irdische Jesus,* 1970, 87f. On the agraphon "Be approved money changers" see the statements above as well as my consideration in *TRE* II, 108f.

125. J. Jeremias, "Die Zuverlässigkeit der Evangelien-Überlieferung," *JK* 6, 1938 (572-82), 580 (I consider this formulation more apt than what was said in the *Unbekannte Jesusworte*[3], 11); cf. also Ropes, *Agrapha* (n. 41), 344b.

the early Church did not set store by the collection and preservation of these utterances of its Lord would be inexplicable.[126]

2. Jeremias has offered the opinion that the agrapha that can be put on a level with the dominical sayings in the synoptic Gospels "almost without exception" stem from the apocryphal gospels.[127] But it seems to me that it is hardly possible to present convincing proof for this opinion. Only from the agraphon passed down by Jerome do we hear something of its origin in the Gospel to the Hebrews (p. 356 above). But about this source we know next to nothing. The script of Oxyrhynchus Papyrus 1224 (p. 356) points toward the beginning of the fourth century, that of Oxyrhynchus Papyrus 840 (p. 351) to the time around 400. The very fragmentary text of the two papyri does not permit us to make a judgment about the character and age of the lost gospels and certainly not about the way they use their sources. With regard to the Coptic Gospel of Thomas the question of sources is still open. I have the growing impression that the Greek prototype,[128] which goes back to the middle of the second century, presupposes a knowledge of the canonical Gospels. Whether Gospel of Thomas 8 (see pp. 352f.) and 82 (see p. 355) stem from a written collection of logia or from the oral tradition cannot be resolved. The issue of provenance and transmission in the case of the saying in Luke 6:5 D and the agrapha passed down by Clement of Alexandria (pp. 353f. above), Origen (pp. 353f.), and in the *Liber Graduum* (p. 347) remains open. One may consider whether the agrapha which withstood critical scrutiny finally go back to the oral preaching and catechetical instruction of the Church, but that is no more than a hunch. So with regard to the question of the tradition to which the nine agrapha belonged we must be content with a modest "we do not know."

3. In the case of none of the nine agrapha which survived the sifting processs can it be made plausible, to say nothing of proving it, that the pronouncement attributed to the earthly Jesus goes back to an original post-Easter prophetic utterance. As far as the extracanonical logia which fall outside the group of those nine agrapha are concerned, here too the personal pronouncements and I-sayings of Jesus are in no way traceable to prophetic utterances. To the extent that we are not dealing with haggadic or heretical inventions, in the overwhelming majority dependence on synoptic or Johannine dominical sayings and, in the remaining cases, dependence on other scriptural passages is evident.[129]

---

126. Whether Papias's five volumes entitled *Explanation of the Sayings of the Lord*, written around AD 130, contained valuable material has to be questioned (cf. E. Bammel, *RGG*[3] V, 47f.: "Genuine traditional material cannot be established" [48]). The skepticism of Eusebius in *HE* 3.39 cannot be ignored. Cf. also the critical comments in Jeremias, *Unbekannte Jesusworte,* 37f., 112. Cf. also B. Altaner and A. Stuiber, *Patrologie* ([9]1980) 53.

127. Jeremias, *Unbekannte Jesusworte,* 45.

128. Witnesses for the Greek version are Oxyrhynchus Papyri 1 (soon after 200), 654 (end of second–beginning of third centuries), and 655 (second or third century).

129. On the pronouncements and I-sayings dependent on canonical dominical sayings, see

These observations by themselves do not, of course, constitute a convincing objection against the form-critical thesis according to which such sayings, uttered originally by early Christian prophets in the name of the exalted Christ, have in no small measure been put on the same level with transmitted sayings of the earthly Jesus. The facts to be noted in the case of each of the agrapha do, however, constitute additional critical arguments alongside the well-founded objections that F. Neugebauer, D. Hill, and J. D. G. Dunn have lodged against that thesis.[130]

4. With regard to the agrapha which originated within the ancient Church—and are therefore nonheretical—and which do not qualify for classification among the group of sayings in section 4 above, we have before us on the whole an astonishing picture: apart from haggadic-legendary pronouncements and deliberate or mistaken attributions, we are dealing predominantly with expansions, with modifications, with blends of synoptic (occasionally also Johannine) logia, and in rare instances with formations modeled on canonical dominical sayings or with the conversion of narrative notations in the Gospels into direct statements by Jesus. *By comparison the number of completely free creations is quite minimal.*[131] This must be noted as a phenomenon worthy of consideration and reflection. The palpable tie-in with the pre-existing tradition of dominical sayings makes it definitely doubtful, in my opinion, that the early Church freely, on a large scale, and without inhibitions, produced sayings of the earthly Jesus.[132] The minting of dominical sayings by the Church ought in no

the examples cited in the present essay; also, for example, the agrapha noted in Resch (n. 30), no. 84, 91 (developed from Matt. 25:35f., 42f.), 93, 107, 108, 110-13, 117-19, 123, and 124. The agraphon cited in Macarius, *Hom.* 12.17 (Resch, no. 104), is indebted to Acts 20:32f.; Eph. 1:18f.; I Pet. 1:4; basic to the agraphon cited by Epiphanius, *Panar. haer.* 23.5.5 (Resch, no. 185), is Isa. 52:6; and basic to the agraphon attested by several authors, Resch, no. 84—despite Resch's objections (pp. 108f.)—is Isa. 24:16. Not agrapha, but free closing formations, are the two I-sayings in Barn. 7:5, 11; on this, see Koester, *Synoptische Überlieferung* (n. 83), 127f.; idem, *Die außerkanonische Herrenworte* (n. 51), 230f.

130. F. Neugebauer, "Geistsprüche und Jesuslogien," *ZNW* 53, 1962, 218-28; D. Hill, "On the Evidence for the Creative Role of Christian Prophets," *NTS* 20, 1973-74, 262-74; J. D. G. Dunn, "Prophetic 'I'-sayings and the Jesus Tradition: The Importance of Testing Prophetic Utterances in Early Christianity," *NTS* 24, 1977-78, 175-98.

131. They are essentially limited to the composite formations discussed in Jeremias (*Unbekannte Jesusworte*, 41ff.) among which also Luke 22:28a D must be classified. Free formations are further (a) the agraphon cited in Macarius, *Hom.* 37.1 (ἐπιμελεῖσθε πίστεως καὶ ἐλπίδος, δι' ὧν γεννᾶται ἡ φιλόθεος καὶ φιλάνθρωπος ἀγάπη ἡ τὴν αἰώνιον ζωὴν παρέχουσα); (b) the dominical saying from the *Apostolic Constitutions*, ch. 26 (τὸ ἀσθενὲς διὰ τοῦ ἰσχυροῦ σωθήσεται); (c) the saying of "the Savior" in the late Acts of Thomas (ed. J. A. Robinson, Texts and Studies V/1, 1897, 28-45; ὁ λυτρούμενος ψυχὰς ἀπὸ τῶν εἰδώλων, οὗτος ἔσται μέγας ἐν τῇ βασιλείᾳ μου [29, 16f.]). A special case is the free formations (though created with the help of older material) in the Syriac *Liber Graduum* (fifth century [?]), which are the responsibility of the unknown author and express his specific theological views.

132. The Gospel of John cannot be adduced as proof of the contrary. The sayings and discourses of Jesus contained in it are in no way intended to be primarily understood as pronouncements of the earthly Jesus. In the understanding of the fourth evangelist, they are ῥήματα ζωῆς

way to be fundamentally called in question by this fact—the agraphon of Luke
6:5 D, as I would think, offers clear proof of this. What we do have to doubt,
however, is that the Church was very productive in the minting of new sayings
of Jesus. If this view corresponded with historical reality, then, analogously to
the state of affairs prevailing in heretical circles, the number of pure creative
Church additions (*Gemeindebildungen*) among the agrapha formulated and
transmitted in the Church would have to be considerably larger. This conclusion
seems to me inescapable—unless one were prepared to reach for the less
plausible thought that in nonheretical early Christianity the free production of
new Jesus-sayings had suddenly ceased with the rise of the canonical Gospels.

Study of the agrapha, as has become clear, has to do with very disparate
materials and with texts of very diverse quality. Here we cannot discuss what
the implications of this study are for study of the history of the early Church and
its theology. If we should inquire into the significance for the study of the
Gospels, then, looking out over the material as a whole, one can only assent
without qualification to the judgment of Jeremias: "The real value of the
tradition outside the Gospels is that it throws into sharp relief the unique value
of the canonical Gospels themselves."[133]

αἰωνίου (6:68; cf. 6:63; 5:24; 8:31f., 51)—the words of the Christ and Son of God who was regarded
as inseparably united with the incarnate, crucified, and exalted One. When the evangelist offers *his*
witness to Christ in the form of sayings and discourses of *Jesus,* he thereby brings to expression the
idea that the apostolic witness to Christ does not constitute a human value-judgment *about* Christ.
The witness can only utter what the Lord who is present in the Spirit has disclosed to him (cf.
14:16ff.; 15:26f.; 16:12ff.); and he can only do this in the certainty that the self-attesting Lord alone
speaking in this witness to Christ is able to convince the reader or hearer of the truth of this testimony.

133. *Unknown Sayings,* 32; cf. *Unbekannte Jesusworte,* 112.

The Gospels and Greek Biography*

Albrecht Dihle

The question concerning the genre (Gattung) to which one can assign the Gospels is complex and therefore hard to answer. Within the sphere of this question, however, one thing seems to be unproblematic: every theological student is warned in his first semester against reading the four canonical Gospels as biographies of Jesus. In this negative categorization of the literary character of our Gospels all schools of New Testament exegesis seem to agree.

Though such a consensus can easily be explained in light of the history of research in the last 100 years, it is worth remembering that it runs counter to an understanding that prevailed for more than 1500 years. This understanding underlies the attempt, made again and again from the second century on, to explain the differences between the four Gospels; and the life-of-Jesus research of the nineteenth century, which steadily distanced itself from the doctrinal tradition of the Church, still shared this understanding of the Gospels.

Indeed, the evangelists quite plainly aim to provide a chronologically ordered account of the earthly life of Jesus, be it in each case with a different degree of completeness and from a different perspective. The avoidance of the term "biography" to describe this fact can only be explained in terms of specific and possibly short-lived concerns of New Testament scholarship. In any case, in my opinion, there is nothing against reading, and hence against describing, the Gospels as biographies, provided one misunderstanding is excluded: by doing this one has not said anything about their peculiar genre in the strict sense of the word.

For a given text to be assigned meaningfully to a literary genre a large number of conditions must be met. If one does not wish unbearably to overwork the concept of genre, it can be applied only to a small fraction of that which people past and present have written.

*A shorter version of this essay appeared in *ZTK* 80, 1983, 33-49, under the title: "Die Evangelien und die biographischen Traditionen der Antike."

Whether a given text belongs to a literary genre and whether the genre in question is therefore represented in that text can be asserted only when over a long period of time the tradition of certain literary procedures has been stabilized in the sense of a genre defined in terms of those procedures. This relates to conventions of language and rhythm, to rules of composition, and to the relationship between the intentions of an author or series of authors and the expectations of a specific public. Not until agreement has resulted and maintained itself over many generations and in all these respects does a literary genre come into being. It proves its vitality, versatility, and productivity by the fact that not infrequently it survives the historical conditions under which it arose and assumed a stable form, and moves from one language into another. A good example of this is the history of tragedy.

The major proportion of the written, indeed even of the literary, communication of a society takes place outside of that which can be subsumed under the concept of genre. This is especially true for biography. Biographical interest tends to make itself felt in every group whose self-consciousness lasts longer than one generation. Lawgivers, military leaders, builders, liberators, tyrants, and many other individuals whose actions have shaped the life of the group have the possibility, after their death at the latest, that people will have an interest in the circumstances of their life. Satisfying this biographical interest are many subliterary and literary forms which have never risen to the status of a literary genre. One only has to think of anecdotes, apothegms, and comparable forms of expression. They all have the potential, given the right occasion, of coming together to form a complete or partial biographical account, perhaps in eulogies or tomb inscriptions, to instruct youth, to serve paranetic purposes in critical situations of the group, and to fortify the awareness of its values and traditions. That full-fledged biographies, in the sense of a literary genre, should grow out of such biographical notices is anything but self-evident and has in fact only rarely occurred.

In the following one must therefore bear in mind that the word "biography" can be used in a technical as well as in a nontechnical sense. There may very well exist biographical accounts for which one does not have to trouble oneself about the "genre" concept in order to place them.

The form and manner of presentation peculiar to gospel accounts developed over a period of almost 200 years, and one presumably has the right to speak in this connection of a genre. If one now asks about a possible relationship between this process and Greek biography, it is natural to focus on Greek biography to the extent that one of its branches evolved into a literary genre with a tradition of distinct forms.

The currently prevailing direction in New Testament studies, a direction characterized by source analysis as well as form and tradition criticism, has proven to be very fruitful and one can as yet in no way predict its import for the future. Although in this manner the peculiar nature of the Gospels, each of them transmitted as a unity and under the name of a distinct author, is explained in terms of the theological Tendenz, the historical evidential value, and the specific selection of preformed pieces of tradition, it is not subjected to literary-historical appraisal. This is already evident from the fact that the usual reference works and textbooks,[1] even those that deal with textual and literary theories, provide, under the heading "literary forms and genres," a wealth of information about the elements of tradition present in the text of the Gospels—parabolic discourses, miracle stories, parenesis, prayers, etc.—but hardly a word about the form of the Gospel account as such in its transformation from Mark to Luke right up to the extensive gospel literature of the second and early third centuries.

That for centuries, right up to "the quest of the historical Jesus,"[2] the canonical Gospels were read as coherent portrayals of the life and activity of Jesus, was not so far off the mark. From the beginning, as certain statements of the apostle Paul show, biographical and prosopographic details constituted fixed components of the Christian message. Precisely at this point the Gospels distinguished themselves from their Jewish environment, which of course possessed very similar doctrinal and ecclesial traditions. How scanty the prosopographic information given in Pirqe 'Aḇōt, and how little one learns of the founder of the Qumran community, the "Teacher of Righteousness"![3]

Amidst the wealth of biographical detail preserved in the synoptic and postsynoptic tradition two events stand out: the baptism by John the Baptist and the passion, the latter handed down with what appear to be at times marginal particulars. From the start these two events clearly marked the beginning and end of the earthly activity of Jesus and provided the framework in which one can fit the sayings, parabolic narratives, and miracle stories. The incontestable fact of the baptism presented certain difficulties to the first adherents of Jesus and precisely for that reason had to be mentioned and explained. In this connection Isaiah 40 and 61 served as welcome aids to interpretation. The passion and crucifixion in their brutal facticity left such an overpowering impression on that first generation, however, that at first all theological reflection and every edifying and didactic purpose fell into the background while the

---

1. This is true, for example, of the pertinent articles in the last two editions of *RGG,* hence "Formen und Gattungen" (RGG³, 1958) as well as "Formgeschichte" and "Evangelien" (RGG², 1928). It is true of more recent literature: see P. Vielhauer, *Geschichte der urchristlichen Literatur,* 1975, 252ff. Also recent textual theory has little to say about the problem of Gattung; cf. K. Berger, *Exegese des Neuen Testamentes,* 1977, 33ff., 78ff., 128ff.

2. Cf. H. Kraft, "Die Evangelien und die Geschichte Jesu," *TZ* 37, 1981, 321-41. On the continuing rejection of the understanding of the Gospels as biographies, cf. G. N. Stanton, *Jesus of Nazareth in New Testament Preaching,* 1974, 118f.

3. Stanton, op. cit., 126ff.

biographical reality remained in the foreground. The literary form of a Gospel account, first attested in the case of Mark's Gospel, seems then to have been constituted by the fact that two chronologically fixed events in the life of Jesus provided the framework for a chronologically neutral body of traditional material that was shot through with individual biographical references, for numerous traditions of individual events in the life of Jesus attached themselves to parabolic discourses or miracle stories.

Now the important thing is that the form which thus originated was continued. This continuation took place in a line which runs from the Synoptists to the apocryphal evangelists of the second century either as a completion of the biography of the Lord or out of aversion to biographical portrayal embodied, for example, in certain Gnostic writings which were called gospels. The fact that contemporaries already saw a problem here is manifest in Origen's long essay about the meaning of the term "gospel" at the beginning of his commentary on John.

This completion of the biography of Jesus necessarily concerned above all two time segments: the period of his childhood and the Easter appearances. The development of the stories about Jesus' origins and birth, childhood and upbringing, relatives and vocation, begins for us in Matthew, in Luke attains approximately three times the scope, and later leads, as for example in the Protevangelium of James and the Infancy Gospel of Thomas, to lengthy creations. In the older version of Mark the tradition of the Risen One covers 8 verses in all, in Matthew it embraces 20 verses, and in Luke—ignoring for now the beginning of Acts—53 verses. The two relevant chapters of John's Gospel are still longer and much more richly developed. In the Encratite and Gnostic gospels of the second century, for example in the Gospel of Thomas, the entire message, preformulated in fixed units of tradition, is put in the mouth of the Risen One. The same thing occurs in the anti-Gnostic Epistula Apostolorum. This situation is particularly enlightening: on the one hand, such a procedure, borne out of a Gnostic-docetic mindset, eliminates the biographical framework, as the corporeal life of the Lord is stripped of its meaning. On the other, granted that sayings collections and the like may have served as sources, this gospel form at the same time stands in the tradition of a progressive development of the post-Easter biography which begins with the Synoptists.

Nor is the effort lacking to give a better order and richer development to the account of the life of Jesus in the period of his public activity—between baptism and passion. This shows, for example, in the varied accents with which the narrative of the beginning of that activity is furnished: hence in the great composition of the Sermon on the Mount in Matthew, in Jesus' appearance in Nazareth according to the report of Luke 4, or in the miracle at Cana in John. Also the arrangement of the events and discourses on the final journey to

Jerusalem points in this direction. This tendency is perhaps clearest in the difference between the three years which John, and the one year which the Synoptics, assume to be the time frame for that public activity. This divergence played a large role in the second century. The problem was enlarged by the fact that there were opinions, perhaps even gospel reports, which assumed a much longer time frame for Jesus' activity and therefore shifted the passion to the reign of Caesar Claudius.[4] The motive for these speculations was at the same time both theological and biographical: God's incarnation as human must occur in the course of a complete life, one that also embraced the higher stages of the age-scale. The reports concerning the appearance, the special character traits, or the vocational activity of the Lord, attested by some very late gospels,[5] doubtless belong in the same context.

Finally to be mentioned is that a number of Jewish Christian gospels similar to John's Gospel obviously deliberately exclude reports concerning Jesus' youth because in the opinion of their authors descent from God occurred at the baptism, not at conception or birth. The same is true for Marcion.[6] In the second century this decision makes sense only as a counter to an already established biographical tradition which includes the infancy narratives.

Accordingly, the conclusion to be drawn from these witnesses is that among Christians of the first and second centuries the description of the life of Jesus became increasingly important but that this significance found expression in a distinct literary form that was enriched from generation to generation. That this distinct form was already available at the turn of the first century is evident from its, in many respects, anti-traditional use by the author of the fourth Gospel.

Since in the same period the adaptation of Christians to the literary conventions of their cultural environment increased, one may well ask whether at some stage of the development of this gospel literature the model of the Greek biography, which was represented at the time by outstanding works, did not influence this process. This would not be unparalleled in the history of other literary genres current among Christians: the apocryphal Acts of the Apostles of the second and third centuries betray the influence of Greek novels, and the early hagiography of the fourth century is modeled, in part at least, on the biographies of philosophers.

In order to give a sensible answer to the question raised herewith one must certainly first define the concept of biography in a way that fits the literary-historical situation of the first and second centuries AD. It must also be noted that such an attempt at historical clarification concerns the rise of a literary form

---

4. Irenaeus, *Adv. Haer.* 2.22.3ff.; *Mart. Petri et Pauli* 18ff.; Hippolytus, *In Dan. Comm.* 4.3.

5. E. Hennecke and W. Schneemelcher, *New Testament Apocrypha* I, ET 1963, 433ff.

6. Adolph Harnack, *Marcion,* [2]1924, 52ff.

or genre, not the phenomenon of biographical interest as such. Mere similarities in the selection, transmission, and portrayal of biographical details, similarities which may be ascertained to exist both among non-Christians and Christians, therefore do not mean too much for the question we have chosen to consider.[7]

Several years ago the historian Arnaldo Momigliano[8] rightly called attention to the fact that the fathers of Greek historiography in the fifth century BC, Herodotus and Thucydides, did not pay too much attention to the life and work of great historical figures in their representation of Greek history. This is in striking contrast with the historiography of the ancient Orient where the focus of the narrative on the deeds of kings can be noted as a persistent feature. As is well known, the Old Testament also contains lengthy examples of such historiography centered on individuals. It is not surprising therefore that in Herodotus the sections devoted to specific persons as a rule reproduce traditions from the Orient and that the first examples of literature which resembles biography, memoirs for example, surface in the eastern part of the Greek world—where there was contact with the Orient.[9] Meanwhile the example of the great historians of the fifth century, who devoted their attention primarily to the suprapersonal factors of history, so marked the whole of the historiography of antiquity that the biography of the individual statesman or military commander could never become a recognized form of historiography. Things are quite different in more recent times: works like the Yorck biography by Droysen or the biography of Richelieu by C. J. Burckhardt are now viewed as specific, even classic, achievements in historiography.

The distinction made here is all the more noteworthy because since the fourth century interest in the outstanding individual in or out of political life had steadily increased also in Greece. One thinks here of Alexander the Great and his successors or of the totally individual ethical goals of post-classical philosophy. As early as the middle of the fourth century BC the historian Theopompus wrote a historical work about his own time in which the person and accomplish-

7. A good example of how the mere registration of similarities in motif cannot be the basis for far-reaching literary conclusions is F. Pfister's attempt to prove that a type of Cynic-Stoic Hercules biography served as model for the synoptic Gospels (ARW 34, 1937, 42-59). From information about the birth, youth, deeds, death, and ascension of Hercules, placed alongside of comparable passages in Luke's account, the author first infers the presence of a religious-philosophical Tendenz in the Hercules biography and then elevates it to the status of a model for the form of the Gospel accounts. Even if one pictures the Hercules literature of Cynic and Stoic provenance, which began with Antisthenes (fragments 22-28, Decleva-Caizzi), as fictitious biographies—which is anything but certain—there is nothing to warrant drawing a conclusion, on the basis of parallels in content, from the structure of Luke's Gospel to his supposed model. The fact that material parallels lose significantly in evidential power through reference to similar motifs in totally different contexts may be noted in passing.

8. A. Momigliano, *The Development of Greek Biography*, 1971.

9. H. Homeyer (*Philologus* 106, 1962, 75ff.) interprets Herodotus's stories of Cyrus and Cambyses as preliminary forms of Greek biography and compares them with the writing attributed to Skylax of Caryanda about the tyrant Heracleides of Mylasa (*Fragmente* [n. 10], no. 709 T 1).

ments of Philip II of Macedon were central and which was therefore titled "Philippica."[10] The notion of history which comes to expression in it can definitely be considered representative for a major part of Greek historiography. Nevertheless, it is to be remembered that such works of history centered on individuals were by no means biographies, in the sense that the character of an epoch was reflected in the life of a great individual as in a concave mirror. The biographical element in postclassical historiography had a different meaning: memorable events were to be made more intelligible by the fact that the reader learned something about the character and circumstances of the main actors. Herodotus and Thucydides, and in the postclassical period Polybius, clearly did not follow this idea, which is so vital in all popular historical and anecdotal traditions: One thinks of the traditions about Henry IV of France or of Frederick the Great. Postclassical historiography, as represented by Theopompus, the historian of Alexander, or by Duris of Samos, with its special focus on the acting individual, makes itself comparable to pre- or extraliterary tradition, as does the historiographic literature of the ancient Orient. One may freely, quite independently of all source-analysis, understand the historical narrative which extends from I Samuel 16 to I Kings 2 as the historical biography of David in which events derive their explanation from the fate and character of the king.

It is precisely at this point, however—namely the elucidation of memorable deeds which continue to affect the present, by means of information about the character and life-circumstances of the actors—that, according to Greek thought, the difference between biography and historiography lies. This distinction kept biography from ever becoming a recognized form of historiography among the Greeks, despite all the attentiveness which was devoted, particularly in the postclassical period, to the role of the individual in the historical process.

Around AD 100 Plutarch expressed himself on precisely this question in the introduction to a biography of Alexander the Great, hence a particularly significant historical figure.[11] Plutarch emphatically made the point that he wrote biographies and not historical works, and no reader should expect therefore to find a complete and correct account of Alexander's deeds. Such a statement is significant if for no other reason than that Plutarch had to rely altogether on historiographic sources which dealt primarily with Alexander's military campaigns.

But the significance of this distinction goes even further. Plutarch assures his reader that plain and insignificant events, often known only from anecdotal stories, illustrate the essence of his heroes much better than the great deeds

10. Fragments in F. Jacoby, *Die Fragmente der griech. Historiker* II[B], 1962, no. 115 F, 24ff.
11. Plutarch, *Alex.* 1.

which concern the historians. The reason that the Greek biographer is interested in the private life of his hero is not that from this source some light can be expected to fall on his historically important accomplishments. This would be the incentive motivating the historian to pay attention to biographical detail. On the contrary, the biographer studies the actions of his hero in order to draw inferences from that source for the understanding of his essential character, and in this regard everyday occurrences are more telling than great deeds.

The idea that inferences can be drawn for the character (τρόποι) of a person from his or her deeds (ἔργα) has become constitutive for the formation, in a formal sense, of the genre of the encomium.[12] To be sure, the concern of the encomiast is not the complete personality but its praiseworthy traits. For that reason the encomiast is interested neither in a complete account of the course of a person's life nor in the chronological sequence of events, and for the appraisal of the greatness of a hero the trivia of every day have little significance. Plutarch, on the other hand, clearly seeks to gain a complete picture of the character of his hero, one that is close to the everyday experience of his reader. Precisely this goal, however, requires the most complete account of the course of a person's private life, and Plutarch seems to be convinced that this is possible on the basis of historical sources even in the case of kings in distant countries or military heroes in much earlier epochs. Precisely for this reason it is more important for the reader of a biography of Alexander to know how he cleared his throat and spat than to remember the story and explanation of his world-shaking deeds.

One can understand the purpose of biographical writing in the sense intended by Plutarch only if one demands of a literary portrayal of a person's life that it entail a moral example which, regardless of all temporal and social differences, fits the everyday experience of the reader and can therefore serve the reader's moral education. Plutarch took this responsibility seriously and saw in it the real purpose of biographical authorship; in the introduction to his biographies of two rather unappealing figures he expressly describes them as negative moral examples[13] and thus justifies the selection made.

If from what older historiographic literature tells about outstanding persons one would gain pedagogical examples for a private morality which the reader is intended to practice in his own life, that cannot be achieved without omissions and additions. Plutarch was well aware of this, the more so since in his day there already existed a rich tradition in the technique of biographical invention—for example, by way of drawing conclusions from the writings of the hero.[14] Thus he makes clear to the reader of his biography of Solon that the

12. Xenophon, *Ages.* 1.6; similarly Isocrates, *Euag.* 65.

13. Plutarch, *Demetr.* 1; similarly *Sertor.* 10.

14. J. Fairweather, *Ancient Society* 5, 1974, 231-75; M. R. Lefkowitz, *Classical Quarterly* 28, 1978, 459-69.

encounter between the wise Athenian and the rich Lydian king Croesus made famous by Herodotus could hardly, on chronological grounds, have happened. Nevertheless, on account of the moral-pedagogical focus of his work he could not leave this incident out.[15]

Hence Plutarch's biographies belong in the sphere of moral theory and parenesis, and the same is true for many other biographies that we know of only indirectly.

The Greek word βίος not only denotes the life span of a person or the course of his life but also a person's livelihood and the form of his existence. A work with the title βίοι or βίος τοῦ δεῖνα can therefore just as well contain portrayals of the course of the life of individuals as the description of certain ways of living, for example of the political or contemplative life. But such a title can also mean that stories will be told of the lives of individuals as examples of a variety of ways of life, as in the lives of Socrates and Pythagoras by the Peripatetic Aristoxenos of the late fourth century BC.[16] The same applies *mutatis mutandis* to the biography which Nicolaus of Damascus, the court historian of Herod the Great, produced of Caesar Augustus.[17] Here, too, the idea is not to provide a historical work on the theme "Augustus and his Age"; rather, the life of the emperor is presented, in this case with an encomiastic intention, as the individual realization of timeless moral values.

Accordingly, one cannot simply define Greek biography as literary genre by saying that it describes lives with an attempt at completeness and with chronological precision. What interests the biographer is not the detailed account of the course of a life but the realization of morally appraised ways of conduct occurring in a human life grasped as a unity only from this perspective.

Basic to the literary category so defined, as one can learn from many expressions in Plutarch, is a most specific view of humankind. Important in this view is, first of all, the assumption that human nature is not affected by historical change. Plato and Caesar, Solon and Sulla, can all be described in the same anthropological and moral categories, because they all shaped their lives on the basis of the same natural prerequisites.

Granted that within this enduring arena nature distributes its gifts very unequally, and therefore individuals also turn out very unlike each other. Though natural aptitudes are the foundations of a structure of characteristics which a person constructs in the course of a lifetime, they themselves elude every moral judgment. Such moral judgments are reserved for good and bad modes of conduct, the ἤθη, of persons. They arise when a person, in the course of living

15. Plutarch, *Sol.* 27.
16. Fragments in F. Wehrli, *Die Schule des Aristoteles* II (Aristoxenos), 1945, fr. 11-41, 51-60.
17. Fragments in Jacoby (n. 10 above), no. 90 F, 126ff.

his life, regularly uses his natural gifts in order to respond to that which happens to him (πάθη) with deliberate, hence intellectually guided, actions (πράξεις). The entire complex of modes of conduct (ἕξεις), formed and established by constant action, then produces what one may call, with a modern word, *character*.[18] For this the Greeks knew only the plural expression τὰ ἤθη, the manners or conduct of persons. For them a person is fully responsible and subject to moral judgment, for nature has given him the capacity to guide his actions by reason.

The social environment in which a human life is lived is not a special object of the biographer's interest. Naturally, in an account of someone's life the relationships which that person sustained with others also come up for discussion. But for biographers like Plutarch they are of interest only insofar as they furnish insight into the character and conduct of the moral personality of the hero. This is precisely in keeping with the ethical individualism of all Hellenistic philosophy. It is true that all schools of philosophy incorporated far-reaching social demands in their ethics. But the rules for a person's social relations were designed to bring the individual closer to his own innately intended perfection, the real goal of moral effort.

Anyone somewhat familiar with ancient philosophy will recognize the handwriting of Aristotle in this doctrine of humakind which undergirds the structure of Plutarchian biography.[19] Consistent with this is what we learn from the adherents of the school of Aristotle in the early period of biographical authorship in the fourth century BC.

For almost all the early Peripatetics, fragments of whose writings have been assembled by Fritz Wehrli (see n. 16), writings bearing the title βίος, βίοι, περὶ βίων, and the like, are attested. It is true that the fragments or title indications do not always show whether they deal with the lives of individuals, with abstractly formulated discussions of certain types[20] or of types exemplified in the fortunes of individuals,[21] or with historical expositions written with the aid of traditions concerning individual persons.[22] At any rate, it is clear that already in the early days of the Peripatetic school the biographical treatment of interesting persons (interesting from a political or literary-historical point of

18. The famous "characters" of Theophrastus contain no personal profiles in our sense of the word at all but rather descriptions of individual, in fact extreme, modes of behavior. For that reason they are closer to comedy and its types than to philosophical ethics and psychology.

19. Cf. A. Dihle, *Studien zur griechischen Biographie,* [2]1970, as well as J. R. Hamilton, *Plutarch's Alexander—A Commentary,* 1969, xxxviiff.

20. So, for example, Theophrastus apud Diogenes Laertius 5.42 and Straton, fr. 18 W.

21. For example, Aristoxenos, fr. 26-32 W, and Dikaiarch, fr. 25-46 W. This type occurs in a particularly distinct form in the Pythagoras tradition, where the story of the biographical Pythagoras legend and the description of Pythagorean ways of life either interpenetrate or alternate.

22. Especially hard to judge in this respect are the pertinent fragments of Clearchus (fr. 37-62 W) and of Hieronymus of Rhodes (fr. 34-49).

view[23]) came up. Thus a wealth of biographical literature by authors unmoved by philosophical interest and by antiquarians of the late third and second centuries BC (Satyrus, Antigonos of Carystus, Hermippus, Heracleides Lembus) emerged which could continue the tradition of such models from the fourth and early third centuries BC. Of course biographical traditions continued in the literature of philosophy, as in the Alexandrian Sotion. It is to his biographies that still valid ideas concerning the inter-academic relationships of post-Socratic philosophy go back. It is also within these traditions that one finds the many sources of the biography of Epicurus in the work of Diogenes Laertius and of various biographies of Aristotle.

Unfortunately the tradition of biographical literature of the Hellenistic and imperial periods resembles a huge expanse of ruins in which only Plutarch's biographies stand out as complete monuments. It is impossible, therefore, with any confidence to undertake a reconstruction of the history of this literary genre and its formal development. All one can say without fear of contradiction is that the *Lives* of Plutarch possess a highly developed literary form and hence that they distinguish themselves from all other extant biographical accounts in Greek literature; further, that this form is inseparably bound up with a conception of human nature which had acquired its theoretical articulation in Aristotelian ethics (which in its basic features, to be sure, corresponds to very ancient ideas common to the Greeks). Add to this that over and over in Hellenistic times literati like Satyrus, who made a name for themselves *inter alia* by writing biographies, were called Peripatetics in our tradition, although in their case no closer connection with the school of Aristotle can be demonstrated. This suggests the conclusion that the close and very specific link between the literary form and the ethical-anthropological conceptions of Peripateticism which gives the *Lives* of Plutarch their distinctive stamp belongs to the tradition of this literary genre and must not just be regarded as the possession of the author.

Precisely the comparison with numerous crude "lives" of poets and philosophers which have come down from Graeco-Roman antiquity throws the exceptional position of Plutarch's *Lives* into sharp relief. However, that this difference in the development of the form does not, or does not primarily, as Friedrich Leo once thought, relate to a fundamentally different mode of treating figures of political-historical and literary-philosophical importance, is already apparent from the crude biographies of Ptolemaic kings which have come to light in a papyrus (P. Haun, p. 37). The predominance of persons of literary prominence in these artless biographies can be very simply explained by the fact that these were, in considerably larger numbers, the objects of learned philo-

---

23. The first is true for Phainias, fr. 20-28 W; the second for the biographies of poets by Chamaileon, fr. 23-43 W.

logical study whose results were preserved and passed on, as a rule, in all simplicity.[24]

In any case the literary genre of a more artistic biography, as documented in the work of Plutarch, is based on the specific fundamental anthropological notions described above.[25] Their unpolitical, unhistorical, private character results from the naturalism and individualism which determine the entire ethics of Hellenistic philosophy, and these conceptual and material attributes of Greek biography of the Plutarchian type influence also the rules for shaping its form.

Such a biography usually pays thorough attention to matters of origin, family, and childhood, since only information of this sort permits conclusions about the natural tendencies of the person presented. These conclusions, then, are expressly drawn over and over in the corresponding sections. The accounts of teachers and training can likewise claim more space because with them the development of moral conduct begins.

As a rule the biographer also provides a lengthy narrative concerning the final phase of the life of the hero and of his death, since here there is occasion to sum up and to take stock of the moral modes of behavior which, good or bad, manifested themselves in the course of this life and which cannot now ever be changed.

Where the sources, and the interest deemed to be present in the reader, permit, the incidents and events occurring between infancy and death are generally narrated in chronological order. Significantly, this is not true for those Greek life-sketches which only fulfill lexicographic, but not moral-pedagogic needs, for instance in the introduction to the edition of the work of a poet or works of reference. There lists of books, systematic accounts of philosophic doctrines, catalogues of friends, and the like frequently confuse the chronological sequence. But even in literary biographies, as Plutarch wrote them, the focus on the genesis and exercise of moral attributes occasionally outweighs chronological precision by so much that episodes which are comparable from a moral perspective are pulled together despite the chronology of events.

The selection and accentuation of the actual events of a person's life in a Plutarchian biography totally serve the purpose of documenting the moral development of the hero. Plutarch even attempts to do this where his sources only furnish him with a record of the main events or actions of a political nature. True: sometimes he cannot deny himself the pleasure of repeating at length the brilliant accounts of battle he has picked up.[26] But he is ever attentive to the manifestation of new ways of behaving in his hero, and also where these are

---

24. Cf. I. Gallo, "Un nuovo frammento di Cameleonte e il problema della 'biografia grammaticale' allessandrina," *Vietriana* NS 2, 1973, 241-46.

25. See also B. Bucher-Isler, *Norm und Individualität in den Biographien Plutarchs,* 1972.

26. So, for example, the account of the battle of Carrhae in AD 53 in Plutarch, *Crass.* 29ff.

primarily military or political in nature he tries to construct a causal nexus with events in the private sphere.[27] Over and over the specific interest of the biographer, whose concern is not the magnitude but the testimonial value of a person's actions, surfaces here. The idea is not that the reference to character traits will explain the deeds of the hero but rather that from his actions the character traits may be inferred.

In the broad field of Greek literature there were, of course, besides this type of biography, many other texts having, in whole or in part, biographical content. We have already mentioned the informative brief biographies which resemble articles about persons in our encyclopedias. They are especially well represented as biographies of poets and philosophers, in which case the traditional story of the life of an individual philosopher, say that of Plato or Epicurus,[28] brings with it devout encomiastic features and thus possesses potential for a higher stylization. In addition, we find biographical excursions in works of history; memoirs and other reports bearing biographical content; panegyrics on the living or the dead in which biographical information ordered in terms of personal qualities is presented; stories of the lives of fictional personages as of many literary and historical persons; an extremely rich anecdotal tradition[29] shot through with biographical references; and more such material.

The great diversity of these kinds of text has always confused those who have been concerned about the classification in literary theory of Greek biography,[30] and not until recently was the proposal made to relinquish the assumption of the existence of a distinct genre called "biography" in Greek literature.[31] This seems to be all the more correct in view of the fact that ancient literary theory seems barely to have taken notice of "biography" as a genre. Plutarch's statements about the distinction between biography and historiography have the status of a rarity. Whereas in the rhetorical-literary works of antiquity there are so many explanations of the different kinds of discourse and historiography, of

27. Thus Dihle, op. cit. (cf. n. 19), 57ff. A. Momigliano is skeptical in *Mededelingen der K. Nederlandse Akademie van Wetenschappen, Afdeling Letterkunde* 34, 1971, no. 7.
28. The biographical-encomiastic Plato tradition in the academy begins with Plato's disciple Hermodorus (Diogenes Laertius 2.106); the Epicurus biography in Diogenes Laertius (10.1ff.) offers insight into a rich tradition both within and outside of the school of this philosopher.
29. On the role of anecdote in the biographical tradition, cf. I. Gallo, *L'origine e lo sviluppo della biografia greca*, 1974, 182.
30. The first to do this was F. Leo, *Die griechisch-römische Biographie nach ihrer literarischen Form*, 1901. His main thesis was that there has at all times existed but one basic form of biography for figures of historical and literary renown. This thesis was very soon disproved by papyrus findings. Cf. Satyrus, *Vita di Euripide*, ed. G. Arrighetti, 1964, 5ff.
31. When Josephus, writing for Greek readers, characterized as "philosophies" the Jewish sects of his time, sects which were distinguished by their different modes of living, he was not at all mistaken by the standards of the first century AD (*BJ* 2.118; *Ant.* 18.11, and other places). On the ancient concept of "philosophy" see A. M. Malingrey, *Philosophia* (1961).

encomiastics and epistolography, fable, ecphrasis, dialogue, and other forms of stylized prose, that the formal designation of the appropriate genres can almost always be easily inferred, ancient rhetorical and literary theory seems never to have granted biography the status of a genre that can be formally categorized as such.

In fact, the major proportion of extant Greek "lives" are marked by the absence of formal structure. A glance at the work of Diogenes Laertius or at one of the "lives" often given prefatorially in medieval manuscripts of the works of poets or prose writers will tell us this. The act of amassing materials of the most diverse provenance usually takes place—with or without indication of the source—completely without any regard to the final form in which these materials existed. We are dealing precisely with the unstructured transmission of erudite materials. For such collections of material there are, of course, ready-made schemes of arrangement: for instance, where the biographical tradition consists primarily of anecdotes, as for example in the case of Diogenes Laertius (6.20ff.), it is natural to place the biographically interesting but chronologically indifferent material within a framework of the birth or origin of the hero, on the one hand, and his death, on the other. (This procedure results in a form similar—at first sight—to that of Mark's Gospel.[32]) However, where the focus of interest was the teaching or literary work of the figure in the title, the dramatic exposition of the teaching, the enumeration of the works, and the discussion of the hero's relationships with his disciples presented itself for the main and center section between origins and youth on the one hand, and death, testament, and burial-tradition on the other. This scheme is very often present in Diogenes Laertius.

But none of the two schemes is followed consistently and slavishly. In Diogenes one sees this, for example, in the *Life of Socrates,* for which precise compliance with the first-mentioned scheme would have been quite fitting. But nowhere is there any indication that such schemes had hardened into rules for the shaping of a biography in the sense that with their help a formal balance had to be achieved, one that satisfied aesthetic demands. The schemes are modified at will, and of the material the biographer communicates, without regard to any formal rules, what he has at his disposal or what he thinks is worth communicating. Especially that which has been preserved in the way of philosophers' biographies is marked by this—one could say, principial—informality and, quite differently from the Gospels, there is nowhere any evidence of a significant continuation or development of the schemes of arrangement referred to.

But this changes with the rise of neo-Platonism. Here the doctrine—emerging first in Plotinus and systematized by Porphyry—of the virtues,

32. I am grateful to Olof Gigon for pointing out these parallels to me.

ordered in graduated steps, became the basic framework for the structuring of
exemplary philosophers' biographies, most impressively in the biography of
Proclus by Marinus. On the other hand, Porphyry's *Life of Plotinus* still stands
in the tradition of the philosophers' biographies that detail the hero's life-
circumstances as part of an introduction to the hero's teaching and literary
legacy, as is also true, for example, of the "Lives" of Aristotle which have been
preserved or can be reconstructed.[33] It is therefore hard to gain indications,
precisely from the biographies of the Hellenistic and imperial periods, for what
could be considered biography in the sense of a literary genre in the first and
second century after Christ. But that Plutarch had such a notion of genre before
him as model when he sharply distinguished his "Lives" from historiography
is very likely, because these works have been composed and stylized very
carefully.

The negative findings in the case of the philosophers' biography, together
with the above-mentioned multiplicity of textual kinds of a more or less
biographical nature, should not, however, drive us to a degree of resignation
such that we would completely relinquish the attempt to define the literary genre
of biography in vogue in the first and second centuries AD.

Among all the textual forms we have mentioned there is none which
owes its existence purely to biographical interest. They share this peculiarity
with the pre- and extraliterary tradition of a biographical and anecdotal
character: here as there the point of interest is the biographical implications
or biographical accounts of memorabilia which are worthy of description also
and especially on other grounds. The anecdotal tradition, which preserves the
memory of great military commanders, lawgivers, poets, philosophers, or
rulers, is consulted because of the lasting significance of their works, not on
account of an exclusive interest in the course of their lives. Biographical
interest is dominant only in the kind of biography we find in Plutarch's
"Lives"—in the sense that the moral phenomena important to the author
could be demonstrated in no other way than in the personal records of the
heroes he depicted. Precisely this stance was significant for the ethics of the
whole of post-Socratic philosophy. From the time of Socrates it had not been
enough in philosophy just to think, teach, or study it; one had to *live*
philosophy and that to the end of one's life, for Plato, following Socrates, had
said that a life without accountability was not worth living (*Apol.* 38A). By
his life and death Socrates had become a teacher of philosophy and, accordingly, philosophy had become the art of living *(ars vitae),* which could only
be put into practice as schools of philosophy became communities where the

---

33. For an overview of this, cf. I. Düring, *Aristotle in the Ancient Biographical Tradition,*
1957.

students lived together. From then on the value of any philosophy could only be demonstrated in the living of it.[34]

This basic moral-philosophical conviction, applied to literary biography, led to principles and rules of composition which conferred the status of a literary genre only on biography of the Plutarchian type.[35] Most other textual forms that are ever and again called biographies or included in the history of biography do not meet the criteria according to which they could be assigned to the category of biography. Occasionally, as for example in the case of the encomiums of Isocrates and Xenophon, the formal criteria and external evidence are sufficient for the recognition of a distinct literary genre but it is precisely not the genre of biography.[36]

But is the literary genre found in Plutarch's work represented for us only by his "Lives"?

As far as the literary composition of a "life-report" is concerned, there are still extant or within reach certain other Greek works which attest this phenomenon. As a result of a papyrus discovery dating from the late third century before Christ, parts of a *Life of Euripides,* written by the Alexandrian man of letters Satyrus, famous particularly for his work in biography,[37] have surfaced. It was stylized as a dialogue and hence sought definitely to satisfy higher literary claims. However, the scope of the material that has been preserved does not allow for an answer to whether the development of a character (ἤθη) through the actions of the hero was active as a formative principle in the same way as in the "Lives" of Plutarch. Of course, one also finds in Satyrus the method of inferring the attributes of the hero from his actions, or, in other words, of making the attributes visible through his actions—but this is not a specific feature of biographical authorship. However, the biographical details which Satyrus selects, details which he derives from the tragedies of the poets or from quotations of the comedy writers, or simply invents, do not really permit the conclusion that it was moral-philosophical interest or interest in character that guided his pen.[38]

The biography of Augustus by Nicolaus of Damascus mentioned earlier (p. 369), composed over a hundred years before Plutarch, is, among all the existing examples of Greek biography, the first to rank with Plutarch's "Lives"—though it must be granted that the scope of the material preserved does not allow us to draw binding conclusions from a comparison.

From the period after Plutarch we have a couple of works with biographi-

---

34. Cf. A. Dihle (n. 19 above), op. cit., 13ff.
35. See ibid., 88ff., for an analysis of a Plutarchian biography of the Spartan king Cleomenes.
36. A. Dihle, op. cit., 27ff.
37. For the latest edition, see n. 30.
38. On this, see M. R. Lefkowitz, *Greek, Roman, and Byzantine Studies* 20, 1979, 187-210.

cal content which likewise show a consistent literary style. We are referring to the accounts which Lucian wrote of the works of Demonax, of Peregrinus Proteus, and of Alexander of Abonuteichos in the second half of the second century after Christ, as well as to the lengthy "Life" of the miracle-worker Apollonius of the late first century AD, which Philostratus published at the beginning of the third century AD. The so-called "Lives of the Sophists" are of less interest because this work deals more with the history of the Second Sophistic than with the personalities of sophists.

Among the aforementioned works of Lucian the *Demonax* is first in line for consideration in the present context, even though the biographical element (biographical in a strict sense) is overlaid by an encomiastic layer, since the great scoffer is obviously sincere in his admiration for this Cynic. A comparison with Plutarch is also made more difficult by the example of Socrates adduced in this *Life* (11) and by flights into the miraculous (1, 11). In any case, what we find is express reference to the purpose of the work as moral example (2f.), the brief portrayal of the genesis and growth of the personality of the hero based on natural talent (3) and education (4f.), and a lengthy narrative of the events surrounding his death (63ff.). By far the largest proportion of the book is filled, however, with chronologically indifferent, though biographically sometimes significant anecdotes and sayings (12-62), among which there are also many travel anecdotes of the Cynic tradition attributed here to the hero of the title.[39] At any rate, the similarity in structure to the Gospel of Mark is undeniable, while the moral-anthropological "directional" values to be inferred, values from which the work draws its legitimation, are reminiscent of Plutarch. True, one learns nothing of the lifelong growth of a personality in action, and to that extent the literary classification of this book as biography is questionable.

The situation is much more difficult in the case of *Peregrinus Proteus* and *Alexander*. In both cases we are dealing with ill-natured polemical writings whose wit lies in multi-layered parody which relates only to a small degree to the literary form of biography. It is precisely in this multi-layered parody that the rhetorical strength of the author lies, as Bompaire (see n. 39) has analyzed it. The similarities between the *Life of Apollonius* by Philostratus and these two works of Lucian are based on the fact that Philostratus, in a serious manner, and Lucian, in a parodic manner, are informed by the tradition of the Pythagoras biography, a tradition in which the amazing stories of the life and travels of the ancient miracle-worker are combined with the exemplaristic description of the Pythagorean lifestyle. But in the *Peregrinus Proteus* it was also the Socrates tradition (12),[40] and in *Alexander* the legendary branch (which had then already

39. J. Bompaire, *Lucien écrivain,* 1958, 514f.
40. G. Anderson, *Lucian,* 1976, 72f.

blossomed for a long time) of the tradition of the deeds of the great Macedonian king that served as points of reference for parody.[41] The linkage of the Pythagoras legends with those of Alexander may definitely have been available to Lucian as a model, because—in a serious and edifying vein—it is present also in the *Life of Apollonius* by Philostratus. Finally, one may not ignore the possible influence of the novel, literary tradition begins, as far as we know, in the late Hellenistic period with works which expanded their fanciful narratives by linking them to historical figures and to which then the motif of long, dangerous, and amazing journeys was added.

Just as this was the case with biographies having a consistent literary form, so also the genre of the novel failed to attract the attention of ancient rhetorical and literary theory, and for that reason we are now dependent for our attempts at classification on inferences and hunches.

Finally, the much-discussed *Life of Apollonius* by Philostratus is so hard to classify as biography because the religiously motivated miracle-and-travel stories completely overshadow the overall structure of the work. The influences and models one can doubtlessly discern here—Pythagoras tradition, cult legend, Alexander legend, travel romance, philosopher's anecdote, dialogue, tyrants' anecdote, miracle story, historiography, geographic-ethnographic report, epistolography—are so numerous that one can only focus on individual passages of the work, and none of them really determines the shape of this monstrous book as a whole. For that reason alone, and not only on account of its late date, this book is unfruitful for the study of the question concerning the origin and development of the form of the Gospels.[42]

Thus our conclusion will have to be that, for the notion of a literary genre called "biography," which deserves this label on conceptual and formal grounds, one can only gain an impression from the parallel "Lives" of Plutarch. The genre present here clearly possessed enough vitality to affect regions beyond the literature of the Greeks. We have already referred to its influence on Christian hagiography. In the first century BC Cornelius Nepos introduced it into Latin, and in the second century AD it was modified[43] by Suetonius to the degree that as "life of the emperor" it could become a recognized form of historiography in late antiquity and the Middle Ages.

After this overview let us return to the issue formulated at the beginning. It must be immediately obvious that the question concerning the possible

41. G. Anderson, *Studies in Lucian's Comic Fiction,* 1976, 89ff.

42. There is a useful inventory and a wealth of references to the relevant literature in G. Petzke, *Die Traditionen über Apollonius von Tyana und das Neuen Testament,* 1970, where, of course, the units of tradition gained by form analysis are treated but without regard for the literary composition and form of the end product.

43. G. Luck, "Die form der suetonischen Biographie und die frühen Heiligenviten," in *Mullus,* Festschrift T. Klauser, 1964, 230ff.

influence of Greek biography on the Gospel literature can be raised meaningfully only in relation to the genre just defined. In the context of preaching
centered in the activity of Jesus of Nazareth, biographical interest in the broad
sense could manifest itself in the most diverse ways without it requiring for this
purpose a literary model in the form of an established genre. That is evident
from the many preliterary forms of anecdotal/biographical tradition in the entire
world. Hence, the drive to complete the account of a person's life, which we
were able to recognize as the significant motive for continued gospel writing
from the first to the second or even third century, therefore in no way implies
an orientation to the genre of Greek biography.

Specific similarities between Greek biography and the canonical as well
as the extracanonical gospels, especially such similarities as might arise from
the commonality of anthropological conceptions, definitely seem to be absent.
Nor is this surprising: the notion that the really important (because morally
assessable) characteristics of a person could only develop in the course of his
life, could hardly be applied to the earthly life of an incarnate God. Regardless
of whether one dated the "sending" of Jesus (or, according to the later dogmatic
understanding, the incarnation) from his birth or his baptism, in any case it
documented itself in a human being who was perfect from the beginning. In this
conviction the infancy narratives of Luke and the story of the wedding at Cana
in John agree with the stories of the Gospel of Thomas. The almost unbridgeable
distinction between gospel and biography becomes clear from a comparison
with hagiography. Athanasius could take over, in its entirety, the developmental
scheme found in the biographical tradition as it had been modified by the
neo-Platonic doctrine of the graded virtues which lead to perfection. This
conception forms the framework of a life of the monastic father Antony which
began the most important branch of Christian hagiography.[44] But for a gospel
account this scheme was useless.

In any case, in the period which occupies us here, the period from the late
first to the second century AD, there is to be noted the adoption of individual
conventions of Greek literature by the new Christian literary tradition. With
regard to the gospel literature then unfolding this means above all a certain
amount of contact with Greek historiography, from which, as we saw, Greek
biography, despite the active interest of both in the individual personality, was
sharply distinguished as a literary genre.

Gospel and historiography are very closely bound up with each other in
Luke, the historian among the evangelists, as this phenomenon has been most

---

44. Still valid, for the problem of the form of the life of Antony, is K. Holl, *Gesammelte Aufsätze*
II, 1928, 249ff. There are fresh viewpoints in A. Priessnig, "Die biographische Form der Plotin-Vita
des Porphyrios und das Antonios-Leben des Athanasios," *Byzantinisches Zeitschrift* 64, 1971, 1ff.

cogently described by Martin Dibelius.[45] The prologues of Luke's Gospel and Acts, the precise datings and other details which remind one of the literary conventions of the Greek world, serve to draw the events reported into a historical context which embraces the entire Gentile world.

However, as compared with the tradition presupposed in Luke there is absolutely no fundamentally new form of gospel account corresponding to the changed historical perspectives present in the work of this most educated of the canonical Gospel writers. This concerns particularly the incorporation of biographical (in the strict sense of the word) information. After all, we were able to show earlier that the completion of the biography of Jesus clearly coincides with a trend which continues without a break from the early synoptic Gospels right through the extracanonical gospel literature. However, though the historical perspective within which the details of the story of the life of Jesus have been arranged has been changed and enlarged in Luke, the existence of such a perspective is definitely not new. From the beginning of the history of the Church's message, this perspective was a given resulting from orientation to the Old Testament as a scheme of prophecy and fulfillment. It is profitable in this context to remind the reader of an observation made a long time ago: the part of the tradition of the life of Jesus which contains by far the most—often quite incidental seeming—details, namely the passion narrative, is also most thickly studded with references to the Old Testament by which events are interpreted as fulfillment of the promised salvation. One only has to call to mind the significance that Psalm 22 has in all the Gospels for the ordering and interpretation of the passion story. Precisely those elements which one could, in the message of the early Church, most quickly describe as biographical acquire a special historical, more precisely, a salvation-historical, meaning. True: the horizon of this historical mode of viewing things may change, as one sees in Luke or John. Then it transcends, without breaking it, the framework given with the tradition of Israel. In any case, the fundamental idea, that of shaping the message of salvation in Christ as the report of the life and works of Jesus of Nazareth, allows itself to be understood only as the outflow of historically oriented thought. On this view the life of Jesus appears as a decisive segment of a salvation history which began in the remote past and continues in the future.

At the beginning we saw how in Mark the baptism and the passion clearly became the constituents of a new literary form, namely that of the gospel as the report of the activity of Jesus, by providing a biographical framework for traditional material that was otherwise chronologically neutral. However, this biographical framework belonged from the very start to a redemptive-historical

45. M. Dibelius, *Die Reden der Apostelgeschichte und die antike Geschichtsschreibung*, 1949.

context given *a priori* with the tradition of the people of Israel. In contrast with this, Greek biography as a literary form was rooted in the philosophical conviction of the immutability of the natural order, which was especially confirmed in the moral phenomena of human life, and before which all historical distinctions paled into insignificance. But the message of divine salvation in the form of a report on the works of Jesus of Nazareth presupposed a confirmed faith in the once-for-allness and incomparability of this life. This once-for-allness could be established only by reference to the broad redemptive-historical perspectives of the biblical tradition. One could, as after Luke also Melito of Sardis or Eusebius of Caesarea did, very well expand or modify this connection or link it with other traditions, but one could not replace it by recourse to an unchangeable order of nature or of creation, at least if one wanted to leave the core of the message intact. The result is that though there could be material and formal contacts between gospel literature and the universal historiography of antiquity there were no bridges leading to the genre of Greek biography and its anthropological foundations.

One must therefore claim the canonical Gospels, and certainly not only the synoptic Gospels, as witnesses for a special kind of historical thought, which separates them from Greek biography, despite the interests of both in biographical details. This interest was historically, and in the final analysis, not biographically, motivated.

However, implied in the canonization of our four Gospels is a recognition of historical thinking which can by no means be assumed for all Christian groups in that early period. This becomes plain especially in light of the question we have posed—hence with regard to a possibly meaningful definition of the Gospels as biographies.

We have already learned that certain Gnostics, when they put the traditions of the early Christian message into the mouth of the Resurrected One, though (unconsciously) they followed the trend toward the completion of the Jesus-biography, at the same time denied the significance of the historicity of his appearance and thus neglected the report of his life. The Gospel of Thomas contains numerous utterances of Jesus without indicating any of the biographical connections which the logia-source visible in Matthew allows us to recognize throughout. Besides this specific Gnostic aversion to the historical perspectives of the Christian message there is a similar loss of history in the later gospels—but from a different set of motives, predominantly those of edification and vividness.

As is well known, the evangelists over and over establish the redemptive-historical significance of individual occurrences in the life of Jesus with the aid of scriptural passages interpreted as prophecies. That this method invited the extension of traditional episodes and the invention of new ones in a rapidly expanding gospel literature is natural. One only has to recall John 19:24: In imitation of the misunderstood parallel formulation of Ps. 22:19 in the style of Hebrew poetry, John's Gospel, in distinction from the synoptic report, tells us that the soldiers divided the clothes of the Crucified but cast lots for the especially valuable tunic, which had been left intact.

Such developments of biographical details, supported in part by the search for Scripture proof, remain within the prophetic perspective, which justifies a formulation of the message as report of the life of Jesus. In addition, especially in the extracanonical gospel literature, there is an elaboration of the life of Jesus without this motivation. This is presumably the place where—we have referred to them before—the infancy and childhood narratives belong, or the history of the correspondence between Jesus and the Essene king Abgar.[46] In such texts of an edifying or anecdotal nature one can only assume the absence of a redemptive-historical perspective. But often one can see very clearly how the formation of biographical legends detaches itself from this framework. John, in his account of the passion of Jesus, based the nonoccurrence of the breaking of Jesus' bones on the prescribed procedure for the slaying of the passover lamb (Ex. 12:46). But a gospel from the second century after Christ picks up this motif and explains it with reference to the cruelty of the soldiers, who thus attempt to prolong the suffering of the Lord.[47] Here biographical legend, presumably from ignorance of the meaning of the tradition, has taken an independent turn. Still, such elaboration serving the purpose of edification already presupposes the canonical formation of the salvation message as redemptive-historically illumined report of the life of Jesus.

The anthropological notions that put a distinctive stamp on the literary form of Greek biography are, therefore, worlds apart from the premises of the gospel literature. The exemplary, morally assessed realization of human potentials in the actions of a human life—this conception could definitely be applied to the life of a Christian saint in the sense that his rise to perfection goes through a succession of stages. But the earthly life of the incarnate God, as a decisive segment of the long road over which the same God takes the world to its goal of its eternal salvation, could not be grasped in these categories. In the framework of the gospel message the events of the life of Jesus did not acquire meaning as evidences for the way a potentially perfect character is formed and unfolds. According to the intent of the evangelists they must rather demonstrate how both great and seemingly insignificant actions in a human life testify, for one who has ears to hear it, to the ever purposeful and gracious action of a transcendent and incomprehensible God.

46. The Abgar legend is translated in Hennecke-Schneemelcher I (n. 5 above), 441ff.
47. Gospel of Peter 4:14; M. Dibelius, "Botschaft und Geschichte," *Gesammelte Aufsätze* I, 1953, 221ff.

If we then, with some justification, call the Gospels biographies of Jesus—for a biographical framework unquestionably determines their literary form and biographical interest shapes the development of their content—we must nevertheless keep the idea of the specific Greek art of biography at a distance. Like the "Lives" of the emperors by the Roman Suetonius they rather attest the historiographical possibilities of a complete or partial "life," possibilities which have been realized on an enormous scale in medieval and modern literature. Here a human life appears as an incomparable and unrepeatable piece of history; in Greek biography, in contrast, a human life appears as individual realization of possibilities which an immutable nature holds in readiness for all times.

The historiographic function one may attribute to the Gospels in fact, in a peculiar way, brings this genre into the vicinity of Roman biography.

We have already mentioned that Greek biography in its Roman adaptation became a widespread means of historical representation in late antiquity and the Middle Ages. In this process Suetonius's "Lives" of the Caesars occupy a key position. They are biographies in the Greek sense to the extent that they attempt to grasp the growth and character of imperial personalities; and at first glance their structure accords with this purpose: the origins, youth, and "development" of the hero are chronologically depicted up until the accession; then follows a description of the activity of the ruling emperor under the rubric of distinct fields of activity and life-spheres; and the conclusion is again formed by a chronologically ordered narrative of the events surrounding the death of the ruler.

The structure of the "Lives" written by Suetonius has occasioned a wide range of literary-historical hypotheses, which we cannot discuss now. In the present context we must only point out that, though the biographical conception of the Greeks was undoubtedly the godparent in the process, this concept, with its individualistic tendencies, did not meet historiographic objectives. The middle sections of the Suetonian "Lives," meanwhile, contain a great deal of historiographic material, which in its value as information points beyond the goal of describing the personality of the emperor under consideration. If one adds to this the fact that the unbroken sequence of biographies of emperors by itself creates a historiographic situation, the transition from biography oriented to individual-ethical concerns to historical biography becomes immediately clear.

It was, of course, no accident that this fateful transition which made biography into a medium of historiography was brought about by a Roman man of letters belonging to the circle of the court at the height of the rule of the Caesars. In established Caesarism events of political importance were much more concentrated around the person of the ruler than was ever the case before. Therefore, a sequence of biographies of emperors could be conceived as an account of the history of the epoch. The same thing, though in another way, is attested by the—in its form quite traditional—historical work of Tacitus. Meanwhile there probably are even deeper reasons why in Rome the individual biography became a medium of historiography.

Among the Greeks, the sense of identity and continuity which every group or society tends to cultivate from an early time acquired traits which point to a concept of nature which dominated the classical and postclassical periods of Greek thought. Kings who were regarded as founders of a *polis* or colony, lawgivers credited with the creation of the political order, warriors or military commanders to whose courage people attributed the preservation of the commonwealth—they were all moved up into an earlier, but still historical, period as heroes in the circle of the powers which upheld the natural-cosmic order. However, as the guarantors of the existing order of state and society, an order which included the marathon contests, were moved into the sphere of the sacred, they lost a good part of their historical individuality, and the social order they had founded or preserved could be freely conceived, together with the natural (divine) order of the world, as an unhistorical, but for that reason all the more venerable, unity. Solon's Athens elegy (fr. 4, West) and Sophocles' ode to the laws (*Oed. R.* 863ff.) are impressive documents of this mindset, one which in its secularized form led to the conviction that within the framework of the eternal cosmic-natural order human nature was also immutable, a fact which demonstrated itself especially in the fortunes of the political commonwealth. Thucydides gave the most exact expression to this view of history (1.22.4), which as a matter of fact provides an unsuitable basis for the development of biography, hence of the description of the course of a person's life, as a form of historiographic presentation.

Among the Romans, too, there was a lively awareness that every political commonwealth needs the protection of, and the undisturbed linkage with, the gods who regulate the processes of nature, and to that extent every social order must be congruent with the (divine) natural order. But the sense of identity and continuity of the Roman people related much more than that of the Greeks to an unbroken chain—going back to primeval times—of persons, deeds, and occurrences, none of which needed to be raised into a sacral sphere and from which as a whole came the *mos maiorum,* the prevailing system of norms for social conduct.

The famous verse of Ennius, *moribus antiquis res stat Romana virisque,* describes this situation with unsurpassable precision. Both the tradition of the Roman state as a whole and that of the great men who were the real subjects of Roman history are composed of innumerable memories, individual and precise, each of which constituted a precedent. The use of *patria potestas* by a certain consul, the capture of a city by a certain proconsul, the legislative proposal of a certain tribune, and numerous other individual events, and thus the recollection of unmistakable—but by no means sacrally elevated—individuals, preserved the collective memory of the Roman commonwealth. This is most vividly illustrated by Polybius's famous description of the ancestral images which, dressed in their robes of office, were brought along in the funeral procession of a great Roman (6.53.4ff.). For all the high regard for individual personalities and achievements which belongs to such a practice, the attribution of the *mos maiorum* to numerous guarantors prevented the excessive presumption of individuals. In protest against the overvaluation of the individual, a tendency arising in his time and imported from the Hellenistic world, Cato the Elder in his historical work avoided all mention of proper names and only referred to "the consul," "the hostile military commander," or "the centurion." The work was nevertheless full of information about the achievements of unmistakable individuals who had to serve as examples of the proper attitude toward the state. In the Roman understanding of history, as in early Roman jurisprudence, the idea of a supply—created by individual precedents—of values and insights was more important than the idea of universally valid systems of law visible in isolation from the historical situation.

Against this background it is not surprising that it has long been noted that from the beginning Roman historiography was characterized by a biographical element. The earliest works of Roman history stemmed from members of the nobility who sought to explain and justify their own politics, and in the same circles, from the same motive, there soon arose an autobiographical literature of memoirs.[48] Caesar's commentaries, for all the apparent distance which the author observes toward the principal heroes of the action, is still an (auto)biographical witness, and the same must have been true for Cicero's works about his period of office. The younger Pliny mentions writings of the genre *exitus virorum illustrium* (*Ep.* 5.5; 8.12), which he half reckons as historiography. The depiction of the events surrounding the death of a person, according to the understanding of antiquity, is a particularly important part of his biography. These works, too—a category which includes Lactantius's *De mortibus persecutorum*—attest to the linking of biographical and historiographic motives, for the illustrious men in question were the victims of tyrants like Nero or Domitian. The settling of accounts with these tyrants, however, was a primary aim of political historiography in Trajan's Rome. Something similar applies to Tacitus's biography of his father-in-law Agricola, probably the most successful transfer of the biographical form into Latin. Here, too, the purpose is not to depict a human life from the perspective of universally valid individual-ethical viewpoints. Tacitus's aim is much rather to show how, under the specific historical conditions of the tyrant Domitian, his father-in-law maintained his moral integrity and, in addition, while occupying a responsible position, performed great and enduring deeds for the well-being of the Roman state. Accordingly, a large proportion of the work is

48. Cf. Momigliano, op. cit. (n. 8), 93f.

filled with the detailed portrayal of the British campaign, which could just as well have been recounted in a historical monograph.

Now, the first series of biographies of emperors, certainly, is a work of the Greek Plutarch who wrote eight such successive biographies, presumably soon after the fall of Domitian in the year AD 96.[49] Unfortunately, only three of the short-lived rulers of the year of the three emperors—Galba, Otho, Vitellius—have been preserved and there, as Syme correctly observes, the focus is more on the turbulent events of that year than on personal sketches. We are not sure, therefore, whether already in Plutarch the succession of "lives of the emperors" was conceived as a presentation of Roman history—as this is undoubtedly the case for the "Lives" by Suetonius from Caesar to Domitian.[50] It is certain that Plutarch, before and during the time he wrote his "lives" of the emperors, maintained close contacts with the Latin world, particularly with the upper classes in the city of Rome. Thus it would not have been strange if the strengthening, based on the circumstances of the Principate, of the biographical element peculiar to Roman historiography, which we just attempted to describe, had influenced him.

For Suetonius this specific Roman tradition certainly had meaning; and one may say, accordingly, that his biographical historiography was not an accident but derived from the Roman conception of the state, society, family, and their transformation. The frequently observed affinity between Suetonius's biographies and historiography[51] definitely corresponds to a biographical perspective from which, from an early time, many Roman historians wrote history. It continues, nevertheless, to be to Suetonius's credit that, despite all inadequacies as an author, he successfully adapted a Greek form of biography to the demands of Roman historiography. His work, and not the much better done Agricola biography of Tacitus, was precedent-setting.

Now, as little as Suetonius and the evangelists had to do with each other, so surprising is it that from the redemptive-historical perspectives of early Christianity, for the first time in the Greek language, the historiographic potential of the life-story of an individual[52] was realized by way of a literary genre—gospel—that developed over a period of several generations, as it did among the Romans as well. However, while among the Romans the influence of the established forms of the traditions of Greek literature is undeniable, a similar statement cannot be made about the literature of the Gospels.

---

49. R. Syme, "Biographers of the Caesars," *Museum Helveticum* 37, 1980, 104-28.
50. Cf. ibid., 110f.
51. Cf. H. Grugel, *Studien zur biographischen Technik Suetons,* Wiener Studien Beiheften 7, 1977, 145f., 154; S. Doepp, *Hermes* 100, 1972, 444-60. New literature on the biographies of Suetonius is in G. Alföldy, *Ancient Society* 11-12, 1980-81, 352.
52. H. Cancik emphasizes the historiographic character of Mark's Gospel ("Die Schriften des Neuen Testamentes und die antike Literatur," *Humanist* Bildung 4 [1981] 63ff., esp. 70-72).

Overview of the Discussion

Peter Lampe and Ulrich Luz

The questions that remained unresolved throughout the symposium and that call for further study are:

1. The *Johannine Problem.* How does the relationship between John and the synoptic tradition develop? As compared with the synoptic Gospels, does John's Gospel represent something genuinely different? Does John presuppose the stability of the synoptic tradition or is this precisely not the case?
2. The problem of *early Christian prophecy.* The ambivalent character of early Christian prophecy began to emerge as a consensus: prophecy and tradition, prophets and teachers appear to be not opposites, but two sides of the same phenomenon.

As the link between the two problem areas stands Käsemann's old thesis: Did John's Gospel perhaps represent the final stage of an early Christian prophetic strain?

On "Jesus' Gospel of the Kingdom" *(O. Betz)*

1. The term "originality," put forward by Betz, a term that qualifies as "original" that which is closest to the Old Testament (in this case deutero-Isaiah), was questioned. At the very least this use of the category "original" does not seem well suited to help in making tradition-historical statements: is it not possible that in the course of the later tradition a secondary assimilation to the Old Testament took place, so that, methodologically, closeness to the Old Testament permits few conclusions concerning that which is early in the history of the tradition (for example, concerning the authentic message of Jesus)?

387

2. Further remaining difficulties for Betz's presentation are: Why does Luke in his Gospel consistently avoid the term εὐαγγέλιον—in fact, even eliminate it from the Marcan prototype and use it only marginally in Acts? Is the expiatory suffering of Isaiah 53 really represented in Luke? If so, why does not Luke use the concept εὐαγγέλιον?

The varied use of εὐαγγέλιον in the Gospels (Mark uses it most often; Matthew less so; Luke virtually not at all; and John totally avoids it) rather constitutes an argument against the tiered arrangement of Luke-Matthew-Mark posited by Betz.

On "The Path of the Gospel Tradition" *(B. Gerhardsson)*

1. How can one define the relationship of the process of gospel transmission to the educational enterprise of wisdom teachers and rabbis, on the one hand, and to the process of transmitting prophetic texts, on the other?

The circle of disciples around the Old Testament prophets constitutes an important analogy to the Jesus-communities. But in distinction from the former, the prophet Jesus had a much stronger language-shaping effect. Early Christian prophets considered themselves much more bound, in content and language, to their teacher Jesus than the Old Testament prophet-disciples were to their teachers (cf. Schürmann: "Christ-language!"). In their utterances the early Christian prophets were bound to the language and content of Jesus' message.

By comparison, Gerhardsson emphasizes the analogy between the Gospels and rabbinical education, though he does not see it as exclusive. As Jesus already shows, one cannot make a strict distinction between the teacher's sphere of action and that of the prophet. Nevertheless, for Gerhardsson the conscious process of interpreting the words of Jesus is at some distance from prophecy. The focus is rather on a further development of existing interpretation of tradition than on the creative formation of new material. Jesus certainly did not found a school in which only recitation took place. The transmission of tradition always meant: "to work with a text!" Matt. 13:51f. shows that scribes not only practice conservation but also innovation. The rule is: In early Christianity people did not simply make things up but *interpreted.* In many cases also the so-called "Spirit-logia" had a traditional core.

2. Although there is no quarrel with Gerhardsson's basic intention to take seriously the analogy of the rabbinical attitude toward tradition, but not to understand it in a way which excludes freedom and change, some questions nevertheless remain:

a) The parable tradition shows a very high degree of change and freedom. At the same time, the parables and similitudes nevertheless necessarily remained the parables and similitudes of Jesus.

b) The Gospel writers display a high measure of freedom in dealing with the tradition. They are teachers with an authority very much their own. What remains unclear is the extent to which the freedom of the evangelists vis-à-vis their sources permits conclusions concerning the freedom of earlier teachers vis-à-vis the oral tradition.

Is it perhaps the case that the degree of freedom grows in the measure in which written texts already exist, texts which in any case insure the continuity of the tradition? This would explain why in the Lucan special material (e.g., Luke 1–2) Luke is more conservative in his transmission than in the case of the material he adopted from Mark. In any case, this presupposes that later evangelists wished to supplement, not to replace, their predecessors.

On the one hand, one must remember that in contemporary antiquity verbatim transmission of longer texts occurred in only two instances: that of the *carmen* and that of the oral tradition in ethics. On the other hand, one must remember that the Gattung is a great mnemonic help in oral tradition: a story-teller only needs to note the basic facts and particulars of a given history. He can then tell a story as the public expects it of him, that is, in accordance with a given narrative framework.

c) Finally, the Johannine tradition constitutes an important challenge to Gerhardsson's model of tradition. Is it to be characterized as "parasitic" in the sense that John can only write because the Synoptics are already there, and he can, so to speak, profit from their existence? Or are we dealing in John's Gospel with a very different, possibly prophetic, model of tradition in which the Spirit creates the tradition? Did John really understand his Jesus-discourses in general as words of the earthly Jesus? However, one must also not absolutize the differences between John and the Synoptics, because there are also synoptic texts with a "Johannine measure" of freedom. At this point the Johannine problem already emerges as the crucial open question of the whole symposium.

On "The Theological Center of the Sayings Source" *(A. Polag)*

1. The essay shows that many open questions exist, even when the existence of a written logia-source is not called into question. Not only the question whether there are perhaps several collections but also the question concerning different recensions of Q (QMatt., QLuke) is completely open. Also open is the question whether Q was not more extensive than can be documented today. For the determination of the literary character of the logia-source one must proceed from the form of the *codex:* the codex, which was also the notebook of antiquity, could be carried on one's person, expanded, or changed. Hence the character of the sayings source is not comparable with that of the Gospels as complete literary units. The introduction of Luke 3–4, which is tradition-historically late,

marks the place, so to speak, where Q develops the tendency to become a literary document. But because Q is not yet a finished literary document in the way that the Gospels are, the existence of various forms of the text, which according to Polag are not conscious recensions, is understandable.

For most of the participants in this discussion it was clear at least that the logia-source had to be a literary document: the common akoluthia which can be reconstructed right up to Luke 12 and possibly in Luke 17 is a strong barrier against all attempts to regard Q as merely an oral stratum in the tradition. This is all the more true when one considers that the preservation of the *akoluthia* in Jewish tradition is not a very important principle.

2. With regard to the literary state of affairs, it is very difficult, in general, to raise the question of the theological center of Q. Polag's formulation, "being struck by Jesus," as the center of Q is in fact the center of every New Testament writing. In any case, the situation is very different from that of the Gospel of Thomas, where a persistent Gnostic interpretation of the Jesus-tradition proves to be the unifying center. If Isaiah 61 is also fundamental for the Q tradition, there are consequences for the determination of the relationship of Q to εὐαγ-γέλιον. At this point a thorough study of the significance of Luke 7:18ff. for the Q tradition would be necessary.

It became clear that a general desire to preserve tradition alone does not explain the existence of the logia-source; there must have been a heightened desire to preserve tradition which can be explained only by the person and effect of the preaching of Jesus. An additional motive for the collection is the existence of the Church. In part Q is an aid to missionary preaching, but according to Polag the greater proportion of the material points to internal use by the Church, perhaps in catechesis; the material is focused on issues of discipleship and on reinforcement of the confession of faith. It is also possible that this collection of material gained special significance in Greek-speaking churches of converts in which there were no longer any eyewitnesses of the earthly Jesus. It must also be remembered that traditions are, as a rule, not collected for one purpose alone but for multiple use.

From everything that was said great caution evinced itself toward the thesis of a special kerygma in Q and a special circle of tradition behind Q. The materials of Q are rather complementary—say, to the passion tradition—than exclusive. But even then the question whether there are special emphases in Q has not yet been answered: striking, by comparison with Mark for example, is the heavy eschatological accentuation in the Q materials and the stress on the demand for decision. The question of who the bearers of the Q tradition were remained open. The thesis that they were Christian teachers and the thesis that they were Christian prophets need not be mutually exclusive. What kind of freedom to reinterpret is there in the teachers' relationship to tradition and what is the constitutive relationship of tradition to the early Christian prophets? Are the prophets at the same time teachers?

On "The Gospel in Jerusalem—Mark 14:12-26 as the Oldest Tradition of the Early Church" *(R. Pesch)*

1. *Mark 14:12-16.* There was general agreement that Mark 14:12-16 is a constituent part of a pre-Marcan passion narrative and also that Pesch's exegesis represents a possible interpretation that must be taken very seriously. Nevertheless, questions remain: Could I Sam. 10:1ff. have played a role as model? Why are we not told of any arrangements between Jesus and the owner of the upper room? Why is it not explicitly stated that the location of the Passover meal must remain a secret? In any case, the detective side of the narrative is not given prominence. Perhaps a historical occurrence was later furnished with miraculous features (Jesus' foreknowledge). Pesch would not consider such an understanding of the story plausible in the case of Mark but only later—in the case of Luke and Matthew. It is important to him that the episode is recounted from the perspective of the disciples, who knew nothing of any arrangements. A synchronous analysis of the narrative shows an extraordinary accumulation of circumstances which call attention to the place of the meal. It is the larger context that furnishes the element of tension—it is better not to speak of a detective component in the episode. After 14:11ff., the reader asks: Will the Jewish leadership succeed in arresting Jesus? From this point of view it makes sense that apart from Jesus and two disciples no one was allowed to know where Jesus would celebrate the Passover.

2. *Pesch's understanding of the Marcan tradition of the Last Supper.* There was far-reaching agreement that Mark 14:22-25 was not a secondary interpolation. It remained unclear, however, to what degree the Passover meal must be divided, by the Passover haggadah, into a preliminary part (Mark 14:17-21) and a main meal (Mark 14:22-25), that is to say, to what degree the entire Passover meal must be understood as a unity, so that the genitive absolute καὶ ἐσθιόντων αὐτῶν simply means: "and as they were eating (the following happened)." It also remained an open question whether it is really possible to contrast the Marcan narrative with a liturgical version of the Last Supper sayings as Paul renders them. The words of I Cor. 11:25 (μετὰ τὸ δειπνῆσαι) could point to history just as well as the parallel Marcan version of the interpretive sayings (where the distribution of bread and wine immediately follow each other) could point to a liturgical text. Pesch, finding his support in Mark, takes Jesus' last meal to be a Passover meal, but is also able to leave the question of the character of the Last Supper open. Decisive for

him is that the Pauline text I Cor. 11:23ff. is a text for liturgical use because (a) it does not mention the original participants of this meal—the disciples; and (b) the phrase ἐν τῷ ἐμῷ αἵματι looks back to Jesus' death while the formulation τὸ ἐκχυννόμενον in the cup-saying in Mark looks *forward* to Jesus' death. Whether the pre-Marcan passion report is really as historically reliable as Pesch assumes remains in dispute. It would also be conceivable that in a Jewish Christian Church the Passover character of the Last Supper had emerged later. An argument in favor of this position could be that Barabbas could hardly have been released after the Passover.

Another question which remained unresolved was the question concerning the relationship of the Marcan Last Supper sayings to the Lucan tradition of the Last Supper. Is Luke 22:15-20 really a secondary combination of the Marcan and the Pauline Last Supper paradosis or should we not rather reckon with a pre-Pauline ("proto-Lucan") narrative strain in Luke? Over against this, Pesch suggests the possibility that Luke bases himself on Mark but, during the composition of his Gospel, already had before his eyes the collection of materials for Acts.

3. Then there is the question of the genre of the pre-Marcan passion narrative. Are there models? Can one really get beyond the very general label of "narrative"? Pesch mentions that the Church's question concerning why Jesus was crucified leads to a new genre, for which there are only rudimentary models. As a possible but speculative hypothesis one may consider whether the passion narrative together with Jesus' "anabasis" to Jerusalem which preceded it was a "founding legend" of the Jerusalem church.

As consensus the debates produced agreement with the postulate that kerygma and history are mutually inclusive and not exclusive. Critical reflection on possible criteria, especially for the determination of breaks and tensions in literary-critical and tradition-critical analyses, was considered an urgent necessity.

On "The Pauline Gospel"   *(P. Stuhlmacher)*

1. In dispute was the question of the degree to which Paul's gospel *developed* during the roughly fifteen years between Damascus and the conflict with the representatives of the Jerusalem church, Peter and James (Gal. 1–2). Why did the conflict break out so late? Was Paul's teaching originally quite similar to that of the men of Jerusalem? Over against this, however, stands II Corinthians 11, where we learn that the Paul of the early period was persecuted precisely on account of his *violations of the law* (table fellowship with Gentiles, etc.) and not only on account of his preaching of the Messiah (the flogging and the attempt at stoning as the synagogue's means of last resort against a lawless person), so

that Paul's basic theological shift, the break with his Pharisaic past, must have occurred in his early years (cf. Phil. 3).

A consensus emerged: The disagreement between Paul and the men of Jerusalem was present *theoretically* and *in nuce* from the beginning but became *practically* virulent and manifest only after and with the Antiochian incident, when concrete Church-political problems began to crop up and there were practical conclusions to be drawn from Paul's theology of justification. How should Gentiles and Jews live together and hold table fellowship in one and the same Church? Was it to be on the basis of the fulfillment by the Gentiles of a legal minimum (Lev. 17–18)—a solution κατὰ νόμον—or on the basis of Christian liberty κατὰ νόμον Χριστοῦ, with the "strong" taking responsibility for the "weak"?

For fifteen years Paul and the men of Jerusalem lived together in apparent peace on the basis of closely related theological presuppositions (cf. I Cor. 15) until the demands of the *concrete praxis* of Church and mission first brought to light that throughout the whole period these presuppositions contained different implications. Therefore, insofar as the practical concretization of the doctrine of justification was accomplished and became the material of conflict, one could speak of *development*.

2. Also in dispute was the constellation of the word-group εὐαγγέλιον-εὐαγγελίζεσθαι-ἀκοή-šᵉmuâ-ῥῆμα Χριστοῦ plus the related but subordinate question whether the call to mission before the walls of Damascus came to Paul only as a *vision* (e.g. I Cor. 9:1) or also as an *audition*, as ῥῆμα Χριστοῦ. Should not a distinction be made, on the one hand, between εὐαγγέλιον = ῥῆμα Χριστοῦ, the word spoken by the Lord himself, and ἀκοή = εὐαγγελίζεσθαι, the apostolic message, on the other? Or is it the case in Paul that εὐαγγέλιον, in bipolar fashion, precisely embraces both: the power of revelation coming over Paul as well as the missionary message (= ἀκοή) to be preached by the apostles (Rom. 10:16f.).

From the direction of Greek philology a semantic differentiation between ἀκοή and εὐαγγέλιον is quite natural, insofar as ἀκοή described the "hearsay" which came to the hearer more or less accidentally without particular reference to the intention of the one broadcasting it. On the other hand, in Jewish usage šᵉmuâ is almost a technical term for the prophetic message originating with God and not that which happens to come to a person as "hearsay." The message which the prophets did not produce themselves, the šᵉmuâ, can then, following the *parallelismus membrorum*, be equated with bᵉsora = εὐαγγέλιον. For the rest, Paul himself does not, in *ad hoc* fashion, in Rom. 10:16 pick up ἀκοή from Greek usage but rather uses the term in the context of Isaiah 53. (The use of ἀκοή in the LXX requires further study.)

3. In dispute, finally, was the extent to which a connection can be

established between the pre-Lucan material of Acts 10 and the genuinely Petrine message. Similar material lies behind Acts 13, which, however, is expressly attributed to Paul. In Luke's work "Peter" and "Paul" preach basically the same gospel. Possibly the comparability of Acts 10 with Mark's outline (insofar as this could be said to go back to Peter) would constitute a completely hypothetical bridge from Acts 10 to Peter.

On "The Gospel Genre"   *(R. Guelich)*

The agreement between the papers by Stuhlmacher and Guelich was not "by arrangement."

1. The Marcan prologue was extended by Guelich up to Mark 1:15; the Isaian tradition serves as "depth-structure" of the text. If the gospel existed in narrative form, as "narrative genre," already *before* Mark, as Guelich maintains, then the question arises: Does Mark 1:1f. (ἀρχὴ τοῦ εὐαγγελίου Ἰησοῦ Χριστοῦ with reference to Isaiah) refer back to this already existing primitive model, in accordance with which people had begun at a very early stage to tell the story of the εὐαγγέλιον θεοῦ as the story of Jesus from the perspective of Isa. 52:7? Thus from the very beginning not only the narrated history of Jesus from John the Baptist to the resurrection but also the characterization of this history as εὐαγγέλιον θεοῦ in line with Old Testament usage was a feature of this pre-Marcan "genre."

2. To be listed as witnesses for this primitive εὐαγγέλιον-genre or proto-type (from the Baptist to the resurrection—in the light of the fulfillment of Old Testament Scriptures) would be a) Mark, b) Acts 10:36ff., and c)—especially controversial—John, so that one has to assume a development with some very early bifurcations:

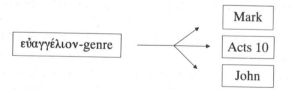

Or does not John presuppose a certain knowledge of Mark? In dispute also was the question to what extent Acts 10 may be enlisted: does not Luke—incorporating traditional elements, to be sure—*himself* consciously formulate matters in archaizing fashion here also to a great extent (cf. e.g. the notion of witnesses, the utilization of Galilee, or for example the prospect of judgment, which does not seem very well suited to function as a basic element for Mark's Gospel)? Hence, the question to what extent Acts 10 actually contains early material (perhaps going back even to Peter) is open and one which must be subjected to even sharper criticism.

3. In the *derivation* of the genre as given in the essay (see the diagram above) it is striking how little is made of the formation and development of tradition within the synoptic tradition itself. For example: How is the relationship between the "gospel" genre and the passion narrative to be defined? Did categories of development arise within the synoptic tradition by themselves? Or: the expansion of the Q tradition shows that the greater the distance in time from Jesus becomes, the greater also becomes the necessity to fix and thus to ground the teaching tradition in the history of the earthly Jesus (cf. e.g. the "apothegm" genre as an attempt to tie doctrine to the earthly Jesus). Was the Jesus-tradition itself thus designed from the beginning to develop, through a continuous process of growing precision, into the genre "gospel"?

4. Contact between the (pre-Marcan) genre "gospel" and the christological kerygma in I Cor. 15:3-5 (traditionally described as εὐαγγέλιον) consists in the fact that the passion narrative also begins with confession of Christ, and the materials in the first half of Mark's Gospel have the express christological function of authenticating the discourse concerning Christ by his words and deeds. This correspondence could suggest in fact that, already from the beginning, the Jesus-tradition (both the kerygmatic, in the style of I Cor. 15, and the narrative Jesus tradition) was called εὐαγγέλιον. Mark himself employs the term εὐαγγέλιον in its bipolarity: it describes not only the narrative genre of Jesus' history (Mark 1) but also the kerygmatic (I Cor. 15), the missionary gospel-message given to the apostles (Mark 14:9/13:10).

5. *The terminological dilemma.* The "gospel" as "genre"? In the domain of philology there is talk of a "genre" only when over long periods of time in historically diverse situations a certain literary procedure appears again and again and maintains itself (e.g., tragedy). In other words, the danger exists that the word usage of New Testament scholarship and that of philology are drifting apart.

There are, in principle, only two ways out of the dilemma: The New Testament scholar either reaches for new terms (but which?) or persists in making a loose, unspecific use of the term "genre," while the philologist reaches back to the ancient term "genus," where the roots of his definition of genre lie.

On "Literary, Theological, and Historical Problems in the Gospel of Mark" *(M. Hengel)*

1. Disputed was the extent to which Mark actually knew of a sayings-tradition (Q!) shaped on the model of wisdom literature, the extent to which he

presupposes knowledge of Jesus-logia among his readers and, in his narrative Gospel, expressly offers that which is lacking in the logia collection! Does this thesis of Hengel's remain an inference from silence? Remaining in dispute also was whether, as compared with Q, the sayings presented by Mark always represented the more developed (= adapted to the Marcan community) forms.

2. In support of the disputed value of the evidence from Papias, which, after all, goes back to the elder-tradition and may reach back at least as far as the year AD 100, it may be added that early Church data about the Gospel writer Mark as pupil of Peter are much more numerous than the data about all the other Gospel authors. One must also bear in mind, however, the observation of E. Schwarz (*Der Tod der Söhne Zebedäi*) that in antiquity there is hardly any trustworthy external information about documents, but that, by contrast, literary-historical legends are numerous indeed.

3. How is the interpretation by the ἑρμηνευτής in the Papias fragment to be taken? Did Peter not know enough Greek (hence: "interpreter" = "translator") or does Mark's hermeneutic function according to Papias also embrace the framework and the context as we see it in the Gospel? Or should Mark's function be understood on the analogy of the rabbis: a rabbi teaches in conjunction with an interpreter, the rabbi himself coining only very brief sayings, which another explains?

4. In dispute, finally, was the value of the Elijah-Moses typology in Mark. Furthermore, if Peter's preaching was in fact behind Mark and his Moses typology, the result would be that already in Peter there was the beginning of a contrast between law and gospel. Then Peter and Paul would not be that far apart after all but only separated in questions of praxis (cf. "The Pauline Gospel" above).

On "Matthew as a Creative Interpreter of the Sayings of Jesus" (*G. N. Stanton*)

Stanton's overall thesis of Matthew as a conservative interpreter who accepted the authority of his sources but carefully organized and clearly profiled his materials found general acceptance. It was considered less certain that Matthew made his redactional activities visible especially toward the end of the discourses. The discussion was especially concentrated, however, on the two textual analyses—Matt. 11:28-30 and 25:31-46.

1. Stanton's proposal to regard Matt. 11:29b as redactional seemed largely convincing. One could also weigh taking καὶ μάθετε ἀπ᾽ ἐμοῦ as redactional; that would make the symmetry of the traditional saying even clearer. In agreement with Stanton's thesis is the redaction of Matt. 11:19:

Jesus as wisdom was justified by his *deeds*. Stanton stresses that the identification of Jesus with Wisdom is not the real interest of Matthean christology but is modified, or interpreted, by Matthew's additions. The connections between Matt. 11:28-30 and Sirach 51 are generally overvalued in the research; only a small number of words are held in common; the material thrust of Sirach 51 is very different from that of Matt. 11:28ff. One might rather consider whether Mark 6:31, omitted in Matthew, could not be a parallel tradition or even a source of Matt. 11:28-30.

2. Matt. 25:31ff. remained controversial. The context of Matthew 24–25, which ends with the judgment over the Church, argues for the universalist interpretation of πάντα τὰ ἔθνη as referring to all people or to all Christians, who in the final judgment will be asked about their works of mercy for the poor and suffering. In the context of Matthew Stanton's proposed identification of the Son of Man with *his* brothers does not signify a climax but an anticlimax. The reference in Matt. 18:3-6, 10 is not to ἐλάχιστοι but to παιδία and μικροί. It is important to consider, however, whether in the course of tradition-historical development the meaning of the text has not shifted. Originally βασιλεύς was most likely a reference to God. Under the circumstances the development must be understood as follows: Jesus understood the text in a universalist sense; the Church in mission later probably restricted it to its own experiences in mission and identified itself with the least of the brethren of the Judge. Matthew, perhaps, thought of it in universal terms and inserted the text with a view to the judgment facing the Church. But there are arguments also for Stanton's position that ἀδελφοί meant the Christian missionaries: "Son of Man" (in the redaction) suggests the idea of the Church ("the saints of the Most High") just as "king" (in the original version) suggests the idea of all people. Vv. 31 and 46, which frame the text, carry clear reminiscences of Dan. 7:13 and 12:1 respectively, where the focus is on the salvation of the people of God. Stanton's thesis does not at all need the unprovable argument that the function of the text was to comfort the Church being attacked in its missionary endeavor: the idea of judgment over those who reject the Christian mission is dominant in the context of Matthew 25. The serious problems of the context of Matthew 24–25 can also be resolved in the case of Stanton's more restricted interpretation, as Lambrecht's attempt shows. Finally, the argument that in Matthew 18 there is no mention of ἐλάχιστοι is doubtful because in the manuscript tradition ἐλάχιστοι and μικροί are interchangeable.

On "Luke and His Gospel" *(I. H. Marshall)*

1. The difference between Guelich and Marshall[1] can be mediated by holding that Luke, after all, also wrote from the perspective of being an εὐαγγελιζόμενος, since even before Luke the tradition had been shaped in the direction of the perspective embodied in the Lucan corpus:

(a) In I Corinthians 15 the gospel had already been extended (by Paul or earlier?) to include the appearances to the apostles, and that means an extension to include a glance at the missionary history of the early Church! In other words: I Corinthians 15 offers an extended summary of the passion tradition, one that moves toward the perspective of Acts. Hence, when in his double work Luke presents not only the message of Christ but also the history of the witness to Christ, he seems only to be utilizing a mode of presenting the εὐαγγέλιον which was already available to him in the tradition.

(b) Mark's concept of the gospel is also not a single-track narrative of the story of Jesus; it is bipolar and fundamentally open toward the missionary message of the Church (see the references to Mark 13:10; 14:9 above).

2. Matthew and Luke offer two types of story, which differ in emphasis and together correspond to the bipolarity of the term εὐαγγέλιον: Matthew relates an "inclusive" story, a story in which the present as embodied in the disciples has been included in the fortunes of the earthly Jesus. Luke's Gospel, on the other hand, presents an "incomplete" story, one that is open-ended and calls for continuation. The Lucan corpus thus represents not only "continuity" (so Marshall), but also development, change, a progressive history. The Christian's relations to law and to possessions change. Even the forms of the kerygma change. Such terms as παῖς θεοῦ, δίκαιος, and ἅγιος, for example, figure as part of the Jerusalem message, in contrast, for example, with Acts 17.

Could it be that this different accentuation in Luke is behind his avoidance of the term εὐαγγέλιον? In distinction from Matthew and Mark (the retrospective reference to the history and message of the earthly Jesus) Luke emphasizes the progressively unfolding nature of redemption history. To be sure, the contrast is only relative—a matter of accentuation.

3. Among the terms in Luke's prologue, ἀσφάλεια was particularly discussed. Does the interpretation of ἀσφάλεια imply a dichotomy between the preached kerygma and the narrative of Jesus? Is it true that Theophilus has already heard the gospel? Is the narrative of Jesus, depicted in all detail and in the correct sequence, by contrast only an added guarantee for the reliability of

---

1. "There was no fixed 'gospel'-genre into which he had to fit his work as a whole. He regarded the works of his predecessors as 'accounts,' not as Gospels. He was not writing a 'Gospel' to which he subsequently added a sequel, but a two-part work" (point 3 of Marshall's Conclusions, p. 291 above).

the "gospel"? In other words, does the narrative itself not really belong to the "gospel" as it is necessary to the faith? Is it only a supplement to the "gospel"? Is Luke, generally speaking, the first to introduce Jesus-material in his diaspora community on a large scale?

There was a clear consensus that for Luke the Jesus-stories themselves already belonged to the kerygma of the gospel and were "gospel," so that the unity of "gospel," both in the sense of the synoptic as well as in the Pauline branch of the tradition, remained in view. Thus we hear again of the frequently mentioned bipolarity of the term εὐαγγέλιον, which includes both the narrated story of Jesus and the kerygmatic missionary message of the apostles.

On "Let John Be John—A Gospel for Its Time" *(J. D. G. Dunn)*

The question concerning the genesis of Johannine christology, that concerning its precise profile and claim and the matter of the relationship of the Johannine to the synoptic tradition, could only be touched upon.

1. Doubts were expressed whether John's Gospel could be situated in the context of Palestinian Judaism. The Ebionites, or James the brother of Jesus, who belong there, represent an essentially different type of Christianity. In Palestinian Judaism the status of Jesus as Son of God is not known until the third century (Abbahu). The assignment of John's Gospel to Palestinian Judaism would also be opposed by the fact that Wisdom played no significant role there. Another argument against Transjordan as the place of origin for John's Gospel (Dunn, Wengst) is that from this peripheral area it is hard to conceive how John's Gospel could so swiftly spread and be known in the Church. It also remains unclear from what time persecution for confession of Jesus as Christ is conceivable (cf. 9:22). Already before AD 70? The few notations about the persecution of Christians by Jews in the earlier period (e.g. Gal. 1:13; I Thess. 2:14) suggest rather that in the earlier period the law was the crucial factor in the confrontation.

2. It was even harder, from a tradition-historical point of view, to define the profile of Johannine christology against the background of Hellenistic Jewish logos speculation (Philo!), Old Testament sophia speculation, and Palestinian traditions of the Son of Man. Could it be perhaps that the real profile of Johannine christology does not consist in the definition of a still-open early Christian Son-of-God christology by the Logos/Son christology, but rather in the completion of the Son christology? The preexistence and Wisdom christology preceded John by two generations, and was present at the latest from the time of Paul (I Cor. 10:4; Phil. 2:6-11; Col. 1:15ff.; perhaps the mission formulas). In contrast, the absolute use of υἱός and the idea of ἑνότης between Father and Son may be specifically Johannine. On the other hand, the placement of the

Logos hymn in the preface of the Gospel seems to belong to the last phase of the history of the Johannine tradition. The fundamental question whether John's Gospel makes at all possible a redaction-historical interpretation (one oriented to the final form of the text) or whether a tradition-historical reconstruction of the development of Johannine christology deserves priority was left unresolved.

3. The question that was decisive for the symposium was that concerning the relationship between the synoptic and the Johannine Jesus-tradition. John had at his disposal reliable traditions that were special but related to the synoptic traditions. How are the Johannine "reproclamation" of the message of Jesus and the doctrine of the paraclete related to these special traditions? The challenge confronting the symposium consisted in the fact that it does not seem possible to understand this Gospel only as a new interpretation of the Jesus-tradition. John appeals to his own tradition, which he anchored directly in the life of the earthly Jesus (the beloved disciple!) and opposes it to other traditions. But how is this relationship to be defined? Dunn's thesis that according to John every christology that does not understand Jesus as Logos/Son misunderstands the Christian faith implies that the Johannine and earlier christologies do not all simply have the same standing. Gerhardsson advocates a counterthesis: John's Gospel presupposes the synoptic Jesus-tradition and uses it just as Gnosticism presupposes the faith of the Church and needs it. Johannine piety and Gnosticism would thus be "parasitic" in similar ways.

On "The 'Memoirs of the Apostles' in Justin"   *(L. Abramowski)*

1. That Justin insisted on the written character of the gospel, a rather isolated phenomenon in the second century, is interesting. The important consideration here is not that in the second century the written Gospels were of course known everywhere but that Justin uses the written character of the Gospels in a specific polemical[2] context as an argument—an argument which constitutes evidence for the historical truth of what happened. It is at precisely that point that Justin distinguishes himself from Irenaeus.

A side note here: An additional motive for Justin's insistence on writtenness could be the apologists' high-literary environment, in which, so to speak, "only books count" and no one can establish anything with a vague, merely oral, tradition. Also, on the assumption of an anti-Gnostic front in the treatise, this

---

2. In dispute was the polemical thrust of the treatise on Psalm 21 (LXX) which was incorporated into the *Dialogue*. Is it anti-Gnostic/antidocetic (cf. e.g. ἀληθῶς) or anti-Jewish, insofar as Jews could acknowledge neither that God could assume flesh and blood nor that he could suffer as a human being? Was the treatise perhaps *originally* anti-Gnostic while in the *present context* it is anti-Jewish?

pointer seems helpful if Justin regarded Christian Gnostics, in part, as educated—hence as influenced by that literary environment—opponents whom he
sought to persuade.

2. Justin's description of the Gospels as ἀπομνημονεύματα of the apostles
seems to be an apt accommodation to the word usage of Greek literary activity.
One aspect in particular is important: In Greek literature ἀπομνημονεύματα also
refers to writing which draws its material secondarily from other writings and
does not represent the personal memories of the authors (cf. Xenophon's
Socrates memoirs). Justin seems to be familiar with this Greek literary state of
affairs and thus is possibly aware that the Gospels also were not the original
notes of the apostles but themselves presuppose written prototypes and thus a
preceding process of transmission.

3. It needs to be established, however, that by his use of the term
ἀπομνημονεύματα Justin is not referring to a general genre (just as there are not
many book titles by the same name, there are also no fixed genres that have the
same name), but appeals to Xenophon's *Socrates,* so that in the choice of
ἀπομνημονεύματα Justin's parallelizing of Jesus and Socrates already comes to
expression.

As a more generic term there is ὑπομνήματα: "rough notes," since they
may, for example, serve as basis for the composition of a historical work (cf.
Lat. "commentarii").

4. In the domain of Greek literary production ἀπομνημονεύματα are notes
without literary form, whereas there is a decided literary aim behind the word
σύγγραμμα. That Justin avoids the terms σύγγραμμα/γραφή to describe the
Gospels could therefore have linguistic, in addition to theological, reasons—
reasons suggested to him from the domain of Greek literary production.

5. "Ἀπομνημονεύματα of the *apostles*" in an antiheretical context is a
phrase which fits the early Christian practice of securing the tradition against
heretical "distortions" by claiming apostolic authorship (e.g. II Peter). There is
correspondence here also to John who, alone among the evangelists, stresses the
written form at the close of his Gospel but, on the other hand, avoids the title
"gospel."

On "'Unknown Sayings of Jesus'"   *(O. Hofius)*

1. Does Hofius's initial definition of the agrapha as sayings attributed to the
earthly Jesus lead *a priori* to too narrow a view, to the extent that it blocks out
an entire realm (especially Gnostic Christianity, the Gospel of Thomas, but also
the Gospel of John) in which the Spirit-sayings of the exalted Lord and those of
the earthly Jesus have become indistinguishable? Can no conclusions be drawn

for early Christianity, say for the phenomenon of early Christian prophecy, in the light of this realm of the tradition in which the revealed sayings of the exalted Lord have started traditions of their own?

Hofius believes that this realm of tradition is relatively unimportant for the question of the transmission of Jesus' sayings: The authors of these sources themselves knew that they "had invented all that material." (The Gospel of Thomas, for example, is not dependent on a Christian source independent of the four Gospels but is rather loosely dependent on the Synoptics, which were known from the public reading in the worship services.) That entire realm of tradition is only relevant as source material to the degree that it furnishes information about the way Christ was understood in the ancient Church or by the Gnostics.

2. The question, "How were the agrapha formed?" remains important. ("Agrapha" now in the narrow sense as defined by Hofius, not in the senes of the revealed sayings of the exalted Jesus.) By what formal process did the agrapha come into being? Was this different from the way sayings came into being in the early Christian tradition (e.g. by early Christian prophets)? Was it different also from how it was with the Johannine Spirit-sayings, where the paraclete is expressly mentioned as coauthor? Hofius expressly rejects the character of I Thess. 4:15ff. as a prophetic saying. Hence the question arises: Was the process by which the agrapha originated less a spontaneous, Spirit-induced process of formulation than a process of interpretation? The latter especially because the Jesus-tradition had already come to be written down? Apart from a handful of new formations for which no tradition history can be given, the overwhelming majority of the agrapha are demonstrably and more or less directly based on written material. Most agrapha seem to have evolved as follows: Synoptic sayings that were in oral use (in sermons and catechesis) and familiar in public worship gave rise to dominical sayings that were new, modified, interpreted (e.g. by the addition of a proverb or other idea) or mixed with other sayings of Jesus. One can observe a parallel here with the formation of sayings of Jesus in the gospel tradition to the degree that in it too expansion, interpretation, combination, etc., took place.

3. How can one explain the surprisingly small number of agrapha for which there is no tradition-historical derivation outside the canonical Gospel tradition? Or do the present findings deceive us? Could there perhaps be more? An indication in this direction could be Acts 20:35: a dominical saying which Luke refrains from using in his Gospel. Also, the Matthean and Lucan redactors simply dropped materials: the gathering process did not take place on the model of the Prussian academy; rather there was traditional material to the left and to the right, a border area in which transmission occurred. Though the likelihood is not great, the possibility exists that this marginal zone of transmission was a wide one.

However this may be, John writes (21:25): "But there are also many other things which Jesus did; were every one of them to be written, I suppose that the world itself could not contain the books that would be written." Does John perhaps have in mind another kind of Jesus-tradition—one devoid of *sayings* of Jesus?

4. In Gnostic writings (e.g. the end of the Gospel of Thomas) the term "gospel" has marginal significance in that the most diverse literary products (frequently modeled on the available Church Gospels) were called "gospel" (e.g. "the Gospel to the Egyptians"). The word "gospel" simply refers to the "good news according to the Gnostics" and is applicable in a number of ways.

On "The Gospels and Greek Biography" *(A. Dihle)*

1.1. Do the biographies of philosophers (Pythagoras, Epicurus—as redeemer-figures) and the biographies of religious mythic figures (Hercules, Romulus, and others) represent a special vein *next to* the biographies of Greek rulers? Not in principle. The private dimension also stands out in Plutarch's biographies of rulers. In *all three* complexes the purpose is to show: this is what human nature is like; this is how it comes to expression in this individual—to this the reader who has the selfsame nature must orient himself. That which has been biographically depicted—a portrayal which lacks genuine uniqueness—can be imitated by the reader because in principle it does not exceed the limits of his experience.

1.2. Though it has a stronger focus on the individual's relationship to the community and state, Roman biography is not distinctive because, when it represents the development in the individual of *general* virtues, it remains bound to the Greek model. (Nepos's *Life of Atticus* illustrates, in Rome, a life that is rich in moral qualities without involvement in political affairs.)

2.1. The comparable New Testament concept of the *imitatio Christi* (Phil. 2, etc.), which in the presentation of the example intends to give parenesis for living and thus a fair measure of repeatability to the life of Jesus, does not stand in contrast with faith in the *uniqueness* of the life of Jesus, a uniqueness provided by redemptive history and not traceable to "nature." In ancient biography it is recourse to nature which destroys uniqueness.

2.2. The difference between ancient biography and gospel can therefore be sketched with notions like "redemptive-historical perspective," an aspect of Dihle's essay that accords unusually well with the New Testament vantage point, which regards the redemptive-historical view (fulfillment of the Scriptures, the scheme "prophecy and fulfillment") as the source of the narrative framework of a gospel presentation (cf. e.g. Acts 10).

3. On the relationship between gospel and the ancient universal history/historical monograph:

Ancient universal history always offers perspectival notations or a cosmo-
logical framework with corresponding historiographic conventions,
conventions which Luke takes over; hence, for example, the multiple
datings, a typical universal-historical convention. What is totally lacking, however, is the specifically biblical scheme of prophecy and
fulfillment.

The historical monograph as a special literary genre does not really
develop a historical perspective; it tends much more to treat isolated
events (e.g. a war) and can at best furnish a view of a separate epoch.

Universal history (from the beginning to the end of the world) came as a
given to early Christianity in an Old Testament and Jewish framework
(e.g. Daniel). Judaism had also learned to take advantage of the
historical monograph (e.g. II Maccabees). The latter can hardly,
however, be compared with the gospel.

Conclusion

The tendency among members of the symposium was to reckon with greater
fidelity in the transmission of tradition than was the case in classical form criticism.
Over against the picture which classical form criticism has produced of the
origination, transmission, and fixation of the synoptic tradition, a picture in need
of revision, there was a willingness to reckon with tradition that was very old and
had been transmitted very carefully. The elements which accrued in the course of
the process of transmission arose as a result of further interpretation and combination of existing materials, rather than through creative formation of new material.

A fine instance of the trustworthiness of tradition came out of the discussion
and is here for the first time written down from the oral stage of tradition. This is
an anecdote about F. C. Baur that Martin Hengel received as oral tradition from
Otto Bauernfeind, who received it from his teacher, Eduard von der Goltz, the
patristic scholar and practical theologian, who in turn heard it from his grandfather,
who heard F. C. Baur lecture: "Around the year 1840, when F. C. Baur was
exegeting ch. 13 of the Apocalypse and came to the number 666, he took off his
glasses, looked up from his lectern and said: 'And Hengstenberg in Berlin says
that is me!' " This piece of oral tradition has been carefully preserved by a chain
of tradents which spans more than 140 years. Quite naturally, and highly illuminating for the character of the transmission process, the story at the same time
acquired in Tübingen a (preredactional) addition with a second point: "I"—said
Martin Hengel—"have presented this anecdote to a group of great critics, Günter
Klein and others. At first they said: 'That can't be!' But after they heard the point
of the story they said: 'That is genuine!' . . ."

Index of Biblical and Other References (Selected)

I. Old Testament

405

V. Rabbinic Literature

VI. Hellenistic Jewish Literature